THE POLITICS OF SOCIAL TRANSFORMATION
IN AFGHANISTAN, IRAN, AND PAKISTAN

Contemporary Issues in the Middle East

The POLITICS of SOCIAL TRANSFORMATION in AFGHANISTAN, IRAN, and PAKISTAN

Edited by
MYRON WEINER and ALI BANUAZIZI

Syracuse University Press

First Edition 1994

94 95 96 97 98 99   6 5 4 3 2 1

The paper used in this publication meets the minimum requirements of American National Standard for Information Sciences—Permanence of Paper for Printed Library Materials, ANSI Z39.48-1984. ∞™

Library of Congress Cataloging-in-Publication Data

The Politics of social transformation in Afghanistan, Iran, and
  Pakistan / edited by Myron Weiner and Ali Banuazizi.
          p.   cm.—(Contemporary issues in the Middle East)
     Includes bibliographical references (p.   ) and index.
     ISBN 0-8156-2608-8.—ISBN 0-8156-2609-6 (pbk.)
     1. Elite (Social sciences)—Afghanistan. 2. Elite (Social
  sciences)—Iran. 3. Elite (Social sciences)—Pakistan. 4. Income
  distribution—Afghanistan. 5. Income distribution—Iran. 6. Income
  distribution—Pakistan. 7. Women—Government policy—Afghanistan.
  8. Women—Government policy—Iran. 9. Women—Government policy—
  Pakistan. I. Weiner, Myron. II. Banuazizi, Ali. III. Series.
  HN670.6.Z9E47   1993
  305.5'2'095491—dc20   93-16345

Manufactured in the United States of America

Contents

PART ONE

Political Elites and the Restructuring of the Political Order

PART TWO

The Political Economy of Redistribution and Social Equity

PART THREE

State Policies Toward Women

   MICHELINE CENTLIVRES-DEMONT   333

9. Power, Morality, and the New Muslim
   Womanhood
   AFSANEH NAJMABADI   366

10. Gender Inequality in the Islamic Republic of Iran
    A Sociodemography
    VALENTINE M. MOGHADAM   390

11. The Consequences of State Policies
    for Women in Pakistan
    ANITA M. WEISS   412

    Bibliography   447

    Index   471

Illustrations

Tables

Figure

Acknowledgments

The editors acknowledge with appreciation the support of the Ford Foundation to the MIT Center for International Studies for a series of workshops at which papers for the present volume were initially presented and discussed. Plans for these workshops were developed with the help of a committee that included Shahid Javed Burki (the World Bank), John L. Esposito (Georgetown University), Farhad Kazemi (New York University), Barbara Metcalf (University of California, Davis), Ann Elizabeth Meyer (University of Pennsylvania), Vahid F. Nowshirvani (Columbia University), M. Nazif Shahrani (Indiana University), and Tony Smith (Tufts University). Suggestions from Gary Sick (Columbia University) and Zalmay Khalilzad (the Rand Corporation) were also helpful in the initial phases of the project.

Comparative discussion papers prepared by Patrick Clawson (the World Bank), Margaret Mills (University of Pennsylvania), Hanna Papanek (Boston University), Tony Smith, and Marvin G. Weinbaum (University of Illinois) were especially helpful to both the authors and the editors, as were suggestions and critical comments by Lucian W. Pye (MIT), Gustav F. Papanek (Boston University), Ijaz Gilani (Gallup Pakistan), Barbara Metcalf, and M. Nazif Shahrani.

Finally, we thank Elizabeth Prodromou of MIT and Timothy Shortell of Boston College for their assistance as rapporteurs, Ramesh Farzanfar for preparing the index, and Lois Malone of the Center for International Studies for her managerial and editorial contributions at every phase in the preparation of the present volume.

Myron Weiner
Ali Banuazizi

Contributors

ANTHONY ARNOLD graduated from Yale in 1950 with a B.A. in Russian area studies. After twenty-six years in the Central Intelligence Agency, including one tour in Afghanistan in the mid-1970s, he became a visiting scholar at the Hoover Institution, which published his *Afghanistan: The Soviet Invasion in Perspective* (1985) and *Afghanistan's Two-Party Communism: Parcham and Khalq* (1983). His most recent book, *The Fateful Pebble: Afghanistan's Role in the Fall of the Soviet Empire*, was published by Presidio Press in 1993.

AHMAD ASHRAF teaches at New York University and is an editor of the *Encyclopaedia Iranica*. He has taught comparative sociology and Middle Eastern social history at the University of Teheran, the University of Pennsylvania, and Princeton University. He is the author of numerous works, in both Persian and English, on Iranian social history and comparative politics, including *Historical Obstacles in the Development of Capitalism in Iran* (1980) and "State and Agrarian Relations Before and After the Iranian Revolution, 1960–1990," in *Peasant Politics in the Modern Middle East* (1991).

ALI BANUAZIZI is professor of social psychology at Boston College and a research fellow at the Center for International Studies at MIT. He served as the editor of *Iranian Studies* from 1968 to 1982. His recent publications include "Social-Psychological Approaches to Political Development," in *Understanding Political Development* (1987), and *The State, Religion, and Ethnic Politics: Afghanistan, Iran, and Pakistan*, edited with Myron Weiner (1986).

SHAHID JAVED BURKI is the director of the China Department at the World Bank and is also in charge of the bank's Mongolia program. His most recent books include *Pakistan: Development Choices for the Future* (1985), *Pakistan: A Nation in the Making* (1986), and *Pakistan under the Military* (with Craig Baxter, 1991).

MICHELINE CENTLIVRES-DEMONT took her M.A. degree in political science from the University of Lausanne and her Ph.D. in anthropology from the

xiii

University of Neuchâtel. She has conducted field work in Iran, Afghanistan, India, Turkey, and Pakistan; and under a grant from the Fonds National Suisse de la Recherche Scientifique, she is presently conducting a study of Afghan refugees. She is the author of *Une communauté de potiers en Iran: Le centre de Meybod (Yazd)* (1971) and *Popular Art in Afghanistan* (1975), and she is coauthor, with Pierre Centlivres, of *Et si on parlait de l'Afghanistan: Terrains et textes 1964–1980* (1988).

PATRICK CLAWSON is a scholar associated with both the Washington Institute for Near East Policy and the Foreign Policy Research Institute's Middle East Council. Previously he was a senior economist at the World Bank and the International Monetary Fund. His earlier work includes *Economic Consequences of Peace for Israel, Palestinians, and Jordan* (1991), with Howard Rosen, and more than a dozen articles on the Iranian economy.

AYESHA JALAL is currently associate professor in the Department of History, Columbia University. Her publications include *The Sole Spokesman: Jinnah, the Muslim League, and the Demand for Pakistan* (1985) and *The State of Martial Rule: The Origins of Pakistan's Political Economy of Defence* (1990).

VALENTINE M. MOGHADAM is a senior research fellow and coordinator of the Research Programme on Women and Development at the World Institute for Development Economics Research of the United Nations University, in Helsinki. She received a Ph.D. in sociology in 1986 from American University. She has taught development studies at New York University, held a postdoctoral fellowship at the Pembroke Center for Teaching and Research on Women at Brown University, and taught Middle East Studies at Rutgers University. Her many articles on Iran, Afghanistan, and the Middle East have appeared in journals and edited books; her book *Modernizing Women: Gender and Social Change in the Middle East* was published in March 1993.

AFSANEH NAJMABADI is associate professor of women's studies at Barnard College. She is currently working on two manuscripts: *Daughters of Quchan: The Forgotten Gender of the Iranian Constitutional Revolution* and *Female Sun and Male Lion: The Gendered Tropes of Iranian Modernity*. Her publications include *Vices of Men* (editor) (1992), *Women's Autobiographies in Contemporary Iran* (editor) (1991), *Land Reform and Social Change in Rural Iran* (1987), and *In the Shadow of Islam: The Women's Movement in Iran* (with Nahid Yeganeh) (1982).

VAHID F. NOWSHIRVANI is a senior lecturer in economics at Columbia University. He has taught economics at Yale University and the University of Teheran. He is the author of several works on the historical and contemporary aspects of the Iranian economy, including "Land Reform in Iran Revisited: New Evidence on the Results of Land Reform in Nine Provinces," in *Journal of Peasant Studies*, vol. 20, no. 3, with Mohammed Gholi Majd.

OLIVIER ROY holds degrees in philosophy and in Oriental languages (Persian). He is presently a researcher in political science at the Centre National de la Recherche Scientifique (CNRS), Paris. From 1980 to 1988 he engaged in extensive fieldwork with the Afghan mujahidin. He is the author of *Islam and Resistance in Afghanistan* (1986) and *L'échec de l'Islam politique* (1992).

BARNETT R. RUBIN is associate professor of political science at Columbia University, director of the Center for the Study of Central Asia, and a member of both the Southern Asia and Middle East Institutes. He is the author of two forthcoming books: *Mirror of the World: Afghanistan's State and Society in the International System* and *From Cold-War Regional Conflict to Post-Cold-War State Disintegration: The Failure of International Conflict Resolution in Afghanistan*. He is also coauthor (with Jeri Laber) of *A Nation Is Dying: Afghanistan under the Soviets, 1979–1987*. He has also written articles on the state, society, political elites, and conflict resolution in Afghanistan, as well as studies of human rights, economic policy, and other subjects in India, Pakistan, and Sri Lanka.

MYRON WEINER is Ford International Professor of Political Science at the Massachusetts Institute of Technology and former director of its Center for International Studies. He is the author of *The Indian Paradox: Essays in Indian Politics* (1989) and *The Child and the State in India: Child Labor and Education Policy in Comparative Perspective* (1991) and is coeditor and author, with Samuel P. Huntington, of *Understanding Political Development* (1987). He is presently working on a study of the international relations implications of international population movements.

ANITA M. WEISS is associate professor in international studies at the University of Oregon. She is a member of the executive committee of the American Pakistan Research Organization, is on the board of the U.S. Council for INSTRAW, and has written on issues pertaining to women, industrial development, and sociocultural change in Pakistan. She is the author of *Walls Within Walls: Life Histories of Working Women in the Old City of Lahore* (1992) and *Culture, Class, and Development in Pakistan* (1991) and is the editor of *Islamic Reassertion in Pakistan: The Application of Islamic Laws in a Modern State* (1986). She is currently studying the social impact of rising female secondary school attendance rates in Pakistan and several other Muslim countries.

Introduction

In spite of their deeply rooted historical and cultural ties, the three non-Arab Islamic countries that are the subject of this book have only recently been viewed as politically interrelated parts of a region. For much of the present century, they were primarily preoccupied in their external relations not with each other but with their other neighbors or outside powers—India and China in the case of Pakistan; the Soviet Union in the case of Afghanistan; and the Arab states, the Western powers, and the Soviet Union in the case of Iran. Since the late 1970s, however, profound changes in the internal politics of each of these countries have reshaped their relations to one another, to their neighbors, and to the major powers beyond the region. Today, the political futures of these countries appear to be more intertwined than at any time in their modern history.

The unprecedented political changes in the region began with the collapse of the old regimes in Afghanistan and Iran in 1978 and 1979, respectively, and their replacement by revolutionary governments with starkly different political ideologies. The Iranian revolution, with its broad popular support, demonstrated the potential of Islam as an overarching ideology for mass mobilization and as a framework for transforming a society's economic, political, and social institutions. Before the Iranian revolution, the notion of an Islamic revolution was an oxymoron. But after Iran, the specter of a religiously inspired social revolution has haunted ruling elites in many Muslim societies.

In Afghanistan, the Soviet invasion in December of 1979, to help prop up a faltering communist regime that had come to power through a coup one and one-half years earlier (the "Great Saur Revolution," according to its supporters), tore the social fabric of Afghan society, turned a third of its population into refugees, and ultimately led to one of the costliest blunders in Soviet foreign policy since the Second World

1

War. Here, too, Islam played a critical role as the unifying ideology of a diverse resistance movement against the radical reforms of the People's Democratic Party of Afghanistan (PDPA) and, later, the Soviet occupation.

For Pakistan, where Islam has been the raison d'etre of the state, the cataclysmic changes in the political fortunes of two of its neighbors, particularly as they involved an intense politicization of Islam, have had far-reaching consequences. They contributed to the fervor of the Islamic revival that was already under way in many quarters of Pakistani society. Furthermore, it was partly in response to these changes that the country's military leader at the time, the late President Zia ul-Haq, fashioned his own Islamization program in the hope of enhancing his political legitimacy and thwarting the spread of a militant Islamic movement at the grass roots.

With the continuation of the civil war in Afghanistan, millions of refugees poured into Pakistan and Iran. The care of this enormous refugee population of more than four million and the channeling of U.S. military aid to the Afghan mujahidin through Pakistan pulled that country further into the Afghan conflict. For its part, Iran, too, hosted well over two million Afghan refugees at a time when its own resources were severely overtaxed by its protracted war with Iraq.

Finally, the breakup of the Soviet Union and the emergence of the six Muslim republics in Central Asia and the Caucasus have introduced a new element of uncertainty in the region. Groups within Iran and Afghanistan—Azerbaijanis in Iran, Tajiks and Uzbeks in Afghanistan—have close ethnic ties with the new republics. The cross-cutting of ethnic and religious ties—Persian-speaking Tajiks are Sunni, and Turkic-speaking Azerbaijanis are Shi ʿites—adds still another complexity to the entire region.

In some respects, the aforementioned developments, particularly in Afghanistan and Iran, have been guided by an even more fundamental idea than Islam: the notion that a whole society—its economic, political, and cultural institutions, the moral character of its people, and its sense of national identity and purpose—can be transformed swiftly by massive *state* intervention. Thus, whereas political elites have differed on such issues as the sanctity of private property, redistribution of wealth and income, or limits of desecularization, most have shared the vision of an interventionist state structure with a decisive transformative capacity. It is to an analysis of this transformative role of the state in restructuring society that the contributions to this volume are specifically directed. Systematically analyzing the similarities and differences in the role of the state in restructuring the political and social institutions of these three societies over the past fifteen years can shed light on the dynamics of change in each of the three, as well as in the region as a whole.

In analyzing the role of the state, we focus on two specific problems. In the first part of the volume, we examine the role of the elites and their relation to the masses, their ideologies and the nature of their authority. In this examination of the elites—both governing and opposition elites—attention is paid to intraelite divisions, the social and ideological bases of these divisions, and the implications these intraelite conflicts have for governance.

In the second part of the volume, we focus on the ways in which the governing elites have sought to use the powers and resources of the state to deal with problems of distribution and social equity. Distributional struggles, as well as ideological debates over which social categories should be considered for different distributional policies, have been central features of all three polities. In the third part, particular attention is given to the women's question, where the issue of equity is closely linked with Islamic norms regarding gender relations and with concerns about the preservation of Islamic values against further Western incursion. And finally, in reviewing these state interventions, we consider not only the redistributive consequences of direct and indirect state policies but also their impact on the legitimacy and viability of the regimes in power.

I

In Iran the weakness of the state and the relative autonomy of the religious establishment enabled religious leaders to use a politicized Islamic theology as the basis for a revolutionary movement against the state. On the surface, the prerevolutionary state appeared to be strong: it had a large bureaucratic apparatus, substantial oil revenues, expanding public enterprises, and a powerful coercive machinery in the police, intelligence apparatus, and military. But in economic terms, the state was weak: its share of the gross domestic product was quite small (8 percent in 1979, excluding gas and oil revenues)—a classic rentier capitalist state whose expansion was dependent on the price of oil rather than on a domestic tax base. The sociopolitical base of the shah's regime was also limited; not only was the regime opposed by sizable segments of the young intelligentsia, the ulama, and the bazaaris, it was also only weakly and intermittently supported by the modern bourgeoisie, the new professional-bureaucratic middle class, and the industrial workers—that is, the very groups that had been the chief beneficiaries of the country's economic development since the early 1920s.

The first and, in retrospect, critical phase of the revolutionary struggle against the regime of the shah, according to Ahmad Ashraf, was the struggle within the religious establishment itself. The charismatic Ayatollah Ruhollah Khomeini acceded to the position of grand ayatollah in the early 1960s and soon superseded the majority of his more conservative clerical colleagues who had accommodated themselves to the Pahlavi regime. Khomeini successfully attracted many of the younger teachers and students of theology and forged an alliance with the bazaaris and sections of the young intelligentsia who were drawn to his militant style. The second phase of the struggle was the revolution itself, during which Khomeini, with the aid of a small coterie of militant clergy, seized the leadership of a broad coalition of forces opposed to the shah's regime. The third phase followed the familiar pattern of earlier revolutions, as an intraelite struggle unfolded among the various groups that had taken part in the triumphant revolutionary coalition. One by one, Khomeini's clerical supporters eliminated or reduced the power of their opponents—the restive ethnic minorities (the Kurds, the Baluch, the Turkomans, the Azerbaijanis, and others), the liberal nationalists, the secular leftists, the bazaaris, and the Westernized middle classes. Concomitant with this consolidation of power, the regime significantly expanded the size of the state apparatus and its role in nearly every sphere of public life.

Ashraf's chapter also provides a detailed description and analysis of the social composition and ideological orientation of the postrevolutionary governing elite. Using data on the social composition of the Islamic Consultative Assembly (Majlis-e Shura-ye Islami), he reports that the ulama were initially dominant but that within a few years the proportion of state managers and professionals increased sharply. The new leaders were young and educated, committed to radical transformation through the exercise of state power. Within the revolutionary elite itself, differences soon arose about what constituted "revolutionary Islam," particularly about the role of the state in the economy and in reshaping the moral and cultural character of the society. Cross-cutting these two divisions were questions of relations with the West and of exporting the Islamic revolution. Arguing against a neat division of the elite, as is often done by many Western observers,

along conservative, radical, and pragmatic lines, Ashraf points out, for
instance, that whereas "conservatives" who believe in the sanctity of
private property are often strict on cultural issues, "radicals" who believe in state intervention on behalf of the poor, nationalization of foreign trade, and confiscation of rural and urban property tend to be
more permissive on cultural issues. Each of these three groups has its
own social base: the conservatives among the bazaaris and some of the
clergy, the radicals among the young intelligentsia (many of whom lean
toward one or another form of Islamic socialism), and the pragmatists
among the new middle classes of white-collar employees in both the
public and the private sectors, the military, and sections of the industrial proletariat. At several crucial junctures during the first decade of
the revolution, Khomeini threw his support to those favoring radical
economic policy, to those who sought stricter state control in cultural
affairs, and to those pressing for a more radical foreign policy.

With the death of Khomeini in June 1989, the revolution entered its
fourth phase, one in which Ayatollah Ali Khamenei, as the chosen successor to Khomeini in his role of the supreme jurist (faqih), and Ali-
Akbar Hashemi Rafsanjani, as president, pursued a more moderate
course, both domestically and internationally. As Ashraf writes, although the paradox of a charismatic leadership of a bureaucratic state
has come to an end, clerical leadership remains well entrenched in the
state bureaucracy and within the various parastatal organs. Unlike the
situation under the shah, ideological and personal factions within the
elite are not only more intense, they also reach more deeply into the
society, thus increasing the likelihood of future conflicts within the society at large.

II

In contrast with the revolution in Iran, the Afghan "revolution"
was entirely from above. In 1978, leaders of a recently united Communist party (the PDPA) overthrew President Daoud, a member of the
ruling Mohammadzai clan of Durrani Pashtuns. Anthony Arnold describes the first phase of this revolutionary movement as a struggle
within the PDPA between the multiethnic Parcham faction, based on
the urban middle class and intellectuals, and the predominately
Pashtun Khalq faction, based on the rural intelligentsia. Neither of the
two factions, nor indeed the PDPA collectively, was particularly strong
until the mid-1970s, when the Khalqis began successfully to penetrate

the military. In April 1978 the Khalqis within the Afghan military overthrew Mohammad Daoud in what was dubbed the Saur (April) Revolution. In the second phase, the Khalqis sought to crush their
opponents, both those within the PDPA (i.e., the Parchamis) and those
outside. Committed strongly to using the state for a revolutionary
transformation of Afghanistan, the Khalqi leaders sought to provide
equal rights for women and to shift resources from larger landowners
to the landless and smallholders through the Khalqi land reform program and debt cancellation. The result was a civil war, a popular armed
resistance in Afghanistan's highly decentralized and well-armed society. The wave of terror then launched by the Khalqis against the
Parchamis and other opponents was soon followed by Soviet military
intervention in December 1979.

In the third phase of the revolution, the Parchamis, supported
by the Soviets, assumed power. The Parchami faction took control of
the PDPA, the secret police, and the military, scaled down the revolutionary program of the Khalqis, halted the land reforms, and
adopted the rhetoric of Islam. None of this won back the social
forces in the countryside, who were implacably opposed to PDPA
rule and to the Soviet presence. Nor did it end the factional struggle
between Khalqis and Parchamis. Unable to consolidate their rule,
the Parchamis after 1985 launched a policy of "national reconciliation," essentially an effort to woo back the private sector, the peasantry, and the tribal leaders. The Soviets replaced Babrak Karmal
with Dr. Najibullah, head of the secret police. Although the PDPA
was still unable to win support in the countryside, the party consolidated its position within the military, sought to win over the youth
(many of whom were sent to the Soviet Union for training), and
attempted to build support in urban enclaves.

The social classes the communists sought to displace, especially the
khans, or local notables, were traditionally concerned with social control, not social transformation. They were less concerned with building
the state than with using whatever resources were controlled by the
state, and a major preoccupation of elites was with succession. Under
Daoud and his predecessors, Afghanistan had been a society with a
low level of political mobilization but a high level of feuds and occasional armed combat.

Whereas in Iran the revolutionary movement mobilized mass participation, in Afghanistan it was resistance to the domination of a self-
designated revolutionary elite that mobilized mass participation. As
Olivier Roy explains, prior to the Saur Revolution and the civil war,

politicization in Afghanistan was largely an educated urban middle-class phenomenon, with political power still mainly in the hands of traditional elites, tribal leaders, and landowners. Only the military and the state bureaucracy provided career opportunities for the newly educated—one reason the young advocated a revolutionary transformation of the society's social structure through control over the state apparatus. Some young people turned to the PDPA; others turned to revolutionary Islam: politically poles apart but based on a similar commitment to the notion of a transformative state.

Roy shows how the struggle against the PDPA was led not by traditional notables and landowners but by this new class of young, university-educated Islamic revolutionaries of urban middle-class origin. The young revolutionaries have been opposed to the traditional elite, as they have been to the Communist regime in Kabul. Mostly of Sunni persuasion, they do not regard the religious leaders as a political elite either. Their organizational model, as Roy explains, is a disciplined political party united around an ideology and concerned with undoing familial, ethnic, and patronage relations. As among the PDPA members, there are also among the Islamic revolutionaries sharp divisions and bitter conflicts over the political future of the Afghan society. Although some of the local notables were prepared to make a deal with the Kabul regime, the Islamic revolutionaries took a hard-line position against compromise with the Najibullah government and have also been opposed to the return of the king, who, in their mind, is tied to the local notables.

The segmented character of Afghanistan's social system, the cleavages among tribes and linguistic groups, and the nature of the terrain all contribute to the development of highly localized elites, armed local commanders with their social base in the local community. The local commanders are not the local notables, however, but belong to a new generation of young Islamic activists. Though supported by some clerics, the Islamic revolutionaries are thus fundamentally different from the revolutionary elite in Iran, whose core leadership comes from within the religious establishment. Roy emphasizes the rivalry among Islamic revolutionaries, the ulama, and traditional khans, as well as rivalries within each group that prevented the development of a unified opposition to the Communist regime. Differences were and continue to be intense, not only over the vision of the future society but over the institutional structures of governance and politics, between those who seek to build bureaucratized party structures and those who prefer the traditional local game of politics. In the war against the Communist regime each group had its own military force and was dependent on foreign assistance rather than domestic resources.

Roy argues that the young educated Islamic revolutionaries, like the young men who supported the PDPA, want a significantly expanded state apparatus, partly for social reconstruction but also because the state is the final provider of employment. Both the Communists and the Islamic revolutionaries rejected the traditional leaders and dreamed of mobilizing popular support for a new expanded state, an outcome rendered more difficult not only by the capacity of traditional elites to resist state power but by the many divisions and rivalries within the emerging educated classes in terms of ideology and ethnicity.

III

Pakistan—the country and the state—was the creation of a political elite: the leaders of India's preindependence Muslim League wanted a country for the subcontinent's Muslim population. Out of that dream—and a bitter struggle against both the Indian National Congress and a variety of regional Muslim political movements—came a country divided into two parts, West Pakistan and East Pakistan, with governing elites who were sharply divided about what kind of state and country they wanted to create. Some of the elites, mainly the Muhajirs, migrants from India who founded the Muslim League and who held positions in the Pakistan civil service, together with many Punjabi leaders who held a dominant position in the military, wanted a strong central unitary government. In contrast, the Bengalis in East Pakistan (who formed a numerical majority of the country) and the smaller linguistic communities (Sindhis, Baluchis, and Pashtuns) favored a more decentralized federal Pakistan in which the provinces would have considerable autonomy. The elites were also divided over what it meant to be a Muslim country, whether Pakistan should merely be a homeland for the Muslims of the subcontinent or should in some special way be "Islamic." Some sections of the political elite, especially portions of the intelligentsia, dreamed of a more egalitarian society in which the state would play an active role in breaking up the large landed estates (especially in the Sind and in portions of the Punjab) and limit the wealth of the business community; the landlord and industrialist elites, the bureaucracy, and the military, on the other hand, sought to protect property rights.

The struggle of contending elites for control of the state and for definition of legitimate authority has led to a succession of major political crises: periodic regime changes from civilian to military rule and back again, two coups, a civil war that broke the country in two, the violent death of three heads of government, persistent conflicts between the central and provincial governments, and violent conflicts among ethnic groups.

Any periodization of postindependence political developments in Pakistan must begin with a description of regime changes based on an alternation of party and military rule. During the first phase, from 1947 to 1958, when the Muslim League was in power, Liaqat Ali Khan served four years as prime minister and was followed in rapid succession by six others. During this first decade of independence, Pakistan was largely led by the Muhajir middle-class Muslims (an estimated six million) who migrated after 1947 to the newly created country. Faced with the awesome task of building a state, the Muhajir-dominated Muslim League, as Ayesha Jalal writes, chose to strengthen the administrative system and the military rather than to build a political party. State building was given precedence over creating a political process that would enable the government to bring together the country's diverse ethnic groups. The state grew stronger, but the governing party grew weaker, and its electoral hold, never strong, soon dissipated.

Fearful that East Pakistan's political elite would win the parliamentary elections in 1959, the military made a preemptive move in 1958 to seize power. The military, predominantly Punjabi and, to a lesser extent, Pashtun, suspected the national loyalty of the Bengalis and believed (probably correctly) that a Bengali-dominated government would reduce the power and resources of the military. This second phase, the period of military rule, lasted from 1958 to 1972, first under General Ayub Khan (1958 to 1969), then under General Yahya Khan.

Faced with growing opposition, in part from the new middle classes in West Pakistan and in part from nationalist Bengalis in East Pakistan, the military agreed to hold elections in 1970. The results were victories of the Pakistan People's Party (PPP) led by Zulfikar Ali Bhutto in the West and of the Awami League led by Mujibur Rahman in the East. Civil war, Indian military intervention, the breakup of Pakistan (the only postcolonial state to have disintegrated), the return of the military to the barracks, and the assumption of office by the PPP under Bhutto soon followed. Just as the Muslim League had earlier failed to transform itself from a nationalist movement to a national party that could incorporate the country's diverse ethnic groups, so too had the military failed to win over the majority Bengali community.

Bhutto proved to be no more successful in building an effective coalition for governing the new Pakistan. Reaching out for support at various points to the urban middle classes, the landlords, and to the religiously more conservative lower middle classes and rural population, Bhutto succeeded only in alienating one group after another. He was particularly keen on reducing the power of the civil bureaucracy. The civil service of Pakistan (CSP), heir to the preindependence Indian civil service (ICS), held a predominant position in making policies and programs during the period of military rule. Bhutto sought to reduce the power of the bureaucracy and to make it politically accountable to the elected government. He abolished the CSP cadre system, limited the tenure of bureaucrats, established a system of lateral entry into the civil service, and dismissed large numbers of civil servants. But, as Jalal writes, Bhutto's combined assault against the military and the civil bureaucracy was not accompanied by a successful effort to build a coalition of popular support or to create an effective party organization.

This third phase of governance, the second period of civilian rule, lasted until 1977, when Bhutto was overthrown in a military coup by General Mohammad Zia ul-Haq. Under General Zia, military personnel moved into key positions previously held by the civil bureaucracy. Paradoxically, the deepening of control by the military elite was facilitated by Bhutto's nationalization of numerous industrial units, which Zia now staffed with retired military officers. Additionally, in an effort to win popular support and to curry favor among new military recruits drawn from lower-middle-class families, Zia pursued a policy of "Islamizing" Pakistani society. Zia's hold on power was consolidated with the Soviet invasion of Afghanistan in 1979 and the injection of American assistance. But, Jalal writes, the rivalry between the civil bureaucracy and the army persisted, while the so-called defunct, or banned, political parties continued to build up popular opposition to military rule.

After eleven years, formal military rule came to an abrupt end when General Zia was killed in a plane crash and national, party-based parliamentary elections were held. In 1988 a fifth regime change took place with the return to power of the PPP and the selection of Benazir Bhutto, daughter of Zulfikar, as prime minister. Although the regime change was widely heralded both as the restoration of democracy and as a rejection of Zia's Islamization, the transformation was limited in its scope and reach. Prime Minister Bhutto's authority was severely constrained by civilian and military bureaucrats who dominated key ministerial appointments and who continued to shape the country's domestic and foreign policies. Ghulam Ishaq Khan, often described as the "dean" of Pakistan's bureaucracy, was president, with the critical power to make appointments to the High Court, and, given his earlier role as finance minister, was reputed to remain a central figure in all matters relating to government finance. The army and Interservices Intelligence (ISI), which handled external intelligence and counterintelligence and which took special responsibility for dealing with Afghan guerrillas, remained central institutions in matters affecting both domestic order and regional security. The prime minister was in no position to cut the defense budget without risking martial law, nor was she able to develop a coherent reform agenda. In a country in which bureaucratic power had been predominant, the aim of elected officials was still largely to influence the bureaucracy and share its patronage rather than to engage in social and economic reconstruction.

By mid-1990, Benazir Bhutto was out, dismissed by President Ghulam Ishaq Khan in what was generally regarded as a constitutional coup. Much of Bhutto's popular support had been dissipated by reports of increasing corruption and cronyism in government, by an upsurge in ethnic violence in the Sind, and by growing antagonism between Bhutto and the military, the bureaucracy, and the president. Little had been done by Prime Minister Bhutto to strengthen the PPP, for she was more concerned with personal loyalty than with impersonal institution building.

Nawaz Sharif, the chief minister of Punjab, proved to be far more effective than Bhutto in creating an electoral coalition. His party, the Islamic Democratic Alliance (IDA), itself a coalition of diverse groups, won a majority of seats in the national assembly and in the Punjab assembly and emerged as the single largest party in the North-West Frontier Province. Bhutto challenged the results, arguing that there had not been a level playing field (during the campaign she was harassed by the courts, her husband was arrested on charges of corruption, the president of the country supported the IDA, and government-run television and radio were opposed to her) and that in many constituencies the results were rigged. Thus, by challenging the integrity of the electoral process itself, Bhutto had cast a shadow over the legitimacy of the elected government.

Political power in Pakistan has alternated between the military and political party elites, with the military taking power through coups and political parties through elections. But such a characterization of the

Pakistan political system belies the critical importance of the civil bureaucracy in the country's governance under both military and party regimes and understates the dynamic interplay of regionalism, ethnicity, class, family, and political institutions in the changing composition of Pakistan's governing elite. The bureaucracy, once Muhajir- and Punjabi-dominated, has become more ethnically diverse. As an institution, however, it has become more politicized and offers a less attractive career choice to young, educated Pakistanis, who are increasingly drawn to business and the professions. The military remains overwhelmingly Punjabi, and many of its leaders continue to regard themselves as guardians of Pakistan, but virtually all of the country's political parties would regard the assertion of military control as an illegitimate exercise of authority. The PPP proved to be a weak and fragmented organization. Its precarious hold on power rested on its base in the rural Sind, but it was besieged by Muhajir opposition in the urban Sind and by a coalition of opposition parties in control of the provincial government in the Punjab. The IDA has its base among the Punjabis, with strong support from sections of the business community (Nawaz Sharif, the prime minister, was himself an industrialist) and considerable support from Islamic traditionalists and those in the establishment who backed Zia ul-Haq. In short, each major institution of Pakistan has its own distinctive ethnically based elite with a claim to societywide support.

Pakistan, like its Afghan neighbor, is a plural but not a civil society. Its pluralism is based on diverse linguistic communities, a feudal land structure, and segmented tribes. But the more fundamental notions of pluralism—that there can be a civil society independent of the state, that elites at the top need not share the same outlook but must share support for an open, tolerant, competitive political process, and that elites do not regard their opponents as disloyal and unpatriotic—are not widely held. The result is a state with considerable coercive authority but, for much of its history, with little popular legitimacy; a country with strong institutions of the state (the military, the bureaucracy, and intelligence organizations) but weak institutions of society (political parties and interest groups); a country where redistribution means a shift in power and resources among elites rather than among social classes; a country where most people regard political life as corrupt and the private domain as virtuous and in need of protection against the state; a country where law is regarded by some as derived from the will of elected bodies and by others as derived from a body of religious doctrine that no ruler can change and that can only be interpreted by those who are experts in religious law.

IV

A comparison of the elites in these three countries reveals striking similarities as well as fundamental differences.[1] In Iran the Islamic elites, while turning to the masses for support, derive their views of what the state should do, not from the will of the people, but rather from the will of God as they interpret that will. In Afghanistan, too, the PDPA elites regarded their interventions in the economy and society as a response, not to popular demands, but rather to their own ideologies. And in Pakistan the military and bureaucratic elites' conception of what is essential for maintaining political order and national unity has often excluded any role for political parties. The concerns of the governing elites, therefore, have been to create institutions that would be able to impose their programs while giving the appearance of having popular support. In Iran the postrevolutionary clerical elite redesigned the state itself as a quasi-theocratic "Islamic republic" in which the highest position within the state was reserved for a supreme religious figure, a *faqih*. In Afghanistan the young Marxist Pashtun intellectuals who created the Democratic Republic of Afghanistan relied on the military, the KHAD (the intelligence apparatus), and the Soviet Army to pursue their transformative goals. And in Pakistan the military under Ayub Khan created a system of indirect elections to enable them to govern with the semblance of popular government but without the political parties.

In all three countries, governing elites have slighted the role of the population in the political realm. Pakistani military leaders were loath to see mass-based political parties and disliked adversarial politics, which they saw as threatening political order. They preferred local elections and systems of indirect representation that would keep the urban middle classes out of politics and prevent the emergence of political parties. General Ayub Khan, in particular, sought to persuade Pakistanis that government should be without politics, without a legislature, without political parties, and without elections. In Iran the clerical elites mobilized the masses against the shah, against the Americans, against the various leftist and liberal-nationalist groups, and against their Iraqi enemies, but their conception of governance has excluded a genuine participatory role in decision making by the masses. For them, "ultimate" sovereignty resides not in the people but in God and his laws, and hence all decisions and policies of the state—including those enacted into law by the legislature (the Islamic Consultative Assembly)—are potentially subject to veto by a clerically dominated Council of Guardians. In Afghanistan, legitimate authority in the pre-Communist regime was exercised by the monarch, khans, or local landlords and by the traditional assemblies of tribal elders (jirgah). For the Marxist-Leninist Afghan leaders, only the party and, by extension, the military exercised legitimate authority. As Anthony Arnold puts it (in Chapter 1), "A vanguard party was to lead an uneducated and perhaps even unwilling populace into a golden future by a way that only the party could perceive." Similarly, according to Olivier Roy, the ideal type of political power as defined by the various Afghan resistance leaders assumed that authority should be exercised by either local notables or an Islamic party organization.

This conception of an elite that is above rather than responsive to society is so deeply and widely held that it has persisted through many changes in the composition and the ideological orientation of the ruling elites. The urban intelligentsia that made up the Parchami faction of the PDPA was no less exclusionary than the rural-based Khalqi leadership that it displaced; in Iran the ulama have been no less exclusionary than the shah's elites; and in Pakistan both the military and the bureaucracy maintain a viceregal view of their role, even when a popularly elected government is in power. The alacrity with which the president dismissed Benazir Bhutto's government is a case in point.

In all three societies, elites have wrestled with the problem of establishing their own legitimacy. In Iran and Afghanistan the largely patrimonial systems of governance were replaced by regimes that sought to win legitimacy by mass mobilization and popular approval. The Afghan Communists pursued ideologically inspired reforms in opposition to popular sentiment, then reversed themselves by emphasizing the personal religious practices of the elite, by avoiding giving offense to public sentiments, and by showing respect for tribal norms, all in an effort to win public support against the mujahidin. Pakistan's military leaders, faced with growing pressures for political participation from party elites, sought legitimacy by emphasizing their attachment to Islamic ideals. Islamization became the ideological justification for military rule.

None of these strategies, successful as they have sometimes been at least for brief periods, entailed any significant element of power sharing or public accountability; on the contrary, they have often been aimed at forestalling political liberalization. Only in Pakistan can one see a gradual shift from a system of popular mobilization to one of popular participation since the elections of 1988. Of the three countries, only Pakistan has a history of participatory politics, elections, and political parties that provides the basis for a modicum of democratic politics. The ideal of liberal democracy has little support among Afghan elites, including the mujahidin, or among Iran's governing elite. In Pakistan the ideal of liberal democracy, though rejected by some as incompatible with Islamic institutions and thought, has the verbal support of most politicians; but this has not prevented sections of the political class from throwing their support to the military on several occasions in order to dislodge their political enemies from power or, when in power themselves, to repress their opponents.

The distrust—and fear—that elites have for one another is at the root of much of the violence and political volatility that has characterized all three countries. In Afghanistan not only the struggle between the mujahidin and the PDPA (later the Homeland Party, Hizb-i Watan) regime was violent, but within the PDPA itself the Parchami and the Khalqi factions were engaged in several devastating conflicts after coming to power jointly in 1978. Differences within the Peshawar-based mujahidin, and between them and those based in Iran, prevented them from presenting a unified front against the Kabul regime; the field commanders at times turned their arms against one another or against the Peshawar groups. Conflicts among the mujahidin continued after the fall of the Najibullah regime in April 1992. The two largest resistance parties, the Hizb-i Islami led by Gulbuddin Hekmatyar and the Jamiʿat-e Islami led by Burhanuddin Rabbani and Ahmad Shah Masud, turned their arms against one another, the former drawing support from among the country's Pashtuns, and the latter from among the Tajiks and Uzbeks.

In Iran the Islamic revolutionaries have turned their wrath not only against those who collaborated with the shah's government but also against those who supported the revolution: for example, the former prime minister, Mehdi Bazargan, his liberal-nationalist colleagues, such prominent clerical leaders as Kazem Shariatmadari and Hossein Ali Montazeri (both grand ayatollahs), the Islamic socialist mujahidin, and the secular Left. Indeed, what most threatens the present government is not a mass revolt but intense intraelite schisms that could prompt one faction within the ruling elite to purge another and to mobilize its mass supporters against dissidents within. Even in Pakistan, where elected parties rule and power has been transferred from one elected government to another, charges of "antinational" are hurled by the IDA against the PPP, while PPP Sindhi supporters and the Muhajir party, the Mujahir Qaumi Mahaz (MQM), once allies against the Zia regime, shoot each other in the streets of Karachi. In all three countries, levels of distrust are so high that competing factions within the governing elites may strike alliances with sections of the counterelites, mobilize popular support, arm their own militants, or turn to foreign powers to enhance their position against factions within the government.

The social and ideological bases of intraelite conflicts vary, of course, among the three countries. Ethnic divisions abound, especially in Afghanistan and Pakistan, where linguistic and tribal subelites vie for political power, but these divisions only partially explain the intensity of intraelite conflict and the low tolerance for opposition. As Olivier Roy points out, the Kabul Communist elites shared many of the same ethnic and socioeconomic characteristics as the Peshawar mujahidin. For that matter, Pakistan's major political parties are not neatly divided along regional or ethnic lines either. Competing visions of the future and of how one should use the state to achieve that vision are important features of intraelite conflict in all three countries, especially in Afghanistan and Iran, but even those with shared doctrinal beliefs have been known to take arms against one another. The high level of intolerance and the unwillingness of elites to acknowledge the value of their opponents may, of course, be related to deep-seated ethnic and ideological divisions, but it is just as likely that these divisions are so acute precisely because of the high level of elite intolerance. The distrust that ethnic groups feel toward one another, the clash of personal ambitions, the bitterness of those with conflicting doctrinal positions—all have a violent edge when elites do not share a consensual framework for the conduct of political discourse. Distrust was a conspicuous feature of elite behavior during the reign of the shah, Mohammad Daoud, and Zia ul-Haq, and so it remains, notwithstanding the changes in regime and in the composition and ideologies of the elites.

V

In our analysis of the role of the state in promoting social equity in Afghanistan, Iran, and Pakistan, we focus on the ideological environment within which state policies have taken shape, as well as on the contents, manner of implementation, and consequences of the policies in question. In the case of each country, furthermore, the impact of macroeconomic factors, at both domestic and international levels, has been considered in some detail.

The quest for social equity was a central concern of the new elites in the aftermath of the Afghan and the Iranian revolutions in the late 1970s. For Pakistan, on the other hand, redistribution and social equity have not been critical policy objectives since Zulfikar Ali Bhutto's government (1971–77). In all three societies, explicitly or implicitly, Islamic laws and traditions have set the terms of the discourse on social justice and equity, influencing both the types of policies pursued and the societal reactions to them.

In Afghanistan, as Barnett R. Rubin shows, the elimination of economic and social inequalities was at the top of the PDPA's Marxist-Leninist agenda of emancipating Afghan peasants and workers from the yoke of exploitation and establishing a classless society. Viewing the problem in highly doctrinaire and narrowly economic terms, the leaders of the first postcoup (Taraki-Amin) regime sought to end what they described as "feudal or prefeudal" relations of production in rural Afghanistan by eliminating the "class enemies" of the peasants—that is, landlords, tribal leaders, and their allies—as well as those traditional institutions and customs that they considered supportive of such relations.

In the Iranian revolution, social justice was one of the major areas of consensus within an otherwise diverse coalition of revolutionary forces. It figured prominently in Khomeini's militant vision of Islam—ultimately the hegemonic ideology of the revolution—which promised the disinherited masses (*mostazafan*) not only an end to their exploitation but also the restoration of their dignity and honor. Beyond social justice, therefore, the revolution was to usher in a new cultural order based on Islamic holy law (the Shariʿah) and traditions, not merely a new set of economic relations.

In Pakistan the composition, values, and interests of the elite have generally precluded the use of state power for the purpose of societal restructuring. And this, as David Gilmartin (1981, 1) has pointed out, has been in spite of the fact that "the movement for the creation of Pakistan was the first and perhaps the most successful of those twentieth-century Islamic movements that sought to bring about an Islamic transformation of the postcolonial state." For the most part, Pakistan's governing elites have wavered among Ayub Khan's efforts to protect the state from popular forces advocating an Islamic state, Zulfikar Ali Bhutto's rhetorical advocacy of Islamic socialism, and Zia ul-Haq's embrace of Islam as a legitimizing ideology for state power. The country's regional elites, particularly those who have led ethnic and regional parties, have been more concerned with regional autonomy than with a centralized Islamic state, and more concerned with the regional distribution of power and resources than with a redistribution of income and assets along class lines (see Amin 1988).

Aside from any differences in their content, the success or failure of particular state ideologies in each of these societies has been closely linked with the question of regime legitimacy. In Afghanistan the relation between the periphery and center has historically been fraught with ambivalence and mutual suspicion, and successive Afghan governments have learned to keep their intervention in the affairs of the countryside to a minimum. The typical Afghan peasant or tribesman is more likely to be suspicious of the government agent than he is the local mullah or khan. In the wake of the April 1978 coup, little or nothing was known about the tiny PDPA outside the secular intellectual circles and the politically active urban middle classes. Subsequently, the identification of the regime as dominated by the Communists and, by implication, as anti-Islamic and dependent on the Soviet Union marred its image. The Soviet invasion of December 1979, which helped replace the "ultraleftist" (as the Soviets characterized them) Khalqi faction with the more moderate Parchami faction of the party, and the active participation of the Afghan government in the brutal war against the Afghan resistance, further undermined the legitimacy of the regime in the eyes of most Afghans.

The PDPA's program of reform for Afghanistan was announced a few months after the April 1978 coup in a series of decrees by the Revolutionary Council. In rural areas, it consisted of a sweeping agrarian reform program, cancellation of peasants' debts to landlords and moneylenders, abolition of traditional marriage contracts involving a bride-price, and the establishment of voluntary cooperatives. As Rubin points out, had these reforms been fully implemented, they would have replaced the traditional relations of authority, patronage, and exchange in Afghanistan with a new relation of production in which nuclear-family-based productive units are linked through market relations under the tutelage of the state. In the cities, the reform included a concerted literacy and educational campaign, various measures to improve workers' wages and benefits, and expansion of educational and work opportunities for women. Resistance to the PDPA's radical reforms came from nearly every segment of the Afghan society, including the vast majority of peasants in whose name the government's rural program had been introduced. The resulting civil war eventually forced the regime to repeal or modify its revolutionary reform agenda and to bring it in line with the Afghan traditions, Islamic customs, and the local political realities—but not before tens of thousands of its citizens had already been killed, more than one-third of its population had become refugees in Pakistan and Iran, and much of the country had been decimated. In the interim, reform measures were used as vehicles for counterinsurgency, as tools for appeasing its opponents, or as incentives for winning new allies.

In Iran, too, the new revolutionary regime began with a series of drastic steps to fulfill its promise of social justice. But with the collapse of the old order, as Vahid F. Nowshirvani and Patrick Clawson point out, the largely unexamined ideological consensus on social justice began to break down. Sweeping changes in the legal-institutional foundations of the state, including its transformation from a constitutional monarchy to a quasi-theocratic "Islamic republic," were effected by fiat, coercion, or electoral procedures, but profound ideological differences surfaced once the new regime began to address the revolution's egalitarian goals. These differences occurred not only between the revolutionary elite and its political opponents on the Left, who for the most part pushed for more radical policies, but also within the elite itself. Islam, the sacred canopy that had unified a diverse coalition of political forces in the course of the revolution, was now subjected to conflicting interpretations and could not provide a coherent basis for a new socioeconomic order. The fundamental debate centered on the limits of state intervention in economic affairs, particularly when state actions violated the sanctity of private property and the freedom of contract. The specific policy questions on which these conflicting points of view focused included land reform, nationalization of foreign trade, and labor legislation. Though cast in theological terms, the positions taken on these issues often reflected the interests of major social groups as they were represented within the political elite itself.

Within six months after taking power, the regime nationalized privately owned banks, the insurance system, and heavy industries, as well as smaller industrial units that were owned by individuals linked to the Pahlavi regime or whose liabilities exceeded their net assets. Other economic assets—including small factories, commercial firms, hundreds of thousands of acres of agricultural land, and private residences and other urban real estate—were confiscated by orders of "revolutionary courts" or through the arbitrary actions of individuals or revolutionary committees (komitehs). Most of the confiscated properties were put under the control of the Foundation for the Oppressed (Bonyad-e Mostazafan), which had been established in 1979 to administer the expropriated property of members of the former royal family and of all persons who had acquired their wealth through their relations with that family, but this was later expanded. In 1982 the holdings of the foundation were listed as follows: "203 mining and manufacturing enterprises, 427 commercial farms, 101 construction companies, 238 trading and other service enterprises, and 2,786 real estate properties" (Behdad 1989). The major impact of this first wave of expropriations by the revolutionary regime "was not, therefore, to distribute wealth and economic opportunity more widely. It was, rather, to further fatten that already overfed leviathan—the government" (Bakhash 1984, 185). Much of the redistributed resources, however, went to the various parastatal "revolutionary organizations" that catered to the needs of the underprivileged groups, thereby bolstering the political base of the regime—a strategy that inevitably enhanced the popularity of the state as the patron of various newly mobilized groups. These included the Foundation for the Oppressed (Bonyad-e Mostazafan), the Martyr Foundation (Bonyad-e Shahid), the Housing Foundation (Bonyad-e Maskan), which helps to provide housing for the poor, and the Jihad for Reconstruction (Jahad-e Sazandegi).

The redistributive program of the Iranian regime, after this initial phase, proceeded through both legislation and the extension of administrative controls. After the establishment of the parliament (Islamic Consultative Assembly), the most important governmental redistribution efforts were directed at land reform and labor reform through legislation. As the chapters by Ashraf and by Nowshirvani and Clawson indicate, the passage of these reforms and other social reform legislation in Iran has involved intense debate, political rifts within the elite, jurisdictional fights among the various legislative and judicial organs of the state, the invocation of theological principles, and, while Khomeini was still alive, several critical interventions on his part. In the countryside, the Islamic regime has committed considerable material and human resources to rural development. The effects of this "rural bias" can already be seen in the relatively high rate of growth in the agricultural sector (4.7 percent per year in real terms between 1977 and 1987) over a period when other economic sectors were experiencing a decline, and in a steady improvement in the standard of living of rural households since the revolution.

Another distributive policy of the Iranian regime has been the rationing of basic necessities: allocation by special vouchers and various other methods of obtaining basic food items and selected consumer goods. The rationing has egalitarian effects, but it is particularly significant for alleviating the hardship of low-income families and for reducing regional and rural-urban disparities. It is also a method by which the government can selectively reward those organizations and groups on whose support it relies.

Compared with postrevolutionary Iran and Afghanistan, successive Pakistani regimes since independence have shown little interest in asset and income distribution. The civil bureaucracy supported the creation of a large public sector first in the 1960s, when the government created the Pakistan Industrial Development Corporation, which invested in the creation of public enterprises, and then in the mid-1970s, when the Bhutto government nationalized private enterprises. But neither this effort nor the various rural development programs initiated by the government had any significant redistributive effects. Indeed, as Shahid Javed Burki points out, some of these measures widened the rural-urban economic gap and increased disparities between the more prosperous provinces (Punjab and Sind) and the poor provinces (Baluchistan and the North-West Frontier). Zia ul-Haq's dismantling of many of Bhutto's socialist policies promoted the growth of the private sector and of the economy as a whole. Little attention, however, was given to the redistribution of resources to less developed regions or to the poor.

Burki identifies a number of distribution crises in Pakistan since its independence. These crises include income disparities between East and West Pakistan, the neglect of agriculture until the late 1960s, the neglect of the North-West Frontier and Baluchistan, the relative decline in the income and power of the Muhajirs, and discontent in rural Sind. Although each of these distribution crises has had political repercussions, in most instances the government did little to correct the imbalances, many of which were the results of its own policies. Some efforts were made to bring about asset redistribution: the award of abandoned property to some of the estimated six million refugees who entered the country following independence, the allocation of government lands to civil and military officers (a policy that exacerbated existing inequalities), and several land reform efforts that had limited impact. The largest asset redistribution was the nationalization under Zulfikar Ali Bhutto of thirty-two large-scale industries and a host of small and medium-size firms. The main effect of this nationalization policy was to enhance the power and resources of the state, rather than to alleviate poverty and improve income distribution. Later, the Islamic policies introduced by Zia ul-Haq—notably the introduction of *zakat* and *ushr* (wealth taxes)—had no significant distributive benefits. Little attention has been given by the government to fiscal and tax policies aimed at greater income distribution. More fundamentally, government expenditures on social services and on human resource development (primarily health care, primary schools, etc.) have been too meager to alleviate absolute poverty.

It is interesting to note that taxation, which is often considered to be the most direct policy instrument for achieving greater income equality, has not been used effectively by any of the three countries. All three countries have had a very low tax base over the years, and the situation has changed only marginally for Afghanistan and Iran since the late 1970s. In 1983, for example, the ratio of tax revenues to GDP was 8 percent for Afghanistan, 7 percent for Iran, and 17 percent for Pakistan; in the same year, the world average was 30.5 percent and the Third World average 20.4 percent.[2]

The capacity of both Afghanistan's and Iran's government to implement and continue their redistributive programs was limited seriously by economic factors well beyond their control. For Iran, the major economic factor was the precipitous decline in oil income, at first (1980–81) because of disruptions caused by the revolution and the war with Iraq, and later (in the mid-1980s) because of the glut in the world oil market. Consequently, as Nowshirvani and Clawson point out (in Chapter 6), "between 1977 and 1987, real GDP fell 23 percent, while population rose 37 percent; the result was that 1987 per capita real GDP was just about one-half of the 1977 level." Another huge economic burden for the government was the eight-year (1980–88) war with Iraq. The war exacted an enormous toll in human life and suffering, and the physical destruction of hundreds of villages and several cities will have long-term economic consequences for the country. Nowshirvani and Clawson, however, believe that the economic consequences of the war have so far been less significant than the decline in oil revenues.

Considerable foreign resources have flowed into Pakistan, mainly from individual Pakistanis abroad, but because remittances were not taxed, the flow has had little impact on government revenues. Moreover, much of the foreign assistance has gone, directly or indirectly, into the acquisition of arms. Indeed, a very considerable proportion of the Pakistan budget has gone into defense, in some years exceeding 50 percent of the national government's expenditures.

For both Afghanistan and Iran, the economic disturbances resulting from war, civil conflict, and a reduction in revenues from oil have significantly reduced the *absolute* level of income and standards of living for nearly all classes of the population. It is within this context of declining GDP that we have examined the relative distribution of assets and income and other resources in these societies.

In Iran the principal outcome of redistributive policies has been a far greater control by the state over the society's productive capacities. As Nowshirvani and Clawson point out, within the manufacturing sector, "by 1984, about one thousand publicly owned and managed industrial units (excluding those in the oil sector) employed 430,000 of the 530,000 workers in establishments with ten or more employees and produced 73.5 percent of the value added. In that year 90 percent of the manufacturing firms employing over five hundred workers were in government hands."

Changes in income distribution are somewhat different for urban and rural areas. In urban areas, income inequalities were reduced in the first two years after the revolution (1979–81) but then moved in the direction of greater inequality. This can be seen in the overall measure of inequality: the Gini coefficient declined from 0.4998 in 1977 to 0.4040 in 1980, and to 0.4205 in 1984. In the rural areas, the Gini coefficient showed an initial improvement in the distribution of household expenditures, from 0.4789 in 1979 to 0.4051 in 1982, but then moved in the direction of greater inequality, 0.4293 in 1984.

In Pakistan, the country's substantial economic growth since 1947 notwithstanding, there has been little "trickling down" to the poor. Consequently, although Pakistan's GDP today is equal to that of many middle-income countries—on a variety of social indexes, such as life expectancy, infant mortality, and literacy—the country is much like the other low-income countries of South Asia. There has been, Burki writes, some improvement since the mid-1970s, but it is almost entirely owing to remittances from workers who have migrated to the Middle East. In general, those who have reaped the financial benefits of state policies have been members of the military and the bureaucracy, landowners (especially an estimated five thousand landed families, including such well-known political families as the Bhuttos, Qureshis, Gardezis, Noons, Kuros, Jatois, Soomros, Tiwanas, etc.), the Punjabi, urban Sindhis, some industrial families (the Saigols, Habibs, Adamjees, Sheiks, Fancys, and Dawoods), some religious communities (Bohra Muslims, Khoja Ismailis), and castes (Memons). Most of the country's leading political figures—such as Benazir Bhutto, Nawaz Sharif, Mohammed Khan Junejo—and senior bureaucrats come from well-off landlord and business families. Military officers of lesser means are often able to improve their income substantially by taking important positions in nationalized corporations, such as fertilizer factories, the airlines, and steel. Power and wealth are inextricably linked in Pakistan, the one leading to or, in some instances, derivative of the other.

VI

Unlike the contemporary West, where much of the debate about the status of women has centered on questions of parity and socioeconomic equality between the sexes, the "woman question" in Afghanistan, Iran, and Pakistan has been inextricably bound with deep religious sentiments and cultural mores, a highly ambivalent stance toward modernity, and, above all, patriarchal norms that justify the seclusion of women and their subordination both within and outside the family sphere. As a result, in the past several decades, reformist policies toward women have often been met with strong resistance and moral condemnation, leading to vacillations between periods of relative progress, on the one hand, and of retrenchment, if not reversal, on the other. The final four chapters in this volume analyze the socioeconomic context, ideological framework, and consequences of policies toward women since the late 1970s in Afghanistan (Micheline Centlivres-Demont), in postrevolutionary Iran (Valentine Moghadam and Afsaneh Najmabadi), and in Pakistan (Anita Weiss).

In all three societies, prior to the upheavals of the late 1970s, measures intended to promote the participation of women in public life and to achieve greater sexual equality were part of modernization programs pursued by their governments. Initiated almost invariably from the top and supported by the intelligentsia and other members of the nascent modern middle classes, these measures were often opposed vehemently by the conservative Islamic clerics and their allies among the traditional middle and lower middle classes on the grounds that they were anti-Islamic and would undermine the moral foundation of the society. With the revival and politicization of Islam in the late 1960s and early 1970s, opposition to women's emancipation—particularly with respect to such symbolic issues as dress, lifestyle, and public behavior—has come not only from religious leaders and the more traditional segments of these societies but also from many young, educated, and urban-based Islamic activists. Among the latter groups, such opposition has been voiced as a form of resistance against Western "cultural imperialism," whose many pernicious effects are believed to include the degradation and corruption of women. Analyzing the contents and the symbolic language of Iran's revolutionary Islamic ideology regarding women, Najmabadi (Chapter 9) rejects the oft-cited reference to the new elite's vision as a "revitalization of an eternal ahistorical Islam, implementing edicts *a*, *b*, and *c* about women," and instead sees Iranian policy as the expression of a fundamentally new, postcolonial amalgam of secular and religious elements that spurns all previous secular ideologies of emancipation and equality in favor of an authentic Islamic sensibility.

Over the past decade, the three regimes have followed distinctly different strategies in dealing with the question of women. Of the three, the course taken by the Afghan regime, particularly in the immediate aftermath of the Saur Revolution, was the most radical and, ultimately, the most disastrous. The core of the new regime's reforms affecting women, as summarized by Centlivres-Demont, was contained in the six articles of Decree Number 7, which was announced by the regime in October of 1978. Among other things, the decree sought "to do away with unjust, patriarchal, and feudal relations between husband and wife and to consolidate sincere family ties." Its provisions included setting an upper limit (three hundred afghanis) on the monetary gift (*mahr*) offered by the groom's family to the bride, establishing a minimum age for marriage for both men and women (eighteen and sixteen, respectively), and abolishing arranged marriages. A parallel decree provided the legal basis for initiating a universal literacy campaign that promised to make all Afghans, including females of all ages, literate in the course of a single year. Although each of these goals may seem laudably progressive from the perspective of an outsider, to the overwhelming majority of Afghan men—and women—they represented an unwarranted intervention by the state in domains that could only be ruled by long-standing cultural mores, customs, and Islamic traditions.

The alien ideological rhetoric with which these programs were imbued, the haste with which they were formulated, and the zealotry with which the local officials attempted to implement them led to a massive resistance among large segments of Afghan society, particularly in the rural areas. Initially impervious to this resistance, the Khalqi leaders of the PDPA continued their campaign with relentless vigor and brutality for more than a year, until they were overthrown in December of 1979 by the more pragmatic Parchami wing of their party, which was put in power by the Soviet army. As Centlivres-Demont points out (in Chapter 8), the "women policies" of the new, Soviet-backed regime, months before the onset of the civil war that followed the Soviet occupation in December of 1979, were among the chief reasons tens of thousands of Afghans fled to Pakistan, where they believed they could "protect the honor of their women and daughters." As originally conceived, then, the campaign failed to produce any tangible improvement in the lives of the Afghan women, particularly in the countryside, where the overwhelming majority of them lived. In subsequent years a far less ambitious set of reform policies has been pursued by the regime, focusing mainly on adult literacy, compulsory education, technical training, and greater access to higher education and public-sector employment for women. Success of these policies has been limited to the urban areas under the Kabul government's control. Centlivres-Demont offers a review of many of these programs and their limited achievements. The final section of her chapter is devoted to an analysis of Afghan refugee women in Pakistan, where they face extreme hardships because of the overcrowded living quarters, economic idleness among the men, forced propinquity with other families with whom they share no kinship ties, and various other restrictive conditions.

In her analysis of the impact of state policies on women in Pakistan, Anita Weiss examines changes in the country's legal structure and its social and economic policies. In 1986 Pakistan had 47.3 million women and 51.9 million men, a sex ratio of 111 males for every 100 females. Life expectancy for women has improved more slowly than in other developing countries; literacy levels remain low (16 percent for women, 35 percent for men); less than a third of all school-age girls attend primary school; and, not surprisingly, fertility rates remain high, giving Pakistan one of the world's highest population growth rates (3.1 percent). Changes in state policies toward women in Pakistan are inextricably linked to the broader issues of Islamization. Quaid-i Azam Muhammad Ali Jinnah, Liaqat Ali Khan (Pakistan's first prime minister), Ayub Khan, and Zulfiqar Ali Bhutto, all Islamic modernists, supported legal reforms providing women with increased rights (involving inheritance, property, divorce, political representation). It was under General Zia ul-Haq's Islamization program that the government of Pakistan introduced a penal code that restricted women's rights. Indeed, much of the debate over Islamization centered around women's rights issues—how women were to dress, whether the state should enforce Muslim personal law, whether the testimony of women in court should count for half of that of men, and whether women should be confined to their homes. With the passage of the Shariʿah Bill in April of 1991, many of the liberal reforms that were enacted earlier seem destined for reversal.

Why the "woman question" has become the centerpiece of Islamic political discourse is the issue explored by Afsaneh Najmabadi. In the 1960s' debates on the pernicious economic, political, and cultural impact of the West on Iran, the Westernized (gharbzadeh) woman was seen as the embodiment of social ills: "She was a superconsumer of imperialist, dependent-capitalist, foreign goods; she was a propagator of the corrupt culture of the West; she was undermining the moral fabric of society; she was a parasite, beyond any type of redemption" (Najmabadi, in Chapter 9). Iranian women—how they dressed, how they walked, how they spoke, their very gestures, their mingling with men—had become, in the eyes of Iranian clerics, purveyors of Western cultural imperialism. "Westoxication" (gharbzadegi) was the enemy of the Islamic revolution. The imposition of the veil by the state was thus not a marginal issue for Islamic militants but a centerpiece in the creation of a new Islamic society. Among the earliest acts of the Khomeini government was the reversal of many legal rights that women had acquired under the Pahlavi regime. The state restricted the kind of employment women could hold in order to restrict contact between men and women. Islamic morality, as understood by the clerics and their followers, required that the state interpose itself between the sexes and redefine literally the space within which women could live their lives.

The above emphasis on the impact of state policies on women should not lead to an exaggerated view of the state's capacity to effect change in this arena. Quite aside from the usual limitations on the state's reach and resources, at least two other factors have tended to mitigate state action. The first has to do with the contradiction between the imperatives of economic expansion and modernization, on the one hand, and the exclusion of women from the public sphere, on the other. Although inequalities abound, the education of women has moved forward, even in Iran, as Valentine Moghadam points out; and the exigencies of war have influenced the place of women in the labor force in both Iran and Afghanistan. The second factor is the active resistance by women themselves, which is expressed more in symbolic than in institutionalized forms.

VII

In all three societies the efforts of governing elites to restructure economic and political institutions must be understood in the context of their legitimacy problems, the persistent tension between local and

central authorities, and—to look forward—the way in which developments in one country and other parts of the region affect developments
in the other two.

In all three countries, elites have looked for ways to legitimize their
authority. Legitimacy in this context has a double meaning: first,
whether elites in and out of power believe that those who have power
have the right to rule and, second, whether the remainder of the society—the "masses"—share that view. Iran's clerical leaders, for example,
are concerned not only with the effectiveness of the income distribution
programs but also with whether these programs can be presented and
justified within an Islamic framework before the masses. From this
perspective, the redistribution policies—and rhetoric—of the Iranian
government contributed to its legitimacy, even though in reality the
result was declining incomes. Suffering does not make for illegitimacy
so long as it is for a righteous cause and is, or appears to be, equitable.
On the other hand, the revolutionary restructuring program pursued
by the Communist leadership in Afghanistan did not enhance their
legitimacy. Indeed, those who might have benefited from the reforms
were among the most disgruntled; the only satisfied beneficiaries were
members of the secular, urban middle class, and their numbers have
been too small to sustain the regime in its present form. Again, whether
programs were effective proved to be less important than whether they
conformed to indigenous traditions and shared moral norms. In the
case of Pakistan, the government has had no explicit commitment to
redistribution, and its emphasis on growth and development, while
yielding considerable improvement in the overall state of the economy,
has done little to contribute to the regime's legitimacy, for the policies
have not addressed the larger issues of power sharing among the
country's ethnic groups, of state-center relations, and of creating procedures and institutions for governance on which the elite could agree.
Even the issue of women in all three countries must be understood in
the broader context of the legitimacy debate. Whereas in the West the
women's issue is largely seen in the framework of social justice and
equity, in all three countries discussed here the women's issue is part of
a different discourse involving Westernization, modernization, and
secularism.

Of the three countries, Iran has been the most successful in having
an elite with some shared notions of how authority should be structured and of what constitutes a moral order. Whether it be the women's
issue, notions of social justice, a conception of what constitutes the
country's cultural heritage, or what the relation ought to be between

central and local authorities, there is more agreement within the Iranian elite than among the elites of Pakistan or Afghanistan.

For Pakistan and Afghanistan, the divisions among elites over how the country should be governed are particularly acute, especially on the question of the relation between central and local authorities. In Pakistan, "local" has meant tribes, pirs, ulama, provinces, linguistic communities, and local powerful families. The center, controlled for much of Pakistan's history by the military and always with the support of the bureaucracy, has maintained control over the territory, but all too often it has resorted to massive force to keep control—unsuccessfully in the case of East Pakistan, more effectively in the case of Baluchistan, and now problematically in much of urban Sind and in portions of the Frontier. For its elite, and for financial and popular support, the center has depended primarily on the Punjab. When the center has been controlled by non-Punjabis, it has not held. However, when Punjabi elites have been in control, they have failed to win support from non-Punjabi elites, thus rendering the country unstable. Whatever institutional arrangement has been tried has lacked legitimacy in some powerful quarter, and whatever regional elites have held power have not had their legitimacy recognized by those who are not in power. Two popularly elected governments with Sindhi prime ministers failed for lack of adequate support from both military and Punjabi elites. The tenure of Nawaz Sharif, the first popularly elected Punjabi prime minister, also proved to be brief, for in mid-1993, after less than three years in office, he was dismissed by the President. Benazir Bhutto was elected prime minister in October to head another precarious government.

In Afghanistan, "local" has meant traditional tribal notables and landowners, and now includes the new local commanders. Their capacity to resist the center is legendary, in part because the resources of the center are so limited. Rural Afghans are dependent on local, not national, leaders, and local leaders have successfully turned to outsiders for support. Whatever central authority emerges from the conflict among the various factions following the fall of the Communist government, one should expect continued tension between the central authority and a variety of armed local forces. The issue of governance is thus reduced to its most elementary level: Who will run the schools, the medical services, repair the roads and canals, and administer justice?

In addition to the many uncertainties about the future of the regimes in Iran, Pakistan, and Afghanistan is the prospect of autonomy-seeking movements in the Caucasus and Central Asia. The major ethnic groups in these regions have their ethnic kinfolk across the borders.

Persian-speaking Tajiks, constituting 59 percent of the Republic of Tajikistan (population 5.1 million), number 3.5 million in Afghanistan. The Turkic-speaking Uzbeks (the largest of the Muslim groups in Central Asia), Turkomans, and Kirghiz have ties with their Sunni kinspeople in Afghanistan. Azerbaijanis are linked to the Shiᶜite Azerbaijanis across the border in Iran. What will be the political consequences of the emergence of new Muslim majority states in the Caucasus and Central Asia for Iran and Afghanistan? Will Azerbaijanis in Iran and the Republic of Azerbaijan build cultural and political links that will shape the relations between Iran's Azerbaijanis and the central government? Will ethnic groups in a fragmented Afghanistan provide support to their ethnic and religious counterparts in Central Asia, particularly in Tajikistan and Uzbekistan? To whom will the various minorities in all of these countries turn for support? The possible scenarios are too numerous to contemplate. But two points are worth making. The first is that in each of these countries ethnic groups that strike out for greater autonomy or secession will look for allies. The ally may be a neighboring state, ethnic kinspeople across the international border, other secessionist groups, or distant powers. Weak groups will try to increase their strength by internationalizing their struggle. Therefore, each state in the region has a keen concern that neighboring states keep their ethnic groups under control and that there not be "interference" in their own internal conflicts. The second point is that the entire region is awash with arms, including billions of dollars worth of arms that are in Afghanistan and could be traded in through private arms dealers. These arms are now readily available throughout Pakistan (which is why the Sindhi-Muhajir conflict has become so violent), and it will be difficult for authorities in Iran and the former Soviet Central Asian republics to keep them out should an underground market develop.

The confrontation between elites and counterelites that has taken such a bitter and violent turn in the past seems unlikely to abate. Moreover, elites and counterelites have often turned to outsiders for support, or turned against outsiders as a means of mobilizing popular support against their opponents. Thus, in Afghanistan both branches of the PDPA turned to the Soviets for support, while the mujahidin obtained economic and military assistance from the United States, Pakistan, China, and Saudi Arabia. In Iran, militant groups played against the United States and its regional allies (Israel, Saudi Arabia, and Egypt) as a means of undermining more-moderate elements. And in Pakistan the power of the military has been enhanced by their success in soliciting economic and military assistance from the United States. In all three societies, elites are strongly disposed to blame outsiders for failure and to define their identity and seek cohesion in opposition to their enemies.

The issues that have violently torn these three countries are ones that touch the recesses of deeply held personal beliefs: Who has the right to govern? Which identities and loyalties most matter? What is the cultural heritage, how can it be sustained, and does it provide a framework for the future? And, above all, what should be the role of the state in shaping that future? The debates, more than ever before, spill across the borders not only east and west, but now to the north as well.

Notes

1. For these comparisons, we are particularly grateful to Professors Tony Smith and Marvin G. Weinbaum for the discussion papers they presented at the workshop on elites in Afghanistan, Iran, and Pakistan.

2. These figures are drawn from a discussion paper prepared for the present project by Patrick Clawson.

PART ONE

Political Elites and the Restructuring
of the Political Order

1

The Ephemeral Elite
The Failure of Socialist Afghanistan

ANTHONY ARNOLD

> I will note that the social bastions taken by the
> people's democratic government have not, perhaps,
> been expanded or even firmly established.
>
> —Soviet writer Lyudmila Shchipakhina,
> "Motherland Meets Its Sons"

Would-be rulers of mountain nations rarely have an easy time of it. The steeper the terrain, the more difficult is the imposition of central authority. Loyalties tend to be local, restricted to the family and the village, and the voice of higher government is rarely heard and even more rarely heeded. Even in modernized alpine societies, such as Switzerland, the heritage of local independence lives on in the cantonal system and the citizenry's deep-rooted individualism.

In Afghanistan, where communications are yet to be modernized, the gulf between state and society is infinitely broader. The country basically consists of some twenty-three thousand village states, traditionally self-governing and largely self-sufficient. In addition, there are a few provincial headquarter towns and one capital city, Kabul, that marches to a different drum. Before 1978 and again under the communists, the government representative in the village lived in a separate house, dressed differently, spoke in his own vernacular, and often communicated with the citizenry only via one village-designated individual. "The relationship between the peasantry and the state official is characterized by a profound and mutual contempt" (Roy 1986, 10).

35

Thus, the term "elite" in the Afghan context does not carry the same connotations that the word implies in less unruly societies. The Marxist-Leninist Afghan leaders indeed considered themselves an elite, but that perception was not shared by the vast majority of those over whom they wished to exercise power. Therefore, most of the chapter that follows deals more with the former Kabul government's intentions than its accomplishments, more with failures in restructuring than with successes.

Another peculiarity of Afghanistan is its ethnic makeup. Until the breakup of the Soviet Union, four of the most prominent ethnic groups—the Pashtuns (about 45 percent of the Afghan population), the Uzbeks (about 10 percent), Turkomans (about 2 percent), and Baluch (less than 2 percent)[1]—were in the strange position of having most of their ethnic kin live across various contiguous borders, where each constituted an ethnic minority in its country of residence: there were more Pashtuns in Punjabi-dominated Pakistan, more Baluch in Pakistan and Iran together, and more Uzbeks and Turkomans in the Russian-dominated former Soviet Union than could be found in Afghanistan. True, the Afghan Tajiks (30 percent) outnumbered Soviet Tajiks, but only the Hazaras (about 7.5 percent) were contained more or less within Afghanistan's borders. Ironically, these only "pure" Afghans have traditionally occupied the lowest rung on the Afghan social ladder.

At the top of that same ladder, again according to tradition, are the Pashtuns. They consider themselves the only true Afghans and have ruled the country almost uninterruptedly since the middle of the eighteenth century, when the modern Afghan state was born, until 1992. Until the Communist coup of 1978, the Mohammadzai family within the Durrani Pashtuns provided Afghanistan's rulers; thereafter, under the Communists, there were three Ghilzai Pashtuns (Taraki, Amin, and Najibullah) and one self-proclaimed Pashtun (Babrak) of unknown ethnic parentage.[2] Only in 1992 did a Tajik leader, Burhanhuddin Rabbani, become president of a shaky post-Communist coalition government.

With the Mohammadzais, rule was indeed a family enterprise, with most levers of power in the hands of trusted relatives. The circle was kept ingrown by the tradition of first cousins marrying first cousins, sometimes an entire generation intermarrying within the family. This did not prevent intrafamily rivalries and the rather frequent violent overthrow of one Mohammadzai in favor of another. Except for Abdur Rahman Khan, who died peacefully in bed in 1901 after two decades of savagely disciplining his subjects, all pre-Communist

Afghan rulers in the twentieth century were either assassinated or violently deposed. Only two out of six survived their departure from office.

The tradition did not die with the Mohammadzais. Of the Communist era leaders, two were murdered, one is reportedly in exile in the USSR, and the last vanished from public view when the regime fell in 1992.

This should not be taken to mean that the average Afghan is politically volatile. On the contrary, Afghans are extremely conservative. Until President Najibullah was deposed in 1992, only King Amanullah (1919–29) had been chased from office by popular unrest; others had been deposed by various coups d'état in which most citizens took neither part nor interest. The Communist regime made history when it fell to full-scale revolution. Until the coming of the Communists, the attitude of most Afghans toward Kabul politics could be summed up in a single word, *padshahgardi* (the king game) (Roy 1986, 11).

Pre-Saur, 1965–1978

Nevertheless, the closing decades of Mohammadzai rule saw a well-meaning effort by King Zahir to diffuse power outside the family. Under his attempt at constitutional monarchy (1964–73), members of the royal family were supposed to be excluded from all important legislative, executive, and judicial posts in the government. Instead, power was to pass gradually into the hands of political parties, with the throne to lose its political significance over time. Because this reform remained largely theoretical (e.g., the king never signed into law his own proposal for legalizing political parties), he has been accused, perhaps unfairly, of hypocrisy. It seems at least as probable that he simply did not have the political strength to abolish his relatives' privileges.

Zahir's failure to legalize political opposition acted as a brake on the development of democratic parties, but it did not prevent the formation of the People's Democratic Party of Afghanistan (PDPA), which dated its formal founding to 1 January 1965. It is indicative of Afghan values that the PDPA came into being more than forty years after the next youngest Communist party in a state bordering the USSR, that of Norway (1923).

From the outset, the party was divided into two basic wings that remained locked in bitter factional struggle until the party dissolved: Parcham (Banner), which found its multiethnic support among the offspring of the small urban middle class of white-collar workers and intellectuals in Kabul, and the almost purely Pashtun Khalq (People) faction, representing the rural intelligentsia. At first, both factions focused their recruiting activity on the tiny artistic-intellectual community, on media specialists, and especially on the academic establishment, including both teachers and students.

Among students targeted for recruitment, the concentration was on Kabul's secondary school system, Kabul University, and particularly teachers' training establishments. Inasmuch as secondary education was divided into day schools catering to local residents and boarding schools that educated out-of-towners, the factional split was maintained and intensified by concentrating the Parcham and Khalq student constituencies in separate institutions. The factional rivalry thus became mingled with interschool rivalries.

In spite of the internal split, the party contributed significantly to the political turmoil during the birth pains (and premature death) of political democracy in Afghanistan. Nevertheless, it would be a mistake to exaggerate the numerical strength of the fledgling PDPA at this early stage. By 1973, after eight years of recruiting, both factions—by now split into distinct parties—had attracted at most a few hundred members each, less in total than the pro-Maoist Shu'lah-ye Javid. Although many nonmember students were sympathetic to one or the other Communist group, their allegiances could be best likened to those of American students toward their alma maters' football teams: vociferous, superficially passionate, sometimes illegally active, but with minimal intellectual underpinning (from interviews I conducted with Afghan émigrés, 1982; see also Arnold 1983, ch. 3; Klass 1987, 142).

The recruitment policies of Parcham and Khalq are indicative of their political intentions at various stages. From 1965 to 1973, during the final years of the monarchy, both focused their attention on long-range molders of public opinion: media figures and teachers. At this stage, the aim was to influence generations of students and to infiltrate the Afghan bureaucracy over a long period of time; the actual seizure of power was a distant goal, to be approached with patience and circumspection. Although during this time both Parcham and Khalq gained a few military officer adherents (a priority target group if either had been contemplating any immediate radical action), these appear to have been handled very gingerly and clandestinely.

The situation changed in 1973, when Mohammad Daoud, aided by the Parchamis, overthrew the monarchy and proclaimed a republic. At first, the Parchamis' privileged position led them to recruit aggressively, but within a few months Daoud let it be known that this activity was not to his liking, and for the next several years Parcham marked time. The Khalqis, however, continued to recruit and by 1978 enjoyed a three-to-one numerical advantage over the Parchamis. More ominously, the Khalqis were focusing their attention on the Afghan military (Arnold 1983, 47).

Although Daoud had come to power with the aid of the Parchamis, he proceeded to eliminate them one by one from his inner councils. By 1977, virtually all had been fired, sent into diplomatic exile, or shifted to positions of minimal influence. Meanwhile, Daoud had also begun edging Afghanistan cautiously away from the Soviet orbit, mending his relations with Pakistan, and actively seeking help from the wealthier members of the Islamic world. He also moved toward internal democratization by promulgating a constitution that provided for eventual establishment of a multiparty system.

Despite the changes that Daoud was trying to engineer, he left the basic political and social structures of Afghanistan intact. A first cousin and brother-in-law of the king he had deposed, he at first kept his distance from promonarchy branches of his clan, the Mohammadzai family. After easing out his Parchami supporters, however, he made up his differences with estranged family members and returned them to the positions of power and influence to which they were accustomed.

None of these external and internal developments was welcome in Moscow.

By 1975, Daoud's intentions had become clear to all. The following year, a temporary reconciliation between Parcham and Khalq was engineered with the aid of the Communist Party of the Soviet Union (CPSU). It soon collapsed in bitter mutual recriminations, but in July 1977 a second effort to merge the two parties, also arranged by the CPSU, was more successful. Less than a year later, in late April 1978, the "Great Saur Revolution"—a coup d'état by Afghan military officers acting on the instructions of the Khalqi Hafizullah Amin—saw the birth of the Democratic Republic of Afghanistan (DRA) and swept Mohammad Daoud and most of his family into history.

Khalqi Rule, 1978–1979

The fragile Parcham-Khalq coalition patched together in 1977 was reflected in the careful alternation between Khalqis and Parchamis in the pecking order of DRA ministers published in May 1978. This balance, however, survived less than two months. By late June, the leading Parchamis were being shipped off into diplomatic exile, while their lower-ranking followers were being hounded from power by the triumphant Khalqis.[3] Later that summer a Parchami coup attempt, possibly Soviet-backed, was detected and thwarted by the Khalqis, who then persecuted their remaining unhappy rivals with renewed vigor. Parchami ambassadors were recalled and, when they refused to obey, were expelled from the PDPA (Arnold 1983, 64–73). They then vanished into Eastern European exile, to reappear on the coattails of the invading Soviet armies at the end of 1979.

The Khalqi victory was a recipe for political disaster, and the Soviets must have known it. Although enjoying a 75 percent majority in the party, the Khalqis were such embarrassingly doctrinaire Marxist-Leninists that they could not fail to alienate the profoundly conservative and individualist Afghan citizenry. Moreover, the PDPA itself, a tiny minority of the population even when united, was reduced in size by the loss of Parchamis. According to official Afghan statistics, the party numbered fifteen thousand at the time of the Saur coup (*World Marxist Review*, Jan. 1988, 37), or about 0.1 percent of the population.[4]

Despite its numerical weakness, the PDPA under Taraki rushed forward with a series of decrees designed to shake the social structure of Afghanistan to its roots. The first three of these, promulgated in May 1978, when the Parchamis were still a political factor, were relatively innocuous. They named Taraki president and Babrak vice-president, abolished Daoud's constitution, and established a new civilian and military court system. For most Afghans this was business-as-usual *padshahgardi*.

Decree Number 4, however, which followed on 12 June, was literally a red rag to the Afghan people. It established the Afghan national banner as a bloodred clone of the Soviet flag. This was also the first decree that was not preceded by the customary Islamic invocation. When the new banner was finally unveiled in October, it produced a groundswell of popular discontent.

Decree Number 5, which took away citizenship from twenty-three surviving Mohammadzais, was probably a relatively minor matter to most Afghans, but Decrees 6 (12 July), 7 (17 October), and 8 (28 November) struck at the core of Afghan society.

Number 6 canceled debts and mortgages owed by smallholders and landless peasants to the larger landowners, but it failed to provide the goods and services that the wealthy had always tendered to the poor as a matter of course, including seed, fertilizer, and the use of agricultural equipment.

Number 7 gave equal rights to women and abolished the bride-price, whereby a groom's family paid a bride's family a negotiated sum for the union. Although this traditional practice lent a more commercial than romantic aura to matrimony, it served a valuable social function: a stipulated part of the money always went directly to the bride and constituted an untouchable reserve on which she could draw in case the marriage ended in divorce.

Number 8 promised land reform. Unlike earlier land reform programs planned by Daoud, the PDPA sought to confiscate and redistribute lands without reimbursing their previous owners. In Afghan eyes this was tantamount to accepting stolen property, and it was vigorously resisted. The accompanying official propaganda in favor of collective farms was greeted with uncompromising hostility by most Afghan farmers.

Although not the subject of a specific decree, traditional Islam was a main target of the new government. By word and deed, the PDPA made no secret of its hostility to the religious establishment.

Accustomed as they were to ignoring Kabul's bombast, the Afghan people would not necessarily have been upset by the decrees and propaganda if the government had not made the mistake of trying to carry them out. Party activists, accompanied by armed military detachments, went into the countryside to enforce the new order. Respected elders and mullahs were rounded up and sent away to unknown fates or, in some cases, executed locally. What had been an acceptable seizure of power was transformed into an unacceptable imposition of Kabul's authority and a violation of age-old Afghan values. In short, the widely proclaimed "revolution" turned out to be real, not the simple coup that most Afghans had assumed but a revolution from above.

Before many weeks had passed, popular resentment had become resistance, and resistance rebellion. Though at first disorganized, sporadic, and on a small scale, armed opposition to Kabul's rule spread from the summer of 1978 until the Soviet invasion of December 1979. Contrary to Soviet allegations, it was neither financed nor encouraged from abroad to any significant degree but was a spontaneous, self-propelled movement reflecting popular outrage against Kabul's intended ends and the means it was using to attain them.

According to a candid assessment in 1988 by Habib Mangal, a Central Committee member and first deputy chairman of the National Front, the primary mistake under the Khalqis was trying to implement land and water reform too hastily. A second error was that "things were carried too far in relation to believers and religious figures," a euphemism for religious persecution. Last, he cautiously backed away from equal rights for women by saying that coeducation in literacy classes had been "intolerable interference in the affairs of Afghan families" (Kholin 1988).

During the period of Khalqi rule, the PDPA probably posted membership gains in the early months. Thereafter, however, a combination of intraparty purges and popular resentment against the party's excesses resulted in a membership that probably grew little, if any. A January 1979 claim that the PDPA had fifty thousand members can be safely discounted.

Although the total membership held static during Khalqi rule, its composition undoubtedly changed. Not only were Parchamis purged, but the violence-prone Khalqis tried to impose "socialism" with the knout. Whereas left-wing politics had once been largely the preserve of intellectuals (Nur Mohammed Taraki, a poet, was typical of the early breed), it now became a promising field for the ambitious, the unscrupulous, and the vicious. The successive waves of terror that swept over the country in 1978–79 (between fifty thousand and one hundred thousand people vanished during this period) not only struck at real and imaginary sources of opposition among the people but also had a callousing effect on the party itself.[5]

The terror was implemented by military detachments under party command, by police (Sarandoy) groups, and by two successive security services, AGSA (Da Afghanistan da Gato da Satalo Adara [Afghan Interests Protection Agency]) and KAM (Kargar-e Astekhbarat-e Muassessa [Workers' Intelligence Institute]). For this era, no figures have been released on the percentage of PDPA members belonging to such punitive groups or on the percentage within such groups belonging to the PDPA. It is safe to assume, however, that the relative weight of security force personnel in the party climbed sharply throughout the tenure of the Khalqi administration and came to be a dominant factor in it.[6]

The policies pursued by Khalqis were classic Marxism-Leninism: a vanguard party was to lead an uneducated and perhaps even unwilling populace into a golden future by a way that only the party could perceive. As Hafizullah Amin said, it might have required "not only years but centuries" for a socialist revolution to occur spontaneously (*Kabul Times*, 15 Mar. 1979, 2). Even building popular prerevolutionary support for the PDPA might take thirty years; better to "seize power first and then build their base" (*International Herald Tribune*, 13 Mar. 1979, 2).

But the vanguard only succeeded in distancing itself ever further from an alienated and hostile population. By December 1979, the Khalqi elite was all but isolated from the people. About half the 1978 army officer corps of eight thousand had evaporated, and the government was fast losing control.

It was then that Moscow launched its seventy-thousand-man surprise attack, occupying the main strategic points, killing Amin, and installing Parchami chief Babrak Karmal as its viceroy.

The Parchamis' Return, 1980–1981

Following its military invasion of December 1979, the USSR faced several politico-ideological dilemmas in forcibly returning the Parchamis to power. On the one hand, the Parchami minority in the PDPA had of course shrunk while the faction was being persecuted under Taraki and Amin; there were simply too few of them to run the country by themselves, especially because they had been all but eliminated from the vital military, police, and security services. This meant that in addition to Soviet advisers, as many Khalqis as possible had to be kept on in the new government, despite their unpopularity with the people and the inevitability of continued feuding between the factions. At the same time, the Khalqis could not be permitted to maintain their monopoly over all the guns in the new regime; the Parchamis had to be provided with an equalizer.

A second dilemma was a contradiction between practical politics and ideology. The only possible way of creating a DRA regime acceptable to the Afghan people would be by renouncing its pretensions to socialism, yet to do so would be to acknowledge that socialism had been a failure. Although the USSR had ceased calling the DRA socialist by mid-1979, the Khalqis had continued to the end to insist that they were pursuing "scientific socialism." Moreover, in early 1979, the leading Soviet ideologue, Mikhail Suslov, had personally confirmed the socialist label for the DRA, and for a while thereafter none of his lesser colleagues dared to contradict him explicitly (Arnold 1985, 90–91).

To achieve legitimacy in the eyes of the Afghan people, the Babrak regime had to pretend to some trappings of democracy, concerning both the composition of the government and the programs it would pursue. Coupled with the renunciation of socialism, this promised to infuriate the remaining doctrinaire Khalqis, thus complicating still further the Parcham-Khalq confrontation. Unless handled with finesse, it might endanger real PDPA control over the government. Nevertheless, there was no other option if the confidence of the Afghan people was to be won.

The Soviets and their Parchami allies attempted to resolve these conflicting considerations as follows:

1. The state and especially the party would be under firm Parchami control, in the person of Babrak Karmal and his closest associates, all of them blooded veterans of the Parcham-Khalq feud.

2. The Khalqis would be represented in token form at the highest party and state levels, but their representatives would not be former factional infighters; instead, they would either be technocrats, opportunists, or individuals who the Soviets felt owed more allegiance to Moscow than to any Afghan faction. The more militant Khalqis would have to be eliminated as a political force.

3. One of the three armed security services (the interior ministry's forces) would remain a Khalqi bastion, one (the secret police) would be turned over to the Parchamis, and the third (the army) would be depoliticized, using some kind of Parcham-Khalq balance.

4. To the extent possible, the new DRA would have to don the garb of an Islamic republic, complete with Qur'anic invocations and the absence of any reference to socialism. To improve the regime's legitimacy, as many prominent non-Communists and crypto-Communists as possible would have to be induced to collaborate directly.

5. Soviet advisers would be posted at all levels of the government to make key decisions and (presumably) to referee factional disputes.

6. Those non-Communists unwilling to take direct part in the government would be pressured to play a role in front activities.

All of these factors bore on the composition of the party and state elites in 1980.

As in 1978, the apparent balance between Parcham and Khalq at the pinnacle of state power was fairly even. Babrak Karmal was both president and prime minister, but two out of three deputy prime ministers were Khalqis. The four most prestigious and politically powerful ministerial posts were evenly divided, with foreign affairs and defense going to Parchamis and communications and interior going to Khalqis. Thus, counting the deputy prime ministers, the apparent score at the top was four Parchamis to four Khalqis, but the reality was an overwhelming Parchami advantage.

Of the four leading Khalqis, three had participated in the coup attempt against Amin in September 1979 and had been forced to flee for their lives to the Soviet embassy, where they were sheltered until the December invasion. If not already Soviet agents (as was strongly suspected at the time), they owed a profound debt of gratitude to their rescuers, who were not known for restraint when presented with recruitment opportunities. The fourth man, Abdur Rashid Arian, who under Amin had served as Afghan ambassador to Pakistan, was almost certainly the Soviets' source for information on how Amin was trying to mend his fences with Islamabad in the preinvasion period.

Thus, although each of the four Khalqis retained some measure of allegiance to his political antecedents (Minister of Interior Gulabzoy in fact ultimately emerged as de facto chief of Khalq), Moscow probably believed that it could exert considerable leverage over them in the interests of preserving intraparty peace.

In positions of lower profile, the Parchamis consolidated their hold on the state apparatus. The most significant such position was head of the secret police, which, though not a ministry until 1986, played as important a role in Afghan affairs after 1978 as its KGB equivalent did in the USSR. The old secret police, the KAM, was abolished and its ranks ruthlessly purged. Rebuilt as KHAD (Khadamat-e Itilla‵at-e Dawlati [State Information Service]) under Najibullah, it became the single most powerful concentration of Parchami strength in the government. The lesser ministries, meanwhile, were divided up into seven for Parchami and three each for Khalqi and for nonparty representatives.

In the upper reaches of the PDPA, the Parchamis made no effort to disguise their takeover. Out of thirty-one Central Committee members in December 1979, six were killed in the invasion or were later executed, seventeen vanished into political and public oblivion for the next nine years, two went into relatively brief, partial eclipse and were then rehabilitated, and only five survived unscathed. Ten Parchamis who had been expelled under Taraki and Amin reclaimed their seats, and seventeen more were appointed, most of them previous unknowns. In all, the Central Committee now numbered thirty-six. In the Politburo, only two out of seven Khalqis survived, and one of these (Sarwari) would be shipped into diplomatic exile before the end of the year. One Khalqi, surprisingly, was promoted—Saleh Mohammed Zeary, who became a secretary (the only Khalqi in Babrak Karmal's secretariat) in addition to retaining his Politburo seat.

The most radical departure from the previous DRA practice, however, was the attempt to provide a seeming non-PDPA leavening to government. In his first public speech after returning to power, on 2 January 1980, Babrak addressed himself first and foremost to such former class enemies and neutrals as the religious constituency, the military, capitalists, landowners, artisans, tribesman, nomads, government officials, the intelligentsia, and youth, in that order. Only at the end did he tack on the "working men and women, peasant men and women" in whose name the PDPA had overthrown Daoud (*Kabul New Times*, 2 Jan. 1980).

This was all part of Babrak's campaign to "broaden the base" of his government in order to win popular support. Over the next few months, he brought on board as ministers or highly placed advisers some eleven persons with no overt connections with the PDPA. Three of these, to be sure, had been known as crypto-Communists before Saur, but the other eight (referred to in the media as "distinguished persons") were genuine non-Communists whose cooperation had been obtained with promises that the Soviet occupation and interference in Afghan internal affairs would soon end. Between March and May 1980, 78 of 191 persons listed in the Afghan press as having received government jobs were pointedly identified as not belonging to the party. Their nonparty status was repeatedly emphasized in DRA media (Arnold 1983, 109).[7]

As further palliatives, Babrak restored the custom of beginning government proclamations with an Islamic invocation, returned the green and black bands to the Afghan flag, expunged the word "socialist" from the Afghan official vocabulary, halted land reform, and gave lip service to promoting private trade and capitalist endeavors.

Regarding front activities, the usual gamut of youth, women's, professional, peasants', and labor unions became a topic of intense media coverage. An umbrella organization, the National Fatherland Front (NFF), had been proposed under various names by both Parchamis and Khalqis before the invasion, and Babrak called again for its formation in his inaugural speech. The NFF, however, did not hold its founding congress until June 1981.

None of the above political maneuvering succeeded in burying the regime's two basic problems: its own lack of legitimacy and its internal factionalism.

The overriding element fomenting revolt in the pre-1980 period had been Kabul's effort to impose control over the traditionally independent villages. After 1980, the overriding element was foreign involvement. No matter what name was put to it, the Soviet invasion was seen as exactly that by most Afghans, and the government that the Soviet troops installed had no more legitimacy in Afghan eyes than did Vidkun Quisling's government for Norwegians in 1940. Moreover, the invasion caused even many Khalqis to abandon the fight and go over to the resistance. Party membership in early 1980 was estimated at only 2,500 to 3,000, of whom only about 600 to 700 were loyal to the Parcham faction (Arnold 1983, 100).

Opposition took many forms, including a general strike by shop-keepers in Kabul in February 1980, street marches by schoolgirls in the following months, wholesale desertions from the armed forces, a mass exodus of civilian refugees to Pakistan and Iran, and an ever more active and better-equipped underground armed resistance.

Within the party, Khalqi recalcitrance remained as unbending as ever, and there were regular reports of armed conflict between the two factions. In May 1980 Parchami army officers sent into the field to relieve their Khalqi colleagues of their commands were unceremoni-ously turned back at gunpoint. That summer and autumn there were three reported coup attempts by the Khalqis (Arnold 1983, 112).[8]

Faced with wholesale opposition, the Soviets and their PDPA allies largely abandoned the political strategy in favor of an outright military victory and the crushing of all resistance.

Military Phase, 1981–1985

The emphasis on a military solution was neither sudden nor total, but it was nonetheless clear-cut. In January 1981 Babrak doubled mili-tary salaries, issued numerous promotions, and bestowed decorations on fourteen colonels and generals. At the same time, he lowered the draft age, extended the obligatory tour of duty, and proffered various incentives to join or extend military and security tours. In June the Politburo dropped one member (Sarwari) and added three: Minister of Communications Watanjar (a former tank commander), Minister of De-fense Major General Mohammed Rafi, and State Security Chief Najibullah. In September, Babrak called up reservists to age thirty-five (Staar 1982, 159, 161).

These moves were prompted in part by the deteriorating security situation and disastrous decreases in army strength and capabilities. From a force of about one hundred thousand before the invasion, the DRA army could only muster about twenty-five thousand troops in 1981, despite the new measures. Desertions continued to be massive, draft dodging was pandemic, and each new means employed to force young men into the army only led to an increase in resistance strength as those vulnerable to conscription took to the hills.

The country was divided into seven military zones, each of which was headed by a PDPA Central Committee member. "Defense councils" were set up at the national, provincial, and district levels to put all security units under direct party command. A law covering local organs of state power theoretically put the PDPA in control of the nominating process for all local councils, although lack of actual control by the government over most of the country left that law largely inoperative.

The decrease in emphasis on a political solution was also gradual. At the fifth PDPA plenum in March 1981, Babrak continued to assert that the new "national democratic character of the present stage of the revolution" was dominant. In June, in a move interpreted at the time as another indication of "base broadening," he personally stepped down from two of his three leading positions, abandoning the prime ministry to Sultan Ali Keshtmand and the presidency of the Revolutionary Council to Nur Ahmad Nur. He retained, however, the most important post, that of general secretary of the PDPA.

But the previous acclaim given to nonparty members of the state apparatus was no longer a feature of state propaganda. In June the Revolutionary Council was expanded by fifteen members, and although the party affiliation of the new appointees was left obscure, as many as five of them might have been nonparty. If so, however, this was not thought worthy of mention in official media.

By the end of 1981, the eight "distinguished [nonparty] persons" in leading positions had ceased to be a matter of DRA pride. Two of them had been posted abroad as ambassadors, two had simply vanished from the media (one subsequently died), three had defected, and only one was known to be sticking it out as a government advisor.

On 14–15 March 1982 a long-heralded PDPA party conference was held at the Kabul Polytechnic Institute. Although surrounded by advance publicity, the time and the place of the conference were not revealed until after it was over. Originally planned as a party congress, the gathering had to be redesignated a conference because of the dangers of Khalqi takeover. (The mechanism for convening a party congress would have given the Khalqi majority a chance to dominate the proceedings and remove the Parchamis from power; by making it a conference, the Parchamis were able to control the selection of delegates and to insure that they held a three-fifths majority. This only infuriated the already outraged Khalqis even further, and not even the explict threat of expulsion via nonrenewal of party cards, which were exchanged from January to August 1982, was sufficient to bring them to heel.) Less than half the eighteen hundred delegates the press had forecast actually attended, and the conference broke up less than one and one-half days into its three-day program, with the factions as mutually hostile as ever.[9]

In terms of decisions, the conference adopted a new set of party rules that differed only slightly from those in effect since 1966, and it approved a draft "program of action," subject to later confirmation by the Politburo. The action program, which was the subject of a tedious media blitz that continued into the summer, reflected an uneasy trade-off in values between Parcham and Khalq: for example, on the one hand it reinstated land reform (a Khalqi obsession), and on the other it approved a mixed economy of both public and private sectors, a step back from pure socialism.

The party rules made it appear that joining the party was a difficult and drawn-out process. An individual recommended by three party members, each of at least three years' standing, had to submit a written application for membership and then serve a year of probationary membership before being admitted to full membership. In the case of workers, peasants, and military servicemen of worker or peasant background, only two recommendations by persons with only two years' membership, plus a probationary period of six months, would suffice. The minimum age for joining was twenty unless one had been a member of the Democratic Youth Organization of Afghanistan (DYOA), in which case it was lowered to eighteen. Interestingly, members of the Central Committee were not acceptable as references for party membership. The degree to which these rules were actually followed is impossible to determine.

If nothing else, however, the conference provided a unique statistical glimpse into the characteristics of the middle and upper reaches of the party, as revealed later by the conference's commission (table 1.1). Although minor discrepancies abound, in part because of rounding but also because the total number of delegates was sometimes considered 841 and sometimes 836, an interesting profile of the middle ranks of the party emerges. (Five delegates, it was explained, were "absent for good reason," a possible reflection of news accounts that five delegates from Kabul University's staff had been killed in intraparty shoot-outs at just this time.) The only contradiction without adequate explanation is the last table (age), where with neither 836 nor 841 delegates is it possible to obtain whole persons with the percentages given.

The most glaring discrepancy in these figures is in the occupation category, where less than 50 percent of the delegates are tabulated. It is

TABLE 1.1

Delegates to 1982 PDPA Conference

(derived figures are in parentheses)

	Number	%
Date of Joining PDPA		
Before 1966	60	(7.0)
1966–78	667	(80.0)
1978–81	114	(13.0)
Total	841	(100.0)
Occupation		
Democratic Youth Organization of Afghanistan (DYOA)	17	(2.0)
Democratic Women's Organization of Afghanistan (DWOA)	11[a]	(1.3)
"Representing state power"	78	(9.3)
Revolutionary Council	64	(7.6)
Students	27	(3.2)
Teachers, scholars, doctors, creative intelligentsia	40	(4.7)
Trade unions	12	(1.4)
Workers and peasants	106	(12.6)
Total	355	(42.1)
Education		
Higher	431	(51.2)
Secondary	274	(32.6)
Primary, partial secondary, or private	109	(13.0)
No education	27	(3.2)
Total	841	(100.0)
Age		
Under 20	—	2.0
21–30	—	36.2
31–40	—	48.5
41–60	—	13.2
Total		99.9[b]

Sources: Except for the derived figures in parentheses, all material in this table came from *Documents and Records of the National Conference of the People's Democratic Party of Afghanistan,* Kabul, 14–15, Mar. 1982. This material also appeared in the Afghanistan Forum, Inc., *Afghanistan Newsletter* 10, no. 4 (Oct. 1982), 25–27.

[a]Out of a total of 56 women (6.7 percent of the delegates).

[b]A token gray panther, Comrade Khalqi, was listed as more than 100 years old.

probable that the missing 57.9 percent were all in the three basic security services: the regular military, the police (Sarandoy), or KHAD. This
would tie in with Babrak's comment in 1983 that more than 50 percent
of the party were "military personnel" (a frequent euphemism for all
security forces combined), and with later reported figures that showed
an increasing proportion of party members with security functions,
from 60 percent in 1984 to 65 percent in 1985 and 1986. With slight
variations, that figure remained constant at least into 1990 (Radio
Kabul, 31 Dec. 1989 [FBIS-NES, 4 Jan. 1990]).

Young army officers reportedly had little enthusiasm for joining
the party at this time, and in 1988 a similar phenomenon appeared in
the regular police, where only 66 percent of the militia were in either
the PDPA or the DYOA (TASS, 5 July 1988 [FBIS-SOV, 8 July 1988]).
These figures were probably offset by the record of the secret police,
where the need for mutual protection probably drove membership up
to nearly 100 percent.

There are other conclusions to be drawn from these data.

> To lend weight to the changes in the party that these statistics
> represent, it is necessary to delete the 60 who claimed pre-1966 mem-
> bership, leaving 781 as the base figure. . . . The conference presumably
> represented the cream of the PDPA crop in 1982, and . . . the qualifica-
> tions and age of the party rank and file would have been lower than
> the conference average. . . .
>
> The proportion of delegates to total members was far lower for the
> trade unions (twelve delegates out of a total claimed membership of
> 160,000–180,000) than for other front groups like the DOAW (eleven
> delegates for 50,000 claimed members) or the DYOA (seventeen for
> 65,000). The relatively high DYOA representation provided yet another
> indication of the party's emphasis on youth.
>
> Unlike the earlier recruitment drive, however, the post-Saur focus
> seemed to be on youth for its own sake, rather than on educated
> youth. . . . What is astonishing is the low representation of teachers in
> 1982 . . . compared with their (previous) dominance (Arnold 1983, 124–
> 25).[10]

In July 1983 the Central Committee received ten new full members,
of whom five had been candidates, and sixteen new candidate members. Among those mentioned in this connection were three corps commanders and the commander of the air force.

Overall, however, the military did not prosper in its fight with the
resistance. Efforts to draft new troops from the Shinwari tribe, which

custom dictated was immune to the conscription, had led to combat confrontations with a group that heretofore had been relatively passive. Morale-building promotions within the military had been carried to such extremes that a four-hundred-man supply unit in Kabul was reportedly being overseen by twenty brigadier generals. Despite a lowering of the draft age to nineteen in April 1983, by the end of the year, the military stalemate was unchanged (Arnold 1983, 189; *Bakhtar*, 8 Apr. 1982 [FBIS VIII, 8 Apr. 1982]).

Things were no better on the political front, despite continuing barrages of optimistic propaganda. Between 1983 and 1984 the number of party committees in the country's 89 cities and large administrative districts actually declined from 70 to 61 (*Kabul New Times*, 24 Apr. 1983, 5 May 1984; Radio Kabul, 12 Feb. 1984 [FBIS VIII, 17 Feb. 1984]).[11]

In March 1984 the military tour of duty was again extended, from three to four years, a move that sparked yet more desertions and set off a mutiny in the Eighth Division. The government then began drafting PDPA members, thus removing one of the few incentives (military service exemption) for joining the party. In April a combined Soviet-Afghan assault force tried to deliver a knockout blow to resistance forces in the Panjshir valley. Some 500 of the 20,000 Soviet troops were killed in the engagement; of the 2,000 DRA soldiers involved, 400 deserted on their way to the front (Staar 1985, 147).

In lining up their forces for this engagement, the Parchami commanders had drafted heavily among Khalqi bureaucrats in Kabul, thus exacerbating Parcham-Khalq enmity. The extent of hostility was indirectly revealed by Babrak in a speech to a Sarandoy (i.e., Khalqi) audience in April: "Fist and sword do not have a place in the party.... The equipment and military means given to you do not have a place in the party" (*Kabul New Times*, 14 Apr. 1984).

Allegedly as a result of heavy Soviet casualties, General Abdul Qader was relieved as minister of defense, but the return of General Mohammed Rafi to this post after extended training in the USSR resulted in no improvement in DRA military fortunes. Through the first three quarters of 1985, both the Soviet-DRA and the resistance sides maintained the stalemate, though at a higher level of combat and with more casualties on both sides. According to a report by a Swedish relief group, 1985 was the bloodiest year of the war for Afghan civilians: more than half the farmers remaining in the country had their fields bombed, and more than a quarter suffered destruction of their irrigation systems or annihilation of their livestock, or both, at the hands of Soviet and DRA forces (*Wall Street Journal*, 24 Aug. 1988, 15).

Sometime between September and November of that year, however, a policy watershed was reached. At that point the USSR appears to have concluded that the war was militarily unwinnable, and it switched over to nonmilitary means. For the PDPA and DRA, this change of posture was fateful. It meant that before too long the protective mantle of Soviet armed assistance was going to end, and the government would have to survive on its own. This forced changes on many fronts, including the adoption of revisionist policies that would have been considered ideological heresy by any Soviet leader before Mikhail Gorbachev.

Retreat and Compromise, 1985–1988

On 26 September 1985 Babrak Karmal gave marching orders to the Revolutionary Council in a manner that left no doubt about that entity's insignificance. Reminding the assembled council members that "no important political or organizational problem can be solved by a state organ without the party guidelines," he went on to inform them that "the state apparatus is there to implement policy" and that there was "need for complete obedience by the state apparatus to party policy" (Radio Kabul, 26 Sept. 1985 [FBIS VIII, 6 Oct. 1985]).

What specific act of Revolutionary Council independence might have sparked the tirade remains a mystery, but only six weeks later, Babrak's address to the same audience signaled a complete change of policy. Prefacing his remarks with an acknowledgment that the PDPA had been suffering from "infantile disorders," especially "leftist-extremist deviations," Babrak outlined ten theses that in effect turned the clock back to 1980–81: (1) "all national questions" (i.e., the ongoing war with the resistance) should be resolved by peaceful means; (2) the government—and especially the Revolutionary Council—should become more representative of "various strata and groups," and "authority will not be monopolized by the PDPA"; (3) the private sector should be encouraged to increase agricultural production, and state farms should be established only on virgin lands; (4) "national traders" and industrial capitalists, essential for economic development, should be encouraged; (5) independent intellectual organizations would be permissible; (6) tribal self-rule for the Pashtuns and Baluch in border areas would be affirmed; (7) the NFF should be expanded, but other organizations (provided they were cooperative and not opposed to the regime) would also be permissible; (8) Islam should be respected; (9) the various armed forces should be consolidated, and after "foreign inter-vention" had ceased, Soviet forces would leave; (10) the DRA's foreign policy should be one of "active nonalignment" and friendship with neighboring countries (Radio Kabul, 9 Nov. 1985 [FBIS VIII, 12 Nov. 1985]).[12]

The most radical element in the list was the second, the PDPA's renunciation of its monopoly of political power in favor of a broader-based Revolutionary Council. Later, Babrak was to reaffirm the party's "organizing and leading" role, but the retreat from the claim to abso-lute authority was a significant watershed. It was the harbinger of the policy of "national reconciliation" that was to be launched late in 1986, after Babrak himself had been ousted.

In the three months that followed Babrak's speech, the apparent complexion of the DRA government changed radically. The Revolu-tionary Council was more than doubled in size, from 69 to 148 mem-bers, and its nonparty representation jumped from 2 to 58. Six of the 18 members of the council presidium were nonparty, as were 9 of 13 newly appointed top-level bureaucrats. Fifteen out of 21 newly ap-pointed ministers and deputy ministers, 10 of 37 members of an Elec-tions Commission, and 27 of 74 members of a Constitutional Drafting Commission were also nonparty (Staar 1987, 420).

The purpose of these changes was to establish the discredited DRA's authority, especially in the countryside, as soon as possible. Babrak was working under heavy time pressure, as revealed in a speech to a Sarandoy audience in late December 1985, in which he pleaded for establishment of state power in "most of the villages and all of the districts" in a two-stage operation "in the course of two and four months" (*Kabul New Times*, 22 Dec. 1985). The Twenty-seventh CPSU Congress, at which Mikhail Gorbachev referred to Afghanistan as a "bleeding wound," coincided with one of these deadlines (late February 1986), and the Saur coup's anniversary (late April) coincided with the second. At the first of these, Gorbachev pointedly snubbed Babrak; at the second, the Afghan leader was in the USSR for a "health checkup"—probably a final accounting for his political failures—and missed the celebrations in Kabul. When he returned a few days later, he was no longer general secretary of the PDPA.

Babrak's replacement, Najibullah, had been head of KHAD ever since the Soviet invasion. Like his late Soviet mentor, Yuri Andropov, he had worked his way into party politics by stages, becoming a full member of the Politburo in 1981. Again following in Andropov's foot-steps, Najibullah resigned as chief of the secret police in November

1985 to become a party secretary and five months later took over the general secretary's seat from Babrak. Clearly, the Soviets did not expect Babrak to succeed and were grooming Najibullah for his job from at least November 1985.

To outside observers, this change of leadership was perplexing. It did not signify any change in policy, for Najibullah did nothing to change the lines that Babrak had been pushing so hard, including the call for broad, nonparty participation in government. Moreover, at just the time when ideological relaxation and glasnost were coming into vogue in both the USSR and Afghanistan, the choice of the detested chief of the secret police as leader of the country seemed particularly unsound.

Seen from Moscow, however, the choice had its own peculiar logic: unlike Babrak, Najibullah had unimpeachable Pashtun bloodlines, an important advantage if he were to survive on his own; his secret police was the most efficient DRA organization, and it almost surely had the highest percentage of party members; the influence of the KGB (whose man Najibullah was) was at an all-time high in the CPSU Politburo; Yuri Andropov, Najibullah's model, had been the most effective Soviet leader between Stalin and Gorbachev, and it may have been assumed that Najibullah had similar qualities; and reports on Najibullah that passed through KGB channels had undoubtedly been more flattering than warranted, just because he was their man.

Implicit in this reasoning is the answer to the main question, Why change leaders at all? The most logical solution is that by the end of 1985 the USSR had made up its mind to withdraw its troops, and it felt that Najibullah stood a better chance of surviving in a post-Soviet Afghanistan than did Babrak. In reaching this conclusion, the Kremlin seemed blind to the contempt that Afghans felt for a man whose record of brutality to his own people was only matched by his slavish adulation of everything Soviet. Compared to Najibullah, even Babrak seemed relatively acceptable.[13] (And yet, events through early 1992 were to bear out Soviet faith in Najibullah's durability.)

When Najibullah took over, he lost no time in consolidating his position. In July 1986 the number of full and candidate members of the Central Committee rose to 147, and in November to 172. Part of the increase can be ascribed to the investment of provincial party secretaries as full or alternate committee members, but most of the other newcomers had never featured in the Afghan press; and it can be assumed that the unknowns were largely drawn from among Najibullah's old KHAD subordinates. Although there were no publicized dismissals from the Central Committee, between March 1986 and March 1987 some five thousand party members were expelled. Some of these undoubtedly were unreconstructed Khalqis who objected to the reformism of the new party policies, but a good many others undoubtedly were Babrak followers unable to adjust to the new chief.

Despite the expulsions, the party continued to report steady growth (table 1.2), and most of the earlier discernible trends in its makeup remained unchanged. The DYOA posted no known gains in membership for the first year of Najibullah's tenure but then claimed an increase of 11,000 in the first two months of 1988. The Soviets continued and intensified their own efforts to influence Afghan children and students. The annual children's exodus to Soviet summer camps, which had seen 9,000 Afghan visitors from 1980 to 1987, was supposed to include 4,000 in the summer of 1988 alone. As of January 1988, there were supposed to be 8,500 Afghan students in the USSR, including 400 in technicums and 350 in technical, vocational, and workers' schools. It was claimed that there were 250 new Afghan students in Soviet masters and doctorate programs each year and that 1,000 students would graduate from various institutions in 1988 (*Bakhtar*, 27 Jan. 1988 [FBIS-NES, 28 Jan. 1988]; *Kabul New Times*, 13 Feb. 1988; Radio Moscow, 3 Mar. 1988 [FBIS-SOV, 4 Mar. 1988]).[14]

These and other statistics released by the government were designed to show that all was well under the new leadership. Nevertheless, none of the problems faced by Babrak was solved by his successor. Among the most serious of these was the failure of the PDPA to take root in the countryside. In December 1981 Babrak had complained about the failure of party leaders to get out among the people, yet he himself became a prime offender in this regard; a November 1985 visit to Kunduz was his first reported domestic foray out of the capital in two years. Najibullah at first made a point of having Politburo members travel often into the provinces, but their presence there did little to improve either the quality or quantity of rural party membership. For obvious security reasons, the visits were never announced in advance, and the reports in Afghan newspapers of enthusiastic receptions for the leaders were more than a little suspect. When the initial campaign of visits began to lose momentum, a somewhat unrealistic rule was adopted in 1987 that required Politburo members to spend twenty out of every thirty working days in the provinces (Staar 1988, 395).

The party's failure to take hold was shown by a number of indirect indicators. For example, local elections were scheduled for late 1985 and the first nine months of 1986, yet by September 1986, they had been

TABLE 1.2

Trends in Claimed Party and Selected Front Membership, 1980–1990

(in thousands)

Year	Party (PDPA/ HP)[a]	National (Fatherland Front[b]	Trade Unions	Women (DWOA, AAWC, WCA, etc.)[c]	Youth DYOA/ AYU)[d]
1980	40.0	—	—	—	—
1981	60.0	—	—	—	—
1982	>80.0	—	94	50.0	90
1983	>90.0	—	—	—	—
1984	>120.0	650	170	19.3	120
1985	>140.0	700	200	39.6	152
1986	170.0	800	285	>55.0	200
1987	185.0	850	300	108.9	200
1988	205.0	>1,000	—	125.0	200
1989	230.0	1,000	305	—	280
1990	173.6	—	>300	—	—

[a]The People's Democratic Party of Afghanistan (PDPA) became the Homeland Party (HP) in June 1990. The figure given for the new party's membership was an unusually precise 173,614.

[b]The National Fatherland Front became the National Front and then passed out of existence in late 1990. Many of its functions appear to have been taken over by the Peace Front, for which statistics never became available.

[c]The Democratic Women's Organization of Afghanistan (DWOA) underwent several name changes and, as of 1990, was known as the All-Afghan Women's Council (AAWC). Especially during its early days, it suffered from hyperinflated claims for its membership numbers. In 1991 some 15,924 women were listed as HP members. Most, if not all, of these were probably AAWC members.

[d]The Democratic Youth Organization of Afghanistan (DYOA) became the Afghan Youth Union (AYU) in late 1990, but no statistics on membership were announced.

held in only 180 of the 628 villages in Kabul Province, the area under tightest government control. Of the 147 full and alternate Central Committee members in mid-1986, only 46 claimed to live in the provinces, and Najibullah was later to confess that in fact there were only 2 workers and 2 provincial party secretaries who lived outside Kabul at that time. In Balkh Province in 1986, less than 1 percent of the artisans and 0.1 percent of the peasants were party members. In 1987 Najibullah acknowledged that 92 percent of all army recruits came from the city of Kabul. Even among teachers, officially hailed in 1978 as comprising a majority of the party, countrywide PDPA membership in 1986 was only 6,691 out of 22,000, and among rural party members literacy was only about 50 percent (Staar 1988, 396; Staar 1987, 418; *Kabul New Times*, 20 Oct. 1987; unpublished notes of Chantal Lobato, who interviewed many resistance leaders in 1986).

Starting in late 1986 and continuing into 1988, the regime made steadily greater concessions in its efforts to reach some sort of accommodation with the resistance. Launched with the phrase "national reconciliation" (coined by Mikhail Gorbachev in his 28 July 1986 Vladivostok speech and soon to become a watchword in floundering Marxist states worldwide), the policy shifted progressively from open insistence on a controlling role for the PDPA to explicit advocacy of real power sharing: "The [initial] intention of the policy was to achieve PDPA unity and discipline and to promote support of the government among noncommunist elements of the Afghan people. As originally conceived, the policy probably envisaged a small, tightly-knit party making all essential decisions behind the scenes, while a figurehead coalition government . . . provided a cover of democratic respectability. The PDPA (and the CPSU) hoped to gain by political means the victory that was being denied them militarily. . . . As Najibullah himself acknowledged, 'it has become clear that we cannot solve our issues through sheer use of force' " (Staar 1988, 396).[15]

Over time, those with whom the regime was willing to share power changed from mere neutrals in the struggle with the resistance to the resistance commanders themselves. As progressively more-conciliatory offers were made and spurned, the impression given was of a regime with its back to the wall, struggling desperately for survival.

Among other elements of national reconciliation were the following:

1. Proclamation of a ceasefire that on paper came into effect on 15 January 1987 and was solemnly renewed in six-month increments the following July and January. (In fact, the periods in question saw the most intensive combat on both sides since the invasion.)

2. An amnesty for some political prisoners, including some seventeen former ranking Khalqis. This move occurred sometime before May 1987, yet in late 1988 there was still no explicit official acknowledgment

that Khalqis had been included in the amnesty, much less their identification by name or their restoration to any position of authority in the government (*Kabul New Times*, 13 May 1987; *Times* [London], 2 June 1988, 10).[16] By 1991, only one former Khalqi, Abdul Quddus Ghorbandi, had made it to the top party ranks, as alternate member of the renamed Homeland Party's Executive Board (former Politburo). Another, Shah Wali, was named to the 145-member Central Council (former Central Committee). But such earlier Khalqi survivors in the party as Ghulam Dastagir Panjsheri and Saleh Mohammed Zeary were in jail for complicity in a 1990 Khalqi military coup attempt.

3. Intensification of the drive to call refugees home from Pakistan and Iran. This program was put under Mohammed Hassan Sharq, an old but unacknowledged Communist who had served as Daoud's link with the Parchamis in 1973–75. According to the official press, hundreds of "freedom hotels" under the administration of mixed party and nonparty personnel were set up to help returning refugees resettle. As of September 1988, even official statistics were only claiming 160,000 returnees, or well under 5 percent of the total in Iran and Pakistan.

4. A reemphasis of the government's dedication to Islam and of its distance from Marxism, Leninism, socialism, or anything related thereto. In 1986 Najibullah had claimed that some ten thousand mullahs were on the government payroll, and in 1987 he appointed 426 "prayer leaders" in the army and another 420 in the police. Though professing personal piety, he conceded to hostile ideologues that religion was contrary to "scientific revolutionary theory," but observed that it was a "practical political necessity" for the time being, given the role of religion in the country. Meanwhile, both the Soviet and Afghan media kept reemphasizing that the DRA was not then—nor had it ever been—socialist (Staar 1988, 394, 396–97, 398).

5. A wholesale relabeling of various DRA institutions and people, starting with the republic itself, which henceforth would drop the "Democratic" and be known only as the Republic of Afghanistan (RA). The leader (and now president) wished to be called by the more religious version of his name (Najibullah instead of Najib), and he felt it was inappropriate for him to be addressed as "comrade" except in intimate party gatherings. The NFF first lost its "Fatherland" designation, becoming merely the National Front, and by November 1990 had been reorganized and renamed the Peace Front. Late in March 1988, the *Kabul New Times* reverted to its preinvasion name, the *Kabul Times*. Most revolutionary of all, the PDPA became the Homeland Party (HP) in June 1990, and its various components lost their Communist-

associated designations, from the "cell" (now called a zone) all the way up to the "Politburo" (now the capitalist-sounding Executive Board). The DYOA became the Afghan Youth Union (AYU) in December 1990.

6. An intensification of propaganda concerning women. In October 1987 Najibullah claimed that membership in the Afghan Women's Association (AWA, formerly the Democratic Women's Organization of Afghanistan [DWOA] and All Afghan Women's Council [AAWC]) had doubled in the past year, and by February 1988, membership was supposed to be 120,000. Nevertheless, only 3.6 percent of the party apparatus, 9 percent of trade union members, and 43 percent of the ministry of education were women. With the expulsion of Babrak's old comrade Anahita Ratebzad from the Politburo, no women remained in the leadership of the party (Kabul Times, 21 Oct. 1987, 23 Feb. 1989). In 1990, in the Homeland Party there were only five women among over two hundred members and alternate members of its Central Council.

7. The continuation of local elections, originally programmed under Babrak but repeatedly postponed beyond several missed deadlines. The reported results of these polls were consistent in their picture of diminishing PDPA control over rural Afghanistan: 60 and 65 percent of the candidates for office in February and November 1986, respectively, were described as nonparty, and 65 and 76 percent of the villages in February and December 1987, respectively, were under nonparty administration. These villages, along with the 24 percent under PDPA rule, were considered to be under government "control," and the total in this category was 8,600, or about 38 percent of all Afghan villages. In short, by the end of 1987 only about 9 percent (24 percent of 38 percent) of all Afghan villages were being governed directly by the PDPA (Kabul New Times, 23 Feb. 1988; Staar 1987, 423).[17]

8. More encouragement to private enterprise. The key element in this drive was provided by the USSR, which made available a fifty-million-ruble fund for loans to private individuals for business purposes. In March 1988 it was reported that twenty-eight loans (out of one hundred applications) had been granted, including money for such enterprises as bicycle assembly shops, bakeries, salt purification plants, and confectionery factories. Another fifteen contracts were said to be pending, including such larger projects as a spinning mill, a rubber footwear plant, a wool-washing factory, poultry farms, and an oxygen-producing facility. In September, the Soviet foreign-trade organizations were in touch with 250 Afghan private traders, whose share of trade had doubled in the past three years and now accounted for 20 percent

of the total Afghan-Soviet turnover (*Sovetskaya Rossiya*, 3 Mar. and 25 Aug. 1988 [FBIS-SOV, 21 Mar. and 7 Sept. 1988]).

9. A political parties law, designed to legitimize opposition parties and provide a mechanism for dissent. The law was proposed in the summer of 1987 and enacted late in the year. As of September 1988 Najibullah was claiming that twelve parties had come into existence, but the only ones named were the PDPA itself, the Organization of the Working People of Afghanistan (OWPA), the Revolutionary Organization of the Working People of Afghanistan (ROWPA), the Peasants' Justice Party (PJP), the People's Islamic Party (PIP), and the Union of God's Supporters (UGS). The PDPA, OWPA, and ROWPA were allied in a "Union of Left Democratic Parties" whose coordinating council was to work out joint activities and programs. Although there is no question that OWPA and ROWPA were no more than PDPA clones, the other three appear to have had some measure of independence, as indicated by Najibullah's complaints about their selfish grasping for advantage and "shortsighted party-political approach" (Radio Kabul, 1 Sept. 1988 [FBIS-NES, 2 Sept. 1988]).[18]

10. A new constitution, completed in draft in July and adopted in December, 1987. If examined out of the context of an alien occupation, this document might well have been acceptable to most Afghans. By the standards of regimes in power even before the PDPA took over, it provides for a relatively democratic government. The president has sweeping powers, including the right to nominate one-third of the senate (another third to be appointed by preexisting local governments) and to name "at least fifty" additional members of the supreme Grand Assembly (Loya Jirga) that would be convened for considering major policy changes. These mandates in effect gave him full control over the legislative and policy-making bodies. On the other hand, the document as finally approved removed his power of absolute veto, providing instead for the possibility of an override by a two-thirds vote of the national assembly (senate and house of representatives combined), unlikely though such a veto might be. It also removed his power in a state of national emergency to extend the term of the national assembly or to move the capital from Kabul.

As the first of these steps were being taken, the PDPA held its second party conference in October 1987. Despite a more than twofold growth in claimed party membership, the 1987 conference delegates numbered only 670, as opposed to 841 in 1982. Like its 1982 predecessor, this gathering was preceded and accompanied by factional infighting, perhaps even more intense because of the regime's retreat from orthodox socialism. Just as before, the principal conference theme was unity, but the reality—in spite of attempted Draconian methods to impose obedience on dissident party members—was the reverse. Najibullah required the delegates to the meeting to sign a pledge of unity; he threatened those who refused with expulsion from the party and illustrated his determination by firing eleven Central Committee members as the conference was about to open. He also upgraded the Central Committee's Control Commission to a committee and specifically tasked it with purging factional elements. Responsibility for purging "unworthy members" over the next two or three months was extended down to the primary party organizations, but to judge from media exhortations that continued through the rest of the year, these measures did not succeed in reamalgamating the party's fissiparous elements. During the conference, a second party congress to celebrate the tenth anniversary of the Saur Revolution was scheduled for April 1988, but—again in a replay of 1982—plans for the congress were quietly shelved when it became apparent that unity was proving as elusive as ever.

In effect, the PDPA's second conference presided over its own funeral as a Communist vanguard party. Such a PDPA role was, in the words of veteran party member Nur Ahmad Nur, "an ideal ahead of its time." The changes in "practically all the chapters of party rules" reflected this transition, said Nur, but in fact the changes were more in mechanics than in philosophy. The new PDPA did away with candidate membership, and it required its members to take an active part in some NF organization. But the basic principle of democratic centralism was to be retained, and the emphasis was to be on centralism. Moreover, the Central Committee Organizational Department was charged with setting up schools for the political education of party members in scientific revolutionary theory (*Kabul New Times*, 25 Oct. 1987). At the same time that it was pretending to be just another political party, the PDPA was demonstrating its Marxist-Leninist essence.

The new constitution became operative in the spring of 1988. After elections in April, the Revolutionary Council held a "last emergency meeting" on 26 April to vote itself out of existence and turn over its functions to the incoming national assembly. By the end of May, the Afghan and Soviet presses were claiming that 1.6 million voters, "representing 74 percent of the enfranchised population," had elected 51 senators and 186 deputies. If accurate, this would indicate that there were only 2.2 million enfranchised voters among an Afghan population estimated at more than 14 million. Some 13 seats in the senate and 48 seats in the house were reserved for "opponents," but they were never filled by resistance figures.

The national assembly's ethnic makeup (48.7 percent Pashtun, 30.2 percent Tajik, 9.4 percent Uzbek, 6.4 percent Hazara, 2.7 percent Turkoman, 1 percent Baluch, and 1.6 percent miscellaneous) was reportedly "compatible with the population proportion of the country." Politically, the assembly was 22.6 percent PDPA, 15.4 percent NF, 3 percent ROWPA, 3 percent PIP, 3 percent PJP, and 56 percent nonparty. In terms of class, it was 65.8 percent "intellectuals" (for which one must probably read all state employees and military officers as well as true intellectuals), 10.4 percent "tribal and influential figures," 8.5 percent workers, peasants, and craftsmen, 4.7 percent nomads, and 2.7 percent "national entrepreneurs and merchants" (*Kabul Times*, 30 Apr. 1988).[19] The remaining 7.9 percent were not accounted for.

The new prime minister, Hassan Sharq, was ostensibly a nonparty figure, and he proceeded to nominate a thirty-one man cabinet, which was approved unanimously by the national assembly. This represented an almost 50 percent cut in the previous number of ministers, and it saw the replacement of many old PDPA figures by heretofore little-known nonparty individuals. The latter took sixteen (or eighteen, depending on which account one read) of the ministries, but their lack of formal PDPA affiliation was not a sign of opposition to the party or even of neutrality. Like Sharq himself, who had been Daoud's principal liaison man for contact with the Parchamis until 1976, they were all believed to be collaborators. According to Sharq, his key demand of each cabinet nominee was support for national reconciliation (as defined, or course, by the PDPA). Only those who accepted that proposition, he said, were acceptable as ministers.

All of the moves toward national reconciliation must be placed in the context of the most important development in Afghanistan since Soviet forces invaded in 1979: the withdrawal of those same forces from 15 May 1988 to 15 February 1989. The CPSU Politburo decision to withdraw has been documented as having occurred on 13 November 1986 (*Washington Post*, 16 Nov. 1992, A-1), but as we have seen, there were strong indications that the Soviets had decided on this course a year earlier, when they began grooming Najibullah to take over from Babrak.

For the Afghan Communist elite, the withdrawal signaled a new sharpening of the Parcham-Khalq split, for without the presence of Soviet occupation forces, Moscow's authority for dampening intra-PDPA squabbles no longer carried the same weight. The first indications of serious difficulties came in October 1988, when one of the most influential Khalqis, Saleh Mohammed Zeary, was suddenly dropped from the Politburo and Secretariat, and the de facto Khalqi leader, Sayed Mohammed Gulabzoy, was exiled to Moscow as ambassador. Only 94 of 163 full and alternate members of the Central Committee took part in the plenum that decided these personnel matters, lending credence. to widespread rumors at the time that a large-scale political revolt had occurred and that between 17 and 50 other Central Committee members had been arrested (Staar 1989, 459).

Although no official explanation of the mini-purge has ever been given, it doubtless represents the reaction to a Khalqi attempt to unseat Najibullah. But his response, after dealing with the main figures, was to try to mend his fences with the remaining intraparty opposition, a move rendered critically important by the impending departure of the last Soviet combat troops. In February 1989, almost before the dust of their last outgoing convoys had settled, Najibullah was circling his political wagons by firing his prime minister, Hassan Sharq, and ten other ministers (seven, including Sharq, were ostensibly nonparty) and replacing all but two of them with party members. As the spring wore on, he even rehabilitated the last Khalqi foreign minister, Shah Wali, who had been under house arrest since 1980, and retrieved Babrak's brother-in-law, Mahmud Baryalai, from jail to become first deputy prime minister under party stalwart Sultan Ali Keshtmand (Staar 1990, 530).

These appointments were spurred by the desperate straits in which the Najibullah government found itself. During the spring of 1989, resistance forces had launched an all-out assault against Jalalabad, a key provincial capital on the road between Kabul and Peshawar, Pakistan, and it was only thanks to a combination of factors—including massive Soviet arms deliveries, the use of Soviet technicians to fire Scud missiles against the resistance, and the resistance's own unpreparedness for set-piece warfare—that the regime held on by a thread.

The common peril did not, however, deter the Khalqis from pursuing their goal of overthrowing the Parchamis. As early as March 1989 (*Times* [London] 8 Mar. 1990, 9), again in July (AFP [Islamabad], 1 Aug. 1989), yet again in December, and finally on 6 March 1990, Defense Minister Shahnawaz Tanai, who had inherited Gulabzoy's mantle as undeclared Khalqi chief, undertook anti-Najibullah coup attempts (Staar 1991, 471). Again displaying remarkable tolerance, Najibullah not only avoided overreacting to the first attempts but in October 1989 appeared to be trying to mollify his opposition by promoting as many as seven Khalqis to high party positions (Staar 1990, 530). The December 1989 attempt, however, resulted in the arrest of 124 military officers, and it was the start of their trial on 6 March that triggered Tanai's final attempt (*Christian Science Monitor,* 9 Mar. 1990, 4).

This time there was no hiding the revolt, as Afghan air force planes bombed the presidential palace in an effort to kill Najibullah. When the coup failed, Tanai and many of his close followers fled to Pakistan, where he revealed that he had long been allied secretly with Gulbuddin Hekmatyar, the mujahidin leader whose devotion to the reactionary aspects of Islamic traditions had placed him on the extreme right wing of the resistance movement. (Given the Khalqis' own reputation for devotion to the most extreme forms of Marxism-Leninism, the union of the two apparent opposites was reminiscent of the 1939 Hitler-Stalin pact.)

In the wake of Tanai's ouster, there was a thoroughgoing purge of Khalqis from the upper reaches of the party and state apparatuses. Six of the expelled had been members of either the fourteen-man Politburo or twenty-man Supreme Defense Council or both, and two others had been Central Committee members (*San Francisco Chronicle,* 28 Mar. 1990, 5). Some 600 arrests of regime officers followed (*New York Times,* 29 Apr. 1990, 1).

Although the purge of Khalqis cut drastically into the PDPA leadership, it did free Najibullah's hands for pursuing the reforms these opponents had blocked previously. In May 1990, he again tried to mask the PDPA's dominant role by appointing a new nonparty prime minister, Fazl Haq Khaleqyar, to replace Keshtmand. (Keshtmand was not only politically incorrect for the times but had also been guilty of too open corruption and nepotism in office, and he was quietly banished to the Soviet Union.) At the same time, Najibullah fired fifteen PDPA cabinet ministers, replacing them with thirteen nonparty "technocrats." But the degree to which most of the latter were truly free from party control remained in question, and the key ministries of defense, state security, interior, and foreign affairs remained firmly in the hands of dedicated Communists (AFP [Kabul], 22 May 1990).

Like previous efforts to put a democratic face on his rule, this one also failed to lend Najibullah and his government the legitimacy they so desperately needed. Soviet military and financial aid continued to pour in from the USSR in unprecedented amounts, enabling Kabul's forces to achieve a temporary stalemate with the resistance, but in April 1991 that stalemate was broken when the resistance finally succeeded in taking the provincial capital of Khost. The blow was rendered doubly bitter to Najibullah because he was from that area and because the fall of the city again involved reported treachery by his officers (*Komsomolskaya Pravda*, 29 June 1991, 4).

Shortly thereafter, Najibullah appears to have made one final swing toward reliance on traditional party values. The visit to Kabul in May of CPSU Central Committee member Yuriy A. Manayenkov (Radio Kabul, 13 May 1991 [FBIS-NES 14 May 1991])—the first officially announced CPSU visit in years—set the tone. The following month, for the first time since 1988, Najibullah was identified in Afghan official media by his party rank of general secretary as he exhorted party activists to more energetic performance of their duties (Radio Kabul, 11 June 1991 [FBIS-NES, 14 June 1991]). Also in June, Babrak Karmal and Keshtmand were returned from the Soviet Union to Kabul.

But if Najibullah was placing any hopes on Manayenkov, or if anyone believed that the return of the two exiles would help stabilize the regime, such dreams were soon dashed. Manayenkov was disgraced after being implicated in the abortive coup attempt against Gorbachev in August 1991, and the return of the two former Afghan leaders did not result in any intraparty healing.

The failure of the August coup resulted almost immediately in the collapse of the Soviet Union and disintegration of the CPSU, and from that point on, the Najibullah regime was clearly doomed. Aid from the Soviet Union slowed to a trickle and then stopped at the end of 1991; not quite four months later, Communist rule in Afghanistan died. On 17 April Najibullah resigned and tried to flee to India but was turned back at the airport by a militia force that had gone over to the resistance. On 27 April 1992, the fourteenth anniversary of the Great Saur Revolution, the exiled politico-religious leader Sibghatullah Modjaddedi crossed the Afghan border at Torkham to take up his post as chief of the interim government. He arrived in Kabul the following day.

But what of the Communist elites that the interim government replaced? In the former USSR, many Communist officials were finding no trouble in making the transition to a non-Communist society. As established figures in their communities, many of them succeeded in winning political posts in free elections, while others were becoming successful private businesspeople. In Afghanistan, by contrast, the stigma of association with communism was far more damaging to one's reputation.

As late as October 1991, the *Economist* was predicting that Prime Minister Khaleqyar and some of his nonparty ministers might stay on as part of a transition government (*Economist*, 12 Oct. 1991, 36). The resistance had been saying for several years that they were willing to work together with "good Muslims" in the Najibullah government, though without specifying who these individuals might be (*Christian Science Monitor*, 1 Dec. 1988, 11). Between Najibullah's resignation and Modjaddedi's arrival, the government was reportedly in the hands of the four vice presidents, the Homeland Party's executive council, and four generals (*Washington Post*, 17 Apr. 1992, A-1). Farid Mazdak had succeeded Najibullah as party chief, and he immediately made overtures to Ahmad Shah Masud to come and take power. But if he or the other surviving Communists thought that such gestures would permit them to stay in office, they were soon disabused of the notion.

Of the forty-three leading figures in the Afghan government in March, there was precisely one survivor in the thirty-six man leadership in July, Abdul Wahed Sorabi. Before 1978, he had been the dean of Kabul University's economics faculty, and he stayed on at the university after the Communists came to power, later (1980) serving as an adviser to the Ministry of Education. He then became minister of higher and vocational education (1987), vice president (1988), deputy prime minister and minister of planning (1990), and again vice president (1991). He survived under the interim government as minister of development and inspection.

Some of the other interim government ministers may have held lesser posts in Najibullah's regime, but an exhaustive search of my own 2400-name data base of known Communist government members and collaborators fails to reveal any positive identifications with the new ministers. Two of the old regime's members, WAD chief Faqir Mohammed Yaqubi and his deputy Abdul Baqi, reportedly died by their own or someone else's hand (*Washington Post*, 22 Apr. 1992, A-23), and two others (Minister of Interior Raz Mohammed Paktin and Defense Minister Mohammed Aslam Watanjar—both Khalqis) were believed to have joined up with Hekmatyar's forces (*Washington Post*, 28 Apr. 1992, A-17).

One other individual with ties to the old regime was Abdul Rashid Dostam, who had served Najibullah as chief of the notorious Uzbek militia, a brutal mercenary unit that had been used as a punitive force to suppress the resistance in various trouble spots. But Dostam stood outside the ranks of the Communist-era elite; as a hired gun (a loose cannon might be a better term), he was loyal neither to Marxism nor to any PDPA leader, and he followed orders only when it suited his purposes. After the fall of the Najibullah regime, he allied himself loosely with the interim government but without submitting to their discipline any more than he had to Najibullah's. The size, equipment, training, and internal discipline of his forces were on a scale that permitted him the luxury of independence; no other Afghan armed units in early 1993 were in a position to impose their will on him.

A few old-regime collaborators, such as Hassan Sharq, fled abroad before the curtain fell on Afghan communism. In February 1993 Najibullah was reportedly writing his memoirs while still hiding in the Kabul U.N. offices, where he had fled after being thwarted in his effort to escape to India. Babrak Karmal was rumored to have crossed the border into Tajikistan.

The rest of the elite had vanished.

Conclusion

When this chapter was first written, in 1988, its title seemed pretentious. Who could know whether the Afghan Communist elite was or was not ephemeral? As late as the paper's 1991 update, there was still reason to be concerned how Soviet influence might continue to be exerted in Afghanistan via present and future elites. Eventual "Sovietization" still seemed a clear danger.

The PDPA, whose membership was suffering from educational degradation (only 50 percent of rural party members were literate according to one resistance source in 1986) and whose concentration of members in the various armed security services was leading to ever greater estrangement from the people, was nevertheless the most cohesive and perhaps largest Afghan organization. Its continued survival in a post-Soviet Afghanistan had already astonished most analysts, including me. Its prospects for underground survival under any post-Communist regime appeared much better than we had estimated earlier.

Individual PDPA leaders, such as the Hazara intellectual Keshtmand, were estimated to have loyal followings among their ethnic kin. Even the hated Najibullah might have been able to call on the loyalty of his fellow Ghilzai Pashtuns to oppose non-Ghilzais.

In the Soviet Union there was a long-term program of educating Afghan youth that had been going on since 1984, when 834 seven- to nine-year-olds were shipped off from Kabul to Soviet boarding schools for ten years of cloistered education. By the turn of the century, these young Afghans could be expected to have returned and to be forming a new ruling, pro-Soviet intelligentsia. Meanwhile, somewhat older Afghan youths were receiving Soviet scholarships for specialized education at higher levels. Their technical skills, desperately needed for rebuilding the war-ravaged country, would probably have outweighed even a post-Communist government's worries about their political reliability. Moreover, Soviet influence threatened to spread via local and even privatized trade links that had been set up between Afghan communities and selected Soviet communities. Soviet support for Kabul regime policies designed to attract women, religious figures, landowners, and businessmen might have encouraged sympathy for Moscow among those groups. Finally, the PDPA/HP's efforts to mask its true Marxist-Leninist essence might have succeeded in the long run, leaving it able to control Afghanistan's destinies from behind the scenes.

But with utter discrediting of Soviet communism and collapse of Moscow's empire, both the organizational structure and ideological cement that might have held the elite together and sustained Sovietization crumbled away. It is perhaps the supreme historical irony in 1993 that a more realistic worry today than the Sovietization of Afghanistan is the ongoing Afghanization—if one takes the term to imply extreme localism and intercommunity hostility—of the former Soviet Union.

Notes

1. Estimates of the relative size of the various Afghan minority groups vary widely. Before 1978, the Pashtuns were commonly believed to hold an absolute majority of around 55 percent, but most contemporary observers agree they are now only a plurality (*Documents and Records of the National Conference of the People's Democratic Party of Afghanistan,* Kabul, 14–15 Mar. 1982). See also note 19.

2. Although he claims to be a Pashtun, Babrak's native language is Dari, and he is reputed to carry more Tajik than Pashtun blood in his veins.

3. The April coup, which had been planned for August, was set off prematurely by the Khalqis, who then successfully outmaneuvered their Parchami rivals to seize complete control.

4. Most Western observers in 1978 were estimating PDPA strength at three thousand to six thousand. For a discussion of conflicting membership claims, see Arnold 1983, 115–19.

5. Roy (1986, 95–97, 103–6) summarizes the terror and its victims. Though generous in its scope, the terror was not total. It was directed against religious figures, landowners, unsympathetic intellectuals, the wealthy, Maoists, Parchamis, and not a few common people with a previous history of personal enmity toward a party member's family. Unlike Stalin's purges of the 1930s, however, it largely exempted the bureaucracy, the military, those with technical skills, and even some persons who had held positions of authority in the previous regime.

6. When the Parchamis later released such statistics, they showed consistent majorities in both party membership among security personnel and security personnel among the PDPA membership at large. This trend was undoubtedly established under the Khalqis.

7. Interestingly, however, the Revolutionary Council, now expanded from twenty-three to fifty-seven members, contained no known nonparty figures except the three ministers.

8. Soviet blindness to the seriousness of the Parcham-Khalq split is reflected in their coequal seating of Deputy Prime Minister Assadullah Sarwari, the man who as head of the secret police under the Khalqis had personally tortured Parchamis, next to one of his most prominent former victims, Deputy Prime Minister Sultan Ali Keshtmand. Before more blood flowed, however, Sarwari was sent off to Moscow in June 1980 "for medical treatment" and from there was posted as Afghan ambassador directly to Ulan Bator.

9. In a remarkably frank article in *Kommunist* (never published in Afghanistan), Babrak subsequently lashed out at "serious weaknesses" that had become apparent as the party prepared for the conference: problems with organizational consolidation, ideological upbringing, and party discipline. These, he noted, were especially noticeable in the army, the militia (i.e., Ministry of Interior), and an unspecified group of other ministries, where an old sickness, factionalism, had broken out again. In blocking the Central Committee's rulings on selecting delegates, certain persons "even went so far as to espouse instituting rotten bourgeois 'democracy' in the revolutionary party" (Babrak Karmal, "O proekte programmy deystviy NDPA i zadachakh po ukrepleniyu partii i usileniyu ee svyazey s narodom" [On the PDPA's projected program of action and the tasks of consolidating the party and strengthening its ties with the people], *Kommunist* 5 (May 1982: 106).

10. The discrepancy between these figures for trade union membership and those in table 1.2 cannot be readily explained except by reference to the occasionally excessive overoptimism of Afghan Communist statisticians. The figures in table 1.2 are more consistent with preceding and succeeding membership claims. Conversely, the much higher claim for DYOA membership in table 1.2 comes from later in 1982. It also is probably exaggerated.

11. Paradoxically, there was supposed to have been an increase in the number of committees in small and medium districts during this period, but resistance control of the countryside casts doubt on this assertion.

12. TASS transmitted praise of the theses within two hours of Babrak's speech, an indication of prior Soviet coordination (TASS, 9 Nov. 1985).

13. Pro-Babrak demonstrations erupted almost immediately after Najibullah took over and continued sporadically until the former leader was shipped off in May 1987 to exile in the USSR.

14. The students were not doing very well, however. Najibullah claimed in late 1987 that most of them were at the 3 (approximately C) level (*Kabul New Times*, 11 Nov. 1987). According to purported official DRA statistics, there were 52,496 Afghan students in Communist countries (46,772 in the USSR alone) between 1980 and 1984 (*Afghan Realities*, 1 June 1985, 5).

15. The same strategy of co-opting even hostile elements into the party in order to deal with them piecemeal and progressively was used by Moscow in Central Asia and the Caucasus in the 1920s (Valenta and Sheikh, 1987).

16. The first source refers obliquely to "former members of the Central Committee included in the amnesty." The second mentions a total of seventeen former Khalqi "ministers" who had been freed and identifies one (former minister Shah Wali) by name. Only

ten Khalqi ministers were replaced, but exactly seventeen Central Committee members, including Wali and all the other vanished ministers, disappeared at the time of the Soviet invasion, and it is these who were probably liberated.

17. These nonparty villages were ostensibly under Kabul's control, but unless there was an armed government presence on hand to enforce federal orders, they were undoubtedly independent. Lip service loyalty to Kabul, an old Afghan tradition, has never counted for much.

18. Of the parties named, ROWPA appeared to be a direct descendant of the old Settam-e-Melli (Against National Oppression), a mostly Tajik orthodox Marxist-Leninist group that was ideologically in line with the Khalqis but opposed to the Khalqis' Pashtun chauvinism.

One party that Najibullah did not name in 1988 (but had been the first non-PDPA group to pledge allegiance to his national reconciliation program) was a self-styled social democratic party, Afghan Mellat (*Kabul New Times*, 29 Oct. 1987). As early as the 1960s, this party, previously known as Tolan-Pal Woleswak, had been renowned for its virulently pro-Pashtun, ultranationalist and racist (some have said proto-Nazi) propaganda. In October 1979, in apparent coordination with an anti-Amin coup attempt by Mohammad Oslam Watanjar, it had tried to overthrow Amin, and its leader, Qadratullah Hadad, had been arrested. Miraculously avoiding execution, he later "escaped" and fled to Pakistan, where he took up a prominent position in Afghan Mellat. There were suspicions at the time that this far-right group, like others uncovered elsewhere, might have been Soviet-sponsored from the outset (Arnold [1981] 1985, 89–90), and its hasty jumping on the national reconciliation bandwagon strengthens such doubts. In June 1991 its leader, Mohammad Amin Wakman, delivered a speech to the Socialist International in which he called his group "the only organized democratic force in Afghanistan," one that since 1987 had been calling for a political resolution of the Afghan conflict (Wakman 1991, 2). He did not add that this had entailed collaboration with Najibullah's national reconciliation program.

19. Although the national assembly is not the same as a party conference, it has some of the same characteristics as a gathering of middle- and upper-level elites. To this extent it is comparable to the conferences of 1982 and 1987. Regarding ethnic makeup, a review of 219 persons directly and indirectly associated with the PDPA on whom ethnic data is available showed 57 percent Pashtun, 23 percent Tajik, 8 percent Hazara, 7 percent Uzbek, 2 percent Turkoman, and the remainder scattered among other nationalities. The relatively heavy representation of socially first-place Pashtuns and last-place Hazaras may carry a message, but the base is too small for far-reaching conclusions.

2

The New Political Elite of Afghanistan

OLIVIER ROY

Afghanistan is a segmented society, with different levels of identification between an individual and segmental groups, from extended family to ethnic identity. The relations between the state and the different groups have always been based on compromise and mutual indifference more than on open confrontation; therefore, two kinds of elites have coexisted: local notables (the khans), who strive for local preeminence and who may use the state apparatus as an ally in local feuds, and urban elites, whose aim is to control the state central power and who tend to despise the rules of the provincial power game (Daoud 1982).

Today, in Afghanistan, war is the main factor of social change, through migration of refugees to Pakistan and Iran, forced urbanization (at least in Kabul), and a new balance of power among ethnic groups and between the central state and the countryside. These are the classic effects of any war, but one of the lasting effects of the 1980s war is the politicization of Afghan society and the emergence of a new leadership. Until recently in Afghanistan, combatants in feuds and wars respected the framework of the traditional society and even its relation to the state: warriors were tribesmen led by their peacetime leaders (except in jihad time, when ulama could become military leaders), who never intended to establish a new regime in the capital; looting the bazaar and making a new king were the utmost desirable achievements. War was part-time (after the crops), and even during the fighting, families could go on with everyday life because women, children, and villages were spared. War and fighting did not bring social change; it was just a way of playing the power game (to fight for preeminence, not to destroy the enemy) with more exciting rules. But from 1980 to 1988 the Soviets waged total war, in which no space, time, or group could be spared; traditional tactics and fighting habits did not fit this new war, which required that fighters become full-time professional soldiers and that a new category of leaders emerge having both political and military skills. What was at stake was not the preeminence of a group or of a leader but the nature of society and state (communism versus Islamism). The old tribal society was not fit for modern warfare; tribal fighters were not necessarily professional guerillas. This explains why so many Afghans left the country, sometimes in whole clans or tribes, and why the traditional tribal leadership had either to emigrate or to join the regime. Afghanistan was mainly a peasant society, but with some five million external refugees and three million internal refugees, the traditional rural way of life has given way to something very new, not only in terms of a way of life but also in terms of leadership.

Traditional society in Afghanistan depends on a fragile balance among khans, clans, ethnic groups, and the like and does not provide a suitable framework for mobilizing civilians and fighters for a protracted war. The introduction of modern warfare has been the main reason for a change in leadership in a traditional society.

The Old Political Order

Before the war, the process of politicization affected only the new urban elite—mainly young, educated middle-class people who did not find status in a society that, although changing through the spread of education, was still dominated by the traditional elite: the Durrani (see glossary at the end of this chapter) tribal aristocracy and the comparatively large (for Afghanistan) landowners. Educated youth had no future except in the civil service and the army, where they would be excluded from top appointments.

These young educated people made up the bulk of the political opposition to the king's and President Daoud's regimes and became mostly pro-Soviet Communists on the one hand and "Islamists" on the other. Maoists were also active in Kabul, especially among ethnic minorities and Shi'ites. Militant Shi'ites had their own cultural and political organizations, but as far as ideology was concerned, they were very close to the Sunni Islamists, except that they never went along with them in common political organizations. In Afghanistan, as in other parts of the Middle East, as far as the Shiʿite-Sunni issue is concerned, sectarian differences supersede common interests.

All these political movements were confined to Kabul. In the countryside the local elite was made up of the khan, the *mawlawi,* and the *hakim* (or *uluswal*)—that is, respectively, a landowner head of a powerful local *qawm;* a cleric trained in a high-level, but generally private, *madrasa;* and the district administrator, an outsider appointed from Kabul, poorly paid and with a term of two or three years.

A *qawm* is any segment of the society bound by close ties: it could be an extended family, a clan, an occupational group, or a village. A *qawm* is based on kinship and client-patron relations; before being an ethnic group, it is a solidarity group, which protects its members from encroachments from the state and other *qawms* but which is also the scene of lively competition between contenders for local supremacy.[1]

For an Afghan, khan and *malek* status means competition with equals, vigilance against encroachments, and constitution of a patron-client relation (and mujahidin commanders promoted through the war tend to adopt the same attitude). Afghan society has a hierarchy but is acephalous and dynamic: as soon as one is in a position to be a leader, someone else (a cousin, a neighbor) challenges the newly acquired position. Wealth is a means, not an end. A rich man is not necessarily a khan if he does not work to convert his wealth into a following of clients. Authority does not follow from one's position in a truly corporate group structure but from a permanent and personal effort to attract followers and to enhance the status of one's own *qawm.* Wealth is just a means to achieve prestige.[2]

The New Leadership

In the course of the war, a new leadership has emerged in Afghanistan. These people are not drawn from traditional landowning families; in fact, like the Communists, they belong to the urban middle-class intelligentsia. Contrary to most of the accounts of the Afghan mujahidin movement, the leadership of the resistance is *not* mainly made up of traditional notables and landowners.[3]

Local administrators, identified with the Communist state, fled or were killed. Whatever the future evolution of the war, there will for years be no state-appointed outsiders as local administrators, first, because the war has stressed the local communities' traditional distrust of the central state and, second, because the mujahidin movement has established a local administration that is either shaped as a would-be state administration or that will oppose any appointment made from the capital, even if the mujahidin win central power. There are today three categories of mujahidin leaders.

The Islamists

Most striking is the emergence of young, educated political activists through the three Islamist parties (Jamiᶜat, Hizb-i Hekmatyar, and Hizb-i Khales). The Islamist movement, whose origins may be traced back to the Egyptian Muslim Brotherhood in the 1950s, was not active before the second half of the 1960s on Kabul campuses; it recruited mostly among young intellectuals who considered Islam more a political ideology than a religion.[4] The Islamists were organized in the loose framework of the Young Muslims Organization (established around 1965).

Born in the 1950s, these men were studying at the state university around 1970, mostly in the faculties of sciences or religious law, or in teacher-training schools; the pro-Soviet Communists were mostly trained in the same teacher-training schools, in the military academy, and in the arts university; and Maoists were dominant in the faculty of medicine. The Islamists originally came from middle-class families living in big cities but with roots in the countryside. Few of them belonged to big landowning families, which either did not care to send their sons to school or, if they did, provided them with a foreign-based education. The ordinary educated youth entered school precisely because this was his only hope of social promotion.

Apart from this shared socioeconomic background (which is very common in the entire Middle East), ethnic bias played a role in political affiliations: Jamiᶜat members were mainly Tajiks, and the two others were Hizb Pashtun. Khales recruits mostly in Nangarhar and Paktya provinces, and Hekmatyar among recently detribalized Pashtuns, mainly Ghilzai and eastern Pashtuns (see my "Observations on the Survey," below). They became politicized in the sixties, fighting against the old establishment; for this reason they still oppose the return of the former king, whom they identify with the old social order.

The Islamist ideology uses an intellectual framework close to Western ideologies, especially Marxism, but filled with Qurʾanic terminology and Islamic historical references. They advocate a revolution (enqelab) to bring about an Islamic state (dawlat); such a revolution is undertaken by a vanguard party (hizb) and not by the corporation of the ulama; that means that a real Islamic society is not the result of the ethical reformation of individual ways of life through ulama religious predications but is achieved through political means; it is a historical process. The state is not just a tool to protect and propagate religion but is the core of the process of Islamization; the truth of any society is in the state, not in the beliefs of the citizens; the ulama and Shari ͨah (holy law) are less important than "party" and "Islamic ideology." Thus, politics wins over mere performance of religious rituals.

For the new Islamist elite, in contrast with the traditional notables and the ulama, the state is worthy of being taken; the state is the key for any transformation of society. Islamist political organizations depart from traditional segmentation and are established along the patterns of any Western revolutionary political party; they are a disciplined congregation of political workers who unite around a common ideology and program to transform society without regard to familial, ethnic, or patronage relations. But in fact such modernist attitudes have proved to be too optimistic.

After an abortive coup in 1975, which drove them into exile, the new Islamist elites came back into Afghanistan beginning in 1979, after the Communist coup and the Soviet invasion. They faced problems in establishing their new power, based on political affiliation and ideological commitment, in a traditional and segmented society where political and ideological references do not play an important role. Among Pashtuns, the transplantation did not work well in the Ghilzai and Durrani tribal areas, but it was more successful among the eastern Pashtuns, mainly through Khales (Zadran and Khugiani tribes). Hekmatyar won the majority of the Pashto-speaking pockets in the Northeast (in Baghlan, Takhar, Kunduz), where tribalism has disappeared as the basis for the social order but not from the memory of the former tribesmen, who still retain the name of their tribe. Hekmatyar himself is a Pashtun Kharut from Kunduz. Jami ͨat has the upper hand among Persian speakers; Rabbani, a Tajik from northern Badakhshan, is the only one among the seven leaders in Peshawar who is a native Persian speaker. Two factors are important here: sociological (tribal-nontribal) and ethnic (Pashtun–non-Pashtun). But none of these parties is merely an ethnic party: there are Persian-speaking military commanders in Hizb-i Hekmatyar (around 20 percent, according to my survey [table 2.1], such as Commander Farid in Kohestan) and in Hizb-i Khales (Mohammed Qol in Baghlan), and Pashtuns in Jami ͨat (24 percent, such as Naquibullah in Kandahar, Arif in Kunduz, and Anwar in Kabul).

TABLE 2.1

A Survey of Mujahidin Field Commanders

(in percentage; particularly significant figures are in italic)

| | Party[a] | | | | | | |
	JIA (39)	HIH (19)	HAR (10)	NIFA (10)	HIK (10)	HIM (3)	Total
Age							
Born before 1938	12	5	16	*55*	0	—	14
Born 1938–48	20	25	*84*	27	40	66	37
Born after 1948	*68*	*70*	*0*	18	60	33	*49*
Education							
Modern high schools and universities	*64*	*75*	*0*	27	40	66	*48*
Modern religious training (state university of Shariᶜah, or Najaf for the Shiᶜites	*7*	0	0	0	*10*	33	5
Traditional religious education, private madrasa	22	5	*89*	9	30	0	30
No education or traditional private education	7	20	11	*64*	20	0	17
Ethnic Group							
Pashtun	24	*75*	63	*80*	*90*	—	*51*
Tajik (more accurately, a Sunni Persian native speaker)	64	20	10	10	10	—	35
Uzbek	10	5	*26*	10	—	—	8
Other (Hazara, Baluch, etc.)	2	—	—	—	—	100	6

[a]JIA   Jamiᶜat-e Islami (Rabbani) HAR Harakat-e Enqelab-e Islami (Nabi)
HIH   Hizb-i Islami (Hekmatyr)   NIFA National Islamic Front of Afghanistan
HIK   Hizb-i Islami (Khales)   (Gaylani)
                              HIM Harakat-e Islami (Mohseni), Shiᶜite party

The exercise of local power has also changed these intellectuals, for whom the important question is how to adapt to traditional society. Few of them had legitimacy according to traditional patterns: they were not the offspring of respected families, either wealthy or religious. Among the exceptions are Fazlullah (Jamiᶜat, Logar, who is a member of the Modjaddedi family), Abdul Wudud (Hizb-i Hekmatyar, Badakhshan, who was the son of a former member of the national assembly), Husseyn Shah Padshah (Khales, Nangarhar, who is a *sayyad* and the son of a respected local cleric). But generally, these commanders are newcomers in the world of the notables: Masud is the son of a petty army officer; Jallaluddin Haqqani in Paktya is not a member of the local dominant tribe, the Zadran. They saw three ways to establish themselves locally.

1. To push for a new political structure, putting aside traditional notables at the risk of an open confrontation with traditional society (as with most of Hekmatyar's commanders).

2. To become self-made notables along the same patterns as the former ones (using patronage relations and sometimes the murder of rivals, a common pattern in the North from Maymana to Nahrin, in Ghorband and in Laghman), access to weapons delivery providing the best guarantee of achieving such a position.

3. To connect a new political structure to a traditional society, as has Masood, who built his Shura-ye-nazar (supervisory council) using respected ulama as a connection with traditional notables, and who appointed young intellectuals as district heads but let villages govern themselves as usual.

So the young Islamist intellectuals are not a homogeneous group, even if they are all reluctant to see the old establishment return.

Traditional Notables

Generally, the former establishment left the country; there was no khan fighting at the head of his tribe, or clan, against the Soviets. Strangely enough, the former establishment still present in Afghanistan had joined the Kabul regime against the mujahidin. Some new governors recently appointly by the regime—who tended to supplant the party secretaries as acting leaders of the regime's forces at the provincial level (such as Wakil Shah Nazar in Helmand)—were former members of the national assembly from the time of the king or President Daoud, as were some prominent members of the National Fatherland Front (e.g., Wakil Naqshband from Zabul Province, Sayyad Abdul Ghyas from Badakhshan, and Mohammad Sarwar Shahi, Husseyn Khadem Beg, and Wakil Abdullah Jan).

In fact, the Communist regime failed to bring about any social change in the countryside, although the parties to the resistance did, at first. Local notables now feel more at ease with a regime that needs them according to the traditional patterns of power sharing between a weak central state and strong local powers, which could hope to become stronger by making a deal with the state. They prefer to compromise with a distant Communist regime that gave up all mention of Marxism than to deal with a new category of ascending rival local leaders: mujahidin commanders, whose authority relies on the totally different patterns of Islam as an ideology for national liberation. These notables could play the game with the regime according to the same rules that worked for centuries; they cannot do that with the mujahidin.

Some categories of traditional notables nevertheless did find their way into the resistance. Local petty notables still play a role at lower levels. Being identified with their *qawm*, they are never able to bypass local divisions or to represent a political alternative to division, because they are systematically opposed by their counterparts from other *qawm*. They usually either find their place in the framework of a dominant party, dealing with it as they used to do with the central government, or they join the rival party to preserve a local sphere of influence, thus helping to undermine the emergence of a modern political framework. Few of them have achieved a leading position at the provincial level (as did Amin Wardak in Wardak). Most of them would of course favor the comeback of the king, but they have few ways of influencing the course of events.

The Ulama

The ulama were edged out of the political scene at the time of the king, but they are now playing a more significant role, especially in areas where the young Islamist intellectuals have not made inroads (tribal areas, but also some northern provinces). Zabul, Paktya, Farah, Ghazni, Samangan, and Faryab have many ulama leading mujahidin *jabha* (a "front," that is, a local mujahidin territory or network); in other provinces, they act as deputies or middlemen for Islamist intellectuals (as in Herat, in the Northeast), dealing mainly with justice. Generally, the ulama are able to overcome local division but do not establish a modern administration; they lead the area both as military commanders and as religious judges. Their attitude toward the old regime depends here on their political affiliation, not on the methods they use to rule the area: when they adhere to an Islamist party, they are reluctant to see the return of the king; when they adhere to Harakat, they favor it.

The Islamist movement recruited only a handful of the clerics who were teaching in government religious schools and universities and were therefore a minority among the Afghan clergy (which used to be trained in private *madrasa*); these modernist ulama (or religious students) account for 17 percent of the ulama registered as mujahidin commanders in my survey, all of whom belong to Jami‘at or to Hizb-i Khales. Before the war, most of the traditional ulama, though reluctant to accept the growing Westernization of Afghan society and the increase of Communist influence, kept aloof from active politics. After the Communist coup and the invasion, they identified themselves with Mohammad Nabi Mohammedi, a cleric who headed a *madrasa* in Ghazni and was elected to the national assembly in the sixties. His party, the Harakat-e Enqelab-e Islami (which is neither very revolutionary, *enqelab*, nor dynamic, *harakat*), attracted the bulk of the fighting ulama in the first years of the war.

The strength of the ulama is that they are not supposed to promote their own *qawm* (and a lot of them are said to be *sayyad*), so they do not identify themselves with the interests of a specific group and can therefore rally a coalition of tribes. They also have an uncontested legitimacy in terms of Islam and not, like the khan, through custom and tradition.

The ideological references of the ulama are those of jihad, which has played an important role in the last 150 years of Afghan history. Jihad means that all Muslims should join to fight infidels, forming a *mellat*, which is a subset of the *umma*, whatever the division of the society into tribal or ethnic groups. Jihad is always temporary: as soon as it is achieved (in fact, before it is achieved), the traditional rules of the power game have always made a destructive comeback. Under these conditions, either the ulama played on the side of the king or opposed the king on the side of a tribal coalition (Hadda Mollah around 1890, Mushk-i Alam in 1879, Mollah-i Lang in 1924) or of an ethnic upheaval (like that of Bacha-e Saqqa in 1928). The only perennial claim of the ulama is the implementation of Shari‘ah, whether by an emir or a king or a tribal leader. Jihad ideology does not provide the framework for building a state, but it could afford religious legitimation to any leader who tried to bypass tribal division for the sake of the war against the infidels. Whether the present coalition between ulama and Islamists would hold after victory is another question (and the question should be, What is an Islamic State?).

The ideology of the jihad nevertheless allowed some ulama to build effective local military and civilian organizations and to bypass tribal divisions, however traditional they might have been. Ulama and

Islamist intellectuals are thus the more representative of the new mujahidin elite, at least inside Afghanistan.

The Politicization of Afghan Society

The Communist coup, followed by the Soviet invasion of Afghanistan, triggered a large-scale politicization of Afghan society. Already existing Islamist organizations found an increased following, and new parties, mostly conservative, were founded in exile in Peshawar. After some ups and downs, the political landscape of Afghan resistance has been the same since 1980: a Sunni alliance of seven parties in Peshawar, and a Shi'ite coalition of eight parties in Qom, of which only four seem to be really established inside Afghanistan.

Politicization of the Afghan resistance was effective through two different trends. First, a certain number of urban political workers, all Islamist, came back from exile in Peshawar to organize the upheavals; they were mainly successful in the North and in the West. Second, usually non-politically minded peasants and local notables joined one or another of the different mujahidin parties in order to get weapons. But the choice of a party was not made at random; according to my field researches, less than a quarter of the field commanders inside Afghanistan changed their political affiliation in the course of the war, and even these changes were made according to some permanent patterns.

In these conditions, one can speak of a new *political* elite in Afghanistan. Political affiliations depend on a nexus of different motivations whose importance varies according to the sociological, religious, and ethnic environment. The trends I identify here do not, of course, mechanically determine political affiliations, any more than political science in the West can predict people's choices in elections. Actually, the connections I have established to explain political affiliations permit many exceptions and do not pretend to explain everything, but sufficient patterns and trends exist to make sense of what at first glance looks like confusion.

The following explain the political affiliation of a local *jabha*:

1. Previous political affiliations of the local commanders. This is the case only among the former Young Muslims, who always joined one of the Islamist parties, although they joined a particular one of the three Islamist parties (Rabbani, Khales, or Hekmatyar) for other reasons.

2. Ideological considerations. The first ideological split among mujahidin is between Islamists, who advocate an Islamic revolution bringing social justice, and traditionalists, who, even if they want an Islamic (that is, merely "Muslim") state, are puzzled by the idea of a revolution and do not see the need for a change in social structures. This split, in fact, embodies the opposition between the notables (either secular, like the former establishment and most of the tribal leaders, who joined Gaylani or Mojaddidi, or religious, that is, the clerical establishment, who joined the religious but conservative Harakat-e Enqelab) and a new generation of young, educated middle-class activists who did not find their way in prewar Afghanistan.

In fact, the ideological split reveals the sociological changes in modern Afghanistan: the decrease of tribalism and the emergence of a new generation of young intellectuals. This trend had appeared before the war but was given an unexpected boost by the war, to the astonishment of both the Soviets and traditional tribal leaders.

In the tribal areas of the South, the change was not so noticeable, because the influence of the vanished khans went mostly to ulama, as traditionally minded as the khans; but in the North, a new category of political leaders appeared in the very first years of the war.

A second ideological split is between the Islamists themselves: moderate Islamists mainly joined Jamiʿat, whereas more radically minded young people joined Hizb-i Islami (Hekmatyar).

3. Preexisting religious networks. There are two kinds of religious networks (not mutually exclusive): Sufi affiliations and madrasa fellowships. Sufi orders are not centralized in Afghanistan: one follows a pir, who could be independent or might himself rely on a more important pir. There are two kinds of Sufi orders: one supposes a client-patron relation between a charismatic family and a tribal segment (this is the case of the Qaderi order headed by the Gaylani family), a relation that has become rather secular in the course of time; the other supposes a personal initiation by a pir who provides not only barakat (charismatic blessing) but also an orthodox religious training. The former kind of Sufism is the basis of Gaylani's National Islamic Front of Afghanistan (NIFA) and is therefore strong in tribal areas. The latter is the basis of most of the Naqshbandi groups, which, except for the Modjaddedi family itself, did not establish a specific party but are very active in Jamiʿat and in Harakat. Sufi networks may have a territorial basis, but not necessarily: two networks could overlap. The biggest networks are centered around Kabul, Purchaman (Farah), Karukh (Herat), and Kunduz. Thus, a Sufi affiliation can explain di-

rectly or indirectly a political affiliation. For example, Amin Wardak, despite his vocal dissatisfaction with delivery of weapons, stood with Gaylani for years because his family, and especially his father, was *murid* of Pir Gaylani.

Clerical networks were established through common studies and teacher-pupil relations in the private *madrasa,* where the bulk of the Afghan ulama have been trained. This explains why the Harakat-e Enqelab, whose influence is based on these networks, was spread throughout Afghanistan, whatever the ethnic and tribal affiliations. But in areas where Islamists were strong, Harakat influence decreased in favor of Jami ʿat, mainly in the North.

4. Ethnic considerations, and sometimes more-parochial communal loyalties (tribal links, client-patron relations, local solidarity groups). It is important to note that in the Peshawar Alliance there is, strictly speaking, no "single ethnic issue" party. True, some small ethnic parties exist (e.g., the Union of the North, headed by Azad Beg, which is an avowed pan-Turk ethnic party), generally infiltrated by the Communist regime, which played the ethnic card. But all seven Sunni parties have followers in different ethnic groups and tribes. There are, however, some permanent trends that give an ethnic or tribal bias to political affiliations. For example, at the beginning Jami ʿat was mainly Persian-speaking, whereas Hizb (Hekmatyar) attracted the majority of the northeastern Pashtuns, the Naqel, or displaced Pashtuns, who came from the South during the last hundred years; Gaylani and Modjaddedi are stronger among Pashtun tribesmen in the South. In Nangarhar province, the Khugiani Islamists joined Khales because he is a Khugiani himself, whereas most of the Shinwari Islamists joined Hekmatyar. In Qandahar, most of the commanders dissatisfied with the moderate parties joined Khales because the other possible party, Jami ʿat, was seen either as Tajik or as Alikozay (the great Jami ʿat commander in Qandahar, Naquibullah, is a Pashtun Alikozay). Only the Harakat-e Enqelab has a uniform mixture of all Afghan ethnic groups, owing to its clerical nature.

More-parochial considerations play a role at the lowest level of fragmentation of the Afghan society, especially among secular petty notables. The fact that a local *qawm* joins a party for one of the motivations cited above could trigger a reactive affiliation by other local *qawm* traditionally opposed to the first. Here, also, affiliations are not made at random; for example, when the Panjshir valley joined Jami ʿat, the Andarab valley, which is sociologically and ethnically close to the former, joined Hizb (Hekmatyar), a similar but concurrent party.

Most of the changes in political affiliations used to occur among Harakat-e Enqelab commanders, mainly Uzbek and Pashtun Durrani; roughly 50 percent of the former Harakat commanders in Faryab and Qandahar provinces changed political affiliation at least once. By contrast, Jami ͑at, Gaylani, and Khales commanders have been more stable, and Hekmatyar's fronts have shown a slow but continuous erosion. Affiliation with the Sayyaf party is purely opportunist, based on traditional client-patron relations and without any ideological or religious consideration but with some ethnic bias. Sayyaf followers are mainly Pashtuns; the Sayyaf-Wahhabi connection in Peshawar has no religious influence inside Afghanistan, but it had considerable financial consequences, at least until 1986.

New and Old Notables

The ambivalence of the process of politicization in Afghanistan is obvious. On the one hand, it gives a new look to traditional divisions, but on the other hand, it introduces political references (e.g., to a specific ideology, which is alien to traditional society) and new structures. Parties tend to create administrations using the prerogatives of the former central state: for example, there are committees dealing with finance, health, culture, and so forth; the party collects taxes and might establish its own judicial power; mujahidin tend to shift from being part-time fighters to being professional soldiers. The notion of state structure is no longer seen as alien to the society; local mujahidin administrators always belong to the local community (except in Hizb-i Hekmatyar) and owe their legitimacy either to their traditional status (as mullah or *malek*) or to their party membership, or to both. Except in the cases of notables who join the government militias, local leaders do not explicitly express the narrow interests of their community but pretend to refer to a new model of state and society, even if the traditional fragmentation always plays a bigger role than they admit. This complexity of their political affiliations makes them stronger than it appears at first glance.

Each of the three categories of leaders in the Afghan resistance tends to define an *ideal type* of political power.

The Islamists use an explicitly Western (or Marxist) model of party organization, the party being seen as a would-be state. Their ideology discards the traditional values—loyalty to the *qawm*, a desire to fight for preeminence among equals, contempt for the central state. The administration they try to implement is supposed to supersede the divisional organization of the society, not because they embody Islam, as the ulama do, but because they represent a would-be state; they think as if they were above family and kinship ties. They try to enlarge their initial stronghold, generally built on a *qawm* territory or network, to a provincial-scale territory, and then to a national dimension.

The ulama use the model of jihad, with two priorities, war and Shariʿah; building a would-be state is not a priority. The typical entity established by warring mullahs is a *markaz* (center), built along the same lines as the traditional *ribat* (Charnay 1986, 232, 250): a military base, far from bazaars and villages, where mujahidin are permanently established in a protected stronghold and from which they launch attacks against the regime outposts or place ambushes on the main roads. In this *markaz*, mujahidin might come from different tribes and even ethnicities, as is the case around Maymana. The *markaz* is generally headed by the staff of a former *madrasa* and is sometimes no more than a fortified *madrasa*. Frequently, the *madrasa* was affiliated to a Naqshbandi order, and so also the *markaz*; in this case, it is easier to bypass tribal and ethnic divisions, the Sufi affiliation being perceived as more important than the *qawm* affiliation. A local *alim* is seldom contested by another local *alim*, because teaching in a *madrasa* and belonging to a brotherhood has established between them an acknowledged hierarchy. This is different from the permanent dynamic of competition that pitches one khan against another.

The *alim* establishes a Shariʿah court but does not interfere in the daily life of the surrounding villages except for meting out justice. He is more interested in reforming the standards of behavior of his mujahidin than in establishing a would-be state. Like the whole muslim tradition of jihad, victory is seen more as God's gift for pious Muslims than as the achievement of a politically minded organization and strategy. So the warring *alim* is less interested in extending a territorial organization than in attracting followers who could enhance his reputation as a pious man. Ulama are not expansionist in terms of territory. Even if they give up the khan's perception of prestige, they still identify success as a patron-client relation turned into a teacher-disciple relation. This is why the ulama were able to establish local strongholds (from Anardarrah in Farah, with Mawlawi Faqirullah of Hizb-i Khales, to Samangan, with Mawlawi Islam of Harakat-e Enqelab) but never tried to extend their territorial influence, in which case the personal relation embedded in both patron-client and teacher-disciple relations would have disappeared in favor of a more anonymous political administration, and this would not have fit with ulama values. But most of the ulama maintain good relations with the neighboring traditional notables and the Islamists, sharing the notables' contempt for any state, their refusal of political revolution, and their definition of influence in terms of allegiance, and the Islamists' acceptance of hierarchy, their perception of Islam as the main motivation for fighting (thus superseding traditional tribal divisions), and their stress on the necessary re-Islamization of a society that has become "corrupt."

The Afghan traditional notable lacks political references; in speech, he uses either the jihad model or a nationalist conception *(mellat)*, but he thinks and acts in the framework of the traditional local game of power. Even if he can sometimes stress the necessity for a technical modernization of the society, he does not advocate new and modern political structures, except for the revitalization of old tribal institutions (like the *jirgah,* an assembly). In fact, today's notables use the political fragmentation (mainly the Peshawar seven parties) to express and enhance the traditional *qawm* fragmentation. Joining a party, the notable strengthens his position by getting weapons or by choosing a party bigger than that of the rival notable or just by preventing the rival from being the sole mujahidin commander. This phenomenon is strengthened by the rivalry between local notables. Thus, traditional notables in the resistance tend to play the new political game along the old rules. The party is like the central state, which is used to enhance local status, not to achieve a nationwide, ideologically minded project. In these conditions, to join a party already having a local commander entails, for a traditional notable or for a newly promoted military commander, a demotion in terms of status and power. To be the leader of a *qawm,* one has to give, not to take (which is why Afghan society is not feudal). Because weapons are channeled through a party, it is important for a local leader either to be the sole appointed commander of a party or to receive weapons directly, without going through the officially appointed emir, the provincial head of the party. Thus, a local commander or notable tends to look for a direct affiliation with a party other than the locally dominant one, but in doing this, he follows the patterns dealt with above. The traditional power status in Afghanistan is an incentive to both political affiliation and political fragmentation. Subordination of local notables and commanders to an emir is possible only if the leader is a charismatic or religious figure or if the level of politicization is so high that discipline exists, which is very rare except in Hekmatyar's Hizb-i Islami. So both external and internal divisions among the resistance parties come not only from the passive division of the society but also from the dynamics of power status.

Rivalry between Islamists and ulama, on the one hand, and traditional khans, on the other, is obvious when they discuss Afghanistan's future. Both advocate free elections but are adamant about the name to be given to the national assembly. The Islamists call it *shura;* the notables, *jirgah.* In fact, this quarrel embodies two perceptions of what constitutes politics in Afghanistan. *Jirgah* is a tribal institution, a gathering of elders to discuss an issue; the word is Pashto and refers to a typically tribal practice that was used only twice at a national level, in 1747 and 1929 in order to provide political legitimization for a ruler. To use this word is to stress the ascendancy of tribal institutions and ideology in Afghanistan. By contrast, *shura* is a Qur'anic term whose signification remains very broad, but it implies that "advice" (*shura* means "the council for advising") must be based on religious wisdom and knowledge. Here, Islam as a political system supersedes traditional tribal institutions.

Actually, the three categories above are not so clearly differentiated. Some intellectuals in the countryside, hence in the traditional society, actually saw themselves either as traditional notables or as ulama and, without changing their discourse, began to play the power game as such. It is not unusual now, specifically from Fayzabad to Maymana, to hear stories of personal feuds and revenge, of competition for women, and of assassinations of political opponents who became personal enemies. To take booty or extort taxes, even bribes, is more important than to destroy the Kabul regime's base of power. Nepotism supersedes political appointments. These new notables, who added the term "khan" to a single name or nickname bestowed during their student days, also adopt the same cautious and static war tactics as the ulama: months in a distant *markaz* followed by some raids on a neighboring bazaar, tactics closer to the former tribal raids than to the methodical harassment of guerilla warfare.

By contrast, some ulama, mainly the ones who were trained in state-sponsored *madrasa,* adapted themselves to the political party system. On the other hand, no traditional khan is able to give up his traditional status for a modern political game.

Paradoxically, the implantation of modern political party structures in Afghanistan could either bypass the traditional tribal divisions (as in the Northeast) or (as in the center North) give a new boost to infrapolitical, infraethnic, and even infratribal fragmentation, that is, to politics at the *qawm* level: a local petty notable, followed by some dozens of parents and tenants, could suddenly regain some power by joining a party that is a rival of the dominant party and that will provide him with enough weapons and money to be above the new law and to act independently. These local petty notables might not have politically expressed themselves before the war, but they now find in political affiliation an access to weapons and a new self-assertion, making it more difficult for the dominant party and leader to assert themselves as a political alternative above the traditional structures. Such petty notables do not necessarily have a territorial basis, so they are neither feudalists nor warlords, but their simple presence as an independent network is enough to block the implementation of a would-be state structure and to destroy the educational benefits of politicization. As an example, a petty notable will ask voluntary or U.N. agencies for direct help on the grounds that the local chieftain is not of the same ethnic, political, religious, family, or geographic background as his; he will generally find a sympathetic ear among one of the private voluntary organizations (PVOs), which, incidentally, are as tribalized and fragmented as Afghan society; but such a fragmentation of help will jeopardize needed coordination. All parties are responsible for letting such petty notables prevent the process of politicization, because they could not resist sending money and weapons into areas dominated by rival, or even friendly, parties. Client-patron relations are very much alive inside Afghan political parties.

The impact of politicization on traditional power patterns differs from one province to the other. For example, political affiliations in the Qandahar area are the most confusing. In Qandahar the majority of the field commanders have changed their political affiliation at least once and have sometimes retained multiple affiliations. Because Qandahar is one of the most ethnically homogeneous areas in Afghanistan, the ethnic link does not provide an explanation for political affiliation as it does in the mixed Northeast. Even if a sociological change is obvious (the former Durrani aristocratic establishment, now in exile, lost ground to clerics and middle notables), tribal affiliations are the key to political affiliations, and tribal traditional institutions (*jirgah*) supersede party structures. The Alikozay tribe in mainly Jami ͨat, whereas Nurzay, mainly Khales, are fighting against Atsekzay, who retain some links with the government. In the absence of a charismatic leader, a tribal council (Ittihadi-i Qawmi) is striving more or less successfully to settle feuds.

In the North, either party structures supersede traditional leadership (in Masud's and Hekmatyar's areas) or any power structures above the level of the qawm have collapsed. Because of the mixing of different ethnic and tribal groups and the larger influence of the central state in previous centuries, no traditional large-scale power structure, such as tribalism, has ever existed in the North. In this case, traditional divisions have been worsened by the war and by the availability of modern weaponry; young intellectuals tend to act as traditional notables more than as spearheads of a new model of the state. The worst of the traditional society wins over the sociological change brought by the war.

In the North, politicization has triggered either the emergence of would-be state structures or a collapse into internecine warfare. In the South, loose political affiliations have allowed tribal areas to find some original patterns of coordination through traditional institutions and customs; traditional structures either remain untouched or, more often, tend to adapt to new patterns of warfare, like the *markaz* headed by a traditional cleric and affiliated with a Sufi brotherhood, mentioned above.

Two Case Studies: Hizb-i Islami of Hekmatyar and Masud's Council of the North

Hekmatyar's Hizb-i Islami tends to carve relatively small pockets into the map of Afghanistan east of the Qandahar-Maymana line, there being almost no Hizb west of this line; these pockets, from which all the other organizations have been expelled, are very strong and homogeneous. Interestingly enough, they generally correspond to local minority ethnic groups (Pashtuns in the Northeast, Uzbeks in Badakhshan). As usual, *qawm* determinations fit with political motivations; party structure supplants traditional patterns of power. This is the best example of implantation of modern political structures at the cost of an open confrontation with traditional society and other parties.

Hekmatyar's influence is decreasing inside Afghanistan and increasing in Peshawar. The reason is that, even if the party cadres are young, it is difficult for Hekmatyar to replace them when they have been killed, mostly by assassination or in battles with other Afghans (Salim in Baghlan; Issa, Sayfurrahman, and Rauf in Ghorband), because the party rules state that the members of the Central Council must have held their party cards since 1970. The number of old hands fighting inside is declining; thus, Hekmatyar now tends to send new appointees from Peshawar, with good party records, instead of the local deputy commanders promoted from the rank and file; this move makes local

Hizb-i mujahidin resentful of the Peshawar headquarters. On the other hand, Hekmatyar is gaining influence in Peshawar among the new intelligentsia, educated abroad and uprooted, which finds in such a heavily centralized, bureaucratic, and authoritarian party its only political future: through the state and not through local influence and spadework. Conversely, many of Hekmatyar's followers with tribal backgrounds have been unable to settle in their original areas and are living in Peshawar as bureaucrats in the party. South of Peshawar the party established an entire camp of officers and bureaucrats; thousands of them, each paid about a thousand Pakistani Rupees a month, live here with their families and, go every morning to the party's offices (Pierre Centlives and Micheline Centlivres-Demont, personal communication, Nov. 1988).

Masud's organization is the best example of how to link a modern organization with a traditional society. At the begi–ing Masud was leading a classical *qawm* territory, the Panjshir valley. But from early times, the adjacent (Shotol and Hazara) and upper valleys (Paryan) joined the "front," even if their inhabitants did not call themselves Panjshiri (in Shotol they were even from a different ethnic group, whose language is Parachi, not Persian). The *qawm* territory was thus immediately enlarged. What made this possible was the sociocultural background of Masud's close followers: most of them were literate and working in Kabul and thus were less influenced by the *qawm* system in the narrow sense of the word. A broader and regional identity (Panjshiri) replaced traditional and narrower affiliations (by village, descent, or ethnic group). A second important factor was the military success of Masud, who was able to convince his people that an efficient military organization must bypass traditional tribal differences in matters of recruitment, command appointments, and distribution of weapons and territory. Thus, local groups, attached to the narrow territory of their own *qawm*, were unable to strike efficiently against the enemy. Only a highly mobile and professional commando force, moving far from its base (hence circulating among different *qawm* territories) could strike decisive blows at the enemy, according to the Clausewitz (and Mao) conception of guerilla warfare.

So through the military, Masud was able to impose a new political structure. In his eyes, political action was only a means for military efficiency. A would-be state set up the ground for a suitable battlefield. But it took him six years to achieve his aim. In 1983, when he invaded the neighboring Andarab valley, he triggered an angry reaction from the local population, who saw his arrival not as an extension of guerilla activities but as an encroachment of Panjshiris against Andarabis and thus joined the government (an example of how one can play the political game during wartime as a mere extension of traditional tribal differences).

Then Masud decided to create a "central group" of mobile units without any *qawm* link. He invited non-Panjshiri commanders and mujahidin who were feeling constrained by the local *qawm* affiliations system. It was only when the Panjshiris numbered less than 50 percent in these units (in 1986) that Masud was able to cross the Hindu Kush on the north and establish his organization in more than five provinces. His system was imposed from above and through the military, but he did not touch local powers in the villages. He created the Supervisory Council of the North to embody the new political framework, and he used the ulama to legitimate this new system through a discourse on Islam, Shari ͑ah and *umma* being more acceptable to peasants and notables than the "Islamic ideology" of the "campus years." A new administration has slowly been established at district level; the newly appointed governors do not necessarily belong to the local *qawm*. At a higher level, the council is working as a would-be state, with committees for health, reconstruction, education, culture, propaganda, finance, and so forth. But *qawm* affiliations did not disappear overnight; they remain a parameter that must be dealt with.

Masud is neither a khan nor a military commander, but an emir: a leader holding both military and political power. This notion of emir is new in Afghan society. It comes from the Qur ͐anic tradition and bases the new power in the history of Islam, not in tribal tradition (the title Khan is not added to Masud's name). Through these means Masud rises above the rules of the game, as does a *pir*, a *sayyad*, or an *alim*, but he is none of these; he is a political leader; here, the process of politicization reaches its highest achievement.

What limits the expansion of this new political-military would-be state model is that it does not encompass the whole social spectrum, but this condition must be accepted; the law is in the hands of the ulama, who are full members of the council. Economic, social, and private life is outside the council framework. Trade is carried on by private traders, the market is free, and schools are established only with the people's consent.

In fact, compared with the one-party, all-encompassing, totalitarian system of most liberation movements, the Afghan resistance is making a strange but genuine compromise between freedom and organization, between would-be state and society, order and anarchy, town and village. Would this fragile balance last after the fall of Kabul, or prevent the fall of Kabul, precisely because balance is more important than victory? Could this elusive would-be state manage to become an effective central state, ruling a whole nation from the capital, above fragmentation and anarchy? That is the gamble of the future Afghanistan.

The Afghan Political Landscape and the Future State

Most successful national liberation movements have built a new state from an existing centralized would-be state structure, already effective, either in exile or in liberated areas. But in Afghanistan, no centralized liberation movement exists inside the country, and any kind of government in exile or based on the Peshawar parties will have to behave like previous central governments, whatever the sociological changes in its elites.

If no strong central government will be in charge for years, the reconstruction of Afghanistan must be done at the local level, working with the de facto political authorities. This does not mean, as superficial observers used to say, that the Peshawar parties are losing their influence, but that there is a growing discrepancy between the Peshawar bureaucracies (a monster built by a combination of U.S. and Saudi money, Pakistan army strategy, and expectations of the Afghan intellectuals in exile and in search of a secure job, far from the killing fields) and the field commanders, who retain their political affiliation and try to combine a modern political structure with a traditionally segmented society.

The alliance in Peshawar gave birth in February 1989 to an Afghan interim government, which pretended not only to embody legitimacy but also to act as a counterstate, with ministries, bureaucracy, and administration. As far as relations between state and society are concerned, it does not matter whether the alliance is made of seven parties or of just some of them, or whether it remains united or splits in two; the problem is the growing discrepancy between a would-be state from below (the field commanders) and a would-be state from above (the Peshawar bureaucracies).

To establish its power inside Afghanistan, the alliance (or its remaining parts) will have to deal with the local field commanders along the same patterns as any state would have before the Communist coup, except that for the first time a large part of rural Afghanistan is now ruled by people who think of themselves as administrators and statesmen, not as warlords or khans.

The Peshawar Alliance resembles previous governments in Afghanistan at least in its financial basis and recruiting patterns. Since Abdur Rahman's rule (1880–1901) no state in Afghanistan has relied on internal resources, that is, the extraction of wealth from the society. Previously financed by booty, governments turned mostly to foreign aid for their financing. The British subsidies of the early twentieth century were replaced in the 1950s by international aid. Taxes, duties, and excises never matched the foreign help. (Etienne [1972, 50] states: "Foreign investments make two thirds of Second Plan Investments.") The Peshawar Alliance relies on the same patterns; there is no domestic financing, first, because the Afghans are very poor (compared to the Palestinians, e.g.) and, second, because they are used to giving, not to any overarching central authority, but to a local commander or for a specific reason. For instance, the Kabul bazaaris have paid duty to Masud in order to keep the Salang road open. Thus, a would-be state is emerging from below, based mostly on domestic resources and not on the distribution of subsidies by Peshawar. Interestingly enough, the more deeply rooted commanders, in political terms, are used to relying less on Peshawar to get weapons than are more ephemeral local leaders: Masud and Ismail Khan for years used to get a lesser share of weapons than Hekmatyar's people; but instead of weakening them, this lack of assistance strengthened them politically, in the sense that they were obliged to acquire their autonomy by finding direct access to the enemy ordinances through successful assaults and by establishing their own tax system.

The sort of bureaucracy established by the alliance in Peshawar is consonant with the trends that were at work under Zahir Shah's regime and that culminated under the Communist rule: the reign of the new, educated middle class, opposed both to the aristocracy and to the local powers.

In fact, foreign donations (American, Saudi, and Pakistani money) have enabled the Peshawar Alliance to create a foreign-based bureaucracy. The people recruited through the parties in Peshawar are mainly young educated urbanites, having generally left Kabul directly for Peshawar, with little or no fighting record. Whatever the party they are affiliated with, they came from the same sociological background as the Islamists. Even in the "moderate" parties, the new bureaucracy is made of young intellectuals, not of khans or ulama. But, naturally enough, most of these educated youths tend to join the extremist, dogmatic, anti-Western, authoritarian, but nevertheless technocratic, Hekmatyar school of thinking. Uprooted people tend to be more extremist than field commanders confronted with the complexity of the political situation. In Hizb-i Hekmatyar, educated refugees can combine their fascination with Western technology and their resentment at being denied the political perks attached to it, by dreaming of an Islamic revolution that will give them political control of the society. It is no wonder that this contradiction expresses itself best among the Afghan "field officers" of the PVOs working in Pakistan. In camps and in towns, thousands of young Afghans are now educated in Pakistan either through Western-sponsored programs or through Wahhabi *madrasa*. But their dilemma is the same as it was twenty years ago: they have no future except as state employees. They are trained as accountants, nurses, teachers, clerks, interpreters, and trainers in different fields. But where will they find a job, if not in a state? And there is a state in Peshawar: the parties and the alliance. More than that, it has been official American policy to turn the Peshawar Alliance into a would-be state to challenge the Kabul regime. But the proof of the state is in the bureaucracy. Rivalry between parties has led to an overloaded administration (every committee has to be multiplied by seven to avoid controversy); decisions are made by consensus, so that no decision is reached on critical issues. Bureaucrats in Peshawar tend to repeat the mistakes of the Communists: ignoring local situations and governing by decree. Perhaps this is because sociologically, and sometimes even ethnically, the bureaucrats in Peshawar are closer to the Communists than to most of the mujahidin.

But the main employer is not the alliance itself but the odd hundreds of agencies working in Pakistan. In Peshawar the educated young Afghans find administration-like structures, where they work as employees but are excluded from top appointments and political decisions, as they were fifteen years ago in the ancien régime in Afghanistan. Western cadres (generally young, and often women) have replaced the aristocracy that blocked their way to power before. It is quite normal that anti-Western cultural feelings are now spreading in Peshawar. Hekmatyar's Hizb-i Islami is the only party that could give a political form to this frustration, because of its radicalism. So the new "elite," trained and employed in Peshawar, is as ignorant and as arrogant as the Communists were in 1978, and could play the same role as the Communists did then. Also, most of the future "civil servants" trained in Peshawar are as reluctant to go to the countryside, now or later, as their predecessors were years ago.

On the Iranian side, among the Afghan refugees, one can witness the same phenomenon but on a smaller scale, owing to the absence of Western help. The nascent foreign-based bureaucracy there does not join the Hizb-i Hekmatyar (which has lost its influence in Iran) but joins either the pro-Khomeini Shi^{c}ite parties, based in Qom, or the Sunni Afzali organization. The latter comprises most of the Jami^{c}at apparatus based in Iran that now opposes Ismail Khan and the field commanders and that is heavily subsidized by Saudi money through Nurullah Emmat (Jami^{c}at's second in command in Peshawar).

The contradiction today is not between town and village, between traditional notables and intellectuals, but between a fledgling state rising from below and an imported state, both manned by young intellectuals. The discrepancy between Peshawar and the inside fronts is growing, not so much politically as psychologically. Even if the alliance takes Kabul and remains united, it will not be able to administer the country. The only possible compromise would be for the new state in Kabul, whatever it is, to make room for the field commanders. Such a compromise could restrain the ambitions of the thousands of foreign-based intellectuals, although it would also create a bitterness among them that could be used by foreign countries to challenge any state power in Kabul (as did the Soviets with the Communists, and Ali Bhutto with the Islamists in the seventies). Traditional notables could be used as referees by both sides, as in the traditional rules of the power game. But the war's uprooting created drastically new conditions for the future of Afghanistan. Nothing will be as it was before, and the new elite will more and more be made from the educated youth; the danger is the same as that which could have destroyed the Communist party: internal infighting may take the shape of tribal and ethnic feuds, despite the ideological formulation of these feuds.

But in case of political chaos, most of the new cadres will revert to traditional affiliations; in case of a general crisis, ethnic identity is the only identity that does not prove to be controversial; in the worst case scenario, what will follow will not be the creation of a modern state but the Lebanonization of Afghanistan: collapse of the central state and emergence of antagonistic communities whose identity is based on ethnic, religious, and historic references, disguised under superficial contemporary political references. Lebanon demonstrated that modern elites could lead their own country into a political collapse. But the worst is not inevitable in Afghanistan, and it is too soon to know what role ethnicity will play.

In 1991 most of the U.S. financial support for Afghanistan was cut. In the aftermath of the Gulf War, in which fundamentalists like Hekmatyar sided with Iraq, the Saudis have also reduced their support for the Peshawar-based coalition. Thus, the financial base for the Afghan government has been reduced, and thousands of its employees and bureaucrats have been laid off. This move worked in favor of mujahidin insiders, particularly Masud, who was able to conquer most of northeastern Afghanistan.

Observations on the Survey

The sample is taken from my own field research, checked with other Westerners accustomed to going inside Afghanistan. I selected 104 names from my list of about 250 field commanders. The criteria for selection were twofold:

1. Military effectiveness or political control of the population. A successful commander is supposed to be able to achieve some influence in the next regime in Afghanistan. The Islamist commanders, being generally more efficient than the traditionalist ones and hence more likely to play a role in the future, are slightly more numerous in the sample than in the field.

2. Availability of biographical data.

The percentages given are not necessarily accurate as far as the ethnic composition and political map of Afghanistan are concerned. The main purpose is to give a profile of the mujahidin elite with regard to political affiliations, not to describe the influence of the different parties and ethnic groups. Distortions inherent in this kind of research are as follows:

1. The Pashtuns tend to be more fragmented, because of tribal influence, than the Tajiks. As a consequence, more Pashtun commanders are listed here than appear to be warranted by the percentage of the Pashtun ethnic group (each commander controlling fewer people than his counterpart in the Persian-speaking area). To compensate for that, I should have added local Tajik commanders under direct authority of Masud and Ismail Khan, but it would have overemphasized the Jami'at influence, so I decided to avoid adding more Jami'at local commanders.

2. Small parties, like Modjaddedi's National Liberation Front, are not represented, because it has not enough commanders to be listed.

3. Gaylani's party (NIFA) and Harakat-e Enqelab are underestimated: the first, because there are so few ranking commanders and so

many local petty commanders that it is difficult to collect biographical data; the second, because there has been a great deal of change in political affiliations since 1983 among its followers, making it difficult to update data.

4. Hekmatyar's Hizb-i Islami, on the contrary, is overestimated in strength. But the political influence it enjoys in Pakistan makes the study of its followers very useful.

5. Except for Mohseni's Harakat-e Islami, no Shiʿite party has been included here, because of the difficulty of field research. Hence the underrepresentation of the Hazaras in this survey. But random surveys show that the pro-Khomeini parties have the same composition as the Hizb-i Islami and Jamiʿat, and the conservative Shura-ye-nazar the same as the Harakat-e Enqelab.

The survey shows that, as a general pattern, the mujahidin elite is young (49 percent under forty) and educated (53 percent from state schools), but with high variations according to their parties. Intellectuals are to be found mainly among the Islamist parties (around 70 percent of commanders of these parties graduated from a high school or from a university).

Among the mujahidin are very few traditional secular notables (generally listed in the "no education" level) or members of the establishment, who used to be educated abroad (none of the listed mujahidin commanders has been educated in Western countries or the USSR). So the bulk of the mujahidin commanders belong either to the new urban and educated middle class or to traditional religious families (the former educated at high schools and universities, the latter educated at *madrasa*). A mixed category is that of ulama trained in state-sponsored *madrasa* after having studied in government high school; almost all of them joined JIA or HIK.

HIH is the youngest and the most modern (75 percent are intellectuals), but it is also the most uprooted party, having little connection with the traditional society. Jamiʿat, though having the same background as the HIH (64 percent are secularly trained intellectuals), has more connections with traditional clerics (22 percent of JIA, 5 percent of HIH). HIK, like Khales himself, is a bridge between the Islamist parties (60 percent are under forty, and 40 percent are secular intellectuals) and the HAR (40 percent are ulama trained either in modern or traditional madrasas).

NIFA is the party of the traditional local secular leaders (*malek*), with little education and tending to be older than most of the other commanders (55 percent over fifty).

HAR of Nabi is the party of the traditional religious establishment. Nabi has lost much influence among Tajiks but remains as well implanted among Uzbeks as among Pashtuns. This is the party of those who have had only traditional religious education.

JIA cannot be said to be exclusively Persian (36 percent non-Persian). HIH is mainly Pashtun, but with a significant Tajik minority (20 percent). NIFA and HIK have the greatest concentration of Pashtuns.

HIM of Mohseni is exclusively Shi'ite; there are not enough data to be conclusive, but it appears to have roughly the same structure as JIA (the greater age of the leaders is owing to their training in Najaf, there being no high-level Shi'ite religious schools in Kabul).

Glossary

alim	Singular of ulama, a learned one.
barakat	Blessing, hereditarily transmittable.
dawlat	State.
Durrani	Name of a confederation of southern Pashtun tribes that seized power in Afghanistan in 1747 with Ahmed Shah Durrani at its head.
emir	Qur'anic term; the head of the whole muslim community.
enqelab	Revolution.
Ghilzai	A tribal confederation of Pashtuns, living between Qandahar and Kabul.
hakim	Local district administrator.
harakat	Movement.
Harakat-e Enqelab	A clerical Afghan party, headed by Mawlawi Mohammad Nabi Mohammadi, seen as "moderate."
Hizb-i Islami	Islamic party, of which there are two: one (the largest and most radical of all the resistance parties) headed by Gulbuddin Hekmatyar, the other headed by Mawlawi Khale.
hizb	Party.
jabha	A "front," that is, a mujahidin military base whose influence extends over a territory or a network of affiliated groups.
Jami'at-e Islami	Islamic Society, the biggest party of the Afghan resistance, Islamist but moderate, headed by Burhanuddin Rabbani.
jihad	Holy war, waged against infidels.
jirgah	Traditional tribal assembly of the elders to resolve im-

	portant issues.
khan	Leader of a local *qawm,* generally a landowner who has imposed his moral authority by his personal skills to attract a huge following of relatives and clients.
madrasa	Religious school to train mullahs.
malek	A village's head, or the head of a small *qawm.*
markaz	A "center," that is, a mujahidin military base.
mawlawi	Afghan colloquial name for an *alim.*
mellat	Nation or society, as opposed to state.
murid	A follower of a *pir* in a Sufi brotherhood.
Naqshbandi	A Sufi brotherhood, very active in Central Asia.
Naqel	Pashtuns incited to emigrate to the north of Afghanistan after the end of the nineteenth century.
Pashtun	The main ethnic group in Afghanistan (from 40 to 50 percent of the population).
pir	The spiritual head of a Sufi brotherhood.
Qaderi	A Sufi brotherhood.
qawm	Term used to designate any segment of the society bound by solidarity ties: an extended family, a clan, an occupational group, a village, an ethnic group, or the like.
ribat	A muslim "monastery" for fighting clerics.
sayyad	A descendent of the Prophet Muhammad.
Shari ͨ ah	Muslim legal and religious law.
shura	A council.
Tajik	The second largest ethnic group in Afghanistan, Sunni Persian speakers.
ulama (pl. of alim)	Religious scholars, trained in high-level schools, who tend to specialize in theology or religious law.
uluswal	The lowest level of local administrator, head of a sub-district.
umma	The whole community of believers.
wakil	A member of the national assembly.

Notes

1. For the definition of a *qawm,* see Roy 1986, ch. 1; Centlivres 1972, 158–59; Azoy 1982, 31–32.

2. For a well-perceived exposition of the rules of the power game among traditional notables in Afghanistan, see Azoy 1982.

3. A misleading account of the resistance leadership is that of Raja Anwar (1988, 146): "As stated elsewhere, there were roughly 400 big landowning families in Afghanistan. These handfuls of feudalists inflicted a humiliating defeat on 100,000 armed soldiers; small though their number was, they were among the country's most influential

2.1), the majority of the mujahidin commanders are young men, educated, and middle-class, almost none of them inside Afghanistan stemming from an upper-class family.

4. For the history and the ideology of the young Islamist intellectuals, see Roy 1986, ch. 4.

3

Charisma, Theocracy, and Men of Power in Postrevolutionary Iran

AHMAD ASHRAF

Ayatollah Ruhollah Khomeini's prophetic mien, the manner of his rise to power, the moving commemoration of his death, and the shrine that was erected over his graveyard leave little doubt that his leadership warrants the attribution "charismatic." Genuine charisma is a rare historical phenomenon, deriving from a conviction that an individual possesses a mysterious and supernatural gift of grace—a belief that the person so endowed and his disciples share. Even though the phenomenon of pure charisma can appear anywhere, it is most evident in the religious realm and thrives with particular abundance in the fertile soil of the Shiᶜite culture. "Television has rarely shown more astonishing sights than the crowds in Teheran literally ripping the shroud from Ayatollah Khomeini. It was a scene from the Age of Belief: mourners flagellating themselves and crushing one another as they grabbed at a helicopter bearing aloft the Imam's coffin. What may also have fed the crowd's awesome grief was awareness that the Ayatollah's authority was unique, that this was the last act of a drama expiring with its dominating character" (editorial, *New York Times*, 8 June 1989, A30).

Khomeini exemplified a multifaceted charisma in the course of his ascendance, first, to the position of the highest Shiᶜite authority and, later, to the theocratic position of the national political leadership. Both positions were achieved through his leadership of rebellious movements. Khomeini's multifaceted charisma led to the assumption of a number of contradictory positions. First, and above all else, he was the most emotional and inventive charismatic leader of recent times; the radius of his charisma spread beyond the boundaries of Iran to reach millions of Muslims all over the world. Khomeini was endowed with a number of character traits that appealed to the hearts and minds of Muslims in times of crisis, including cunning, creativity, youthfulness, asceticism, militancy, radicalism, and the will to power. Khomeini gave the masses a sense of personal integrity, of collective identity, of historical rootedness, and feelings of pride and superiority. Second, Khomeini acquired an "office charisma," a religious office with traditional charismatic authority, namely, the traditional office of the Shi ͨ ite source of emulation, which granted him religious authority and entitled him to receive religious charities and financial obligations, including the tithe of the Hidden Imam. Third, Khomeini introduced the new theocratic institution of the divine commission of the jursiconsult to assume political authority and sovereignty as the vicegerent of the Hidden Imam. Fourth, Khomeini assumed the position of the supreme leader and commander in chief of the armed forces of a modernizing state apparatus, while as a supreme theocratic ruler he transcended the constitutional constraints of an apparently legal-rational order. Finally, Khomeini assumed the title of the Imam, the position reserved in the Iranian Shi ͨ ite community exclusively for the twelve infallible Imams. Even though his position as one of the Imams, or a sort of imam with infallibility and supernatural qualities, was, evasively, neither confirmed nor entirely ruled out by his disciples during his lifetime, it was declared immediately after his death that he resembled the prophets and infallibles sufficiently that one could believe he was the "fifteenth infallible," following the Prophet Mohammad, his daughter Fatimah, and the twelve Imams. The shrine of his graveyard is identified as the sacred shrine (haram-e motahhar), an expression used for the shrines of the saints in the Shi ͨ ite tradition.

Personal charisma is the power relation of command and obedience, based on the belief of both leader and followers in the leader's extraordinary qualities and on the identification of disciples and followers with that leader.[1] Therefore, two conditions are necessary for the charismatic relation to emerge: the claim by the leader that he or she is the carrier of the "gift of grace" and the acceptance of that claim by the community of disciples and followers. Personal charisma, in its genuine and pure manifestation, is characterized by a number of properties. Above all else, it is an innovating and revolutionary force, challenging and disrupting the established authority. As a revolutionary force, personal charisma is distinct from office charisma. The latter is based on an established religious, or temporal hierocratic, authority. Personal charisma is also different from other types of established authority, that is, traditional authority and legal-rational domination. Personal charisma is transitional; office charisma, traditional authority, and legal domination are well-established matters of everyday life. By its "extraordinary" nature, personal charisma creates a number of conflicts within the social and political environment.

For Weber (1968, 1115), the prototype of the charismatic leader is a person who "in a revolutionary and sovereign manner . . . transforms all values and breaks all traditional and rational norms." Such a person challenges the authority of the established order, without regard for whether such challenge is traditional or legal-rational. The charismatic leader is not bound by administrative organs, rules of conduct, or legal wisdom oriented toward judicial precedent. Charismatic leadership is prophetic; the leader demands obedience from his disciples and followers on the basis of the mission he feels called upon to perform. The genuine prophet, Weber (1968, 243) says, "demand new obligations—most typically by virtue of revelation, oracle, inspiration, or of his own will."

Four analytical and empirical issues must be addressed in applying the concept of charisma to the case of Khomeini: (1) the definition of Khomeini's personal charisma and its distinction from and interrelations with his charismatic authority as a religious and political leader; (2) the genesis of Khomeini's charisma in the crisis situation under the old regime; (3) the problem of transformation or routinization of Khomeini's personal charisma in his lifetime and the problem of succession in post-Khomeini Iran; and (4) the relation between Khomeini's personal charisma and Iran's religious, social, economic, and political structure.

The White Revolution

In the period of the 1960s and 1970s, the Iranian state developed an elephantine bureaucratic apparatus and took an active role in shaping the civil society in the course of the "White Revolution of the Shah and the People." The White Revolution was designed and implemented under mounting pressures from the shah's patron state, the United States. The land reform and revolution from above was recommended by the Kennedy administration to forestall the peasant revolution from below (Ashraf 1991, 278–84). Although this view of the revolutionary potential of peasantry in no way reflected the political realities in the Iranian countryside, it worked as the driving force of the White Revolution and engendered drastic changes in the Iranian society and economy. In this period the state gained excessive power at the expense of the civil society, many of the links between the state and civil society eroded, cultural and intellectual polarization was intensified, and the regime lost the allegiance of intellectuals of both the old and the new breeds. These developments provided favorable conditions for the rise of a charismatic leader.

The ideological foundation of the shah's White Revolution was the old Iranian and Islamic conception of "organic benevolent statism"; its economic basis was the increasing oil revenues and expanding public enterprises; its political and coercive power base was the rapidly expanding public and military bureaucracies; and its social base was built on maneuverings and mediations among conflicting forces in the civil society. The accumulation of vast political and economic resources within the public domain made the state the supreme social mediator among the major social forces, including the dominant classes of the public and private sectors, the modern and traditional middle classes, as well as such popular classes as peasant proprietors, privileged workers in the modern industrial sector, and urban poor and rural migrants. Under these circumstances the state acquired great bargaining power and relative autonomy vis-à-vis the civil society, thus subordinating all social forces to its selective and often arbitrary developmental policies and strategies.

The rapid growth of sprawling public bureaucracies in the 1960s and 1970s is illustrated by some selected indexes of the size of the state work force and of the share of the state in total expenditure and capital formation compared with that of the private sector. During 1956–76 the number of public-sector wage and salary earners in urban areas rose from approximately half a million, or one-fifth of the economically active urban work force, to nearly 1.5 million, or more than one-third (SCI 1976, 33; 1981, 68). The average share of the state in total consumption leaped from 10 percent in 1959 to 35 percent in the mid-1970s. The average share of the public sector in capital formation increased from 36 to 54 percent in the same period (Central Bank of Iran 1981, 126–27, 406, 416–19, 422–24). As a result, in the mid-1970s more than 50 percent of the GDP was created in the public sector, and a substantial portion of the remainder came from trade, construction activities, and other services that were mainly generated by the state's expenditure of oil revenues. The state emerged the largest capitalist in this period; it tightly controlled the banking system and owned many major industrial establishments and all major transportation networks and agro-industries. It had developed into a rentier capitalist state.

The process of intellectual and cultural alienation reached its climax in the 1960s with the emergence of a new Westernized intelligentsia that boasted about its contempt for and ignorance of religion and traditional Persian culture. A segment of this group, many of whom were educated in Western universities, replaced the old-guard political elites in the course of the White Revolution in the 1960s and 1970s. Meanwhile, the religious establishment at Qom showed resilience and experienced a drastic intellectual change, which paved the way for the impending rise to power of its militant and modernizing segment.

Under these circumstances, the main societal role of the state became that of uncomfortable mediation among major conflicting forces in civil society. The selective mode of the state's social mediation—with its strong statist and bourgeois-capitalist biases—led to increasing grievances between civil society and the state. The state managers were bitterly critical of the windfall capital accumulation by the private-sector magnates and the influence-peddlers operating around the royal court. The entrepreneurs and the nouveaux riches of the private sector were discontented with their powerlessness vis-à-vis the arbitrary decision making of the state, with the authorities' support of privileged labor, with the competition of state-owned enterprises, and with the lack of political power and an autonomous organizational base. The rapidly growing intelligentsia, although it had acquired a handsome share of the petrolic pie, was discontented with its political powerlessness and the repression of human rights. The bazaar-mosque alliance was dissatisfied with the state's increasing interventionist policies (including state-owned and -operated chain stores, rising taxes, and the launching of a campaign against price gouging) as well as with the encroachment of a Western mode of life, which was considered a threat to their traditional urban Islamic life-style. Fixed-income wage and salary earners, including industrial workers and government employees, aspired to increase their human rights, which they measured in terms of "human salaries." This experience derived from a conflation of the two meanings of the term *huquq*: first, salary; and second, an obscure notion of rights. The state's clear objective was to prevent the transformation of the covert class conflict into an overt class struggle. To this end, it relied on benevolent distributive policies as well as repressive measures and prevention of the formation of autonomous class-based organizations, including those of the grande bourgeoisie and the industrial proletariat.

The Iranian regime in this period may be characterized as a neopatrimonial authority that was imposed on a rentier state under the command of the shah. The shah proved himself time and again to be an incompetent, autocratic ruler in times of political strife. Such a regime was susceptible to challenge and collapse in a time of crisis. Rentier states in general tend to be vulnerable because they are the center of resources and thus monopolize the mechanisms of economic development with increasingly paternalistic distributive, accumulative, and extractive policies.[2] In Iran, these circumstances led the state to assume excessive responsibilities, thus encouraging, if not forcing, the privileged classes to retreat from responsibility, weakening the internal cohesion of the dominant classes and the inarticulate links between the rulers and major social classes and groups in the society.[3]

With the regime organized around a network of patronage relations, "political immaturity" and the lack of ideological commitment came to be a significant characteristic of the dominant classes under the tight control of the shah. The political culture of the power elite, top bureaucrats, army commanders, state managers, grande bourgeoisie, intellectuals, and the new middle classes was essentially one of idleness. As individuals, they were given opportunities for social mobility and promotion of their material interests, but as a group, they were systematically denied the opportunity to protect their class interests through organized and independent political action. They were ignorant of Persian culture and the living conditions of the traditional strata and the masses of villagers, urban poor, and rural migrants. Moreover, as even many loyal members of the establishment were "suffering from a profound malaise, from lack of conviction in what they [were] doing, from doubts whether the regime deserve[d] to endure" (Herz 1964, 7). The shah's style of leadership and patronage increasingly weakened the ability of the leading elites to develop ideological commitment to the regime, to forge alliances among themselves, or to guide, mobilize, and control others in support of the regime at times of political turmoil. Thus, while political and operational feebleness of the bureaucratic elites and entrepreneurial classes limited their symbolic and institutional autonomy, their lack of ideological commitments helped to undermine the regime's long-term stability.

The White Revolution eliminated the old landowning class and alienated the ulama, who together with them had constituted the traditional foundation of patrimonial authority and had served the regime by maintaining links among the old oligarchy as well as between them and the masses of urban, rural, and tribal communities. They were replaced by new classes and groups—the infantile grande bourgeoisie and the young, Western-educated bureaucratic elites and new middle classes—who had weak links among themselves and who were unable to develop a strong connection with the core of the state or with the intelligentsia and other key elements in the civil society. Having no independent political base, the new elite rarely had any significant input in the major economic and policy decisions, whereas the old elite, by virtue of its traditional patron-client relations with the local populations, had provided a point of articulation between the regime and the civil society and had participated more actively in regional and national politics. Because of the shah's fear of the emergence of independent power centers, members of the new power elite and the grande bourgeoisie were denied the opportunity to organize themselves into effective political groupings.

Finally, the character of the ruler in autocratic rentier states is an important factor in crisis management. At a time of crisis, a ruler's lack of a will to power would, of course, be detrimental to the system as a whole.[4] In the mid-1970s the shah began to lose his will to fight, especially after the victory of Jimmy Carter in the presidential race of November 1976, as he was pressed on human rights issues by the new Democratic administration in Washington. The political pressures to accord human rights created opportunities for mass mobilization of the opposition. When the political upheavals of 1977–79 came, the feeble character of the shah, combined with the structural weaknesses and lack of ideological commitment of the dominant and new middle classes, led to the collapse of the Pahlavi regime.[5]

The pressing interests, grievances, and aspirations of conflicting groups in civil society were not yet at the point of explosion in the last years of the shah's regime. Both a crack in the regime and firmly entrenched organizational networks and solidarity groups in the civil society were needed as catalysts for the mobilization of an effective protest movement. The major urban social forces, with the exception of the bazaar-mosque alliance, lacked the preexisting structures, organizational networks, and workable solidarity groups necessary for a protest mobilization when an opportunity for collective action presented itself. The intelligentsia of teachers and students possessed far more revolutionary potential than the bazaar-mosque alliance, but by themselves they were not able to mobilize effectively their huge human and institutional resources; they needed the social support of other forces in the civil society. When the opportunity for collective action arose, students and teachers who had already formed a coalition with the militant ulama were able to use the facilities of the schools and universities in the course of their protest movement. Thus, a nucleus of revolutionary organization was formed from a small group of militant ulama, their bazaari followers, and activist intelligentsia, who together had ready access to the extensive human, financial, and institutional resources of the bazaar, the mosque, and the school-university networks. They exploited these resources to mobilize the ulama, the bazaaris, students, government employees, industrial workers, and the urban poor.

Under these circumstances Khomeini was inspired to politicize Islam, to set in motion a revolutionary breakthrough, a "reformation," in the Islamic world, to instigate a crusade against the Christian West, to mobilize the masses of impoverished Muslims throughout the world against Western imperialism, and, finally, to establish an Islamic empire. He had dreamed of this for half a century.

Khomeini's Ascension to Leadership

The basis of Khomeini's legitimation, and of his claim that he, and only he, had the mission he believed called upon to perform, was the mystical charisma he felt within himself. This feeling was reinforced by his deep-rooted belief in the Gnostic and pantheistic ideas of Ibn al-Arabi and Mulla Sadra. These leading Gnostic figures in the history of Islamic thought had a powerful impact on Khomeini's ideas—on his conception of the world, of Islamic law as the shell of truth, and of charisma's role in the realization of the ultimate goal of historical development, the Islamic state.[6] The idea of the absolute authority of the jurisconsult as the embodiment of the Islamic state, an authority that equals the absolute sovereignty of the state itself, appears to have derived from Khomeini's personal belief in a pantheistic mission for the Islamic state as the vehicle for revolutionizing the world and preparing the ground for the fulfillment of God's design in history. This idea of the Islamic state is similar to the pantheistic Hegelian notion of the modern state as the embodiment of the ultimate goal of history. Khomeini's disavowal of the routine and unbearable world of traditional and conservative Islamic jurisprudence originated in his condemnation of the orthodox and ultrafundamentalist jurisprudent Muhammad al-Ghazali and the latter's debate with Ibn al-Arabi. He commented on al-Ghazali that "he was a most knowledgeable jurisconsult, yet the light of truth had never enlightened his heart" (Khomeini 1983, 1:124; all translations are by the author unless otherwise noted). In the last months of his life, Khomeini cried in a mystical love poem—with a pantheistic mood of dealienation:

> Freed of the self, I claimed "I am the Truth" as mine.
> Just like Mansur, I bought the secret of the gallows tree.
> My lovers' grief set fire to my soul, it drove me wild,
> And I became the scandal of the marketplace.
> Swing wide the tavern door before me, day and night,
> For I've grown weary of both mosque and madrasa.
> (*Resalat*, 15 June 1989)

Ironically, Khomeini's mystical ideas differed sharply from the pacifism and quietism of the Sufi saints and their disciples. His Gnostic experience was a militant and radical mysticism. In a poem he composed in the 1930s, Khomeini reveals his dream of a militant Islamic revolution—a revolution that he eventually mobilized and led to a victorious conclusion half a century later. The dream is millenarian; it envisions the reappearance of Mahdi and the coming of his revolution, when the ultimate goal of history is realized and the world becomes the eternal heaven. At this time Khomeini was immersed in dreams of an Islamic state that would solve human problems. Apparently, Khomeini projects himself onto the spirit of spring and the personage of Mahdi and expresses his own vision of the Islamic state.

> It is New Year's Day, the first day of spring [the national Iranian religious feast and ritual]. The spring conquers the world from the West to the East in its first month. Its will dominates from Arabia to Iran, from India to Mongolia, from Caucasia to Bulgaria, from central Asia to Ethiopia and Sudan. It will erect a state so great and glorious that it resembles the Sasanian Empire. It will command the thunder to play the marching music for the warriors and will lead the field marshals to the front. The bombardments and shootings will split the hearts of two hundred million warriors; their blood will flood the earth; the guts of Caesar will split; the heart of Napoleon will explode. Yet from that bombardment the whole world becomes the eternal heaven.
> (Runahi 1979, 55–59)

During his long life, Khomeini witnessed four waves of attacks on the Shi ᶜite religious establishment, all of which came from one mode of modernization and Westernization or another: the constitutional movement of 1905–11; Reza Shah's drive for modernization in the 1920s and 1930s; the years of social, cultural, and political mobilization and popularity of atheism and Marxism among the intelligentsia in the period 1941–53; and the era of the White Revolution of the 1960s and 1970s. These times were grievous for the ulama. Their first great challenge came from the constitutional revolution of 1905–11. The anticlerical nature of the ideas of liberalism and national sovereignty, with their humanistic undertones, weakened the overall status of the religious hierarchy in society. More specifically, the transfer of the judicial and educational functions of the ulama to the secular forces of the modern state caused further deterioration of the political and economic position of the ulama. The constitutional revolution also split the leadership and the rank and file of the ulama into a minority, who advocated constitutionalism, and a majority, who either retreated from politics or supported absolutism.

Khomeini could never forget the devastating blow dealt to the ulama during the reign of Reza Shah (Khomeini 1944, 271–74, 302–3). He remembered the painful day of 21 March 1926, when Reza Shah rushed furiously to the holy city of Qom, entered into the shrine with his military boots on, and whipped an outspoken cleric who had protested the improper veiling of the women of the royal family during their visit to the holy place a day before (Razi 1953, 1:31–36). He also recollected with pain the mounting hostilities of the regime toward the ulama and the students of theology, the repressive measures of the police state against their uniform, and the forced unveiling of women (Khomeini 1981, 333–34; Khomeini 1983, 1:269; 5:153–54). And he never forgot the black day in July 1935, when the armed forces invaded the Gowharshad Mosque, adjacent to holy shrine of Imam Reza in Mashhad, and massacred a score of religious protestors (Khomeini 1983, 1:46, 168, 247, 269). But the most galling memory for Khomeini was the erosion of the esteem of the ulama in the eyes of the populace. It grieved him that the prestige of the ulama had so deteriorated that bus drivers often would not give a ride to men in religious attire, on the grounds that their cars might get a flat tire because of the inauspicious presence of a turbaned passenger (Razi 1953, 1:46–52). He was painfully aware that as a result of the fragmentation of the ulama and the decline of their esteem, the number of applicants to the religious academic center of Qom had decreased. During the whole period of harassment of the ulama by the state, Khomeini's mentor, Grand Ayatollah Abd al-Karim Ha'eri, who founded the religious center of Qom in the early 1920s, remained almost silent and refrained from protesting the assaults of the state against the religious establishment and the ulama. Throughout these troubled years, Khomeini was primarily absorbed in classical Persian poetry, mysticism, and theosophy.[7]

The third great blow to the ulama and the religious establishment came during the twelve years of relative freedom, 1941–53. The antagonism between the old and new (or religious and lay) intelligentsia widened during this period, when Marxist ideology dominated the modern intellectual circles. Most of the major poets, writers, artists, politically minded university students, and committed intelligentsia were among the Marxist sympathizers. Condemning religion as superstition and rejecting traditional culture as outmoded became fashionable in intellectual salons and in the universities. Nevertheless, in this period the majority among the political elites and many intellectuals were still acquainted with Islamic ideas and traditional Persian culture.

Khomeini began to participate actively in the politics of the ulama in the 1940s. Although Khomeini's participation in politics in the period of the 1940s and 1950s was mostly covert, he managed nevertheless to gather supporters and build his position as the political cleric in the Qom religious center. He rallied around himself a group of dedicated, politically minded theology students and awaited an opportunity to engage in overt political action and to enter onto the scene of national and international politics. During the same period, breaking its isolationist orientation, the Qom religious center gradually adopted a more receptive attitude toward modern political, economic, and intellectual issues. Two major changes in the Qom religious center occurred in the 1950s. First was a relative consolidation and centralization of the position of the source of emulation (marja 'iyyat) at Qom, made possible by the expansion of modern means of transportation and communication. Second was a greater acceptance of a modern school system parallel to the madrasa system and the establishment in Qom and Teheran of a number of modern schools that offered a curriculum combining modern and religious studies. Now many graduates of modern· schools were accepted to the Qom academic center. Thus, in the early 1960s there emerged in Qom a new generation of young theological students who were acquainted with modern sciences and humanities at least at the high school level. A score of these young clerics continued their education at the modern universities in the late 1950s and the 1960s. As a result, a new breed of ulama made their appearance on the stage, those prepared for the demands of a new society and removed from the outmoded traditionalist jurisconsults at Qom and Najaf, as well as from the provincial religious leaders who served as regional patrons (Hojjati Kermani 1988–89). Grand Ayatollah Borujerdi was, however, a highly conservative and apolitical leader who forbade the young theology students to get involved in political controversies. His death in 1961 opened up the Qom center to new ideas and allowed a relatively liberal figure, Ayatollah Sayyid Kazem Shariatmadari, and a militant charismatic leader, Ayatollah Ruhollah Khomeini, to rise to the highest position of the source of emulation.

In the post-Borujerdi era of the 1960s and 1970s, the clerical establishment was divided into three conflicting factions. The largest segment, centered at Qom, followed the general accommodationist tradition of peaceful coexistence with and de facto recognition of the state. This segment had been established by the founder of the Qom center, Ayatollah Abd al-Karim Ha'eri, in the 1920s and 1930s and was continued by Ayatollah Borujerdi for the following two decades. Most sources of emulation in the post-Borujerdi era followed, more or less, this accommodationist orientation. The grand ayatollahs Shehab al-Din Najafi Mar'ashi and Muhammad Reza Golpayagani of Qom and Sayyid Abu al-Qasem Khu'i of Najaf, for example, eschewed political involvement with the state, though Khu'i was overtly critical of the regime and Golpayagani covertly and quietly criticized the wrongdoings of the state and prayed for the authorities to follow the just path. Others, including the grand ayatollahs Sayyid Kazem Shariatmadari of Qom and Sayyid Ahmad Khwansari of Teheran, followed the path of the fathers of Qom center and maintained some relations with the authorities.

The second segment of the ulama assumed a collaborationist stance toward the Pahlavi regime. Some members of this group, appointees of the shah, served as leaders of Friday prayers in Teheran and other major cities. Others were attached to the Organization of Religious Endowments (*awqaf*), which was a part of the state apparatus of custodianship for the holy shrines, and to other religious establishments. Still others served as advisers and officials of the religious corps institution, which was founded as a part of the shah's White Revolution program of the 1970s. Most members of the Mashhad religious center, including leading popular figures like Ayatollah Ahmad Kafa'i and the rank and file of the religious hierarchy and students, may be placed in this collaborationist category. Also included among the members of this group was such an influential religious leader as Ayatollah Sayyid Mohammad Behbahani of Teheran, who played an active role in the making of the 1953 coup d'état as well as in the antiregime movement of the early 1960s, representing the vested interests of the landowning classes. Most members of the large collaborationist group of ulama were supported by the prime minister's secret budget. These elements have often been stigmatized by Khomeini and his circle as "clerics of the palace" (Khomeini 1978, 199–204).

The third group within the religious establishment began to form after the 1963 antigovernment riots led by Ayatollah Khomeini and a small group of his students. Capitalizing on the resentments of the entire religious establishment—including the collaborationist and accommodationist factions—toward the regime's policies in such areas as land reform, women's suffrage, and the extension of diplomatic immunity to American military advisrs in Iran in the early 1960s, this group achieved prominence within the religious hierarchy. It was at this time that Khomeini emerged as a charismatic religiopolitical leader and assumed the position of source of emulation and the title of the grand ayatollah. The manner of his accession to the latter position was itself significant, indeed unique, in Shiʿite history. Never before had a member of the ulama risen to the high office of source of emulation through political mobilization of the masses. Khomeini was determined to appear on the political scene as a leader, not as a follower or even as a second-rank figure in the movement. Thus, he waited for years for the propitious moment to commence his overt political leadership from the top of the ulama's hierarchy, that is, from the charismatic office of the source of emulation. This not only brought spiritual leadership, office charisma, enormous social status, and political power to Khomeini, but also placed at his disposal considerable financial resources, consisting of one-fifth of the profits of the merchants and other wealthy individuals. The control of such resources allowed Khomeini to establish a wide informal network for both the collection of religious dues and the distribution of stipends among theology students throughout the country. The same network could, and did, serve as a political and organizational base from which Khomeini and his lieutenants could mobilize, even from exile, members of the bazaar-mosque alliance, the overwhelming majority of whom were apolitical.

This new militant image of the Shiʿite ulama's role in politics and government has, as in the case of the constitutional revolution, led some scholars to attribute an inherently oppositional stance to all members of the ulama's hierarchy, while neglecting the accommodationist and collaborationist stance of the overwhelming majority of the ulama in the modern history of Iran. Nearly all religiously inspired antiregime activity under the direction of the ulama, both within and outside of Iran, was carried out by Khomeini's faction. That only one small segment of the ulama was involved in oppositional activity is often ignored by those who present the entire Shi‘ite ulama as having been engaged in militant action against the state.

Meanwhile, Khomeini rallied around himself a group of young and dedicated students of theology who were concerned with problems of the modern world, with the modern sciences of man and nature, and with militant and radical Islam. They were bitterly critical of the antipolitical orientation of the leading figures of the Qom center, including the sole source of emulation, Ayatollah Borujerdi. Outside of Khomeini's circle of disciples, most religious students at Qom would not even read newspapers and would look down with contempt at those few students who did (Rafsanjani 1980, 19). The label "political cleric" was used pejoratively against Khomeini and his disciples at Qom and Najaf. The disciples of Khomeini began to approach students and teachers outside of Qom in the early 1960s. The publication of two major journals, *Maktab-e Islam* and *Maktab-e Tashayu’* in Qom, and such anthologies as *Marja’iyyat va Ruhaniyyat* and *Goftar-e Mah* in Teheran, from the late 1950s onward, marked the opening of a new era in the history of the Iranian religious intelligentsia. Interesting articles on current political, social, economic, cultural, and religious issues were presented in a language familiar to the new lay intelligentsia. The new political and religious discourse led to the convergence of a segment of the ulama and a segment of the modern secular intelligentsia. The convergence was stimulated by the urban uprisings of 1963, when Khomeini rose to prominence and became the religiopolitical leader of the opposition forces and contenders for political power. The militant and committed intelligentsia were attracted to the militant discourse and political style of Khomeini and found a potential ally among the militant ulama.

Enjoying the leading position at the core of major social forces in the civil society, including the bazaar-mosque alliance, the middle classes, intellectuals, and the popular classes, Khomeini managed to unify all under the canopy of his charismatic leadership and to lead them to a victorious revolution.

Consolidation of Power

The immediate aftermath of the February 1979 revolution was a short period of collective ecstasy and revolutionary honeymoon. In this period the liberal faction in the revolutionary coalition, including Mehdi Bazargan's Liberation Movement and veterans of Mosaddeq's National

Front, occupied most upper- and middle-echelon positions within the public bureaucracy. The bazaaris were well rewarded for their contributions to the making of the revolution and enjoyed a short period of esteem and political power. Radical students became the masters of the universities and high schools. The young students and teachers, along with lower bourgeois and subproletarian elements, armed and organized themselves under the militant ulama in the neighborhood revolutionary committees, often located in the mosques. Government employees and industrial workers organized numerous staff and workers "councils," in effect exercising a period of active self-management at the workplace. The urban poor were championed by the revolutionaries and were referred to by the Qur'anic phrase the "impoverished of the earth," and they were given a variety of token material and symbolic rewards. The middle peasants demanded rural services and mobilized protest movements to that end. At the same time, the young radicals mobilized a small segment of peasantry and helped them to confiscate and distribute agricultural land in some areas.

The February revolution unleashed many covert class antagonisms that had been repressed under the old regime, including different forms of intergroup conflict, class and ethnic warfare, factional rivalries within the regime, ideological quarrels, and religious oppression. Of all these groups and strata, the middle and upper middle bourgeois classes of different types and levels of economic power managed at least partly to protect their collective class interests, which they had never been able to accomplish under the old regime. Middle-level industrialists, commercial farmers, and bazaaris were engaged in a life-or-death struggle for economic survival. Industrialists formed an Islamic association of owners of industrial establishments and also used the organizational network of the Chamber of Industries and Mines to protect their interests. The commercial farmers established agricultural councils and waged a full-fledged campaign to forestall or emasculate the Islamic land reform. The bazaaris were organized in the Islamic Association of Guilds and stood firmly against excesses of the state. All three groups were supported by the conservative, traditionalist faction of the ulama, including the majority of the professors of the Islamic academic center of Qom, the militant Ulama of Teheran, the conservative deputies in the Majlis, and the Councils of Guardians. The wage and salary earners, including the state employees and workers who did not possess autonomous organizations and preexisting ordinary structures, were left helpless, and their interests were represented only by the benevolent action of the radical forces in the regime.

The period of the people's honeymoon in the aftermath of the February revolution was soon over; it was replaced by a long period of internal friction, repression, and violation of human rights. This latter period began with the takeover of the American embassy in Teheran and the resignation of Bazargan's liberal cabinet in November 1979. The hostage crisis was used by Khomeini and his disciples to consolidate their power through, first, discrediting and eliminating the liberal elements from the regime and, second, winning over and disarming the Left. The regime achieved both goals and rallied behind its leadership the support of a large number of leftist groups. The Left split: one group supported the regime for its anti-imperialist posture; the other criticized it for its conservative and reactionary orientation. The regime labeled the movement "second revolution." Khomeini's march to total power culminated, however, in the events of June 1981, when he dismissed President Abu al-Hassan Bani-Sadr and ordered a crackdown on all organized opposition forces, which in turn led to the massacre of thousands of leftist students, mainly from the mujahidin organization. The regime labeled the move the "third revolution."

Although the regime eliminated the challengers from the organized Left, the legacy of the Left and the presence of a strong radical faction within the regime led to the emergence of internal factional politics. A prime example of overt class conflict organized by the radical forces within the regime was that stirred up by an Islamic land reform provision that imposed a ceiling on the size of landownership. The commercial farmers, along with traditionalist and liberal grand ayatollahs and the majority of the ulama, launched a rigorous campaign to suspend that measure. After years of bitter struggle, a truce was arranged. First, it provided for granting the ownership of some eight hundred thousand hectares of agricultural land whose ownership had become a matter of mounting dispute in the course of the revolution; second, a proposed ceiling on the size of landownership was suspended, a decision that must be regarded as a concession to the commercial farmers and the traditionalist ulama (Ashraf 1991, 299–304).

The bazaaris who participated in the revolution had the illusory expectation that they would be liberated from state intervention in the internal affairs of the bazaar, that they would be exempted from state taxes and excessive custom duties, and that they would regain the communal respect that they had once enjoyed. They were among the first groups to become deeply disappointed and disillusioned in the aftermath of the revolution. Merchants and the more prosperous shopkeepers were increasingly threatened by puritanical, if not opportunistic, elements from the lower petite bourgeoisie. Much like their counterparts in the French Revolution—the sansculottes—the lower bourgeoisie organized themselves in revolutionary committees, took arms, and vied for a share of power, prestige, and wealth. The bazaaris, however, were fundamentally threatened by members of their own younger generation, many of whom moved into the ranks of the militant and radical intelligentsia of students and teachers and assumed the leadership of the emerging Islamic state. Now the bazaaris were confronted with an overgrowing state apparatus with a set of policies to nationalize the foreign trade, to expand consumer cooperatives, and to set in motion a ruthless anti-price-gouging campaign. The bazaaris resorted once again to their old allies, the traditionalist and conservative ulama, to wage a struggle against an overexpanding modern state. The traditional ulama came to the support of the bazaaris and objected to the nationalization of the foreign trade. They prevailed, and the bill was vetoed in the Council of Guardians. Furthermore, the conservative ulama who served as judges in ordinary tribunals declined to issue court orders against the bazaaris who were indicted for price gouging. The bazaaris were thus increasingly caught in a situation of uncertainty, in many ways more menacing than what they had experienced under the old regime. Their gain in the revolution was primarily cultural: their values, behavior, and lifestyle, as traditional urban ideals of behavior and appearance, received greater recognition and respect after the revolution than at any time in the recent past. But the economic position of the bazaar vis-à-vis the state has eroded and become even weaker than what it had been under the Pahlavis. The ordinary structure of the bazaar-mosque alliance, however, has survived and has served as the organizational network for protecting the interests of the bazaaris as a collectivity.

The Westernized middle class, including intellectuals, professionals, educated government employees, white-collar workers, and the majority of the young intelligentsia, were the main losers among the groups that formed the core of the revolutionary coalition. The fundamental antagonism between the new middle class and a large group of the traditionalist and conservative supporters of the regime has been cultural. The Western orientation and life-style of the new middle class—particularly of middle-class women—has been under severe attack by the traditionalists and the lower bourgeoisie of the old urban culture. The new middle class has been denied any autonomous organization: the revolutionary strike committees and staff councils established in public agencies in the course of the revolution were forcibly dissolved and their leaders purged by the regime, and they were subsequently replaced by Islamic associations, a move supported by only a slight minority of government employees.

Tens of thousands of professionals, white-collar workers, students, and teachers, of both liberal and radical persuasions, supporters of the revolution, were purged, imprisoned, executed, or fled to exile in Western countries. For example, the number of university instructors dropped from 16,000 in 1978–79 to 9,000 in the 1981–82 academic year. More than 10,000 members of radical groups, most of whom were students and teachers, were executed or simply massacred after the events of June 1981. More than 80,000 professionals, intellectuals, and those with managerial skills have left the country; they constitute a large group of "cultural asylees," a new type of refugee. The middle classes, disillusioned with the Islamic revolution, have increasingly supported a variety of political groups with liberal, nationalist, and monarchist ideologies. Nationalism, particularly the idealization of pre-Islamic religion and civilization, has once again become prevalent among the intelligentsia and the new middle classes.

The industrial working class, particularly privileged labor, has also been severely repressed since the events of June 1981. In the aftermath of the February revolution, the working class organized workers' councils in many workshops and factories and mobilized hundreds of protest strikes to bargain for higher wages, better working conditions, self-management, and a larger share of the profit. After the June movement, the workers' councils were dissolved, and were replaced by Islamic councils, which functioned essentially as the regime's secret agents in the workplace.

Khomeini and his disciples established their theocratic domination in two phases. In the first phase, they mobilized the resources of the bazaar-mosque alliance and the school-university network to destabilize the Pahlavi state, to lead the popular movement toward dual sovereignty, and eventually to dislodge the shah's regime. The second phase was a ruthless struggle to eliminate all other constituents of the original revolutionary coalition and to consolidate the central power of the state under their own ironfisted control. It was after this latter phase that the whole state apparatus was brought under direct control of Khomeini and his confidants, confronting them directly with the problems of the public bureaucracy and the modern economy. Also in this phase, and particularly since the mid-1980s, Khomeini began openly and vigorously to promote the radical camp within the regime by waging a campaign against the traditionalist ulama. During the first phase and a good part of the second one, Khomeini's personal charisma operated effectively and with no internal contradiction. Following the consolidation of power and total capture of the state apparatus, however, he had to contend with the leviathan state bureaucracy and its administrative and economic burdens.

During the period of dual sovereignty, in the last months of the old regime (December–February of 1978–79), Khomeini began to establish his authority by appointing the Central Strikes Committee, particularly to oversee the oil industry. At the same time, Khomeini's followers established the Revolutionary Council, local committees for organizing demonstrations and strikes, and a committee for welcoming Khomeini on his triumphant return to Teheran (Khomeini 1983, 4:111, 207, 245). In his first speech upon arrival, he said, "I will punch this government [of Prime Minister Bakhtiar] in the mouth; I will appoint a government" (Khomeini 1983, 4:285). Thus, in the final days of the old regime, Khomeini appointed Mehdi Bazargan as "his own" prime minister to form a provisional cabinet (Khomeini 1983, 5:27). At the same time, he seized the opportunity to make a number of other much more important appointments. The weak cabinet had only loose authority over some of the bureaucratic and technical organs of the government, a fact that Bazargan (1983, 165–75) himself often acknowledged and complained about by referring to "multiple centers of power." Thus, Khomeini, from the moment of his arrival in Teheran, made it clear to everyone who the boss was.

Building the Islamic state has been achieved, stage by stage, through a number of moves. With victory in the revolution assured, Khomeini was determined to place the repressive state apparatus under the control of his own lieutenants and confidants. To that end he formed revolutionary tribunals and appointed judges and prosecutors, while establishing direct control over prisons and the revolutionary committees. He commanded the first executions of the old regime's elites, which were carried out on the roof of his own residence. The establishment of the Revolutionary Guards was the next step in the consolidation of central authority. The state agencies, however, were brought under control gradually, through a series of continuous purges by Islamic committees. To recruit new supporters for the regime, the Islamic Republican Party (IRP) was established. The newspapers, radio, and television, the news agency, and the political-ideological offices were all brought under the tight control of Khomeini's confidants (Bazargan 1984, 116–63, 183–88).

Iran's revolution of 1977–79, like other major revolutions in modern times, has led to further consolidation and expansion of the central state apparatus under the new men of power, who come primarily from the traditional middle and lower middle classes. One index of such expansion is the sharp increase in the percentage of public-sector employees from one-third of the total urban work force in 1976 to approximately one-half in 1986 (SCI 1981, 68; *Resalat* 19 Mar. 1989). Another index is the leap in the ratio of public to private industrial establishments. The number of large state-owned industries with 100 workers or more rose from 130 units, or 18 percent of the total in 1976, to about 600 units, or over 75 percent of the total, in 1982. The number of workers in these units rose in the same period from 70,000 to 350,000 (SCI 1982, 433–36; SCI 1985, 444, 464). In the aftermath of the revolution, the legacy of a "petrol economy" combined with the new revolutionary institutions furthered the superordination of the state and its leading functionaries over the civil society.

Iran's New Men of Power

The Islamic revolution of 1977–79 led to the overthrow of the dominant class and the new middle classes of the previous regime and set in place a new group of men with power and privilege. The shah's large retinue and thousands of top bureaucrats, big industrialists, farm capitalists, big traders, and leading contractors were executed, imprisoned, purged, or forced to flee the country, and their property was confiscated. Their place on the top of the state hierarchy was taken by Khomeini's disciples of both clerical and lay backgrounds, who gradually occupied the key state positions. The leadership and middle-layer elites of the new regime are predominantly educated young men from middle and lower middle classes, mainly from bazaar, mosque, and village backgrounds. In addition, tens of thousands of teenagers from both urban and rural lower classes have been mobilized and organized within various revolutionary organizations.

Several hundred younger members of the intelligentsia, indoctrinated in Islamic political ideology, have gradually occupied the primary and secondary positions in the state apparatus over the ten years of revolutionary struggle. They have served as cabinet ministers, governors of provinces and districts, mayors of large cities and small towns, prosecutors and judges in both revolutionary tribunals and ordinary courts, Majlis representatives, commanders of revolutionary guards and revolutionary committees, and directors of revolutionary organizations such as the Jihad for Reconstruction, the Foundation for the Oppressed, and the Martyr Foundation. They have also served as commanders of the armed forces, directors of state agencies, and managers of hundreds of nationalized enterprises.

The new men of power who have replaced the old dominant class are primarily ulama, teachers, students, and young professionals. In terms of their social origins, both the ulama and laymen come from old petit bourgeois families. This is clearly reflected, for example, in the social composition of the deputies in the first session of the Islamic Consultative Assembly (Majlis). The relative proportion of different groups in the First Islamic Majlis was as follows: ulama, 50 percent; teachers, 30 percent; professionals and government employees, 17 percent (table 3.1). They came from three old strata of the Iranian society: peasant farmers, 31 percent; bazaaris, artisans, and shopkeepers, 31 percent; and ulama families, 29 percent (table 3.2). In other words, the First Islamic Majlis representatives were mostly from the traditional intelligentsia of the ulama and *madrasa* students and a new intelligentsia of secular students, teachers, and professionals.

But later the composition of Majlis deputies changed, to the disadvantage of the old and new intellectuals and in favor of state managers. The ulama's representation rose to 54 percent in the second session but was cut in half (27 percent) in the third session. Teacher representation also slightly increased in the second session, to 32 percent, but decreased to 21 percent in the third session. The proportion of state managers and professionals first decreased to 10 percent in the second session but later leaped to 47 percent in the third session. As a result of these changes, the power of state managers, bureaucrats, and professional elements increased sharply in the legislative body (table 3.1).

The social origin of Majlis representatives before and after the revolution is indicative of changes that occurred in the structure of the country's dominant political class after the revolution. In the Twenty-first Majlis (1963–67), which was formed after the land reform program of the early 1960s, 42 percent of the representatives still came from landowning families and only 2 percent represented the peasant farmer families. This representation of landowning families dropped to 20 percent and that of peasant farmers increased to 8 percent in Twenty-fourth Majlis (1975–79). In the First Islamic Majlis, no one represented the landowning families, whereas peasant farmer representation leaped to 31 percent. The proportion of those from ulama families increased from 2 percent in the Twenty-first Majlis to 10 percent in the

TABLE 3.1

**Distribution of Representatives of Three Sessions
of Islamic Majlis by Social Standing**

(in percentage)

Social Standing	First	Majlis Second	Third
Ulama	50	54	27
Teachers and professors	30	32	21
State managers	17	10	47
Other	3	4	5
Total	100	100	100
Number	(216)	(269)	(260)

TABLE 3.2

**Family Background of Majlis Representatives
Before and After the Revolution**

(in percentage)

Father's Occupation	Twenty-first Majlis	Twenty-fourth Majlis	First Islamic
Old strata			
Landowners	42	20	0
Merchants	16	8	5
Ulama	2	10	29
Peasant farmers	2	8	31
Guildsmen	2	4	26
Subtotal	64	50	91
New strata			
Bureaucrats	28	6	5
Professionals	6	2	—
Other	2	6	4
Unidentified	—	36	—
Subtotal	36	50	9
Total	100	100	100
Number	(192)	(263)	(216)

Sources: Shaji°i 1965; Majlis-e Shura-ye Islami 1981; and a survey of the Twenty-fourth Majlis by the author.

Twenty-fourth and to 29 percent in the First Islamic Majlis. The bazaaris' representation shows a decline for merchant families and a sharp increase for artisan and shopkeeper families: merchant family representation decreased from 16 percent in the twenty-first session to 8 percent in the twenty-fourth and to 5 percent in the First Islamic Majlis, whereas representation of shopkeepers and artisans increased from 2 percent to 4 percent and to 26 percent in the First Islamic Majlis. The proportion of representatives from the families of government employees decreased substantially over the same period: from 28 percent to 6 percent and to 5 percent in the First Islamic Majlis. The representation of professional families was slim, and declined further over this period. In general, there was a shift from old and new upper classes of landlords, merchants, and government functionaries to petit bourgeois families from the bazaar, the mosque, and the village (table 3.2).

The new men of power and privilege are educated people. For example, an overwhelming majority of the Islamic Majlis representatives have had some college education. The level of educational attainment, however, has declined in the three successive sessions of the Majlis: 92 percent of the lay deputies in the First Majlis, 76 percent in the Second, and 78 percent in the Third Majlis had received some college education. The educational level of the clerics also declined over the same period: those with *ijtihad* (doctoral degrees) declined from 25 percent in the First Majlis to 14 percent in the Third, and those with intermediate education *(sath)* declined from 21 percent in the First Majlis to 17 percent in the Third, whereas those with elementary religious education rose from 2 percent to 17 percent in the same period. The level of educational attainment of bureaucratic officials and state managers was much higher than that of Majlis representatives; 93 percent of the cabinet members, for example, had some college education; 41 percent of them held doctorates (table 3.3).

The age structure of men of power is an important factor influencing their political orientation. It is largely acknowledged that the younger the political actors, the deeper their radical and revolutionary zeal. The Iranian revolution shows, on the surface, a diversion from this pattern of behavior. Khomeini was in his late seventies when he led the successful revolution. Many of his disciples also were old members of the ulama, including his two prominent aides, Hossein Ali Montazeri and Mortada Mutahhari, who were in their early sixties; a number of provincial ulama were even older. Two main factors, however, gave a youthful character to the revolution: first was the vividly youthful character of Khomeini himself, and second was the presence of a large corps of young revolutionaries at the heart of the movement.

TABLE 3.3

Distribution of Cabinet Members and
Islamic Majlis Deputies by Education
(in percentage)

Type and Level	Cabinet	Majlis First	Majlis Second	Majlis Third
Religious, ulama				
Ijtihad (doctoral degree)	40	25	19	14
Kharej (doctoral candidate)	60	52	64	52
Sath (A.A., B.A., M.A.)	—	21	13	17
Moqaddamat (high school)	—	2	4	17
Total	100	100	100	100
Number	(5)	(108)	(144)	(70)
Modern, lay				
Doctorate	41	25	8	9
M.A., M.S.	30	20	16	8
A.A., B.A.	22	47	52	61
High school	7	8	24	22
Total	100	100	100	100
Number	(59)	(108)	(125)	(190)

Khomeini often showed radical, inventive, ruthless, resourceful, and ascetic tendencies that are generally the character trait of young revolutionaries. In all phases of his activities, he supported the young radical components of the regime. This may be seen, for example, in his support for hostage taking, suicide missions, and the juvenile slogan "War! War! to Victory." Furthermore, the men of power in Iran are fairly young. Most of the cabinet members, state managers and bureaucratic officials were in their late twenties and thirties when they assumed their new responsibilities; most army generals were in their thirties and early forties when promoted to that rank.

The average age of the Majlis deputies has been considerably higher than that of the cabinet members, provincial governors-general, ambassadors, and state managers; the age structure of the three sessions of Majlis was rather constant. Approximately 30 percent were under 35 years old, from 37 to 46 percent were in the middle-aged

TABLE 3.4

Distribution of Cabinet Members and
Islamic Majlis Deputies by Age Group
(in percentage)

Age Group	Cabinet	First	Majlis Second	Third
25–34	24	31	28	28
35–44	64	37	40	46
45–54	12	25	23	20
55 and over	—	7	9	6
Total	100	100	100	100
Number	(64)	(216)	(269)	(260)

Sources: Majlis-e Shura-ye Islami 1981, 1985; *Kayhan,* 29 May, 26, 27 July, 9 Aug. 1988.

group 35–44, from 20 to 25 percent were in the age group 45–54, and only 6 to 9 percent were 55 and older (table 3.4).

These demographic characteristics have influenced the general orientation of the men of power in postrevolutionary Iran. For example, changes that have occurred in the occupational structure of Majlis deputies in the three sessions are indicative of two significant trends in the Islamic regime: the first is a shift from the clerical to lay elements, and the second is a switch from members of the intelligentsia to state managers and bureaucratic elements. These trends may lead to a transformation from the traditional and charismatic revolutionary orientation of the earlier period to a more bureaucratic, mundane, and pragmatic attitude in the future.

Another example of the relation of differential demographic characteristics to political behavior is the case of radical and conservative advocates in the Majlis. An analysis of these advocates in the second session of the Islamic Majlis illustrates that the proportion of the ulama was higher among the traditionalist deputies (60 percent) than among the radical ones (50 percent). The ulama of the traditionalist camp were better educated than were their counterparts in the opposite camp. The lay deputies who advocated the cause of the poor were better educated and held higher degrees in the modern educational system than their counterparts in the opposite camp. The median age of the traditionalist deputies was higher than that of the radical deputies. The lay radical deputies included a greater number of the former revolutionary students and teachers (80 percent) than did the deputies of the opposite camp (60 percent). Further, the radical deputies were less frequently from the civil service and small business backgrounds (20 percent) than were the traditionalist deputies (35 percent). The proportion of re-elected ulama of both factions was about 40 percent. The proportion of reelected lay deputies, however, was higher among the traditionalist deputies (44 percent) than among the radical ones (26 percent). Thus, 74 percent of radical lay deputies in the Second Islamic Majlis were newcomers. The newcomers were younger (mean age, 36 years) than the relected ones (mean age, 43 years).[8]

The available information for cabinet members, governors, and other leaders of revolutionary organizations shows a similar trend. The cabinet members form a new breed of young professional intelligentsia. Eighty-eight percent of them range in age from 25 to 44 (table 3.4). The cabinet members are specialized primarily in applied sciences: 43 percent in engineering and 13 percent in medicine, followed by the social sciences (20 percent) and Islamic studies (11 percent) (table 3.5). They have studied at both Iranian and foreign institutions of higher education. Of the cabinet members, 41 percent have received the doctorate, 30 percent M.A. degrees, 22 percent B.A. degrees, and 7 percent hold only a high school diploma (table 3.3). The presence of ulama in the cabinet (only 8 percent) is minimal; however, they occupied such key cabinet positions as ministers of interior, of intelligence, and of Islamic guidance.

An examination of cabinet members' educational and political backgrounds shows that most of them have combined technocratic skills with proven dedication to the cause of the regime: nearly 50 percent of ministers served in revolutionary tribunals, committees, the Revolutionary Guards, and other revolutionary organizations; 30 percent had served directly under Khomeini; and the remaining 20 percent were known more for their technocratic background.

An examination of the background of the power elite in postrevolutionary Iran, including cabinet members, deputy ministers, governors-general of provinces, state managers and directors of the revolutionary organizations, officials of the public bureaucracy, and members of the parliament, thus reveals the emergence of a new status group among men of power in Iran. Of the members of the Iranian political and managerial class dominating national politics in the 1980s, a large number of individuals received their primary political socializa-

TABLE 3.5

Distribution of Cabinet Members by Field of Education

Field	Number	%
Engineering	28	43
Social sciences	13	20
Medicine	8	13
Islamic studies	7	11
Military and other	8	13
Total	64	100

Sources: Kayhan, 26, 27 July, 9 Aug. 1988.

tion within the system that evolved under the shah's White Revolution in the 1960s and 1970s. They began their political life in the course of urban revolts of the early 1960s under the leadership of Khomeini and continued their activities over the following fifteen-year period. Though they constituted only a small minority, they were a well-organized and dedicated group in the Qom religious center. Some of his followers were even granted a sort of benefice, that is, the privilege of collecting a portion of the Imam's share on behalf of Khomeini and appropriating it for certain purposes, including the support of underground and guerrilla organizations (Khomeini 1983, 141–42, 179, 221). Thus, a select group comprising Khomeini's faithful students among the ulama and a handful of lay confidants, who were jointly called the Imam's loyal apostles, was formed in the course of the two decades of his political struggle. These people constituted the core of Khomeini's lieutenants in the course of the revolutionary mobilization and, later, the power magnates of postrevolutionary Iran. They lived clandestinely for many years, were prosecuted, imprisoned, tortured, expelled from the cities of their residence, and sent into exile. When they were detained because of their antiregime activities under the shah, they formed the commune of Khomeini's followers in the prisons, where they learned about politics and political ideologies, particularly those concerned with the dictatorship of the proletariat. After the success of the revolution, they were appointed to such influential and powerful bodies as the Revolutionary Council, the Council of Guardians, the

Assembly of Experts (which serves as the constitutional assembly), other revolutionary organizations, and the Majlis. Others among them were posted as the imams of Friday prayers and Khomeini's representatives in the provinces, as well as his personal representatives in the various revolutionary organizations and state agencies. Thus, members of the dominant class of postrevolutionary Iran either were among Khomeini's disciples and were active in the protest movements before the revolution or served in one or more of the revolutionary organizations in postrevolutionary Iran. Serving in revolutionary institutions has often been used as a stepping stone for upward mobility and promotion to higher offices.

Khomeini and his disciples began to learn the rules of the bureaucratic game in the first three years of the revolution. The leading figures of the regime, including Ali-Akbar Hashemi Rafsanjani and Sayyid Ali Khamenei, took their in-service training as deputy ministers in the Ministry of Interior and the Ministry of Defense. The circulation of middle- and lower-level officials and state managers took place later, after the bureaucratic network was brought under total control of Khomeini's confidants. In these new roles, both Khomeini and his disciples vacillated between revolutionary charisma and the requirements of a rational bureaucratic order.

Khomeini began his leadership career in Teheran with no experience in running the day-to-day affairs of a gigantic modern state. Mentally, he still lived in a small preindustrial Islamic town such as Qom or Najaf. Furthermore, as a pure charismatic leader, the specifics of economic considerations were foreign to him. His revolutionary, charismatic want satisfaction was, from the point of view of rational economic activity, antieconomic. He repudiated the predominance of the routine economic issues by asserting, for example, that "economy is the preoccupation of animals" (Khomeini 1983, 9:71–72). On his arrival at Qom in March 1979, Khomeini promised the inhabitants of that city, and by implication the inhabitants of all other cities, free electricity, gas, and water. He also issued an edict proscribing on religious grounds the import of frozen meats, an edict that he revoked a few days later (Khomeini 1983, 5:139). On another occasion Khomeini expressed astonishment when he was informed by the minister of agriculture that a number of owners of dairy farms in the vicinity of Teheran possessed hundreds and even thousands of cows. He advised the minister to distribute the cows among the discontented workers, letting them take home a few cows each instead of encouraging them to cooperate with the owners and managers of the farms.[9] Later, however, he not only became an ardent advocate of statism but, in mediating the rivalry between two revolutionary organizations (Jihad for Reconstruction and the Martyr Foundation) over the control of Caspian Sea fisheries, also issued an order in his last year in office favoring the former organization on the ground that it was the more efficient and profitable of the two. Yet, again, as in the question of bureaucratic rationality, Khomeini vacillated between the antieconomic requirements of pure charisma and economic rationality.

The new men of power who conquered the huge state apparatus in postrevolutionary Iran share similar social origins, generational experience, educational background, and life-style; together they form a "social status group," in Weber's (1968, 302–7) sense of *ständ*, which has a potential to develop into a social class. The members of the new class are young educated people who come predominantly from the traditional and modernizing petit bourgeois families. They are mainly of the emerging lay professional-bureaucratic intelligentsia. They are in the process of shedding the traditional village and Bazaari attitudes of their class of origin and are assuming the outlook and life-styles of their new, state managerial class. They are less traditionalist and conservative and more reformist or radical in their orientation. They are less interested in revolutionizing the world and more involved with matters of everyday life. Finally, they are more concerned with the Iranian nation-state than they are with an international Islamic republic or the export of the revolution. Most of them advocate a normalization in foreign relations and reconstruction at home.

Ideological Configurations of the Power Elite

No monolithic "Islamic ideology," even in the course of the revolution itself, could unite the major forces of rebellion. Instead, there existed a variety of Islamic ideologies, each attractive to particular social classes and groups. Five distinct and different versions of Islam furnished idealized visions of future society as well as the means by which the existing society should be transformed.[10]

Two significant variants of revolutionary Islam were the radical Islam advocated by Ali Shariati and the militant Islam expounded by Ayatollah Khomeini. Both had made bold innovations in the interpretation of Shiʿite doctrines, particularly as these doctrines applied to the relation between religion and politics. Moreover, both supported the use of violence to transform society into an Islamic utopia. Shariati's version of such a utopia was a classless community of Moslens ruled by enlightened thinkers, a dictatorship of secular intellectuals with no room for the ulama. Khomeini's utopia, on the other hand, was an Islamic state ruled by the ulama as vicegerents of the Hidden Imam. Shariati's ideology was a blueprint for a radical transformation of the social order; Khomeini's was primarily a design for the political and cultural transformation of the existing order. The agenda for Shariati was a social revolution; for Khomeini it was a political revolution aiming at the establishment of his own brand of theocracy. The followers of Shariati's ideas were almost exclusively the young intelligentsia.

Khomeini's position changed in the course of revolution and of establishing of his theocratic authority over a bureaucratic mass society. In the process, he became radicalized and ceased to exclude some of the basic ideas of Shariati. The radicals within the regime were allowed to preach Shariati's ideas despite his constant rejection of the ulama in general and of the conservative traditionalist forces in particular.

A third variant of revolutionary Islam was "liberal Islam," contesting for political power through nonviolent means and seeking an accommodation of Islam to the modern world. A segment of modern bourgeoisie, some enlightened merchants, a segment of the modern middle class, some students and teachers, and a tiny group of the ulama, including the Grand Ayatollah Shariatmadari, followed this liberal orientation. The organizational network of this variety of Islamic ideology became Bazargan's Iran Liberation Movement (Chehabi 1990). The fourth variant was "traditionalist conservative Islam," which appealed to the overwhelming majority of the ulama and the bazaaris. These were groups that yearned for a past in which the dictates of their faith were strictly carried out, when as a group they enjoyed greater respect and wielded more power in the community, and when they were required to pay only religious taxes. The bazaar-mosque alliance served as the social and political basis of this traditional Islam. This ideology was closely connected to the last variant of Islamic ideology, the popular Islam of the masses in the cities and the countryside. The popular Shiʿism of the masses was marked by such religious practices as commemorations of the "passion" of Hossein, which included the rituals of self-mutilation and flagellation. The ulama patronized, watched, but did not participate in these popular practices of the masses.

The distance separating all these groups was far less in the late 1970s than it has been among roughly comparable groups in other Moslem societies. This is because Shiʿism provided an overarching ideology that accepted difference in religious consciousness as a natural part of life. With the appearance of Khomeini, a militant charismatic figure who combined personal charisma with office charisma, the different groups—and with them virtually the entire urban society—rallied to his support. All variants of Islam found a place in and were united under the canopy of Khomeini's charismatic leadership.

The advocates of all these brands of Islamic ideology have contributed, in various ways and in different degrees, to the establishment of the Islamic state, and many of them have made their way into the emerging elites of the new regime. The basic ideological differences and conflicts among the major forces of the revolution, however, were transformed after the revolution into a set of coalitions and counter-coalitions among their advocates.

The Islamic regime has subdued virtually all major forces of opposition, including a variety of Marxist-Leninist organizations, the Islamic socialist mujahidin, Bazargan's nationalist and Islamic-oriented Liberation Movement, and such Moslem dissidents as the late Grand Ayatollah Shariatmadari and the Hojatiyyah religious association. In spite of such victories over its various challengers and opponents, the regime has suffered increasingly from intense internal rivalries and infighting that could potentially lead to serious problems for its future stability.

In the years since the victory of the revolution, various groups, organizations, and factions within the ruling party, as well as advocates of different brands of Islamic ideology, have reorganized themselves into three major camps in the Islamic regime: (1) those who support the interests of the old strata of the traditionalist ulama, as well as the interests of the bazaari merchants, shopkeepers, and master artisans, and who advocate the traditional Islamic jurisprudence are referred to as conservatives, rightists, or first-liners; (2) those who support a pragmatist approach and are concerned with the survival of the regime in the modern world are called centrists, reformists, or second-liners; and (3) those who support the cause of the deprived, or "mostazafan," and advocate an innovative, dynamic, and progressive Islamic jurisprudence are called radicals, leftists, the followers of the Imam's (i.e., Imam Khomeini's) line, or third-liners. The first camp backs up the active participation of the private sector in economic activities and underlines the sanctity of unrestricted private ownership and economic liberalism in Islam, while taking a reactionary line on cultural issues. The second faction represents the pragmatist line of the new middle-class professional and bureaucratic elements who attach the highest priority to the reconstruction of postwar Iran on the basis of a mixed

TABLE 3.6

Ideological Configurations of Factional Politics

Ideological Orientation	Economic Issues		Cultural Issues		Foreign Relations	
	Public	Private	Permissive	Strict	Aggressive	Normal
Conservative	–	+	–	+	–	+
Radical	+	–	+	–	+	–
Pragmatist	+	+	+	–	–	+

Sources: *Kayhan*, 26, 27 July, 9 Aug. 1988.

economy with appropriate accommodations to the requirements of the modern world. The third camp champions statism and distributive justice, and hence supports nationalization of foreign trade, ceilings on the size of agricultural landholding, a progressive labor law, and a tighter control of the state over the private sector.

Broadly speaking, there are four sets of internal and external questions with respect to which the different ideological and political factions can be distinguished. The two internal issues are (1) the degree to which the state should intervene in economic life of the society and (2) the degree to which the Islamic modes of behavior should be imposed on Westernized middle classes—particularly regarding women, music, films, sports, and even chess. The two external questions relate to (1) the degree to which Iran should normalize its relations with the United States, the West, and Russia and (2) the mode of exporting the Islamic revolution in the Near East and North Africa.

The economic issue has become the center of mounting controversies and has served as the major dividing point among the three factions. The economic controversies are focused on four issues, including private ownership and freedom of economic activities: land reform, foreign trade, urban real estate, and labor laws. The conservatives, who have the support of the bazaar-mosque alliance, underline the sanctity of private property in Islamic jurisprudence; they support the unlimited freedom of commercial and industrial activities. They even oppose setting a minimum wage or any control by the state over economic enterprises, arguing that capital and labor are interacting in the Islamic free market and that labor accepts the proposed wage of its own free will; thus, no intervention by the state in the economic life of the community may be permitted. On the other side are the radicals who represent revolutionary organizations and the cause of the impoverished. They advocate the imposition of a ceiling on agricultural land, confiscation of the lands in urban areas, nationalization of foreign trade, progressive labor laws to protect the interests of labor against the owners of capital, and ultimately a form of statism, or state socialism. The pragmatists, representing the new middle classes, are located in the middle of this spectrum. They support a mixed economy in which there will be a peaceful coexistence of the public and private sectors.

The main issue in the postwar era is the strategy to be followed in the reconstruction of the country. The conservatives support a cautious strategy of reconstruction without excessive foreign presence and with minimum disturbance of the traditional values. The radicals, on the other hand, categorically oppose the opening of Iran's economy to the capitalist world, arguing that the reconstruction should be achieved by the native human, financial, and natural resources—independence first, development second. The pragmatists want rapid economic development with foreign participation and assistance.

The cultural issues are focused on overt behavior of men and women in the Islamic society, including the appearance of women in public and in the movies, employment opportunities for women, and men's wearing of neckties or short-sleeved shirts or shorts (on the playing field). Performing music and playing chess, which are forbidden according to the opinion of the majority of the jurisconsults, are also among the current controversial issues. Conservatives are highly rigid on all these issues: no music, no chess, no unveiled women on the streets or in the movies, and no men with shorts or short sleeves should be permitted; they resist the "cultural invasion" of the West. Radicals and pragmatists, on the other hand, are relatively more permissive on these cultural issues.

At the core of the foreign relations controversy are the problems of normalizing relations with the West and the export of the Islamic revolution to other Middle Eastern countries. Most conservatives are interested neither in the export of the revolution by force nor in isolationism; they support normalization without the excessive presence of foreigners. Most radicals are highly suspicious of the West, particularly the United States, and of conservative states in the region; they advocate the export of revolution by supporting liberation movements. The pragmatists support normalization of foreign relations and the export of revolution through example.

The origin of the above three factions can be traced, first, to the polarization of factional politics since the mid-1980s and, second, to the postwar and post Khomeini political situation. During this period the state managers and bureaucrats have been influenced by two sets of processes: first, the process of bipolarization and radicalization in the course of the war and, second, the process of normalization in the postwar period. In the course of the war itself, the hardliners rose to prominence and assumed leadership of the new radical camp in the regime. Significant shifts in factional alliances resulted. As the moderates and radicals split, a large group within the IRP and the Majlis joined the traditionalists, and a number of leftist or opportunistic elements merged with the new radical camp. The traditionalists gained more resources within the IRP. Thus, the dissolution of the IRP in 1987 was a blow to the traditionalists, significantly reducing their ability to mobilize the IRP's political resources in the summer election of 1988.

These two camps were far from being internally homogeneous. They were formed by coalitions and countercoalitions of loosely organized individuals, subfactions, political groups, and revolutionary organizations that are in constant intra- and interfactional competition and rivalry. The main social basis of the conservative and traditionalist camp is the old bazaar-mosque alliance. The overwhelming majority of the leading ulama, including all sources of emulation, the prominent ulama, the majority of jurisconsults, doctors of Islamic jurisprudence, and instructors of religious schools, and rank and file of the ulama, belong to this traditionalist camp. The bazaari merchants, master artisans, and shopkeepers, both within the bazaar and outside of its boundaries, also belong to this camp. The physical proximity and interdependence of the mosque and the bazaar in the structure of the Islamic town and the latter's enclosed physical space reinforce their alliance as a closely knit community. Paying one's religious taxes, contributing to charitable funds, and maintaining a generally good relationship with the ulama are all signs of piety and as such help to sustain one's respect and honor in the bazaar (Ashraf 1988).

The organizational bases of the conservative camp are the well-established preexisting structures of the bazaar-mosque alliance, including all major professional and political associations of the ulama and the bazaaris. The Association of the Instructors of the Qom Religious Center, the Society of Preachers of Teheran, and the Militant Ulama of Teheran are some of the more important conservative organizations. The Society of the Islamic Associations of Teheran's Bazaar and Guilds has been active in promoting the interests of the bazaaris. The

TABLE 3.7

The Social Bases of Factional Politics

Factions	Bazaaris	Ulama	New Middle Classes	Workers	Rural Urbanites
Conservative	+	+	−	−	+ −
Radical	−	−	+	+	+ −
Pragmatist	+	−	+	+	+ −

Society has closely cooperated with the conservative group of the Militant Ulama (Ruhaniyyat-e Mobarez) of Teheran. *Resalat*, the main daily newspaper of the conservative camp, represents and supports the cause of the bazaaris and serves as the joint organ of the bazaar-mosque alliance. The first decade of the revolution witnessed a concerted effort by the united front of the ulama and the bazaaris to preserve their traditional privilege. They have organized national seminars to expand the bazaaris' awareness of their class interests and to find practical ways to protect these interests. In all elections, the bazaaris have supported the candidates of the bazaar-mosque alliance. They also have grass-roots support among numerous Islamic associations of white-collar workers. The conservative camp also enjoyed a fairly large block of votes in the first and second sessions of the Majlis, but it lost its previous power base in the Third Majlis and regained a large majority of the seats in the Fourth Majlis. The Council of Guardians from its formation in 1980 has consistently protected the conservative forces and the private sector from intrusion by state managers.

The radical camp is composed of the young intelligentsia of students and teachers who were active against the shah's regime in the 1970s. They were influenced by the ideas of Ali Shariati and advocated the promotion of a classless society. Their organizational bases of support used to be the revolutionary organizations and ordinary organs of the state, including the Bureau of Promotion of Unity Between Religious Center and University. The leaders of this group organized the students who occupied the premises of the American embassy during the hostage crisis. The radicals claim to represent the interests of the peasantry, the industrial proletariat, and the urban poor.

TABLE 3.8

Shifts in the Leadership's Position from
the Khomeini Era to the Post-Khomeini Period

	Khomeini Era 1979–89	Post-Khomeini Period 1989–93
Supreme leader	proradical	conservative
Head of cabinet	radical	pragmatist
Speaker of Majlis	proradical/pragmatist	conservative[a]
Chief justice	proradical	conservative

[a]The Third Majlis Speaker, Mehdi Karrubi, was a radical; he was replaced in the Fourth Majlis (1992–96) by an ardent conservative, Ali Akbar Nateq Nuri.

The pragmatists' social bases of support are the new middle classes, the industrial entrepeneurs, the modern commercial bourgeoisie, government employees, and the intelligentsia. In the postwar and post-Khomeini era, even the industrial proletariat and the peasantry support the reconstruction agenda of the pragmatists. The regular army officers whose loyalty is primarily to the nation-state also constitute a base of support for the pragmatist camp.

Following Khomeini's lead, particularly after his message to the pilgrims to Mecca on 10 August 1987 (dubbed the regime the "manifesto of the Islamic revolution"), the cabinet has managed to increase significantly the authority of the executive branch to punish those who, in its judgment, act against the interests of the community, including the profiteers and price gougers. This was achieved through the enactment of a series of bills that were spurred by Khomeini's edict. Conservative Islamic judges had often refused to prosecute the price gougers on the ground that it would be un-Islamic.

On 7 December 1987 the radical minister of labor requested Khomeini to issue his opinion on the extent of the government's authority to impose various requirements on the operation of the private sector. Khomeini's initial edict was positive, but rather vague and evasive. The radical camp launched a propaganda campaign for legitimation of unlimited authority of the state to intervene in all spheres of economic life of the community. The response of the conservative ulama was relatively inarticulate and ineffective. Ayatollah Safi, the secretary of the Council of Guardians, asked Khomeini to express his opinion on the question of the extent of the Islamic state's authority. In response, Khomeini extended the scope of his earlier declaration, although he still left room for different interpretations, perhaps in order to assess the potential political capabilities of the two rival factions in resource mobilization. At this point, President Khamenei, championing the cause of traditionalist ulama against the radicals, interpreted Khomeini's edict in favor of traditionalist ulama in his sermon at the Friday prayer. Assured of the weakness of the traditionalist ulama and the conservative camp to mobilize effectively their political resources, Khomeini delivered his final blow to the traditionalist camp and issued his historic edict that gave unconditional authority to the Islamic state to make all manner of decisions concerning the affairs and interests of the Islamic community.

Furthermore, to facilitate the enactment of radical measures, Khomeini created a Discretionary Council to review the controversial bills in the event the Majlis and the Council of Guardian failed to reach an agreement on theological and legal points. The new members, in addition to the conservative members of the Council of Guardian included the president, the prime minister, and the heads of the legislative and judicial branches. Khomeini's chief of staff, another staff member and his son Ahmad, who were registered among the supporters of the radical measures, were also included.

The limitations of the Shi^{c}ite jurisprudence in the management of the daily affairs of a highly complicated secular society in the modern age had been apparent for quite some time. The only available Shi^{c}ite principle was that of the overriding necessity *(zarura)* for preservation of the system; it allowed for deviation from the primary rules of Shari^{c}ah under circumstances of emergency that would require the adoption of secondary rulings to guarantee the survival of the regime. In Sunni Islam the Islamic ruler *(vali-yi amr)* is authorized to ratify government rulings according to the principle of the best interest of the Islamic community *(masleha)*. Following a number of abortive attempts to apply the principle of *zarura* during the ten years of Islamic rule, the Islamic regime was forced by circumstances to adopt the Sunni principle of *masleha*. Substituting for the Shi^{c}ite principle of *zarura*, the Sunni principle of *masleha* required a legal loophole. Khomeini, as the ruling *faqih*, was faced simultaneously with God and the community. Absolute power in relation to the polity and the civil society had already been secured for him in the Islamic republic's constitution; he did not need more power or domination. By inventing the principle of the absolute authority of the ruling jurisconsult (i.e., Khomeini), he directed attention to the other side of the equation, that is, in relation to God, the prophet, the Imams, and Islamic jurisprudence. This removed the constraints that Articles 72 and 96 of the constitution had imposed on the Majlis and the Council of Guardian: "The Islamic Consultative Assembly cannot pass laws in contravention of the principles and precepts of the constitution and the official religion of the country. On the basis of Article Ninety-six, the determination of this principle is the responsibility of the Council of Guardian."

The absolute authority of the *faqih*, it was argued, would expand and enrich the power of the legislature, including both the Majlis and the Guardianship Council. It was thus a pragmatic move to solve the basic problems of the legislature, but not to eliminate the role of the legislature. Besides its pragmatic orientation, the principle of *masleha* was adopted because of pressures from below and from the revolutionary organizations. Meanwhile, the radicals used these developments to pave the way for a sweeping victory over their rivals in the 1988 Majlis elections. The radical and pragmatic factions managed to win the majority of the seats, with traditionalists and conservatives becoming a small minority in the Third Majlis.

At least four factors have contributed to the radicalization of a segment of the power elite in postrevolutionary Iran. First, Khomeini himself was basically a militant person and at times adopted radical positions, although he often managed skillfully to conceal his intentions in order not to alienate the mainstream segment of the ulama; furthermore, charisma is primarily a revolutionary phenomenon and as such is antitraditional and extraordinary. Particularly since the mid-1980s, Khomeini's drive for radicalization has corresponded closely to the position of the young radicals within the regime and with pressures from below.

The legacy of the Left, the influence of Marxist-Leninist ideas and practices, has been a second factor in the radicalization process. The Iranian Left, in the last two decades, has organized itself in three different groupings: Marxist-Leninist organizations, the Islamic-socialist Mujahidin, and the left wing of the Islamic regime. Each of these groups, in its own way, has applied pressures toward radicalization on the regime. Furthermore, the leftist groups within the regime have successfully managed to dominate revolutionary organizations, hoping for an eventual takeover in the post-Khomeini era.

Third, the war has been instrumental in the promotion of the radical camp. Arguing that the dissemination of such traditionalist ideas of

Islamic jurisprudence as the sanctity of private property could lead to the demoralization of young volunteers for martyrdom at the front, Khomeini, on several occasions, curbed some of the initiatives of the traditionalist camp. For example, the traditionalists were for a long time denied access to the media, including the state-owned radio and television, the two major daily newspapers, the daily newspaper of the IRP, and the morning daily newspaper *Abrar* (organ of the militant faction of the radical camp). Not only did these media decline to publish news and articles that would favor the traditionalists cause, they also missed no opportunity to attack the traditionalists as "agents of capital and the enemy of the impoverished." Furthermore, the decline of productive activities because of the war forced the state to resort increasingly to redistributive measures in order to respond to the rising expectations of youth for a greater share of societal resources and for a mobilization of the masses in the postwar period.

Fourth, the popularity of Ayatollah Khomeini among militant students and masses in the Moslem world has led the Islamic regime to look at itself with the eyes of activists in the Islamic movements outside of the country and hence to behave according to their expectations.

The demoralization and subsequent defeat of the Revolutionary Guards on the war front, their retreat from the Iraqi territories, and the acceptance of peace negotiations were blows to Ayatollah Khomeini and his radical supporters. Ayatollah Khomeini accepted the cease-fire with deep agony, comparing it to "swallowing a chalice of poison." Furthermore, the war economy, destruction of cities and infrastructures, and shortages of the necessities of life increased the grievances of the people from all walks of life. Under these circumstances a new centrist and pragmatist faction—located between the conservative and the radical camps—was boosted up. Now it enjoyed the leadership of Ali-Akbar Hashemi Rafsanjani, the Speaker of Majlis, and the support of Ayatollah Hossein Ali Montazeri, the chosen successor to Khomeini, and President Ali Khamenei. Furthermore, the bazaar-mosque alliance tactically supported the more moderate camp against their common enemy, the radicals.

The radical camp has been under mounting pressures from all sides. The tenth anniversary of the revolution, on 11 February 1989, gave the rising pragmatist camp a chance to launch a propaganda campaign against the radicals. Ayatollah Montazeri urged the authorities to "make up for the past mistakes" and to create an "open society." He called for freedom of foreign trade and regretted that "the people of the world thought our only task here in Iran was to kill" (*Teheran Times*, 13 Feb. 1989).

On 14 February, two days after Pakistanis protested against Salman Rushdie's novel *The Satanic Verses*, Ayatollah Khomeini, apparently acting out of mixed motives, issued his edict for the execution of Rushdie. It was for Ayatollah Khomeini an antidote to the "chalice of poison" that he had to swallow earlier by accepting U.N. Resolution 598. His anti-Rushdie edict was well received by masses of Moslems everywhere, and he emerged as the leader of the world's Islamic community. Heartened by this support, he mobilized the radicals, attacked his domestic foes, and as a result redeemed the radical camp from an impending demise. Five weeks later Ayatollah Khomeini dismissed Montazeri as his deputy leader and successor.

Ayatollah Khomeini's death on 3 June 1989 posed the question of charismatic succession. Leaders with genuine charisma, particularly those who are endowed with both personal qualifications and prophetic calling, do not have true successors in the totality of their charismatic performance. Ayatollah Khomeini was considered by his followers a renewer of the faith, an imam; he was a jurisconsult, a source of emulation, the vicegerent of the Hidden Imam, the commander of *umma*, and the *vali-yi amr*. He was believed to be the leader of the mass rebellion in 1963 and of the successful revolution in 1977–79; he was believed to be the founder and the great leader of the Islamic Republic; and last, he was the redeemer and the hope for the wretched of the earth and for millions who still live in the Age of Belief. It is true that these extraordinary images of the charismatic leader were partially fabricated by rational planning and the propaganda machine of the regime. Yet Ayatollah Khomeini was endowed with some exceptional character traits, including brutality, ruthlessness, and determination, as well as a number of acquired religious, social, and political stations that, combined, facilitated the inflation of his charismatic image by generating a hybrid of genuine charisma and spurious pseudo-charisma. The person who was selected as Khomeini's successor enjoyed merely one of Khomeini's qualifications and titles, the position of "supreme leader." The regime will certainly make an attempt to enhance the office charisma for the position, but how it will work remains to be seen, Sayyid Ali Khamenei, then the president, reflected, in the same way as argued above, on the occasion of his selection to the office of the supreme leader of the Republic, "Imam Khomeini was so great that among the great men and world leaders in history, one could hardly imagine a man with such characteristics, except among prophets and the infallibles. Neither I, as a humble theology student with all shortcoming and defects, nor any other man in the Islamic Republic

CHARISMA, THEOCRACY, AND POWER   141

can reach the summit of that distinguished and exceptional personality" (*Teheran Times*, 10 June 1989).

Khomeini's death led to an exacerbation of factional conflict. A major shift of power took place from the radical left, which had enjoyed Khomeini's support, to the conservative forces and a pragmatist group of bureaucratic and professional elements. The first major gain of the conservative camp was the election of president Sayyid Ali Khamenei as the successor to Khomeini. He swiftly appointed Shaikh Mohammad Yazdi as the head of judiciary. Given that the 1989 amended constitution dissolved the Supreme Judiciary Council and transferred its extensive power to the office of the chief justice, the new conservative chief justice has much more constitutional power than his predecessors. Most religious judges since the beginning of the republic have espoused conservative policies and have often had differences of opinion with a quasi-radical chief justice, Musavi Ardabili, and a radical prosecutor general, Musavi Khoeiniha, the leader of the radical students following "Imam Khomeini's line." These moves brought the judiciary under the tight control of the conservative camp. Meanwhile, the radicals maintained their power base in the Third Majlis. They reached a compromise with the conservatives and suspended the constitutional power of the new supreme leader to dissolve the Majlis.

The pragmatist's major gain was the election of Hashemi Rafsanjani to the presidency in August 1989. Empowered by the amended 1989 constitution to form the cabinet and preside over its meetings, the new president rose to prominence and with considerable constitutional power. However, the pragmatist cluster that enjoyed the support of the modern middle classes had no active groups to fight for its cause and thus had to rely increasingly on the support of the conservative camp in its struggle against the radical Left. Enjoying the full support of the Council of Guardians—which was empowered to supervise the elections and approve the credentials of the candidates—the conservatives managed to deny any seat to the radical clerics in the elections of the Assembly of Experts in 1991. The Council of Guardians rejected the credentials of most radical candidates on the ground that they did not have sufficient knowledge of Islamic jurisprudence. The council also rejected the credentials of many ardent radical candidates in the 1992 Majlis elections on the ground that they lacked sufficient commitment to the tenets of Islam. These interventions secured an overwhelming majority of the 270 Majlis seats for the conservatives and some forty seats (approximately the same number as in the Third Majlis) for the pragmatists. An uneasy coalition of the Right and the

Center ended soon when the conservative majority began to obstruct President Rafsanjani's pragmatist policies just as their radical predecessors had done in the Third Majlis.

In sum, the support of Khomeini, the legacy of the revolutionary left and, above all, the exigencies of the war gave a major boost to the radical camp in the 1980s. Khomeini's death, the end to the war, and the dissolution of the Soviet Union set a blow to the radical camp: they lost the supreme spiritual leader, the chief justice, and the speaker of the Majlis to conservatives, and the chief of the cabinet to pragmatists. They also lost their grip on the revolutionary organizations and were eventually pushed to the margin of Iran's contemporary politics.

The Genesis and Legacy of Charismatic Leadership

The drama of the Islamic revolution in Iran could be portrayed as a dialectical process of contradictions and conflicts among various social forces and cultural expressions that was thrust onto Iran's historical stage by two personages: the shah and the Imam. These two characters were endowed with different personality types and were committed to very different agendas for action. They were characterized by contradictory ideas for historical development and by distinct images of the world and of the future of their society, and above all, they enjoyed dissimilar social bases of support. The shah was a fragile and vulnerable character who lacked the will to fight yet played the role of a dictator. He appeared on the stage as a leader of a Westernizing client state with a demoralized and politically immature dominant class. Khomeini was "an extraordinarily bold, inventive, and ruthless politician"[11] who, while representing popular classes, acted as the antithesis to the shah and his established order.[12]

The dichotomy of the shah's and Khomeini's distinct modes of cultural expression and political discourse and of their bases of support prepared the way for the genesis of charisma. Charismatic leadership typically arises at times of crisis, when the basic value orientation, institutional setting, and legitimation of the established order, as well as the dominant classes who are identified with that order, are questioned by intellectuals, middle strata, and popular classes. Like other great charismatic figures in history, Khomeini personified the crisis charisma. The emergence of charisma is not a random incident; it depends on certain intense external social and cultural crises or great internal psychological distresses.

Social and economic developments of the 1960s and 1970s in Iran brought about a cultural polarization and civilizational crisis. More specifically, they shifted the social bases of the regime, weakened the cohesion of the dominant classes, changed the allegiance of the intellectuals to the political contenders, corroded the links between the regime and the civil society, alienated the life-style and basic values of the dominant classes from the popular classes, and undermined the legitimacy of the existing political order. Furthermore, Iran shares with other Islamic societies a source of strife in the critical period of the 1960s and 1970s, naemly, the ideological crisis of humanism and its twin offspring, liberalism and Marxism. The ideological crisis deepened with the indictment by Western intellectuals of the malaise of their own culture and civilization and with the failure of several attempts at applying those Western models of progress in Islamic societies. The advocates of Western ideologies were discredited and demoralized. A favorable condition emerged for the revival of Islam. These circumstances in the late 1970s intensified the need for an extraordinary leader who had to fulfill his charismatic mission and to assuage the fears and anxieties of the people. This situation provided Khomeini with a favorable precondition for mobilizing the people from all walks of life if they were faced with an opportunity for rebellious action and rise to power.[13] Thus, one may say metaphorically that there was no Khomeini without the shah, that there was no popular revolution without the revolution from above, and that there was no Islamic revolution without Khomeini.

Khomeini's rise to the theocratic leadership of the bureaucratic apparatus of a modern state with a sizable surplus-producing economic sector confronted him with a very complex situation in the period 1979–89. He found himself caught between the pressures coming from the major conflicting forces in the state and civil society. He had to modify his personal and traditional arenas of leadership and adapt himself to the new situation. In doing so he had to cope with three challenges: (1) to modify his antibureaucratic orientation, (2) to alter his antieconomic stance, and (3) to adopt a radical stand that deviated significantly from conservative Islamic jurisprudence.

Genuine charisma is antibureaucratic—it does not get along with officials. Khomeini, therefore, was faced with a number of problems transforming his inexperienced clerical and lay disciples into the officials of the bureaucratic state, bringing under his control a large number of modernized officials and state managers, leading a huge and complicated state apparatus, and bridging the hiatus between the two inherently contradictory political entities of theocracy and modern republican democracy. The men of power who emerged had to learn through trial and error and in-service training how to run the modern state. The confidants of the leader were superimposed on major revolutionary and ordinary bureaucratic agencies. A mode of democratic centralism was developed in which the elected representatives, councilmen, and officials of the state could express their views and even stand against the will of the leaders, but the final voice in the key decisions was that of the leader. At the same time, the constitution gave the supreme charismatic leader the authority to appoint the members of the Council of Guardians, who had veto power over legislation passed by the Majlis. When Khomeini became dissatisfied with the conservative and traditional stance of the council in vetoing several radical bills, he did not hesitate to institute a Discretionary Council to overrule the veto power of the former council.

Economic factors were even more significant and pressing in shaping the behavior of the new men of power and privilege than were the workings of the bureaucracy. The economics of charismatic revolution, as an independent variable, directs the process of transformation (Weber 1968, 254).

Khomeini was fairly successful in revolutionizing Shiʿite world views, but he was limited by the requirements of the modern state and its economic base. Thus, he succeeded in making a revolution in Qom because in "traditionalistic periods charisma is the great revolutionary force," but he was forced to modify his attitude and assume an adaptive orientation in Teheran because of overwhelming bureaucratic and economic constraints. In the end, Khomeini became an ardent advocate of the central state and its superordination over the civil society. He also accepted the principles of rationality, efficiency, and profitability in administering the public bureaucracy and state-owned capitalist enterprises.

Khomeini exemplified, apparently, a rare case of a genuine charisma in modern times. Most modern charismatic figures, including Lenin, Mao, Castro, and Nkrumah, argue Bensman and Givant (1975, 599–604), do not have genuine charisma in the classic Weberian sense of the term. They are at best pseudocharismatics. Their charisma is nonpersonal and rational; it is fabricated by rational planning, by mediation of the impersonal mass media, by the propaganda machine of a bureaucratic mass society. By operating in the modern world, Khomeini's genuine charisma was thus contaminated by rationality, by impersonality, and by accommodation to the modern bureaucratic and economic order. He combined, however, tradition and modernity, personal relations of *Gemeinschaft* with personal relations of *Gesellschaft*. He increasingly used the mass media, particularly television, for communicating with the masses. As a matter of fact, the mass appeal of his charisma emerged at this stage through the use of newspapers, cassettes, radio, and, later, television. Furthermore, tens of thousands of believers who were seduced by the regime's propaganda officers and the mass media were brainwashed and dispatched to the war front for suicide missions and martyrdom.

Even at this stage of his mundane leadership, Khomeini remained consistent with his genuine charismatic calling in sticking to the charismatic dimension of arationality in such important acts as waging a political war against both superpowers, the West, and the regional powers, and particularly in his insistence on victory at any cost in the Iran-Iraq War. It may be equally argued, however, that these tendencies exemplified value-rational actions of an uncompromising ascetic revolutionary; they were neither traditional nor emotional.

Most observers of modern charisma recognize the central role of the mass media in the making of modern charismatic politics. Bendix (1968, 172) notes that "modern means of publicity can give such leadership all the appearance of charisma." Loewenstein (1966, 86) observed that "mass media can produce a reinforcement and deepening of an originally spurious but artificially promoted charisma attributed to the ruler." Bensman and Givant (1975, 604, 606) say that "modern charisma . . . rests upon the conscious selection of themes, appeals, slogans, and imagery that is based upon the systematic study of audiences, target populations, constituencies, and strategic public. . . . Modern charismatic leaders may rationally select irrational themes, motifs, and values to personify those themes and values and a sense of pseudo-*Gemeinschaft* to distant publics." Although Khomeini was endowed with personal charisma, he and his disciples used the mass media consciously for the expansion and sustenance of their charismatic community in the 1980s. They were well aware of the praxis of modern politics and the legacies of Machiavelli, Marx, and Lenin.

Khomeini's charisma, as a typical case, was also a dramaturgical phenomenon. It was created by symbolic representations in the Shiʿite community and involved the selective and purposive mobilization of human, physical, and financial resources as well as manipulation of rhetorical tools and strategies. The drama and the passion play of Hossein, the commemoration of his death, and the notion of martyrdom in Shiʿite culture were manipulated for the purpose of political

mobilization of the masses. These rhetorical symbols served as significant *cultural resources* for the purpose of mass mobilization. Furthermore, to appeal to the intelligentsia, Khomeini's disciples adopted an
innovative modern political discourse as early as 1960. By mastering
contradictory discourses of the traditional elitist language of Islamic
law, the popular rhetorical sermons and passion plays that focused on
the drama of Hossein, and the modern political discourse of the intellectuals, Khomeini's groups succeeded in manipulating and deceiving
individuals from all walks of life.

What Khomeini did at Qom was reform and rationalize Shiʿite
Islam by introducing a set of new ideas and the requirements of the
modern world. He went well beyond the boundaries of the Shiʿite
world in Qom and Najaf. Khomeini often showed his support for the
radicals and their cause in economic, political, and cultural realms. He
did not hesitate to express his disdain for the traditionalist and conservative segment of the ulama. He called them "reactionary and stupid
asses living in the old age!" Thus, Khomeini's mission was an "Islamic
reformation." The return to political hegemony of traditionalist and
conservative forces of the bazaar-mosque alliance after Khomeini's
death, however, has largely blocked a charismatic reformation and
eliminated progressive forces within the movement.

Khomeini's charismatic revolution in Iran was the culmination of
recent Islamic revivalist movements and provided them with a new
perspective and hope. Khomeini's movement was, at the same time, an
Iranian national movement. It was a religious revolution that served,
though tragically and at a great human cost, the arena of political development and nation building. It has led to an expansion of national
identity that goes beyond loyalty to small groups. The Protestant Reformation occurred in the West much earlier than the processes of industrialization and nation building began. These three major processes
have occurred, argues Ernest Gellner (1985, 1–3), simultaneously in the
Islamic society. The combination of these giant processes has profoundly affected and complicated the processes and goals of the Islamic
movements; it has constituted the heart of "the Islamic dilemma."

A significant consequence of Khomeini's charismatic revolution
was the process of further integration of the state through mass participation in the course of rebellious activities and particularly via the
mass mobilization of hundreds of thousands of villagers, tribesmen,
and urbanites to fight in the eight-year war with Iraq. Even though the
motives for fighting mixed patriotism and a religious duty to wage a
holy war, they led to the intensification of feelings of both national

identity and political participation. Unintended consequences of what Ali Banuazizi (1988) has called the "democratization of martyrdom" may further the national identity and even enhance democratic processes. The primary loyalty of individuals has shifted from village, tribe, clan, neighborhood, status group, class, or profession to the Islamic state. Furthermore, the revolution has advanced the level of political awareness and the political maturity of major social classes and groups and brought them to the arena of national politics. Thus, it is fair to say that the charismatic legitimation has led to further political integration and that the process of national integration has, to some extent, reduced the intrasocietal tensions and led to further cultural-ideological consensus.

Khomeini's charismatic revolution was, however, a double-edged sword. It also led to the exacerbation of a number of salient internal tensions, which could potentially lead to instability of the regime and deter the progressive integration of the state. One major area of tension and conflict was the grave human cost and destructive physical effects of the arational charismatic pursuit of a futile war abroad coupled with an oppressive policy at home. On the occasion of the commemoration of the tenth anniversary of the revolution, on 11 February 1989, almost all major leaders of the regime spelled out their grievances in response to the directives of the supreme leader on major issues. They believe, for example, that from the beginning they "had to make an effort to prevent war" from breaking out or at least "to refrain from prolonging the war after the retreat of Iraqi forces from Khorrmashahr" (*Iran Times*, 17 Feb. 1989). More specifically, Ayatollah Hossein Ali Montazeri's evaluation of the balance sheet of the revolution tells what has happened in the volatile sphere of the "giant charisma."

> Have we succeeded in keeping up the revolution in accomplishing its goal and in fulfilling the promises we have given the people? Let's see what happened to all the unity, coordination, and devotion that we enjoyed at the beginning of the revolution. . . . Let's see whether we did a good job during the war or rather the enemies who imposed the war on us emerged victorious. . . . Let's count how many people did we lose, how many splendid young men were martyred, how many towns were destroyed . . . and then repent after realizing that we made these mistakes. . . . Social and political mistakes too must be remorsed for. . . . To admit a sin is remorse and it is incumbent upon us to notify each other of our mistakes. . . . Let's see what slogans we gave (over the past ten years) that made us so isolated in the world and turned the people pessimistic towards us. . . . On many occasions, we shouted

obstinacy, shouted slogans and frightened the world. . . . The people of the world thought our only task here in Iran was to kill. . . . To fill the prisons would not heal any wounds. . . . Prisons must be emptied. . . . When my statements as a humble student of theology and a sympathizer to the revolution are censored let alone others whose voices can be more easily suppressed. . . . A free press is essential for a more humane Iran. . . . The authorities should pave the way for the return of nearly four million Iranians abroad who intend to return to Iran but are scared. . . . If we care for Islam, the revolution, and the country and want the ideals of the revolution be safeguarded, we must create unity, optimism, and confidence among the people, just like the beginning of the revolution. . . . All forces must be mobilized for reconstruction. . . . We must work to create an open society in the real sense of the word.

(Teheran Times, 13 Feb. 1989)

A major event with disintegrative effects, the mass exodus of hundreds of thousands of well-educated and prosperous members of the new middle classes has created a brain drain at home and a sizable hostile Iranian community (about one million) in exile abroad. Together with those members of the middle classes who still reside in Iran, they constitute a threat to political integration and to the stability of the regime. Another source of conflict is the status of religious minorities in a predominantly Shiᶜite theocratic state. Armenians, Jews, Zoroastrians, and Bahaᵓis have been increasingly excluded from the public domain, alienated from the society, purged from offices, persecuted, and even executed in postrevolutionary Iran. A more severe area of strife and antagonism that may cost the very geographical integrity of the nation-state is the problem of ethnolinguistic groups. The ambivalent attitude of the theocratic regime toward the question of Iranian nationalism and Islamic internationalism has, ironically, fanned the nationalist feelings of both Persian-speaking Iranians and other ethnolinguistic groups. The Persian-speaking intelligentsia have increasingly resorted to their pre-Islamic historical roots and mythologies. Azerbaijanis, Kurds, Turkomans, Baluchis, and Arabs who have been alienated from the Islamic state have been encouraged by the Islamic internationalist ideology to denounce the overarching Iranian nationalism, on the one hand, and to resort to their own secessionist local chauvinism under the oppressive measures and ambiguous signals of nationalism-internationalism of the Islamic state, on the other. This tendency has been particularly enhanced as they have become the targets of mounting propaganda campaigns by neighboring states with claims over these groups.

Above all, the major disintegrative legacies of Khomeini's charisma are the exacerbation of internal strife within the religious hierarchy, the factional politics within the regime, and increasing antagonism between the state and the civil society. The split and the antagonism between the state and the Shiʿite establishment emerged at the beginning of the post-Khomeini era; the regime is separated from the source of emulation, and thus its theocratic basis of legitimation is under question. The division among the followers of Khomeini in supporting two sources of emulation, Grand Ayatollah Mohammad Reza Golpayagani and Ayatollah Mohammad Ali Araki, marks the beginning of a long road of strife and antagonims within the regime. The radical elements within the regime have supported Aytaollah Araki, whereas the traditional force of the bazaar-mosque alliance has supported Ayatollah Golpayagani. The roots of some of these tensions, with disintegrative potential, could be traced into the very politics of Khomeini's charismatic revolution and the symbolic manipulation of the rhetoric of the Shiʿite movement, on the one hand, and the canopy of his leadership that temporarily united conflicting social forces against the old regime, on the other. In this way, Khomeini's charismatic revolution has had both integrative and disintegrative effects, both constructive and immensely destructive consequences for modern state building in Iran. Thus, it would be premature to assess the effects of the revolution as essentially integrative or to characterize the charismatic movement of Khomeini as simply "the turban for the crown."

In post-Khomeini Iran many of the original ideas of Khomeini for the permanent revolution until the time of the appearance of the Mahdi, the Lord of the Age, are unlikely to be followed by his successors. Both international and internal developments that have occurred in the late 1980s and early 1990s are likely to lead to a more moderage regime in Iran. The sweeping changes that have rolled the socialist world and the new relations that have developed between the West and the former Eastern bloc have drastically altered the old geopolitical role of Iran as a buffer state. Iran has already lost most of its capability for playing a militant role in the region and is likely to follow a more moderate foreign policy in the future. Furthermore, the failure of the state socialism will lead to demoralization of the radical groups within the regime—the groups who have preached an Islamic variant of state socialism for Iran—and will strengthen the position of more moderate groups. However, the traditionalist forces of the bazaar-mosque alliance, occupying key state positions in the post-Khomeini era, have repeatedly obstructed the centrists' modernizing efforts to promote economic reconstruction and normalization of foreign relations. In all, those who are succeeding Khomeini are far less preoccupied with his charismatic mission. They are men who are concerned mainly with the day-to-day problems of the country. Their goal is not to change the world but to accommodate themselves to it. As Weber (1968, 1120) noted, "Every charisma is on the road from a turbulently emotional life that knows no economic rationality to *slow death by suffocation* under the weight of *material interests:* every hour of its existence brings it nearer to its end."

Yet, the shadow of Khomeini's charismatic revolution and the bolstering of the sense of self-esteem, collective identity, and historical rootedness that it gave to the masses, with all its productive and destructive repercussions, seem to remain in Iran and in the Islamic world of the future.

Notes

1. I follow in this paper, with some modifications, the original Weberian conception of charisma. The distinction between *personal charisma* and charismatic authority was first underlined by Robert Bierstedt (1954, 71–72) and later followed by Reinhard Bendix in his lucid presentation of Weber's ideas. This distinction, Bendix says, "is also embedded in Weber's analysis but is not clear from his terminology" (Bendix 1968, 616–29). For an application of the Weberian conception of charisma to modern times and a typology of fifty-five charismatic leaders, as well as a comprehensive bibliography of charisma, see Schweitzer 1984.

2. For the vulnerabilities of rentier states and a discussion of the Iranian case, see Mahdavi 1970.

3. For an account of the vulnerabilities of the neopatrimonial regimes at times of unrest, see Eisenstadt 1978, 273–310.

4. For an account of this issue, see Zonis 1991.

5. See also Ashraf and Banuazizi 1985.

6. In a letter to Gorbachev, Khomeini underlined his preoccupation with Ibn al-Arabi's ideas and recommended that the Soviet leader learn the ideas of the great Sufi thinker.

7. See Algar 1988, 271–76, for a few instances of Khomeini's sympathy with the ulama's antigovernment actions during the Reza Shah era.

8. Major demographic characteristics of the two main factions of the Second Islamic Majlis are drawn from a survey of Majlis representatives based on the data on individual deputies presented in a publication of Majlis-e Shura-ye Islami (1985) and the list of the supporters of the candidate of each faction from the daily newspapers *Resalat, Abrar,* and *Kayhan,* 30 and 31 July 1986.

9. From an interview with the deputy minister of agriculture, who was present at the meeting of Khomeini and the minister.

10. This part of the chapter, on four variants of Islamic ideology, is taken from Ashraf and Banuazizi 1985, 30–31.

11. Michael Walzer (1965, vii) says the puritan and ascetic Calvinist saint "is the destroyer of an old order . . . is the builder of a *repressive system* which may well have to be endured before it can be escaped or transcended . . . is, above all, an *extraordinarily bold, inventive, and ruthless politician,* as a man should be who has 'great works' to perform, as a man, perhaps, must be for "great works have great enemies' " (emphasis added).

12. Khomeini's personality traits have shown similarities to those presented by a number of political psychohistorians as a profile of the "revolutionary personality," including asceticism, autocratic tendency, unwillingness to compromise, and identity with the masses though avoiding close personal relations. Bruce Mazlish (1976, 212–13), "taking Weber's notions of asceticism and charisma, and Freud's notions of displaced libido, masochism, sadism, and narcissism," has introduced the ideal type of "revolutionary asceticism." He shows that "traits of asceticism and displaced libido, originally placed in the service of religion, were displaced first to the service of economic activity, and then to the service of revolutionary activity." E. Victor Wolfenstein (1971, 309–13) sees revolutionaries "as rebels against the father who, once in power, experience 'the return of the repressed.' " In this vein, one may argue that Reza Shah played the role of the generalized father for Khomeini by humiliating his family profession and his status group. Thus, Khomeini, who was a hyperactive, intelligent, and proud child, suffered deeply from low self-esteem based on strained relations with Reza Shah, who was called the father of the Iranian nation. He turned to politics, then, in order to overcome the low estimate of his own worth that was constantly engendered by the Pahlavis. He was determined to kill and devour the "nation's father" and to take his place.

13. One should not overstate the magnitude of crisis in Iran under the shah and lose sight of the fact that Khomeini, his disciples, and the lay intelligentsia played, as agents provocateurs, a central role in fabricating and fanning a political crisis by using both the traditional communicative network of the pulpit and passion play and the modern mass media when they were given an opportunity to mobilize a collective action. Furthermore, one should not overlook the Machiavellian manipulation or preexisting ordinary structures of the bazaar-mosque alliance by Khomeini's disciples and followers and the role it played in their successful mobilization of the masses.

4

The State and Political Privilege in Pakistan

AYESHA JALAL

Assessing the nature of the state by focusing on the location, complexion, and ideological leanings of the "dominant elites" raises a number of imponderables. For one thing, it obfuscates, even if unwittingly, the vital role of the modern state in defining and redefining the category "elites." Yet if the state is as much the creator as the creation of dominant elites, then how useful is the approach of elite theorists in analyzing the complex hierarchy of power relations? The assumption that differences between the dominant elites are less significant than the common ground between them and that the role of largely unorganized nonelites in determining the course of social change is marginal at best seems too stark a depiction of horizontal and vertical relations in any society. This is especially true for linguistically and culturally heterogeneous societies where the intensity of the scramble for economic resources and political power between provincial and national elites tends to be in direct proportion to the threats emanating from below. Put differently, since provincial elites are generally not the co-equals of national elites in terms of access to state authority, can they be dubbed subelites or counterelites when they are in fact the fiercest upholders of the status quo in local society? Even if "elites" is considered a relational concept, which is how it is best deployed, one cannot altogether justify referring to political and economic tensions between dominant and subordinate provinces or between the wielders of local and provincial power and state authority at the center as manifestations of elite cleavages, pure and simple. So it is perhaps better to resist

152

the temptation to use shorthand concepts like "dominant elites" and concentrate instead on identifying the actual bearers of social, economic, and political power, on the one hand, and their differential access to state authority, on the other.

Such an approach aims at disaggregating economic power blocs, ascertaining their relative political strength vis-à-vis each other as well as vis-à-vis the underprivileged strata, and in this way providing a more holistic view of the factors shaping the nature of the state in the contemporary world than that proffered by a study of dominant elites alone. It is premised on a clear recognition of the initiative of the state in the processes of social formation as opposed to its mere derivation from the social structure. But stressing the magnetlike quality of the state is not to endorse in any unqualified way specific state-centered approaches to the study of politics that of late have become fashionable in political science literature. It is different from these other approaches because the metaphor says as much about the qualities of key groups in civil society as it does about the state. By helping identify segments of society that are likely to develop closer links with the state apparatus than others, it serves to emphasize the crucial bearing that the changing nature of the state's links with different elements among the privileged strata has on its political, economic, and ideological posturing in relation to society as a whole.

In analyzing these links, one must be as wary of the Marxist conception of the "ruling class" as that of the "ruling" or the "power" elite. Whereas elite theorists accommodate societal complexities and change by acknowledging that the ruling elite is not the preserve of any particular social group, the Marxist idea is that of an economic group exercising political power on the basis of its dominant location in the social mode of production. Both in their own way try to relate the exercise of state power to identifiable classes or groups in society. Yet the equation between class and state power has never been an easy one, particularly in those parts of the developing world where the aftermath of formal or informal colonialism has seen the military and the bureaucracy assuming dominance over the elected institutions of the state. The dominant role of a military and civil bureaucracy selectively recruited from certain provinces favored by the colonial state has large consequences for the nature of the state in the postcolonial world. Although frequently drawn from the dominant social strata, military and civil officials in the immediate aftermath of colonialism have often given primacy to their own institutional interests by equating them with state imperatives rather than with those of any specific class, "elite," or sociocultural group. This has often led to sharp disjunctions between the domestic structures of economic dominance and social control and the actual wielding of state authority. Any analysis of relations between state and civil society in countries where state authority is a projection of institutional interests demands a scrutiny of the international dimension because the relative autonomy of the military and the civil bureaucracy from the internal class structure is frequently made possible by their closely nurtured connections with the erstwhile colonial metropolis and with the emergent centers of the postcolonial international system.

The key analytical task, therefore, is to identify the ways in which the domestic and regional factors combine with the international dimension to mold the structure of the state. Elites, in the sense of privileged social groups, undoubtedly play a role in channeling or deflecting forces operating at all three of these levels. Yet they are as much the creations as the architects of the kind of state that these forces combine to forge. The formation of the state, in the postcolonial world at least, more often than not precedes the formation of elites in analytical sequence. Empirical investigations of the interplay of domestic, regional, and international factors in state formation can help to explain why the institutional balance of power within the state apparatus can become a more important variable in shaping the processes of state consolidation and reconstitution than simply the socioeconomic background of privileged groups.

The case of Pakistan affords rare insights into the problem of state formation, consolidation, and reconstitution and, by extension, into the nature of social elites, or classes, jockeying to position themselves advantageously in relation to the state structure. An analysis of the first decade of Pakistan's independence is important for a number of reasons. First, it helps to clarify the open-ended relation between the state and elites during the process of formation. Second, it provides an opportunity to examine the construction of a central state apparatus where none existed before. Third, it illuminates how the flux in the balance of power between elected and nonelected institutions resulting from the lack of a preexisting center gave way to the dominance of the military and civil bureaucracy that has proven to be so enduring in Pakistan's subsequent history.

State Formation and Consolidation

Unlike India, which inherited British India's unitary center, Pakistan began its independent career having to create a wholly new central government over territories that not only were separated by over a thousand miles but also had been ruled from New Delhi until 1947.[1] The Muslim League's organizational machinery was weakest precisely in those areas that became part of Pakistan. The initiation of hostilities with India soon after independence entailed the diversion of very scarce financial resources—inevitably extracted from the provinces— into the defense procurement effort at a time when the political process had yet to be clearly defined. While Pakistan's early managers sought to use its strategic location to acquire British and, subsequently, American military and economic aid, the increasing costs of maintaining the defense establishment set the imperative of state formation on a collision course with the political process. As tensions between the center and the provinces weakened the political leadership, top echelons of the civil and military bureaucracy attempted to gear the state to sustaining a political economy of defense.

The origins of Pakistan's political economy of defense can only be elucidated by probing the balance between elected and nonelected institutions while they were still in flux. In the initial years of independence, the provincial arenas continued to serve as the main centers of political activity. Yet those who set about creating the new central government apparatus were either landed or middle-class émigré politicians from the Muslim-minority provinces of India, with no identifiable bases of support in the Pakistani provinces, or civil servants trained in the best colonial tradition of the British Indian administration. In the absence of a preexisting central government, the choice that presented itself to the Muslim League leadership at the center was either to concentrate on the twin processes of constitution making and party building or to establish the mechanisms of an effective state administration. The need to raise revenue for the defense procurement effort as well as for the construction of a wholly new central government saw administrative reorganization and expansion taking precedence over building a political party system that would reflect Pakistan's linguistic and cultural diversities.

One largely unforeseen consequence of the administrative expansion was that in many instances it pitched civil bureaucrats at both the central and provincial levels against the very groups who dominated the political arena—landlords in West Pakistan and middle-class professionals in East Pakistan. Clashes between centrally appointed civil bureaucrats and provincial politicians did not augur well for a healthy equation between state formation and the political process. This was especially so because the refugee status of Pakistan's most prominent politicians at the center had given senior civil bureaucrats far greater autonomy of action than might otherwise have been possible in a context where the "national" leadership had real bases of support in society. More to the point, Pakistan was very far from possessing a government machinery reflecting the linguistic and cultural heterogeneity of its people that could even remotely justify the autonomy enjoyed by senior civil bureaucrats.

The beneficiaries of recruitment policies adopted by the colonial state for purposes of its own, Punjabis from the middle and upper economic strata not only dominated the military but also had a stranglehold over the most important civil jobs at the center. Despite the existence of a quota system to ensure representation from all the provinces, non-Punjabis—with the exception of migrants from the United Provinces of northern India, now known as Uttar Pradesh— were underrepresented. The decision to continue with the colonial policy of posting members of the central superior services (the Civil Service of Pakistan, or CSP) to the provinces, though consistent with the centralization policy, soon became a major source of friction, not only between the central and the provincial services but also between the provinces themselves. So the drive for administrative centralization left the Pakistani state at a double disadvantage. While it created sources of internal tension within the government structure, it also provided greater space for power struggles between administrators and politicians at the central, provincial, and local levels. Politicians in the provincial and the central arenas were incapable of overriding the administrative services, certainly not without a countervailing force in the form of an organized political party. The result, exceptions at the local levels granted, was a decisive shift in the balance of power from the political to the administrative arms of the state.

This power shift was to have dire implications for the political process and consequently for relations between the center and the provinces as well as between the Punjab and the non-Punjabi provinces. By the end of 1951, Punjabi civil bureaucrats-turned-politicians began to dominate the central executive. For Bengalis, Sindhis, Baluchis, and even the somewhat better-off Pashtuns, the mutuality of interest between the Punjab and the center seemed palpable. But despite similarities in their socioeconomic and educational backgrounds, no love was lost between state bureaucrats and the landlord politicians of the Punjab. Familiarity bred contempt as frequently as it encouraged alliances based on intermarriages, economic interest, or just pure convenience. Only when class and occupational interests tended to converge, which was not too often or too long-lasting, could the Punjab's landed politicians expect their fellows in the state apparatus to serve their provincial, or even class, interests. The relation between the Punjab administration and the provincial leadership was strewn with as many instances of rivalry as of collaboration. Though able on occasion to threaten bureaucratic and military purposes, Punjabi politicians were not better placed than their non-Punjabi counterparts to dictate the terms of central policies. For much of the fifties, the Punjab's landlord politicians could do little more than bicker about state policies aimed at laying the foundations of an industrial infrastructure by turning the terms of trade against the agrarian sector. Moreover, while some Punjabi families like the Sheikhs and Chinotis succeeded in exploiting the Pakistani state's industrial bias, the main beneficiaries were the Karachi-based Memon and Khoja merchant capitalists who had recently migrated from Bombay and Kathiawar. It might be argued that the failure of the predominantly Punjabi state bureaucracy to implement land reform or impose an agricultural income tax, strongly demended by the nascent industrial groups and also by Bengali middle-class professional politicians, is proof positive of its "organic alliance" (as Alavi [1986] implies) with Punjabi landed families. But such an argument confuses the politics of compromise with the politics of "organic" collaboration. Above all, it underestimates the extent to which state officials are prepared to sacrifice direct economic control for the sake of perpetuating and enhancing state authority.

During the fifties the exercise of state authority had, willy-nilly, to coexist with a political framework based on a parliamentary and federal system of government. Under such a system, East Pakistan's predominantly middle-class professional politicians could expect to use their majority in parliament to dominate the central government. This was anathema to an already dominant civil bureaucracy and military establishment and those among West Pakistani landed and nascent industrial families who had been won over as junior partners through the politics of compromise and patronage. Having largely succeeded in dismantling what there was of a political process, the top echelons of the military and the bureaucracy were not minded to rely West Pakistan's wily landlord politicians to prevent a Bengali majority winning elections that were due to be held in 1959. And so, in October 1958, the Pakistan army under General Ayub Khan preempted the result by assuming direct charge of the political arena.

Since 1958, recurring cycles of military intervention, consolidation, and collapse have plagued Pakistani history. Yet even the first instance

of intervention was preceded by a phase of military-bureaucratic dominance that can be dated to 1951. This decisive and what has proven to
be most enduring shift in the institutional balance of power occurred
within a context of the passing of hegemony in the international system
from British to American hands. Skillful manipulations of international
connections contributed to the success of the military and civil bureaucracy in registering their dominance over parties and politicians within
the evolving structure of the Pakistani state (see Jalal 1990b).

Yet in the absence of organized channels for the articulation of
sociopolitical and economic interests, except through a highly centralized administrative structure, the legitimacy and effectiveness of state
authority in a society riddled with economic disparities and a multi-
plicity of ideological beliefs was perpetually at risk. On the face of it,
Pakistan's early managers showed an almost equal interest in the problems of building a state structure and in the need for a legitimizing
ideology. But "legitimacy," far from being an abstract concept, is a loose
label for the complex web of realities that orders and defines relations
between state and society everywhere in the world. So although it
seemed natural to point to the unifying principles of an "Islamic ideology," which they never cared to define, Pakistan's senior civil and military officials, with their secular orientation and frank aversion for the
religious guardians, could not expect to legitimize authority without at
least appearing to bend in a direction suited to the interests of society
as a whole. Yet this confronted them with contradictions inherent in the
role of any state: the need to square diverse socioeconomic interests
while furthering their own institutional concerns. Unable to resolve the
contradictions, much less the dilemmas posed by a contrived deference
to the religious galleries, Pakistan's first crop of bureaucratic and military officials inadvertently laid the basis for a lasting correlation between anxieties about the legitimacy of the state structure and
obsession with the supposed panacea offered by Islam.

But the resounding defeats of "Islamic" parties at the ballot box in
Pakistan's subsequent history suggest that the main contribution of the
bureaucratic-military axis of the fifties was not in shaping the state's
ideology but rather in distorting its institutional structure. Grossly un-
derestimating the need for popular bases of support, civil and military
officials in the fifties concentrated on manipulating their international
connections in the hope of molding the administrative machinery and
pursuing development strategies aimed at creating a political economy
of defense. But the military takeover in October 1958 indicates that in
spite of the dominance of the civil bureaucracy and the army, the inter-

nal structures of the state were still fluid enough to be threatened by regionally based political groups seeking to better their prospects in the general elections by capitalizing on the widespread social and economic grievances of the late fifties. Severe domestic resource constraints and regional and international security concerns had combined to undermine the relative autonomy of the state, persuading an already dominant military and civil bureaucracy of the urgent need to depoliticize Pakistani society.

Between 1958 and 1971 two different military rulers tried consolidating state authority and implementing externally stimulated development strategies. Both relied on the support of a predominantly Punjabi army and civil bureaucracy and, through the extension of differential patronage, on social and economic groups with political bases that were neither so extensive nor so independent of the state apparatus as to pose a serious threat to the stability of the regimes. Ayub Khan's basic democracies order of 1959 was a less-than-subtle attempt to consolidate the state's control over the political process by extending the scope of bureaucratic patronage to rural localities, thus releasing the exercise of central authority from constraints imposed by parties and politicians with provincial bases of support. The professed aim was to create a new rural "middle" class, carefully selected by the members of the CSP, who would promote capitalist farming, counter the influence of the bigger landlords, and facilitate a partial, as opposed to a mass, mobilization of the rural areas. But although there was a statistical decline in landlord representation in the national assemblies during the sixties, partly owing to the entry of business interests, bigger landlords did much better economically than most middle-level landlords under the basic democracies system. Relative autonomy in the economic domain was the price bigger landlords extracted for their relative deprivation in the political sphere.

Providing differential economic patronage was essential for the depoliticization sought through the basic democracies system. Once the logic of functional inequality had been accepted, it was natural for the regime to adopt economic policies emphasizing growth rather than redistribution. Scholarly concern with the growth and redistribution issue has distracted attention from an examination of the state's role in the formation of elites as well as classes. Those who lament the state's lack of interest in policies of redistribution have concentrated on investigating the location of vested interests within the state structure. But given the dissonance, if not divergence, between institutional interests and those of particular socioeconomic groups, it may be more worthwhile to investigate the location of functionaries of the state within key economic sectors. State-sponsored links with socioeconomic structures generally prove to be less tenuous than the organic links between dominant social groups and the state, although even these might weaken in time. The Ayub Khan regime's attempts at socioeconomic engineering—foreshadowing the magnetic quality of the Pakistani state in determining elites and nonelites, irrespective of inherited background, during the seventies and the eighties—are particularly instructive in this respect.

The land reforms of 1959 were ostensibly intended to break the hold of the landed gentry in West Pakistan. But in actual fact they were specifically aimed at ingratiating the regime with middle-sized landlords, many of whom were former military and civil officials. A good part of the resumed land was handed over to these former officials at throwaway prices. Newly irrigated land in Sind was allotted to state functionaries, Punjabis in the main. Under the Veterans' Settlement program, an estimated three hundred thousand acres of land in Sind as well as rice acreage along the Indian border in West Pakistan was parceled out to military personnel (Rizvi 1986, 132). Military and civil officials were also given plots of land in the urban areas that would fetch fantastic prices in the open market. Retired military officials were given top jobs in both the public and private sector; others were absorbed into the various central and provincial services. Some of the more enterprising were able to use their access to state authority to join the ranks of the regime's other most favored groups—business and industrial entrepreneurs.

But despite an increasing stake in preserving the existing state structure, neither the newly enriched functionaries of the state nor Ayub Khan's Basic Democrats—with their bases of support limited to the localities and districts—could muster sufficient mass support effectivly to counter mounting opposition to the regime. After the mid-sixties the politics of exclusion and the economics of regional and class disparity had turned the logic of functional inequality on its head. Against a background of labor militancy and student radicalism, provincial politicians led by Sheikh Mujibur Rahman, the leader of the East Pakistan-based Awami League, called for an immediate devolution of power to the constituent units. His six-point program for provincial autonomy, justified on the grounds of growing economic disparities between the two wings and inadequate representation of the Bengali majority in the civil bureaucracy and the army, was seized on by an array of disaffected elements in West Pakistan. By 1967, parties belonging to the Left and the Right in both wings of the country were demanding universal adult franchise and the reintroduction of parliamentary government.

Between November 1968 and March 1969 voluntary associations representing students, industrial labor, professional groups, low-ranking government employees, and the ulama staged massive demonstrations against the Ayub Khan regime in key urban centers (Ahmed 1978). Sensing doom, Ayub Khan handed over power to General Yahya Khan, the commander in chief of the Pakistan army. Also dependent on the support of the military and the civil bureaucracy, Yahya Khan agreed to hold the first-ever general election on the basis of adult franchise. But he had no intention of transferring power to any political configuration, whether from the eastern or the western wing, that aimed at restructuring the state with a view to undermining the dominance of the military and the bureaucracy. So although the Awami League and the Pakistan People's Party (PPP) won the 1970 elections in the eastern and the western wings respectively, their regional bases of support gave Yahya Khan an opportunity to delay the transfer of power in the hope of extracting the concessions needed to perpetuate the existing state structure and with it the long-standing dominance of the military-bureaucratic axis. The fierce resistance of the nonelected institutions of the Pakistani state to accepting the verdict of the people, rather than the supposedly irreconcilable differences between East and West Pakistani electorates, goes some way toward explaining why no political formula could be found to prevent the disintegration of Pakistan in 1971.

Reconstruction and Reform: The Populist Interlude

The breakaway of East Pakistan provided Zulfikar Ali Bhutto, the leader of the PPP, with an opening to reconstitute the state by tilting the balance firmly against the nonelected institutions. But for a man who claimed to have been swept into power by a popular wave, not by a temporary loss of military nerve, Bhutto's stolid resistance to building up the PPP's organizational machinery has confounded political analysts. Attributing his neglect of the PPP's grass-roots organization to a voracious appetite for power, they understate both the resilience of unegalitarian social structures and the constraints that a preexisting state structure can impose on the policies of a populist, as opposed to a revolutionary, party. Bhutto unleashed storms of expectations and counterexpectations and yet failed to deliver all the matching goods. He failed not merely on account of a spurious commitment to reforms, as some of his most trenchant critics argue, but also because of the enduring institutional imbalances within a state structure officiating over a deeply polarized society and because of the disparate nature of the PPP's social bases of support—a product of Ayub Khan's politics of exclusion and the peculiar blend of populism Bhutto had bandied about in order to take political advantage of the mass discontents of the late sixties and early seventies.

In any case, reconstituting a state structure is just as difficult as creating one anew. At the helm of a party with the largest number of seats in the Punjab and Sind assemblies but no influence in either the North-West Frontier Province or Baluchistan, Bhutto had a measure of the limitations and potential brittleness of his social bases of support. He had won the 1970 elections by cobbling together a loose coalition of divergent social and economic interests: middle-level Punjabi farmers, landed notables from Sind and the Multan district of the Punjab, Punjabi urban middle-class professionals, newly organized industrial workers in Karachi and the Punjab, new rural-urban migrants, and the Punjabi rural underprivileged—small landlords cum tenant farmers, landless field laborers, and menials. Moreover, the PPP's electoral victory was restricted to the relatively prosperous, more urbanized, and semi-industrialized parts of the Punjab (Baxter and Burki 1975). So although it made a dent in the old structures of the agrarian Punjab, breaking down the *biraderi* (clan), caste, or tribal affiliations that had been the determining factor in all previous electoral contests, the dominance of rural notables was by no means at an end. Indeed, in Sind the PPP relied on the very *biraderi* and tribal ties that it was trying to rupture in many districts of the Punjab.

Those who somewhat idealistically bemoan Bhutto's apparent lack of reformist zeal in office and the PPP's manipulation of *biraderi* linkages in the 1977 elections would be well advised to reassess the extent to which the 1970 elections had ushered in a new era of social relations in the Punjab and Sind countryside. Soon after the 1970 elections, rural lords reacted to the PPP's promise to give land to the tillers by allying with local state functionaries to carry out a series of tenant evictions. Attacks on the PPP's rural bases of support, matched by a wave of worker retrenchments in large and medium-scale industries in the urban areas, aggravated the ideological differences that had been apparent within the PPP ever since the beginning of the election campaign (Jones 1979). It was only by performing a delicate balancing act that

Bhutto managed to keep a tenuous hold on both the left and the right wings of the PPP and to realize his claim to state power.

Once in power Bhutto showed a clear preference for the moderate middle-roaders and began distancing himself from the extremists and self-styles Galahads and Lancelots in the party (*Viewpoint* [Lahore], 13 Oct. 1975, 30). This was hardly surprising. The role of any party after the assumption of office, especially one in a state structure long dominated by nonelected institutions, is dramatically different from that of a party seeking the trappings of power. The purge of the extremists and the shift in the balance of power within the PPP in favor of influential landed families after 1972 is generally seen as proof of Bhutto's lack of commitment to the PPP's socialist economic program. But no sooner had Bhutto announced his first spate of land and labor reforms than a systematic campaign was launched by landed and industrial groups to bring down the regime, and "this campaign started long before the PPP Government had adopted tough policies towards those who opposed it" (*Viewpoint*, 17 Oct. 1975, 6). Pressures from the privileged groups the PPP had vowed to cut down to size may seem a lame excuse for the "betrayal" of the radicals within its midst; after all, the 1970 elections were a watershed in Pakistan's history precisely because they threw up elements from the lower and middle social strata who, having been radicalized by the politics of exclusion and the economics of functional inequality, now wanted to capture the PPP and, by extension, the political arms of the state. The fate of the PPP's radicals, however, has quite as much to be with the weakness of Pakistan's left wing as with the metamorphosis of Bhutto the populist politician into Bhutto the authoritarian statesman. For one thing, lacking any sort of commonality of interest, the radical strata had joined the PPP severally rather than jointly. For another, their conflicting demands and often disruptive methods meant that they were plainly incapable of thinking or acting coherently. So it is not too difficult to see why, in the face of a concerted challenge from an ideologically consistent, determined, and powerful landlord lobby both within and outside of the party, Bhutto decided to phase out this confused medley of radicalism from the PPP. In so doing he was not abandoning his party's socialist economic program as much as co-opting the very landed elements who were most likely to undermine them. Facilitating access to state authority, as Bhutto knew from experience as minister in Ayub Khan's cabinet, was the best way of controlling those most anxious to destroy his party's populist appeal.

This may have been a dangerous way of dealing with a world he was out to reform. Yet Bhutto was convinced that his ability to continue

holding center stage depended on a reformism punctuated by modera-
tion. Without some such mixture he could not forge the tacit under-
standings he needed with the civil bureaucracy and the army—the
discredited but by no means disabled wielders of state power. The
cooperation of the bureaucracy was essential for the implementation of
the PPP's reform programs, and the support of the military was crucial
for the continued survival of his regime. Pakistan might have entered
the era of mass participation, or populism, but the structure of the state,
though reflecting some of the tensions generated by the changes, had
not with the mere advent of the PPP government adapted itself to new
social realities. A highly talented and skillful political operator, Bhutto
was well aware of the need to reform key state institutions. But he
confused reforms enabling him to deploy state resources to his own
political advantage with reforms specifically aimed at altering existing
institutional imbalances. Seeing easy advantages in using the magnetic
power of the state to broaden his constituency, Bhutto made the grave
error of failing to recognize the need to build an independent base of
support. His inability to accept the mildest criticism from party loyalists and his failure to hold elections within the PPP had more to do
with his deep distrust of the civil bureaucracy and the military than
with an insatiable appetite for power. In perceiving his own party as a
potential vehicle for challenges to his authority at the center, Bhutto
missed the chance to create the popularly based institutional counterweight he so desperately needed to check the civil bureaucracy and the
military's dominance of the state apparatus.

An analysis of Bhutto's attempts to reform state institutions underlines the striking contradictions of his rule. A variety of steps were
taken to neutralize the military's threat to his regime. Debates criticiz-
ing the military's involvement in politics were encouraged; a special
commission was established to inquire into the cause of the 1971 military debacle; several senior officers were removed from office; the military high command was restructured; the post of commander in chief
was abolished; the tenure of the seniormost member of the army, the
chief of staff, was reduced; and a firm decision was taken not to grant
extensions to any of the chiefs of service. And most significant of all, a
special clause introduced into the 1973 constitution at Bhutto's behest
made the military's participation in politics punishable by law (Rizvi
1986, ch. 10). But no steps were taken to cut military expenditures,
which continued to swallow more than 40 percent of the center's annual budget, despite the fact that his agreement in July 1972 with Indira
Gandhi at Simla was a conceivable prelude to recasting the state's re-

gional defense imperatives and restricting the influence of army head-quarters on domestic politics. Instead, the cost of maintaining the coercive arms of the state increased appreciably under Bhutto. A paramilitary force—the Federal Security Force (FSF)—was created with the explicit intention of minimizing the regime's dependence on the military during times of civil unrest. Army headquarters' adverse reaction to the FSF saw Bhutto sanctioning successive increases in salaries, allowances, and other benefits for senior and junior members of all three services (Rizvi 1986, ch. 10).

The regime's administrative reforms were intended to be of a more far-reaching nature. Within months of the PPP's assumption of office, some thirteen hundred civil servants were dismissed. In 1973 Bhutto abolished the CSP cadre—referred to by some as the Central Sultans of Pakistan—and merged it into a linear all-Pakistan unified grade structure. Special constitutional privileges extended by Ayub Khan in 1962, practically guaranteeing permanence of service, were abolished. This gave Bhutto considerable leverage over civil servants suddenly denied the comforts of tenure. The lateral entry system, introduced to attract talent into the civil service and the police, proved to be an invaluable instrument for the distribution of political patronage. Bhutto personally encouraged the entry of middle-class Sindhis into the junior and middle levels of the civil service and the police. Between 1973 and 1977 an estimated 1,374 new recruits entered the civil service; most of the senior-level appointees were either relatives or close friends of central government ministers (Noman 1988, 62–63).

The rapid expansion of the public sector necessitated by Bhutto's most popular policies—land reforms, new legislation safeguarding the interests of labor, the nationalization of thirty-one heavy and capital-intensive industrial units, and later the extension of state control over the banking and insurance sector as well as over selected educational institutions—provided immeasurable opportunities for graft and corruption. Ironically, civil servants were able to exploit the expansion of the state apparatus following Bhutto's nationalizations to increase their economic role and job opportunities. Despite low salaries relative to managers in certain nonnationalized firms in the private sector, the perks of office and the gains from bribery, nepotism, and manipulation of rules had become so extensive that the economic status of many senior state employees was almost commensurate with that of landlords and industrialists (see *Viewpoint*, 12, 19, 26 Nov. 1981). This was especially true for those who had already acquired land in rural or urban areas through state largesse during the Ayub Khan era.

For those whose fortunes began changing only under the PPP regime, access to state authority and the political patronage of the ruling party held out promises of a quick and smooth passage into the upper economic strata. With a "few exceptional cases of rags to riches, most of Pakistan's nouveau riche had access to state power in one way or the other" (*Viewpoint*, 12 Nov. 1981, 10). But by the same token, the allegiance of emergent socioeconomic elites, whether occupying positions within the state apparatus or possessing access to it, is rarely to the party or government under which rags were turned to riches. Simply put, those who are able, by virtue of their access to or location within the state, to amass private fortunes misappropriating public monies are more likely to switch loyalties with a change of government than the vast majority of the underprivileged who support a mass party in the hope of improving dismal standards of living.

These were subtleties Bhutto was prepared to ignore, not because he had naïve notions about the sincerity of the fortune seekers clambering onto the PPP's bandwagon but rather because he took the dictum that "power corrupts and absolute power corrupts absolutely" as the best insurance of his ability to keep tabs on the PPP's multicolored opportunists. This can be seen in his use of reforms as a way of rewarding and punishing his supporters and opponents while using the socialist rhetoric of each wave of nationalization to widen his base of popular support. But Bhutto pushed his Machiavellian methods beyond the point of ingenuity—by throwing open the PPP's gates to all comers he alienated loyal party workers anxious to capitalize fully on the impact the PPP's land and labor reforms and promises of allotments of state land to slum dwellers were having on the psyches of the rural and urban downtrodden. To the barrage of criticism from an urban intelligentsia that had hailed him as the harbinger of a new popular social order, to say nothing of the criticism from those preparing to launch a serious challenge to his regime, Bhutto responded by relying increasingly on the coercive instruments of the state—the FSF as much as the army. In February 1973 he rid himself of the non-PPP governments in Baluchistan and the Frontier and began showing a calculated disregard for the 1973 constitution, which had granted more provincial autonomy than its predecessors. By December 1973 he had set the army against Baluchi tribesmen in armed revolt against the federal government.

During the remaining three and one-half years of the regime, Bhutto was more often reacting to his opponents than steering his party on the road to a new popular order. Proud of portraying himself in the secularist traditions of Pakistan's founder, Mohammad Ali Jinnah, Bhutto might have simply shrugged off charges by religious parties that his rule was "un-Islamic." But during the oil boom of 1973, the national economy took a nosedive and an externally financed religious opposition grew in both confidence and strength. Bitter about the adverse effects on the constituencies they represented, the Islamic parties—most notably the fundamentalist Jamaʿat-e Islami—had been awakening the religious sensibilities of a people dispirited by military defeat (Lodhi, n.d., 150–51). Their claim that it was not the ineffectiveness of religion in welding together Pakistan's diverse constituent units but the state's lack of Islamic morality that had led to the disintegration of the country touched sympathetic chords across broad sections of society. It provided consolation for the more religiously oriented segments of the lower middle classes—the small shopkeepers and petty merchants, teachers, and semiprofessional and educated unemployed (Ahmad 1986, 18–19).

The calls for an "Islamic revival" provided an opportunity for a wide spectrum of social groups to target their disaffections against the regime. Industrialists and big business hit by nationalization and the implications of the PPP's labor legislation, fearing similar measures in the future, had been contributing handsomely to the opposition's coffers. They were, and have remained, Bhutto's most strident and implacable opponents. In March 1976 the announcement of a national charter for peasants, followed in January 1977 by the promise of new reforms aimed at lowering land ceilings and introducing an agricultural income tax, spread panic among the landed groups. In the summer of 1976 Bhutto's nationalization of some two thousand agro-processing industrial units radically altered the mood in the *mandi* (market) towns of the Punjab. Designed to bring the state into direct dealing with the growers, it completely alienated the *arthis* (middlemen), who provided the main bases of support for the religious parties. But perhaps most disconcertingly for Bhutto, even sections of the urban middle classes, incensed at the steady etiolation of civil liberties and curbs on the press, on the one hand, and rising prices of basic commodities, on the other, began looking for alternatives to the PPP.

Instead of addressing the real causes of opposition to his regime, Bhutto, not least because nearly 66 percent of the PPP's top leadership were by now members of conservative landed families (Lodhi, cited in Noman 1988, 104), cynically pretended to be concerned about establishing his regime's Islamic credentials. A number of concessions were made to appease the religious parties, thus giving more significance to the Islamic umbrella than the discordant and materially based interests accommodated under it warranted. These concessions further alienated the Left without winning Bhutto very many leading lights from the religious Right. But this did not worry him unduly. He had taken care to offset his political accommodations with bigger landlords. Granted the nominal impact of the 1972 land reforms, an estimated 53,458 small farmers and tenants had nevertheless been the beneficiaries of the re-distribution of vested land (*Viewpoint*, 23 Jan. 1976, 21). In 1975 he had waived land taxes for the smaller peasant proprietors and in 1976 had promised proprietary rights to tenants on state land. In the urban areas also, the PPP had tried to keep the wage increases of lower-income groups above the rate of inflation. Moreover, in addition to providing fringe benefits, the wages of industrial labor were kept on a gentle upward climb (cited in Noman 1988, 95). As even his critics admit, the PPP's popular measures were immensely popular among the rural and urban underprivileged, largely skeptical of the Islamic wave that was being promised by the opposition. Above all, entire *biraderis* of leading landlord families were continuing to join the PPP, not for ideological reasons of course, but because that was the best way of minimizing the impact of the agrarian reforms that were in the offing.

Warning Bhutto of the consequences of the growing disjunction between the PPP's composition and its ideological posturing, one im-passioned supporter implored him to stop currying favor with the landlord lobby and mobilize the peasantry and the working classes instead. The trade union movement was in "shambles," and as for the "young ones [students] who merrily faced the dictator's henchmen," the "Jama ʿat claimed to have bought the souls of most of them." What was needed was a disciplined and motivated PPP, "not a motley crowd in which landless tenants rub shoulders with jagirdars [large landown-ers], in which unreformed advocates of theocracy constantly browbeat the fighters for a free, egalitarian society" (*Viewpoint*, 13 Aug. 1976, 7–9). Needless to say, the message was lost on Bhutto and his key advisers, who were apparently content to accept the "flabbiness of mere num-bers as a sign of strength" (*Viewpoint*, 12 Nov. 1976, 4). By December 1976, the deadline for the preelection enrollment drive, millions had joined the PPP (Syed 1977, 185). In 1977 Bhutto decided to renew his mandate in the obvious hope of improving the PPP's position in parlia-ment and the provincial assemblies. He was taken aback by the unex-pected show of unity by nine opposition parties—the Pakistan National Alliance (PNA)²—which had nothing in common except the objective of dismantling his regime. It was the most ambitious attempt at opposition unity in Pakistan's history—an indication of the PPP's perceived electoral strength. Bhutto's response to the formation of the PNA was to farm out tickets for an estimated 192 of the seats in the National Assembly to members of influential landed families, many of whom had been defeated by the PPP's relatively unknown candidates in the 1970 elections. A mere fifty of the sitting members of the assembly were given tickets. The virtual absence of known party workers at the local and district levels in the PPP list suggested that Bhutto had opted to fight the elections by exploiting *biraderi* ties (*Viewpoint*, 21 Jan. 1977, 9–11). The initial shock among PPP workers and members of the intelligentsia turned to despair upon their discovery that the high command had literally "unearthed" a number of political "fossils" among the landed families solely because of the successful coming-together of mainly right-wing opposition parties (*Viewpoint*, 21 Jan. 1977, 11). "Set a Rightist to catch a Rightist" seemed to be the "general idea" (*Viewpoint*, 4 Feb. 1977). Preelection statements by opposition politicians that the elections would be grandly rigged hinted at the nature of things to come.

Bhutto won. But there were few signs of rejoicing. Although no one had really doubted that the PPP would sweep the polls, the margin of victory was nonetheless astonishing. According to official figures, the PPP bagged 58.1 percent of the popular vote to the PNA's 35.4 percent. It was the election result in the Punjab, however, that cast the die. In the 1970 elections, the PPP had secured sixty-two out of the eighty-two seats to the National Assembly from the Punjab, and 75 percent of the total vote cast. In 1977 the total popular vote cast for the PPP was declared to be 93 percent! Charging Bhutto's regime with extensive rigging and calling for a Nizam-i-Mustapha (the system of the Prophet Muhammad), the opposition PNA launched an amazingly well-planned and well-financed postelectoral campaign. Political commentators did not miss noting the curious phenomenon of the Pakistan rupee rising against the dollar during the election campaign, and an all too visible abundance of cash in the opposition's hands (*Viewpoint*, 27 May 1977, 5). This was seen as Washington's way of punishing Bhutto for his attempts to limit Pakistan's dependence on the West and, more specifically, for his determination to proceed at all costs with a nuclear program. Bhutto himself accused the United States of conspiring with his opponents to overthrow the PPP regime (*Viewpoint*, 13 May 1977, 23). In the absence of documentation, it is impossible to establish the validity of the allegation. But, as usual, the international factor was casting a shadow on the perceptions of some political analysts of

Pakistan's domestic politics, who were confident that "no known, overt source" could conceivably have financed and planned the PNA's operation (*Viewpoint*, 27 May 1977, 5).

Between March and July 1977 Pakistani cities and market towns were rocked by violent demonstrations. A broad cross-section of Pakistani society was represented, although industrial labor was mostly conspicuous by its absence. Its place, however, had been more than adequately filled by commercial and trading groups, the main constituents of the religious parties. Unable to meet the PNA's demands that he step down, and still less able to control the organized fanning of passions in the streets, bazaars, and *mohallas* (wards) of Pakistan, Bhutto the great political conjurer was falling prey to the populism he had done so much to promote. But street power per se did not sweep Bhutto from office; it merely pushed the half-closed doors wide open for a military intervention. On 5 July the Pakistan army was in the political arena for the third time, and Bhutto was in military custody.

Bhutto had been caught in the classic dilemma of a populist politician in power. Needing to use the state as a vehicle of reforms for the underprivileged, he had chosen to deploy state authority to bully sections of privileged social groups to join his political bandwagon. In doing so he had failed to erect a political-institutional counterweight powerful and organized enough to withstand the military-bureaucratic onslaught, in alliance with industrial and commercial groups, once he himself was ejected from the central arena and was consequently shorn of the state's magnetic power to attract uncommitted adherents.

Restructuring or Islamic Posturing?

General Zia ul-Haq, Pakistan's new military ruler, lost no time dispelling the view that his was just another takeover of the state apparatus. A devout Muslim, Zia claimed to be single-minded about returning a "degenerate [Pakistani] society" to the pristine purity of Islam (cited in Sayeed 1980, 183). Suggesting that his rule was part of a divine plan, he argued that Pakistan and Islam were two sides of the same coin, and the protection and integrity of both the geographical and ideological frontiers was a task the military establishment alone was capable of performing. But it was easier to assert and proclaim than to maintain and establish the legitimacy of his regime. The device of promising elections in one breath and postponing them in another, while keeping the country firmly under martial law for nearly seven and one-half years, proved invaluable. Zia's designation as the "cancel my last announcement" president instead of chief martial law administrator is a measure of the humor that unrelieved social repression can sometimes generate. An investigation of the ways in which Zia selectively and systematically went about stifling incipient populist urges and co-opting those frightened or alienated by Bhutto's reforms exposes the qualitative changes his eleven years in office wrought on relations between the state and society in Pakistan.

Nine days after assuming office, Zia admitted in an interview with United Press International that although there was evidence of large-scale rigging in certain constituencies, especially in the Punjab, electoral irregularities were not as widespread as alleged by the PNA. He absolved Bhutto of direct responsibility and instead blamed his lieutenants and administrative staff who in their "eagerness to show loyalty" had rigged the results even though the PPP would have "won the elections anyway" (British Broadcasting Corporation and the Voice of America, 13 July 1977). But by the closing hours of 8 August 1977, the general's perceptions changed dramatically. On that day Bhutto, released from military custody to lead the PPP's electoral campaign, returned to Lahore only to be greeted by millions of enthusiastic supporters chanting the slogan "Gharibun ki majboori hai, Bhutto boohat zaroori hai" (The poor have no choice, Bhutto is very essential). To the utter dismay of his opponents and especially the top brass in military headquarters, nervously running their fingers through the article in the 1973 constitution that prescribes the death penalty for a military coup, the PPP seemed poised as never before to make a triumphant return to state authority. As one observer grimly noted, there was "more to this phenomenon than the mere under-dog syndrome." Despite the well-orchestrated "charges of corruption and abuse of power," massive retrenchments by owners of industrial units and factories had persuaded organized labor in Lahore," which had remained neutral during the PNA movement," to rally around Bhutto (*Viewpoint*, 25 Sept. 1977, 7).

Much the same feeling had taken hold of the underprivileged in rural Punjab. In Sargodha small peasant proprietors, tenants, and field laborers believed that Bhutto had released them from the grasp of oppressive landlords who, while managing to evade the PPP's land reforms, had nevertheless been forced to "part with some of their feudal perks" and "overlords mentality," which was "by no means a small achievement." Although Bhutto's accommodations with the bigger landlords alienated the "hard core of the party," the "harassment" and

172   AYESHA JALAL

eviction of tenants after the imposition of martial law was bringing the
dissenters back into the PPP fold. But—and this needs stressing—they
were doing so with a clear view of forcing the PPP into adopting an
agrarian reform program more radical than that offered in 1970 (*Viewpoint*, 28 Aug. 1977, 16).

Pro-PPP sentiments in Sind were of an altogether different magnitude. Bhutto, himself a Sindhi, had channeled more development resources into the province—excluding Karachi—than any previous
regime in Pakistan's history. As even the Sindhi middle-class opponents of the PPP conceded, Bhutto's policies had created "some employment opportunities [for] the educated unemployed" in the
province (*Viewpoint*, 18 Sept. 1977, 9–10). After the coup, members of
the Sindhi middle class recruited to the provincial civil service were
dismissed on the grounds that they were political appointees. By February 1978, some 1,746 Sindhis had been thrown out of the provincial
service; "even clerks ha[d] been listed as political appointees and sent
home" (*Viewpoint*, 12 Feb. 1978, 4). Indigenous Sindhis, who constitute no more than 2 percent of the armed forces and a mere 5 percent
of the federal service, control five hundred out of some two thousand
industrial units in the province (Sayeed 1984, 221). The inflow of
Urdu-speaking migrants at the time of partition and of footloose
Punjabis, Pashtuns, and Baluchis during the sixties has reduced the
Sindhis to a minority of 45 percent in their own province. Considering that Punjabi- and Urdu-speakers (Muhajirs) dominate not only
wholesale and retail trades but also transportation, construction, and
credit services in the province, and that it was largely Punjabi civil
and military officials who were allotted newly irrigated agricultural
land in the fifties and sixties, it is possible to understand the inherent
antipathy among Sindhis from the bottom up to being ruled once
again by a non-Sindhi military-bureaucratic-industrial alliance.
Threatening the PPP's landed notables with federal investigations
into their assets, the military regime tried keeping some sort of a lid
on this potentially most restive of the Pakistani provinces. It was a
typically ill-conceived ploy. Delighted by the new regime's firmness
in reversing the trends of the Bhutto period, retired state functionaries
in possession of land in the irrigated areas of Sind celebrated by carrying out large-scale evictions of tenants (*Viewpoint*, 25 Dec. 1977, 15).
Provincial landlord politicians could not for long ignore the resentments and the matching upsurge of provincial feeling among Sindhi
middle classes and the rural underprivileged without jeopardizing
their own dominant positions in local society.

Once the extent of the PPP's support was evident, Zia promptly decided to postpone elections. Zia needed time to break the back of the PPP and co-opt those for whom access to state power remained the only constant in political affiliation. By attracting constituent parties of the PNA such as the Muslim League and the Jamaᶜat Islami with the lure of office at the center, Zia sought to give his regime a semblance of legitimacy. It provided the cover the regime needed to place Bhutto in the dock. A number of cases had been registered against the PPP leader, including treason, but the one that was chosen, because it carried the prospect of his total elimination from the political scene, was the murder of a political opponent's father. Bhutto was convicted and, despite an international outcry that drowned domestic protests conducted under a veil of batons and riot gear, was hanged in early April 1979.

With Bhutto out of the way and the PPP's amorphous organizational structure largely crippled, Zia concentrated on consolidating his existing support base in the military and the civil bureaucracy and on building a broader constituency for his regime. He had not neglected to do the necessary spadework while the murder case was *sub judice*. Soon after Zia's assumption of office, the Jamaᶜat-e Islami was given clearance to position its cadres in strategic positions within the coercive, administrative, and ideological arms of the state. Studding the state-controlled media with religious ideologues helped insure that the use of Islamic symbolism by the three religious constellations in the nine-party alliance—the Jamaát-e Islami, the Jamiát-i-Ulama-i-Pakistan, and the Jamiát-i-ul-Ulama-i-Islami—would be the best-remembered expression of the movement against Bhutto. So there was ample justification for the general to woo their main constituencies and in this way strengthen his own case for the "Islamization" of the Pakistani state, economy, and society.

In the Punjab, support for the religious parties came primarily from urban middle- and lower-middle-class groups engaged in trade and commerce—traders, merchants, small shopkeepers, and middlemen—thus the common view of the PNA movement as a "mercantile revolt" (*Viewpoint*, 2 Oct. 1977, 7). Migrants from the eastern Punjab in the main, these trading and commercial groups had replaced western Punjabi Hindu and Sikh traders and moneylenders after partition (Jones 1979, ch. 11; Lodhi, 151). Zia himself was a migrant from the eastern Punjab and so a beneficiary of the close *biraderi* ties that are a distinguishing feature of these groups; thus, he was well placed to lay claims on this ready-made constituency. The fact that they were also the most conservative strata in the country perfectly fitted the general's grand design to Islamize Pakistani society. Yet although their money and influence could help in bringing down governments, these were not the groups who could turn Pakistan's electoral arithmetic to Zia's advantage, in spite of the generally correct scholarly notion that the declining role of the commodity-producing sectors in relation to the service sector in Pakistan's gross domestic product in the seventies and eighties is the best explanation for the growing support of fundamentalist parties such as the Jama ʿat-e Islami.

More to the point, too close an association with religious ideologues could alienate those in the senior and middle echelons of the military establishment who, with the obvious exception of the Jama ʿat's supporters, did not share the enthusiasm with which Zia was seeking to establish an Islamic ethos within the army as well as in Pakistani society at large. But just as the ideological differences in society could be manipulated by the Jama ʿat's penetration of the state-controlled media and educational institutions, the party's long-standing policy of encouraging its supporters to join the armed forces could now be turned to good advantage. Since the 1965 war with India, there had been a noticeable shift in the social background of new recruits to the officer corps. Instead of belonging to landed and middle-class families, the majority were now drawn from lower-middle-class families (Hussain 1985, 208–13). It would be erroneous to conclude that there is a neat equation between the former groups and secular, liberal, or even left-wing leanings, and between the latter group and an Islamic orientation; nevertheless, the Jama ʿat's success in placing its supporters within the armed forces, both before and after the 1977 coup, had much to do with Zia's success in curbing or weeding out officers opposed to his Islamization campaign. But the fact that Zia survived two separate coup attempts, one in 1980 and another in 1984, is as much a commentary on the persistence of ideological differences within the army and the other two services as it is an indication of the growing strength of the religious ethos in Pakistan's military establishment.

Well aware of the dangers from within his main constituency, Zia not only confirmed support among the trading and commercial groups but sought to curry favor with the industrial and business groups— whom he liked to call the "third force" in order to distinguish them from the military and the civil bureaucracy. Loud assertions that his regime would bury the socialist hatchet through deregulating the economy and protecting life and property won him the support, but not the confidence, of the industrial and business groups. Although agro-processing industries were denationalized, the larger nationalized industrial units were not returned to the owners. The expansion of the public sector in the seventies and consequently the state's enhanced ability to distribute patronage continued to hold out attractions for a regime committed to the principles of a free market economy. Despite the decline in public-sector investment as a proportion of the GNP, from 12 percent in 1976–77 to 8.6 percent in 1983–84, private-sector investment averaged around a disappointing 5 percent during the same period (Hussain 1988, 5–6). The regime's almost brutal repression of industrial labor and efforts to co-opt trade unions with money or, in some instances, with doses of Jama ʿ at ideology, could not persuade the financial magnates to undertake long-term investments in new industries. In fact, by 1981 as many as twenty-one industrial units in Karachi alone had been sold by established industrial families who saw brighter futures in trading, construction, and real estate (*Viewpoint*, 20 Aug. 1981, 13).

Of course, no amount of catering to industrial and business groups could assist the regime in overcoming its electoral handicap. Pakistan was no longer a purely agricultural economy, but in the rural areas where the vote banks were still bunched, electoral contests could not be won without the support of one landed faction or another. But although Zia blocked the new land reforms that were in the pipeline, he faced an uphill task weaning sufficient numbers of landed groups away from the PPP. Even after Bhutto's execution, landed families, surprised by his continuing support among their social subordinates, were still calculating the dangers of leaving the PPP. Yet martial law was a potentially constraining influence on local privileges and could mean a possibly prolonged exclusion from direct access to state authority at the provincial as well as the national levels. So in September 1979 Zia tried co-opting the landed groups by resorting to the Ayubian device of holding nonparty elections to the local councils. The expectation was that the elections would be fought along wholly *biraderi* lines. Instead, the PPP's candidates, in the guise of *awam doost* (the friends of the people) routed the *fauji* (military) candidates. The regime was understandably shocked by the results. With the lone exception of Baluchistan, the *awam doost* candidates won convincingly in the Punjab, Sind, and the North-West Frontier Province.

Significantly, after the local polls, Zia not only postponed national elections indefinitely but announced a total ban on parties and politics along with curbs on the press and draconian powers for the military courts. He declared that "from now on Martial Law would operate as real Martial Law," adding with nonchalance that the military had come to stay (cited in *Viewpoint*, 21 Oct. 1979). In December 1979 the Soviet invasion of Afghanistan proved to be a boon for the general's tottering regime. Apart from raising the all too familiar specter of an external threat to Pakistan's survival, it once again entitled the Pakistani state to morale-boosting injections of American military and economic aid. But it took the general another two years to announce the setting up of a selected, as opposed to an elected, federal advisory council—the Majlis-e Shura. The original plan was a nominated assembly of 350 members; of these, the general managed successfully to co-opt 288, mainly landed groups. Some hundred of them were drawn from "defunct" political parties, including over sixty from the PPP. Various occupational groups were represented. But the most striking entry into Zia's "Islamic" legislature was that of some forty religious leaders, most of them men who could never have expected to win access to the state in a straight electoral contest (Weinbaum and Cohen 1983, 127).

The ostensible purpose of the Shura—a showpiece of "Islamic" democracy with no effective powers over the executive—was to give the regime the appearance of support in civil society. But the hidden agenda was to extend state patronage generously for as long as it took to convert the Shura members into the regime's loyal agents for the national and provincial elections that, with each passing year of martial law, Zia was finding more and more awkward to postpone. This might seem surprising in view of Zia's solid support from the military and large sections of the federal bureaucracy as well as his efforts to gain legitimacy through his Islamization program. Yet no amount of support from the nonelected state institutions or of resort of Islam could solve the problem of legitimacy. Zia had to seek some sort of mandate from civil society through a slow and selective mobilization of key social groups.

Although the general scored some successes in his forays into certain sectors of agriculture, industry, and trade, he met with sullen, if muted, opposition from substantial sections of the urban intelligentsia and the professional groups. But these groups were the would-be islands of enlightenment in a sea of illiteracy and so could safely be ignored in the general's scheme of things. The deprived and marginalized groups, in the rural as well as the urban areas, were potentially more of a threat. The general's Islamic prescriptions to create a society free of class tensions seemed irrelevant to what they needed and, in any event, were too outworn to erode the hold on their psyches of the PPP's catchall "roti, kapra aur makan" (bread, cloth, and shelter) and the proclamation "all power to the people."

Clearly, then, so long as the government remained in the hands of a military ruler with limited popular support, the Pakistani state, for all its Islamic posturing, could not register its claim to be serving the general interests of society, least of all in the economic realm. Polarization had by now enveloped all levels of Pakistani society. Social divisions, especially among the dominant interest groups, could temporarily increase the state's relative autonomy of action, but in the Pakistani context they proved to be a double-edged sword. Although martial law gave an uneasy sense of stability, the prolongation of the political stalemate made the legitimacy of the state shakier than ever. The difficulties were compounded by the fact that the state's internal structures were affected not only by the broader social tensions but by a distinct sharpening of rivalries between its two main institutions—the civil bureaucracy and the army. Martial rule had been accompanied by grafting military officers onto top positions within the civilian administration at both the provincial and central levels as well as in quasi-government and autonomous organizations. Appointment to ambassadorial posts was another way of making retirement more palatable for senior military officers and in the process avoiding bottlenecks in the rate of promotions. Between 1980 and 1985, 96 army officers were given plum jobs in the central superior services on a permanent basis, and 115 signed new reemployment contracts. Another 10 percent of the civil jobs were reserved for former servicemen (Rizvi 1986, 243–44). The intense bitterness among members of the central superior services who had made their way up slowly after passing a competitive examination and undergoing rigorous training was well conveyed by a federal employee serving in the Punjab government. "We can control the politicians," he quipped, "but not these army wallahs" (from a conversation with author).

Placing military men in strategic positions within the state apparatus was not simply intended to help army headquarters keep better watch and ward over the affairs of government. Rather, holding senior jobs within the civilian administration and in public corporations was a first step to placing men with proven loyalties to the military institution in the upper strata of key sectors of the economy. There was nothing new about the Pakistani state's attempts at socioeconomic "elite" formation. One estimate in 1985 suggested that since 1950 some 6,150 military officers had acquired 444,024 acres of land in the Punjab alone (Rizvi 1986, 243–44). Considering that over 300,000 acres of the most productive land in Sind was also allotted to former military personnel during the Ayub Khan era, there seemed small cause for alarm about

Zia's use of state authority to burnish the fading stars of the military establishment. But there was a qualitative difference from similar attempts in the sixties and the seventies. Instead of civil servants and progovernment politicians, exceptions in both categories notwithstanding, the main beneficiaries of state patronage in the eighties were army officers. Moreover, it was now the industrial and especially the service sector—trading, transportation, construction, and real estate, not to mention defense contracting—rather than agriculture, that were the most sought after by enterprising army officers, some of whom began taking early retirement in order to make hay while the sun was still shining. To expedite their entry into the service sector, the Zia regime resorted to a variety of measures. Serving and retired military officers were given lucrative assignments in Saudi Arabia and the Gulf states on a rotating basis. Those who could not partake of the oil bonanza to quadruple their incomes were allotted residential and commercial land in the urban areas. These could be sold at astronomical prices to those suddenly enriched by the emergence of a parallel arms and drugs economy following the Soviet invasion of Afghanistan or, more acceptably, by money earned in the oil-rich Middle Eastern states. One rough estimate of the hoard of black money circulating in the economy was Rs 70 billion, "twice as much, if not more . . . [than] required to arm and develop [Pakistan] without the U.S. being bothered and Americans in hundreds of thousands getting unemployed" (*Viewpoint*, 3 Dec. 1981, 12).

The military's stranglehold on the state apparatus and, by virtue of legal and extralegal privileges, also on society made the regime's search for legitimacy increasingly desperate. Turning nonissues into issues of national importance was one way of easing the pressures on Zia's beleaguered regime. Making women the centerpiece of his campaign for an Islamic moral order, Zia sought to gain legitimacy by fiddling to the chauvinistic strains in Pakistan's male-dominated society. Vowing to restore the sanctity of the *chador* (the veil) and the *chardivari* (the home)—those well-known bastions of female honor and the security of the Muslim family—the general pronounced a series of discriminatory "Islamic" laws for women.[3] Zia also tried dabbling with Islamic economics, but promptly abandoned the effort in the face of stringent criticism. Although there was much excitement about the creation of Shariʿah courts in 1980, the general made sure to exclude all matters relating to the economy from their purview (Alavi 1986). The brunt of Zia's Islamization, therefore, has mainly been borne by women and religious minorities.

Clearly, Zia's state-sponsored Islamization program cannot be seen as anything more than a token effort, and a highly spurious one at that, to establish his own legitimacy without having to court mass popular support. There was never any sign of a groundswell of feeling for the general's policies outside a very narrowly based political constituency and certain segments of the military and civil establishment. His Nizam-i-Salat, or enforced prayer plan, was damned for what it was—a blatant attempt to invade the private sphere merely to enlist the support of an estimated fifty-five thousand imams for the government (*Viewpoint*, 7 Feb. 1985, 12). But the cruelest cut for the general came in December 1984, when he held a referendum in which he hoped, by equating himself with Islam, to get a mandate for another five years. Despite government claims to the contrary, the turnout was embarrassingly low.

Zia's palpable lack of popularity explains his stubborn resistance to the demands of the opposition's movement for the restoration of democracy—a conglomerate of parties as disparate as the PNA but lacking its financial clout—that he hold free elections on a party basis. In 1985, when he finally decided to hold national and provincial assembly elections on a nonparty basis, he was faced with an opposition boycott led by the PPP. But by then there were enough Shura members anxious to retain their privileged access to state authority and others for whom staying on the margins of a system based on differential patronage seemed nothing short of political and economic suicide. Confident that he had won the war of attrition and ready to use the state machinery to deliver the "positive" results that for so long had eluded him, Zia surprised many by not canceling the announced elections.

The list of candidates and winners points to the persisting qualities of the Pakistani state as a magnet determining both the shape and the scope of the political field. Apart from existing members of the Shura and of the local governmental bodies, federal and provincial ministers, political nonentities who had amassed private fortunes in recent years through dealings in the service sector, the sons and grandsons of veteran landed political families, more than ninety of the PPP's supporters in the Punjab and Sind as well as members of smaller opposition parties contested the elections. Despite the prominence given to local as opposed to national and provincial issues, the turnout was just a little below that in the 1970 elections. But here was the twist: although *biraderi* ties dominated the voting patterns in a number of constituencies, the electorate showed circumspection by casting negative votes against some of the regime's staunchest loyalists. Five out of the nine federal ministers, sixty-three members of the Shura, and as many as forty-one of the fifty candidates put up by the Jama ʿat-e Islami—the only significant party contesting the elections—suffered defeats (Noman 1988, 128). The result was nevertheless a parliament dominated by landed interests, with business groups in the second place.[4] It was familiar story. The lure of state patronage and protection had thrown up a new string of politicians, albeit from the same socioeconomic strata that had always dominated the political areans of West Pakistan. Delighted at what he understandably interpreted as an endorsement of his political system by the dominant interest groups, Zia appointed a Sindhi landlord, Mohammad Khan Junejo, as prime minister and in December 1985 finally lifted martial law.

The costs of maintaining a dependent and subservient political system, however, proved to be exorbitant. To keep the wheels of state patronage well oiled, the regime resorted to the extraordinary measure of handing out huge sums of money to members of the National Assembly to be spent in their constituencies, ostensibly for purposes of development. The burgeoning of a "grants economy" has had dire implications for the fiscal health of the state (*Viewpoint*, 4 Apr. 1985, 18). Deficit financing reached unprecedented levels between 1985 and 1988 amounting to Rs 56 billion, according to the state bank's conservative estimates (*Herald* [Karachi], Jan. 1988, 61). Having already borrowed to the hilt in foreign money markets, the government had now to sell off its savings schemes and to draw money from the banking sector in order to pour funds down the channels of state patronage. When Zia seized power in 1977, the government's debt-servicing charges had been roughly equal to its revenue receipts; already in April 1985, interest payments outstripped receipts by Rs 6.9 billion to Rs 4.8 billion; this gap only widened as military rule put on a civilian mask (*Viewpoint*, 4 Apr. 1985, 19). The regime was clearly falling in debt to a small affluent crust of Pakistani society and could ill afford to ignore the interests of this stratum, yet the dominant military and bureaucratic institutions kept the balance firmly tilted against the political clients. Junejo could only be as powerful as Zia wanted him to be. The moment the prime minister began to "jump his traces" he was sent packing.[5]

For all of Zia's expensive political engineering, his ability to perpetuate his rule for eleven long years was as much, if not more, owing to the shifts in the regional balance of power triggered by the Iranian revolution, followed soon after by the Soviet invasion of Afghanistan. After December 1979 the military regime became a major recipient of crucial international support as it came to be seen by the United States and the Western allies to be on the "front line" between the Soviet Union and the "free world." The Zia regime's support of the Afghan resistance movement based in Pakistan won it billions of dollars in American military and economic aid. The social costs of using its strategic location to obtain Western support for the regime have proven to be staggering. The presence of some three million Afghan refugees on Pakistani soil has fueled intense social conflict and, more alarmingly, created a parallel and pernicious arms and drugs economy that is run by syndicates allegedly linked to the military's Interservices Intelligence. Massive kickbacks for military and civil defense contractors and the narcotics kings won the regime ardent supporters it was in no position to offend. If the fifties had seen senior civil servants and army officers adopting a blueprint for a state structure geared toward a political economy based on defense, the interplay of domestic, regional, and international factors in the eighties enabled the Zia regime to bring the scheme to virtual fruition.

Conclusion

In August 1988 the death of Zia and key senior military officers in an air crash opened up a chink of hope for a people long denied the right of free and fair electoral choice on a party basis. But the general's use of the state apparatus to carry out political, economic, and social engineering hitherto unparalleled in Pakistan's checkered post-independence history had left an awesome legacy. The ban on parties encouraged the politics of *biraderi*, the monetization of the electoral process, and the use of the state apparatus at all levels of society to ensure the success of candidates favored by the upper echelons of the military and the civilian establishments. The bankruptcy of the state exchequer and the mushrooming of new pockets of private affluence that had resulted from efforts to build a constituency for the regime posed formidable obstacles to a major recasting of economic priorities and to the redistribution of resources needed to dampen grievances of entire provinces and various linguistic groups within them. During the Zia era the situation in Sind was particularly alarming. Its rural areas simmered with popular discontent against the federal government, there was armed conflict between Sindhis and Muhajirs in the city of Hyderabad; and the slums of Karachi—ruled by coalitions of gunrunners, narcotics dealers, and their associates in military intelligence and the local police—provided the backdrop to deepening tensions between Sindhis and Punjabis, Muhajirs and Punjabis, and Muhajirs and Pashtuns. Zia, that great social tactician and soldier of Islam, had left behind a country that was virtually ungovernable.

Remarkably, two general elections held in rapid succession, in November 1988 and October 1990, escaped being sabotaged by a recrudescence of the violent conflicts that have so badly scarred Pakistani society. Yet this did not mean that the political process had managed to extricate itself from the stranglehold of the state structure. A powerful determining influence on the results of both elections was the access to state power enjoyed by one of the main contenders, the Islamic Democratic Alliance (IDA)—a motley collection of nine pro-Zia political groupings, including the Muslim League and the Jama'at-e Islami. In the 1988 elections the PPP, led by Benazir Bhutto, resorted to expedient accommodations with landed notables, thinly disguised by populist rhetoric, in an attempt to counterbalance the IDA's control over the institutionalized channels of patronage. Although the PPP emerged as the largest single bloc in the National Assembly, far ahead of the IDA, it did not win the majority needed to form a stable government. The entrenched institutional dominance of a mainly Punjabi army and of the federal bureaucracy cast the democratically elected government of Benazir Bhutto, whose principal power base was in Sind, in the role of loyal opposition to the preexisting state structure. The formation of an IDA government in the Punjab led by Mian Nawaz Sharif, an industrialist chosen to do the military's bidding in Pakistan's largest province, and the instability of coalition ministries in the smaller provinces were simply the headlines detracting from some of the other hurdles Benazir Bhutto had to overcome in order to consolidate her government. With a tenuous majority and facing a severe resource crunch, she was acutely vulnerable to the blackmailing tactics of her own supporters in parliament, many of whom sought to extort government monies on threat of defection. This was what contributed to the deluge of allegations by critics that the Benazir Bhutto government had broken all previous records of jobbery and corruption. The PPP's supporters were a deeply disappointed with Benazir Bhutto's inability to deliver on the socioeconomic front or even to fashion a new style of politics, one that would substitute for the well-worn strategy of using the state's magnetic power a measure of genuine democratic practices.

After her unceremonious dismissal in August 1990 by President Ghulam Ishaw Khan, the IDA, led by Mian Nawaz Sharif, was able to deploy its privileged access to the institutionalized channels of state patronage and manipulation to generate the votes needed to defeat the

Pakistan Democratic Alliance (PDA) led by Benazir Bhutto. Unused as well as newly discovered "development" funds were distributed to IDA candidates; the administrative machinery galvanized to undertake the most rapid sanitation, road building, and electrification exercises ever witnessed in the localities; and selected voters were treated with jobs and notes to pull tricks out of the ballot box. The PPP government's well-advertised failure in office and the party's organizational disintegration in the electorally vital province of the Punjab certainly contributed to a critical swing in certain key constituencies, but it was access to state power and patronage that was ultimately responsible for the IDA's winning performance at the hustings.

Democratically elected heads of government in Pakistan's parliamentary system have so far found it tempting to continue using the state's magnetic power to attract political support rather than to engage in the more daunting task of real party building. Until 1988 the enduring imbalances between the elected and nonelected institutions had enabled successive regimes to extend and refine the state's capacities to transform elites into nonelites, and nonelites into elites, irrespective of socioeconomic background. The 1988 elections had made clear that a substantial section of the Pakistani electorate was sophisticated enough to flout the state machinery while selecting their representatives. Less than two years later those in control of the state machinery succeeded in manipulating the electoral system to change the political configuration at the top but could only marginally alter the voting patterns at the base. Despite a dramatic drop in the number of seats in the National Assembly, the PPP managed to retin much of its popular vote bank. The weakness of democracy in Pakistan stems not from the absence of a discerning electorate but from the lack of a concerted effort to build a strong parliament and popularly based, institutionalized counterweights to the military and the civil bureaucracies. Until that happens, the centrality of the Pakistani state in the making and unmaking of elites is unlikely to be replaced by the complex social dynamics underlying the political process.

Notes

1. For a more detailed analysis of state construction in Pakistan, see Jalal 1990b.

2. Representing the entire political spectrum from the extreme Right to the Left, it included the Jama'at-e Islami, the Jami'at-i-Ulama-i-Pakistan, the Jami'at-i ul-Ulama-i-Islami, the Convention Muslim League, the Tehriq-e-Istiqlal, the Pakistan Democratic party, the National Democratic party, the Khaksar Tehriq, and the Muslim Conference.

3. The Hudood ordinance of 1979 blurred the distinction between adultery and rape. It was followed by the *qisas* (retaliation) and *diyat* (blood money) ordinance in 1980, which provided that the compensation for a woman who had been beaten or murdered would be only half that for a man. But the real affront was the law of evidence; it reduced the weight of a woman's evidence to half that of a man's. For a fuller discussion of the Zia regime's policies toward women, see Jalal 1991.

4. For the occupational background of the members of the National Assembly, see Noman 1988, 129.

5. As one political analyst had predicted soon after Junejo's assumption of office (*Viewpoint*, 9 May 1985, 11).

PART TWO

*The Political Economy of
Redistribution and Social Equity*

5

Redistribution and the State in Afghanistan
The Red Revolution Turns Green

BARNETT R. RUBIN

The experience of the past decade in Afghanistan provides an extreme test case of the thesis that state autonomy combined with the political will of the rulers suffices for the implementation of a program of redistribution. The People's Democratic Party of Afghanistan (PDPA), a tiny Marxist-Leninist party, took power through a military coup on 27 April 1978 and within several months introduced a series of reforms that, if implemented, would have destroyed the social basis of class power in the Afghan countryside.[1] The PDPA state evinced not merely autonomy from but open hostility toward every previously powerful social group in Afghanistan, and it could back up its hostility with the political, military, and financial support of the major superpower in the region, the Soviet Union. Furthermore, its leaders showed themselves willing and able to adopt the most extreme measures of repression to meet or even preempt opposition to their redistributive policies.

The result was a countrywide revolt leading to a collapse of much of the state structure and the undoing of most of the reforms. Although the initial leaders of the revolt were sometimes the targets of the state's reforms (the "class enemies"), the reforms' intended beneficiaries actively supported the revolts. The state retained its autonomy from

Research for this chapter was supported in part by grants from the Yale Social Science Research Fund and the Yale Council on International and Area Studies. I received invaluable help with data collection from Anita Bhatia, M. S. Noorzoy, and Marianne Siegfried.

Afghan society but lost its autonomy in the international system, as it was transformed into an occupation regime nearly totally dependent on the Soviet Union. Furthermore, in its struggle with the revolt, the PDPA made important changes in the reform decrees, so that they became as much instruments of counterinsurgency as of social transformation. The state thus recognized the social power of the classes it had tried to dislodge and, in effect, became more "penetrated."

The attempted revolution did initiate a process of social transformation in the Afghan countryside, but—in another irony of the historical dialectic—the landlords and tribal chiefs have been displaced not by the PDPA but by the Islamic political parties who have mobilized and armed the small landowners and tenants to fight the jihad. Many of the assets of Afghanistan have been destroyed rather than redistributed. The income produced using the remaining assets, however, appears on the basis of anecdotal evidence to be distributed more equally than before. For now, this redistribution is an unintended consequence of mass guerilla mobilization rather than a result of deliberate policy. It has not been institutionalized, and future trends depend on the shape of the new Afghan government and the return of refugees.

Several tentative conclusions emerge from the study of this experience. First, like all areas of policy, redistribution requires not only political power but also *knowledge of society*.[2] The PDPA's reforms failed partly because their net effect was to worsen the conditions of their intended beneficiaries. The policies were conceived on the basis of an oversimplified, ideological view of the structure of Afghan society and hence did not have the intended reformist effects.

Second, the lack of knowledge of the society is related to the social conditions that gave rise to the autonomy of the state. The Afghan state and the social strata dependent on it (including the strata that created the PDPA) had weak links to most of the society of Afghanistan. Neither political pressure nor information crossed the boundary between rural society and the central state. Too much, or the wrong kind, of autonomy may impede effective policy formulation and implementation.

Hence the concept of "autonomy" of the state should not be used in too general a way without specifying what the state is autonomous from. The coup of 1978 made the state more autonomous from the social groups that had dominated it previously, but the state came in turn to depend on a faction of another social group, the secular intellectuals. The ideology of this faction was as determined by its social and class position as that of the other social groups. Redistribution by the state was also redistribution to the state and hence to this group as much as, if not more than, to the claimed beneficiaries.

Finally, and with some caution, the apparent redistribution of resources toward the poor in the resistance-controlled areas emphasizes the decisive importance of empowerment of the disadvantaged, even in the absence of an explicitly redistributionist program. Whether that redistribution continues after the war that gave rise to it depends on whether the empowerment of the beneficiaries is institutionalized in postwar Afghanistan.

State, Autonomy, and Redistribution

The debate about redistribution has become part of the effort to elaborate a state-centered approach to the study of politics.[3] Redistribution is a key issue for any debate about the state and society because, as usually conceived, it entails the state using its power to reshape the distribution of goods in society. If state policies resulted from a stable, socially produced distribution of power, this could never happen; and, indeed, thoroughgoing programs of redistribution are rare. Some government, however, *have* implemented them, and these cases can provide great insight into the relations of politics to social power.

The debate about state- versus society-centered paradigms of analysis presupposes, of course, a distinction of state from society, or civil society. Society includes relations of kinship, gender, culture, and property; the state is a territorial bureaucracy, coordinated by executive power, claiming a monopoly of legitimate legislative and coercive power. In the modern world there is a one-to-one correspondence between societies and states because the nation-state system itself defines the boundaries of societies. As Giddens (1987, 17–28) argues, the sociologist's bounded society is the nation-state. Thus, an essential characteristic of the nation-state is that it is also, and necessarily, a member of a worldwide system of such states, which have structured relations to one another and mutually define certain characteristics of states.

The relation between society and state in the modern nation-state system, then, is not a relation of two separate entities but of a whole to a part. The social "whole," however, is in turn a part of a larger whole, the nation-state system, and the state is that part of society through which much (not all) of the society's relations with the rest of the system are mediated.

Redistribution means a change in the distribution of goods produced by kinship and property as a result of action by the state.[4] The
state itself, however, also has property and other rights. Any redistribution of goods and power in society also reallocates the goods and
power of the state. The state-centered paradigm rightly criticizes con-
ventional pluralist and Marxist views for seeing the state as transpar-
ently representing social forces. Analysts using a state-centered
paradigm, however, can err in seeing the state as *above* social forces
rather than a social force in itself. Indeed, much redistribution has as its
primary purpose the enhancement of state power and penetration.

Furthermore, it is necessary to distinguish redistributive policies
from redistributive outcomes. As noted in the case of Afghanistan, redistributive policies may fail to produce the intended outcomes, and
redistribution can occur through a political process in the absence of
policies intended to bring it about. Indeed, Skocpol (1988) has pointed
out that redistribution is a consistent outcome of mass military mobilization, such as has occurred in Afghanistan.

Recent empirical research has concentrated on the specifically political
mechanisms that may enable a political elite to act relatively independently of other dominant groups. The central controversy is over whether
the autonomous power needed for redistribution is more likely to come
from the imposition of a form of authoritarian regime or from the mobilization, often through democratic means, of the program's beneficiaries. In
theory, a socialist revolutionary regime combines these two characteristics
(that is the meaning of "proletarian democratic dictatorship").

Much of the debate has centered around land reform, which long
appeared to be the most effective redistributive reform for the countries
of the Third World. Huntington (1968) and Tai (1974) both argued that
"concentrated power" was necessary to achieve land reform, and that
parliamentary regimes were unlikely to bring it about because of their
dependence on clientele networks dominated by landowners. Recent
research on South Asian cases, however, has argued that the actually
successful cases in the region largely resulted from mass mobilization
within a democratic framework (Kohli 1987; Herring 1983). The successful cases most often cited were the land reforms enacted by governments led by the Communist Party of India-Marxist (CPI-M) in the
Indian states of West Bengal and Kerala.[5] In these cases the state became autonomous specifically from dominant interests and also
achieved the capacity to formulate and implement effective reforms
because the CPI-M succeeded in organizing the beneficiaries. Furthermore, Kohli emphasizes the importance of not just organization but

disciplined organization, which enables the party to control and limit the reforms, preventing a violent reaction and maintaining a predictable environment for private-sector economic activity.

Kohli's analysis of the importance of particular forms of political organization is a variant of a more general development in the study of the relation of state autonomy to policy. Evans, Rueschemeyer, and Skocpol (1985) have argued that the right kind of autonomy is necessary but not sufficient; a state may formulate policy autonomously but be unable to implement it. A state's *capacity* to implement policy is a dimension separate from that of autonomy.

The Afghan case also illustrates the relation of capacity to legitimacy. In Afghanistan the redistributive policies involved a great extension of the scope of the state apparatus (Roy 1986). Hence, this case clearly demonstrates that redistribution of resources *by* the state also constitutes a redistribution of power *to* the state. In such a case the legitimacy of the state itself is at issue, and this issue, rather than the redistributive policies, may come to dominate politics, as it has in Afghanistan.

Background: State and Society in Afghanistan

The PDPA had redistributive policies aimed at both the rural and urban sectors of society. The main programs aimed at the former were debt, land, and marriage reform, combined with a heavily ideological literacy program.[6] In the urban society linked directly to the state, the PDPA combined expanded education (including programs in the Soviet Union) with high wages and subsidized consumer goods for state employees and members of the party and mass organizations. In both areas the explicitly redistributive policies were combined with effectively redistributive policies of repression and deprivation of opponents of the government, although these policies redistributed resources along political rather than class lines.[7] The government has not, however, financed these programs through taxation and has not tried to introduce a progressive tax system. To understand these policies it is necessary to know something of Afghan society and the structure of the state, especially its fiscal basis.

Kinship: Family, Qawm, Tribe

The most important political and economic institution in Afghanistan is the patriarchal, patrilineal, patrilocal family. The "family" in

Afghanistan shades off into larger kinship groupings. It is common in casual writing on Afghanistan to describe this phenomenon by calling Afghanistan a "tribal" society, but the overly general use of this term confuses several different, though related, realities. The term "tribe" refers to kinship groups with specific political institutions (councils or chiefs) and a legal or a customary code distinct from that of the state. A tribe is thus not simply an extended kinship group but a political institution that claims authoritative jurisdiction over a set of persons bound by (possibly fictive) kinship relations.[8]

Even though many, perhaps most, Afghans do not belong to tribes as defined above, and some of the tribes have preserved their institutions better than others, all Afghans do belong to more extended kinship-based solidarity groups known as qawms. A qawm may be a tribe, a linguistically based ethnic group or "nationality" in the Soviet sense, a lineage, a clan, or an occupational group similar to a caste. (Mullahs and barbers, for instance, may come from specific qawms.) There is a norm of solidarity within qawms and competition among them. The structure and extent of the qawm varies among different ethnolinguistic groups in Afghanistan.[9]

Material Production and Class

The major economic activities in prewar Afghanistan were agriculture and pastoralism, which accounted for nearly 60 percent of domestic product and employed about 60 percent of the labor force. Including rural handicrafts and trade, 85 percent of the population made their living from the rural sector (DRA 1982, 39, 74; Mathonnat 1984, 146). The agricultural population included around 2.5 million people (of a total population estimated variously at 15 to 19 million) living primarily from nomadic pastoralism.[10]

Within agriculture, water rather than land is the major scarce resource. Although only about 12 percent of Afghanistan's surface is arable land, only about half of that is cultivated in any given year for lack of water (DRA 1982, 76). There is a distinction between irrigated (abi) and rain-fed (lalmi) land.

Techniques of cultivation remained traditional until the 1960s, when the Afghan government introduced improved seed varieties, chemical fertilizers, an extension service, and tractors (Etienne 1972; Anderson 1978). Agriculture requires five major factors of production: land, labor, water, seed, and draft animals (or tractors). Lalmi land relies on rain; on abi land, water rights and land rights are generally conjoined. Each village has a *mirab*, an official chosen by the elders or village council who regulates the sharing of water among landowners. The landowner also usually provides the seed. The major variables in the allocation of factors of production are thus land, labor, and draft animals.

The most common types of relations of production are the family-owned-and-operated farm, where the family provides labor and animals for its own land; sharecropping, where the tenant receives a portion of the crop; and commercial farming, which is common only on the peripheries of the cities, where the owner pays cash wages for labor. There are two main types of sharecropping. Where the tenant owns his own draft animals (and, very likely, some land as well, though not enough to occupy him fully), he receives perhaps half the crop. Where the tenant uses animals provided by the landlord, he is often landless, and receives as little as one-sixth of the crop.[11] Owner-operators and sharecroppers alike may employ hired labor by the day during peak seasons.

Nomadic pastoralism requires flocks, labor, and pasture. Pasture originally belonged to entire tribes or clans, but the Afghan government introduced private property in both summer and winter pasture in the 1920s (Barfield 1981, 33–42). Pasture can be either owned or rented. In pastoralism as in agriculture, much labor is family labor. Shepherds without flocks formerly received a portion of the flock they brought to maturity in a type of sharecropping arrangement with large flock owners, and this arrangement could provide the start of a private flock. Since improved transport raised sheep prices in the 1970s (as livestock from north of the Hindu Kush could be brought to market in Kabul), some flock owners began paying shepherds cash wages (Barfield 1981, 110–11).

Land ownership is a favored way of converting temporary income into long-term secure gains in wealth. More liquid forms of wealth storage are animals (which multiply, but also sicken and die) and precious metals and cash. At times of marriage, family crises, or major investments, families may need extra capital. Debt is thus ubiquitous in rural Afghanistan. Relatively wealthy individuals such as landowners or shopkeepers, as well as nomads, may make loans, sometimes at interest rates as high as 50 percent, despite a clear prohibition in the Qur'an. Peasants can also place their land in a type of mortgage, *geraw*, in which the lender receives a portion of the crop in lieu of interest and takes over the land if the principal if not repaid after a certain number of years.[12]

TABLE 5.1

Village Social Structure in Afghanistan:
Distribution of Households into Classes in
Provinces Surveyed, 1970

(in percentage)

	Bag	Gha	Kun	Lag	Nan	Par	Qan
Landlord	10.2	9.8	6.4	19.5	23.4	1.1	14.9
Owner-Operator	55.2	53.2	60.6[a]	63.4	54.1	86.2	36.4
Landless	34.6	37.0	33.6	17.1	22.5	12.7	48.7
Renter	2.9	0.6	2.4	—	2.7	2.3	1.6
Sharecropper	22.2	36.4	16.0	17.1	19.8	2.3	35.5
Agricultural workers	9.5	—	15.2	—	—	8.1	11.6
Number	(796)	(173)	(125)	(41)	(111)	(87)	(121)

Source: Survey of Progress 1970–1971, 32–58. The *Survey of Progress* does not explain how the categories were defined. In particular, it does not explain how it dealt with the very common mixed cases, such as that of a household owning a small plot of land that it supplemented by sharecropping another plot.

[a]This figure should probably be 60.0.

Abbreviations:

Bag	Baghlan	Nan	Nangarhar
Gha	Ghazni	Par	Parwan
Kun	Kunduz	Qan	Qandahar
Lag	Laghman		

The distribution of ownership of the means of production (primarily land and animals) and other assets, and the relation to those assets of those who labor in the production process, define the distribution of the population into social classes. Whether this theoretically defined class structure becomes relevant politically depends on a number of factors discussed below.

A 1970 agricultural survey of selected villages in seven provinces (table 5.1) showed landlessness ranging from 12.7 percent of households in Parwan to 48.7 percent in Qandahar, with a median of 33.6 percent (Kunduz). This survey is roughly consistent with estimates given by a Soviet scholar and an Indian Communist journalist that about a third of rural households were landless in the late 1970s.[13] In

TABLE 5.2

**Estimates of Size Distribution of Private
Landholdings in Afghanistan**

	Families Owning Land		Land Held	
	Number	%	ha	%
Recalculated on equivalent of first-grade land				
Size of holding (ha)				
<1	470,000	39.1	520,000	26.3
1–2	450,000	37.5	—	—
2–6	230,000	19.1	660,000	33.3
>6	51,600	4.3	800,000	40.4
Absolute landholdings (unadjusted)				
Size of holding (ha)				
<2	805,000	67.1	1,100,000	24.2
2–4	161,000	13.4	738,000	16.3
4–6	125,000	10.4	702,000	15.5
>6	109,000	9.1	2,000,000	44.1[a]

Sources: Glukhoded 1981, 241–42; Mukherjee 1984, 176–78. Based on table in Shahrani 1984, 19.
[a]Percentages total 100.1 because of rounding.

none of the provinces surveyed does the proportion of agricultural workers, that is, of those without any year-long guaranteed access to land, exceed 15.2 percent. The median is 8.1 percent. Furthermore, in every province but Qandahar more than half of the households were owner-operators.

Table 5.2 shows some available date on the size distribution of landholdings. Two aspects of this structure are worth noting. On the one hand, almost 40 percent of the landowning households had the equivalent of less than 1 hectare (2.5 acres) of irrigated orchards (Glukhoded 1981, 241). Compare this, however, with the 60.3 percent of Indian landowners in 1970–72 with plots less than 1 hectare, regardless of quality (Kohli 1987, 81). On the other hand, extremely large holdings are on the whole unusual. According to Mukherjee (1984, 177), out of 1.2 million landholdings, only 370 were of more than 100 hectares. By way of comparison, in Iran in 1960 (before the shah's land reform), out of 1.9 million holdings, 4,086 were of more than 100 hectares (Iran 1960, 32). Mukherjee (1984, 177) also notes that "the landholdings [of the big landlords] were by no means huge, compared to the zamindaris India had, but these were big in the context of Afghanistan."

A more systematic comparison with Iran and India shows that Afghanistan's distribution of landholding was more egalitarian than that of either one, although it was rather similar to that in Pakistan in 1980 (see fig. 5.1). Note that landholding in "feudal" Afghanistan was more egalitarian than in India *after* the abolition of the zamindari feudal landholdings.

Thus, the characterization made by Montstuart Elphinstone ([1815] 1972, 1:389), the British emissary to the Afghan court in 1808–9, remains valid: "The estates of the proprietors are, of course, various in their extent; but, on the whole, the land is more equally divided in Afghanistan than in most other countries. There are a great number of small proprietors who cultivate their lands themselves, assisted by their families, and sometimes by hired labourers and Buzgurs [sharecroppers]." Since Elphinstone's time, population pressure on the land has grown, and the extent of landlessness has probably increased. Rural Afghanistan is a poor, predominantly small peasant society without a polarized class structure.

The distribution of assets is in turn a major determinant of the standard of living. Rural Afghanistan is poor on a world scale, but it had not developed the grinding poverty of South Asia. Elphinstone ([1815] 1972, 1:391) calculated that the standard of living of agricultural laborers in Afghanistan "must be very superior to that of the same class in India, even if the difference of climate be allowed for." Gilbert Etienne, who has considerable experience in rural India and Pakistan as well, echoed this finding over a century and a half later. "Traveling through the countryside, speaking with different types of peasants, one does not encounter poverty in its most acute form. Of course, the diet [of poor and landless peasant families] is too monotonous to be well balanced, and there is no lack of quantitative deficiencies. Nevertheless, we do not find the exterior forms of deprivation that characterize certain regions of India and Pakistan. The landless peasant . . . does not have that self-effacing attitude, as if he were mentally and physically crushed by poverty to the point of merely surviving" (Etienne 1972,

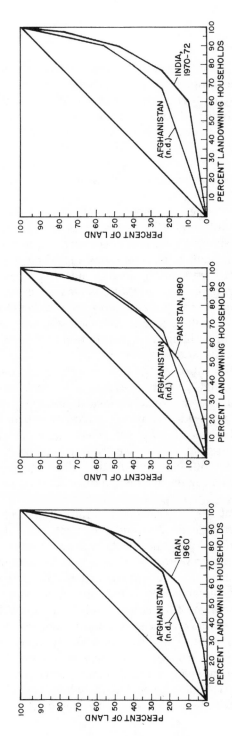

Fig. 5.1. Inequality of distribution of landholdings: Afghanistan compared to Iran, Pakistan, and India.

Sources: Mukherjee 1984; Iran 1960; Pakistan 1981; Kohli 1987.

Note: The diagrams are Lorenz curves. The farther a curve is from the diagonal, the more unequal the distribution.

102; all translations are by the author unless otherwise noted). Despite this slight but meaningful advantage, the margin of security of the poor peasantry is small enough that bad harvests in the early 1970s caused tens of thousands of starvation deaths, which the government did little to prevent. This disaster had serious political repercussions.

Political Conflict and Leadership

The social relations defined by institutions of extended kinship and material production define and distribute resources such as ownership of land, flocks, and cash; seniority; family connections; and relations with outside forces (the state or empire, today including the Afghan resistance as a quasi-state transmitting foreign aid). Aspirants to local power or influence may deploy any of these, as well as Islamic knowledge, piety, or charisma, in the political process. A successful leader consolidates a corporate following out of dyadic relations built up through various forms of exchange and distribution of these resources (Barth 1959, 4).[14]

The most prevalent form of village politics in normal times is the competition and occasional conflict of leaders who manipulate relative wealth and kinship ties to create political followings. Power in villages or tribes does not reside in any one person or structure but in fluidly structured networks of influence. These networks are not based on any single principle: neither wealth nor kinship suffices to assure a man influence.[15] But class within the village has never become a focus of political struggle, even when the state tried to make it so in 1978 and 1979.

The society of rural Afghanistan has several different elites that provide different types of leadership and organization. Within each village are distinct wards, or neighborhoods, that are often the homes of different qawms. Each such ward has its own mosque and council of elders. Most villages also have a council of elders, consisting of the leaders of various lineages or wards in the village, and may have a large mosque where the men of the entire village pray on Friday. The councils may settle disputes or organize economic cooperation in, for instance, the sharing of water. These leaders settle the daily affairs of the village and may also be responsible for relations between the village and the state (or the resistance). In tribal areas, where the villagers are mainly or wholly of a single tribe or clan, the village council may be equivalent to a tribal jirgah. One of their number may be designated by the government as *arbab*, or *malek*, the official representative of a village, ward, or *qawm*, but the *malek* is not necessarily or even usually the most powerful person.

The khan is the typical leader of rural society in most of Afghanistan. As in many tribal societies, and in other societies where commercialization is still at a relatively low level, a khan mainly becomes recognized as a leader through patronage, that is, through redistribution of his wealth, especially through hospitality. Indeed, Anderson (1983, 134) reports that among Ghilzai Pashtuns one of the most common sayings about khans is that they "feed the people." This patronage establishes networks of reciprocal obligation that knit the group together or, as Ghilzai say, "tie the knot of the tribe." The ability to obtain and distribute resources from the state or from other outside sources, such as smuggling, is an important factor in the struggle to become recognized as a khan.[16] The main object of politics as practiced by khans is to be recognized as "bigger" than other khans by both villagers and the state.

Views of khans differ. For some Marxists, the khan is simply the landlord, and his patronage or tribal relations with other villagers, including his tenants and hired laborers, are mechanisms of domination creating a hegemonic ideology of "tribalism," which "divides the oppressed from each other" (Halliday 1978, 35).[17] This was the conception of khans that underlay the land reform program of the Khalqi government in 1978 and 1979.

Khans do indeed make loans and employ tenants on their lands. Thus they use their resources to build up a dependent clientele within the qawm. Villagers, however, do not see such relations solely or mainly as exploitation but as what Tabibi (1981, 53–66) calls "asymmetrical reciprocity." Anderson (1983, 137) found that "in a sense that is quite real to Ghilzai, a khan is a self-financed public servant, expending his own wealth for the aggregate good of a community," and he noted that "khans emerge as social creditors and not as lords." Another anthropologist found that the Sheikhanzai Durrani Pashtuns wished to have *bigger* khans in order to have stronger collective organization, in particular to protect themselves from the state (Glatzer 1983, 224). The anthropologists confirm that Elphinstone ([1815] 1972, 1:217) had it right, at least for the Pashtun tribes, when he wrote, "In their notion of their Khaun, the idea of a magistrate set up for the public good is certainly mixed with that of a patriarchal and natural superior, yet the former impression will always be found to be strongest."[18]

Poorer villagers undoubtedly do engage in everyday forms of resistance against those who are more powerful; for instance, landlords
have to devote much energy to supervising sharecroppers who do not
own their own draft animals and who therefore receive as little as one-
sixth of the crop, because they do not work efficiently and may engage
in petty theft or encroachments. Nevertheless, it appears from the little
available research that villagers do not see wealth in land as in itself a
source of oppression. Furthermore, the patterns of circulation of wealth
in the village indicate that this perception is not simply the result of
domination and false consciousness.

The wealth and power of khans may serve the social ends of providing public goods, such as irrigation, or of protecting the village from
the predatory forces outside it.[19] Villagers distinguish between khans
who use access to state power to oppress people, in collusion with
corrupt government officials, and khans who organize and protect the
village or tribe, often against those same predatory officials (Shahrani
1986a). Khans, unlike state officials, belong to the village and share
cultural and life-cycle activities with fellow villagers, and are often
bound to them through kinship and other networks of obligation (Roy
1986, 20–29). The pattern of hospitality and marriage prestations are
mechanisms of redistribution along lines of kinship and community
and across class.

These social arrangements are owing both to geography and to
the lack of colonial conquest, which limited commercialization of
the agricultural economy. As a result, the best investment of surplus
production in the village has often remained political redistribution
rather than commerce, so that the bonds of reciprocity in the village
remained more intact than elsewhere. With the construction of the
first nationwide road network, the increased commercialization of
farming, and the introduction of modern agricultural technology
mainly in the 1970s, this arrangement had begun to change in a few
areas but had yet to have a major impact on political relations.[20] As a
result, there have been no known cases of peasant movements
against landlords in the Afghan countryside. The Khalqi minister of
agriculture during the early land reform said in 1979 that the aim of
the land reform was to introduce class struggle to a society with no
such tradition (Saleh Zeray, quoted in Gille 1984, 195–96). Conflicts
in the village have been either between corporate followings based
on kinship or ethnolinguistic ties or between the village and the
state, whose corrupt servants have been perceived to be the main
agents of exploitation.[21]

REDISTRIBUTION AND THE STATE

The State in Afghanistan

"The relation to the state traditionally maintained by the various Afghan communities is a relation of exteriority and compromise, not of exclusion," writes Olivier Roy (1988, 1; see also Roy 1986, 10–29). The village communities recognized the state as legitimate; they sent sons to the army and paid at least some taxes. In return, they benefited from some government expenditures on roads, schools, and agricultural development. At the same time, the villagers attempted to prevent the agents of the state from interfering in the internal life of the village. The *malek*, or *arbab*, was a member of the community, not a state employee. Villagers tried to settle internal disputes within the community rather than in the state court system, and the village council system of self-government was their own tradition rather than a part of the official state structure. Representatives of the state coming to the village found themselves isolated behind what Dupree has called the "mud curtain" (Dupree [1973] 1980a, 249).[22] Thus, the peasants try to establish an equilibrium between their community and the external state.

This pattern is not simply the result of Afghanistan's being at a "low" level of development or state formation along some continuum. It is rather the result of the struggles over the national and international role of the Afghan state that have occurred since Afghanistan was integrated into the modern state system in 1879, when the Treaty of Gandamak signed by Emir Ya'aqub Khan with the British made Afghanistan into a buffer state between the British and Russian empires.[23]

From 1880 to 1919 British subsidies in cash and weapons (in return for British control of Afghanistan's foreign affairs) enabled Emir Abdul Rahman Khan and his son and successor Emir Habibullah to build up a central state capable of extracting increasing direct taxes from the landlords and peasantry. Abdul Rahman's state-building activities gave rise to forty disturbances, including ten major rebellions, four of which he called civil wars, but British support (and his considerable acumen at tribal and Islamic politics) gave him the resources to defeat them (Kakar 1979).

Emir (subsequently King) Amanullah won Afghanistan's full independence in the Third Anglo-Afghan War in 1919, which cost him the British subsidies. He was thus the first Afghan ruler to face the problem of developing a domestic economic base for the state. He launched Afghanistan's first development programs, financed mainly by increased direct taxes on agriculture, which reaped as much as one-fifth of the harvest (Barfield 1981, 163). He also tried, but failed, to create a disciplined professional army. It is important to note that progressive redistribution played virtually no part in Amanullah's reform programs.[24] He tried to redistribute resources and power from rural, tribal, and religious leaders to the state, the embryonic modern intelligentsia, and an as yet nonexistent capitalist class. His main concern was the nationalist one of raising the stature of Afghanistan in the world, rather than of raising the status of the deprived within Afghanistan.

Amanullah's policies, if successful, would have increased state penetration of the village community and would have expanded capitalist development. His defeat in 1929 by a set of tribal and Islamic revolts was his most durable legacy; it led his successors, until the Communist coup of 1978, to conclude that they could not effect global social transformations in Afghanistan but should instead establish and expand a nation-state enclave insulated as much as possible from the traditional society. The villages succeeded in restoring their strong position in the compromise with the state, reversing the policies aimed at ending its "exteriority" (Poullada 1973; Gregorian 1969, 227–92; Dupree [1973] 1980a, 441–57; Gankovsky et al. 1985, 212–25; Adamec 1974, 77–172; Roy 1986, 62–68; Shahrani 1986b, 45–50).

This was the context in which the various rulers of the Musahiban dynasty that came to power in 1929 elaborated the fiscal system that the PDPA inherited. The Musahiban shared with Amanullah the goal of "modernizing" Afghanistan, but they concluded from his experience that the balance of forces in the country precluded a state-imposed global transformation. Instead, while compromising with the traditional forces that had brought them to power, they forged links with the international state system and market that enabled them gradually to enlarge a state-dominated export enclave centered in Kabul. This mini-nation-state depended less and less on the remaining peasant-tribal society.

The break was clear in the fiscal basis of the state. Direct taxes on agriculture and livestock continually diminished in importance during the period of Musahiban rule. As shown in table 5.3, they had been 62.5 percent of domestic revenue in 1926; in 1952–53 they were 18.1 percent and fell to about 7 percent by 1958; in the 1970s they were less than 2 percent.[25] The Musahiban relied instead on taxes on foreign trade, foreign aid (after 1957), and profits of government enterprises, including sales of natural gas to the Soviet Union (after 1968). The sources of finance illustrate the extent to which the government relied on its links to the international system and market as a counterweight to its inability to penetrate rural society directly.[26]

TABLE 5.3

**Resource Base of the State in Afghanistan:
Selected Years, 1926–1975**

(in percentage)

Resource	1926	1953	1957	1963	1968	1972	1975
Government domestic revenue as % of GNP	—	3.2	3.9	5.7	6.5	6.6	9.5
Shares of domestic revenue							
Taxes on land and livestock	62.5	18.1	7.0	5.7	2.2	1.3	0.7
Taxes on foreign trade	—	39.7	57.6	49.9	45.5	45.7	40.0
Profits of government enterprises	—	9.8	4.6	18.4	22.6	15.1	7.8
Sales of natural gas	—	—	0	0	9.6	11.8	14.0[c]
Government expenditure as % of GNP	—	4.4	4.0	8.9	8.8	8.3	12.8
Development expenditure as % of total expenditure	—	20.5	61.7	71.3	48.9	44.8	40.1
Foreign aid as % of development expenditure[b]	—	—	84.8	70.9	80.3	81.6	66.0

Sources: Guha 1967; Fry 1974, 170–71; DRA 1979; DRA 1981b.

[a]Some of the years are Afghan (Islamic solar) years, beginning about 21 March of the given year of the Gregorian calendar, and others are the indicated standard calendar years.

[b]Includes both project aid and commodity assistance

[c]Estimated from physical quantity exported using later price data and the official exchange rate.

Progressive redistribution was not a consideration in the elaboration of the financial system or the pattern of government spending.[27] First of all, the lack of state penetration was reflected in an extraordinarily weak tax effort. Of fifty developing countries studied in the early 1970s, only Nepal had a lower tax effort than Afghanistan.[28] This result shows that the weakness was not simply a result of the low level of economic development but was of political orgin. Another comparison showed that in 1968, public-sector net savings as a proportion of national income were smaller in Afghanistan (at a mere 0.8 percent) than in fourteen other representative underdeveloped countries (Fry 1974, 188).[29]

Such a small public-resource base can have only a small redistributive impact. The overall effect of state fiscal policies could better be characterized as *distributive* rather than redistributive. The state, tightly controlled by the Musahiban lineage (Nader Shah's brothers and their sons), acted more or less like a tribal khan, obtaining resources from outside (foreign aid and trade) and distributing them through patronage networks in order to enhance its status and power. In this respect, Afghanistan might be classified a rentier state living off incomes derived from the position of the state elite in the international system. These incomes, however, were still small relative to total income, so that whereas oil income made the shah's Iran into a powerful rentier state, Afghanistan became a weak one.

An incidence-benefit analysis in purely economic terms shows that the government taxed the producers of traditional agricultural exports (cotton, karakul, and wool), and subsidized wheat production and road transport. The subsidy of wheat production took the form of large (and often wasteful) investments in dam and irrigation projects such as the Helmand-Arghandab Valley Authority. The subsidy to transport, which was largely in the private sector, took the form of large investments in road construction with no user fees (Fry 1974, 178–79). The government also spent foreign aid heavily on the education and employment of the new middle class.

Such a sectoral analysis does not provide an explanation for the pattern of distribution. The explanation is most likely ethnic. The beneficiaries of most of the irrigation projects were tribal Pashtuns and, in particular, Durranis. Eastern Pashtuns dominated the trucking industry, especially because much of the profits to be made derived from smuggling across the Pakistani border, where they lived. Many of those recruited into the new middle class were also tribal Pashtuns; indeed, the Musahiban made a concerted effort to Pashtunize the predominantly Persian-speaking civil service. The producers of traditional exports, however, were predominantly non-Pashtuns (Turkomans, Tajiks, and Uzbeks) as well as some detribalized Pashtuns, as, for instance, in the cotton-growing areas of Kunduz. The Musahiban rulers thus used the resources they obtained from their international connections to create a patronage network to strengthen Pashtun nationalism, which was a major ideological support of their rule.

The Rural Reforms of the PDPA

Although President Taraki initially indicated that the PDPA would take a cautious attitude toward the implementation of its program, within three months after taking power the new government began to introduce a series of unprecedented sweeping reforms. The reforms were introduced by decree of the Revolutionary Council without any prior public discussion. Except for those party members involved in drafting the decrees, no one in Afghanistan knew of them until they were read over the radio and published in the official gazette, whereupon they took immediate effect.

The decrees containing the redistributive measures affecting the rural sector were Decree Number 6 (12 July 1978), dealing with rural mortgages and debts; Decree Number 7 (17 October 1978), dealing with marriage and bride-price; Decree Number 8 (28 November 1978), dealing with land reform; and the statute governing agricultural cooperatives, issued on 21 September 1978.[30] If implemented, these decrees would have transformed rural Afghan society from one of asymmetrical reciprocity, with the state kept at arm's length, to one of economically more-equal nuclear families linked through market relations and tied directly to the state. These decrees would have destroyed the economic and social basis of the exchanges—marriage prestations, loans, mortgages, tenancy, hospitality—that enabled khans to "tie the knot of the tribe." The network of clientage that held extended families together and knitted them into a *qawm* would have been replaced by direct dependence of nuclear families on the government bureaucracy. Where collective efforts were needed, they were to be organized by state-sponsored cooperatives rather than khan-sponsored patronage.

Decree Number 6 provided relief for a broad category of debts. Sharecroppers and agricultural laborers (*bazgar* and *mazdur*) were freed of all debts (principal and interest) to the landlords for whom they worked or to moneylenders.[31]

The other provisions applied to landless tenants or peasants owning less than ten *jaribs* (two hectares) of first-quality land or the equivalent.[32] According to the minister of land reform, Saleh Mohammed Zeary, "larger landowners usually borrow for reinvestment in buildings, in farm improvement, for trading, and the like, and when they borrow they are likely to get richer [rather] than poorer."[33] These provisions also distinguished between debts contracted more than five years before and more recent ones. This provision was connected to the drought of 1971 and 1972, which drove many peasants into debt and forced them to mortgage their land (Tabibi 1981, 165–66).

For these categories of peasants, all debts more than five years old for the purchase of seed or on which any interest was charged were canceled. Any land that had been placed in *geraw* five years or more before the decree was introduced was to be returned to the owner after the harvest of the standing crop, without any payment to the mortgage holder. Land placed in *geraw* more recently was also to be returned to the owner after the harvest, but the owner had to repay a portion of the principal on a sliding scale and according to a schedule determined by the age of the loan. These small landowners also had all interest payments and portions of the principal of other debts less than five years old canceled, with a similar sliding scale and repayment schedule.

An important provision of the decree was that its enforcement depended on the claimants' being able to produce legal documents attesting to the loan. To administer the decree the government published a regulation providing for district *(uluswali)* and provincial committees to resolve the problems of the peasants (Vercellin 1979, 106–7). The district committee, presided over by the *uluswal*, or district commissioner, was composed of bureaucrats from five government ministries, plus two "representatives of the peasants," who were generally village schoolteachers as well as members of the party (Anwar 1988, 142). The provincial committee, headed by the *wali* (governor), was to be composed of representatives of six government ministries and three "peasant representatives." The district committee was responsible for recommending peasants for loans from the Agricultural Development Bank. The only appeal from the decision of the district committee was to the provincial committee, whose decision was final.

Decree Number 7 dealt with marriage and bride-price. It established minimum ages for marriage (sixteen for girls, eighteen for boys) and stated that marriage could occur only with the free consent of both parties. It outlawed all marriage prestations except the Islamic bride-price *(mahr)*, which it set at the level determined by the Shariʿah, 10 dirhams, or Af 300 (less than $9 at the official rate of exchange). The decree also forbade the groom's family to demand expenditures for the wedding ceremonies. The cost of both the bride-price and the ceremonies could be exorbitant and, hence, sources of debt. The decree stated, employing neologisms *(pidarsalari, fiyudali)* unknown to the Afghan people, that its purpose was to end "oppressive patrarichal and feudal conditions." If implemented, Decree Number 7 would have transformed marriage from a social and economic transaction between two extended families (sometimes within one extended family) to a private decision of two individuals.

The statute for the organization of cooperatives was unexceptional because it did not obligate anyone to join cooperatives. Cooperatives were to be open to peasants owning up to twenty *jaribs* of first-quality land or the equivalent. Their elected officers were to deal with the collective affairs of the peasants and act as mediators with the administration as khans and *maleks* had done. The true meaning of the cooperatives only becomes apparent when they are viewed in conjunction with the subsequently announced land reform measures. These measures would have created a rural society of smallholdings, many of which would have been uneconomical, and none of which would have been adequate as an economic base for the provision of collective goods. The cooperatives would provide an alternative to the traditional role of the khan as a "public servant" and that of the *malek* as an intermediary with the government. They also might have been a first step toward collectivization, as they were in China.

Decree Number 8 aimed at eliminating "feudal and prefeudal conditions" by establishing a land ceiling of thirty *jaribs* (six hectares) for first-quality land or the equivalent for each "family." The "family," defined as husband, wife, and unmarried children aged less than eighteen years, was to be the basic unit of land ownership. This definition was consistent with the intention of the marriage reform. The reform would thus have eliminated the joint family and larger kinship units as economic entities (these were considered "prefeudal" relations).

Land above the ceiling (as well as state land and the lands of the former royal family) were to be confiscated by the state and distributed to landless laborers and tenants, small peasants (those owning less than five *jaribs*), and propertyless nomads. Each beneficiary was to receive enough land to bring his total holding up to the equivalent of five *jaribs* of first-quality land. The beneficiaries were divided into six grades of priority, from tenants who were to receive the land they were already cultivating (highest priority) to tenants and propertyless nomads from other provinces (lowest priority). Since all landholdings would then be between five and thirty *jaribs*, this ceiling would have virtually eliminated tenancy ("feudal" relations).

The decree would also have given the state an altogether new, intrusive role in agriculture. The state was to expropriate the surplus lands and, in the first instance, place them under the authority of the Land Reform Department. It would then decide who was to receive the land and require all new landowners to register their deeds with the state (something Afghan peasants had not traditionally done), cultivate the land within three months, participate in a cadastral survey, and pay the land tax. In order to prevent the emergence of new inequalities, the state then forbade the new owners to sell or mortgage the newly received land. The owners could give it in tenancy only if it were inherited by a minor or woman who could not cultivate it. Contrary to the Islamic law of inheritance, land could not be subdivided among heirs into units smaller than five *jaribs*.[34] The decree also placed the operation of all irrigation canals under the authority of the Ministry of Water and Energy (Article 6) and required the peasants to cultivate the land in accord with the "suggestions and instructions of the Ministry of Agriculture and Land Reform" (Article 34). A later regulation (6 June 1979) also provided for "special popular committees" to resolve legal disputes arising from the land reform. There were to be committees at both the *uluswali* and provincial levels, each composed of four bureaucrats and three peasant representatives, the latter being elected "under the control [or supervision]" of the previously mentioned committees to resolve the problems of the peasants, which were, of course, dominated by the government administration.

The implementation of the land reform began in the warm provinces in January 1979 and spread through other areas of the country. By July, the government announced that the land reform had been completed.[35] Nine years later, however, a Soviet general with extensive experience in Afghanistan stated, "The pace at which the land and water reform is being carried out is extremely slow. So far, approximately 30% to 35% of it has been carried out." The Soviet journalist interviewing him (who also had spent much time in Afghanistan) commented, "And only pro forma at that, in many instances. After all, approximately one third of the land the peasants have received has returned to the hands of its former owners, and almost half of the land in the peasants' hands is not being tilled" (Borovik 1988, 2). If these estimates are approximately accurate, on the eve of the Soviet withdrawal, peasants in Afghanistan were cultivating only about one-ninth of the land they had supposedly been allotted nine years before.[36]

Of course, the major result of the attempts to implement the reforms in 1979 was the spread of armed revolt through much of the country, leading to the Soviet decision to intervene.[37] The Soviets and the Parchamis called the reforms "ultraleftist." They argued that their overly egalitarian nature did not take into account economic requirements of agriculture; that the attempt to move directly to "socialism" did not take into account the backward condition of the country and the need for capitalist development in agriculture; that the distribution of land took on a "self-contained character" (Glukhoded 1981) without adequate attention to the needs for credit and other factors of production, especially water; and that the method of implementation was too fast and relied too much on violent repression rather than political methods.

The most fundamental critique, however, was enacted by the insurgents. After the Soviet invasion the resistance became so widespread that most of the countryside was no longer under the government's control or even accessible to it.[38] Hence, the main priority of the Soviet-Parcham alliance was to reestablish state power. In practice, this goal took priority over the government's redistributive program and, indeed, often contradicted it. Aggressive pursuit of revolutionary policies, which the government was unable to implement, in fact strengthened the resistance and weakened the state. The rural counterinsurgency strategy concentrated on winning traditional notables, usually landlords, to the side of the government, a strategy in direct contradiction to the government's redistributive program. As Roy (1988, 4) put it: "The Communist state, which at first was perceived as the quintessence of the state in general, now plays the traditional tribal game; thus it again plays by the rules and loses the 'Martian' aspect that had led to its rejection. But if this evolution of the Communist state allows an opening of the political game, it also deprives the USSR (and the Communists in general) of any political discourse about Afghanistan."

The amendment to the land reform decree passed in 1981 illustrates this process (DRA 1981b). Whereas the original decree mentions the abolition of "feudal and prefeudal" relations, the amendment speaks of "observing the principle of legal property, respecting the religious and tribal traditions and customs and enhancing the living standards of the people" (Article 1).

Four categories of persons were allowed to retain the land they owned over the original ceiling: "religious ulemas, preachers of mosques, mullahs and the spiritual leaders of the country" (Article 3);[39] "leaders and elders of tribes who fight and have rendered prominent services against the domestic and external enemies of the revolution" (Article 4); "officers who are serving in the armed forces" (Article 5);[40] and "persons who expand production, use mechanization in agriculture and sell all their agricultural produce to the state" (Article 6). Other landowners "who have escaped abroad as a result of the hostile propaganda of the counterrevolution" but who return home would receive back any land expropriated from them or its equivalent, up to the legal ceiling (Article 7). The state promised to pay cash compensation to any of the members of the above categories whose land had already been distributed (Article 8). The decree also gave priority in the distribution of land to "landless peasants and those with small plots of land, whose sons are voluntarily serving in the armed forces and in units of the Ministry of Interior" (Article 10).[41]

This decree effectively transformed the "land reform" into a counterinsurgency measure. It continued the policy of making the society more directly dependent on the state: Islamic leaders had to have their exemptions approved by the Department of Islamic Affairs (subsequently the Ministry of Islamic Affairs), which was responsible for the government's Islamic propaganda; tribal leaders' exemptions required the approval of the Ministry of Tribal and Nationality Affairs and the Supreme Council of the Tribes, which, in collaboration with the State Information Services (KHAD; subsequently, the Ministry of State Security [WAD]) ran the progovernment militias; and service in the security apparatus brought direct economic benefits.

The method of extending the dependence, however, was different from that of the Khalq.[42] Rather than introduce revolutionary measures to reduce the qawm to a set of nuclear families dependent on the state, the government now offered inducements to khans to bring their clienteles over to the side of the government, whom they could serve as militias. The clergy could retain all of their property if they agreed to cooperate with the Islamic policy of the government.[43]

The government also tried to promote commercial farming tied to the state sector in order both to increase the dependence of the agricultural sector on the government and to strengthen the shaky fiscal base of the state. This reflected the Soviet belief that state-guided capitalist development was a necessary part of the "national democratic" (as opposed to socialist) revolution. Large capitalist farmers could retain all their land if they sold all produce to the government. The government placed increased emphasis on the technical requirements of such farming, paying attention to the need for water, credit, and fertilizer.[44] It established Soviet-style agricultural mechanization centers (FBIS VIII, 5 Mar. 1985, C2) and also provided subsidies and higher procurement prices to encourage farmers to raise karakul and to plant cotton and sugar beets, which would have to be sold to the state-owned processing plants.[45]

The government's distributive policy was not based on class but on manipulating the segmentation of Afghan rural society. The purpose of the manipulation was to create a base for a state power that was imposed from above with the help of the powers in the international system, in this case, the Soviet Union.

Fiscal Policy of the PDPA

Even more than previously, the government's fiscal policy was distributive rather than redistributive. Table 5.4 shows fiscal developments in the years before and after the coup. Before commenting on these figures, a few words of caution are in order. During the best of times, Afghan government statistics had to be treated with some skepticism. During a period when the state itself had broken down in much of the country and the government was engaged in a war for its own survival, little faith can be placed in estimates such as that of GNP. Both the number and quality of Afghan government publications declined, especially after the Soviet intervention (the reason that the table stops after 1982).[46] The government may, however, have had the capacity to calculate its own receipts (although it may not have reported them honestly) and to monitor government-sponsored foreign trade with the Eastern bloc and its associated revenues and taxes. Nevertheless, the reporting of government revenues and expenditures is far sketchier than in past years—there is no itemization of different taxes—which impedes comparison. Table 5.4 is as similar in format to table 5.3 as was possible with the available data.

Agriculture remained the major economic activity in Afghanistan, but except for the cultivation of export goods and raw materials for government industries, it contributed virtually nothing to the fiscal base of the state. In theory, the land reform, by creating wider registration of land deeds with the government, would have enabled the government to collect the existing land tax more fully, but there was no attempt made to raise the tax rate over its existing low level. In fact, with the loss of control over the countryside, the government could hardly collect land tax at all. In a 1983 speech, Prime Minister Sultan Ali Keshtmand stated that whereas the government had collected Af 280 million in land tax in 1978–79, it had collected only Af 16 million in 1981–82.[47] This is about 0.01 percent of estimated GNP, about $350,000 at the official rate of exchange, a derisory sum for an agrarian nation of about fifteen million people. Despite the low level of tax collection, the government repeatedly announced the cancellation of both back taxes and fines for their nonpayment.[48]

TABLE 5.4

Resource Base of the State in Afghanistan: 1975–1982

(in percentage)

	1975[a]	1976	1977	1978	1979	1980	1981	1982
Development expenditure as % of total expenditure	40.1	43.0	50.9	53.1	44.4	38.2	34.2	30.7
Foreign aid as % of development expenditure[b]	66.0	68.3	67.3	63.6	80.2	72.4	75.4	92.2
Shares of domestic revenue								
Direct taxes	9.9	12.3	15.2	15.4	15.6	9.0	11.2	10.1
Indirect taxes	46.8	44.2	45.8	42.0	41.8	31.9	18.9	23.6
Profits of government enterprises	7.9	6.4	9.8	<12.3[c]	<15.1[c]	<1.4[c]	<0.1[c]	<-2.6[c]
Sales of natural gas	15.6	13.5	12.8	13.9	23.9	40.1	45.6	47.3

Source: DRA 1979, 1982, 1983, 1986.

[a]The years are Afghan (Islamic solar) years, beginning about 21 March of the given year of the Gregorian calendar.

[b]Includes commodity assistance.

[c]Estimated as income of government and mixed enterprises (including subsidies) less expenditures. Some profits of mixed enterprises are paid to private investors.

Under the PDPA, government expenditure increased, but the proportion of "development" expenditure declined. This indicates greater expenditures for military purposes as well as for various distributive policies designed to win support for the government. The increase in expenditure was not accompanied by greater extraction from the domestic economy of Afghanistan. Tax revenues declined as a share of total revenue. Despite occasional exhortations to increase the efficiency of state enterprises, their profitability declined.[49] Foreign aid paid for increasing amounts of both development and nondevelopment expenditure. This foreign aid came almost entirely from the Soviet Union and its allies.[50]

Not all of this foreign aid was labeled as such. For instance, the increase in the government's domestic revenue in 1980–81 over 1979–80 comes almost entirely from an increase in revenues from sales of natural gas to the Soviet Union. The natural gas fields were developed with Soviet aid and by Soviet experts. The gas was piped directly across the border into the Soviet Union and was metered on the Soviet side of the border. Furthermore, the reported increase in revenues appears to be owing to an increase in the price paid by the USSR for essentially the same amount of gas.[51] Thus, although the increased revenue is listed as "domestic revenue," it is in effect a transfer from the USSR.[52] This pattern apparently continued, as isolated statements indicated. In January 1984, for instance, an official spokesman said that in the past few years gas prices "have grown several times over," to the point where they equaled Western European prices, and that gas sales to the USSR provide "close to 50% of the state budget income."[53]

In addition to its military and police expenditures, the government also made transfer payments to politically key sectors. Many of these programs involved the free or subsidized distribution of commodities (especially food and fuel) supplied by the USSR. Again, these payments are better explained as part of a counterinsurgency strategy than as a policy of social transformation. Only isolated figures on transfers are currently available, but they give an idea of the types of transfers the government engaged in. Monetary figures give some idea of their total amount.

Statements by the government focused on transfers of two major types: those to Islamic institutions and those to the urban population in their varying capacities as government employees, cash-paying consumers, and students. After 1987 the government also announced a series of benefits for those returning to the country under the policy of national reconciliation. Substituting the printing press of the central bank for Soviet bombs and bayonets, it also paid large sums to commanders of government militias and to resistance commanders.

Grants for Islamic purposes included those for building new mosques, amounting to Af 70 million in Kabul and Af 14 million in the provinces during 1981–84. The government announced it had spent Af 130 million on the repair of existing mosques in 1981–82. It allocated Af 3.7 million for fuel and firewood for mosques in 1983–84. It also subsidized participation in the hajj. The government gave the amount of the subsidy as Af 85 million in 1983, Af 180,000 or Af 196 million (reports differ) in 1984, and Af 172 million in 1985. (Another report states that the 1985 subsidy was Af 28,000 per hajji, making for a total of 6,143 pilgrims.)[54]

The urban population, mainly composed of government employees, received various benefits consistent with the government's policy of trying to build up a loyal, or at least neutral, body of state employees in order to secure its base in Kabul. Given the high rate of inflation, however, these policies may not have succeeded in keeping the urban standard of living from falling, except for the most privileged groups.

First of all, members of the security forces had their salaries raised many times. For instance, Prime Minister Keshtmand announced that the salaries of soldiers would be raised by a factor of five to ten during 1988–89. One might speculate that this increment was connected to the Soviet pullout. Other government employees had also had salary increases, though not on the same scale. In 1983, government employees' salaries were increased an average of 26 percent, with increases ranging up to 50 percent in the lower brackets (*Bakhtar*, 16 Mar. 1988, cited in *Afghanistan Forum* 16, no. 3 (1988): 35; FBIS VIII, 19 May 1983, C1).

The government established a system of subsidized consumption for its employees. Food prices shot up throughout the country as a result of the destruction of agriculture in the war, the disruption of transport and marketing systems, and the emission of large quantities of currency. An important tool of social control was the offer of free or subsidized food to the urban population.[55] Thus, in his 1988 budget speech, Prime Minister Keshtmand announced, "State assistance to food allowance of government employees has been increased one and a half times. The free distribution of flour, wheat and edible oil to state workers and employees, disabled veterans of revolution and work as well as the families of martyrs against coupons has been generalized. Currently 340 thousand coupon holders receive 56 kg of flour or wheat and six kg of edible oil." The government has also established special stores, similar to those under the Soviet *propusk* system (or U.S. Army PXs), "where the personnel of the armed forces and their families can buy foodstuffs and industrial products at low price" (*Kabul New Times*, 16 Mar. 1988, cited in *Afghanistan Forum* 16, no. 3 [1988]:35). The government also made low-interest loans available to civil servants and military officers, mainly for the building of homes.[56]

The government introduced other policies aimed at winning over the urban population as consumers. Electrical rates in Kabul in 1984 were subsidized by 26 percent (or perhaps 600 percent; there are two incompatible sets of figures).[57] In 1988 the government decided to give free uniforms, stationery, and breakfast to all primary and secondary school students and to increase the monthly allowances of university students (*Bakhtar*, 16 Mar. 1988, cited in *Afghanistan Forum* 16, no. 3 (1988): 35). Finally, as part of the national reconciliation program, the government announced that all debts and back taxes of returning refugees would be canceled and offered various other benefits as well (FBIS VIII, 7 May 1987, C1).

So great were these transfers, especially those to resistance and militia commanders, that a new term developed for money, "containers." The author was told in 1990 that commanders sometimes received whole "containers" of Afghanis, which they did not bother to open. Instead, the container became a unit of measurement. The overall quantity of the redistribution can be estimated through data on currency in circulation.[58] According to these data, the amount of currency in circulation from 1973 to 1986 rose at a rate of 13 percent per year. From 1986 to 1989, however, after the start of national reconciliation, the money supply rose at a rate of 34 percent per year; it increased by 57.5 percent in the first year of the program.[59]

Failure of Red Redistribution

The failure of the land and debt reform is the key to the failure of the PDPA. The party's attempt to intervene in rural society led to the disintegration of the state and the rise of the insurgency. Combating the latter dominated all other policies, which is why the government never attempted to impose inevitably controversial extractive policies and piled disbursement upon disbursement, despite its precarious financial situation. As a Soviet journalist (now a leader of Russia's reactionary Right) who had previously written much egregious nonsense[60] on Afghanistan put it, a mere week after Gorbachev had made it clear that he would withdraw Soviet troops:

> Since those December [1979] days when USSR troops entered Afghanistan, the political course of the Kabul government has been changed repeatedly. State forums are now preceded by a mullah's prayers. The flag is no longer red; it now includes a green Islamic segment. The star has disappeared from the country's seal. The party has stopped talking about the construction of a socialist society. It has

renounced a monopoly on power. It has declared pluralism. It has invited the bellicose opposition abroad to participate in the government, and the possible return to the country of the aged Shah, who was overthrown not by Taraki but by Daud—a return to a vestige from 15 years in the past—is under study. Most important, it has announced a policy of national reconciliation, an unprecedented compromise with its enemies, a willingness to see them not as enemies but as patriots, as collaborators in the future of a traditionally Islamic, nonaligned Afghanistan, slowly healing the wounds inflicted by war.

Taken together, all this makes it possible to say that the original goals proclaimed by the PDPA have not been achieved. The party itself, the revolutionary government itself, has renounced them. (Prokhanov 1988, 1)[61]

Why, then, did the redistributive reforms fail? Four different, though not mutually exclusive, lines of argument merit consideration:

1. The reforms failed because the reformers had insufficient *knowledge* of the society they were trying to reform. They did not understand that water, rather than land, was the major constraint on Afghan agriculture and hence distributed land without providing for adequate irrigation. They did not understand that there were relatively few large landholdings in Afghanistan and that hence there would not be nearly enough surplus land to distribute to all the supposed beneficiaries. They did not understand that peasants needed a source of credit and that abolishing debts to landlords and moneylenders would be counterproductive without providing alternative sources of credit. They did not understand that the landlords generally supplied seed and, sometimes, draft animals, so that landless tenants and laborers who received land needed an alternative source of these factors of production. They did not understand the culture of asymmetrical reciprocity and therefore assumed that the peasants could be mobilized immediately along class lines. This line of argument is valid to a certain extent, although lack of institutional knowledge of the society is a manifestation of low state capacity, the second explanation. Furthermore, the reformers were indeed aware of some of the above problems but were unable to devise means of dealing with them, pointing again to the importance of state capacity.

2. The Afghan state did not have the *capacity* to carry out the reforms. There were no accurate land records. The administration that was supposed to carry out the reforms had no experience in such activity. The Khalqis did indeed understand the need for alternative sources of credit, but the state could not come up with the financial or institu-

tional resources to make the Agricultural Development Bank work as envisaged. In the absence of effective administration and trained cadres, those charged with carrying out the reforms resorted to brute force, which alienated the peasants. The political purges of the administration eliminated many of the few existing trained specialists. Hence, the reforms could not actually be implemented.

Both of these first two explanations imply that the actual effect of the attempt to implement the reforms was to *worsen* the condition of the peasantry in general and the beneficiaries in particular. For instance, the *musallis* of Laghman in eastern Afghanistan, an impoverished *qawm* of grain cleaners, were allotted land in far-off Helmand, in the Southwest. Thousands of them moved there by truckloads, only to find that there were no tents or houses for their accommodation, no one to demarcate the plots, no water, and no tools. After subsisting for a few months on World Food Program handouts, they returned home "more disillusioned than ever" (Ølesen 1982). Other explanations do not rely on the simply defined interest of the peasants.

3. According to the government itself, *external intervention* deprived it of the chance to correct its "mistakes." Aid from Pakistan, the United States, and a host of other reactionary powers consolidated the hold of the "counterrevolutionaries" on the peasantry, who remained in the grip of false consciousness. Yet even the Soviets abandoned this as the primary explanation for the failure of the PDPA. The truly massive aid to the mujahidin did not begin until the war was several years old and was more the result than the cause of their successes. External aid to the Nicaraguan contras or to the National Union for the Total Independence of Angola (UNITA) did not comparably weaken the state, because the Sandinistas and the Popular Movement for the Liberation of Angola (MPLA), despite their mistakes, had far greater legitimacy.

4. Finally, according to one argument, the reforms failed because the government that carried them out lacked legitimacy. When the government attacked Islam and visibly allied itself with the Soviet Union, it lost any possibility of winning the confidence of the people (Shahrani 1984). Of course, the reforms were also badly designed, in accord with an ideology that did not accord with the reality of Afghan society, but the revolts were mainly directed against a state that was *illegitimate* because it was *kafer* (unbelieving) and *zalem* (tyrannical), rather than simply ignorant or incompetent.

A different formulation can unite elements of explanations (1), (2), and (4), while adding something different that is related to the theoretical point made at the beginning of the chapter: that redistribution *by* the state is also redistribution *to* the state. The proposed reforms would have amounted to an allocation of power in the rural areas from the khans and *maleks* to the state and the ruling party. Most analyses have ignored the extent to which the reforms did not simply rearrange rural society but inserted specific, new social actors—the Marxist intelligentsia staffing the state administration—into the key positions in that society. The peasants were thus not given a choice between domination and exploitation, on the one hand, and freedom and equality, on the other. They were given a choice between the leaders they knew, with whom they shared much, and leaders they did not know, who believed in an alien ideology and who showed by their actions that they could not be trusted. Indeed, long experience had taught the peasants that, harmful as some khans could be, others were useful in protecting the village from the state administration, even when the state administration was Muslim (Shahrani 1986a). The ignorance behind the formulation of the reforms and the incompetence and brutality of their implementation only served to further convince the peasantry that the proposed changes would not be in their interest, as, indeed, they turned out not to be.[62] The revolt was thus not against the "state" as such, nor was it against "reforms" as such; it was against the imposition and extension of an illegitimate state power that in fact (and not in false consciousness) worked against the interest of the peasants and most other social groups in the country.

The Red Revolution Turns Green

Whether or not the resistance to the PDPA government started as a "counterrevolution," it turned into something else. The social dislocations caused by the PDPA's programs combined with those created by the requirements of mass mobilization for modern warfare and the extraordinarily destructive counterinsurgency strategy of 1980–86 to produce massive social change in the resistance-held areas (Roy 1986, 149–71; Roy 1988).[63] The main redistributive impact of the war was to remove or kill many of the population from resistance-held areas and to destroy much of the assets in those areas, including irrigation works, orchards and vineyards, animals, farmland, houses, roads, and tools. Within those areas, however, some anecdotal evidence indicates that the existing production was distributed more equitably than before.

Before drawing far-reaching conclusions from this, a word of caution is in order. The war has greatly reduced the labor force through emigration, fatalities, and participation in the war (part-time mujahidin or militia members are less available for farm labor, and full-time mujahidin or government soldiers are not available at all). Opportunities for nonagricultural activities such as smuggling and gunrunning have also increased. As a result, labor has become relatively scarcer in relation to land. Hence, the return to labor should increase and that to land decrease, and, in fact, it appears that the wages of agricultural laborers have gone up and that sharecropping tenants are paying significantly less of the crop to the landlords. It is impossible with existing data to test whether the results can be interpreted strictly as a market response that will return to the previous situation if the refugees return and the economy is restored.

The resistance, of course, opposed the government's land reform on ideological grounds. According to Islam, property lawfully acquired may not be expropriated from the owner without compensation. Some property of landlords may be *haram* (Islamically invalid) if, for instance, it was purchased with money earned from interest on loans, which is forbidden in Islam. Such land could be expropriated, but it is difficult to prove that a particular piece of property was purchased with money from a specific transaction. The resistance *would* favor canceling payment of interest on loans as contrary to Islam.

The reality on the ground, however, was that the resistance relied for its manpower on the support of the small peasants and tenants. Indeed, as Roy (1986) has shown, the big landlords and khans were generally absent from the struggle, having chosen to leave the country or to go to one of the more secure urban areas. Furthermore, he argues, although the peasants, tenants, and workers as well as the ulama generally oppose expropriation as contrary to the right to property, they have no such objection to reforms in tenancy relations. Indeed, a redistribution of the product in favor of the tenant and worker is the type of reform favored by the ulama and the peasantry. In those areas where subsistence farming continues, the resistance has thus been favorable to what Herring (1983) has called the "venerable tenancy reform model."[64] Tenancy reform, or regulation of the maximum share a sharecropper can be required to pay the landlord, is also the model used by the CPI/M in its Operation Barga in West Bengal (Kohli 1987).

The context in which the resistance began favored such developments. As Roy (1986, 92) observed, "Opposition to the reforms not only strengthened the feeling that the ownership of land was sacrosanct, but it also caused the landowners to offer more favourable contracts to those who farmed their land (except in Hazarajat [where no land reforms were carried out and the society is more hierarchical]) and it ensured that the resistance movement could not avoid coming to terms with the social question."

Furthermore, the arming of the small tenants and peasants by the Islamic parties has given them a power they never had before. This is key, because the weakness of tenure reform, as Herring shows, is that it is generally impossible to enforce. In India, for instance, it is up to the tenants, generally impoverished and powerless members of lower castes, to take their landlords to court. The net result of such action generally is further impoverishment through the legal process plus ex-tralegal reprisals by the landlords against whom the tenants have no effective recourse. The CPI-M was able to overcome these obstacles in West Bengal through its organization of the tenants into village coun-cils under the guidance of its disciplined party apparatus and with the support of the state government. The resistance base (*markez, qarargah,* or *komiteh*) may be able to perform a similar function.

Roy (in a personal communication) recounted a specific case that illustrates how this works. In the summer of 1987 he was in an area of Baghlan Province where the detribalized Pashtun wheat farmers were mainly organized by Hezb-e Islami (Hekmatyar). Most of the mujahidin were smallholding peasants and tenants; the larger landlords had emi-grated to Pakistan. For several years the tenants and peasants had been cultivating the abandoned land without paying any rent to the land-lord. While Roy was in the area, a delegation arrived from Pakistan with a message from the landlords. The landlords requested that the tenants pay the accustomed share of the crop in return for farming the land. The tenants, who were armed mujahidin, held a meeting of the village, together with local ulama, to discuss the dispute. They ac-knowledged that the landlords were in fact the owners of the land. On the other hand, the landlords had abandoned the jihad and gone to live abroad, for which they ought to be fined. Rather than fine them, the mujahidin would continue to cultivate the landlords' land without pay-ing rent. If the landlords returned, the mujahidin would negotiate a just compensation for the use of their land.

Of course, the Islamic parties are not "disciplined, left-wing par-ties" of the type that Kohli (1987) argues are necessary for carrying out redistributive reform. Like left-wing parties, however, they have mobi-lized the potential beneficiaries of redistribution. They are not disci-plined, but the need for discipline in Kohli's theory is to prevent the movement from becoming overly radicalized and attacking the institu-tion of property to the extent that capitalists disinvest and ruin the economy. The Islamic parties, however, are ideologically committed to the protection of legally acquired private property. Their followers accept the same view.

The main effect of the war, however, was not to transfer power but to fragment it. By the end, the only instrument the state had to redistribute income or assets was to print money. The resistance parties could also redistribute money they received from abroad or from the drug trade. No political force, however, has the power to formulate policy for the transformation of society. All are likely to be consumed by power struggles and little else for the foreseeable future.

Notes

1. The Communist Party of the Soviet Union (CPSU) did not publicly recognize the PDPA as a fraternal party until after the coup. After 1988 both the CPSU and the PDPA claimed that the PDPA was not a Marxist-Leninist party, but a member of a major institute in Moscow told the author in June 1988 that the CPSU still considered the PDPA a Communist party but would not say so because the term was so unpopular in Afghanistan. At its second congress in June 1990, the PDPA changed its name to the Homeland Party (Hezb-e Watan). It renounced Marxism-Leninism, socialism, and the monopoly of power, and endorsed Islam, market economics, and democracy.

2. Charles Edward Linblom, in many conversations and seminars, did much to impress this on me.

3. For an attempt to integrate hypotheses about redistribution into the state-centered approach, see Kohli 1987, 15–50.

4. Ahluwalia (1974), for instance, provides a typology of areas of redistribution, including factor markets, ownership and control of assets, taxation of personal income and wealth, provision of public consumption goods, and commodity markets, all of which, he notes, are related to the state of technology.

5. The CPI-M is the party that split from the CPI over the Sino-Soviet conflict in the early sixties. Whereas the CPI remained dogmatically pro-Soviet, the CPI-M became independent rather than pro-Peking. Its ideology is uncompromisingly radical, but Kohli (1987) finds that in practice it is a "disciplined social-democratic party." Kohli studied the party's policies in West Bengal, and Herring (1983) those in Kerala.

6. The major redistributive effect of the government's policies in the countryside was the destruction through bombing and other military means of assets belonging to communities supporting the Islamic resistance.

7. The government has also undertaken to transform gender and ethnic relations, which are also redistributive policies. These policies are addressed in other chapters in this volume.

8. Hager (1983, 84) defines the tribe as a polity with jursidiction over persons rather than territory.

9. For a particularly illuminating discussion, which I follow here, see Roy 1986, 10–29. See also Tapper 1983, Beattie 1982, and Anderson 1975. The latter defines *qawm* among Pashtuns as "any category of common patrilineal descent that persists through time as a distinct identity from a particular community to the totality of Pashtun." Thus *qawms*

may be nested inside one another. Barth (1959) describes a structure of *qawms* among Pashtuns in Pakistan that resembles the Indian caste system.

10. An estimate based on the available returns of the never-completed 1979 census was that 2.56 million (16 percent) of a total of 15.96 million population were "nomadic" (DRA 1982, 4). This is consistent with Ferdinand's (1962, 123) estimate that one-sixth of the population was "more or less nomadic." Dupree ([1973] 1980a, 164) estimates there were about two million "nomads or semi-nomads" in 1973. Tapper (1974, 127–28) notes a "generally quoted . . . figure of between 2 and 3 million nomads out of a population of over 15 million persons, but specific estimates of 'full-nomads'—that is, tent-dwelling pastoralists with no agricultural occupation—vary from 200,000 to 2,741,488. For nomadism so defined, the former figure is more realistic while the latter would probably be exceeded by the number of nomads defined by the broader criterion, which I shall use, of tribally organized, tent-using transhumants with a primary interest in pastoralism." Barfield (1981, xvii) estimates that 10 to 15 percent of the population of Afghanistan were "nomads."

11. Several writers report a traditionally sanctioned system of product distribution that grants one-fifth to whoever provides each of the five factors of production, but they report that in practice the distribution follows a variety of formulas, depending on the region and the crop (Etienne 1972; Barry 1984, 103; Centlivres-Demont and Centlivres 1984; Centlivres 1972; Tabibi 1981, 53–55). Kakar (1979, 188–89) provides a survey of sharecropping systems in the late nineteenth-century Afghanistan. The types of farm given in the text are abstract categories; in actual cases the types are considerably mixed up.

12. Etienne (1972) has many observations on rural debt. The best general discussion is in Tabibi 1981, 57–60. Ferdinand (1962) discusses *geraw*, especially as a form of loan from nomads to peasants. No reliable information on the total indebtedness of the peasantry in Afghanistan before 1978 is available.

13. According to Glukhoded (1981, 242), 26 to 36 percent of the agricultural households were landless. Mukherjee (1984, 177) claims that "over 30 percent" were landless. Both these sources apparently use figures supplied by the Kabul government, although neither cites sources.

14. As Ahmed (1976) points out, the one form of leadership to which this does not apply is charismatic religious leadership in moments of crisis.

15. Barth (1959, 74) wrote that influence proceeds from the "control of the sources of livelihood, distribution of wealth, [and] martial valour in defence of family honor." Tapper (1984, 259) wrote, "Generally, organization and cooperation at the local level are unstructured by segmentary opposition or any other single principle, but instead by a combination of agnation, cognation, alliance, and friendship, forming shifting clusters around wealthy and ambitious men."

16. On the political process among khans, see the classic, though disputed, study by Barth (1959). A partial critique of Barth is found in Ahmed 1976. See also Barry 1984, 96–116, Roy 1986, 25–29, and Anderson 1983.

17. Halliday fails to note that tribalism also divides the "oppressors" from one another. Indeed, it is such division that leads the khans to recruit followers.

18. See also Anderson 1978, 170–71. Barfield (1981, 63–64) describes leaders called *bai* who play a similar role among the Arabs of Kunduz. Shahrani (1986a) suggests an interesting way of looking at khans in relation to both local society and the state.

19. Dupree ([1973] 1980a, 249–50) notes that villagers do not cooperate voluntarily for projects of mutual benefit but have to be paid or forced to work on them. This is a

common characteristic of real, as opposed to romanticized, peasants, as the Chinese revelations about bogus stories of voluntary labor during the Cultural Revolution and the Great Leap Forward also confirmed. Dupree also notes that the village tries to isolate itself behind a "mud curtain" because "sustained relations with the outside world have seldom been pleasant, for outsiders usually come to *extract* from, not bring anything *into* the village."

20. On the moral universe of the peasant, see Scott 1976. On the beginnings of breakdown of reciprocity, see Barfield 1981, which describes the effect of a rise in sheep prices on relations between shepherds and herd owners, and, especially, Anderson 1978. The latter article is frequently cited by defenders of the PDPA, who seem to have read only one page (171) of the article (see Male 1982). The article describes the effect of the introduction of tractors in the early 1970s on agriculture among the Ghilzai of Ghazni. Those wealthy enough to purchase or rent them could make a lot of money by plowing others' (and their own or unclaimed) *lalmi* (dry-farmed) land. One tribesman waiting at a bus stop with anthropologist Jon Anderson remarked that, as a result, "there are no khans anymore," pointing to a local landowner who preferred to invest his money in tractors and moneymaking rather than in feeding and helping his followers. However, the same tribesman went on to contrast that (bad, fake) khan with his own, genuine khan, who used his tractor to plow the fields of his followers without charge. Anderson concludes that the effects of the tractor would work themselves out through conflicts within the culture of reciprocity, rather than destroy it. The incident illustrates that villagers use the standards of reciprocity and hospitality to distinguish good and bad landowners, not to oppose them as a class.

21. Shahrani (1986b) and Kakar (1978) both argue that government corruption rather than exploitation by landlords was the major source of rural oppression in Afghanistan. Kakar (1978, 205) noted that Afghanistan was a relatively egalitarian society in which the landlord-peasant cleavage was not significant. "Revolts of peasants against landlords are exceptions to the rule. Revolts of both, often joined by religious leaders, against the state are the norm." In a later work (Kakar 1979, 123), published a year after the start of armed revolt against the Communists and three years before his own arrest in Kabul, he wrote, "Although such an action was clearly to their disadvantage, landless peasants, *hamsayas* [clients], and the socially disabled artisans have defended the status quo in critical times, if not with the same zeal as the small and large farmers, at least with enthusiasm. Instances are numerous in which, instigated by landowners, landless peasants have risen against the government, but there are none in which they have risen against the landlords." Perhaps such actions were not, in fact, clearly to the disadvantage of the poor groups; landlords may be oppressive, but the state may be more so.

22. See also Tabibi 1981, 64. "For the upper stratum [*Oberschicht*] in the village, but also for its dependents, the state is and was a foreign [*fremde*] power."

23. For a discussion of state formation in Afghanistan, see Rubin 1988.

24. One possible exception is that as part of his attempt to stimulate agricultural production, he sold off state land to cultivators. Soviet analysts (Gankovsky et al. 1985) claim that only merchants and richer landlords benefited from this measure.

25. Land and livestock tax amounted to 0.6 percent of GNP in 1952–53 and 0.08 percent of GNP in 1973–74, in an economy where "the agricultural sector is thought to contribute about 50 percent of the total value of Gross Domestic Product" (Fry 1974, 49).

26. A very interesting analysis of this period, from which I have greatly benefitted, is Ghani, n.d.

27. The only explicitly redistributive policy of the entire Musahiban period was the land reform measure introduced by President Daoud in 1975, which was relatively mild and was hardly implemented. See Tabibi 1981, 137–46, and Dupree 1977.

28. Fry (1974, 181–89) calculated Afghanistan's tax effort using the same method as the study of forty-nine countries in Bahl 1971. Tax effort is defined as the ratio of actual tax revenues to an estimated taxable capacity. The scores range from 1.63 (Ivory Coast) to 0.32 (Nepal), with a median of 0.995. Afghanistan scores 0.44. Iran ranked twenty-eighth out of fifty, with a tax effort of 0.97, and Pakistan ranked forty-third, with an effort of 0.72.

29. Chile was the highest with 9.6 percent. Iran and Pakistan shared the median score of 4.1 percent. The latter figure actually represented gross rather than net public-sector savings. Gross public-sector savings in Afghanistan were 0.96 percent, which is still less than the *net* savings of any other country in the study.

30. These decrees were published in English in the *Kabul Times*. The only publication of the complete texts in the West appears to be the Italian translation from the Pashto and Dari originals in Vercellin 1979, 99–132. The most detailed and careful analysis of their contents and implementation is in Tabibi 1981, 150–95. Critical analyses which formed my thinking on these matters were Roy 1980, Roy 1986, 84–97, and Shahrani 1984. An inside story on their failure is in Anwar 1988, 125–50. The most intelligent defense of the reforms (and the would-be reformers, especially Hafizullah Amin) is in Male 1982.

31. Tabibi (1981, 167) and Halliday (1980, 24) both claim that loans from bazaar merchants were not included, although, according to Tabibi, "the bazaar generally represented the most important source of indebtedness." Halliday also claims that moneylenders were not included, which appears to be a mistake. Male (1982, 123) calls Halliday's assertion "quite wrong." Tabibi (1981, 168) recounts conversations with peasants in his native province of Herat and around Kabul who were supposed to benefit from these provisions but found that their debts to the bazaar were not affected.

32. The traditional *jarib*, the unit of land area in Afghanistan, equaled 1,952 m^2 according to a Dari–Russian dictionary cited by Vercellin (1979, 131). Article 11 of Decree Number 8, however, defined a *jarib* as 2,000 m^2, which exactly equals one-fifth of a hectare. (A hectare is 100 meters squared, 10,000 m^2, or about 2.5 acres.) All conversions in the text and tables assume that 5 *jaribs* = 1 hectare. The land reform decree divided agricultural land into seven grades and assigned coefficients to each grade for conversion to first-grade equivalents. First-quality land was defined as "irrigated orchards or vineyards." The lowest quality land was nonirrigated land cultivated less than once every two years. The latter was assigned a coefficient of 0.10, so that ten jaribs of the lowest quality land is the equivalent of one jarib of first-quality land.

33. *Kabul Times,* 20 July 1978, cited by Male (1982, 110).

34. Of course, the Shariᶜah provisions on inheritance create a widespread problem of parcelation of the land in all Islamic countries. Under the decree, the heir who actually cultivated the land would become the owner, and the other heirs were to receive plots of one hectare from the government. This, like other provisions of the land reform, did not confront the reality that the supply of land is limited.

35. Tabibi (1981) summarizes the full chronology of government claims about the progress of the reform.

36. In a 1988 interview with Borovik, General Kim Tsagolov said that about a third of the land reform had been carried out, which may be interpreted to mean that a third of the land had been distributed. Borovik claims that a third of that land had been returned to the owners, leaving two-ninths of the original surplus in the hands of the beneficiaries. Of that, only half was being cultivated.

37. The relation of the insurrections to the introduction of the reforms, a subject discussed below in analyzing the causes of the PDPA's failure, has been taken up in Roy 1986, 98–109, Shahrani 1984, and Beattie 1984.

38. Reports from the resistance side unanimously claim this. In an interview, an exiled Afghan career civil servant, a former provincial governor who in 1980 and 1981 was the highest official responsible for municipalities in Afghanistan, stated that throughout this period the central government frequently lost both telephone and ground contact with provincial (not just district) centers and could not even transport the payroll to pay local government employees.

39. Land belonging to mosques, *madrasas,* and shrines was also exempted (Article 2).

40. Unlike the other three categories, military officers had some limitations on the use of the land they held above the ceiling. They could not sell or lease it, and their heirs could not inherit it unless they were also serving in the "professional cadre" of the armed forces.

41. Article 9 stated that the decree did not affect the right to land of small and landless peasants working on land exempted from expropriation under the decree.

42. Roy (1986, 23) distinguished "two possible options" for the Afghan state in dealing with the village community: "Either the community is made into an abstraction, and the state imposes order upon the patchwork of qawm, assisted by the fact that it alone is able to transcend tribal fragmentation (which has been the policy of the kings and the Soviet Union); or the village community is crushed, and the government deals directly with individuals with no group-consciousness (the policy of Amanullah, the Khalq, and perhaps the radical Islamists)."

43. This inducement was not particularly powerful, because Emir Abdul Rahman Khan and King Amanullah had nationalized most of the *awqaf* of Afghanistan, and because the ulama were not major landowners. This was a major difference from Iran, where the Shiᶜite hierocracy had an independent economic base.

44. For one example among many, see the speech by Prime Minister Keshtmand in FBIS VIII, 23 May 1983, C2–C3.

45. *Bakhtar,* 21 Mar. 1984, cited in *Afghanistan Forum* 12, no. 3 (1984): 33; *Bakhtar,* 21 Mar. 1986, cited in *Afghanistan Forum* 14, no. 3 (1986): 38. In 1983 the procurement price of cotton was raised by 60 percent and that of sugar beets by 40 percent (*Kabul New Times,* 28 Dec. 1983, cited in Gupta 1986, 124). They were raised again in September 1988. According to a mujahid from Baghlan Province interviewed in Peshawar in September 1984, the Soviet authorities in the base at Kilagai told the farmers in the area that they would not receive any irrigation water unless they produced cotton. He said that there was a tractor station in the area that rented tractors to cotton farmers. The mujahidin had commandeered one tractor until the farmer who had rented it pleaded that he would get in trouble with the Russians unless they returned it. The mujahidin pressured the farmers to plant rice rather than cotton. Rice fields were more difficult for Soviet tanks to drive over, and production of food crops made the peasantry more independent of the government and national market and enabled them to supply the mujahidin. The author received reports from Laghman and Kunduz provinces, as well, of peasants being pressured to produce cash crops by the government and subsistence crops by the resistance.

46. For instance, DRA 1982 gives figures that claim to be GNP at constant prices, but the figure for 1977–78 GNP in 1975–76 prices is virtually the same as the figure for 1977–78 GNP in 1979–80 prices, despite reported inflation of over 10 percent a year. There are many other such absurdities.

47. "Keshtmand Addresses Financial Seminar," *Bakhtar,* 12 Apr. 1983 (FBIS VIII, 12 Apr. 1983, C1–C4). According to *Afghanistan Forum* 11, no. 4 (1983), *Kabul New Times* of the

same date gave the figure for 1981–82 as Af 13 million.

48. For one example, see FBIS VIII, 21 Mar. 1986, C1.

49. For typical exhortations to "financial discipline," see Keshtmand's speeches in FBIS VIII, 21 Mar. 1983, C1, and again five years later, in *Bakhtar,* 16 Mar. 1988, cited in *Afghanistan Forum* 16, no. 3 (1988): 35. At times, the government stated that 50 percent of state domestic revenues came from government enterprises (*Bakhtar,* 1 Jan. 1986, cited in *Afghanistan Forum* 16, no. 2 [1986]: 3). The available data as well as other statements cited below make it clear that these revenues derive almost entirely from the export of natural gas to the USSR, which can be called "domestic revenue" only by a considerable stretching of the term.

50. In 1988, 97 percent of Afghanistan's foreign aid came from countries belonging to the Council for Mutual Economic Assistance (CMEA), with 81 percent from the USSR alone (*Bakhtar,* 16 Mar. 1988, cited in *Afghanistan Forum* 16, no. 3 [1988]: 35).

51. Afghanistan exported about 2.2 billion cubic meters of gas per year to the USSR in 1978–79, 1979–80, and 1980–81, for which it received $34.3 million, $97.6 million, and $253.8 million respectively (DRA 1981a, 66; DRA 1982, 62). In 1989 a former minister of mines stated that Afghanistan sold 2 billion cubic meters of gas per year to the Soviet Union, so the quantity remained unchanged (*Washington Post,* 24 Apr. 1988). The gas wells were capped for security reasons after the Soviet withdrawal. In 1991 there were reports that gas exports were set to resume.

52. Patrick Clawson pointed out at the seminar where this chapter was first presented that the price increase was a belated response to the increase in the world price of gas and had been under consideration before the Soviet intervention. According to M. S. Noorzoy (personal communication), after 1980 the foreign exchange earnings from natural gas were simply accounting figures used to offset the imports of weapons and the expenses of the Soviet military contingent in Afghanistan, for which Afghanistan was charged.

53. *Bakhtar,* 25 Jan. 1984, cited in *Afghanistan Forum* 12, no. 2 (1984): 37. In April 1988 an Afghan official claimed that sales of natural gas paid for "a quarter of [the Afghan government's] annual budget" (*Washington Post,* 24 Apr. 1988). No comprehensive budgetary figures were available to help evaluate this claim.

54. *Kabul New Times,* 10 Dec. 1983, cited in *Afghanistan Forum* 12, no. 3 (1984): 32; *Kabul New Times,* 12 Dec. 1983, cited in ibid., 33; *Bakhtar,* 14 Mar. 1984, cited in *Afghanistan Forum* 12, no. 3 (1984): 32; *Bakhtar,* 9 Aug. 1984, cited in *Afghanistan Forum* 12, no. 4 (1984): 34; *Bakhtar,* 2 June 1985, cited in *Afghanistan Forum* 13, no. 5 (1985): 33.

55. A woman living in Kabul who left the country temporarily to receive medical treatment in 1986 stated that those in her neighborhood who joined mass organizations such as the Committee for the Defense of the Revolution received special food coupons valid in government stores.

56. It reported an allocation of Af 46 million for this purpose in 1983–84 (*Bakhtar,* 10 Jan. 1984, cited in *Afghanistan Forum* 12, no. 2 (1984): 36).

57. The cost in 1984 was Af 1,218 million but the revenue was Af 900 million (*Bakhtar,* 17 June 1984, cited in *Afghanistan Forum* 12, no. 4 (1984): 33). If *Afghanistan Forum* quoted this article correctly, it also stated that electricity cost Af 7 per kwh but that consumers paid only Af 1. It would be more consistent with the previous figures if the cost were Af 1 per kwh and consumers paid Af 0.70.

58. These data are reported to the International Monetary Fund and published in *International Financial Statistics.*

59. These figures are continuous time-growth rates estimated through a semilog regression with dummy variables.

60. See Prokhanov 1983, a tractor novel set in Afghanistan.

61. Prokhanov concludes: "Given that fact, the presence of Soviet troops in the country loses its point. Their departure is inevitable and logical."

62. The major exceptions to this were tribal areas in which the land reform, in effect, allocated land from a major to a minor clan. In these cases, the reform actually strengthened the *qawm* (the minor clan), which generally became a government militia. This accorded with the tribal code *(pashtunwali)*, although it contradicted the Islamic respect for private property (Roy 1986, 92).

63. On the destruction wrought by the counterinsurgency strategy, see Laber and Rubin 1988.

64. In at least one area (Helmand) where mass cultivation of opium has enabled traditional leaders to accumulate cash and weapons, fragmentary evidence indicates that a kind of tribal warlord despotism has emerged.

6

The State and Social Equity in Postrevolutionary Iran

VAHID F. NOWSHIRVANI
AND
PATRICK CLAWSON

Income and wealth patterns in Iran have undergone several sharp changes since 1960. The early 1960s saw a land reform, as part of Mohammad Reza Shah's White Revolution, and a considerable expansion of industrial output. A transformation from a rural, agriculturally-oriented society to urban industrialism seemed to be underway. Then the oil boom began, at first in 1971 in a tentative way and then after 1973 in a spectacular fashion. Income levels rose sharply for many groups in society, but at the same time so did the disparities between the extraordinary income of the well-to-do and the modest living standard of the vast majority. The traditional elite saw its status decline and its wealth eclipsed by the modern industrial and commercial bourgeoisie. Farmers and unskilled laborers without a permanent post in the modern industries benefited much less from the boom; the considerable rise in costs eroded (or in some cases erased) the effect of higher income. Resentment over the income distribution pattern established during the boom was certainly an element in erosion of support for the imperial system in the late 1970s.

The first decade of the Islamic Republic, 1979–88, saw continuing economic upheaval. Per capita national income declined steeply. This was only partly the result of political turmoil and the policies of Islamic Republic. Several external factors, chief among them the drop in oil revenue end the war with Iraq, adversely affected the course of Iran's economy. The revolutionary movement did not have a clear and coherent economic program, but the regime gave high priority to redistributive measures. There was by no means a monolithic ideological basis for these policies, many of which remained highly controversial. Furthermore, the external shocks to the economy complicated the policymakers' task. Concern for equity influenced the government's macroeconomic responses to the shocks but the way the regime reconciled the competing demands for resources and its expenditure and taxation policies did not always improve the distribution of income.

The net impact of these policies on the income of various groups can be gleaned from the available statistics. The picture that emerges is one of mixed achievements. Some groups made significant gains, at least in relative terms, while the overall distribution of income within the rural areas became less equal. In the urban areas, part of the earlier movement toward equality was reversed by the mid 1980s. An examination of a number of redistributive measures reveals some of the reasons why the final impact of the complex chain of effects of these policies may have been quite different from that intended. We confine our analysis to the period under Ayatollah Khomeini. In the final section of the chapter, we describe briefly how some of the earlier developments were reversed by the policy changes that were instituted after his death in 1989.

The Ideological Setting and Controversies

The Islamic revival movement in Iran consisted of a broad coalition of socioeconomic groups without a unified interpretation of Islam. The ideological differences, which encompassed both economic and cultural issues, were not so divisive while the movement remained in opposition and while there was no need to translate the various underlying tenets into social and economic programs and specific policy measures. What masked the divergence of interests was the common moral outrage against the perceived corruption of the regime and the society under the Pahlavis. The various groups generally agreed on what constituted the blatant excesses of Pahlavi rule: the extremely unequal distribution of wealth and income, the growing gap between urban and rural living standards, the blind imitation of Western cultural norms and consumption patterns, and economic and political subservience to foreign powers. The role of Ayatollah Khomeini as the charismatic leader of the movement was also a unifying force. On the whole, he was influential in downgrading the economic dimension of the Islamic revolution and defining it primarily in cultural and moral terms.

The underlying principles of the envisioned Islamic economic order are set forth in the Constitution of the Islamic Republic of Iran, drafted and ratified while the structure of political power was still in a state of flux. According to the constitution, one of the means of achieving the objectives of Islamic government is "the planning of a correct and just economic system in accordance with Islamic criteria" (Article 3). The constitution stipulated that such a system in order to secure the economic independence of the country, uproot poverty, and satisfy "the needs of man in his process of growth and advancement" would be based on, among others, the following criteria set forth in Article 23:

> a. the provisions of basic necessities to all citizens: accommodation, food, clothing, health care medicine, education, and the necessary facilities for the establishment of a family;
> b. assuring conditions and possibilities of employment for everyone, with a view to attaining full employment; placing the means of labor at the disposal of everyone who is able to work but lacks the means, in the form of cooperatives; and granting interest-free loans or recourse to any other legitimate means that neither results in the concentration of wealth in the hands of a few individuals or its circulation among them nor turns the government into a major or dominant employer . . . ;
> c. preventing the exploitation of another's labor;
> d. forbidding the infliction of harm upon others, monopoly, hoarding, usury, and other evil and forbidden practices;
> e. the prohibition of extravagance and wastefulness in all matters related to the economy, including consumption, investment, production, distribution, and services.
> f. prevention of foreign economic domination over the country's economy;
> g. emphasis on the increase of agricultural, livestock, and industrial production in order to satisfy public needs and to make the country self-sufficient and independent.

Article 44 posits that "the economic system of the Islamic Republic of Iran is to consist of three sectors: state, cooperative, and private." Respect for legitimate private property is affirmed in Article 47, which also stipulates that the relevant criteria would be determined by law.

The different tendencies represented in the Assembly of Experts managed to include some of their own particular concerns. For example, the assertion that the exploitation of labor will not be permitted bears the mark of radical factions, whereas the proviso against the government turning into a dominant employer is a concession to libertarian tendencies. Some of the provisions, such as the ban against usury and hoarding and the injunction against extravagance and wastefulness, are commonly accepted Islamic principles about which there could be little disagreement. Otherwise, on economic issues, the Islamic Republic's constitution is not significantly different from the charters and constitutions of the Arab socialist states.

The constitution clearly affirms two of the basic goals of the revolution, namely, social justice and self-reliance, without giving a concrete definition of either; envisioned welfare statism as a basic component of social justice. These concerns have been integral to the religious discourse of activist Islam. Algar (1986, 17–35) has claimed that justice was the central theme of the ideological consensus that had emerged by the time of the revolution. Even if for the movement as a whole there was a "consensus" about the centrality of justice to the Islamic order, there was no agreement on what constituted social justice and how the application of Islamic tenets and injunctions would ensure distributive justice. Despite Ayatollah Khomeini's assurance that after the establishment of an Islamic government "the entire system of government and administration, together with the necessary laws," would be ready (Algar 1986, 40), legislating social justice has not turned out to be an easy task.

The principles of the constitution are couched in such general terms that there remains considerable latitude for varying interpretations. Indeed, the revolutionaries quickly found that the constitution had not resolved the controversial questions and that they remained divided on many issues. The main areas of contention have been the nature and limits of private property and the proper sphere of government intervention in the economy. There are, of course, also other dimensions to the conflict. For instance, since the cease-fire in the Iran-Iraq War, there has been a heated dispute about the extent to which Iran should rely on foreign resources for its postwar reconstruction. Although this debate touches on the issue of social justice—who should bear the burden of austerity measures—it really concerns the other rallying cry of the revolution, that is, the call for self-reliance. The controversy had not surfaced earlier because as long as Iran was at war, this was an academic question.

The tendency has been to divide the contending factions into two camps: (1) the radicals who advocate strict limits on private property and a large role for the state, supporting legislations on foreign trade nationalization, land reform, and urban real estate; (2) the conservatives who champion the cause of unfettered private enterprise and call for the repeal of most government controls and the return of expropriated assets. In reality the division is not bipolar; there is a whole spectrum of positions, which in the absence of political institutionalization has meant shifting coalitions that form over particular issues. Now a third faction, which Ashraf (Chapter 3) calls the pragmatist, has emerged. This new coalition is concerned with expediency and the survival of the regime, rather than doctrinal and ideological issues.

Although the ideological conflicts had clear socioeconomic roots, the controversies were cast in religious terms. Paving the way for their resolution has required doctrinal innovations that are still not acceptable to many of the ulama. The historical evolution of Shi ͨite jurisprudence *(fiqh)* had not provided it with a ready set of rulings and ordinances that could deal effectively with the social and economic problems that any contemporary government, particularly one concerned with revolutionary change, would face. Recognizing that this deficiency would hamper their attempts to restructure the society, the radical elements have emphasized the need for a dynamic and progressive jurisprudence that is more relevant to the basic goals of the revolution. The conservatives, the followers of traditional jurisprudence, have maintained that the existing rulings and general precepts can guide the formulation of policies and the enactment of social and economic legislation. This debate has not been merely scholastic but has reflected intense struggles in the political arena.

The accepted principles of the sanctity of private property and of freedom of contract have been used by the conservatives to block much redistributive legislation. The initiative for such legislation has come from the radical faction, which based its case on the Shi ͨite principle of overriding necessity for the survival of the system. According to this principle, in a situation of overriding necessity, secondary rulings could supersede and suspend the primary rulings of Shari ͨah. It was clear that the two factions could agree that in certain situations property rights could be restricted. Two problems remained, however. First, the conservatives argued that the suspension of primary rulings had to be limited in time and space. They reasoned, for instance, that the proposed nationalization of urban land to ease the housing shortage was not of overriding necessity in small towns. Second, it was unclear who could decide what constituted an overriding necessity (Bakhash 1984, 206–16; Ashraf, Chapter 3).

These difficulties and Ayatollah Khomeini's reluctance to rule personally on the overriding necessity for particular legislation caused long delays in resolving issues. The Council of Guardians repeatedly overruled bills it considered at variance with the primary rulings of Shariʿah. Many of the bills dealing with economic matters, such as the land reform bill, the foreign trade nationalization bill, and the labor law, were rejected and sent back to the parliament to be amended because they were said to infringe on the right of property and freedom of contract.

Late in 1987, after a series of questions of clarification addressed to Ayatollah Khomeini, edicts issued by him, and an exchange of letters, the controversy was apparently settled in favor of the radical faction. He first ruled that the government, by virtue of public services it provides, can impose conditions on private contracts to which it is not a party. Later he declared that government in the form of the God-given absolute mandate was "the most important of the divine commandments . . . [It is] one of the primary commandments of Islam and has priority over all derivative commandments" (translation provided in Arjomand 1989, 541). Thus, if it were in the best interest (maslahat) of the community, the Islamic government could suspend any primary rulings (Ashraf, Chapter 3).

Previously, a few Shiʿite jurists, notably Ayatollah Baqer Sadr, had come very close to this position, but the concept of best interest of the community was alien to the traditional Shiʿite jurisprudence. Sunni ulama, having been more closely connected with political authority, considered maslahat a source of Islamic legislation (Enayat 1982, chaps. 4 and 5). Its acceptance as a basis for Shiʿite jurisprudence was a major doctrinal innovation. In effect, the whole debate about primary and secondary rulings became irrelevant because government ordinances now had the authority of primary rulings of Shariʿah. A council, in which the executive branch was strongly represented, was appointed by Ayatollah Khomeini to determine the best interest of the community whenever the parliament and the Council of Guardians could not agree on an issue.

These developments did not merely settle some jurisprudential controversy but also signaled the emergence of the radical tendency as the dominant faction. Ayatollah Khomeini, as the charismatic leader of the movement, had for long tried to stay above the factionalism, but the change in his position was not as sudden as it appears. A number of economic, political, and international factors had strengthened the hand of the interventionists. Ayatollah Khomeini might at heart have

234 VAHID F. NOWSHIRVANI AND PATRICK CLAWSON

been inclined to support this group from the beginning, but he came out openly in favor of the side that had already won the contest—at least at that time. The setbacks at the war front and the humiliating manner in which the cease-fire was accepted weakened the radical tendency. The tide turned, not necessarily to the conservative faction, but away from the radicals. By the last year of Ayatollah Khomeini's life (1988–89), the thrust of the debate shifted from issues of redistribution to those of reconstruction and self-reliance. Of course, there were still constant warnings against the rise of dependent capitalism, against the division of the society between the haves and have-nots, and against those who had amassed fortunes during the war. But although the doctrinal obstacles to legislating redistributive measures were removed, there were few concrete proposals.

In addition to the lack of consensus on the issue of public versus private ownership, there have been many other dimensions to state redistributive policies. The fiscal role of the government, its expenditure and welfare program, its development strategies, and its regional and sectoral policies can have substantial distributive impact. In these areas there has been far less disagreement; the guiding principles have been a more equitable distribution of income and greater self-reliance. There have been few dramatic results, but one can point to a whole array of measures that were intended to promote equity. At times, however, certain policies, such as the foreign exchange policies and the industrialization programs, have worsened the distribution, though not intentionally.

Macroeconomic Context

At the time of the revolution, the widespread expectation in Iran was that the Islamic government could, through a more rational use of the country's considerable oil wealth, achieve a rather painless reallocation of resources to meet the urgent needs of society. The accepted view, quite justifiably, was that the Pahlavi regime had squandered the oil income on armaments, useless showcase projects, and luxury consumption. Indeed, the new government believed it could achieve its goals even with reduced dependence on oil, which was to be an essential component of the goal of self-reliance. Economic dislocations, an unavoidable cost of attaining economic independence, were expected to be short-term.

Reality turned out to be much less accommodating, forcing the regime to reconsider its early optimism and greatly limiting its ability to fulfill the promises of the revolution. Part of the explanation lies in the shortcomings of government policy, especially the failure to mobilize resources commensurate with needs. In addition, the war with Iraq had a demoralizing effect and a dreadful human cost. The war was not such a major *economic* drain, however, despite the government's emphasis on the importance of the war as an explanation for its economic difficulties. As analyzed below, military spending fell during the war because Iran was blocked from access to equipment from the major arms exporters. A large army of low-paid, low-skill soldiers was not a particularly heavy burden on the Iranian economy.

The most significant factor underlying the decline in income in Islamic Iran was the profound oil shock of the mid-1980s. Table 6.1 shows that oil receipts declined in two periods, 1980–81 and since 1984. The causes for the two periods of lower revenues were quite different. The decline in the early years of the Islamic Republic resulted from a combination of the initial disruption from the revolution and the war with Iraq, as well as the deliberate policy to limit the volume of exports because the new government initially felt that Iran did not need more revenue and that more-efficient use of oil receipts could allow it to achieve its goals with an income of $11 to $12 billion per annum. The government was able to sustain a relatively high level of domestic expenditure during 1980–81 by drawing down $6 billion of its foreign exchange reserves and by cutting spending on prestige imports, especially sophisticated arms and overly complex capital goods. As a result, personal income did not fall much, even though national output was down. The reserves that provided this cushion of security were, however, greatly depleted by the end of 1981, especially following the repayment of foreign loans under the Algiers Accord that settled the U.S. embassy hostage issue. In 1982 and 1983 Iran resumed exporting higher volumes, and oil income rose to the prerevolutionary level. It appeared that the crisis was over and that the revolution could now turn to its economic goals, including income redistribution. The mood was one of optimism, fed as well by the victories on the front that expelled Iraqi troops from nearly all Iranian soil. The initial disruptions from the revolution and the war seemed to have passed.

Then disaster struck: the world oil market weakened in 1984 and then collapsed in 1985–86. Iran felt the full brunt of the oil glut and consequent price collapse. Its oil receipts fell from $20.5 billion in 1983 to a mere $5.6 billion in 1986. The loss of oil revenues after 1984 was almost entirely independent of the actions of the government. World oil markets moved into structural surplus as energy conservation mea-

TABLE 6.1

Total and Per Capita Foreign Exchange Receipts from Oil Exports

Year	Total (billions of dollars)	Per Capita Dollars	Real Per Capita 1974 Dollars[a]
1972	2.46	83	131
1977	20.99	604	497
1978	18.11	502	365
1979	19.38	510	326
1980	11.85	299	171
1981	12.45	302	174
1982	20.05	468	280
1983	20.46	460	284
1984	16.66	361	228
1985	13.97	292	187
1986	5.98	121	69
1987	9.19	180	94
1988	7.60	144	70

Sources: Central Bank of the Islamic Republic of Iran, *Economic Report and Balance Sheet,* various years; International Monetary Fund, *World Economic Outlook,* various issues.

[a]Deflated by the index of import prices for oil-exporting developing countries (1974 = 100).

sures spread and more producers were attracted by the high prices of the early 1980s. It is hard to see how any Iranian government could have avoided the income loss that the Islamic Republic experienced. Indeed, the income drop in some of its Arab neighbors in the Gulf Corporation Council countries was as steep as in Iran, despite the very different orientation of the governments.

The bitter result for the revolution was that it had to operate in an environment of decline in foreign exchange resources. Distributing income losses is a much more difficult task than sharing a rising income. Many in the population blamed the government for the drop in their income, even though that drop was inevitable. Any evaluation of the population's reaction to the policies of the Islamic Republic must bear in mind the extremely unfavorable external environment with which it had to cope.

When oil revenues are adjusted for inflation in the prices of goods Iran imports and the growth in its population, the extent of the resource crisis becomes strikingly evident. In 1987, per capita real earnings from oil exports were about two-thirds the level of 1972, when oil was still well below three dollars per barrel. Furthermore, in the intervening fifteen years, Iran had become more dependent on oil income, as the other sectors of the economy had adapted to the high oil earnings of the boom years: consumption standards had risen, the increasingly urban population had become dependent on food imports, and economic activity had shifted to providing service to complement imports financed from oil revenues.

The decline in oil revenues was certainly a major element in the fall in per capita GDP. Between 1977 and 1988, real GDP fell 15 percent, while population rose 52 percent; the result was that 1988 per capita real GDP was just over one-half of its 1977 level (table 6.2). The effect of the loss of oil income was felt throughout the economy. Lower incomes meant a practically stagnant service-sector output. Owing in part to the shortage of imports, industrial (including construction) and mining output rose at an average rate of only 0.6 percent per year. On the other hand, agriculture is reported to have done quite well, growing in real terms at 3 percent per year in 1977–88. Because population was rising at 3.9 percent, agricultural output per capita actually fell. Overall, however, the real non-oil GDP rose only 12 percent over the period, which meant a 26 percent drop in per capita terms.

These data must be interpreted with considerable caution. The Islamic Republic has moved far from a pure market economy, and as a result, prices no longer fully reflect economic reality. In particular, the wide gap between the official foreign exchange rate and the various parallel market rates (some legal, some tolerated but illegal) distorts all economic statistics. It would be inappropriate to use the parallel rate as the "true" rate, because the parallel rate moved in response to government pressure to stop arbitrage between the markets. The following simple example illustrates the extent of the distortion. At the official exchange rate, Iran's per capita income in 1988 would have been more than $6,000, whereas at the parallel rate, its per capita income would have been about $500. Neither number is credible, but it is hard to tell exactly where the truth lies between two such different numbers. The effect of the low exchange rate used in the official date is to distort the importance of the different economic sectors. The oil exports were re-

TABLE 6.2

Macroeconomic Data

(in thousands of rials, 1974 prices)

Per Capita	1972	1977	1980	1983	1986	1988[a]
GDP	84.8	100.4	61.2	71.2	61.7	56.4
Non-oil GDP	40.8	63.9	54.7	58.9	53.5	47.1
Consumption	29.1	42.7	36.8	43.9	39.2	34.6
Public consumption	12.0	23.3	14.7	13.5	9.6	8.3
Investment	13.6	31.0	14.6	18.2	10.3	6.8

Sources: Central Bank of the Islamic Republic of Iran 1991; Iran, Ministry of Planning and Budgets, *Annual Economic Report,* various years.

[a]Calculated from 1987 figures and the 1987–88 growth rates using data in 1982 prices.

corded at the low official exchange rate, which understated their importance for the economy. Correspondingly, the revenue that the government earned from oil was converted at the low official exchange rate, which understated the resources that the government had at its command.

Various other shortcomings in economic data flow mostly from the same cause, namely, the replacement of market relations with extensive government regulation. The growing informal economy, spurred by the mushrooming of such regulation, was not covered fully in the official data. The statistics on prices appear to be more or less a blend of the small changes in official prices with the much larger changes in free market prices; in effect, each consumer faced a different price change, depending on how much he or she relied on the free market. The volunteer military personnel did not show up in the government budget; because they were missing from the national income accounts, those accounts understate government consumption and value added in government services. Such distortions have rendered the data on national income in real (price-adjusted) terms and on the distribution of output among sectors particularly questionable.

Because the Islamic regime chose to, or had to, rely on the country's own resources, the various items of national expenditure had to absorb the fall in the GDP. In other words, there was no repetition of the experience of 1980–81 in which foreign resources (in that case, foreign reserves) were used to cushion consumption from the effects of the drop in production. Private consumption, a politically sensitive item, did not decline proportionately as much as the other components of expenditure. Nevertheless, on a per capita basis, private consumption in 1988 was only 80 percent of its prerevolution peak and a mere 19 percent above the 1972 level. Owing to the more equal distribution of income, however, the top 20 percent of the households bore much of the brunt of the decline in real private consumption.

The burden of adjustment fell largely on public consumption and gross investment. The decline in these items from their peaks in 1977 to 1980 was not surprising, insofar as it reflected cutbacks in the extravagant programs of the previous regime. Their continued reductions throughout the 1980s, however, were a matter of serious concern. The shortage of foreign exchange and the need to maintain food and military imports resulted in strict limits on imports of capital goods. Manufacturing firms postponed replacing their worn-out equipment. The government cut back development spending to minimal levels, despite periodic announcements of plans for new facilities. Per capita investment in 1988 was at less than two-thirds of the 1972 level. If the investment necessary for future growth is being kept so low, the likely result will be continuing stagnation or declines in per capita income. A prolonged period of declining per capita income could have grave implications for the future of Iran's poor.

The Changing Pattern of Government Expenditure

The changes that occurred in government expenditure were the result of a number of factors. First was a deliberate decision to abandon the profligate programs of the previous regime. The oil wealth was to be conserved for future generations. The constituency to which these programs catered had been eliminated; therefore the cutbacks encountered no political opposition. Presumably, some of the funds would later have been applied to projects more in keeping with the priorities of the regime. Second, the fall in the availability of resources would have required some adjustments even if the government had been willing to rely on outside sources of finance. Even the conservative governments of the oil-producing countries adjusted to the new realities. Third, the war with Iraq substantially altered the demand on government finances. Last, the state failed to mobilize the necessary resources, and the adjustment process involved substantial cutbacks in total government spending and large changes in the relative shares of the various categories of state expenditure.

Every category of government spending declined in real terms, although in current prices, nonmilitary expenditure as a percentage of current government spending did not fall drastically compared to the prerevolution levels (from 64 percent in 1977 to 55 percent in 1988). It may appear that the war did not have a major impact on reducing the share of other current government services, but because of the exchange rate problems, this conclusion is not warranted. Military expenditure was considerably more import-intensive than the rest of current government spending, which consisted primarily of salaries.

In a comparison of development expenditure to military spending, the distortions are much less. The relative fall in development outlays is startling. From 165 percent in 1977, which was the peak year of military expenditure before the revolution, the ratio dropped to less than 50 percent in 1988. Obviously, it was easier in the short run to cancel development projects than to fire government employees. The long-run implications of failing to invest in productive capacity and social infrastructure already proved to be quite serious by 1989.

The Cost of the War

A number of authors have already written on various aspects of the cost of the Iran-Iraq War (e.g., Clawson [1988] and Amirahmadi [1988]). Patrick Clawson has suggested that although the real current cost of the war was lower than the level of military expenditure under the shah's regime, the war might have absorbed as much as 18 percent of the GDP in 1986 (owing to the kind of exchange rate distortions we have discussed here).

The budgetary allocations for the war are reported in table 6.3. Even though the nominal allocations show an increase during the 1977–88 period, when properly deflated they would show a fall in real terms. The resource costs, however, are not properly reflected in the budgetary figures. Apart from the regular members of the army and the Revolutionary Guards, the war was fought primarily by conscripted soldiers and the volunteer (baseej) forces that received no payment. The impression that most of the volunteers were unemployed young people is not accurate. Many of the volunteers were employed and continued to receive their wages from their employers, both private and public, as long as they served on the front. In fact, in many instances they were paid at the overtime rate. In 1985, in order to attract

TABLE 6.3

Military and Other Costs Associated with the Iran-Iraq War
(in billions of rials)

	1972	1977	1979	1981	1983	1986	1988
Special allocation for the war	—	—	—	381.0	503.0	433.3	858.9
Reconstruction of war-damaged areas	—	—	—	0.0	91.1	26.4	102.0
Shahid Foundation	—	—	—	10.5	40.0	57.3	110.0
Foundation for War Refugees	—	—	—	0.0	40.0	44.5	48.0
Recurrent defense, army, and Revolutionary Guards	90.0	558.8	312.6	371.2	430.1	470.2	515.8
Total expenditures for military and war-related items	90.0	558.8	312.6	762.7	1,104.2	1,031.7	1,634.7
Total military expenditures as % of total government expenditures	21.9	22.4	15.2	28.2	30.1	32.6	38.8

Source: Majlis-e Shura-ye Islami, Annual budget bills, various years; Central Bank of the Islamic Republic of Iran, *Economic Report and Balance Sheet,* various years.

more volunteers, the government decreed that workers would receive a 5 percent raise for every six months of service. A company with 3000 employees, 541 of whom had been to the front over a period of six and one-half years, reported that the financial cost of this government decree was R 74 million in 1987.[1] Assuming this factory is typical of the large industrial firms, the total cost in that year to these firms alone could have been about R 10 billion. The minister of education announced in 1988 that one-fifth of the male teachers of the country had served on the front.

Another source of finance for the war was the "voluntary" contributions of cash and provisions. These went far beyond the symbolic gifts of jewelry by women. A systematic network for their collection existed. Naturally, it is difficult to make even a rough estimate of their magnitude. They ranged from a day's salary donated by a government employee to multimillion-rial gifts of wealthy guild members. A few examples would give an idea of the extent of such contributions. The Foundation for the Oppressed announced that it had donated R 10 billion over a three-year period. In 1982 the Jihad for Reconstruction collected nearly R 2 billion in addition to recruiting nearly ninety thousand volunteers. The Ministry of Education claims to have contributed nearly R 100 billion over the course of the war.

The various trade associations and procurement and distribution cooperatives *(ta 'avoniha-ye tahiyyeh va tozi ')* provided one of the most systematic sources of contributions. They elicited wide participation because they conferred significant economic benefits. The state dispensed its favors in the form of goods in short supply to be distributed among guild members. In return, guild officials were expected to persuade their members to contribute to the war effort and mobilize political support. The executive board of the Cooperative of Service Stations in Teheran stated in 1988 that they had donated R 180 million for the front. There are thousands of such cooperatives in the country. In 1987, when at the height of the fiscal crunch Ayatollah Khomeini made a symbolic gift of R 10 million to cover the cost of maintaining twenty fighting men on the front for three months, every guild and cooperative called on its members to increase their contributions. An unofficial tax system was put in place.

The state certainly extracted resources through such contributions, but they were minor compared to the government's own allocations for the war and the mobilization of manpower for the front. The war, of course, had no distributive objectives, but it had both short- and long-term consequences for such issues. It is unlikely that the state can duplicate this level of resource mobilization for redistributive ends.

One of the first acts of the Islamic regime was to cut the shah's military budget by nearly one-half. The savings from this reduction would have been ample to fulfill many of the promises of the revolution. The war destroyed this hope while it was being fought, and by changing the priorities of the regime, it raised the level of military expenditures even after the cease-fire. There were rumors in Teheran after the cease-fire that the foreign exchange allocation for defense would be raised. Iran did not spend more on the war, because no country would provide it with the expensive high technology equipment, such as fighter planes, it wanted. After the cease-fire there were more willing suppliers.

The war continues to be expensive even after demobilization, not only because of reconstruction costs but also because of the needs of the veterans. When Ayatollah Khomeini announced the guidelines for the postwar reconstruction, the first principle was to give the veterans and the families of martyrs priority in "all social, economic and cultural privileges" (*Kayhan*, 14 Oct. 1988). The government set up an office to coordinate the employment of veterans in the public sector. There were also demands to admit them to universities without the competitive entrance examination.

Taxation and Resource Extraction

The nominal value of taxes collected by the government more than doubled in the first decade after the revolution, and the share of taxes in total state revenue rose from one-fifth in 1977 to an average of about one-half for 1985–87 (table 6.4). In a period of high inflation, the rise in nominal tax receipts was hardly surprising. The apparent growing reliance on taxes was largely owing to the fall in oil revenues rather than to greater tax effort. The artificially low foreign exchange rate at which oil income was converted simply raises the share of taxes. A better measure of the tax effort of the government is the ratio of taxes collected to the non-oil GDP. This ratio showed a marked decline after the revolution, dropping to about 60 percent of its prerevolution level. Clearly, the government has failed in mobilizing resources through taxation. Neither did it succeed in raising the share of its revenues from quasi-tax sources, such as government monopolies and the sale of goods and services. In the last category the increase after 1984 was primarily owing to the sale of gold and foreign exchange at rates above the official rate. For example, in 1984 the income from this item alone amounted to R 121 billion (Central Bank 1984, 83). Obviously, this source of revenue was dependent on the availability of foreign exchange from oil exports. Indeed, because of the decline in foreign exchange earnings, the government did not achieve the budgeted revenue from this source in 1985–88 (Iran 1988, 10).

The lack of political cohesion within the ruling elite and the low level of the administrative capacity of the government were the most obvious of many reasons for the failure of the state to increase its non-oil revenues. The reluctance, owing to equity considerations, to increase indirect taxes limited the government's options. The proliferation of controls pushed many economic transactions into the

TABLE 6.4

Government Revenues

(in billions of rials)

Source	1972	1977	1980	1983	1986	1988
Government revenue	302.1	2,126.7	1,348.7	2,600.2	1,781.8	2,098.9
Oil revenue	178.2	1,590.3	888.8	1,585.3	416.8	667.9
Oil revenue as % of government revenue	59.0	74.8	65.9	61.0	23.4	31.8
Tax revenue	99.4	442.8	340.4	796.5	1,024.5	986.5
Direct taxes	39.2	230.8	129.2	331.9	579.8	645.9
Indirect taxes	60.2	212.5	211.2	464.6	444.7	340.6
Tax revenue as % of non-oil GDP	10.7	11.0	5.9	6.8	6.6	4.4
Government monopolies, and sale of goods and services	14.8	54.9	29.3	116.3	168.6	342.6
Budget deficit	113.2	365.5	903.1	1,072.1	1,374.9	2,111.7

Source: Iran, Ministry of Planning and Budget, *Annual Economic Report,* various years.

informal and black economy where they were impossible to monitor and tax. The monetization of budget deficits eroded the value of taxes through inflation. This effect was specially relevant for corporate and business taxes, which were always collected with a lag. But inflation also reduced the real value of indirect taxes to the extent that they were specific, that is, fixed in rials rather than as a percentage of value. Even the real value of tariff revenues fell, as imports were paid for with increasingly overvalued exchange rates.

The relative proportion of direct and indirect tax receipts shifted after 1984 in favor of direct taxes, which by 1988 constituted about 65 percent of the total tax revenue. This movement would in many countries indicate that the tax structure was becoming more progressive, although such was not necessarily the case in the Iranian context. Nearly two-thirds of the direct taxes collected were on corporate profits. But about three-quarters of corporate taxes were paid by state enterprises and other public-sector corporations, including those owned by the various foundations. In effect, every person paid a tax on his or her equal share of public income, which was equivalent to a poll tax that was variable over time.

The least-taxed sector of the economy was that comprising unincorporated businesses, the professions, and shopkeepers (*kasabeh*). Taxes from this group, still about 14 percent of all direct taxes, increased rapidly after 1984. By 1987, they accounted for nearly one-half of the revenue from the income tax and for the first time exceeded the taxes on salaries and wages. To increase the collection of taxes from this group, the government, after 1987, allowed any contributions to local development projects to be credited to taxes owed.

As we have indicated, the overall extractive function of taxes was minimal after the revolution, and their distributive impact was questionable. An examination of the tax legislation enacted since the revolution reveals that the policymakers always had progressive aims, raising taxes on luxury consumption and high incomes and lowering them on moderate incomes. But what looked good on paper was not necessarily realistic and effective in practice.

Soon after the revolution, the tax schedule for salaries was changed to raise the minimum exemption level and increase the marginal rate on higher brackets. At this stage the top rate was raised from 30 percent to 38 percent. About a year later an extremely steep schedule was introduced raising the top marginal rate to 90 percent. The rates on lower incomes were reduced on several occasions to counter bracket-creep but also for redistributive reasons. The government legislated the same kind of schedule change for inheritance taxes, increasing the top marginal rate from 40 percent to 90 percent, applicable to estates above R 20 million. The net impact of these reforms on resource extraction was inconsequential, and therefore their redistributive effects were also limited, though certainly progressive.

A major revision of the direct tax law was enacted in 1987, introducing for the first time a current wealth tax, one that was not collected only at points of transfer (asset sales and inheritance). This tax was primarily applicable to real estate not used by owners as their place of primary residence. The top rate was quite steep, being 8 percent of the value above R 100 million. The new bill also lowered some of the irrelevantly high marginal rates on income (from 90 percent to 70 percent) in order to reduce tax evasion. It is significant that the Council of Guardians chose not to express its opinion on whether the bill was in accordance with the ordinances of Islam, thus avoiding the need to put the

TABLE 6.5

Fiscal Operations as Percentage of GDP

	1972	1977	1980	1983	1986	1988
Expenditure	34.9	48.3	34.8	28.4	20.3	18.3
Revenue	25.4	41.3	20.8	20.1	11.4	9.1
Deficit	9.5	7.1	14.0	8.3	8.9	9.2

Sources: Iran, Ministry of Planning and Budget, Annual Economic Report, various years; Central Bank of the Islamic Republic of Iran 1991.

issue to the Council for Determining the Best Interest of the Community. So the bill became law without an explicit endorsement of the ulama.

The parliament passed a bill in 1988 imposing a one-time wealth tax to generate revenue earmarked for the reconstruction of war-damaged areas. This tax, which had a steep marginal rate of 40 percent, was levied mainly on real estate assets in excess of R 100 million. Apparently, only R 15 billion was collected in 1988–89 instead of the budgeted R 245 billion. The budget for 1990–91 forecast revenue of R 100 billion from this source but merely R 12 billion was collected.

The Inflation Tax

The government budget consistently showed a deficit that, as a ratio of the GDP, fluctuated over the period, registering higher values in those years when oil revenue was low. The state largely covered the deficit through a variety of means including drawing down on its foreign assets. The main source for financing the deficit, however, increasingly became borrowing from the central bank. In effect, the government imposed an inflation tax that in many years exceeded the proper tax receipts of the state (see tables 6.4, 6.5). The redistributive consequences of the inflation tax could hardly be progressive, although the government tried to redress, through controls on prices and distribution channels, some of the most blatant inequities. The burden fell mainly on salaried employees, especially in the private sector. Government employees who mockingly call themselves the new *mostas' alin* (the desperate) also experienced a marked decline in their living standards.

The state used inflation to extract resources from the society at large, but the inflationary process had distributional implications from which the state drew no benefit. Indeed, inflation was one of the causes of the emergence of a new group of well-to-do, who opposed the redistributive measures of the regime. The Islamic government was perhaps unique among modern revolutionary regimes for its reliance on inflation as a mechanism for reconciling competing demands on resources. The regime showed a puzzling combination of the attributes of both "soft" and "hard" states.

The Statistics of Inequality and Redistribution

The most systematic long-term series that allows an examination of the changes that occurred in income distribution after the revolution is the household expenditure surveys conducted by the Statistical Center of Iran. Some simple measures of inequality calculated from the findings of these surveys are presented in tables 6.6 and 6.7. The pattern that emerges indicates on the whole that income disparities narrowed during the revolutionary period, although there are also some instances of worsening distribution since then. These improvements contrast favorably with the deteriorating trends that were evident before the revolution. The most dramatic reduction in inequality occurred in the urban areas immediately after the revolution. There was a partial reversal in 1982, but the disparities appear to have stabilized thereafter. The bottom 40 percent of the households experienced such a proportionate increase in their share of total expenditure that despite falling average expenditure, their expenditure was higher than before the revolution. The top 20 percent of the households bore the brunt of the decline in consumption.

In the rural areas, there was a worsening of income distributions in 1979 that was more than reversed by 1982. The rural disparities then widened until the mid-1980s, with the bottom 40 percent of the households losing out to the top 20 percent. By 1986, rural income distribution was slightly worse than in 1977 and significantly more unequal than in 1972. The extent of inequality within rural areas in 1985 was comparable to that in the urban centers.

The reported data for the postrevolution period probably exaggerate the degree of inequality, especially in the more recent years. The figures were obtained from household expenditure surveys during a period of rampant inflation, but basic goods, which compromise a large share of the family budget of the lower strata, were provided by the

TABLE 6.6

Measures of Inequality of Urban Household Consumption
Expenditures: Percent Share in Total Expenditure

Year	Bottom 40%	Middle 40%	Top 20%	Gini Coefficient
1972	16.7	36.2	47.1	0.4032
1977	11.7	32.8	55.5	0.4998
1979	12.7	35.8	51.5	0.4702
1980	15.2	39.9	45.0	0.4040
1982	14.5	38.8	46.8	0.4168
1983	13.9	39.3	46.8	0.4282
1984	14.7	38.4	46.9	0.4205
1985	14.4	38.1	47.4	0.4215
1986	14.6	37.5	48.0	0.4193

Sources: Behdad 1989; Statistical Center of Iran, *Urban Household Expenditure and Income Survey,* various years.

TABLE 6.7

Measures of Inequality of Rural Households' Consumption
Expenditures: Percent Share in Total Expenditure

Year	Bottom 40%	Middle 40%	Top 20%	Gini Coefficient
1972	18.4	38.0	43.6	0.3659
1977	14.7	35.4	49.8	0.4375
1979	13.9	32.3	53.8	0.4789
1982	15.8	38.9	45.4	0.4051
1983	14.8	38.5	46.7	0.4161
1984	14.4	37.6	48.0	0.4293
1985	14.6	38.5	46.8	0.4194
1986	13.3	37.6	49.1	0.4472

Sources: Behdad 1989; Statistical Center of Iran, *Urban Household Expenditure and Income Survey,* various years.

government through rationing or other controlled distribution channels. Thus, the distribution of real consumption was likely more equal
than the distribution of nominal expenditures. This conclusion is borne
out by the fact that despite the generally falling level of per capita
consumption, the ratio of food to nonfood expenditures fell in most
years after the revolution.

Evidence from the annual household expenditure surveys also provides data on how various social groups (according to criteria other
than expenditure) changed their relative position. Table 6.8 shows the
distribution of urban households, according to the occupational status
of the head of household, among the three expenditure groups. Five
employment categories are given in the data. First are employers, who
suffered a decline in their relative position after the revolution but by
1985 were more likely to be in the top 20 percent of households than
before the revolution. It must be noted, however, that household surveys do not cover the extreme tails of the distribution, so data are
lacking on the impact of the expropriations of assets of top businessmen and on the wealth accumulated by those who made their fortunes
after the revolution. Second are independent workers, who include the
liberal professions, artisans, many merchants, and the informal sector
in general. Because of the heterogeneity of this category, its distribution
among the three expenditure groups has always been close to the overall sample distribution. With the share of independent workers in the
sample households growing from 22.7 percent in 1977 to 28.3 percent in
1985, it is not surprising that the distribution within this category in
1985 resembles the overall distribution even more closely. On the
whole, those in this group had a slighly better chance of being in the
top 20 percent of households in 1985 than before the revolution.

The third and fourth categories are public-sector and private-sector
employees, respectively. It is hard to interpret the data for these categories, because not much is known about the impact of the state takeover
of industrial enterprises, which probably accounts for most of the shift
from private to public employment. Public-sector employees are on the
whole among the better-off segments of the urban population. Even
with a 37.5 percent increase in their share of the sample households,
still 75 percent of them remained in the top 60 percent of the households. There was, however, a tendency toward equality within this
category, with greater concentration in the middle 40 percent of the
households. The private-sector employees appear to have suffered, in
contrast to owners of private businesses. A possible explanation is that
the state takeover of many of the larger private enterprises left the

TABLE 6.8

Distribution of Urban Households Among Different Expenditure Groups by Occupation of Head of Household, 1977, 1980, and 1985

(in percentage)

| | Share in Sample Households | | | Expenditure Rank | | | | | | | | |
| | | | | Lowest 40% | | | Middle 40% | | | Top 20% | | |
	1977	1980	1985	1977	1980	1985	1977	1980	1985	1977	1980	1985
Employers	5.3	4.4	5.2	17.4	20.0	16.6	42.7	44.1	38.4	39.9	35.9	44.9
Independent workers	22.7	26.4	28.3	39.7	40.4	40.0	43.0	42.2	41.8	17.4	17.4	18.2
Government employees	21.3	23.7	29.3	25.5	24.9	25.3	44.9	47.5	46.9	29.5	27.6	27.8
Private sector employees	34.2	26.2	18.2	49.1	51.0	52.4	37.7	36.5	37.4	13.1	12.5	10.2
Unemployed	16.4	19.3	19.0	47.7	47.5	56.4	33.4	31.7	29.5	19.0	20.8	14.0

Source: Behdad 1989; Statistical Center of Iran, *Urban Household Expenditure and Income Survey,* various years.

sector with the smaller establishments that had proportionately fewer better-paid office and skilled workers. The fifth and final category comprises those not employed, which may include retired household heads as well as unemployed. Unemployment was clearly becoming a prime cause of poverty, and with the rise in the unemployment rate, the jobless were without work for longer periods. As their savings dwindled, they were forced to cut back their expenditures.

The change in the relevance of education to income status is rather striking. The figures in table 6.9 show that there was a systematic delinking of educational attainment and income. This effect is more pronounced the higher the level of education. In the Islamic Republic the illiterate had a better chance of being in the top fifth of the distribution, and the more educated had a greater likelihood of being in the bottom 40 percent. For heads of households with high school diplomas, part of this shift may be explained by the increase in their number in the sample. The figures for university graduates reflect the dramatic loss of the social and economic status of the modern middle class. Despite their declining share in the sample, from 3.7 percent in 1977 to 3.1 percent in 1985, they were nearly six times more likely than they were before the revolution to be in the bottom 40 percent. Although the rest of the sample was more educated, the falling share of this group is itself an indication of their deteriorating situation. Many chose to migrate. It is clear that the exodus of this class was for economic as well as sociocultural reasons. Of course, not every member of this group suffered economic hardship: the dwindling number of doctors that remained in Iran did well.

Another dimension of inequality that changed after the revolution was the urban-rural disparity. This gap, which had been widening until the revolution, narrowed appreciably. Table 6.10 shows the ratio of the average rural household expenditure to that of urban households. The relative position of rural households improved sharply. If the nominal ratios are adjusted for the differential rates of inflation (data for which are available only since 1982), the improvement becomes more pronounced. The rise in rural living standards is not only in relative terms, which could have been owing to the fall in average urban consumption; other measures indicate that the proportion of rural households that own modern consumer durables and have access to electricity and piped water has been growing steadily (see table 6.11).

The rise in rural income disparities becomes less puzzling in the context of growing average incomes. The rural areas were becoming increasingly integrated into the national economy. This process would

TABLE 6.9

Distribution of Urban Households Among Different Expenditure Groups by Educational Level of Head of Household, 1977, 1980, and 1985

(in percentage)

	Share in Sample Households			Expenditure Rank Lowest 40%			Middle 40%			Top 20%		
	1977	1980	1985	1977	1980	1985	1977	1980	1985	1977	1980	1985
Illiterate	45.9	43.6	42.5	55.3	55.4	54.3	35.0	33.6	34.9	9.7	11.0	10.7
Literate no high school diploma	41.1	41.6	40.8	30.9	32.2	33.1	47.1	45.6	44.8	22.0	22.2	22.1
High school diploma	7.9	10.6	13.5	16.1	18.4	22.5	42.8	45.8	43.2	41.0	35.9	34.3
University graduate	3.7	3.2	3.1	2.0	5.3	11.6	19.6	35.0	30.7	78.4	59.7	57.7

Sources: Behdad 1989; Statistical Center of Iran, *Urban Household Expenditure and Income Survey*, various years.

TABLE 6.10

**Average Rural Household Expenditure as Percentage
of Average Urban Household Expenditure**

	1977	1979	1982	1983	1984	1985	1986	1987	1988
Rural household expenditure as % of urban household expenditure	47	55	57	55	54	53	58	61	59
Adjusted for differential inflation rate	—	—	57	57	58	57	66	70	71

Source: Statistical Center of Iran, *Iran Statistical Yearbook*, various years.

TABLE 6.11

Rural Living Standards
(in percentage)

	1979	1983	1986	1988
Households with				
Refrigerators	14.5	32.0	44.1	48.0
Television	8.1	21.6	31.1	37.5
Piped water	19.9	42.4	50.1	56.6
Electricity	27.7	51.8	64.5	68.5

Source: Statistical Center of Iran, *Rural Household Expenditure and Income Survey*, various years.

have occurred naturally, but the "rural bias" of the regime accelerated it. The concern with achieving food security favored the rural areas, and as a result, the agricultural sector has fared relatively well. While the other sectors of the economy experienced cutbacks in development funds, credit, and imported input, the government tried to increase the flow of resources to agriculture. Although the overvalued currency may have had detrimental effects for some agricultural products, it was also used to subsidize agriculture through the increased provision of imported inputs to the sector, mainly fertilizer and machinery. On the whole, the sector's terms of trade improved. In this context it is not surprising that those farmers with more land would be the main beneificiaries. But these were no longer the huge agro-businesses of the Pahlavi period (Karimi 1986; and for a less favorable view, see Mojtahed and Esfahani 1989).

The increasing inequalities within the rural areas were not simply the result of the agricultural policies of the government. The rural economy became less homogeneous, and an increasingly diversified employment structure emerged. The number of service-sector workers rose from less than 10 percent of the rural work force in 1976 to 20 percent in 1986. The bulk of this increase came from the growth of government services, primarily teachers, administrators, and development officers. The ratio of public-sector employees to total rural employment grew from less than 6 percent to 17 percent over the period. The revolutionary state has certainly established itself in the villages. Because government employees would be relatively high on the rural income scale, the widening rural disparities may partly be owing to the expansion of public-sector employment.

State Policies and Redistribution

Practically every government policy had as its stated purpose the fulfillment of the goals of social justice and economic independence, although in practice these objectives were not always compatible. It is true that state policies had profound impact on the redistribution of income and wealth in the society. Some of this redistribution narrowed income disparities, but in other instances new privileged groups have replaced the old. On the whole, the redistributive consequences of the state's fiscal role were limited. More often they were effected through government legislation and the extension of administrative regulations and controls. It was not always possible to enact the necessary legislation, but the executive branch through bureaucratic mechanisms often achieved many of its desired objectives.

The Expansion of Public Ownership

Much of the debate about social justice has revolved around the issue of public versus private ownership. Even without a final resolution of this debate, public ownership in the country expanded dramatically. Much of this expansion came soon after the revolution and involved assets that were allegedly acquired illegitimately. The story of the early confiscations, nationalizations, and public takeover of the management of private businesses in a wide variety of fields has already been told in rich detail elsewhere (Bakhash 1984, 175–94). We need only to recount the highlights here. Within six months of the establishment of the provisional government, the legislation for the state takeover of a major segment of the large-scale private sector was already in place. This included laws for the nationalization of the banks and insurance companies, for the appointment of managers, and for the protection and expansion of industry. Concurrently, revolutionary courts, organizations, and committees carried out their own expropriation and seizures, mainly outside the framework of these laws and often without any authorization in law. With the exception of some agricultural land and many residential buildings that people took over for their own use, the sequestered properties eventually came under the control of the government or parastatal organizations such as the Foundation for the Oppressed (Bonyad-e Mostazafan) and the Martyr Foundation (Bonyad-e Shahid). It is impossible to provide a complete list of state takeovers, but their extent was clearly vast. The banking and insurance sector, in which the state already had a large presence before the revolution, was entirely nationalized. In the manufacturing sector, the state attained a nearly total control of the larger companies. By 1984, about one thousand public owned and managed industrial units (excluding those in the oil sector) employed 430,000 of the 530,000 workers in establishments with ten or more employees and produced 73.5 percent of the value added. In that year, 90 percent of the manufacturing firms employing over five hundred workers were in government hands.

The extension of public control was not confined to the financial and manufacturing sectors, many companies in other sectors, such as agriculture, trucking, construction, engineering consulting, real estate, warehousing, and commerce were also taken over. A 1982 list of the holdings of the Foundation for the Oppressed included 149 manufacturing plants, 64 mines, 60 agricultural companies, 412 orchards, 101 construction and real estate development firms, 25 cultural establishments (cinemas and amusement parks), 238 trading companies, and 2,786 buildings (Central Bank, n.d., 270).

The expansion of state ownership in postrevolutionary Iran has had several features of particular relevance to the redistributive role of the state. First, the extent and speed of the takeovers paradoxically reflect both the breakdown of state power after the fall of the shah and the still considerable financial autonomy of the government based on its continued control over the huge oil revenues. For example, the appointment of government overseers to troubled firms was not always prompted solely by the flight of previous owners and managers. Worker militancy, often instigated by leftist and radical Islamic groups, was equally responsible for the financial and management crises that many companies faced. The breakdown of the normal functioning of the bureaucracy, particularly by delaying payments, was another cause of financial insolvency. Local revolutionary organizations, more responsive to local demands and in many instances penetrated by different political factions, were inclined to seize property even without a legal basis. The simplest way for the government to reassert its authority was to sanction these takeovers and control them through the power of the purse. Furthermore, the desire to prevent the establishment of a base by the leftist groups, rather than the threat from the economic power of a privileged group, moved the government to take immediate action. So to some extent the expansion of state control was in response to societal pressures rather than state initiative. In other areas, the government took action to restore confidence and revive the economy. Justice, not necessarily in the distributive sense, was of course an important consideration. Control over economic resources per se was not a significant motive. Indeed, after the revolution public enterprises became a huge drain on government finances. For instance, the National Organization for Industry, which took over many of the newly nationalized manufacturing firms, incurred a loss of nearly $1.5 billion in the first three years, and its sister organization, the Industrial Development and Renovation Organization, lost $3.5 billion (Central Bank, n.d., 169; Middle East Economic Digest, 17 June 1983). Even though by 1989 these public enterprises were functioning more normally and were earning profits, they were not a significant instrument of resource extraction.

Second, certain elements within the bureaucracy, acting from political and ideological motives and economic self-interest (many were appointed as managers of the firms taken over) pushed government ownership further than the various legislations originally intended. The implementation of the Law for Protection and Expansion of Industry provides an interesting case in point. Clause C of this law stipulated that companies that had obtained "considerable loans for their establishment and expansion from the bank" were to surrender a part of their equity, equal to the ratio of the loans to their total assets, to the government. By including working capital loans and appropriately defining "considerable," the ministry of industry brought practically every large company under the provision of this clause. Later, government accountants, using some imaginative techniques, showed that nearly all such firms had negative net worth, which would make them wholly state-owned.

Third, because of the concentration of industrial ownership in a few hands, generally in the form of diversified groups with interests also in banking and other sectors and often linked to the shah's regime, nationalizations were not resisted by the property-owning classes. This contrasts with the extensive mobilization that took place to oppose the land reform bills. The industrialization policies of the previous regime had created a bimodal industrial structure with relatively few independent midsize firms. When the industrial nationalization law expropriated the holdings of fifty-one families and individuals, a significant portion of the country's manufacturing sector came under state control. One could hardly call them an industrialist class.

Fourth, although every legislation reaffirmed the sanctity of legitimate (mashru) private property, and although there was no blanket seizure of all large businesses, some relatively small holdings were sequestered. Many large fortunes remained in private hands, and many more were amassed after the revolution. There was no well-defined criterion for distributive justice.

Last, the expropriations transferred the assets of a segment of the rich to the state; as a result, many of the public-sector managers became the new rich. They may not be as wealthy as the previous owners, but that is partly owing to the fact that the country is less wealthy today. What is disturbing about the concentration of wealth in their hands is that their capital accumulation is less likely to be invested in domestic productive activities.

The Extension of Government Regulations

Administrative controls such as direct distribution of goods, rationing, and price controls proliferated under the Islamic Republic. They were all intended to ensure an equitable distribution of scarce resources, and on the whole, this aim was served by many of the controls; but they also had significant adverse effects on efficiency and sometimes benefited specific groups among the rich or middle class more than they helped the poor.

The system of controls consisted of a host of mechanisms and channels. In broadest outline, the main components were

1. Simple rationing of the basic necessities such as cooking oil, sugar, detergent, kerosene, and meat.

2. Allocation of goods by special vouchers (in effect, in-kind-payment), limited to public-sector employees and industrial workers.

3. Sporadic distribution of some consumer goods by ration stamps from the "Economic Mobilization Booklet," which every household had to have.

4. Controlled distribution of products by manufacturers, importers, wholesalers, and various retail outlets, often with government permits. Producer goods and consumer durables were primarily distributed in this fashion. This mechanism was different from simple rationing in that there remained an element of administrative discretion in making the allocations.

5. Distribution by special outlets, mainly consumer cooperatives that presumably imposed some informal rationing among their members.

6. Regulation of the prices of many of the items not distributed by rationing or special permits. Without a clear legislative basis for the imposition of price controls, the government enforced them by virtue of special powers granted by Ayatollah Khomeini.

The administrative apparatus for the allocation of goods and the oversight of the distribution network was the Economic Mobilization Command, which was set up soon after the start of the war. The various agencies of the Ministry of Commerce were more directly involved with the actual distribution of goods, but they functioned primarily through existing outlets. There were no fair-price shops (the cooperatives to some extent filled this role), and except for the shops catering to the families of martyrs, there were no special-privilege stores.

For some goods, the government controlled the entire market, but for others, it supplied or regulated only a segment of the market or imposed no controls at all. For instance, in the late 1980s only between 30 and 40 percent of the rice consumption was distributed by the government; similarly, extensive free markets for meat and dairy products existed alongside the controlled network mainly supplied from imports.

In the late 1980s there was a growing realization that the goal of equity could be more effectively achieved by more-limited but better-targeted controls, and therefore there was a greater acceptance of parallel markets. Regulations concerning the operation of parallel markets changed from time to time and according to locality. After 1987, open sales of meat were banned in Teheran, but in the nearby towns there were no such restrictions. In 1988 the government began the unrestricted sale of gasoline at double the price of the rationed allocations. Besides these legal markets, illegal black markets also existed, for example, in ration stamps. On the whole, the most extensive black markets were not in the rationed basic commodities but in the price-controlled and government-allocated goods.

Another instrument for income distribution was the foreign exchange regulations, which were originally introduced to stop capital flight after the revolution. The failure to adjust the official exchange rate and the consequent growing overvaluation of the currency entailed ever stricter administrative allocation of foreign exchange and more controls all along the production and distribution chain in every sector of the economy. Although the immediate aim of all these controls was a more equitable distribution of resources, there were unintended adverse effects on equity as well as significant losses in economic efficiency. For example, the detrimental impact of an overvalued exchange rate on exports and import substitutes may well have depressed employment, which would have had a negative effect on the poor. Furthermore, the implicit subsidies were general, rather than targeted to the neediest segments of the population, and thus were not the most appropriate mechanism for redistribution. At the very least, they had a strong urban bias.

The redistributive consequences of the various measures discussed above differed considerably. Simple rationing was an effective mechanism for egalitarian redistribution. It was an important element in maintaining the real income of low-income households, and it helped narrow regional and rural-urban disparities. Its efficacy stemmed from the absence of administrative discretion. In contrast, most of the other programs favored the better-off segments of the population even when they helped improve the overall distribution of income. For example, the voucher program was mainly for public-sector employees, most of whom were not in the bottom ranks of the income distribution. Supplies of building materials at controlled prices primarily subsidized middle- and upper-class groups.

The government allocation of goods other than the rationed items on the whole benefited the urban consumers even though the regional allotments were reasonably equitable. The provincial allocations of the various goods bore some relation to the population of each province, although they were not in exact proportion to it. Generally, for consumer durables, Teheran got more than its proportionate share, in good part because of the higher rate of urbanization in Teheran Province. That province had 17 percent of the country's population but 30 percent of the urban population. In 1984 it received 46 percent of color television sets, 32 percent of desert coolers, and 36 percent of water heaters. There were instances of even greater inequalities: 58 percent of government-distributed imported meat went to Teheran's consumers. For construction materials, the per capita regional allocations were more equal. Teheran received 11 percent of the cement, 18 percent of the glass, and 12 percent of the construction steel distributed by the government.[2] Although no published data on the intraprovincial allocations of goods are available, given the differential consumption patterns of the urban and rural consumers, there is no doubt the former benefited more from the implicit subsidies even if the latter were not completely ignored.

The exercise of administrative discretion in the allocation of resources in short supply had undesirable consequences for income distribution and efficiency. Much effort was spent on what economists refer to as rent-seeking activities, in contrast to productive economic effort. In other words, businessmen spent their time and money trying to manipulate government regulations instead of producing goods and services. The spread of corruption in government and public enterprises, which became a major social issue, was a direct consequence of the mushrooming of administrative controls and the widening gap between official and market prices. Wolfgang Lautenschlager (1986) has argued that the merchants were the main beneficiaries of foreign exchange and other government controls, but although some merchants profited from the administrative controls, government officials and managers of public enterprises and the private industrialists that remained also benefited. Government officials, well aware of the value of the permits they issued, often demanded to share it with the recipients. Purchasing managers in public enterprises usually asked for kickbacks from foreign suppliers—a practice common everywhere in the Third World. In Iran it was also the domestic sales managers who asked for side-payments. Private industrialists could relatively easily obtain either direct allocation of raw materials or foreign exchange to import them, thanks to the Islamic Republic's policy of encouraging self-sufficiency. Selling a portion of their raw materials in the black market was the main source of their profit. In other words, the government's policy meant to promote industry instead encouraged industrialists to spend their effort at becoming black market merchants. Data from household expenditure surveys are not likely to reflect these types of income transfers, which could hardly have been equitable.

Did the government use the extensive regulation of the system of distribution as a mechanism for political control and mobilization? The evidence is mixed. Consider the "Economic Mobilization Booklet," which was required of citizens for nearly all dealings with the bureaucracy and for most officially recognized transactions. Because a holder's place of residence was specified in the booklet, internal migration to the large cities became more difficult and costly. It was, however, a far cry from an internal passport that could strictly regulate movements within the country. Furthermore, booklets were readily issued to all citizens irrespective of political or religious views, with some exceptions. To be sure, the government to some extent used the administrative allocation of goods, both formal and informal, for political ends. We have already mentioned how the government elicited both financial and political support from trade associations. In the rural areas, the Jihad for Reconstruction often rewarded loyal villagers with more-generous allocations of agricultural inputs and credit.

State Policy on Cooperatives

Small-scale private property combined in some form of cooperative arrangement appeared to be the form of ownership acceptable to all factions in the regime. This form of economic organization seemed most congruent with the principle of social justice, which all Islamic tendencies advocate, and yet it was not based on social ownership of all means of production, on whose rejection there was broad agreement. Ali-Akbar Hashemi Rafsanjani has repeatedly said that although Islam does not favor the concentration of wealth, it encourages private initiative. According to him, this apparent contradiction can be resolved through cooperative production.[3] The constitution of the Islamic Republic stipulates that the cooperative sector is to have a prominent role in the economy. It does not, however, specify what constitutes a cooperative. The minutes of the Assembly of Experts indicate that in addition to consumer and marketing cooperatives, they envisioned employee-owned or -managed productive units (*Majlis-e Shura-ye Islami* 1985b, 2: 1555–68). The various attempts to promote this type of cooperative, such as the distribution of public land for joint farming and the provision of credit for groups of high school graduates to form manufacturing units, were not very successful, and there was not much enthusiasm for them by the late 1980s. By 1986 there were only thirty-two manufacturing cooperatives comprising about a thousand workers.[4]

The government also revived the previous regime's program for distribution of stocks to workers in large firms, but this was hardly more than a political gesture. The scheme was resurrected when there was some talk of returning a number of government-managed factories to their original owners. Officials in the Ministry of Industry were naturally not very receptive to such plans and advanced worker share participation as a counterproposal. It is unlikely that worker-owned factories will become widespread or that workers will have much actual say in management of factories they nominally own.

The numerical expansion of the more traditionalist kinds of cooperatives, such as consumer, housing, and distribution and marketing cooperatives and credit unions, was quite large. Because an extensive cooperative network already served the rural population before the revolution, the increase occurred mainly in the urban areas, where the number of cooperatives rose from 2,893 in 1977 to 14,783 in 1986. Among them were 3,618 (202 in 1977) procurement and distribution cooperatives that were in effect trade cooperatives closely associated with their respective guilds. In order to eliminate the large importers and exporters and the wholesale merchants, the government favored these cooperatives with import and export licenses and allocations of scarce raw materials. One such cooperative for pistachio growers, which happened to be headed by a cousin of a prominent political figure, became the largest business concern outside the public sector.

The government's advocacy of the cooperatives had an egalitarian effect on redistribution, but it was not a policy directed toward the poorest segments of the population. Discriminating against the large merchants and in favor of tradesmen shifted income from the very wealthy to the merely well-off; many cooperatives formed to take advantages of various implicit or explicit government subsidies. The most effective organizations were those set up by the employees of the modern sector, both public and private, who were unlikely to be among the bottom economic strata.

Housing

One of the most pressing and emotionally charged issues of social equity was the provision of adequate housing, especially in the urban areas. In the 1973–78 period, the oil boom raised the demand for housing because it led to higher incomes and increased migration to the cities. Land prices skyrocketed and building costs rose steeply. Great fortunes were made from speculation in urban real estate at the same time that access to affordable shelter became increasingly difficult for large segments of the population. Even though the housing stock was improving, there was a perception of a growing shortage.

Housing was one of the first problems the Islamic regime tried to tackle. The various policies adopted have contributed little to the wider availability of low-cost housing, but some of the measures had potentially significant impact on the distribution of wealth. The Housing Foundation was set up with much fanfare as a revolutionary organization to provide housing for the poor. By itself, the foundation hardly made a dent in the problem; it completed only a few thousand units each year, and a substantial part of its activities was directed toward rebuilding war-damaged areas and regions struck by natural disasters. The foundation, however, was the first government organization to undertake residential construction in rural areas and became the conduit for the provision of mortgage credit for rural housing. Other public bodies were also involved in building houses, but the government's total share, with about 9,000 units out of 160,000 to 170,000 units completed in the urban areas in 1986, was minor (Iran, MPB 1987, vol. 2, ch. 21). In fact, public investment in housing was well below its prerevolution level, which is not surprising in light of the general cutback in development expenditures. The thrust of state policy shifted to changing the structure of demand for housing and to changing the price of land.

Real estate and urban land were and still are the largest source of private wealth in the country. The redistribution of these assets was bound to be an important component of wealth and income distribution program. At first, government policy was almost exclusively concerned with nationalization and distribution of urban undeveloped land, but by the late 1980s, it shifted to one of higher taxation of all urban real estate. In 1979 the provisional government passed a law for the nationalization of undeveloped urban land. Despite opposition from some ulama, a modified version was later enacted by the parliament in 1982. Delays in the full implementation of the law notwithstanding, by 1986 the Organization for Urban Land, having taken over much of the urban land above the permissible ceiling, was providing nearly two-fifths of the residential building plots. Although the sequestration of urban land, some of it paid for at prices based on tax assessments, was an egalitarian measure, its resale at less than market price did little to improve housing conditions for the neediest segment of the society. On the whole, the relatively well-off—government employees, industrial workers, and cooperative members—were the main recipients of state housing assistance, in the form of subsidized land, credit, or actual construction. When the poor benefited, their numbers were limited.

In the first decade after the revolution, the average size of new homes built in the urban areas varied between 127 to 149 square meters, not appreciably different from that of the homes built before the revolution. Average new home size in Iran was 80 percent of that in the United States, despite a difference in average household income that might have been eight to one. Because fewer very large homes were built after the revolution and because the size distribution of the new dwellings was more even, one can conclude that little of the new investment was in low-cost, small housing. Clearly, the more prosperous elements of the society had an inordinate claim on the limited resources of the economy. There was a growing realization that any viable solution to the housing problem would entail a significant reduction in the average size of dwellings. In 1988 the government imposed a progressive annual property tax that rises steeply for homes over one hundred square meters (*Kayhan*, 24 Sept. 1988). This measure, together with the wealth taxes mentioned previously, could have significant redistributive impact if fully implemented, but the capacity and will to put these laws into practice is low.

Government Development Expenditure and Redistribution

The cutback in the development budget following the general resource crisis and the diversion of funds to the war effort caused the postponement of much-needed social and productive investment. Lower development expenditures enabled the government in the short run to moderate the decline in consumption, but their longer-term impact on income distribution was unfavorable. The high rate of population growth (variously estimated at 3 to 3.9 percent per annum) aggravated the problem. Consequently, the Islamic regime failed to deliver on its promise to provide employment and meet basic education and health needs. The unemployment rate was about 15 percent in 1988, and it would have been considerably higher had not many women dropped out of the labor force because of poor prospects. The rise in the unemployment rate was particularly steep in the urban areas—from about 5 percent in 1976 to over 18 percent in 1986. Moreover, there was a change in the structure of unemployment. Whereas in 1976,

70 percent of the urban unemployed were less than twenty-five years old, by 1982 this ratio was less than 50 percent. In 1976 only 28 percent of the urban unemployed had held jobs previously, but in 1982 this ratio had risen to 40 percent (Iran 1983). These figures suggest that a higher proportion of heads of households were suffering from unemployment, which raises the likelihood of their being in the low-income groups.

The decline in the development budget was an obvious cause of the higher unemployment rate, but the government did little to compensate for the decline by changing the composition of its investments. A large portion of government investment was earmarked for highly capital-intensive projects in the electricity, oil, and manufacturing sectors, which create little employment per rial invested. Of the development budget for the manufacturing industry, more than 80 percent was allocated for a few large-scale capital-intensive steel and petrochemical projects, about the same as in the prerevolution period, when the country faced labor shortages.

Under Ayatollah Khomeini the regime was unable to formulate a long-term development and employment strategy consistent with the available resources.[5] Various ministries announced plans for their sectors, and periodic national expenditure programs were formulated (e.g., the priority projects for the tenth anniversary of the revolution). All these programs were, however, overly ambitious in light of the country's limited resources, especially financial resources. Furthermore, some of the policies for job creation, such as the program to encourage self-employment in handicrafts production, were quixotic at best. The urgency of the unemployment problem was not fully appreciated, partly because planners were making unrealistic projections about the rate of growth of the labor force. Whereas the official projection was for only a net annual addition of 350,000 to the labor force, in the fifteen-to-nineteen-year-old group each age cohort consisted of 1.2 million people (Iran, MPB 1987, ch. 14). It appears that the existing unemployment situation will not improve perceptibly in the near future.

The rise in the population put severe pressure on social services, and the cutback in the development budget affected such services even more than the other sectors. The nominal allocation for social affairs was maintained at about 20 percent of the development budget, although, the real share of this sector was less. Because projects in other sectors had a higher import content and because the cost of inputs was kept low by the artificial exchange rate, other sectors received more real resources than the budget shows, leaving less than 20 percent for social affairs. The deteriorating situation is nowhere more apparent than in the education sector. In 1987 most schools were run in two shifts, and three- and four-shift schools were common in some areas. For example, out of 2,170 schools in Teheran, 1,975 operated in two shifts and 100 in three or four shifts (*Kayhan*, 9 Nov. 1988). Despite the overcrowding, the ratio of school enrollments to the school-age population, assumed to be from six to nineteen years, fell from 0.71 in 1976 to 0.66 in 1986. The number of university students barely rose between 1978 and 1986, which, given the large increase in the population, implies a corresponding fall in the proportion of the population attending university.

Medical care did not fare much better. In 1986 there were 690 people for each hospital bed, nearly 10 percent more than before the revolution; over the same period the number of people per physician had risen from about 2,400 to 3,400. The distribution of both health and education services may have been better in 1986, but the basic needs of large segments of the population were still not being met. The very poor were most affected by the unavailability of social welfare services. The expansion of public services, historically one of the most important policy tools for long-term redistribution of income by states, was not a significant instrument for greater social justice in the Islamic Republic's first decade. The regime did not institute the welfare state envisioned in the constitution, but Ayatollah Khomeini himself never promised "a rose garden" in this world.

Conclusion

During Ayatollah Khomeini's life, the main political tendencies in the Islamic republic were strongly committed to more-egalitarian income redistribution, in part as a reaction to serious income discrepancies during the oil boom of 1973–78. The government put in place a variety of measures, mostly through direct distribution of goods and services, to improve the lot of the poor. Opposition to redistributive policies, from those committed to a laissez-faire vision of Islam, however, blocked most initiatives for redistribution of wealth other than industrial nationalization.

The lot of the poor did not, however, improve during the Islamic Republic's first decade. The main problem was the severe constraints under which Islamic Iran operated, especially the tremendous loss of oil income and the war. Per capita real GDP fell by half during this period. The burden of lower income fell primarily on the modern educated upper middle class, which saw a precipitous decline in its living standard. It may be cold comfort for the poor, but they suffered less income loss than did the professionals.

Within the context of the difficult international situation and the declining living standards, the Islamic Republic saw considerable changes in the patterns of income distribution. The most notable trends were (1) relative improvements for rural areas, including higher levels of access to many consumer durables; (2) declining living standards for civil servants, especially in cash income, as government spending plummeted in real terms; and (3) the emergence of new privileged groups, especially those enjoying access to government-rationed imports and credit.

The redistributive policies unfortunately had some negative implications for Iran's growth prospects. The distribution of goods at artificially low prices, without effective taxation of the rich to cover the true economic cost, led to an increase in consumption as a proportion of GDP, leaving less for investment. The drop in investment, from 31 percent of GDP in 1977 to 12 percent in 1988, will almost certainly lead to declining per capita incomes in the future because Iran would need investment of about 20 percent of GDP to get the 4 percent growth required to match population growth. Furthermore, government policy had the unintended effect of discouraging "investment" in human capital: the narrowing of the gap between incomes of the well-educated and the poorly educated meant a lower return from education.

Islamic Iran continues to face the quandary economists are wont to cite between equity and efficiency. Although efficiency certainly could be improved without a sacrifice in equity, the necessary policies—such as effective taxation of the rich—would exacerbate tensions between the political trends. The most likely prospect is for Islamic Iran to continue to pursue politics that aid the poor today at least in part at the expense of the growth that would aid the poor tomorrow.

Epilogue: Post Khomeini Developments

During Hashemi Rafsanjani's first term as president of Iran (July 1989–June 1993) there were substantial changes in economic policy. The general character of those changes was to give more play to market forces and less to government regulation. The government relaxed most price controls, removed some state subsidies and targeted others more effectively, liberalized imports, and privatized some public enterprises. Most important, the allocation of foreign exchange went from a complex system with multiple exchange rates to, after March 1993, a simpler system with most transactions (except for a few basic goods and government inputs) conducted at an exchange rate more or less determined by market forces. With the move to a more realistic exchange rate, the government's rial income from oil exports soared, simultaneously allowing sharp reductions in the budget deficit, increases in development spending, and salary increases for civil servants.

The reform process has been championed by the Western-educated technocrats who control most government posts. It is not clear to what extent this group has benefited from the reforms. Perhaps the reforms have benefited more those businessmen who produce and market efficiently. It is our impression, from anecdotal evidence, that one effect of the reforms on income distribution has been to reverse some of the postrevolution rise of the traditionally educated and the decline of the Western-educated. The losers have been those who used their good political connections to gain preferential access to government-controlled resources, such as foreign exchange. The government has been careful not to abandon all its concerns for equity. In particular, it has continued to provide a safety net for the "vulnerable strata" through subsidizing basic consumer products. Yet, if conspicuous signs of wealth are any indication, the overall distribution of income has worsened.

The years 1989–92 were a period of rapidly rising living standards. We estimate the GDP per capita to have risen by about 20 percent. Imported goods became much more widely available; imports rose from $10.6 billion in 1988 to $25.0 billion in 1991, before declining subsequently in 1992 and 1993. To some extent, the boom resulted from improved oil income, thanks to the price bubble during the Iraq-Kuwait crisis and to increasing Iranian oil production. However, a larger source of foreign exchange during the boom was borrowing, which may have been over $20 billion during Rafsanjani's first term, much of it in short-term trade debt.

It is not clear what direction policy will take in the middle 1990s. The early 1990s' boom will not be sustainable unless Iran has access to continued large-scale foreign financing, or unless oil income increases unexpectedly, or unless the recent investments prove to be more productive than what past experience would indicate. The pace of reforms is a subject for vigorous debate, with those politicians opposed to more scope for market forces still having substantial support.

Notes

1. Figure reported in the annual report of Rey Textile Mill, Teheran, 1988.

2. For details of the provincial allocations, see the Statistical Center of Iran, *Iran Statistical Yearbook*, 1984.

3. For an expression of this view, see Rafsanjani's speech to the National Congress of Extension Centers and Cooperatives, reported in *Kayhan*, 16 Oct. 1988.

4. The data in the section on cooperatives are from the Statistical Center of Iran, *Iran Statistical Yearbook*, various years.

5. Upon assuming office in 1989, President Rafsanjani made the formulation of a five-year plan his first priority. The plan, approved in January 1990, was extremely optimistic but on the edge of the plausible on most matters.

7

The State and the Political Economy of Redistribution in Pakistan

SHAHID JAVED BURKI

The political economy of redistribution in Pakistan cannot be studied without reference to the country's past. Unlike Afghanistan and Iran, Pakistan is a young state still trying to find its national identity, and a number of questions remain unanswered. Was Pakistan created to become an Islamic state or a state that would provide a homeland for the Muslims of British India? Was Pakistan to be a loose confederation of Muslim provinces in British India, or a federal state that allowed considerably autonomy to its constituent parts, or a unitary state with an all-powerful central authority? What should be the role of the civil bureaucracy in statecraft? Was the civil service meant to implement the policies of political governments, or did the underdeveloped state of Pakistan's polity permit the civil bureaucracy to play an autonomous role? Similarly, what was the appropriate role for the armed forces? Were the armed forces to be the guardians of Pakistan's frontiers, and to provide assistance to civil authority for maintaining law and order during periods of exceptional disturbance? Or did the low level of Pakistan's political development permit the military to play a role that went much beyond its principal purpose? Different answers were given to these questions at different times, but even after four decades of independence and many trials and errors, national consensus has still to emerge on these issues.[1]

Pakistan's many distributive crises had political as well as economic causes. To understand them it is necessary to analyze in particular the role of Islam in the Pakistani state, the roles of the military and the civil bureaucracy in economic decision making, and the conflict between the provinces of Pakistan and the central government. Thus my focus is not on the period of President Zia ul-Haq but on the evolution of distributive concerns in Pakistan and the development of approaches to deal with them.

If in terms of most measures of economic change Pakistan's economy has performed well in the forty-year period since independence in 1947,[2] and if much of this achievement cannot be attributed to medium- or long-term planning but was instead the outcome of clever and resourceful day-to-day management, then it is useful to look at the credentials of the people or the groups of peole who were these managers. During most of Pakistan's history, economic decision making was either in the hands of the members of the powerful civil service of Pakistan or in those of the expatriate Pakistanis brought back to the country to help with economic management.[3] Neither group was well disposed toward redistributive issues. Over time, they evolved what I call the bureaucratic model of economic management. This model was developed to handle economic crises rather than to deal with the economy's long-range problems.

Through the years, the nature and scope of redistributive concerns have changed from the incorporation of refugees from India (who now identify themselves as the Muhajirs) into the mainstream of Pakistan's economy, to the widening of income disparity between East Pakistan (today's Bangladesh) and West Pakistan, to the plight of the Sindhi and Baluchi rural areas. Because the composition of the groups demanding redistributive attention changed quickly, policymakers in Pakistan failed to develop a consistent approach toward the political economy of redistribution. A series of six "redistricutive episodes" occurred, each with its own special features and each with its own causes and consequences. Of the six crises identified, only one—the growing income disparity between East and West Pakistan—was resolved by East Pakistan's winning independence and becoming Bangladesh. The remaining five are yet to be resolved.

Fifteen redistributive programs and policies have been tried in Pakistan over its forty-year history (twelve are described here). Most of these policies and programs were politically motivated to provide wider support for the politicians who initiated them. It is not surprising, therefore, that the programs had no profound impact on any of the major redistributive crises confronting the country.

From 1977 to 1988, General Mohammad Zia ul-Haq was in almost total political commands, first as the chief martial law administrator and later as president. During this time, Pakistan emerged from the ranks of poor nations and joined the middle-income countries. A number of socioeconomic groups benefited from this transition. The redistributive impact of the economy's rapid growth and structural transformation was impressive; but once again in keeping with the country's history, it happened more by accident than by deliberate design.[4]

If the run of good luck that helped Pakistan join the ranks of middle-income nations should not continue, the country may no longer be able to postpone the resolution of the main distributive problems that continue to affect its political and economic development.

Pakistan's Economic History

In large measure Pakistan owes its birth to the perception that in a united India without external (British) arbitration, the Muslim minority would be discriminated against by a Hindi majority. This fear was manifested by a group of Muslim fundamentalists who chose migration to Afghanistan and Muslim Central Asia over assimilation into a predominantly Hindu India; by Sayyid Ahmad Khan, who focused on human resource development as a way of providing the Muslims of British India with the same intellectual equipment that had become available to the Hindu subjects of the British raj; by such provincial bosses as Fazle Husain, Sikandar Hayat, Khizar Hayat Tiwana, Khan Sahib, Ghaffar Khan, and Fazl-e-Haq, who believed that the Muslims in the Muslim-majority province of Punjab and in the North-West Frontier Province and Bengal, by practicing the policies of isolation, even within a Hindu-dominated India, should be able to protect the economic and social interests of their community; and by Muhammad Ali Jinnah, who believed that without an explicit central agreement on power sharing, the Muslims of India could not expect fair treatment at the hands of the Hindus once the British departed from the subcontinent. As it turned out, the partition of British India was the only solution that was acceptable to the three parties engaged in this discourse—the British, the Hindus, and the Muslims. The partition, therefore, was a political solution to a problem that was perceived essentially in economic and social terms. But the redistributive concerns that created Pakistan did not disappear with the partition of British India along communal lines—a predominantly Hindu India and a predominantly Muslim Pakistan. These concerns remained on both sides of the border, although only in India were they handled as political problems (Rudolf and Rudolf 1987).

Pakistan turned out to be an economic success but a political failure, despite the belief of leaders of the Indian National Congress that Jinnah's Pakistan could not be economically viable. In the 1940s what is Pakistan today was a predominantly agricultural economy with only three industrial units of any significance. Its infrastructure—railways, roads, and the irrigation system—were all designed to make it a part of the larger economy of British India. Partition created daunting problems. Not only was the territory awarded to Jinnah and his Muslim League much smaller than they had demanded, it also had to accommodate millions of refugees who poured in from India, to fight a war with India over the state of Kashmir, and to come to terms with the severance of all economic links with India. Even so, this "moth-eaten"[5] Muslim state has not only survived as an independent economic identity, it has overtaken the rest of India and, in terms of the purchasing power of its currency, now probably belongs to the category of middle-income countries. In making this transition, Pakistan has also eliminated the worst forms of poverty (Burki 1988b), having fewer people living in absolute poverty than have other countries of South Asia. Today it has a smaller proportion of absolute poor in its population than, say, Indonesia and the Philippines; it no longer belongs to what the Brandt Commission, in its first report, labeled the "Asian belt of poverty," which stretched from Afghanistan in the Northwest to Vietnam in the Southeast (Brandt Commission 1980, 78).

Tables 7.1–7.3 provide some measures of the changes that have occurred during the 1949–88 period. Table 7.1 provides pictures of the structure of the economy in 1949–50 and in 1987–88. The transition during this forty-year period has been spectacular. At the time of independence, Pakistan was an underdeveloped economy dependent almost entirely on agriculture, from which came more than one-half of the GDP. In the forty-year period since then, the share of agriculture has declined by one-half, from 53 percent to 24 percent, while that of industry has increased two and one-half times, from 8 to 19 percent of the GDP. A number of other indexes not presented in table 7.1 reinforce this picture of dramatic change: in the proportion of people employed and the contribution to export earnings, agriculture is no longer the predominant sector. A third of the population lives in urban areas; six cities now have about one million inhabitants each. Table 7.2 uses the statistics generated when national income accounting is done in terms of purchasing power rather than in terms of national income converted

TABLE 7.1

Structural Change in Pakistan's Economy
(in percentage)

Proportion Contributed to GNP by	1949–50	1987–88
Agriculture	53.3	23.8
Construction	1.4	5.4
Manufacturing	7.8	19.4
Public Administration and Defense	7.1	9.8
Services	7.7	6.9
Transportation and Communication	5.0	7.1
Trade	11.9	14.4
Other	5.8	13.2
Total	100.0	100.0

Source: Government of Pakistan, *Pakistan Economic Survey, 1991–1992* (Islamabad: Ministry of Finance, 1992), Statistical Appendix.

into U.S. dollars at the prevailing rate of exchange (Kravis, Heston, and Summers 1982). According to these statistics, Pakistan belongs to the group of countries such as the Philippines, Sri Lanka, and Indonesia, rather than to the group represented by India and Bangladesh; it has already made the transition from the group of poor countries to that of middle-income nations.

Curiously, during this period of economic restructuring and transformation between 1948 and 1988, when Pakistan's GDP grew threefold and the average per capita income of its population increased twofold, Pakistan remained a socially underdeveloped society. For instance, as shown in table 7.3, male life expectancy at birth in Pakistan in 1986 was fifty-two years, equal to that in poor countries but five years less than the average for lower-middle-income countries. Female life expectancy, at fifty-one years in Pakistan, was lower than that for both poor and lower-middle-income countries. Maternal mortality (number of women who die at the time of childbirth per hundred thousand births) in Pakistan is slightly lower than the average for poor countries but considerably higher than that for lower-middle-income countries. The infant mortality rate, at 111 per thousand live births, is nearly 5

TABLE 7.2

Pakistan's GNP Compared to Other Developing Countries, 1985
(in $ millions)

Country	Atlas Methodology[a]		Kravis Methodology[b]	
	$	Ratio	$	Ratio
Pakistan	377	100	1,664	100
Brazil	1,640	435	4,266	256
India	246	65	873	52
Indonesia	525	139	1,551	93
Korea	2,181	578	4,509	271
Philippines	609	162	1,955	117
Sri Lanka	377	100	1,891	114

Source: World Bank, *World Development Report, 1992* (New York: Oxford Univ. Press), table 30.

[a]Atlas methodology refers to the methodology used by the World Bank to calculate national incomes of its member countries in dollar terms. Domestic currency estimates of national income are converted into dollars by using three-year averages of dollar exchange rates.

[b]The Kravis methodology uses purchasing power of basket of consumption goods consumed by an average citizen in dollar terms.

percent higher than the poor country average but 44 percent higher than the average for low-income countries.

These statistics point to a low standard of general health that is hard to explain in terms of the availability of health "inputs." For instance, daily caloric consumption in Pakistan is nearly 4 percent higher than in low-income countries; the number of persons per doctor is six times lower than in low-income countries; and there are 20 percent more nurses available per hundred thousand of the population than in poor countries. The only way to reconcile these statistics with those that suggest a low standard of health for the general population is to conclude that health coverage and food availability must be highly skewed in favor of the more privileged segments of the population. The fruits of extraordinary economic growth during the four decades of Pakistan's existence appear to have been available mostly to the more privileged people in the population. Pakistan prospered without the benefit passing to the poor.[6]

TABLE 7.3

**Pakistan's Social Development Compared
to Other Developing Countries**

Category	Pakistan	Low-Income Countries	Lower-Middle-Income Countries
Demographic (1986)			
Crude birth rate per thousand	47.0	43.0	35.0
Crude death rate per thousand	15.0	15.0	10.0
Total fertility rate	6.8	6.0	4.7
Education			
Primary School Enrollment			
% of Total	47	110[a]	104[a]
% of Male	61	75	109[a]
% of Female	32	56	100
Secondary School Enrollment			
% of Total	17	22	42
% of Male	24	45	57
Health			
Daily caloric supply per capita (1985)	2,180	2,100	2,511
Population per physician (1981)	2,910	17,670	7,880
Population per nurse (1981)	5,870	7,130	1,760
Life Expectancy (1986)			
Male (years)	52	52	57
Female (years)	51	54	61
Infant mortality (per 1,000 live births)	111	106	77
Maternal mortality (per 100,000 live births)	600	607	586

Source: World Bank, *World Development Report, 1992* (New York: Oxford Univ. Press, 1992), various tables in World Development Indicators.

[a]An enrollment rate of more than 100 percent means that the education system is reaching older children as well who, for a variety of socioeconomic and cultural reasons, were not able to attend schools when they were of primary school age.

This conclusion is warranted for the first three decades after independence, from 1947 to about the mid-1970s. During this period the poor neither gained material wealth nor did they see much improvement in their social well-being. From the mid-seventies onward, however, Pakistan's poor began to benefit from the flow of remittances sent by the workers who had gone to the Middle East. The impact of this flow on the incidence of poverty was dramatic. Today, some fifteen years after the migrants began to go to the Middle East in large numbers, Pakistan shows few signs of the extensive absolute poverty that characterizes other countries of South Asia. Malnutrition is less visible than in India and Bangladesh. The cities of Pakistan do not have people living on the streets in the numbers seen in Bombay, Calcutta, and Delhi. Both unemployment and underemployment are less in evidence in the urban areas. The quality of life in the countryside is better than in most other countries of South Asia.

The flow of funds from the Middle East has improved the lot of the poor, and health and educational statistics should begin to reflect this change. But Pakistan's ability to deploy the remittances sent by the workers in the Middle East for alleviating absolute forms of poverty contrasts sharply with its failure to bring about an equitable distribution of a rapid increase in national income during the first three decades after independence. Only an analysis of the forces that shaped Pakistan's political history and that influenced the structural transformation of its economy can explain this disparity.

A series of mostly political circumstances in the early years of Pakistan's independence shaped the leadership's attitude toward economic development. In 1949, as a direct consequence of global economic realignment following the conclusion of World War II, the United States emerged as the principal economic power, and the U.S. dollar became the main currency for international exchange and commerce. Both Britain and its currency, the pound sterling, suffered a decline in importance during this period of adjustment. In September 1949 Britain decided to devalue the pound with respect to the dollar, and with the exception of Pakistan, all other countries of the sterling area followed Britain in realigning the value of their currencies. Pakistan's leadership, confident of being able to sell its exports in the international market without lowering the value of its currency, chose not to devalue the rupee. This decision changed the rate of exchange between the Indian and Pakistani rupees from parity to one hundred Pakistani rupees for 144 Indian rupees. But India refused to test the Pakistani exchange rate in normal trade; starting in October 1949, imports from India declined rapidly, leaving the Pakistani population without a number of goods basic for daily consumption. Up until then Pakistan was a part of the customs union the British had left in place after they had departed from the subcontinent. Not only was Pakistan dependent on India for all forms of basic consumer goods, it also did not have local control over the monetary situation; goods, people, and money flowed freely across the new border.

The Indian decision suddenly to bring down the curtain on trade and other forms of exchange between the two countries might have crippled Pakistan if a sharp increase in world cotton prices, as a result of a short crop in the United States, had not helped to improve Pakistan's export earnings in 1949–50. But the squeeze applied by India persuaded the leadership in Pakistan to establish an industrial base of its own. An industrial policy had been drafted in 1948 demarcating the roles of the public and private sectors; the policy now began to be implemented with exceptional vigor by a bureaucracy that had excellent training in handling crises of all kinds.

The breakup of the Indo-Pakistan customs and exchange union was to have a profound impact on Pakistan's economic development. It caused Pakistan to depart from what was then the orthodoxy of development: the belief that carefully planned and insulated economies are good for developing countries. India practiced the orthodoxy. It undertook long-term development planning, assigned the public sector a prominent role in economic management, closed its economy to outside influences, and began to generate enough domestic resources to meet most of its requirement for investment. Pakistan, in a desperate bid to establish domestic industry, went the other route. In 1949 the newly organized government in Pakistan was still in the process of settling down to govern. It was too preoccupied by dealing with some of the unanticipated aftermath of British India's partition to think of involving itself in any significant way in the task of economic development. Consequently, the government in Pakistan paid little attention to planning; it was prepared to allow the private sector to occupy the commanding heights of the economy; it was willing to accept a relatively open economy if only to let imports meet some of the domestic shortages occasioned by the cessation of trade with India; and it was content to let foreign savings pay for a good proportion of the domestic investment bill. This approach to development, with two exceptions, was pursued throughout Pakistan's history. The exceptions were the first seven years of Ayub Khan's presidency and the five-year period when Zulfikar Ali Bhutto was in power. Ayub Khan made an effort to institute medium-term development planning, and Zulfikar Ali Bhutto attempted to increase the role of the government in economic management. These attempts were, however, aberrations in the Pakistani approach to development, the foundations of which were laid within two years of independence.

The Pakistani approach succeeded in delivering a high rate of economic growth, first, because external resources fortuitously continued to flow into Pakistan and, second, because economic management became the responsibility of the civil service, whose members were exceptionally adept at handling crises, which have occurred with unrelenting frequency during the country's four-decade history.

In the early 1950s President Eisenhower's administration began to recruit countries on the periphery of the Soviet Union and China as members of defense alliances dominated by the United States. In 1954 Pakistan and the United States signed a mutual defense agreement, which opened the way for Pakistan's membership in the Central Treaty Organization (CENTO) and the Southeast Asia Treaty Organization (SEATO). In return, the United States began to provide Pakistan with large amounts of concessional capital flows for military purchases and for reequippings its armed forces (Brown 1963; Burke 1973; Venkataramani 1984). Consequently, from 1955 to 1966 Pakistan received external capital at a rate equivalent to 3.5 percent of its GDP on an annual basis, with the United States by far the most significant contributor to this capital flow. This amount of capital assistance was important for maintaining a high rate of economic growth, as evidenced by the recession when the flow of external assistance was interrupted following Pakistan's 1965 war with India. Pakistan had to wait another fourteen years before official foreign capital in any significant amount would become available again.

Also fortunate for ·Pakistan were the economic booms in the Middle East that followed the sharp increases in the price of oil, first in 1973 and again in 1979. Pakistan was one of the few oil-importing developing countries not to be hurt by the increase in the price of oil; the increase in its oil bill was more than counterbalanced by remittances from its workers in the Middle East (Burki 1980b). Starting with 1974, a constant stream of migrants flowed into the Middle East, and by the early 1980s, a pool of nearly three million migrant workers had been built by the Pakistanis in the Gulf states. These workers earned handsome wages and had a very high propensity to save, and because they had gone to the Middle East without their families, they remitted back to Pakistan almost all of their savings. Between 1974 and 1988 the workers sent back a total of $25 billion to Pakistan through official banking channels. Perhaps another $10 billion came into the country through nonbanking channels. These savings became available at a time when official capital flows to Pakistan had stagnated. Without them, the country would not have been able to produce a high rate of growth in its GDP.

The Middle East boom began to subside about the time the Soviet troops moved into Afghanistan and bestowed on Pakistan the status of a "frontline state." The United States and other Western countries responded quickly with economic assistance to Pakistan and financial aid to the Afghan refugees. With the signing of a six-year U.S. program of economic aid in 1981, Pakistan became the third largest recipient of American bilateral assistance after Israel and Egypt. It received more than $3 billion in the six-year period from 1981 to 1987. Another package of assistance valued at more than $4 billion for another six years was negotiated in 1987 but was suspended in 1990.

These helpful developments in Pakistan's external fortunes not only made it possible to maintain high growth in GDP, they also suited the bureaucrats who managed the economy during most of Pakistan's history. The bureaucracy was not inclined to generate domestic resources beyond those needed for the day-to-day running of the government and those required for complementing the copious amount of development assistance coming in from abroad. The proportion of total domestic investment financed from domestic resource generation therefore continued to decline, and Pakistan's foreign financiers were not disposed to urge use of the resources they provided for social development or the provision of basic needs.

A development effort financed mostly from abroad, an approach to economic development that provided the private sector with a great deal of room for maneuver and the government with only a facilitating role, and an economic leadership that paid only lip service to medium-term planning—all combined to permit a very low level of concern for redistributive justice. The bureaucrats who had become managers of the economy were not well equipped to handle latent distributive problems that did not surface as political and social crises. Accordingly, although Pakistan made rapid economic strides during the 1947–75 period, the impact of this progress was not very profound on redistribution and poverty alleviation.

This situation was corrected in the 1975–85 period, when billions of dollars worth of remittances flowed into Pakistan from the Middle

East. A country with a different set of traditions and following a different model of economic management than the one pursued by Pakistan might have mobilized a part of these capital flows for use by the government. One such attempt was made by the administration of Prime Minister Zulfikar Ali Bhutto when it levied a tax on the remittances received from abroad by families in Pakistan. The imposition of this tax had the effect of lowering the rate at which the remitters exchanged their foreign savings for Pakistani rupees. But the lowered rate was not considered attractive enough by the expatriate Pakistani community to warrant continued use of the official banking channels for sending money to their families, so they switched a good proportion of their remitted savings to nonbanking, informal channels. Because the greater use of the informal *hundi* market (informal transactions in foreign exchange) deprived the government of the foreign exchange brought in by remittances, the administration withdrew the tax.

Evidence remains inconclusive concerning the use to which the remittances were put by those who received them. Some surveys carried out by the Planning Commission and individual scholars suggest a great deal of waste in the use of the windfall gain this resource flow represented for the families that were its direct beneficiaries (Gilani, Khan, and Iqbal 1981; Asian Employment Programme 1983). At the same time, growth in the consumption of a number of important consumer items from 1975 to 1985 indicates a considerable improvement in the common welfare. By the mid-1980s, Pakistan had not only advanced into the ranks of middle-income countries, its population had also been freed from the worst forms of deprivation that continued to characterize the societies of other South Asian countries.

The state in Pakistan, therefore, helped both economic growth and poverty alleviation by not interfering with the process of resource generation and deployment. With the exception of brief interventionalist periods in the early 1960s and again in the early 1970s, it generally allowed people to use their incomes and their savings in the ways that suited them. This attitude of the state ensured rapid economic growth in the quarter century following independence and a pronounced improvement in economic well-being of the poorer segments of the population in the decade following the oil boom in the Middle East. But because the decision-making apparatus was dominated by individuals who had neither the political mandate nor the disposition to occupy themselves with redistributive concerns, the state refrained from playing a prominent role in redistributing either wealth or incomes.

Bureaucratic Control over Economic Policy-Making

The emergence of a noninterventionist economic state in Pakistan was the consequence of poor political development, and even after four decades of independence, the state's political apparatus remains underdeveloped. The process of political development suffered an early setback in Pakistan because the political party that led the movement for the creation of Pakistan was not well equipped to govern the new country. The task of creating an independent Muslim state for the Muslim population of British India was entrusted to the All-India Muslim League at the annual session held in Lahore on 23 March 1940. The league's impressive performance in the provincial elections of 1946 reconfirmed that mandate. But with the emergence of Pakistan in 1947, the league's mission was accomplished; and with no new mandate from the people, it simply collapsed under the weight of its several factions. In August 1947, after the successful campaign for the creation of Pakistan, the All-India Muslim League was rechristened the All-Pakistan Muslim League. But despite this change in name, the league lost its mandate and its influence over the people of Pakistan. Perhaps it might have survived the creation of Pakistan had it gone quickly to the people to renew its legitimacy as a political organization. But the party's leaders had, at best, weak support in the religions that now constituted Pakistan. Instead of risking their political lives at the hands of the electorate, the governing elites decided to indulge in the politics of manipulation. Old governments fell and new ones were formed to accommodate the rapidly shifting sands of Pakistani politics. Into this situation of virtual chaos, the bureaucracy stepped forward and took firm control of the economy.

In managing the economy, the civil servants developed an approach that, with some changes, persists to this day. This approach has three distinct features. First, and in keeping with their training, the civil servants took no interest in long-term planning. They dealt with the economy as they had handled problems of law and order during the period of the British raj: crises were solved as they appeared; long-term solutions were only applied when, in the eyes of the civil servants, the crisis warranted such a handling. Applying this approach to economic management, the civil service scored a number of early successes. To accommodate millions of refugees who had poured into urban Pakistan, they quickly distributed to them the properties left by the migrating Hindus and Sikhs. Within months of the unanticipated havoc that accompanied the partition of British India, Pakistan once again had a functioning urban economy. Similarly, the shock waves generated by the Indian decision in 1949 to stop trade with Pakistan were handled by the civil servants by reinstating the import controls and consumer rationings that they had used during the days of World War II. At the same time, private entrepreneurs—mostly traders who had profited from the commerce associated with British India's war effort—were invited to set up consumer industries in Karachi's Sindhi Industrial and Trading Estate.

In later years the bureaucracy scored a number of other successes. For instance, in 1972, following the separation of Bangladesh, the Ministries of Finance and Commerce, under the direction of senior civil servants, were able to find new export markets for the goods and commodities that had previously been sold in Pakistan's east wing. Again in 1972, under the political direction of Zulfikar Ali Bhutto's administration, the civil bureaucracy was able quickly to bring under public control large segments of the industrial sector that had hitherto been privately owned. And following the Soviet incursion into Afghanistan in December 1979, the civil servants, working as district officers, helped to resettle millions of refugees who poured into Afghanistan. In other words, the civil service responded quickly, and most effectively, whenever they were called upon to handle economic crises; they had little training, and even less taste, for working within the framework of medium- or long-term development plans. Pakistan's distributive problems, however, could only be addressed by such planning, and the fact that they never were is testimony to the power the civil servants wielded over economic management.

Decentralization was the second important feature of economic management as practiced by the civil bureaucracy. This approach also was in keeping with their training. Most civil servants who wielded power in the economic arena and helped shape the country's economic history came from the Indian civil service (ICS) or the civil service of Pakistan (CSP), the ICS's successor in Pakistan. The members of these services had been trained to act on their own within the loose administrative framework that the British had developed in India and that Pakistan adopted for its own use following independence. With poor communication of all kinds—poor roads and even poorer telecommunications—it made sense for the British government in Delhi and in the provincial headquarters to leave their trusted field representatives to their own devices. The field officers were required to maintain law and order, handle crises of all kinds, and collect taxes to pay for government expenditure. There was little reason for the central authority to intervene in their work. Deputy commissioners who were put in charge of the districts constituted the centerpiece of this machinery. More often than not, this machinery worked smoothly, maintaining peace for the British raj and collecting resources to pay for its administration. The British administration's ability to pay for itself was the result of the enterprise and dedication of the civil service (Mason 1969).

The needs of an independent Pakistan were necessarily different from those of the colonial administration, but the administrative machine the British had created for maintaining law and order and generating revenue should have been quickly adapted to suit the circumstances of a self-governing developing country. What was needed was a strong political entity at the center to redirect the powerful civil bureaucracy away from procedures it had used during colonial times. Such a political entity did not come into being for nearly a quarter century, not until 1971, when Zulfikar Ali Bhutto took command in Islamabad. In the meantime, the civil servants were left alone to reorient their approach toward governance. The bureaucracy recognized that the citizens expected the government to work for their economic and social improvement, not for administrative control of their affairs.

The civil service applied its belief in the efficacy of decentralized management by supporting the creation of a public development corporation and the transfer of significant sums of money to local administrations for development purposes. The Pakistan Industrial Development Corporation (PIDC) was the first such entity to be set up; its purpose was to establish industrial enterprises that required investments of capital too large for the private sector of that were considered risky undertakings by private entrepreneurs. The PIDC experiment was considered a success; in the 1960s the government of Ayub Khan set up public-sector corporations to develop power and irrigation (Water and Power Development Authority, or WAPDA) and to promote investment in agriculture (Agricultural Development Corporation, or ADC).

At the same time, a number of rural development programs centered around the civil bureaucracy were started by successive governments in Pakistan. The Village Aid Program in the 1950s, the East and West Pakistan Rural Works Programs in the 1960s, and the Rural Marakaz (centers) Program in the 1970s followed the same model: the local administrator, who was a member of either the civil service of Pakistan or one of the provincial civil services, was given public funds to expend on development, with some guidance from the village council, which he nominated himself, as in the case of Village Aid Programs, or from the elected union and district councils, over which he had considerable influence, as in the case of the Rural Works Programs.

The public corporation as a device for undertaking development had a mixed record in Pakistan, as in other developing countries.[7] The developmental and distributive impact of rural development programs, however, if not negative, was at best marginal. The West Pakistan Rural Works Program, for instance, was captured by the landed aristocracy soon after its inception and made no contribution whatsoever to redistributing incomes or alleviating rural poverty.[8]

The third feature of the bureaucratic model was its political flexibility. Civil servants were quick to adapt themselves whenever a firm political hand appeared at the center, as happened three times in Pakistan's history. The first was in 1958, when Ayub Khan carried out his coup d'état and became the first military president of the country. Ayub Khan was keen to promote economic growth and was persuaded by a number of foreign economic advisors to adopt medium-term economic planning as an important way of achieving this objective. Accordingly, a group of foreign and Pakistani economic experts were engaged to formulate a five-year development plan. The plan, the Second Five-Year Plan (1960–65), was launched after Ayub Khan had been in office for less than two years. It was the first of the two development plans that were to succeed in meeting their overall goals. Growth, rather than redistribution, was the explicitly stated objective of the plan's program. "There exists a functional justification for inequality of income if it raises production for all and not consumption for a few. . . . The road to eventual equalities may inevitably lie through initial inequalities," wrote Mahbub ul-Haq, then chief economist of the Planning Commission (ul-Haq 1974, 1).

The second time a firm political hand appeared in Pakistan was in December 1971, when Zulfikar Ali Bhutto sent the military out of power and became president. Bhutto and his associates moved quickly to restructure the country's economy by bringing most large-scale industries under government control, by nationalizing banks and insurance companies, and by sharply increasing public-sector development expenditure. A second wave of nationalizations followed in 1976, when the government took over most agro-industries. These measures were carried out in the name of socialism and for the economic well-being of Pakistan's poor citizenry. But instead, income disparities increased in the cities, the economic gap between rural and urban areas widened, and incomes in Punjab and Sind, Pakistan's prosperous provinces, increased much more rapidly than in the poor provinces of the North-West Frontier and Baluchistan.

Zia ul-Haq's coup d'état in 1977 placed Pakistan for a third time in the control of a strong leader. With one difference, General Zia reintroduced the model of economic development that had been tried with some success by Ayub Khan in the early sixties; instead of taking personal command of the economy as Ayub Khan had done in the early years of his rule, Zia delegated all economic authority to Ghulam Ishaq Khan, who began his public life in the Zia administration as secretary general and went on to become the minister in charge of finance, planning, economic development, and commerce. Ishaq Khan, a civil servant, turned to his colleagues for help, and the civil service busied itself correcting what in its judgement were the mistakes made by Prime Minister Zulfikar Ali Bhutto. Zia had directed that medium-term planning, suspended during the Bhutto period, should be reinstated. This was done in 1978, and the Fifth Five-Year Plan was launched to cover the 1978–83 period. The plan's main objective was to bring the private sector back into partnership with the government to help with the country's economic growth. Whereas the private sector had been scared by Bhutto's policies of nationalization, it became active again within the framework of the fifth plan. The fifth plan was the second time that a five-year program of development had succeeded in achieving most of its objectives, although redistribution of national income in favor of the underprivileged segments of the population or toward the less developed regions of the country was not included among them.

The model of bureaucratic economic management practiced by Pakistan during most of its history helped to achieve rapid growth in gross domestic output. The civil service was well equipped to handle crises; and left to its own devices, as it was most of the time in Pakistan, it managed to handle a number of problems that left unattended would have taken a heavy toll. Through efficient crisis management, the civil service created an environment in which the economy could grow rapidly, but it eschewed long-term development planning. In that respect it differed from the military, which put greater store in planning, as was made clear when Generals Ayub Khan and Zia ul-Haq instructed the civil service-dominated Planning Commission to prepare five-year development plans.[9]

By leaving the economy in the management of the civil bureaucracy for most of Pakistan's history, the politicians more or less ensured that the country's deep structural and distributive problems would remain unresolved. The civil servants were not ill disposed toward structural change or disclined to deliver benefits of growth to the less privileged sections of the society, but the bureaucracy was neither well equipped nor trained to concern itself with the problem of distribution. Accordingly, all the major distributive problems faced by Pakistan remained largely unattended because the instruments of redistribution deployed were not designed specifically to address these crises.

Pakistan's Six Distributive Crises

Pakistan owes its birth to a redistributive crisis: the widespread feeling among the Muslims of British India that they had been economically, politically, and socially discriminated against by their rulers. As the time for the transfer of power from the British approached, the level of political agitation increased among the Muslims, who were persuaded that independence would further deteriorate their situation if the British were unable to provide special safeguards to protect their political and economic interests. The British failed to define these safeguards to the satisfaction of either the Hindus or the Muslims within the context of a united India; thus, Pakistan was born to allow the Muslims of British India to shape their own destiny.

The creation of Pakistan divided the Muslims of British India into three broad groups: those who live in today's Pakistan, those who stayed behind in India after the partition of 1947, and those who now live in Bangladesh. Although economic data do not exist for the separate religious groups of India, the fact that the Muslims in that country are concentrated in the poorer provinces (Madhya Pradesh, Uttar Pradesh, and Bihar) suggests that they have not done as well as their coreligionists in Pakistan (Bhattacharya, Chatterjee, and Pal 1988, 89–117). Pakistan's average per capita income is perhaps twice as high as the average for the Indian Muslims and two and one-half times that of the people of Bangladesh.[10] In other words, the establishment of an independent Muslim state in British India seemed to have solved the economic concerns of only a third of the Muslim population that lived under the raj. However, aggregate statistics—the rate of growth in Pakistan's GDP since its birth and Pakistan's GDP per capita compared to that of other developing countries—hide a number of distributive problems that remained even after partition (see table 7.4).

The Hindu-Muslim conflict that led to the creation of Pakistan suppressed for some time the wide differences within the Muslim community of British India. Once Pakistan appeared on the political map, these differences surfaced and brought a number of new redistributive crises to the fore. These crises, not unlike the Hindu-Muslim conflict in

TABLE 7.4

Six Distributive Crises in Pakistan's History

	Periods				
	1947–58	1958–69	1969–71	1971–77	1977–78
1. Deepening rural poverty	Cause: • Terms of trade change against agriculture Approach: • None	Approach: • Change in terms of trade in favor of agriculture Consequence: • No visible political manifestation		Approach: • Encouragement of migration of rural poor to the Middle East	
2. East Pakistan/ West Pakistan income disparity	Causes: • Disproportionate use of foreign exchange earnings in W. Pakistan • Emphasis on industrial develop-ment in private sector	Cause: • Use of foreign exchange earnings continued to be skewed up to 1965			

TABLE 7.4

Six Distributive Crises in Pakistan's History *(continued)*

	Periods				
	1947–58	1958–69	1969–71	1971–77	1977–78
	Approach: • Problem largely ignored Consequence: • Level of resentment began to build up in E. Pakistan: the Muslim League was defeated in 1954	Approaches: • Provision included in the constitution of 1962 to narrow the disparity • Ambitious rural development program was initiated Consequence: • Rapid buildup of Bengali resentment against W. Pakistan after 1965 war with India	Approach: • General political paralysis among W. Pakistani leaders on the issue Consequence: • Civil war in 1971 and emergence of Bangladesh resolved the issue for Pakistan		
3. Rural-urban income disparities	Cause: • Deliberate government policy to advance industrialization by turning intersectoral terms			Cause: • Slowdown in the flow of public resources to agriculture	

TABLE 7.4

Six Distributive Crises in Pakistan's History (*continued*)

		Periods			
1947–58	1958–69	1969–71	1971–77		1977–78
of trade against the countryside					
Approach: • Problem largely ignored	Approaches: • Large-scale investment in irrigation undertaken • Government encouraged development of agriculture		Approach: • Migration of rural poor to the Middle East encouraged		Approaches: • Government encouraged development of agriculture • Economic relations with the Middle East further strengthened
	Consequences: • Some improvement in income distribution • Some correction took place in rural-urban terms of trade		Consequence: • Income distribution worsened somewhat		Consequence: • Worst forms of rural poverty eradicated from the Punjab and the Frontier Province

TABLE 7.4

Six Distributive Crises in Pakistan's History (continued)

	Periods				
	1947–58	1958–69	1969–71	1971–77	1977–78
4. Growing income disparities between smaller/larger provinces	Cause: • Public sector neglect of investment in the small provinces, exacerbated by formation of "One Unit" of W. Pakistan	Cause: • Further strengthening of central authority		Causes: • Further strengthening of central authority • Military action in Baluchistan • Dissolution in Baluchistan and the NWFP	Causes: • Centralization trend maintained
	Approach: • Problem not recognized	Approach: • Some recognition of problems, but no overt action taken	Approach: • W. Pakistan's One Unit dissolved	Approach: • No specific programs or policies developed	Approach: • Sixth Plan allocated a large share of development resources to the smaller provinces
	Consequence: • Resentment on the part of smaller provinces against central leadership surfaced but not clearly articulated	Consequence: • Further buildup of frustration in smaller provinces		Consequence: • Sharp buildup of resentment against central authority	Consequence: • Smaller provinces remained dissatisfied with situation

TABLE 7.4

Six Distributive Crises in Pakistan's History (continued)

			Periods		
	1947–58	1958–69	1969–71	1971–77	1977–78
5. Muhajir's dissatisfaction	Cause: • Concentration of economic and political power in the hands of the muhajir community Approach: • Problem not recognized Consequences: • Considerable flow of economic benefits to muhajir community • Resentment surfaced in Punjab	Cause: • Indigenization of politics Approach: • A number of administrative steps taken to bring indigenous groups into political structure Consequence: • Established social and economic groups reentered the political arena		Cause: • Further consolidation of power by the indigenous groups, esp. in the areas in which the muhajir community strong Approach: • Strong administrative action to contain muhajir resentment (military deployed to curb the language riots) Consequence: • Sharp increase in the dissatisfaction of muhajir community	Cause: • Relatively insignificant presence of the muhajir community in a power structure dominated by the military Approach: • Problem not recognized Consequence: • Mahajir Qaumi Mahaz came to power in Karachi and Hyderabad

TABLE 7.4

Six Distributive Crises in Pakistan's History (*continued*)

			Periods			
	1947–58	1958–69	1969–71	1971–77	1977–78
	and Bengal toward the muhajir				
6. Disaffection among the rural Sindhis	Causes: • Settlement of non-Sindhis on the evacuee land vacated by Hindu landlords • Formation of W. Pakistan Unit	Causes: • Allotment of newly colonized land to military and civil officials, mostly from Punjab • Settlement of Punjab; peasants on the newly colonized land			Cause: • Use of the military to control the movement of "dacoits" in Sind
	Approach: • Problem not recognized	Approach: • Problem not recognized	Approach: • Unit of W. Pakistan disbanded	Approach: • Land reform of 1972 and 1977 aimed at reducing the size of landholdings	Approach: • Problem largely ignored
		Consequence: • Some Sindhi resentment began to surface; contributed to triumph of PPP in 1970 elections	Consequence: • Anti-Punjab sentiment continued to grow	Consequence: • Anti-"non-Sindhi-Settler" sentiment turned into strong secession movement	

294   SHAHID JAVED BURKI

the days before partition, were to have profound political consequences. The distributive crises that shaped Pakistan's political history
included the neglect of the countryside during the first
postindependence decade, the widening of the economic disparity between East and West Pakistan from 1947 to about 1965, a sharp deterioration in the terms of trade for agriculture from 1947 to about 1967, the
perception that the provinces of Baluchistan and the North-West Frontier were left behind as economic growth regained momentum in the
Punjab and Sind following the separation of Bangladesh, the feeling of
deprivation among the Muhajir communities in the large cities of Sind,
and the impression on the part of the people of rural Sind that they had
lost the control of their productive assets to entrepreneurs from the
Punjab.

Superimposed on these six problems of skewed distribution of
wealth and income was the frustration felt by the society's underprivileged, by those in the society who were not satisfied with their economic situation. The poor in Pakistan, like the poor in most developing
countries, were able to exert influence only when they were granted
some sort of a political voice. They raised their voices in the general
elections of December 1970, when Zulfikar Ali Bhutto's Pakistan
People's Party (PPP) won a surprising victory in West Pakistan over the
more established political parties (Burki 1988b). The poor acted again
in November 1988, when they returned the PPP to power, this time
under the leadership of Benazir Bhutto.[11] Otherwise, the poor were mobilized politically only when other economic or social groups were
prepared to provide them with leadership, as happened, for instance,
in 1969–71, when Mujibur Rahman led the Bengalis out of Pakistan; in
1987–88, when Altaf Hussain's Muhajir Qaumi Mahaz (MQM) won the
local and national elections; and during most of the 1980s, when many
influential landlords of Sind mobilized support of the peasants to create problems of law and order for the government. With these exceptions, the political role of the poor remained marginal.

It is paradoxical that Pakistan, itself the product of a redistributive
crisis that was solved too late, should have paid such scant attention to
similar problems of distribution and redistribution once the country
gained independence. This complacency was the consequence of the
assumption made by the political and economic elites that once the
Muslim community was left to its own devices, it would somehow
produce a society unmarred by serious problems of economic and social abuse. This assumption was, of course, naïve, resulting in part from
the influence of the Islamic groups that attached themselves to the

Pakistan movement and convinced many of the movement's followers that the organization of an Islamic state would solve the economic
and social problems of the Indian Muslim community. It was a deeply
held conviction of this group that a return to the form of government
practiced by the first four caliphs of Islam would produce the perfect
society that is said to have then existed. In spite of a number of attempts, such a society could not be created. Pakistan failed to found
an Islamic state for two reasons: first, it was not clear whether the
country was created to establish an Islamic system or was simply to
provide a homeland for the Muslims of India;[12] second, the debate
over the role of Islam in politics and economics delayed the attention
the leaders in Pakistan could have given to the problems of distribution of economic wealth.

Deepening Rural Poverty

Pakistan was born a poor country with the bulk of its income coming from agriculture. The countryside was dominated by large landlords; the majority of the population was engaged in agriculture either
as landless peasants or as small proprietors. The urban sector was
small, made up mostly of small businesses. There was very little large-
scale manufacturing. The structure of the economy at the time of independence suggests extreme income inequality, the extent of which
probably worsened as the country began to industrialize. The observation by Simon Kuznets (1955) that economic growth, at least in its early
phase, produces economic inequality was true for Pakistan in the period immediately following independence, as it is valid for a number of
other developing countries.

This episode of maldistribution of income was not marked by political or social unease, because the poor did not have a voice. In
Pakistan's early years, the only explicit recognition of the worsening
situation in the countryside appeared in the report of the Hari Committee, in which Masud Khadrposh, one of the committee's members,
wrote a note vividly describing the destitute state of the peasants of
Sind (Masud 1949). The committee's report did not produce any government action. Pakistan had to wait nearly twenty-five years—until
the electoral campaign of 1970—before redistribution as a general concern became a political issue. Zulfikar Ali Bhutto's PPP won the election in West Pakistan on the basis of a potent political slogan, "roti,
kapra aur makan" (bread, cloth, and shelter), and went on to implement a program of deep structural change in the economy, involving

the nationalization of a number of privately held assets. The program served to redistribute economic assets in favor of the state but did not directly help the poor. In fact, evidence points to some deterioration in the distribution of income during the Bhutto period. According to one study, "it appears that inequality increased in both urban and rural areas in Pakistan during 1969–70 and 1979 and that, according to all indicators, inequality is higher in urban areas than in rural areas" (de Krujk and de Leeuwen 1985, 411).

East Pakistan–West Pakistan Income Disparity

Income disparity between Pakistan's two parts was the first distributive concern to attract political attention after independence and led to the civil war between East and West Pakistan and to the emergence of Bangladesh as an independent state in December 1971 (Jahan 1972, 9–50). The rapid industrialization of Pakistan in the early 1950s was paid for by the windfall profits generated by the Korean War boom, which increased commodity prices, including that of jute—Bengal's golden fiber; more than two-thirds of the increase in Pakistan's export earnings during this period of commodity boom came from jute sales. The government could have captured this windfall through export taxes and spread the proceeds evenly across the country, but it chose not to adopt this approach, and profits were allowed to go into the pockets of the traders, who were mostly from West Pakistan and operated out of the port city of Karachi. The traders showed an extraordinary capacity to save—according to one study, as much as four-fifths of their earnings were put into industrial investment (Papanek 1967, 172). The government facilitated the use of traders' money for industrial investment by providing tax incentives and by investing its own revenues in building the infrastructure needed by private entrepreneurs. For instance, in the vicinity of Karachi a huge industrial estate was set up that contributed to the development of the city as one of the great industrial centers of the Third World.

The government's bias in favor of the private sector aggravated Bengal's resentment against West Pakistan, which escalated into an unstoppable movement of secession in the late 1960s. Before resorting to political action, the Bengalis labored hard to correct the imbalance in economic development that, according to their assessment, was the consequence of the government's discriminatory policies. The approach recommended by the leaders from Bengal was simple: increase the role of the state in economic development and management, give the people of Bengal a prominent place in government, and let the government raise the resources it needed to increase economic activity in Bengal by taxing West Pakistan. Pakistan's political system, however, could not accommodate these Bengali demands. Some half-hearted attempts to placate East Pakistan were made by the administration of President Ayub Khan, including a provision in the constitution of 1962 for the removal of economic disparity between East and West Pakistan and the launching of an ambitious program of rural development. The Rural Works Program was financed by the United States; it was launched in part to move into Bengal a larger proportion of the external resources that flowed into Pakistan. The Bengali leadership was unimpressed by these gestures and made East-West economic disparity a central issue in its political program. Sheikh Mujibur Rahman's "six-point plan" for gaining economic and political autonomy for East Pakistan followed the strategy Muhammad Ali Jinnah's Muslim League had pursued with such success in the 1940s. It ultimately led to the establishment of Bangladesh as an independent state.

Neglect of Agriculture

Pakistan's next distributive crisis was also a consequence of the effort to industrialize quickly. In the 1950s the government instituted a program for procuring surplus agricultural commodities to provide food to urban dwellers and raw materials for the newly established industries. This program was in effect a heavy tax on agriculture. Wheat, rice, jute, and cotton were procured well below international prices; food grains and industrial raw materials were provided on highly concessional terms to the people in large cities and to the private industrial entrepreneurs. This sharp movement in the terms of trade against agriculture affected investments and income in the countryside. It also had an effect on the distribution of incomes between rural and urban areas. In 1949, average rural income per capita was 69 percent of the average urban income. By 1958, this ratio had dropped to 62 percent. This change was felt by all income classes in the countryside, including large landowners. The landed aristocracy became politically restive; having lost its position to the industrial and commercial classes, it was no longer the dominant economic group in the country.

The losses suffered by the Muslim League in the provincial elections held in Bengal in 1954 and the large-scale defection from the party by the rural leadership of West Pakistan were in part the results of the benign neglect of the agricultural sector in the first postindependence

decade. Ayub Khan recognized the problem that the governments before him had created for themselves. He initiated a program aimed at
encouraging private- and public-sector investments in agriculture. His
government significantly increased food-grain procurement prices,
thus reducing the tax on commercial farmers. The farming community
responded by significantly increasing the level of investment, particularly in the exploitation of groundwater resources. These investments
enabled farmers to adopt high-yielding food-grain technology in the
Punjab and Sind. "They [the farming community] have introduced
mechanization, fertilizers, and better seeds. A whole class of young
people after finishing college are going back to the land. All this makes
for a healthy agricultural community," wrote Ayub Khan in 1967, looking back at the reforms his administration had introduced in the agriculture sector during the 1960s (Ayub Khan 1967, 92). The sharp
productivity increases that resulted from these developments produced
Pakistan's first Green Revolution. The revolution began in the late sixties, in spite of a sharp increase in population, and brought the country
back to food self-sufficiency by the mid-eighties. Ayub Khan's popularity with the commercial farmers won him the presidential election in
the winter of 1964–65, although his inability to placate Bengal almost
resulted in the loss of East Pakistan in that election.

The reduction in the amount of resources extracted by the government from agriculture, for investment in industry, improved the economic situation of Pakistan's commercial farmers, but it did little to
improve the lot of the rural poor. The rural poor had to wait another
decade before seeing a significant improvement in their economic situation. They benefited, not from a government-engineered program
aimed at increasing their incomes, but from the opening up of employment opportunities in the Middle East.

Economic Backwardness of Small Provinces

Although the dispute between East and West Pakistan received a
great deal of political attention for over a decade, it was not the only
regional redistributive crisis Pakistan was to face. Pakistan's smaller
provinces—in particular Baluchistan and the North-West Frontier—to
this day believe that they have been discriminated against by the central authority. This perception has deep historical roots. Baluchistan
and the North-West Frontier were reluctant recruits to the Pakistan
movement in the first place. Even after Pakistan gained independence,
the North-West Frontier was governed by a coalition of the Khudai

Khidmatgars and the Indian National Congress, two parties that had opposed the creation of a separate Muslim state in India. Baluchistan in 1947 was not a province; it was made up of a number of princely states and the centrally administrated territories around its major cities. It took a military action to persuade the khan of Kalat, the ruler of the largest of the princely states, to accede to Pakistan, and some further arm-twisting was needed to get the smaller princes to surrender their territories to the province of Baluchistan (Harrison 1981, 21–40).

This historical background should have made the central authority sensitive to the economic development needs of Baluchistan and the Frontier. Economic activism by the provincial government of Abdul Qayyum Khan for a while allayed the Frontier's fears about being swamped by Punjabis. But Qayyum Khan fell victim to political intrigue in 1953, giving rise once again to fears in the Frontier of receiving indifferent treatment from the central authority. Meanwhile, during the half dozen years the Frontier stayed quiet immediately following independence in 1947, the situation in Baluchistan remained politically restive.

Rather than divert resources from the relatively prosperous provinces of Punjab and Sind for discretionary use by the leaders of the poorer regions of Baluchistan and the North-West Frontier, the center sought instead to further consolidate its political and economic control. In 1955, for instance, the government merged West Pakistan's four provinces into one administrative entity. Thus was born the One Unit of West Pakistan, with its capital in the Punjab city of Lahore. The provincial elites who had initially resisted the creation of Pakistan in the belief that they would lose power to a central leadership now saw their fears justified. Lahore was not only far from their seats of power, it was also able to exercise much greater economic and political authority than the British rulers had ever done from New Delhi. Ayub Khan's system of "basic democracies," which incorporated administrative decentralization as one of its major features, did not fully compensate for the loss of effective power the provincial leaders suffered as a result of the creation of the One Unit. The basic democracy structure was built around the system of district administration Pakistan had inherited from the British raj. The deputy commissioner and commissioners were the main players in the system; they considered themselves the representatives of the government based in Lahore, not necessarily the spokesmen for local interests.

The Bengal secessionist movement headed by the Awami League joined forces with the leadership of Baluchistan and the North-West

Frontier to put pressure on the government to dissolve the One Unit of
West Pakistan and grant greater political economic autonomy to the
provinces. The One Unit was dissolved in 1970, but the measure of
authority granted to the provinces remained limited. The smaller provinces, buoyed by the return of civilian authority in 1971, worked with
Zulfikar Ali Bhutto's PPP to write a federalist constitution that would
allow them greater control over their people. In theory the constitution
of 1973 allowed considerable autonomy to the provinces; in practice,
however, the central government under Bhutto managed to exercise
even greater control than it had done in the 1950s (Kardar 1988, 177–
94). Promulgation of martial law in 1977 did not help matters, especially in Baluchistan, many of whose leaders chose political exile rather
than incorporation into the political system Zia engineered in the 1980s.

Political devolution, had it been practiced, would have helped the
poorer provinces to persuade the central government to use
macroeconomic levers at its disposal for redistributive purposes. But
the provinces did not gain political power and were not able to use the
government's extractive authority to direct more resources toward
them. The smaller provinces continued to lag behind Sind and Punjab
in terms of income per person of their populations.

Loss of Power by the Muhajirs

Pakistan's fifth distributive crisis grew out of the massive population movement that took place after independence. The partition of
British India brought eight million Muslim refugees into Pakistan,
while six million Hindus and Sikhs moved in the opposite direction.
Two distinct streams of migrants that flowed into Pakistan were the
Muslims from the rural areas of the Indian Punjab and the Muslims
from Delhi and the urban centers of the Ganges Valley. The first stream
went to the Pakistani part of the Punjab; the second, mostly to the large
cities of Sind. The rural migrants, settled on the properties left behind
by the Hindu and Sikh peasantry, were absorbed fairly quickly, the
urban migrants, however, had to look for new jobs and income opportunities in government, commerce, industry, and the service sector. The
migrants profited handsomely in the early days of Pakistan because
they had an influential voice in the central government that operated
out of Karachi.

From about the middle of the 1960s, the tide turned against the
urban refugees, the Muhajirs. The Muhajir community was already
affected by a number of actions taken during the Ayub period. The

consolidation of political power by Ayub Khan eventually led to reassertion of the authority that had been traditionally exercised by the Punjab's landed aristocracy over the province's countryside. As Punjabi landlords regained power, the Muhajir community began to lose its influence. President Ayub Khan's 1959 decision, taken a year after he came to power, to move the country's capital to Islamabad created a distance of a thousand miles between the urban refugees and the central authority and further diluted the power of the Muhajir community. Ayub Khan did not fully comprehend the political significance of these developments. His government and those that succeeded him remained unaware of the resentment that was building up among the urban Muhajirs against the central authority. The ferocity with which this resentment burst on Pakistan's political scene surprised the government of President Zia ul-Haq and for a while paralyzed economic and social life in the major cities of Sind.

It took the Muhajirs more than a decade to react to these challenges to their power and influence. In the mid-1980s the more articulate sections of the community organized the MQM, which went on to win the local elections of November 1987 and to a spectacular electoral triumph in the national elections of November 1988 and October 1990. The MQM won eleven out of the thirteen National Assembly seats from Karachi and two from Hyderabad and became the junior partners in the PPP government of Benazir Bhutto that took office in December 1988. It won thirteen seats in the 1990 elections and joined the coalition federal (in Islamabad) and provincial (in Karachi) governments.

Discontent in Rural Sind

The sixth distributive problem to have had an important effect on Pakistan's political development was also the product of the partition of India and the migration of millions of Muslim refugees from India to Pakistan. As discussed above, the rural migrants were initially settled on the land vacated by the Hindus and Sikhs who had left Pakistan for India. But the number of Muslim immigrants was much larger than the Hindu and Sikh emigrants, and the Punjab's agriculture became very crowded once the newcomers were finally accommodated. The government responded by opening new areas for cultivation, but most of these were in the province of Sind. As the Punjab was relieved of some of its pressure, the density in rural Sind increased significantly. In 1960 the average size of an agricultural farm in the Punjab was 87 percent of the national average; in 1980 the Punjab's average was very close to the average for the country. This improvement of nearly 30 percent in the Punjab's farm size was achieved at the expense of Sind and Baluchistan. In the two latter provinces, average farm size declined by 20 percent over a period of two decades.

Although the redistribution of land in favor of the people from the Punjab was encouraged by the government, it was also the outcome of aggressive entrepreneurial activity on the part of the Punjabi peasants. These peasants, brought to Sind by the new landlords, were prepared to battle difficult conditions in the inhospitable deserts of the province to bring life to the virgin land. But the political price of this economic adventure was very high. The Sindhi landlords and peasants resented this encroachment by Punjabis. Their restiveness, when combined with that of the urban Sindhis, produced a very difficult political situation, the full consequences of which have yet to be felt (Mirza 1987).

Clearly, successive Pakistani governments have failed to take full notice of these crises of distribution, and this lack of attention has invariably produced unpleasant political consequences. The neglect of the agricultural sector and the deepening of rural poverty contributed to the demise of the Muslim League. The landed interests, cast adrift by the urban bias of Pakistan's first administration, abandoned the league in favor of political alliances that could protect their interests. In making this move they were helped by their poor constituents, who were unhappy with the deprivation caused by the government's pricing and food procurement policies. The failure to address East Pakistan's disaffection with the government's approach toward development led to civil war in 1971 and to the emergence of Bangladesh as an independent state. The perception on the part of the people of Baluchistan and the North-West Frontier Province that they were being discriminated against fueled separatist sentiment in the two provinces. The loss of political and economic power by the Muhajir community sowed the seeds of ethnic violence in Karachi and other parts of urban Sind, and the extensive colonization of rural Sind by the new landlords from the Punjab produced strong separatist tendencies in that province. With such a history of almost continuous disaffection on the part of deprived groups, why did Pakistan's decision makers persist with distributive policies that produced such negative results?

First, the groups that wielded power could without much difficulty extract benefits from those with only a marginal status in the society. Institutional means were not available to those who felt discriminated against to communicate their displeasure to the privileged groups. During the Korean War boom, Karachi-based traders bought jute and cotton from the highly segmented markets at cheap prices and were able to reap handsome windfall profits. When these traders turned into industrialists, the government came in with procurement schemes that lowered their raw material prices and the price of food for their workers. In the first decade after independence, the urban Muhajirs obtained economic privileges at the expense of their host community; later, the Muhajirs suffered at the hands of powerful groups that operated from the Punjab. A number of irrigation schemes opened new land in Sind, but large chunks of it went to the farmers from the Punjab, many of whom held high positions in civil and military bureaucracy. The new settlers brought in cultivators from the Punjab and seriously disturbed the social and ethnic balance in Sind's countryside. In all these situations, the groups that were hurt—the farmers of East and West Pakistan in the 1950s, the Muhajir community in urban Sind, the peasantry of Sind, the political elites of Baluchistan and the Frontier—were unable to evoke a suitable response from the government to correct the imbalance its policies were creating. The deprived groups did not have a political voice and, as such, did not possess a place in the political system.

Second, even when the underprivileged groups found a voice, as they did in the elections of 1970 and 1988, the government did not possess the policy instruments with which to induce change. The government now had the mandate and was put in the position to redistribute wealth and income in favor of its constituencies. The most appropriate way to bring about redistribution would have been through a combination of asset redistribution and fiscal policies; it tried the former but neglected the latter. The asset redistribution policies did not work for the reason that they were not radical enough in their design. The fiscal and tax policies were not even put to use, because the institutional structure that was needed to make them effective did not exist.

Programs and Policies of Redistribution

The programs of asset and income redistribution launched by various governments during Pakistan's forty-year history can be viewed from three different perspectives. They can be analyzed in the context of the categories to which they belonged, in the context of the political periods in which they were undertaken, or in terms of the motives of those who adopted them. The programs fall into four broad categories

TABLE 7.5

Redistributive Programs and Policies in Pakistan, 1947–1988

	1947–58	1958–71	1971–77	1977–88
Asset redistribution				
Refugee resettlement	1947–58	1958–62		
Colonization of new land	1947–58	1958–71		
Land reform:		1959		
			1972	
			1976	
Nationalization of industries and financial institutions			1972	
Nationalization of agro-industries			1972–76	
Three-marla, seven-marla scheme				1985–88
Income redistribution				
Fourth Five-Year Plan		1970		
Labor reform			1973	
Zakat				1981
Income enhancement and economic development				
Rural public works program, East Pakistan		1962–69		
Rural public works program, West Pakistan		1963–69		
Human resource development				
Family planning program		1961–69		
Nationalization of private schools and colleges			1973	

(table 7.5): asset redistribution, income redistribution, income enhancement and economic development, and human resource development.

Asset Redistribution

The preponderance of asset redistribution programs—in particular the efforts to redistribute agricultural lands from large landlords to small peasant proprietors and the landless—is curious in light of the low priority assigned to redistribution by policymakers throughout Pakistan's history and the unceasing opposition to such redistributive policies from landed interests. Nevertheless, three important reasons for the attention received by asset redistribution stand out. First, the country inherited tradition—one firmly anchored in the Qur'an and hence in Islamic history—according to which ownership of property is a legitimate personal right. There is no limit to the amount of assets that may be owned as long the owner contributes to the general welfare by using the assets productively and by surrendering a part of the income produced by the assets to aid the society's underprivileged segments (the *mustaikheen*). This tradition acquired further strength during the British rule of India. The British administration in India distinguished between good and bad landlords; it benefited the former through state attention and penalized the latter by constraining their activities. This notion of good and bad landlords was developed further by the socialist leaders of the Indian National Congress. According to them, most landlords had displayed a lack of social consciousness and were bad landlords. "To our misfortune, we have zamindars everywhere, and like a blight they have prevented all healthy growth," wrote Jawaharlal Nehru in 1928 (cited in Herring 1983, 87). In the congress's political idiom, zamindari (landownership) became a pejorative term. The left wing of the All-India Muslim League, though not fully subscribing to this analysis, did not recommend the abolition of zamindari but suggested instead a limit on the amount of land that could be owned. According to this view, which found expression in a report prepared by some progressive elements in the Muslim League, a ceiling on the ownership of land was one way of constraining bad landlordism (Pakistan Muslim League 1949b, 17, cited in Naqavi, Khan, and Chandry 1987, 91–132). Given this tradition, it became difficult for Pakistan's political leaders not to attempt some form of land reform.

Second, Islam considers it legitimate to own property as long as it has been acquired legally and rightfully. In the eyes of those who opposed the British raj in India—the Muslim religious groups were prominent among them—a fairly significant proportion of landownership at the time of partition was the result of government patronage in the form of *jagirs*, land grants that led to the establishment of large landed estates. Not only were the *jagirs* suspect, there was also considerable skepticism about the legitimacy of the large landholdings bestowed by the British on some of their favored subjects. Large amounts of virgin land had become available to the British crown as a result of the extension of irrigation to the desert areas of the Punjab and Sind; the British awarded large tracts of this land to their loyal subjects, a number of whom became politically important during the fading years of the raj. Some of them vigorously supported the continuation of British rule. Accordingly, "the word zamindar literally means 'one who holds the land,' but in political rhetoric [it] came to mean a category of proprietor created by the British" with disdain for Muslim nationalist politics (Herring 1983, 87).

Third, asset redistribution was politically expedient. During most of Pakistan's history, the governments did not possess sufficient power and political will to use fiscal instruments to extract resources from the haves for distribution to the have-nots, and yet some state action was often expected to redress income inequality. Certain land redistribution schemes could satisfy the demand for action without inflicting heavy damage on the propertied classes.

The first program of asset redistribution to be pursued in Pakistan involved the resettlement of the eight million refugees who arrived in the country following independence and the partition of British India.[13] The refugees were settled over time on the lands and properties left behind by the six million Hindus and Sikhs who left Pakistan for India. The task of redistributing the "evacuee property" was cumbersome. It involved the filing of "claims" by the new settlers in Pakistan, the verification of the claims by specially designated officials, award of "compensation units" to the claimants, and the settlement of the units awarded against evacuee property. Although firm estimates are not available, the value of the property left by Hindus and Sikhs in Pakistan is believed to have been greater than the real value of the assets Muslims vacated in India. The award of the entire evacuee property to the newcomers in Pakistan, therefore, redistributed assets in favor of the settlers as against the locals, and consequently, the locals' unhappiness with this approach slowed the process down. Martial law was imposed in 1958 to expedite the process of resettlement even though only 7.5 percent of the claims filed by the refugees were recognized as accurate (Ayub Khan 1967, 94). "I checked up with a large number of people affected," wrote President Ayub Khan in his political autobiography. "Many confessed, now that the matter was over, that they had got three times more than they were entitled to on the basis of what they had actually left behind in India" (1967, 88). Nevertheless, Ayub Khan believed that some large landlords may have been unfairly treated by the way evacuee property was distributed to them by his officials. He therefore allowed the transfer of state land to those whose full claims could not be settled from the available amount of evacuee property. This program created landed estates of significant size in the southern Punjab and Sind. Because they were owned by non-Sindhis, their creation was to have serious political consequences in later times.

The British had extended irrigation into the Punjab and Sind not only to help solve India's food problem but also to reward loyal clans and tribes with dispensation of land. "Without the modern irrigation system inaugurated by the British in the nineteenth century, there would have been scarcely twenty million persons in West Pakistan [today's Pakistan] by the time of the partition, instead of the thirty five million in 1947" (Ayub Khan 1967, 94–95). Pakistan continued the tradition. New canals opened up land in the Thal Desert of the southern Punjab and in Sind; the area under surface irrigation increased from twenty million acres in 1947 to twenty-eight million acres in 1965. Of this increase of eight million acres, four million were in the Punjab and another four million were in Sind. More than half of the area that was brought under irrigation by government canals was virgin land and under state control. Instead of using the land at its disposal for correcting skewed distribution of holding, the government chose to reward civil and military officers for what was considered to be dedicated service to the state. This practice was followed throughout Pakistan's history by civilian as well as military administrations. It created a new class of "gentleman farmers" who added their influence to the considerable political weight of the landed aristocracy and managed to blunt the impact of even moderate land reforms that were carried out in the 1960s and 1970s.

Governments in Pakistan made three attempts at land reform; the first was implemented in 1959 by the administration of President Ayub Khan, who was of the view that "nothing much will be gained unless we carry out land reforms in a scientific fashion" (Ayub Khan, cited in Michel 1967, 12). A Land Reform Commission, appointed in 1958 for this purpose, worked diligently, interviewed a large number of people, and studied the numerous proposals that had been made previously to reform the system of landownership. But the commission's recommendations as adopted by the government were conservative. The government opted for the establishment of fairly generous ceilings on ownership—500 acres of irrigated and 1000 acres of unirrigated land. The owners of land to be resumed by the state were to be compensated by the award of long-term interest-bearing bonds. Under the reforms, about 2.5 million acres were surrendered to the government, equivalent to 5 percent of the total farm area in the country. Over 183,000 tenants and small owners received 2.3 million acres of redistributed land. The remaining 200,000 acres, being *banjar* (wasteland), stayed in the ownership of the state.

The second episode of land reform occurred in March 1972, when the government of Zulfikar Ali Bhutto sought to implement the "land to the tillers" pledge it had made in the foundation papers of the PPP. A new ceiling on ownership was prescribed—150 acres of irrigated and 300 acres of unirrigated land—but the affected owners were not to be compensated. A total of 1.3 million acres was surrendered to the state, of which 900,000 acres were distributed among 76,000 small cultivators. The third government attempt to address persistent inequities in asset distribution in rural Pakistan was made in January 1976. This reform reduced the ceiling of ownership to 100 acres of irrigated land and allowed compensation in the form of long-term bonds. About 1.8 million acres of land were handed over to the government, of which 900,000 acres were distributed among 13,000 persons.

The three reforms together benefited a tiny proportion of rural households: 272,000 out of a total of some 10 million. In all, 4.5 million acres of cultivated land—less than 10 percent of the total—was redistributed. As shown in the data of table 7.6, despite these reforms, landownership has remained skewed in the country. Farms of less than one acre in size (1.7 million farms out of a total of 10 million) constitute only 2 percent of the land (0.9 million acres out of 47.1 million acres), whereas farms with more than twenty acres (3 percent of the total) comprise 23 percent of the total land.

Although the efforts to redistribute land in order to create greater income and wealth equality were inconsequential, the nationalization of industries and financial institutions undertaken in three phases by the government of Zulfikar Ali Bhutto was of considerable significance. The impact of these decisions not only on redistribution but also on the pattern of industrial and economic growth continues to be felt to this day. Bhutto assumed office in December 1971; in January 1972 his administration nationalized thirty-two large-scale industries. In Septem-

TABLE 7.6

Size and Number of Private Farms

Size of Farm (acres)	Farms		Farm Area		Cultivated Area	
	Number (million)	%	Total Acres (million)	%	Total Acres (million)	%
Under 0.5	0.82	8	0.25	—	0.22	—
0.5–< 1.0	0.91	9	0.69	1	0.62	2
1.0–< 2.0	1.70	17	2.40	5	2.20	6
2.0–< 3.0	1.68	17	4.03	9	3.73	9
3.0–< 5.0	2.27	23	8.82	19	8.10	21
5.0–<10.0	1.75	17	11.61	25	10.18	26
10.0–<20.0	0.64	6	8.37	18	6.87	17
20.0–<60.0	0.25	3	6.92	15	5.01	13
60.0 and above	0.02	—	4.00	8	2.27	6
Total	10.04	100	47.09	100	39.2	100

Source: Government of Pakistan, Agricultural Census 1981 (Islamabad: Ministry of Agriculture, 1990), table 34.

ber 1972 he surprised even his own supporters by bringing under government control small and medium-scale vegetable oil mills. In January 1974 all domestically owned banks, petroleum marketing firms, and shipping companies were nationalized. And finally, in July 1976 some two thousand rice, flour, and cotton-ginning mills came under the direct control of the government. This massive redistribution in favor of the government was motivated in part by politics; Bhutto, a landlord, did not feel fully at ease with the commercial and industrial classes (Burki 1988a, 142–68). The "twenty-two family" speech given by Mahbub ul-Haq (1974, 2), the chief economist in the administration of President Ayub Khan, provided sufficient reason for Bhutto to move against the industrial and commercial interests. Mahbub ul-Haq's analysis suffered from a number of conceptual flaws; for one, it equated ownership of shares in the firms quoted on the Karachi Stock Exchange with control of industrial wealth. "Depending upon the measurement used, there were twenty, twenty-two or thirty-seven family groups in Pakistan which controlled a significant amount of industrial capital (and management) of certain firms in Pakistan. Although some accounts attribute 80 percent of banking, two-thirds of the industrial capital and 97 percent of the insurance business to these families, a more realistic figure appears to have been 20 percent of industrial wealth in the country" (LaPorte 1975, 109). Notwithstanding the problem with the analysis offered by the chief economist, its political consequences were impressive. In announcing the first series of nationalizing measures, Bhutto used the "twenty-two family" speech as justification. In the socialist order he was seeking to introduce, such accumulation of wealth could not be tolerated, he said (Bhutto 1976, 74–78).

The Bhutto administration followed up these actions by expanding in other ways the role of the public sector in economic management. A number of new government corporations were set up in the sectors of construction, commerce, and finance. In addition, the government secured assistance from the Soviet Union to construct Pakistan's first large steel mill. The consequence of all this was a dramatic expansion in the scope of government in economic matters. Public-sector enterprises in 1985 employed well over half a million workers. This was equivalent to nearly 4 percent of the total labor force in nonagricultural employment.

The growth of the public sector in Pakistan during the 1970s was in keeping with trends in many parts of the Third World. For example, in Africa, some three thousand state-owned enterprises were established by 1980, more than half since the late 1960s. But in general, the experience with state enterprises has been disappointing. In Pakistan, as in other developing countries, operating subsidies for these enterprises have constituted a serious drain on the government budget. To accommodate this leakage, governments curtailed expenditures in social sectors, including the programs aimed to help the poor. The purpose behind the creation of these enterprises was often laudable—employment creation, regional development, technological advancement, breaking the hold of the private sector over critical parts of the economy—but there is now consensus among development economists that if these objectives were achieved at all, their realization was at a tremendous social cost.[14]

The main consequence of the nationalization measures taken by the Bhutto regime was to redistribute assets from the industrial and commercial groups to the government. They did not help with income redistribution; in fact, income distribution worsened during the period, largely because of the slowdown in the growth of output of the industrial and agricultural sectors and the attendant increase in unemployment.

Income Redistribution

Although the governments in Pakistan gave considerable attention to the question of asset redistribution, they did very little to promote income redistribution. An income redistribution policy, to be effective, must make use of fiscal and tax levers at the disposal of the state to generate revenues for alleviating poverty. Throughout Pakistan's history, tax and fiscal management was weak for the reasons already discussed above. The bureaucratic model of economic management that guided economic decision making during much of Pakistan's history did not have a prominent place for tax and fiscal reforms; to carry them out would have required the possession of much greater political authority than could be mustered by the bureaucracy. Without these instruments, the state did not have the means directly to bring about income redistribution. Although there was an improvement in income distribution during some political periods in Pakistan's history, this cannot be attributed to policies designed directly to achieve these results.

Income inequality arises for different reasons. It can be the consequence of highly unequal distribution of such physical assets as agricultural land or industrial capital, or it can result from significant differences in the skills possessed by the labor force. To understand the social, economic, and political dynamic that produces income inequality, it is useful to "decompose" income into its sources. According to de Kruijk (1987, 668), "the bulk of income inequality in Pakistan is generated by labor income inequalities within occupational groups rather than by inequalities of income from other sources such as landed property." The importance of inequality in property incomes was estimated by this study at less than 10 percent of the total in the 1969–79 decade. And yet, as indicated above, governments have tended to put much greater emphasis on asset distribution than on income redistribution.

A combination of fiscal and expenditure policies is required to improve income distributions; tax policies alone will not bring about a significant change. Herberger (1977, 261) states that "the conclusions emerging" from an analysis of poor countries' ability to use their fiscal systems for redistributive purposes "will probably be disheartening to those who believe that a major assault on the problem of inequality can be effected by fiscal means." An exclusive reliance on fiscal means cannot be very productive for a variety of reasons, including the propensity of capital to shift to other sectors, such as agriculture, or to migrate from the country altogether. Pakistan's fiscal system, by not taxing agriculture, has already provided a haven for those who consider present rates onerous. And, as Pakistan's industrialists demonstrated during the Bhutto period, they and their capital can take flight as rapidly as the industrial capital in other countries.

Although these responses are important, they remain only theoretical possibilities in Pakistan because of the relatively low tax base. As the tax system has evolved over time, there has been a marked shift in favor of indirect taxes: a move away from direct taxes on income and toward those on import and production. Such a move was prompted by political expediency insofar as indirect taxes were easier to levy than those on income or on wealth. Nontax government revenues (for example, the profits earned by government-owned enterprises, payments for services provided by the government, interests earned on loans advanced by the government), from the civil servants' point of view, were even better than taxes. As shown in table 7.7, the government's fiscal policy, under the management of the civil service, moved in the direction of these easy options. The share of direct taxes declined from about one-sixth of total government receipts in the early 1980s to about one-eighth in 1987–88, the last year of the Zia period. In the total revenues yielded by taxes, the share of indirect levies (import and export taxes, excise duties, stamp duties, motor vehicle taxes) increased from 80 percent in 1980–81 to 82 percent in 1987–88. But at the same time, the share of all taxes in total government revenues declined significantly, from over four-fifths to slightly more than two-thirds of the total. This was possible because of the economic restructuring undertaken by the government of Zulfikar Ali Bhutto. The Bhutto administration—by acquiring industries, banks, and finance companies and by nationalizing some forms of export trade—vastly expanded the state's asset base. During the Zia period, the civil servants busied themselves improving the productivity of the properties and businesses owned by the government. Thye succeeded remarkably well. Between 1979–80 and 1987–88 profits of government trading companies increased threefold, that of the post and telegraph office sixfold, and that of public-sector enterprises tenfold. Although this was an impressive performance, such reliance on the government's nontax revenues created some serious long-term problems. From 1979–80 to 1987–88 the GNP increased by 183 percent in current prices, but tax revenues grew by only 141 percent. Total government revenues, however, kept pace with the increase

TABLE 7.7

Consolidated Federal and Provincial Revenues

(in percentage)

	1979–80	1980–81	1981–82	1982–83	1983–84	1984–85	1985–86	1986–87	1987–88
Revenues									
Federal	93.8	93.9	93.4	94.4	94.7	94.4	94.4	95.0	95.7
Provincial	6.2	6.1	6.6	5.6	5.3	5.6	5.6	5.0	4.3
Sources of Revenue									
Direct taxes	14.3	16.0	17.1	15.6	12.7	12.5	11.4	11.0	12.0
Income tax	13.4	14.9	16.0	14.8	11.9	11.9	10.8	10.2	10.9
Property tax	0.9	1.1	1.1	0.8	0.8	0.8	0.6	0.8	1.1
Indirect taxes	70.1	66.6	65.7	67.2	61.4	59.7	58.8	55.2	56.4
Non-tax revenue	15.5	17.4	17.2	17.2	25.8	27.7	29.8	33.9	31.8
Revenue as percent of GDP									
Total revenue	16.4	16.9	16.1	16.3	17.3	16.2	16.4	16.4	16.4
Tax revenue	13.9	14.0	13.4	13.5	12.8	12.7	11.5	10.8	11.4

Source: Government of Pakistan, *Economic Survey, 1987–88* (Islamabad: Finance Division, 1988), Statistical Appendix, tables 8.1 and 8.2.

in national income. This low level of tax buoyancy has posed a serious resource issue for the country. Pakistan must make a serious domestic resource mobilization effort, but the bureaucracy that has managed the economy until now is not equipped to extract a large proportion of national income.

Table 7.8 provides a consolidated picture of public expenditure in Pakistan. A number of trends, significant for this chapter, stand out from the data. For instance, current expenditures have risen rapidly in the last ten years, from 60 to 70 percent. The bulk of this increase is the result of the deficit-financing policies followed by the government. Budget shortfalls were financed by domestic borrowings; consequently, interest payments on domestic debt now account for nearly 16 percent of government expenditure as against 9 percent at the beginning of the 1980s. Government expenditure on social services has also increased, from 8 percent of the total in 1980–81 to 10.5 percent in 1987–88. As already indicated, however, this increase in government expenditure did not produce an improvement in social development; in fact the larger government outlay on social development was largely the result of the nationalization of educational institutions undertaken during the Bhutto period.

Tables 7.7 and 7.8 point toward two important conclusions about the government's distributive role in Pakistan. First, government finances are not elastic enough to accommodate large outlays on social development and poverty alleviation programs that may be needed to sustain the improvement that has occurred in recent years in alleviating absolute poverty. Second, the weak financial situation of the government imposes a serious constraint on increasing public-sector expenditures on social development, a problem compounded by the fact that defense and debt servicing leave little room for such expansion.

Table 7.5 identifies three programs in the category of income redistribution tried or actually implemented in Pakistan. The first—the Fourth Five-Year Plan (1970–75)—was an attempt to use the central government's fiscal authority to transfer additional resources to East Pakistan. The central government intended to provide East Pakistan with a flow of resources greater than the taxes collected from the province. The Bengalis were not impressed with the offer. Instead, they put forward their "six-point plan," which called for self-administration for the province in financial, monetary, and economic affairs. The second program for income redistribution, launched during the Bhutto period in the spring of 1973, aimed at improving the economic and social situation of industrial labor. The measures introduced, taken together,

TABLE 7.8

Government Revenues and Expenditures, 1980–1988

(in percentage)

	1979–80	1980–81	1981–82	1982–83	1983–84	1984–85	1985–86	1986–87	1987–88
Expenditures									
Federal		76.9	78.0	76.5	76.5	77.1	76.4	75.7	76.4
Provincial		23.1	22.0	23.5	23.5	22.9	23.6	24.3	23.6
Expenditures									
Current	60.1	59.5	62.7	66.3	72.0	71.7	70.4	71.5	72.1
Development	39.9	40.5	37.3	33.7	28.0	28.3	29.6	28.5	27.9
Expenditures									
Defense	23.2	24.1	26.2	26.7	26.8	27.3	25.5	25.7	25.3
Interest	9.3	9.3	10.8	12.8	14.1	14.1	14.7	15.2	15.8
Current subsidies	5.5	4.5	4.8	4.8	6.0	5.6	5.5	4.9	5.0
Social services	7.3	8.0	7.6	7.6	9.8	9.0	9.2	9.9	10.5
Other current	7.8	9.8	9.8	9.8	10.6	11.1	10.3	0.7	10.9

Source: Government of Pakistan, *Economic Survey, 1987–88* (Islamabad: Finance Division, 1988), Statistical Appendix, 97–99.

were labeled the "labor reforms"; their main purpose to was to transfer incomes from industrial owners to industrial wage earners. But the reforms were conceptually flawed because the industrial labor in Pakistan, as in other developing countries, was not economically underprivileged. The reforms had two consequences. They introduced rigidities in the labor market and they adversely affected the financial situation of publicly owned industrial enterprises.

Income Enhancement and Economic Development

The category of income enhancement and economic development includes two programs, both launched by the government of President Ayub Khan, one in East Pakistan and the other in West Pakistan. Both programs used foreign aid to provide employment to the unemployed workers in the countryside. Workers were to be hired by local councils, created under the system of basic democracies, to create a rural infrastructure by building schools, clinics, community centers and village-to-market roads.

Although the redistributive impact of the East Pakistan Public Works Program was the subject of some academic dispute (Thomas 1968, 92–103), the main consequence of the program in the western wing of the country was to strengthen the economic and political position of the already powerful landed class (Burki 1971, 167–206).

Human Resource Development

The role of human resource development—improved education, health, nutrition, shelter—in promoting economic advance and improving income distribution is now well recognized. "Over the past decade, views have changed substantially," wrote the World Bank in 1980 (46). Universal literacy was a political objective in many countries, but money spent on primary schooling was often regarded as diverted from activities that would have contributed more to economic growth. The same was true for primary health care, minimum nutrition, and adequate shelter. But the value of general education, improved health and nutrition for all segments of the population, and better shelter is now more widely recognized. It is also recognized that the only way to alleviate poverty is to provide for these basic needs. "Human development is . . . transmitted from generation to generation in a virtuous circle; but equally, there is a vicious circle that sentences the children of deprived parents to deprivation themselves. Breaking out of the vicious circle into the virtuous one is the essence of human development" (World Bank 1980, 70).

This realization has yet to come to Pakistan. Admittedly, all five-year plans—in particular, the first plan drafted in 1955–58 and the seventh plan that began to be implemented in 1988—have underscored the importance of human resource development. The economic development approach that has advocated human resource development and provision for basic needs, an approach promoted by such international organizations as the International Labor Office (ILO), the World Bank, and UNICEF, was fully reflected in the analysis put forward in the sixth plan (see Burki and ul-Haq 1981, 167–82). Mahbub ul-Haq, the plan's principal author, was one of the members of the group who had worked on the development of these approaches when he was a World Bank official. But none of the plans—not even the sixth plan—developed a detailed blueprint, including financial and management requirements, for the realization of these objectives. Levels of social development remain low and will continue to affect future economic growth.

Nationalization of public schools by the regime of Zulfikar Ali Bhutto was undertaken to improve educational opportunities for the poor as well as to upgrade the quality of education being provided in the privately owned institutions. As with a number of other distributive measures adopted during this period, the consequence was very different from that originally intended. Extending public-sector control over private institutions, without a significant increase in budgetary commitment to education, stretched the available resources. Public-sector resource commitment per student enrolled in government schools in the mid-1980s was lower in real terms than in the early 1970s. At the same time, by banning the participation of the private sector in education, the nationalization policy increased the burden on the government.

As mentioned above, the redistributive programs and policies that were adopted in Pakistan can also be viewed from a political perspective, which would underscore that most of the government's action in the area of redistribution was taken during the Ayub and Bhutto periods. These actions reflected the personal assessments by the leaders that dominated decision making at that time; they did not represent a consensus reached among different economic and social groups. Without such broad support, there was little chance of success for these measures.

Pakistan's Economy under Zia

General Mohammad Zia ul-Haq's eleven years of political control—from 5 July 1977 to 17 August 1988—saw significant economic change in Pakistan (see table 7.9). The size of the GDP more than doubled, and income per capita increased by one-half. Pakistan's GDP increased at the rate of 6.7 percent a year and per capita income grew at the rate of 3.5 percent a year. The performance of the economy during this period was comparable to that during the presidency of General Ayub Khan, when GDP growth exceeded 6 percent a year. The increases in national product and personal income were accompanied by a profound change in the structure of the economy. In 1976–77, the last year of the administration of Prime Minister Zulfikar Ali Bhutto, agricultural output accounted for one-third of the GDP at factor cost. Eleven years later, agriculture's contribution had declined to less than one-fourth of the total. At the same time, the contribution of manufacturing to national income increased by more than one-quarter, from 15.8 percent to 20 percent. Other modern sectors of the economy fared as well as the manufacturing sector: the increases in the output of electricity and gas, banking and insurance, trade, and construction were higher than the growth in the national product.

This performance was all the more impressive in light of the inhospitable global economic situation faced by Pakistan during this period. The early years of the Zia period coincided with a severe recession in the global economy that left a deep impression on the economies of most Third World countries. From 1980 to 1984 combined GDP of developing countries increased at the rate of only 3 percent per year, a shade above the 2.3 percent increase in their population (World Bank 1988, 187–89, tables A.2 and A.4). And although Pakistan was not seriously affected by the global economic downturn, its economy benefited from the expansion in global trade that took place after the recession had run its course.

The Zia period also saw a significant improvement in economic welfar. Although data on income distribution are not available for this period, some secondary evidence suggests considerable benefits accruing to the less privileged segments of the population. For instance, the wages of skilled workers in the large urban centers increased by 3 to 4 percent in real terms; those of unskilled workers may have increased by as much as 18 percent. Wage differentials between different parts of the urban economy alos narrowed. Wages of the unskilled workers in Lahore in 1977 were 72 percent of those in Karachi. Ten years later,

TABLE 7.9

Structural Change in Pakistan's Economy
Under General Zia ul-Haq

	1976–77	% of Total	1987–88	% of Total	% Increase Per Year
GDP at constant factor 1959–60 (Rs million)	42,401	100.0	86,166	100.0	6.7
Agriculture	14,004	33.0	21,124	24.5	3.8
Banking and Insurance	1,124	2.7	2,508	2.9	7.6
Construction	2,076	4.9	4,820	5.6	8.0
Electricity and Gas	1,143	2.7	2,927	3.4	8.9
Manufacturing	6,707	15.8	17,201	20.0	8.9
Mining and Quarrying	206	0.5	548	0.6	9.3
Ownership and Dwellings	1,418	3.3	3,028	3.5	7.1
Public Admin. and Defense	4,135	9.8	8,715	10.1	7.0
Services	3,060	7.2	6,137	7.1	6.5
Trade	5,875	13.9	12,836	14.9	7.3
Transportation	2,653	6.3	6,322	7.3	8.2

Source: Government of Pakistan, Economic Survey, 1987–88 (Islamabad: Ministry of Finance, 1988), Statistical Appendix, 16–17.

wages in Lahore were 85 percent of the Karachi wages. This change represented a 46 percent narrowing of the differential between two major industrial centers of the country. Although it may be premature, in the absence of reliable household and expenditure data, to come to a judgment, it appears that income distribution during the Zia period may have improved significantly.

That economic change during the Zia period helped improve income distribution is a conclusion also supported by statistics on the consumption of some basic goods. For instance, per capita milk consumption in the ten-year period between 1977 and 1987 increased by 6 percent, from 117 kilograms per capita per year to 124 kilograms. Consumption of beef increased by 20 percent, from five to six kilograms per capita. Domestic availability of cloth per capita improved by over 5 percent.

These positive indicators of economic performance, however, hide a number of negative developments that occurred during the period. For instance, Pakistan's dependence on external capital flows increased considerably, while the already low rate of domestic savings declined even further. Pakistan ended the Zia period with public and publicly guaranteed long-term debt of over $13 billion, equivalent to nearly a third of its GDP. Reliance on short-term debt increased; in 1986 there were $790 million of outstanding short-term obligations. Debt servicing was more than a quarter of the value of exports of goods and services. The terms on which these external obligations were obtained deteriorated considerably: in 1970 average maturity of outstanding debt was thirty-one years; in 1986, this had declined to twenty-six years. The period of grace allowed by foreign creditors also decreased, from twelve to six years between 1970 and 1986. Average interest carried by outstanding debt increased nearly threefold, from 2.8 to 6.6 percent a year (World Bank 1988, 256–60). In the fall of 1988, Pakistan's external reserves could finance less than one month's worth of imports.

This sharp increase in external flows counterbalanced the decline in the domestic savings rate. During 1973–80, gross national savings in Pakistan averaged only 6.4 percent of the GNP. The average for 1980–86 declined by 18 percent, to only 4.6 percent. Because gross domestic investment was maintained at 17.5 percent of the gross national income, the decline in investment had to be counterbalanced by capital flows from the outside (World Bank 1988, 193). The impressive performance of the economy noted above, therefore, may have been obtained at a high, long-term cost. It was this feature of the economic situation that persuaded Finance Minister Mahbub ul-Haq to declare in his budget speech, delivered to the National Assembly in June 1988, that he was dealing with a bankruptcy situation.

In spite of the significant increases in national and per capita incomes and in spite of in the indication that the people in 1988 were generally better off than in 1977, there was not a significant improvement in social development. Life expectancy at birth in 1986 was estimated at 52 years, 5 years less than in India and 16 years less than in China. Both India and China have lower per capita income than Pakistan. The relatively low life expectancy was the consequence of relatively high rates of infant and maternal mortality. In 1986 Pakistan lost 111 infants within the first year of birth out of every one thousand that were born alive. Infant mortality rates in India and China were estimated at 86 and 34 respectively. Maternal mortality in Pakistan was 800 per 100,000 live births; the comparable figures were 500 in India and only 44 in China (World Bank 1988, 286). Educational statistics also point to a low level of social development. In 1985 only 47 percent of the children were attending primary school as against 92 percent in India and 124 percent in China.[15] As in the area of health, educational statistics also point to a very low social status of women in Pakistan. Only 32 percent of the girls were attending schools in 1985, whereas 61 percent of the boys attended (World Bank 1988, 280).

This brief overview of economic performance during the Zia period points toward two contradictory conclusions. First, during the 1977–88 period, Pakistan produced an enviable economic record; its GNP and income per capita grew at rates significantly higher than the average for the developing world, and the benefits of this growth were distributed widely among the people. In fact, during the Zia period, Pakistan may have finally graduated into the ranks of middle-income countries and may have succeeded in banishing the worst forms of poverty from its society. The country's economic structure at the time of Zia's death had more in common with middle-income countries than with poor nations.

Second, the remarkable performance of the economy might have been secured at a high cost and may not be sustained over the long run. The ability to generate domestic savings to pay for only a third of the total investment has produced a debt overhang that would have to be serviced at the cost of future domestic capital formation. Also, the impressive distributive impact of growth implied by aggregate data hides the low social status of Pakistani women. The improvement in the situation of poverty and in income distribution may prove to be a temporary one, subject to a complete reversal in the not too distant future.

Both conclusions point to the vulnerability of the present situation. Pakistan's economy fared well during the Zia period, and large segments of the population benefited from the developments that took place during this time. Those developments notwithstanding, a number of structural weaknesses were not addressed, exacerbating the economy's vulnerability. These weaknesses included excessive dependence on foreign savings, inability to put into place programs that would address the problems faced by the more underprivileged segments of the society, and the willingness to allow widespread economic and social discrimination against women.

To obtain a full appreciation of the performance of the economy during the period when General Zia ul-Haq was in control would require answers to the following questions:

1. What was Zia's economic inheritance and in what way did this inheritance affect the policies his government pursued?

2. Did the several administrations under Zia ul-Haq follow a distinctive model of economic management?

3. What is Zia's economic legacy to his successors?

Zia's Economic Inheritance

General Zia ul-Haq's assumption of political control on 5 July 1977 interrupted the process of structural transformation that was initiated by the administration of Prime Minister Zulfikar Ali Bhutto. The Bhutto administration had sought to expand the economic role of the government by giving it a prominent place in external commerce and by allowing it to determine the direction of social change. This expanded government role was made possible by a series of actions taken between 1972 and 1974. Large industries, commercial banks, and insurance companies were nationalized. Public-sector trading corporations were created to handle export of rice and cotton. Private schools and colleges were brought under government control. Public-sector enterprises were set up to manufacture a number of basic consumer goods including vegetable oil, garments, and bread. Although such a deep encroachment of the public sector into the economy had no precedent in Pakistan, it was based on an approach popular in the late 1940s and early 1950s in several academic circles in England and the United States, when Zulfikar Ali Bhutto was at Berkeley and Oxford. Along with other Third World intellectuals, Bhutto was obviously influenced by Fabian socialism. These ideas were tried in India in the fifties and sixties (see "India by Design," *The Economist*, London, 27 Feb. 1989) starting with the Second Five-Year Plan (1956–61).

By the time the Bhutto administration brought this approach to Pakistan, however, the basic economic philosophy on which they were based had few adherents left in the development community. This belated experiment in statism and socialism did not inspire confidence on the part of Pakistan's donor community, which, because of the country's continued dependence on foreign flows, had considerable influence on domestic economic decision making. Also, the swift turn toward a prominent economic role for the state was not especially appealing to the important economic interests in Pakistan who were the product of the capitalist approach followed by the earlier regimes. When Bhutto fell from power, it was obvious that the direction his administration had taken could not be maintained. The new managers, called in to change the course of the economy, quickly dispensed with Bhutto's socialism. They and their predecessors had developed the bureaucratic model of economic management under Generals Ayub Khan and Yahya Khan; they reapplied this model and returned Pakistan basically to the style of management that had been practiced in the 1960s.

Zulfikar Ali Bhutto and his party had made a strong political commitment at the time of the National Assembly elections in December 1970 to alleviate poverty and improve income distribution. These redistributive promises were not fulfilled, and when Zia assumed power, he had to contend with this legacy of the Bhutto period. The bureaucratic management of the economy to which Pakistan reverted, however, was not well equipped to handle this problem. Although the worst forms of poverty were alleviated and although income distribution improved during the Zia period, it was not because of deliberate government policy; it was the consequence of the large amount of capital flows that came to Pakistan, sent by the workers who had gone to the Middle East.

Bureaucratic Management of the Economy under Zia

Unlike General Ayub Khan, Pakistan's first military president, General Zia ul-Haq had little interest in economics. He admitted to little knowledge of, or interest in, economic management. From July 1977 onward, the economy was put under the charge of technocrats. A group including some civil servants (Ghulam Ishaq Khan, Aftab Kazi, and Vaseem Jaffrey) and some industrialists (Habibullah Khan and Mustafa Gokal) was initially appointed to manage the economy, although the industrialists departed after a brief period, disillusioned by the reluctance of the civil servants to return most publicly owned assets to private ownership. From 1979 to 1985, Ghulam Ishaq Khan was in complete control; helped by his civil service colleagues, he went back to the model of economic management that, at least in the eyes of the civil servants, had produced highly satisfactory results in 1960s.

An attempt was made by Mahbub ul-Haq to break away from the bureaucratic model of management when he was reappointed finance minister in May 1988. But ul-Haq was a technocrat; he needed a politi-

324   SHAHID JAVED BURKI

cal framework within which to institute his program of fiscal reform, which had a high redistributive content. Such a framework
did not work for him, especially after the dissolution of the National
Assembly.

In the minds of Ghulam Ishaq Khan and his civil service associates, the loss of confidence in the health of the economy by two important groups—Pakistan's industrial class and Pakistan's external
donors—was by far the most important economic crisis faced by the
country. With an extremely low domestic savings rate, Pakistan could
not afford the disaffection of either the industrial entrepreneurial
class or the donor community. Both groups had been important in
providing the savings needed by the economy for investment. Accordingly, when General Zia ul-Haq persuaded the civil servants to
return to planning, they made regaining the confidence of the entrepreneurial class their principal objective. The Fifth Five-Year Plan was
formulated quickly; it was announced in June 1978, less than a year
after political control had passed back to the armed forces. The plan
was to cover the 1978–83 period; its objectives were reminiscent of
those of the Second Five-Year Plan adopted by the government of
Ayub Khan in 1960. "The broad objectives of the industrial strategy in
the Fifth Plan are commendable," wrote the World Bank in 1979. "Perhaps the major factor in a sustained revival of private investment—
and thus a major consideration in achieving a number of the major
Plan goals for industry—is a revival of business confidence. This is a
complex issue, tied to the country's political stability and political
future" (World Bank 1979, 50).

As was the case with their predecessors in the administration of
President Ayub Khan, the framers of the fifth plan did not intend a
more equitable distribution of wealth and income. Although the plan
was conceived as a "comprehensive national effort to overcome economic difficulties and correct the insufficient spread and quality of
social services" (Pakistan 1978, 2), it did not suggest policies or provide an adequate amount of resources for the realization of this objective. This approach was in keeping with the model of bureaucratic
management of the economy that was being practiced once again.
Successful long-term planning entails the adoption of goals supported by a broad consensus among different segments and sectors of
the society. Realization of these goals entails the adoption of redistributive policies that aim to move resources from the static to the
more dynamic sectors of the economy, or from the more prosperous
to the less prosperous segments of the population. As was the case in

earlier times, the civil service during the Zia period was ill equipped
to define long-term economic and social objectives or to generate resources for achieving them. These responsibilities could only be
handled by the decision makers who had the political mandate to be
so concerned. Accordingly, in the Zia period, as in the period of General Ayub Khan, the government did not concern itself directly with
redistributive policies.

The only exception to this was the introduction of *zakat* and *ushr*,
two forms of wealth taxes that were introduced during the Zia period
with the purpose of Islamizing the economy. In promoting Islamization and thus falling in line with one of General Zia ul-Haq's major
objectives, the civil service was running true to form. The bureaucratic model of economic management allowed civil servants to absorb the objectives of a powerful political authority whenever one
emerged on the scene. In keeping with this approach, the bureaucracy
had implemented rural development programs under Ayub Khan
and, under Zulfikar Ali Bhutto, had implemented the program of
nationalization of industrial and financial assets. Under President Zia
ul-Haq, the administration put together a program for Islamizing the
economy.

The program had two important features. It incorporated the introduction of a "profit and loss sharing" scheme in commercial banking to
replace *riba* (interest) forbidden by Islam (Shafi Khan 1987). And it
included the introduction of such Islamic taxes as *zahat* and *ushr*. The
program did not, however, encompass land redistribution, although
the Shari ͨah courts had "upheld previous land reform and nationalization measures under the governments of Ayub Khan and Ali Bhutto,
citing in their decisions Islamic teaching that all land belongs to God
and that the right of private property is limited by the demands of
social justice" (Esposito 1986, 351).

The Islamization of the financial system was carried out not only
for "eliminating that which is forbidden and establishing that which is
enjoined by Islam" (Pakistan, FBS 1985a, 2). To the government of
President Zia ul-Haq, it was also clear that such a system by its very
nature could bring about a better distribution of assets and income and
thus address the problem of persistent poverty. But the results were
modest. A government report issued in 1985 estimated that the funds
generated by *zakat* and *ushr* were providing Rs 330 per household per
year (about $34 at the rate of exchange prevailing at that time). About
2.71 million households, or 10 percent of the total, were receiving this
stipend (Pakistan, FBS 1985a, 14).

326   SHAHID JAVED BURKI

General Zia ul-Haq's Economic Legacy

General Zia ul-Haq's personal influence on Pakistan's economic history was marginal at best. In that respect he was different from Pakistan's other major political figures, President Ayub Khan and Prime Minister Zulfikar Ali Bhutto. Ayub Khan's legacy was a robust economy in which commercial agriculture became its most dynamic part; Prime Minister Bhutto significantly expanded the role of the state in economic management; both influences continue to be felt to this day. Commercial agriculture remains the dominant influence on the Pakistan economy, and state ownership of industrial and financial assets continues to be an important feature of the economic landscape. Islamization of some parts of the economy is perhaps the only long-term legacy with which General Zia ul-Haq will remain associated.

During the period of General Zia ul-Haq, however, the bureaucratic model of economic management may have reached the stage beyond which it would be unable to extend itself. It is doubtful whether Pakistan's economic problems can be handled any longer with the tools most often employed by the bureaucrats who were called upon to manage the economy: short-term crisis management and long-term dependence on foreign capital flows. The economy is now faced with a number of critical shortages and bottlenecks—electric power outages and crowded roads and highways have begun to take a heavy economic toll. These obstacles cannot be removed by crisis management; they will need large amounts of capital investment that, to be made efficient, will need long-term planning. Moreover, Pakistan may finally have run out of external sources for an ever-increasing capital flow. The country's external environment is likely to become less favorable over time in terms of its ability to obtain transfers of foreign resources. The withdrawal of Soviet troops from Afghanistan now makes Pakistan a less attractive candidate for aid from the United States, and continuing economic difficulties in the Middle East are already affecting the amount of remittances being received by the country from its workers. In other words, Pakistan will need to rely increasingly on its own resources.

This recognition dawned on the "caretaker" government sworn into office by General Zia ul-Haq following the dismissal of Prime Minister Muhammad Khan Junejo on 29 May 1988. Mahbub ul-Haq, the finance minister in the caretaker administration, proposed a significant restructuring of the government's financing and the country's fiscal structure in order to reduce Pakistan's dependence on external resources. The proposals met with a storm of protest from a number of powerful economic constituencies. Mahbub ul-Haq, a technocrat, had clearly gone into the territory reserved for politicians. He did not have a political consensus to support his proposed measures; he was, after all, a caretaker finance minister. Most of his proposals were not implemented, demonstrating the constraints under which the bureaucratic model of economic management must function.

Pakistan is also vulnerable on one additional county: its ability to sustain the progress it has made in alleviating the worst form of poverty. It was the flow of remittances rather than the government's distributive policies that brought about an alleviation of poverty. But with remittances declining, population continuing to increase, and the government without a viable distribution program, the progress made by Pakistan in the 1975–85 decade could be reversed. That the poor and the not-so-poor may fear such an outcome may explain the electoral victory of the PPP in the election of November 1988 and its defeat in the elections of October 1990. Pakistan's growing economic problems have clearly made its people politically restive.

Pakistan, therefore, stands at an important crossroads; the model of economic management that has brought it to a comfortable state of development may no longer be able to sustain the former pace of growth and development. This model certainly does not have the capacity to sustain the improvements in income distribution that occurred over the last decade. With the country faced with a less hospitable external economic environment, Pakistan's new economic managers will have to call domestic resources into play to improve the welfare of the underprivileged sections of the society. There is no precedent in Pakistan's history for this type of redistribution occurring successfully. Countries have been known to slip back from the ranks of middle-income countries into those of poor nations and to experience a significant increase in the incidence of poverty. This reversal has occurred in Africa, and it may happen in Pakistan if a political solution cannot be found for its economic problems.

Notes

1. A rich and growing literature deals with these issues. On the motives that led Mohammad Ali Jinnah and his associates to demand the creation of Pakistan, see Ali 1967, Sayeed 1968, and Jalal 1985.

2. Pakistan's economic history has not received much academic interest. Noman 1988 is the only recent book that attempts to analyze economic developments since 1947,

the year of Pakistan's birth. The author, however, concentrates much of his attention on the more recent period of Zia ul-Haq (1977–88). Andrus and Mohammad (1958 and 1966) provide an extensive analysis of the immediate postindependence period and of the economic reforms introduced by the government of General Ayub Khan. The Ayub Khan period (1958–69) was studied extensively from several different perspectives by a number of foreign academics who worked as economic advisors in Pakistan's Planning Commission and in the Pakistan Institute of Development Economics. Papanek (1967) analyzes the role of the private sector in shaping Pakistan's economy under President Ayub Khan. Lewis (1969) and White (1974) assess the contribution of the industrial sector. Falcon and Gotsch (1968) look at the contribution of the agriculture sector. Burki (1980a) analyses economic developments during the Bhutto period.

3. For an analysis of the political and economic roles of the civil service of Pakistan, see Goodman 1964, Ahmad 1964, and Burki 1969. A blueprint for reforming the civil service was developed by the Planning Commission (1958), which drew heavily on the work of Rowland Egger (1953).

4. For a treatment of this subject, see Burki 1988b.

5. This term was used by Mohammad Ali Jinnah to describe the country the British offered to separate from their Indian empire (see Mujahid 1981, 315). After some hesitation Jinnah accepted the British offer (see Hamid 1968, 175–96; Jalal 1985, 241–93).

6. This theme is developed in a number of articles by Akbar S. Zaidi. For instance, see Zaidi 1985 and 1986.

7. Robert LaPorte, Jr., and Muntazar Bashir Ahmad (1989) provide valuable insights into the motives that led to the establishment of public-sector corporations in Pakistan and the contributions they made to the country's economic development. For a comprehensive analysis of the performance of public-sector enterprises in developing countries, see the World Bank 1984, which carries an extensive bibliography of current literature on this subject.

8. I worked as the director of West Pakistan's Rural Works Program from 1964 to 1966. For an analysis of the program's distributive impact, see Burki 1971, 167–206.

9. The need for strategic as well as long-term planning occupies a prominent place in the curricula of the training institutions that have shaped attitudes of the military-officer class in Pakistan. The Pakistan Military Academy (PMA) at KaKul, the staff college at Quetta, and the war college and the national defense college at Rawalpindi train military officers as they make their way up the command ladder. See Cohen 1984, 15–85, 134–62.

10. According to the World Bank, GNP per capita of Bangladesh in 1987 was $160 and that of Pakistan, $350. The Indian per capita income was estimated at $300. See the World Bank 1989.

11. For some insights into the impressive performance of the PPP under Benazir Bhutto, see Rizvi 1988.

12. The so-called secular point of view—that Pakistan was meant to be a state with a Muslim majority rather than an Islamic state—is powerfully argued by Munir (1981). Maududi (1955, 1960a, 1960b) is among the more important exponents of the opposite point of view, that the main purpose behind the creation of Pakistan was the establishment of an Islamic state.

13. The estimate of eight million refugees who came to Pakistan soon after independence is based on a district-by-district analysis of the census data for the years 1941 and 1951 (see Burki 1974). Other estimates have also been made, however. President Ayub Khan (1967, 94) cited a figure of nine million.

14. The literature on the performance of public-sector enterprises is well summarized in the World Bank 1983. The World Bank has been engaged in advising the governments on improving the performance of these enterprises. For a brief overview of the bank's work in this area, see International Development Association 1989.

15. An enrollment rate of more than 100 percent means that the education system is reaching older children as well who, for a variety of socioeconomic and cultural reasons, were not able to attend schools when they were of primary school age.

PART THREE

State Policies Toward Women

8

Afghan Women in Peace, War, and Exile

Micheline Centlivres-Demont

The subject of women's condition has become a theme à la mode par excellence when discussions turn to the relations between East and West. In the Middle East since before World War I, but especially after it, the position of women has been one of the criteria of the modernity and maturity of a nation, especially (with the nascent movements of emancipation) for reformers, for modernists—Amanullah in Afghanistan, Ataturk in Turkey, and Reza Shah Pahlavi in Iran—and, of course, for the West, from which they drew their inspiration even while struggling against it.

In Afghanistan the conflict between modernists (the intellectual and university elites and government circles) and those opposed to change (the mullahs and urban lower middle class) has been recurrent since the 1920s. Both Amanullah and, fifty years later, Taraki attempted to impose their authority in order to accelerate changes they saw as too slow to effect the envisaged modernity. But their efforts were more successful in modernizing appearances and the legal system than in transforming entrenched traditions.

A conservative orthodox conception of the role of women, defended by the ulama and mullahs, has always opposed emancipation plans proposed by Kabul, whether they concerned questions of custom (girls in miniskirts were shot at in 1970) or of proposed legislation (progressive decrees have met with conservative opposition in the national assembly and with demonstrations). The two positions harden today within the context of war and exile, where they are propagated and discussed. At first glance, the reformist tendency is dominant in Kabul, whereas the orthodox one is dominant among the resistance in exile and among the resistance groups in Afghanistan.

Such transformation of habits and mentalities as has taken place under different regimes and through legislative reforms takes time to pass from the city to the rural areas or to affect any segment of the Afghan population other than a fraction of the urban dwellers. When the condition of woman is evaluated, usually it is only her legal status and the position she occupies (or does not occupy) in the urban public and private domains that are considered. Too often woman's actual role within a rural context (where the large majority of women live), notably her role in production and within the domestic unit, is ignored.

To speak of "the situation of Afghan women" is to generalize unconstructively. Women's roles and status in society and the division of productive activity between men and women vary according to region and ethnic group. Agricultural labor, including plowing and harvesting, is usually masculine, although certain feminine activities such as picking cotton and gardening within the enclosure complement the masculine activities. In Nuristan, however, almost all agricultural activities are carried out by women, while men care for the flocks. Among pastoral nomads, men are responsible for guarding, driving, and caring for the herds and flocks; women are responsible for the production of dairy products and for setting up and taking down their mobile dwellings—tents, or yurts.

In the case of the Durrani Pashtuns from Qandahar and from northwestern Afghanistan, women milk the animals and weave the awnings for tents, whereas men are responsible for these activities in the Ghilzai Pashtun populations of the southeast. Finally, in large towns, men provide crafts, commerce, and services when these activities are carried out as professional occupations in the context of the public market; women ply crafts within the home, where only rudimentary technology, tools, and investment are made available. Beyond these regional and ethnic differences, certain values and practices are common to both sexes. The cultural models of Islam, the great civilizations of India and of the Middle East, have left their mark on the Afghan populations. On the eve of the military coup of 1978, the situation of women in Afghan villages resembled that of women in rural societies of the southern Mediterranean area and the Middle East.

But the roles and status of women are, before everything else, based on women's reproductive functions: physical reproduction and social reproduction. At the center of a system of exchange that is based not on the individual but on entire families, wives are acquired by a transfer of goods from the husband's family to the bride's, a transfer that ensures to the former the young women's reproductive functions.

In fact, it is through motherhood that the Afghan woman fully attains her status. She is in charge of the domestic sphere and is responsible for those who live within it: children, daughters-in-law, and domestics. Very often the wife of the eldest brother of the family or the wife of the deceased head of the family runs the family affairs, including its financial interests.

According to Islamic law, a daughter inherits only half of what a son does when their father dies. In practice, however, landed property is only handed down to men. A wife is considered totally integrated into the husband's family, with no need to inherit property from her own family. She does, however, have the right to possess, and even to direct, a business, such as trucking or carpet making. Custom keeps her out of the public eye; thus, she practices her commercial activities through a representative *(wakil)*, usually a brother or an uncle. Within the domestic group, she has full rights of use to dairy products, chickens, garden products, and of course to her handiwork (e.g., embroidery and weaving).

Divorce is very rare in rural Afghanistan, and polygamy is limited to barely 5 percent of marriages. It is considered shameful for a widow to have to return to her own family or to remain alone; thus, she often claims the levirate (in which the widow is married to the dead husband's younger brother). Of course, it is also considered shameful for the deceased husband's family not to take charge of the widow, and the levirate is considered to be in conformity with the honor of both parties.

Women pay a heavy tribute in deaths from childbirth and infant mortality. The population of Afghanistan at the end of the 1970s was 48.6 percent female and 51.4 percent male, in contrast to the Western European model, 51.3 percent female and 48.7 percent male.

In large towns, however, differences between men and women, and the situation of women in general, already appeared archaic and abnormal at the time of the reign of King Amanullah (1919–29). Immigrants to towns, rural women were often cut off from their networks of solidarity with other women and were isolated within a husband's family. The risks and unknowns of urban life and the example of the middle classes encouraged them to stay in purdah (veiled, in seclusion). The development of a modern economy that accentuates the separation between the activities of production and of domestic life has further segregated women. And finally, for high school and university students, parental customs such as arranged marriages can create traumatic situations or worse.

A First Attempt at Emancipation and Its Failure

At the beginning of the century, Kabul, the capital, was the only city where foreigners—usually English—could be found. The city's population numbered between 150,000 and 160,000 inhabitants.[1] Women's customs were largely copied from those of Indian Moslem women. The *burqa*, or *chadri*, was the garment worn by the greatest part of the population.[2]

In 1919 Afghanistan had just gained its independence. According to the political elite and to King Amanullah, who was greatly influenced by the ideas of Mahmud Tarzi, his father-in-law and a journalist and modernist, development and progress in Afghanistan could only be realized through Westernization.[3] For the king and his counselors, the models to choose from were either Western or Soviet. Woman as a category stood in need of an emancipation that could only result from modernization led by the upper class; the queen and the sisters of the king served as models and examples. Because Amanullah was obsessed by the image of modernity rather than by modernity itself, he attached considerable importance to appearances and in particular to clothing (Centlivres-Demont 1983, 113–114). In the same way that attempts at modernization were to emanate from the upper class, with the royal family setting the example in a court that was supposed to act as the model for the wealthy, Kabul as a capital and as a privileged center for radical change was to set the example for other Afghan cities, then for the whole country. The symbolic value of appearances was to function not only for the modernists but also for the adversaries of modernization, who opposed the signs of modernization with those of modesty (ample clothing, the veil, the turban) and treated partisans of change as agents of licentiousness and immorality.

Even in the early years of his reign, Amanullah would have liked to have women unveiled, yet it was only after his return from his 1928 tour of Europe, and after he had forced men to wear Western clothes in Kabul, that he ordered that no woman should walk in parks of Paghman and Dar-ul Aman wearing the old-fashioned head-to-foot veil (Stewart 1973, 377). In October 1928 Queen Soraya appeared in public unveiled, to set the example; her lead was followed by some one hundred Afghan women.[4] But the importance of the mass media was underestimated; photos of Queen Soraya in décolletage during the trip to Europe or unveiled in Paghman were not only tales, they circulated into even the most remote regions of the country (Viollis 1930, 166; Gregorian 1969, 244; see also Poullada 1973, 70). In 1928 Amanullah also took a direct position against the seclusion of women, or purdah, which had been officially discouraged though never prohibited by law or decree, and suggested that polygamy be outlawed. But this attempt at modernization through appearances was later turned against Amanullah because the adversaries of modernization considered the reform of appearance a threat against modesty.

Legislation granting women's rights appeared in the 1923–24 *Nizamnamah-ye arusi, nikah wa khatnasuri* (11 Nov. 1923, 23 Aug. 1924), the code concerning engagements, marriages, and circumcision. It assured "Afghan women certain hitherto denied rights such as the freedom to marry a man of their choice" (Poullada 1973, 85) and also placed "tight restrictions on wedding expenses, including dowries" (Gregorian 1969, 243).[5]

Following the example of her father, Mahmud Tarzi, and his nationalist bimonthly newspaper *Seraj-ul Akhbâr* (The light of the news, 1911–18), Queen Soraya in 1921 founded the first women's magazine in Afghanistan, the weekly *Irshad-e Naswan* (The guide for women), edited by Asma Rasmiya Tarzi, which ran articles "on the rights of women, child care, home economics and etiquette" (Rahimi [1977] 1986, 44); it appeared until 1925.

In the mid-1920s women were encouraged to organize their own association. One of Amanullah's sisters created the Women's Protective Association (Anjuman-e Himayat-e Naswan).

Education and schools were necessary to improve the position of women; girls' education was stressed, and girls' schooling was initiated as early as 1921 with the founding of Esmat School (later renamed Malalai), patronized and guided by the king's wife and Asma Tarzi. By 1928, about eight hundred girls were attending schools in Kabul. In the autumn of 1928, on the initiative of Amanullah, twenty-eight young women left for Kemalist Turkey to study to become nurses or teachers (Viollis 1930, 166).

To impose women's emancipation legally and socially, Amanullah had to oppose the ulama and the tribal leaders, who founded their opposition on the authority of Shari ͨah, the Pashtunwali tribal code, and the decisions of the *jirgah* (councils). The Khost rebellion of the Mangal tribes (1924–25) was a direct and first reaction against the Emir's reforms, including the family code and public schools for girls. Amanullah's reforms came much faster than the society could absorb them. Rural society and a large part of the towns' inhabitants were far behind the reforms of Kabul and therefore rejected them. Public education for girls, sending some of them to foreign countries, and giving them the right to unveil in public and to cut their hair encountered an enormous opposition, which caused Amanullah to cancel most of his social reforms in January 1929. Among other things, the schools for girls were closed. In October 1929 Amanullah was overthrown.

The Evolving Relation Between Emancipation and Development, 1929–1963

After the events in 1929, when the brigand king Bacha-e Saqqa overthrew Amanullah and was then eliminated himself by Nader Shah (1929–33), all customary and religious laws relating to social position and women's appearance were reintroduced. Women in the urban areas who had experienced the reforms of Amanullah were especially affected, now having to submit to heavy veiling and seclusion.

Girls' schools remained closed, although Malalai was finally reopened in 1931; but to appease the mullahs, it was used only for training nurses and midwives. Only in the mid-1950s did Malalai become a true school again, though only to ninth grade (Gregorian 1969, 309, 356).

For Abdullah Aziz, an observer of the life of the upper classes in Kabul just after the Second World War, strict separation of the sexes only heightened the romantic impulses and unavowed desires between adolescent boys and girls. Secret notes and little poems passed by sisters and cousins played their role, but in the 1950s "the telephone . . . had become the media par excellence for amorous conversations—when it was available and when parents were absent" (Aziz 1987, 84). Women went to a "women's cinema" (*sinema-ye naswan*) during the period 1946–58, to which they alone had access and which was included in the activities offered by the Women's Welfare Association.

In 1950–51 university faculties reserved for women were created in medicine, the sciences, and the humanities—parallel to those exclusively for men—in the newly founded Kabul University (1947). There was no question of women competing with men, particularly in the medical field, but the measures were aimed at improving the condition of women, who could be cared for or taught only by other women. It was, in a way, an attempt to conciliate modernization and *purdah*.

Whereas the movement for emancipation under Amanullah had been initiated by close relatives of the king—his wife, daughters, and sisters—that of the 1950s was supported by a wider circle of the intellectual elite, men who had been educated in other countries and women who had accompanied their husbands abroad. But it was still not the aspiration of the majority; emancipation was not a popular movement, nor was it adhered to by tribes, rural populations, or urban lower middle classes.

After the relatively democratic parliamentary phase of government led by Prime Minister Shah Mahmud Ghazi (1946–53) under Zahir Shah (who had come to power after the assassination of his father in 1933) came a period of authoritarian technocracy. During this period, from 1953 to 1963, Prime Minister Daoud (cousin of the king) and other nationalists and modernists, disciples of the reformers under Amanullah, did not oppose Islam but did consider religion a distinct domain that should not intrude into the prerogatives of the state and its reforms. Failing popular demand, these reforms could only be imposed as before, from the top down, in the form of decrees.

On 25 August 1959, the second day of the observance of the independence celebration (Jeshn), Prime Minister Daoud, encouraged by the queen, succeeded in imposing the "voluntary" removal of the veil and the abolition of the *burqa* for those attending official ceremonies. This authoritarian measure of emancipation perhaps did not correspond to the feelings of the majority of Afghans, but contrary to the measures taken during the era of Amanullah, it was a success, at least in the city. Within a few months almost ten thousand women had appeared in public with their faces uncovered (Sérignan 1960, 52). One of the elements contributing to these high figures was the much larger number of educated women in the city. In the provinces the response was more reserved; in Qandahar, in December of the same year, there was a short uprising after the local governor tried to force the elders to bring their wives to a public occasion.

These measures had been dictated partly by a growing need within the Afghan economy and administration for women to exercise semipublic functions: office employees, airline hostesses, saleswomen in state stores, and traditionally feminine occupations in certain sectors of industry. During this period the first female volunteers started working alongside men in the Kabul china factory (Dupree 1959, 3). Access to public areas of the Kabul airport was forbidden to women in *chadri*. This garment, which was abandoned by the upper middle class, tended to be adopted by the lower middle class in the towns, at least during visits and on festive occasions. In the same year the unveiling of women was required for official occasions, coeducational high schools appeared.

From the Constitutional Period, 1963–1973, to
the Republican Period of Daoud, 1973–1978

A relatively liberal period, from 1963 to 1973, followed the era of Daoud. The promulgation of the 1964 constitution was accompanied by the first women's entry into the national assembly.[6] Kubra Nurzai was the first Afghan woman to become a cabinet minister (minister of health, 1966–69, in the Maiwandwal and the Etemadi cabinets), a woman was elected senator, and several were voted into positions as civil servants at different levels.

This first experience did not last: only two women ran in the elections for the next (thirteenth) national assembly in August–September 1969, and neither was elected. Between 1971 and 1977 there were no female ministers, except for Shafiqa Ziayi, a minister without portfolio (1969–72); nor were there any highly placed women civil servants.

In the early 1970s in Kabul, the Western model of dress (e.g., miniskirts) and behavior was periodically adopted by the daughters and sons of bourgeois classes. Depending on the case, the reaction of the traditional element was sometimes violent. In 1970 two conservative mullahs shot at the legs of female teachers and girl students dressed in Western clothes, protesting the public display of female liberation in the form of Western dress and mores. In April 1970 five thousand girls demonstrated in the streets of Kabul "fearing that the legal system, dominated by males who were often conservatives, would prove too lenient" in prosecuting the guilty parties (Dupree [1981] 1984, 3).

During President Daoud's second, republican term, however, women felt a wave of liberation. The girls went to school and to university unveiled, although they wore headscarves.[7] The popular image of Afghan schoolgirls would seem quite proper to a Westerner: a black dress and white scarf. Teachers outside of Kabul, however, wore the *chadri*. In 1974 girls represented 7 percent of the students in professional schools, 11 percent (of 9,175 enrolled) at the different universities, and 15 percent in primary schools. For comparison, the total number enrolled from primary school to university in 1933 was 1,350; in 1974, 803,141 (Knabe 1977, 167). Figures for 1967–70 are given in table 8.1.

The first women's demonstrations took place within the international women's associations to which a radical elite belonged. In the center of Kabul, unveiled women—though with headscarves—demonstrated with red banners, especially on 8 March, International Women's Day.

TABLE 8.1

Afghan Enrollment from Primary School to University, 1967–1970

School Year	Village-Lycee		Kabul University	
	Boys	Girls	Boys	Girls
1967–68	429,549	68,433	3,531	733
1968–69	469,606	71,131	4,647	798
1969–70	503,594	76,361	4,913	844

Source: Dupree 1971, 29.

Note: For comparison, the total number enrolled from primary school to university in 1933 was 1,350; in 1974, 803,141 (Knabe 1977, 167).

These women's associations traced their heritage back to the reign of Anamullah, under whose auspices the first association was founded and upon whose fall the first association was disbanded. In 1946 the Women's Welfare Association (Anjuman-e Khairia-ye Naswan) was founded at the initiative of French-born Naim Ziai and others close to the government and at court. In 1947 this nonpolitical organization was officially recognized and subsidized by the government. In order to awaken all women of the country, to encourage solidarity, and to create the necessary conditions for their emancipation, the association offered schooling up to the twelfth grade for married women and training for employment such as kindergarten teaching and social work. They also proposed employment opportunities and other support programs for women. A kindergarten, opened in 1957, served as an example. Although the association aimed at protecting mother and child, it involved only a small percentage of the population and above all the urban elite. After 1953 it also published a magazine entitled *Merman,* which was devoted to managing family affairs, to history, and to women's literature. In 1959 the association was attached to the Ministry of Education under the title De Mirmuno Tolanei (Women's Institute). In 1971, De Mirmuno Tolanei declared a Mother's Day and, beginning in 1975, offered an award to the "mother of the year." The new charter of 1975 converted the Women's Institute "from an administrative unit for women to a women's movement planning to reach women in villages even in the far-flung areas of the country. . . . Priority [would] be given to campaigns against illiteracy among women, forced marriages and superstitions" (*Kabul Times*, 15 June 1975, 3, cited in Knabe 1977, 188–89; see also Knabe 1977, 178–89; Grevemeyer 1987, 260, 396).

The constitution of 1964 established a multiparty system. Among these parties, the People's Democratic Party of Afghanistan (PDPA) represented the far Left. Several members of the PDPA were elected to the first legislature, among them Anahita Ratebzad, who had been educated in the United States, was a graduate of a nursing school in Chicago, and was related on her mother's side to Mahmud Tarzi. In order to provide a left-wing alternative to the official organization, at the instigation of her party she founded the Democratic Organization of Afghan Women (DOAW) in 1965. This organization had close ties with the International Union of Women for Peace. Ratebzad presided over the DOAW from 1967 to 1978. From only seven members in 1965, the DOAW grew to claim a thousand members in June 1978.[8]

In the domain of health, the Afghan Family Guidance Association (AFGA) was created on 22 July 1968 as a private voluntary organization dedicated to family planning. Because of fear of hostile reactions from the conservative milieu, however, its charter makes no mention of the true purpose of the association. Ratified by the king, it was approved by the Council of Ministers without passing through the legislature, in order to avoid all discussion or controversy. Officially, the AFGA's purpose is to give better guidance to families and persuade and advocate improved ways to educate and train their children correctly and give them good health and soundness. But through the counseling services in the maternity wards in the cities, and through ambulatory counseling in rural areas, the association tried to offer women (at least those who could be reached) the means for birth control: IUDs, condoms, and pills (see Knabe 1977, 189–94; Dupree 1971, 14).[9]

Mention should also be made of the Afghan Girl Scout Organization, which lays "groundwork for voluntary female youth associations" (Knabe 1974, 157).

These associations intended to develop the Afghan woman's consciousness, but the politically emancipated circles that promised these reforms were narrow and elitist. The initiators were all from the same social category, the aristocratic bourgeoisie and educated urban circles, from which also came the women of the Parcham and those of more traditional parties.[10]

Within this emancipation movement, one must distinguish between the transformation of customs (unveiling of women, Western clothing, mixed classes, and meetings between young men and women), on the one hand, and institutional change, on the other, including laws, associations, and women's place in production, administration, and teaching. The transformation of appearance often acted as a visible sign both for those who perceived it as emancipation and those who saw only decadence, and it was often mistaken for women's liberation.

Until 1978 and beyond, the role of women within marriage and family was never really questioned, although there were a few cases of marriage without the parents' consent.

Legal Maneuvers of the Communist Regime (1978–1992)

When the Communists came to power in 1978, a new phase of emancipation for women began, although it was again an authoritarian liberation imposed from the top. The government, reinforced by the PDPA, had more means at its disposal than had the preceding ones. Not only did it decree measures and announce programs, it also wanted to penetrate all of Afghan society and transform it, something neither Amanullah nor Daoud had succeeded in doing. Through party members and official organs in the provinces, the government had the means at its disposal to ensure that the decrees and campaigns that had been announced would be carried out. No longer content to act through example, those who carried out the new laws sometimes used force. The orders from Kabul concerning the application of the decrees and of the literacy programs, for example, were sometimes interpreted with an excess of zeal by regional and local functionaries. As was the case under Amanullah, the intensity of uprisings and revolts corresponded to the level of ambition of the programs to be carried out. This time, however, the protests came not only from the religious quarter and tribal leaders but from very large sectors of the Afghan population.

Even Soviet authors emphasized the brutality of the reforms, as did the government of Babrak Karmal (Parcham), which succeeded that of Hafizullah Amin (Khalq) from the beginning of 1980. From then on, the government backed away somewhat, first in applying the measures, then in lessening activism in the countryside, and finally in agreeing to ignore the decrees, especially those concerning the condition of women. But it was too late.

A few days after the coup in April 1978, the Democratic Republic of Afghanistan (DRA) abrogated the 1977 constitution and proclaimed the Revolutionary Council's "Basic Line of the Revolutionary Duties of the Government of the DRA," whose Article 12 ensures "equality of rights of women and men in all social, economic, political, cultural and civic aspects."[11]

In the Fundamental Principles of Afghanistan (21 April 1980), which served as an interim constitution, Article 28 guaranteed "equality among Afghan citizens both men and women, before the law, and in economic, political and social life" (DRA 1984, 73); also guaranteed is "the right to marry and form a family." In the constitution of November 1987, Article 14 (Article 38 in the constitution amended in June 1990) reaffirms the equality of men and women, and Article 15 stipulates that "the State will adopt the measures necessary to ensure health for mother and child and the education of children."

In 1978 the DRA promulgated a group of decrees aimed at profoundly modifying Afghan society through a series of reforms: agricultural reform, the reduction or elimination of mortgages and usury in rural areas, equal rights for women, and the abolition of arranged marriages and bride-price.

In only six articles, Decree Number 7 (17 October 1978) seeks to bring profound changes to women's condition and to male-female relations, in order "to do away with unjust, patriarchal and feudal relations between husband and wife and to consolidate sincere family ties." Specifically, Decree Number 7 sets an upper limit of three hundred afghanis on the *mahr*, the gift from the groom's family to the bride herself to ensure some economic independence in marriage, but more generally payable to the wife in case of dissolution of the contract. Decree Number 7 forbids forced marriages and establishes a minimum age for marriage (sixteen years for women and eighteen for men), under penalty of imprisonment of up to three years. In the commentaries on the decree, as in political discourse, traditional marriage appears as a symbol of backwardness and dependence.

Many men protested against Decree Number 7, as was understandable; many women joined in the protests. Indeed, this decree did seem to intervene unduly in a domain already covered by Shariʿ ah (Muslim law). Afghans do not always distinguish distinctly between social custom and Islamic law. Lowering the *mahr* to almost nothing seemed to be a threat to the status, or value, of women, as if the need for her and her role within the system of exchanges between families had been reduced to insignificance.

The superimposition of a Western conception of marriage had little chance of a favorable reception. As Nancy Tapper (1984, 305) put it, "Given that the marriage reforms are themselves derived by an Afghan elite from a First World ideology of production and gender roles, it is unlikely that these goals will be realized even if linked with substantial reforms in other areas. Rather, given the comparative scarcity of resources within the country, it is more likely that any such transformations of Afghan society would result in an inferior imitation of First World society in which poverty and discrimination against women remain integrally connected."[12]

Even in the Kabul of Najibullah, girls questioned by a journalist of the *Washington Post* (1987) declared they would accept an arranged marriage with the condition that they be consulted.

The Literacy Campaign and Programs for Education

One of the first objectives of the PDPA was, as of 1978, immediately to organize a comprehensive literacy campaign that would involve children, adults, and the aged, of course including girls and women. All of the population was to have become literate within a year, through courses designed to last 150 hours (Roy 1985, 123). That campaign, organized by the DOAW,[13] began in May 1978, although the 18,500 instructors, including 16,000 volunteers, had not yet been recruited. Disguised as a literacy campaign, a veritable political education campaign had been initiated that advocated urban, "modern" mores and behavior that were in fact Occidental. The Western model—clothing, body language, and the like—had already appeared in the school books under the monarchy, but without entirely replacing the traditional models and without phraseology concerning backwardness, progress, and feudalism (Centlivres 1983).

On the subject of the literacy campaign, Roy (1985, 123) stated, "Le Livre n'est plus le Coran, mais le livre de classe, . . . slogans et mots d'ordre du régime s'étalaient sur un tiers des pages [The Book is no longer the Qur' an but the class book, . . . slogans and creeds of the regime cover a third of the pages]." Marxist ideology dominated the curriculum.

From the beginning, the campaign raised disapproval, opposition, and revolt. It was, however, neither knowledge nor literacy that was rejected; at the end of the 1960s, although education only reached 5 percent of the girls, it was well received even in rural areas for the boys and also tolerated for girls. Education had progressed, in fact, with the collaboration of the population (particularly in the construction of school buildings). But in 1978 it was the content of the courses and methods of application that caused reaction and resistance. These methods were seen by the population as authoritarian on the part of the instructors, humiliating for adults, and immoral in the eyes of the religious leaders, who considered obligatory participation for girls and women non-Islamic because courses, in the absence of women instructors (and for ideological reasons as well), were often mixed. And why send children to learn to read and write texts that praised communism and revolution? What confidence could be placed in teachers who came from Communist Kabul?

By conducting its campaign for adult and female literacy without taking into account traditions and religious beliefs, the governments of Taraki and Amin ignored one of the most sensitive points in Afghan society. The results of the campaign (1978–79) were almost nil. In 1980, at the beginning of the Babrak era, the PDPA recognized its errors. As for the Soviets, they were just as severely criticial of the "inadmissible methods of Amin who falsified the progressive contents of the revolution" (Muradov 1981, 196).

The "women policies" of the revolutionary government, particularly the obligatory education of women, had much to do with making that government unpopular with the people. Beginning with the winter of 1978–79, a major reason Afghans departed for Pakistan was to protect the honor of their women and daughters from just this policy of the Afghan government. The negative effects of the campaign were felt for a long time within the refugee population; among the traditional elements it bred doubt and rejection of all teaching imposed by the government, and it caused considerable damage to the project of literacy for girls.

In the first years following 1978, secondary school students in Kabul revolted several times against these measures, offering the resistance its first "martyrs." One of the bloodiest demonstrations took place in Kabul on 22 February 1980. Young schoolgirls protested against the forced conscription of young men and the translocation of a large number of students to the USSR. On that occasion a large number of girls were killed, including the two most outstanding figures, Nahid and Wajiha.

By 1980 the literacy campaign was being carried out only in urban areas under the control of Kabul. Within these narrower confines Kabul's campaign succeeded, at least at the beginning, even if the figures given by the government—one million people having finished a literacy course between 1978 and 1983—are certainly exaggerated. And by what standard was this "literacy" measured?

In a brochure dating from 1985, the Democratic Youth Organization of Afghanistan (DYOA) points out that its purpose is to "struggle against illiteracy" and to wipe it out before the year 1991. Twenty thousand courses (of unknown duration and content) were supposedly organized from 1978 to 1985 (DYOA 1985).

It is impossible to say how many women profited from these courses. I found in the press only fragmentary or imprecise figures pertaining to the period concerned. For example, in the province of Badghis "over 210 women are . . . acquiring literacy in 13 literacy courses conducted by members of the Provincial Women's Council" (*Afghanistan Today*, Jan.–Feb. 1988, 15); in the province of Kabul "over 250 housewives of Sorobi district are admitted to 22 literacy courses, taught by volunteer teachers and 2 preachers" (*Kabul Times*, 11 Sept. 1988).

These campaigns are always carried out through voluntary activity or by militant male and female instructors. After the arrival in power of Babrak (1980), however, the regime began to be less antireligious and even made room for the teaching of Islam. In the literacy campaigns and in school programs, the mention of religious teachers guaranteed the government widespread attendance for religious instruction. By abandoning exclusively secular teaching, Kabul indicated its willingness to introduce not only into teaching but also into the government certain ulama who were sympathetic toward the regime. The government also claimed its allegiance to Islam, which permitted it, in propaganda efforts, to deny the resistance a monopoly on Islamic authenticity.

In prerevolutionary Afghanistan hardly 10 to 15 percent of the population had ever been to school, and females only represented a tenth of this small elite (table 8.2). After the coup d'état in 1978, and because of the war and the "antischool" reaction of the population, the percentage of those who attended school diminished. In fact, the number of primary schools in rural areas fell as a result of, among other things, conflict with the mujahidin.[14] Elsewhere there was a feminization of the student populations of high schools and even universities, perhaps owing less to the success of the educational policies for women than to the obligation for young men to carry out their military service. New departments were created in Kabul, and a university in Herat opened in June 1988; and thousands of students, both male and female, were sent to the USSR for higher education.

In the cities controlled by Kabul until the collapse of the regime in April 1992, the government was confronted with the often contradic-

TABLE 8.2

Number of Village, Primary, and Kabul Schools
for Girls and Boys, 1968 and 1973

Year	Village		Rural Primary		Kabul Primary	
	Boys	Girls	Boys	Girls	Boys	Girls
1968	1,191	153	782	89	34	24
1973	1,653	229	1,123	145	34	29

Source: Frommer 1981.

tory demand to train technical and administrative personnel and to recruit future officers for an army plagued by desertion. Several times the government resorted to measures such as university enrollment without examination for all high school students who had fulfilled their military obligations. The number of years of education required to enroll in the university was reduced from twelve to ten; the length of time for medical studies was changed from seven to five years; and professional training was encouraged, with programs modeled on the Soviet system, apart from Qur'anic instruction, which was diminished. At least up to 1989, the Russian language was taught from the fifth grade up; the teaching of mathematics and biology was strongly developed; philosophy (Marxism-Leninism) was taught two hours weekly from the seventh to the tenth grades. From the beginning to the end of schooling, the distinction between courses for girls and those for boys was eliminated, and specific courses for girls, such as home economics (ninth to twelfth grades) and needlework (sixth to ninth grades), disappeared.

Because schools in rural areas were often closed or had been destroyed, and because thousands of families had fled to Kabul, the schools there were crowded. Male teachers were killed, defected to the resistance, or fled to foreign countries; the number of female teachers in Kabul therefore tripled (Elmi 1986, 91). In a secondary school in Mazar in 1990, forty-three teachers of forty-six were female. In Kabul in the autumn of 1990, the level of education was rather low because of frequent interruptions and school closures at all levels.

The official statistics in Kabul mention 634,000 students at all levels in 1985, as against 800,000 in 1980, for a population declared to be nearly 15 million. In 1973, five years before the coup d'état, there were 110,887 girls out of a total of 803,141 students (Frommer 1981, 299). Kabul University had 7,600 students in 1988, fewer than in 1978. Counting the other university institutions such as the polytechnic school and the faculty of medicine in Jalalabad, there were around 13,000 students. The university was highly politicized; all students were obliged to be members of the DYOA. Most of the students were girls because, as of 1983, boys could be admitted to Kabul University only after completion of their military service. In 1976, 1,734 male and 316 female students (15.4 percent) were admitted to the university; in 1984, 753 male and 1,030 female students (57.7 percent) were admitted (government sources taken from *Nouvelles d'Afghanistan* 19–20 [Oct.–Nov. 1984]).

The sovietization process included the education of thousands of Afghans in the USSR and Eastern Europe.[15] The *Kabul Times* published interviews with Afghan girl students in the USSR (see, e.g., *Kabul Times*, 15 May 1988, 4). But no general statistics have been published showing the number of women studying in the USSR.

Since the new Afghan government came to power in April 1992, we still do not know what place the female graduates have or will have. For example, will women students in veterinary studies—a total of 80 percent of all students in that branch in the late 1980s—be able to exercise their profession? How much latitude is the Islamic government allowing women who have been trained in professions which are, under Islamic tradition, reserved for men? It appears that academics occupying technical posts have been maintained in their positions, but what about women? For the moment, their latitude seems extremely narrow. Women newscasters on TV were banned in July 1992, even though they began to wear "Islamic dress" after the establishment of the Islamic government; moreover, the number of women working in administrations clearly declined.

Large Organizations and Their Role in the Emancipation of Women (1978–1992)

"Soviet Holiday: An Unforgettable Experience" is the title of an article in the *Kabul Times* of 11 September 1988 that tells of the marvelous vacations of three hundred boys and girls from Kabul, city and province, who made one-month visits to Frunze (now Bishkek, in Kirghizstan), where they joined other "children from Mongolia,

America, and other countries." Around 1,200 members of Afghan Young Pioneers or of Watan Nurseries were sent every year to summer camps (BIA, 18 Feb. 1985, in *AF* XIII/3: 31), a figure that corresponds to data for the preceding two years: "3,325 children of working people have visited the Central Asian Republics of SSR for vacation and rest" (DRA 1984, 54).

Directly dependent on the PDPA, youth organizations and women's associations (DOAW, WDOA, NCAW, AAWC)[16] have played an essential role in the propagation of party ideology, recruitment, and training of their members and future leaders (this was the case with the DYOA). They were said to struggle for the eradication of social injustice and illiteracy. They established official relations with similar national organizations in Communist and Western countries.

In 1984 the DYOA numbered 100,000, with more than 17,000 young women; the WDOA united more than 30,000 Afghan women in 28 provincial, 34 district, and 77 precinct councils and had 669 primary organizations.[17] "The WDOA has worked among and mobilized more than 80,000 countrywomen in social production, of whom 17,000 are trade union members" (DRA 1984, 61–62).

Women's clubs were established by the WDOA in 1983. In that year there were eleven in Kabul and seventeen in the provinces. In 1987 there were 160 clubs all over Afghanistan. Their purpose was to mobilize the "toiling women in socio-economic activities and to raise their professional skills" in handicrafts, typing, household affairs—and makeup. The clubs helped women to become economically independent and to enter the job world. They organized exhibition-sales to help needy women, particularly those from families of martyrs of the revolution (*Kabul Times*, 12 Nov. 1987). It is the woman as wife and especially as mother who was lauded.

Apart from ideology, the activities proposed by the Women's Welfare Association in the 1950s and 1960s did not differ greatly from those described above. What difference there was resided in the means used and the number of people affected. Of course, the associations of the 1980s never referred to what had been done before 1978.

Two new organizations were created after 1978: the Peace, Solidarity, and Friendship Organization, whose president, Anahita Ratebzad (1982–86), founded its bimonthly magazine, *Afghanistan Today* (first issue, September 1985); and the Union of Martyrs' Wives and Mothers, founded at the end of 1985, for women who have lost their husbands, sons, brothers, and children "in the path of the revolution" (BIA, 12 Dec. 1985, in *AF* XIV/2 [1986]: 3). Communist Kabul also had its *shahid* (martyrs).

Women and the Labor Market

One of the rights of women, according to the Communist regime, was the right to work, guaranteed by the Fundamental Principles of Afghanistan. The Labor Law (1984) ensured equal job opportunities for all, set retirement for female workers at fifty-five (men at sixty), and offered three months' maternity leave to mothers (before the revolution, only forty days). Workers had the right to continue their education, to travel, to benefit from coupon privileges; they received medals, badges, and honorary titles as well (*Kabul Times*, 14 Sept. 1988), which were considered "concessions unprecedented in the history of Afghanistan" (BIA, 26 June 1986, in *AF* XIV/5:4).

But how many women were affected by these measures? Before the revolution the industrial working class numbered fewer than 40,000 members, of whom 2,806 were women (Wiebe 1984, 108). In an interview appearing in the *New York Times* (10 Dec. 1988, in *AF* XVII/1:16), Masuma Asmati Wardak said that 270,000 women had "outdoor jobs" and went to work in offices and factories.[18] In Kabul, before the collapse of the Communist regime in April 1992, women constituted up to 50 percent of the work force in the lower administrative positions. They also work—side by side with men—in textile mills, prefabricated housing complexes, hospitals, laboratories, libraries, and in the armed forces tailoring department, as the photos regularly published in the *Kabul New Times* have shown. For instance, Ayesha has worked fifteen years in the spinning section at the Guzargah textile mill in Kabul. She is one of 550 employees, "most of whom are young female workers, some of whom have earned the title of heroes of labor in the post-revolutionary years." An active member of the AAWC (All Afghan Women's Council) of the textile factory, she felt "prosperous and happy in the post-revolution years, for now I own the great wealth of freedom and literacy" (*Kabul Times*, 14 September 1988, 1).

Women did not work at heavy tasks in construction or in roadwork, nor were they occupied in dirty jobs such as street sweeping, as is seen in Eastern European countries or in India. If they had a place in industrial production, it was within the walls of the factory. The case of a few female trolley drivers in Kabul was so exceptional that it was mentioned by the BIA, 5 January 1984 (in *AF* XII/2:35). The BIA (20 Sept. 1986) reported that 582 women were serving in the army, but in what capacity was not known; there were no women's corps in the Afghan army, in contrast with the militia. About five thousand women served in the police and in the Revolution Defenders. The *Kabul New*

Times (20 Sept. 1986) gives the example of Bibi Marjan of Gulzar (Charasiab, Kabul Province), "Revolution Defender," who collaborates with the armed forces and presides over the Union of the Martyrs' Wives and Mothers.

The Kabul Government followed up and increased the efforts made in the 1960s within the domains of family guidance and of health care for mothers and children and has extended services to provincial cities under its control. These efforts included increased training for nurses and midwives, courses in health care, and family planning centers of the AFGA (thirty-six in Kabul and thirty-two in the provinces in 1988). Concerning family planning, a women's organization publication commented that "there has been a slow, but decidedly significant change in women's attitude over the years. Today none of the women who visit the Mother and Child clinics for guidance are resistant to the idea. Despite the sensitive nature of the programme, the 138,000 women who have adopted various techniques in 1986, are a small increase over that of 1985" (*Afghanistan Today*, Mar.–Apr. 1988, 20–21). Oral contraceptives remain the most popular device at all clinics, added the journalist.

Women in the Ranks of the Government and of the PDPA

In active policies and the management of the affairs of state, women were present within all the ranks of the party and the government, with the exception of the Council of Ministers, although there were few in the higher ranks.

Anahita Ratebzad, for a short time minister of social affairs after the coup of 1978, was the only woman in the government in January 1980, when she was minister of education. She left that office in 1986. Appointed to the Politburo in 1980, she was relieved of her functions on 18 October 1987. In 1980, Jamila Palwasha, vice-president of the Publicity and Extension Department of the PDPA Central Committee, was appointed as alternate member of the Central Committee. She became a full member in July 1986. In the government departments in 1987, the only position of any importance held by a woman was that occupied by Masuma Asmati Wardak as president of the All Afghan Women's Council.

In 1984, according to official sources, the PDPA numbered 115,000 members, of whom 12,650, or 11 percent, were women (DRA 1984, 57–58), but the percentage was much lower where positions of responsibility and decision making were concerned. In the summer of 1986, the PDPA Central Committee had 147 full and alternate members, of whom twelve (3.4 percent) were workers, characterized as seven farmers and five women (BIA, 20 July 1986, in *AF* XIV/5: 7); in the elections of October 1986 for the people's representatives to local organs of state power, only 56 women were elected (0.4 percent) to help fill 14,190 positions (BIA, 30 Oct. 1986, in *AF* XV/1: 3).

At least from a formal point of view, the Kabul regime obtained certain results: in its political training of women, their education, in the roles women play within associations, to a certain extent in women's participation in the job market, and in the domain of health and welfare.[19] The influence of Kabul remained principally a phenomenon of the cities, where educational and health programs had been successfully introduced and where an extensive supervisory and framing effort had been directed at every social category and every domain of social and civil life, for instance, through the constitution of associations, trade unions, and organizations.

Those institutions created or developed by the late Afghan Communist regime, especially the ones devoted to the women, have been suppressed since April 1992. Even if the new regime has not yet found its basis and does not control much of the national territory outside of Kabul, the measures it issued mostly concern morality (prohibition of alcohol, "Islamic dress" for the women, intentions to reform the women's educational system, etc.) and an attempt to "Islamize" society.

Afghan Refugees in Pakistan

The case of the Afghan refugees is unique in the twentieth century. Until the establishment of an Islamic government in Kabul, bringing a large number of refugees back to their home country, they made up the greatest population of the same origin ever transplanted outside of their own borders. From approximately 1,500 under the government of President Daoud (1973–78), the number of Afghan refugees in Pakistan rose to 109,000 in April 1978, following Taraki's Communist coup, and to 500,000 in mid-January 1980, following the arrival of Soviet forces and Babrak's accession to power in Kabul. At the end of 1991, according to official Pakistani figures, there were about 3.2 million Afghan refugees in 345 refugee villages. What follows applies to the situation previous to 1992 as well as to the refugees who had not yet returned to their home country.

In the Afghan refugee villages of Pakistan, the majority of settlers have built houses of earth, smaller than their village houses in Afghanistan, more exactly hovels surrounding an interior courtyard, or compound. For women, this is a great change. Not only are their activities reduced to tasks of domestic subsistence, such as cooking, washing, and sewing, but their other movements are also restricted to a minimum, within tighter quarters and over a much smaller area.

In Afghanistan, dwellings may have two courtyards, strangers being barred from the second and larger compound, which is surrounded by several rooms—perhaps one or two per family unit. During the daytime, the men of the family, unless they are very old or ill, do not enter this area except in case of absolute necessity and even then only momentarily.

In the Afghan refugee villages, the tight and overcrowded living quarters, on the one hand, and the inactivity of part of the men, on the other, have led to daytime contact between men and women. The latter strongly feel and resent this masculine presence and authority, which renders even more slender the margin of liberty left to women in the domestic sphere. Relations with neighbors are almost nonexistent because neighbors are no longer family or kin, as in Afghanistan, but often strangers who, through the situation of exile, are placed there in a context of interethnic promiscuity, insecurity, and poverty. In the refugee villages it is rare to find compounds with a guest room. Thus, during the visits of strangers, women are sent out of the courtyard. They are either sent to a room or into a tent or shelter, or else to a neighbor's, and have to wait until the visitors have left before coming back.

In the refugee villages the family group is constantly crumbling because of the war and the scattering of men, who are away looking for work in Pakistani cities. In an environment where families are dispersed, a married woman or a widow sometimes lives with her own family again and not necessarily with her in-laws (as custom would have had it previously). Thus, there is a new distribution of family members living within the same compound.

Women have hardly any occasion to leave their close quarters to go anywhere else, as they had gone in Afghanistan to the garden, the orchards, or the brook, on pilgrimage to the tomb of a saint, or to visit neighbors or kin. These were all occasions for women to meet outside the home. In the camps, of course, there are reunions for burials, celebrations, and weddings. Women, who are the fundamental link with their culture and traditions, try hard to reproduce the social life they knew in Afghanistan, at least as they imagined it to be, in order to preserve and transmit their identity. Marriages still occur, but the back-and-forth negotiations between two families are no longer as extended as previously, and the wedding meals are less abundant, with fewer guests (Centlivres-Demont 1981; Centlivres and Centlivres-Demont 1988c, 135–47).

The bride-price is undiminished, in spite of the high proportion of women in the refugee population. According to the statistics, women make up the majority of Afghan adults who have left their country (28 percent, as against 25 percent men and 47 percent children). It is not possible to be certain to which age groups these women belong, whether young marriageable women are present in the usual proportion or have in large numbers been left behind with relatives in Afghanistan. One possible explanation for the undiminished bride-price is that whereas marriages in Afghanistan were coupled with other arrangements that were not always financial, and whereas certain debts for the bride-price were spread out over a period of several years, in Pakistan nonfinancial arrangements are hardly possible, and the context is such that only cash counts. In addition, the political parties help young resistants to find a spouse. Some of them even put up the bride-price for their mujahidin.

For most women, the only place to go or to meet others is the Basic Health Unit or the NGO (nongovernmental organization) dispensary. When physically ill or in need of psychological treatment, women have found a haven of counseling and attention there; it is the only outing authorized by husband and family. Crouched in the shelter of an awning or behind the building or tent of the dispensary, they spend hours talking among themselves before the consultation. Afghan women quickly learned how to use these services as an excuse to get out of their quarters. It is, of course, out of the question for the women to be physically examined by male doctors; a woman can only, while veiled, describe her symptoms. Female doctors are rare, although "Lady Health Visitors," having benefited from three years' medical or paramedical training, are sometimes available.

"Strictly speaking, there are no health problems which are specific to the Afghan refugee woman" (from a conversation with Dr. Evelyne Marry, who worked for several years in the Surkhab camp in Baluchistan). Thanks to better medical supervision in the refugee villages, however, sanitary conditions for women—and in particular after childbirth—have improved greatly. Infant mortality has not only diminished in comparison to that in Afghanistan (and not only in comparison to the first years of exile) but is also lower than that of rural Pakistani populations. Women still give birth at home, but in case of complications, medical advice from the dispensary or even hospitalization for a cesarean is more quickly accepted.

For the women, as for the men, tuberculosis remains the major health problem; the necessity for frequent, regular, and long-term treatment is poorly understood by the family. Other recurrent illnesses are diarrhea, dysentery, skin diseases, malaria, and anemia. Some women suffer from the emotional problems caused by stress and anxiety owing to the absence or death of their husbands or sons, to uncertainty about the future of the family and children, to the strange environment, to the lack of activity, or to worries about the future. This depressive state is manifested, for example, in a general lassitude and indifference toward a newborn, who may be undernourished, weak, and vulnerable. But these cases fortunately are rare. The great majority of Afghan women demonstrate a remarkable capacity for adaptation as well as an exceptional physical and psychological resistance.

For some Afghan women, exile has been a learning experience. For the first time, large-scale education and training programs in health care have been addressed directly to Afghan women, without any of the central governmental restraints. Although only a minority of the refugee women have access to these programs, vaccination campaigns and rudimentary courses in hygiene and infant care have managed to motivate many and help them take responsibility for themselves.

Apart from health and hygiene, however, training activities for women are rare. A few "training courses" have been conceived to teach women and girls how to use sewing machines, to enable them to earn their own income as tailors, or to participate in the workshops of "income generative projects" in the refugee villages. In the latter case, their skills in embroidery or sewing are used in making quilts, school uniforms, bags, and so forth. Organizations in charge of these programs redistribute the products to newly arrived refugees or to distributors who specialize in the embroidery and local handicrafts trade in Peshawar or abroad.

These activities are only possible to the extent that they can be carried out within the homes of the women or near the camps, where purdah and transportation can be guaranteed. Certain populations have easier access to remunerated activities because of their tradition of feminine crafts, which include carpet making by Turkoman women and embroidery by Qandahari women. In the camps where refugees from the north of Afghanistan live, the craft of carpet knotting has continued to be handed down. Women belonging to the Uzbek, Tajik, Hazara, and Pashtun ethnic groups emulate the Turkoman women, sometimes securing the assistance of a widow, for example, who is well trained in carpet making. Following an informal apprenticeship within their homes, these women become carpet producers and place their wares on the market in Pakistan.

In addition to the money earned, these activities are positive experiences because of the contacts established between the Afghan women of rural origins and those from urban areas (usually from Kabul) who, because of their former education, are indispensable intermediaries between the producers and those in charge of the international aid organizations. These more educated women help somewhat in pulling back the curtain that separates the rural Afghans from those of the urban middle upper classes.

Certain educated refugee women and girls in Peshawar and Quetta work in the NGOs only to the extent that conditions to preserve their Muslim identity are met. These conditions include proximity to the workplace, or adequate transportation, and absence of contact with men. The *chadri* is obligatory; it protects their reputation in Pakistan and in the eyes of the ulama and political leaders.

Women who were students in Kabul before the war (at the university they represented 11 percent of the total before 1974) and who had walked in the streets without any headcovering whatsoever or had gone to the cinema with girlfriends find it very difficult to adapt to the constraints imposed by purdah. The relative liberty experienced in Afghanistan disappeared completely in exile. For these women, as for the village women of the camps, there are few occasions in their new environment to remain in contact with groups outside of the family. They fall back into the domestic environment and under social pressure submit themselves to, accept, or even reinforce their own seclusion. Their fathers and brothers (especially the latter) exercise severe control over their comings and goings. Of course, women from Kabul and from the former urban upper classes have the greatest difficulty in accepting the situation.

In addition to *mujahidin* (resistance fighters) and *mohajerin* (refugees), the critical war situation has also caused the emergence of other categories: widows and orphans. Of course, there were widows and orphans in Afghanistan before the war, but this bitter conflict has made them categories apart, groups encountering special risks, needing particular attention, treatment, accommodations, and protection. They have drawn the attention of the international organizations, nongovernmental organizations, and the political parties of the resistance.

The organization of a "widows' camp" at Nasir Bagh near Peshawar, run by a foreign organization, drew heavy criticism from fundamentalist groups. In response, the Hizb-i Islami has established a huge private camp at Nasrat Mina (not far from Peshawar) for its staff and also for the widows and the orphans of its mujahidin martyred in Afghanistan. Of the two thousand families of the camp, 80 percent are families of *shahid*, martyrs, according to a Hizb-i Islami staff member. A special department is devoted exclusively to their interests. In one office, closets marked according to provinces contain files of the names of the Hizb-i Islami widows, orphans, and handicapped veterans who receive aid from Muslim countries and other through the Association for the Heirs and Descendants of the Martyrs and the Handicapped. The widows are helped financially, of course, but the party also assists them, when they desire, to find a partner and remarry. The large number of widows leads certain members of the staff to reconsider the levirate and even polygamy as solutions to the crisis, in order to assure the security of the helpless and familyless widows.

In prewar Afghanistan a widow had hardly any choice other than to stay with her in-laws and sometimes to marry a brother or a cousin of her late husband. Today a *shahid*'s wife has the right not to marry again; in many cases widows go back to their own (father's or brother's) families if they can, but in that case they usually do not marry again.

There has been a great deal of discussion on the "reinforcement of purdah," which is generally understood in Western countries as the result of Islamic intolerance. This reinforcement should, however, be seen as an attempt to preserve the family, a cultural and ethnic nucleus in a context of deconstruction. The extreme sensitivity of the Afghan refugees—both men and women—to the question of purdah is a response to the presence of people who are neither kin nor neighbors; it can be seen in the refugees' rejection of schools for girls that expose them to the gaze of outsiders; it reflects their ambivalence toward visiting experts or foreigners, functionaries responsible for the administration of the villages, and photographers passing through. When an Afghan refugee family settle in a village and duly register, one of their first acts will be to reestablish the screen between the outside world and their private life; they are taking back their dignity. The most conspicuous signs of that dignity are represented by purdah: the physical purdah composed of the walls, screens, and a little guest room or tent outside the dwelling; but also the social purdah, protecting one's daughters, sisters, and wives from the gaze of strangers and refusing to expose them to contacts with administrative personnel in charge of distributing aid.

The education of girls remains a sensitive issue. Two parallel school networks were put into place, both with limited success: one organized by the United Nations High Commission for Refugees (UNHCR) and the other by the political parties of the Afghan resistance. Among the Afghan refugees there is a very strong aversion to secular schools, which are help responsible for the rise of communism and atheism leading to the coup d'état of 1978. Part of the refugee population has expressed this antipathy in a violent reaction against education for girls. Similarly, the education for girls and mixed classes imposed by the Kabul government had also elicited great hostility from the rural populations.

The Afghan political parties, however, cannot be accused of being hostile to education, even for girls, and one of their slogans is "Ilm bara-ye mard o zan farz ast [Knowledge is obligatory for both men and women]." All of these parties have insisted on compulsory education according to Islam, the condition being that it be carried out separately for boys and girls. Schools set up by the resistance parties, called *madrasa*, not only offer religious education but also teach Dari and Pashto, arithmetic, science, geography, and drawing.

Thus, several schools for girls were set up both by the UNHCR and by the political parties. At the end of May 1988 the schools financed by the UNHCR and dependent on the Pakistani Commissionate for Afghan Refugees (CAR) were educating 112,000 children, though only 7,800 girls. Of 729 schools, only 74 were for girls, and even these only offered education up to the primary level, a sign that education for girls remains a sensitive issue with the refugees.

The number of students registered in the schools of the Afghan political parties was, according to my estimates, slightly smaller than that of the UNHCR schools. In reality, however, absenteeism is very high in both types of schools, and the percentage of girls who continue their education drops sharply after the third grade. In addition, the farther one goes from the cities of Peshawar and Quetta, the fewer are the schools for girls. The number in all of the camps of Baluchistan, for example, can be counted on the fingers of one hand.

For adolescent girls whose education was interrupted by the war, there is hardly any possibility to continue. The CAR, though supported by the UNHCR, was unable to implement any secondary or higher education for girls. The rare secondary schools for girls are in Peshawar and Islamabad and have been founded under the auspices of the political parties of the resistance or by the Muslim Sisters of Afghanistan or through private patronage. For example, the two high schools for girls, Malalai and Zarghuna, were created through the initiative of Tajwar Kakar, a former director of a school for girls in Kunduz, with the support of the International Rescue Committee.[20] They offer complete secondary education: languages, social sciences, physical sciences, mathematics, religion, art, domestic economics, sewing, and cooking, till the eighth grade. Presently they number almost two hundred students. In Quetta, four schools, including one girls' school, were begun by Shiʿ ite organizations, from which their name is derived: Maktab-e irani. But these are available only to girls whose parents live in the city—in other words, outside of the refugee villages and the centers of aid distribution—and already believe in education. A few girls whose parents live in the camps of Mohammed Khel or Surkhab live in a boarding school in Quetta in order to continue their education.

In everyday life and in social integration, women's position has regressed. It is as if the development of their "emancipation" had come to a halt. Begun first under Amanullah, this emancipation—after some slowing down—began again under Zahir Shah when Minister Daoud was in office, even if it was limited to participation in education and to urban life. Life in exile permits men to continue their productive activities, but only rarely does it permit women to do so. This does not mean, however, that at some level women have not become irreversibly aware of their role in Afghan society.

Political Resistance Parties and the Place of Women

The affirmation of a position specifically for women and the theory of women's position appear episodically in the declarations and writings of the Islamist resistance movements, like faint echoes of the discussions that had been held on the subject of women during the Iranian revolution (see Muttahhari 1981). These subjects are less present within the moderate parties. Afghan resistance parties based in Peshawar undergo pressure from Western influences (interviews, aid organizations) that forces them to specify their position on the question of women and feminist claims.

The Hizb-i Islami, represented by its leader Gulbuddin Hekmatyar, publicly proclaims adherence to notions of equality: In Islam, there is no difference between men and women; both have the same rights except in particular cases, which is due to natural differences in constitution.

The parties of the resistance also created women's organizations. Less discreet than others on this subject, the Hizb-i Islami claims to have been, from the beginning, alone in promoting the emancipation of Afghan women. This is exemplified by the creation of the Islamic Organization of Afghan Women. This organization, now independent of the party, has created schools and training centers (for embroidery, sewing, carpet making) in the area of Peshawar (*Résistance/Renaissance Afghane*, no. 2, Mar.–Apr. 1988, 5). Another women's organization, the Shura-ye Zainabiya of the (Shi'ite) party of Mohseni, collaborates with the resistance in the city of Kabul.

A left-wing women's association called RAWA (Revolutionary Association of the Women of Afghanistan) was founded in 1977 by Kishwar Kamal, who was known as Mina and was assassinated in Quetta in 1987. Based in Quetta, that organization has been in conflict with the seven Peshawar parties from the beginning, and in particular with the Islamists. It has established schools and hospitals for children and women refugees and has published since 1987 *Payam-e Zan* (Woman's message). RAWA claims to be active inside Afghanistan as well and to organize strikes by women workers in the Bagram textile mills in Kabul (see RAWA, 28 Aug. 1987). RAWA is the only women's resistance organization that promotes armed struggle for women. In the summer of 1992, some of its members created a separate organization called the Revolutionary Organization of the Women of Afghanistan (ROWA).

The majority of the parties of the Peshawar Alliance are favorable to women's suffrage. In the summer of 1987, however, a contradictory discussion appeared in the newspapers *Shahdat* of the Hizb-i Islami of Hekmatyar and the *Al-Noor* of the Hizb-i Islami of Khales. The first proclaimed that "nobody can deny women the right to vote from an Islamic point of view"; the second maintained that "in Islam women are not allowed to vote."

For the Islamist parties of the resistance, "the emancipation of the Afghan woman is not synonymous with the emancipation of the Western woman. The Afghan woman has her own culture and specific problems. . . . We consider that as long as the real Islamic status for women has not been accorded to the Afghan woman, it is vain to believe in a positive evolution of our society" (*Résistance/Renaissance Afghane*, no. 2, Mar.–Apr. 1988, 5). All the parties insist unanimously on seclusion and segregation.

At the Conference on Afghanistan held at the Institute of Political and International Studies in Tehran (15–16 January 1989), attended by Shi'ite and Sunni leaders and Western experts, Sibghatullah

Modjaddedi, leader of the Nejat-e Melli, spokesman for the alliance of the seven parties based in Peshawar, and since February 1989 president of the Afghan interim government, mentioned the role of women in the conference's final communiqué. Point 8 of this communiqué states, "With due consideration to experiences in the past, the Seminar proposes that the role of the women in the resistance and the victory of Afghanistan's Jihad and the future reconstruction be reviewed in special gathering."

When they deal with the subject of women, the parties try to make a distinction between a Western-style "shameful emancipation," which is contrary to a woman's dignity, and a status that only Islam can confer, conforming to that dignity as well as to her rights and duties.

The parties are waging the war, and women are not present on the front. The parties, absorbed by their organizational and supply tasks and occupied by the war, accord relatively little importance to women. To the extent that they are forced to think of reconstruction not only as a material but as a political and social reality, greater thought and attention will have to be paid and a larger role accorded to women within Afghan institutions.

"We have no women fighters—thank God we still have enough men," wrote the biophysicist-mujahid Shah Bazgar (1987, 174; translated by the author). Women participate in the struggle as wives, mothers, and sisters of the mujahidin; they hide resistants or occasionally fire on the enemy to protect home and family. Under the *chadri*, they carry arms and tracts sometimes even to the center of Kabul. But in comparison to the women heroes of the Anglo-Afghan wars, the woman in the resistance remains in the background. There are no women like Malalai, whose heroic behavior in 1880 in the Battle of Maiwand (near Qandahar), where she lost her life, made her a symbol of the armed struggle against all invaders. For the English who fought in the Afghan wars of the nineteenth century, the Afghan woman was frightening; her image haunted the battlefield at nightfall, finishing off the wounded and snatching bloody trophies.

Nothing similar exists now. The participation of a woman in the struggle against the enemy is indirect. This does not mean she is excluded from the jihad; even without fighting there is a jihad accessible to her as an auxiliary to the fighters, and she reaps some of the rewards. But she is no longer found on the battlefield.

For Maulana Muhammad Ali (n.d., 647), quoting the *hadith* (tradition about the Prophet Muhammad), woman is above all "the bringer-up of children and manager of the household." She has a large number of duties to perform such as carrying water to the battlefield (El-Bokhâri, titre LVI, chs. 65 and 66), taking care of the wounded (ch. 67), and removing the wounded and the slain from the battlefield (ch. 68). It is only in extreme circumstances that she can take part in actual fighting (chs. 63 and 65). To Ayesha, who asked the Prophet if she could take part in the holy war, the Prophet said, "Your holy war is the pilgrimage" (ch. 62).

Nor did the Communist government of Kabul integrate women into the regular fighting units. Even the youth organizations were given a role in the defense of the country; but although in certain cases armed women could be seen within the ranks of the militia, their guns were probably empty (television documentary, TSR/Swiss Television, 5 Feb. 1989).

Until April 1992, for the thousands of women living in zones controlled by the resistance or in refugee camps under the influence of Islamist or traditional parties, the measures of emancipation in Kabul were marked with the ineradicable stigma of a shameful regime. The policy of Kabul, which seemed relatively moderate and reasonable, was thus fouled at the core by the very nature of those who created it. Between 1978 and 1992, for the government in Kabul, a certain liberalization of customs and behavior went along with reform and the progress of women's status in society. Kabul's policy toward women was following the path opened by Amanullah in the 1920s. But contrary to Amanullah's policy, it did not insist on Westernized emblems, which could have been considered anti-Islamic.

After the resistance took power in Kabul, there was a relative withdrawal of women from the public scene. This does not mean that the resistance parties should be considered altogether backward, old-fashioned, or conservative, but that they have a very strict definition of the role and the condition of women, based on an interpretation of the Qur'an that puts the accent on separation, modesty, and the veil. Everything recalling the image of a Western-style evolution is to be avoided as contrary to the "true" condition of women according to religious belief and thus remains banished.

Notes

1. On the eve of the coup d'état of 1978, Kabul had 600,000 inhabitants; it is said to have had about 2 million at the end of 1988.

2. The *chadri*, or *burqa*, is a sacklike garment covering the entire body from head to toe, with a small embroidered "window" in front of the eyes. In the rural areas or among

very poor people, the women wear a veil over the head and the shoulders; they do not veil their faces. In 1903, Habibullah (1901–19) took measures to impose specific colors for the *burqa:* khaki for Muslim women, red or mustard yellow for Hindu women, and slate for the others. He also condemned excessive embroidery (Hamilton 1906, 384).

3. Mahmud Beg Tarzi lived in Damascus, then under Ottoman domination, for some thirty years, where he was greatly impressed by the Young Turks movement.

4. In 1936 "the abolition of the veil in Iran was done by law. It was the result of a decree by the shah; the ladies of his own house initiated the change" (Hansen 1983, 162).

5. See Decree Number 7, 1978, of the Communist regime of Taraki, discussed on p. 344 of this chapter.

6. Anahita Ratebzad, Ruqia Abubakr, Khadija Ahrari, and Masuma Asmati Wardak.

7. The scarf has not disappeared; schoolgirls appear in white headscarves in photos published in the *Kabul Times.*

8. According to Najibullah, they numbered fifty thousand in April 1982 (Arnold 1983, 228, quoting Foreign Broadcast Information Service (FBIS) VIII, 30 Apr. 1982, C-1).

9. According to Knabe (1977, 194), in 1971, 18,000 women received oral contraceptives, 1,000 had received IUDs, and 36,000 condoms had been distributed.

10. Parcham (flag), one of the two constituents of the PDPA, recruits among the Kabul bourgeoisie; the other faction, the Khalq (people), recruits its adherents from provincial and rural Pashtun families.

11. "Afghanistan's first Constitution promulgated in 1923 guaranteed equal rights to all citizens of Afghanistan without specific reference to women. . . . No specific mention of women was made in the 1931 Constitution, nor in the 1964 Constitution [art. 25]. . . . Article 27 of the 1977 Constitution, however, states 'The entire people of Afghanistan, women and men, without discrimination and privileges have equal rights and obligations before the law.' " (Rahimi [1977] 1986, 96).

12. In the Democratic Documents adopted after 1980 (DRA 1984, 70), Decree Number 7 no longer appears. For commentaries on Decree Number 7, see Dupree [1981] 1984, 10–12.

13. The literacy campaign was headed by Shah Mohammed Hussain with a woman, Dil Ara Mehak, as his deputy (Anwar 1988, 146).

14. In 1983 Shah Mohammad Dost, foreign minister of the Kabul regime, stated in the United Nations that 50 percent of the schools in Afghanistan had been destroyed (Elmi 1986, 90).

15. The figures obtained from different sources vary widely. In 1982 Sarwar Mangal, deputy minister of high education, stated that 12,000 Afghan students were in the USSR, in addition to 1,200 children sent to summer camps (Elmi 1986, 91); *Afghan Realities* (no. 34, 1 June 1985) cites 2,322 students and 19,920 children four to eight years old for the period 1980–84; Bazgar (1987, 153) claimed that 30,000 children had "departed" for the USSR; Elmi (1986, 93) claimed that 4,000 every year, "that is to say 16,000–20,000 young Afghan boys and girls in the past 5 years have been sent to Russia."

16. From 1965, the year of its foundation, until today, this organization has changed names several times: 1965–78: DOAW—Democratic Organization of Afghan Women (president: Anahita Ratebzad); 1978–80: KOAW—Khalq Organization of Afghan Women (Dilara Mahak, former principal of Amana Fedawi School, was president during Taraki's time. After September 1979, the president was Miss Aziza); 1980–August 1986: WDOA—Women's Democratic Organization of Afghanistan (president: Anahita Ratebzad); August 1986–Autumn 1986: NCAW—Nationwide Council of Afghanistan's Women (president: Feroza, an alternate member of the Central Committee of the PDPA and commander of a

Revolution Defenders group in Kabul); Autumn 1986–: AAWC—All Afghan Women's Council (president since June 1987: Masuma Asmati Wardak; vice president: Sultana Omed).

17. In April 1982 Najibullah claimed 65,000 members for the DYOA and 50,000 for the DOAW (Arnold 1983, 228).

18. It is difficult to determine the exact number of women who work outside of the home. BIA (9 Mar. 1986, in *AF* XIV/3: 55) refers to "over 300,000 women working in the production and social affairs areas." Some months later, the same BIA (21 Aug. 1986, in *AF* XIV/5: 9) says "22,000 women are working in production enterprises; 11,000 are engaged in educational, cultural and social affairs."

19. I do not know of any independent study to verify the female condition in Kabul under the Communist regime; most of my sources are official quotations, except for some very short journalistic articles. A visit to Kabul and Mazar-i Sharif in the autumn of 1990 allowed me to witness certain aspects of the women's condition.

20. Tajwar Kakar, threatened by some of the fundamentalist groups, was later forced to leave Pakistan.

9

Power, Morality, and the
New Muslim Womanhood

Afsaneh Najmabadi

Women in the ideology and the policies of the Islamic revolution and the Islamic Republic of Iran have held a very prominent, if not central, position. In a significant incident early in 1989, the broadcast director at the Teheran Radio was sentenced to five years in jail, three directors of the station's Islamic ideology group were sentenced to four years each, and all four received fifty lashes (*Iran Times*, 3. Feb. 1989; *New York Times*, 10 Feb. 1989). The sentences, levied by a Teheran court, were prompted by a letter addressed by Ayatollah Khomeini to the director of Iranian Radio and Television, Mohammad Hashemi, following the broadcast of a radio program on 28 January 1989 (coinciding with Fatimah's birthday, the official Woman's Day in Iran).[1] In the program, an interviewer had asked women about their "ideal role model." One woman had said that she considered Fatimah to be an old image and that she found Oushin (a female character in a highly popular Japanese television serial) a more appropriate model for herself. In his letter of 29 January, Ayatollah Khomeini expressed shame over the broadcast and demanded expulsion of the person who had broadcast the program and imposition of Islamic

The work on this paper was carried out while I was a research associate at the Women's Studies in Religion Program at Harvard Divinity School and a fellow at the Pembroke Center for Teaching and Research on Women. Both occasions provided me not only with financial support, but, more important, with an invaluable atmosphere for exchange of ideas. I would like to thank Ali Banuazizi and Myron Weiner for inviting me to present a paper to the workshop on Women and the State in Afghanistan, Iran, and punishment *(ta ʿzir)* on all those responsible for the program. "If it is proven," the letter continued, "that there has been any intent to insult, the person guilty of insult undoubtedly is condemned to death. If such an incident recurs, severe and serious punishment of higher level officials will follow" *(Zan-e Ruz,* 4 Feb. 1989).

Although it may be tempting to dismiss the whole incident as an amusing expression of the fanaticism of an old and possibly senile man, one may ask what was so dangerous in the simple imagination of an Iranian woman that required such a harsh, instantaneous intervention on the part of the supreme political and religious authority of the country. Exactly two weeks before the tenth anniversary of the Islamic revolution, a woman came very close to losing her life over a seemingly trivial comment. She may have indeed lost her life had she "erred" ever so slightly in one or another direction; for instance, had the intonation of her voice conveyed mockery or intent to insult, or had she referred to a less desirable character than a hardworking Japanese woman (a recent migrant from the countryside to the big city), she would have then had to go into hiding as Salman Rushdie has had to do.

The most evident reading of this incident would be that the woman's view constituted an insult to the sacred images of Islam; and thus, as the supreme religious authority in Iran, it was incumbent upon Ayatollah Khomeini to intervene. But there was more at stake. Through such seemingly trivial incidents, a restructuring of power, creation of new culture, and the emergence of a different state and society has been taking shape in Iran over the past decade.[2] A study of changes affecting the position of women in Iran over this period, therefore, cannot be carried out as a "routine" listing of measures adopted by the new regime with respect to employment, legal rights, education, and social welfare. Iranian society in this period has been going through a rare historical moment, a moment of revolution and of restructuring of state and society in the aftermath of that revolution. It is in that context that the lives of women have been affected and women have affected the course of these revolutionary changes.

Pakistan. I owe special thanks to Ali Banuazizi for his sustained encouragement as well as helpful editorial suggestions. An earlier draft of this chapter received critical reading and comments from a number of friends and colleagues whom I would like to thank here: Kirstie McClure, Margaret Mills, Shahrzad Mojab, Hanna Papanek, Nayereh Tohidi, and Nahid Yeganeh. I would also like to thank Nahid Yaganeh for generously making available for my use her Persian archives of women in Iran.

Islam as Politics

To insist on the political context of seemingly trivial incidents as relevant implies a rejection of a tendency that has marked much of the interpretation and many of the studies of the contemporary Middle East, a tendency that attributes these events to the implementation of a given set of doctrines, Islam, and views the rise of Islamic movements as religious revivalism.

The rise of the Islamic movement in the 1970s in Iran signified above all else the emergence of a new political sociability and the dominance of a new political discourse, a shift to a new political paradigm.[3] Several processes went into the production of this new sociability: delegitimation of secular politics of the old (liberal nationalism, statism, socialism, and communism—all in one way or another identified as politics of modernization, Western or Eastern), producing a shift toward Islamic politics as represented by such figures as Al-e Ahmad coming out of the Communist movement and such currents as Nehzat-e Azadi coming out of the nationalist movement; politicization of Shiʿism, as expressed in the political writings of Khomeini, the growth of the prominent network of theologians around him, the rising activism of an important section of the Shiʿite clergy, and the speeches and popularity of a figure such as Shariati.

A central place in the emergence of this new sociability was occupied by "the woman question." Although "the woman question" has been prominent in the political and cultural confrontations in Iran (as in the rest of the Middle East) since the mid-nineteenth century, as demonstrated by the recurrent symbolic and actual battles over veiling and unveiling, the new Islamic politics positioned this question at the heart of its moral and ethical claims.

The political discourse of the late 1960s and 1970s had crystallized around the concept of *gharbzadegi*—Westoxication or Weststruckness —popularized by Jalal Al-e Ahmad. The concept was accepted by a whole generation of Iranian radical youth in this period regardless of secular or Islamic sympathies. Al-e Ahmad's book, with the same title, was read and acclaimed by every oppositionist.[4] Also, the concept and the sentiment to which it gave such powerful expression called for a thorough break with the past politics of whatever color. It was posed, from the start, not as a critique of "excesses of modernization" but as a critique of the whole project. It not only opposed the rise of the "authoritarian benevolence" of the shah but also viewed the political experience of the country from the constitutional movement itself through the experience of the National Front and the Tudeh Party as politics of alienation and subjugation. In other words, it became a rejection not only of politics and policies of the Pahlavi state but also of oppositional and reform politics of the whole previous century.

Perhaps nowhere did this total rejection touch popular as well as intellectual imagination more acutely than in the rejection of the *gharbzadeh* woman. The *gharbzadeh* woman came to embody at once all social ills: she was a superconsumer of imperialist, dependent-capitalist, foreign goods; she was a propagator of the corrupt culture of the West; she was undermining the moral fabric of society; she was a parasite, beyond any redemption. The woman's body, in its interaction with the man's, became the presentational symbol of the bad—and the key location for imposition of the good.[5] Everything associated with her body seemed to make a crucial statement about society as a whole: what she wore ("too much" makeup, "too short" a skirt, "too tight" a pair of pants, "too low-cut" a shirt) and how she expressed herself (with "too loud" a voice, "too frivolous" a laugh, "too loose" gesturing of arms, torso, and legs, "too direct" an eye-contact). She smoked in public and mingled with men. She was everywhere: on the streets, eye to eye; in the crowded buses, breath to breath; in schools, side by side; in offices; on telvision. She seemed to have taken over the whole social space. As Ali-Akbar Hashemi Rafsanjani, speaker of the Majlis, put it, "A cleric could not walk through the university with those scenes on the grass, in classes, in streets. We could not go to government offices. If you stood in front of a desk, you would commit a sin, because there was a nude statue [an unveiled woman] behind the desk" (*Kayhan*, airmail edition, 12 Feb. 1986).

Within the new Islamic paradigm, where imperialist domination of Muslim societies is seen to have been achieved through the undermining of religion and culture—rather than through military or economic domination as the earlier generations of nationalists and socialists had argued—and where moral corruption is viewed as the linchpin of imperialist designs, "the woman question" acquired a singular centrality.

This new vision is amply expressed in an editorial that appeared in the 7 April 1984 issue of *Zan-e Ruz*, a weekly women's journal published in Teheran. In this editorial many of the important tenets of the new ideology are formulated. It begins by reiterating that the "hegemonic aims" of colonial powers in modern times were not achieved through force but, in the first instance, through subversion of culture. Women's liberation is presented as one such subversion.

Colonialism was fully aware of the sensitive and vital role of woman in the formation of the individual and of human society. They considered her the best tool for subjugation of the nations. Therefore, under such pretexts as social activity, the arts, freedom, etc., they pushed her to degeneracy and degradation and made of her a doll who not only forgot her human role, but became the best tool for emptying other human beings from their humanity.

. . . In Western societies where capitalism is dominant . . . women's liberation is nothing but the liberty to be naked, to prostitute oneself. . . . Women's freedom, means the freedom to use women for all the dirty and ominous aims of the powerful and the rich. . . . The depth of the tragedy is that this same woman, through sickening and horrible films, fashion magazines and deviationist and lowly journals, is presented to the rest of the world as a model for women to copy.

In the underdeveloped countries, in addition to the above role, women serve as the unconscious accomplices of the powers-to-be in the destruction of indigenous culture. So long as indigenous culture persists in the personality and thought of people in a society, it is not easy to find a political, military, economic or social presence in that society. . . . And woman is the best means of destroying the indigenous culture to the benefit of imperialists.

The editorial then continues by discussing the specifics of Islamic societies in these words:

In Islamic countries the role of woman is even more sensitive. Islamic belief and culture provides people of these societies with faith and ideal. . . . Woman in these societies is armed with a shield that protects her against the conspiracies aimed at her humanity, honor and chastity. This shield is verily her veil. For this reason, in societies like ours, the most immediate and urgent task was seen to be unveiling, that is, disarming woman in the face of all the calamities against her personality and chastity. Then she became the target of poisonous arrows of corruption, prostitution, nakedness, looseness, and trivialities. After this, she was used to disfigure the Islamic culture of the society, to erase people's faith and push society in her wake toward corruption, decay and degradation.

After detailing the "political, cultural, economic and social dimensions" of the impact of women on Iranian society during the reign of the Pahlavis, the editorial turns to the significance of the Islamic revolution: "It is here that we realize the glory and depth of Iran's Islamic Revolution. This revolution transformed everyone, all personalities, all relations and all values. *Woman was transformed in this society so that a revolution could occur*" [emphasis added]."⁶

The moral purification of the corrupt Pahlavi society and state begged a new construction of "the woman question": transforming the woman in order to revolutionize the society. This transformation is evidently a postcolonial, postnationalist project rather than a mysterious revitalization of an eternal ahistorical Islam, implementing edicts *a*, *b*, and *c* about women. Moreover, Islamic politics, as the new emerging social order, constructed in a particular historical context, became the dominant language in the Iran of 1970s, not through a violent elimination of other political discourses, but through many sensibilities shared with these previously dominant, seemingly secular discourses. An integral part in the construction of shared political sensibilities was occupied by "the woman question." By the 1970s, the historically distinct voices of secular anticolonialism and traditional religion were singing in unison the condemnation of the Weststruck woman.⁷

Within the political context of building a new power in postrevolutionary Iran, the new regime's seeming obsession with such issues as the exact dress code of women, with whether a woman's voice should be heard from radio and television, with trivial rebellious acts of wearing colorful veils, showing off strings of hair, wearing Michael Jackson T-shirts and punk haircuts, listening to "vulgar" music, acquires significance. These issues point to the battles over the shaping of a new power in society, of domination of a new culture, of emergence and consolidation of a new state. To be sure, the new state is an Islamic state; the new culture and society are to be Islamic ones. But the harshness with which transgressions are punished cannot be attributed simply to their being viewed as un-Islamic acts. The breakdown of moral behavior has acquired the connotation of political subversiveness; the enactment of Islamic codes is seen as essential for rooting out imperialist cultural values; those not sharing the dominant moral preoccupations are viewed not simply as un-Islamic but, more seriously, as fifth columnists of "cultural imperialism."

Morality and Power

In the postrevolutionary decade no issue related to women has been as frequently and seriously contested as the veil. Before the overthrow of the old regime, women's public appearance had already become a contentious issue. In the fall of 1978, on several university campuses, Islamic militant students were reported to have attacked unveiled women.[8] In mass demonstrations, women were asked to appear veiled or at least to wear large scarves. Extra scarves were at hand to be offered to those who had come uninformed or had not conformed. The offer could be rejected only at great risk. At issue was not simply a matter of Islamic modesty; through the imposition of the Islamic dress code a new power in society was already being built. As Hunt has noted about the French Revolution, "Power... was not a finite quantity possessed by one faction or another; it was rather a complex set of activities and relationships that created previously unsuspected resources" (1984, 72). Through the imposition of the veil, among a thousand other activities, Islamic forces were creating and testing their power.

Since February 1979 the veil has been the subject of numerous government bills and religious edicts, from Ayatollah Khomeini's first statement on 6 March 1979 to the executive bylaw "to confront mal-veiling" that went into effect on 21 April 1989 (see Appendix A for a full text of this bylaw). Indeed, every year around 7 January, the date of public unveiling enforced by Reza Shah in 1936, several seminars are held across the country on the subject of "the veil and women's rights in Islam."

On the other side of the contest, through their resistance (8 March 1979 and subsequent occasions), women opposed to compulsory veiling had discovered their own, albeit scant, resources and power.[9] At least momentarily, in March 1979, they delimited the boundaries of Islamic power. Another year passed—during which Islamic forces, through a number of other battles, had created and consolidated their power—before a new, more successful imposition was decreed. Since then, at every turn of events, state authorities and their supporters, as well as dissident women, have battled over the boundaries of the veil as an issue of power. For instance, when Ayatollah Khomeini issued his eight-point statement on 15 December 1982—a statement that did not concern the veil but cautioned against arbitrary attests and confiscations of property—it was immediately tested by breaking the strict ordinance on the veil. While women attempted to create a minimal space for their power by wearing colorful veils and inventing new fashions of veil, the state created, extended, and consolidated its domain of power by insisting on specific types and definite colors of veil—neither of which could be justified as an Islamic requirement.

The continued resistance of some women against the strict enactment of the dress code has been likened to a sickness, such as cholera, against which the rest of society must be vaccinated through ever more strict demands for veiling and moral public behavior: "This [proper veiling] is a kind of social vaccination, vaccination of the Muslim man and woman, vaccination of our pure and virtuous sisters. One cannot say that there should be no microbes in the world, that there should be no diseases. . . . What shall we do against diseases? We must preserve ourselves. We must quarantine ourselves."[10] And in the same manner that vaccinations are compulsory for the sake of public health, that the state does not need anyone's consent for compulsory vaccination, veiling cannot be consensual.

In *Gharbzadegi*, Al-e Ahmad had defined the general phenomenon he was to write about as a sickness: "I speak of being afflicted with 'westitis' the way I would speak of being afflicted with cholera. If this is not palatable let us say it is akin to being stricken by heat or by cold. But it is not that either. It is something more on the order of being attacked by tongue worm. Have you ever seen how wheat rots? From within. The husk remains whole, but it is only an empty shell like the discarded chrysalis of a butterfly hanging from a tree. In any case, we are dealing with a sickness, a disease imported from abroad, and developed in an environment receptive to it. Let us discover the characteristics of this illness and its cause or causes and, if possible, find a cure" (Al-e Ahmad 1981, 3).

The metaphors used by Al-e Ahmad for what he thought of as a general social illness have now collapsed onto the body of the woman, on her public physical appearance. Moreover, this illness is viewed as a sickness of the will, and as a willful sickness.[11] Not only is the society to be quarantined against the contaminated agent, the agent needs to be cured of her willed disease; she is to be "disciplined and punished." Women who have resisted total conformity have been fired from jobs, punished with Islamic punishment (seventy-four lashes), subjected to physical attacks on the streets, excluded from social space (shops refuse to sell them goods; banks, government offices, taxis, and airplanes refuse to deal with them), and threatened with transfer to "rehabilitation camps" at their own expense.

The unsettled power struggle has required the invention of new language. Between veiling and unveiling, a new word has been coined because of the insistence of some women to test the limits of the new power again and again, "mal-veiling." When it became too dangerous to appear unveiled, some continued to pose problems for the government and for the more religiopolitically committed through smaller infringements of the dress code. It became necessary to launch a new campaign every few months to eradicate mal-veiling.

Several important points are at issue in these campaigns and the resistance against them. First, the uprooting of what is seen as imperialist culture, embodied in non-Islamic, or Western-influenced, female behavior, is viewed as essential to the very definition of the Islamic revolution. Second, through the insistence on "proper veiling," as through many other similar details, the overall *Islamic* character of the new state and culture is again and again insisted upon.[12] "If anyone insults or is disrespectful of the veil, not only has he/she insulted a veiled woman, all Islamic values and the Prophet of Allah have been insulted," declared Dary-E Najafabadi in the 1986 seminar on *hejab* (veiling).[13] Third, the implicit religiopolitical message is that the men of the state and religious authority have the prerogative to define what is truly Islamic: *hejab* is in the category of religious exigencies *(zaruriyat),* the argument goes; it is not up to individual taste or interpretation. "When God or His Prophet issue an order, it is not worthy of any believing man or woman to deal with it on the basis of taste. God's decrees are absolute. There is no dispute on the issue of *hejab.* It is not worthy of believing men and women to make a choice in a matter commanded by God or His Prophet."[14] Fourth, the veil and "proper veiling" have become definitional symbols of a woman's faith and loyalty. Although in traditional Islamic discourse the veil is related to modesty and morality, its transformation into a central symbolism of power has imbued it with a total religiopolitical significance. The most important definers of the symbolism have been Islamic activist women themselves. Writers such as Zahra Rahnavard, Shahin Tabataba'i, Fereshteh Hashemi, and Soraya Maknun have produced extensive writings and given public speeches on the broader meaning and significance of the veil. In some cases the original intent of the writer may have been to change the level of public discussion and policy away from strict and narrow concerns over chastity and clothing and toward more general and symbolic discussion of what constitutes a truly Islamic womanhood. The transformation, however, far from reducing the significance of the actual piece of clothing, gave it an even more essential and vitally contested meaning.

Fatimah: The Ideal Muslim Woman

Closely related to the veiling campaign has been the choice of Fatimah's birthday as Woman's Day and the ongoing ideological campaign to establish Fatimah as "the ideal role model" for all Muslim women.

Shortly after the overthrow of the old regime, various women's groups and political organizations initiated a series of activities to commemorate International Woman's Day on 8 March 1979. The activities turned into demonstrations against compulsory veiling after Ayatollah Khomeini, in a 6 March speech addressed to a group of clerics and students from Qom religious center, had stated, "In Islamic ministries women should not appear naked: women can go there, but they must wear the veil. There is no problem with their going to work, but it must be with religiously legitimate veiling, with observation of religious norms." The slogans of International Woman's Day were carefully selected to emphasize its belonging to the culture of the revolution. One of them insisted that "Woman's Day is neither Western nor Eastern; it is universal." This kind of universalism—which in fact meant that Woman's Day was both Western and Eastern—was not what one of the main mottos of the Islamic revolution—neither Western nor Eastern, but Islamic—had in mind. The correction came two months later. On 16 May 1979, speaking on the occasion of Fatimah's birthday—which happened to be Khomeini's birthday as well—Khomeini repeatedly referred to the day as Woman's Day. A year later the Islamic Republican Party (IRP) officially adopted it as Woman's Day, organizing rallies and demonstrations in several cities, and the day has been commemorated every year since.

The timing and the choice of the day are significant. Once 8 March had been celebrated and in part turned into demonstrations against Islamization measures, the issue could not be ignored. An Islamic alternative had to replace the international date in order to disassociate Islamic women from Western and Eastern concepts and dates and to symbolize Islamic values for womanhood. It is also significant that between the two early Islamic female "role models" that had been projected frequently over the previous years, Fatimah (the good daughter of the Prophet, the faithful wife and companion of Ali, and the exemplary mother of Hossein and Zeynab) and Zeynab (the courageous sister of Hossein, who is said to have stood up against Yazid and who, after the Karbala massacre, delivered an eloquent speech of condemnation), Fatimah's birthday was given preference over Zeynab's.[15] Before the overthrow of the old regime, Zeynab's image had predominated, as the embodiment of courage and faith; the black-veiled Iranian women demonstrators were perceived as enacting the stand of Zeynab at the battle of Karbala against the Yazid of the time. Now that the Islamic government had been formed, Zeynab had exhausted her value; her place was vacated, to be occupied by her mother. Fatimah is mostly associated with a quiet, constructive character from whom the Prophet drew inspiration, who unfailingly stood by Ali's rightful claims, and in whose lap Hossein and Zeynab were raised and educated. The symbolic choice could not have been clearer.

Legal Construction of the New Ideal

There have been two distinct phases in the policies of the Islamic Republic toward women. In the first phase, in the immediate aftermath of the revolution, policies toward women were shaped by the exigencies of eliminating what was seen to be the corrupt legacy of the past, including annulment of many laws seen as un-Islamic, elimination of women from the judiciary, segregation of women in public places such as buses, sports venues, and beaches, and the campaign to impose the veil. The central theme of this phase was purification of society and of women. Because this purification meant an attack on what significant numbers of urban women felt were their gains over the previous fifty years, to them it looked as if the new regime wanted women, all women, pushed back to the domestic sphere.

As early as 3 March 1979 the Ministry of Justice refused to issue confirmation orders for women judges who had completed all their requirements. They were told to look for administrative positions within the ministry. By November 1979 all women judges were transferred to other government jobs. Women were not legally barred from other professions, although many were purged on political, religious, or moral grounds. Many more, finding the pressures of conformity unacceptable and not actually needing the income, resigned or opted for early retirement (Moghadam 1988, 226–28).

The most important piece of legislation affected in this early phase was the Family Protection Law of 1967 (modified in 1975). Before the passage of this law, special notary officers handled all marriage and divorce registrations. This law referred all matters related to the family to courts. According to its provisions, either the wife or the husband could ask for divorce; the court would then investigate the case and decide whether to issue an "incompatibility decree" and allow the divorce to proceed. The court would also decide who should have the custody of children. Previously, the custody of all female children over the age of seven and male children over the age of two would automatically go to the father, and except in certain unusual situations, only husbands could obtain divorce, by simple referral to a notary registration. The family courts would also determine the amount of alimony.

The law stipulated that a married man needed court permission to take a second wife and that the court would investigate each application to establish if the first wife consented, if the man could afford a second wife, and if he could be fair in his treatment of all wives. It also stated that a wife had the right to divorce her husband if he took a wife without her prior consent. The exercise of other prerogatives of a husband, as codified in the Iranian Civil Law, such as his right to stop his wife's employment if he considered it harmful to his honor, was made conditional on the court's ratification. The law was revised in 1975 to remove mutual consent as a condition of divorce.

Barely two weeks after the overthrow of the old regime, on 26 February 1979, a letter was issued by the office of Ayatollah Khomeini, suspending the Family Protection Law because it had been determined to be against the Shariʿah. A government spokesman, however, later stated that the old law would remain in effect until new legislation was drafted. Much confusion and debate ensued over the following months. On 21 April 1979, for instance, Mahdavi Kani reiterated that the Family Protection Law had been voided by Khomeini and that therefore husbands could divorce their wives with no hindrance. On 9 August 1979, Sadr Hajj Seyyed Javadi, minister of justice, declared that family matters would henceforth be referred to religious courts and that although family courts had not yet been dissolved, they were no longer issuing decrees that countervened the Shariʿah. New family legislation was proposed by the Ministry of Justice to the cabinet and approved by the Revolutionary Council on 2 October 1979.[16] This new law gave the right of divorce exclusively to the husband, unless at the time of marriage a woman specified in the marriage contract that under certain specified conditions she could divorce herself on her husband's behalf (those conditions giving her power of attorney). The law also reinstated a husband's right to forbid his wife to take employment, lowered the official age of marriage for women from eighteen to thirteen, entrusted the custody of female children after seven years of age and of male children after two years of age to the father in case of divorce and to his relatives in case of his death, and permitted polygamy (up to four wives) and temporary marriages without any legal restrictions. The new law immediately became the subject of protest and discussion, not only on the part of secular women. Muslim women reformers, writing extensively in the pages of *Zan-e Ruz* and "lobbying" influential clerics, used every possible argument in support of a more enlightened legislation. By early 1984, twelve conditions were printed into the official marriage contract as grounds for the wife to

acquire divorce, assuming the husband agreed to these conditions before the marriage ceremony. All clerics were instructed to read these
conditions one by one and to get the signature of the prospective husband and wife on each of the conditions before they would officially
marry them (see Appendix B for the full text of these conditions).

The new legislation recognized special civil courts (*dadgah-e khass-e
madani*), rather than husbands or individual clerics, as the legitimate
body that would make the final judgment and decision regarding family disputes. This had been one of the main points of contention between the old regime and the clerics and one of the grounds for
considering the old Family Protection Law un-Islamic. These courts
were also empowered, through a different piece of legislation, to make
all the child custody decisions.

Also, the twelve provisions under which a wife could divorce herself included all the provisions of the old Family Protection Law.

Last, in the new legislation the courts were given the prerogative of
allocating up to half the properties generated during the years of marriage to the divorced wife if she was divorced against her wishes.

What does all this mean when, on the one hand, the clerics opposed the old legislation as un-Islamic and, on the other, hailed the
new as an Islamic consolidation of women's rights? Put simply, it indicates that the dispute was never over some essentially Islamic set of
laws but over who—the state or the Islamic jurisprudent—makes the
decisions. Once the dichotomy between the state and the jurisprudent
was dissolved, through the establishment of an Islamic state under the
supervision of the jurisprudents, the contest shifted to competing interpretations of Islamic Shariʿah. Moreover, once certain changes in the
law had been made under the old regime—all of which could easily fit
some sort of Islamic reinterpretation—it was not so easy simply to
discard them; precedents had been set, and there was a sizable and
vocal group of Islamic women (and men) advocates not only for preserving those changes but indeed for enhancing them through more
favorable legislation.[17]

Social Location of the Ideal

Subsequent to the initial phase of eradicating "the vestiges of the
Pahlavi era," there have been incessant debates over the role of women
in the construction of the new order. The debates revolve around the
tensions between women's domestic role and their social responsibilities in an Islamic order. These tensions arise from a certain

hierarchization of women's social roles, as expounded by religiopolitical leaders of Iran. Women's employment and social involvement, in this view, are not prohibited by Islam, except in three domains: becoming judges, issuing binding religious opinion, participating in jihad (the latter restriction is waived when the Islamic community is under attack). Otherwise, female employment and social activities are not prohibited but are conditioned by four criteria: social expedience, family interest, individual morality, and natural appropriateness.[18] The four criteria are presented as an intimately connected whole. Social expedience, for instance—which in earlier years had been invoked as grounds for exclusion of women from certain employments and higher education disciplines, such as mining, geology, and agricultural engineering—is closely linked to the importance of preserving the health of the family and the primary responsibility of women in caring for husbands, raising children, and managing the home. Thus, women cannot hold employments that require absence from the conjugal household; training them in such fields is therefore a waste of social resources.[19] Training of female veterinarians, on the other hand, is excluded on the grounds of the delicate female physique. Social and individual moral concerns have prompted the fixing of a 50 percent female quota in the university students' admission procedure in medicine and in many of the related disciplines, and midwifery and family hygiene accept only female students. For women to be eligible for government scholarships to study abroad, they must be married and accompanied by their husbands (*Ettela ͨat*, 13 July 1987).

Several measures have also affected high school education for female students. Married women are prohibited from attending day schools. Considering their domestic priorities, they are hardly in a position to attend night schools. And the legal lowering of the marriageable age for women to thirteen could lead to higher levels of female dropouts over the coming years. Abolition of coeducational classes in private institutes that prepare students for university exams or teach foreign languages has also had adverse effects for women. Many such institutes do not have a large enough number of female applicants to hold separate classes for them, which in effect restricts their availability to women. Since 1982, new courses have been introduced into high school curricula to train students in practical skills for future employment. These courses are limited to the following subjects in girls' high schools: first year, knitting and needlework; second year, sewing; third year, hygiene, safety, and first aid; and fourth year, nutrition and child care (*Zan-e Ruz*, 17 Dec. 1988). As Sister Zamani, who is in charge of the nationwide implementation of this project in girls' high schools, observed:

> The aim of this project for boys is to insure that they do not go unemployed after graduation. If they do not enter universities, they can be absorbed into the labor force or do productive work on their own. But for their sisters, it is not based on the notion that they should not go unemployed in the future. . . . but that they fill their spare time at home. . . .
>
> The primary need of a man is employment; his principle work is to provide for the family. But for a woman, her primary work is the family and the improvement of family life. (*Zan-e Ruz*, 24 Dec. 1988)

The Economic Imperative?

To make woman's priority as mother and wife compatible with her social involvement, the government introduced legislation, passed by the Majlis in early 1983 and modified in late 1985, making half-time employment in government services formally open to women and eligible for certain benefits.[20] Contrary to the initial assault against day-care as an imperialist plot to separate mothers from children, all government offices are now required to provide on-the-job child-care facilities (*Zan-e Ruz*, 16 July 1988).

The overall employment pattern of women since the 1979 revolution is not encouraging. According to Moghadam (1988, 229), although economically active women as a proportion of the total female urban population aged ten and above has declined from 9.5 percent in 1976 to 7 percent in 1982 and although employed women as a proportion of economically active women has declined from 8.5 percent in 1976 to 5 percent in 1982, corresponding drops in activity rates for men have been even more drastic. Moreover, women continue to constitute roughly the same proportion of government employees in 1983 as they did in 1974–75 (Moghadam 1988, 230). Female employment in modern industry, however, has decreased sharply from over 20 percent in 1976 to 7 percent in 1982–83 (Moghadam 1988, 232–33). An article in *Zan-e Ruz* (22 Aug. 1987) painted a rather gloomy picture. The cover of the magazine was a collage of employment advertisements, all explicitly requiring only men to apply. An expert on labor force planning and development, Dr. Hedayat, is quoted as saying that a woman of equal qualification has one-sixth the chance of a man to be employed for the same job. Women civil engineers, oil engineers, communication engineers, architects, and mechanical engineers were interviewed in this article, all complaining that they had been refused employment specifically because they were women. Hojjat ol-Islam Motebahheri, director of the politico-ideological section at the government-owned Defense Industries Organization, explained the reasons for their refusal to employ any women.

> Basically I am against women working outside the home. Of course teaching in girls' high schools or working in hospitals are exceptions. . . . In some of our factories . . . we do have women workers on the production line. But generally speaking women moving into these jobs is unnatural. . . . Woman's mission is to bring up children. This is no mean mission. Western patterns must be eradicated in the Islamic Republic. . . . If women abide by Islamic norms, they can participate in social activities, . . . but there is no need to have women here or in some of the ministries: What I insist upon and want to emphasize is that these workplaces must become healthy places, where not only would they not be sites of sins, the thought of sin would not arise either. One way to achieve that would be to prohibit mixed interactions. Naturally when at a place, at a social, woman and man, girl and boy mix together, no matter how much they abide by divine virtue, there will be grounds for deviation and corruption, . . . this has to be prevented. . . . It is because of these considerations that when women ask to end their services or when they retire, we fully cooperate with them and in their place we bring in young, active, and interested males. (*Zan-e Ruz*, 22 Aug. 1987)

According to the same report, institutes and corporations that function under the general umbrella of the National Industries Organization received directives in 1985–88 prohibiting them from hiring women. The Industrial and Mining Bank argued that the nature of their investment projects required long periods of travel and that therefore women could not possibly fill their posts. Another government organization, the General Accounting Office, reported that they had not hired any women since 1979–80 under specific directives. As reasons for this policy, the associate director gave the necessity of trips lasting over several days at a time and the necessity of groups of employees working together on projects in the same room, which involves mixing of female and male employees, a practice prohibited on religious grounds. He also emphasized that this latter problem is a particular hazard in a higher-level management post, where the person in authority receives thirty to forty clients a day, all of them men; such a job could not be given to woman because it would put a woman alone with a man in the same room many times a day.

Like many other social issues, women's employment has thus continued to be subject to contradictory orientations. Whereas many in authority have shown a general reluctance toward, if not outright policy against, women's employment in many industries and government jobs, others, such as Rafsanjani and Khamenei, have emphasized the necessity of tapping women's time and energy as a resource for the consolidation of the revolution and the general progress of the country. Much of the emphasis, however, has been on mobilizing women for volunteer social projects.

To account for the emphasis on women's social involvement, in contrast to the more traditional Islamic emphasis on confinement of women to domesticity, Moghadam (1988, 238) has proposed the following factors: "(1) the imperatives of economic development, which the Islamic Republic has not totally abandoned, and the exigencies of the war with Iraq; (2) economic need on the part of some women and the resistance to total subjection on the part of others, including educated women with prior work experience; and (3) the ambiguities in the discourse and policies of the Islamic political elite and the conflicting cultural images of women, allowing some room to maneuver within the confines of the Islamic system."

But "the imperatives of economic development" need to be argued much more persuasively for a period that has not been marked by any kind of "labor shortage" in the economy. Moreover, the prominent social profile of women in the last decade has not been as much in the economy as in volunteer activism. Educated professional Islamic women activists, themselves the product of state building and modernization under the Pahlavis, have been vocally instrumental in charting out the regime's attitude and policies affecting women. And the regime is under the pressure of precedence not to be conceived as less attentive to its female citizens' legitimate needs and demands, because it views itself as a world model for the solution of all social problems and tensions. Despite its own likings, it does feel the challenge of modern feminism.

A more immediate and conjunctural factor was of course the exigencies of the Iran-Iraq War. Women were mobilized in a whole series of activities: They staffed the mass laundries and kitchens servicing the war front, and they served as nurses and doctors in the military hospitals. After Khomeini's directive for a general national mobilization of an army of twenty million, women volunteers were also formed in special units and received training in military know-how, first aid, and chemical weapons neutralization. They worked behind the battle lines; no women's units were actually used in combat.

It might have been expected that if the Islamic regime was in need of absorbing more women into the labor force, into social work, and into war-support activities, it would have relaxed its regulations on the veil and its strictures on the moral codes of public behavior. The contrary has been the pattern. The more women have become involved in social life, the more necessary has it become to enforce the moral codes to ensure that such increased contact between men and women does not unwittingly undermine the moral fabric of the Islamic community and thus open it up to alien penetration. Thus, over the past two years numerous campaigns have been waged to root out the smallest infractions of the moral code, while prominent spokesmen and politicians of the regime, such as Rafsanjani and Khamenei, have expounded the necessity of women's involvement in social tasks, within such limits as not to damage their roles as mothers and wives.

With the war over, what will happen to women's social activism? Will they be persuaded, cajoled, into a return to domesticity, as has happened in other countries after wars? Already a new debate is taking shape on women's role in the reconstruction period, as reflected in the pages of the woman's weekly *Zan-e Ruz*. There is no way of predicting the outcome of the new debate. One indication does not bode well: in 1989, around Fatimah's birthday—Woman's Day—there were fresh discussions about readopting that day as Mother's Day.

Appendix A

The Executive Bylaw Concerning the Struggle Against Mal-veiling
Translated from *Zan-e Ruz*, 22 April 1989

Following the decision of the National Security Council concerning the necessity of decisiveness of the executive and security forces in actively encountering and dealing with the phenomenon of mal-veiling, the Social Council of Teheran Province ratified an executive bylaw against unveiling, mal-veiling, and vulgar clothes. The bylaw went into effect as of 21 April 1989.

According to the decision of the Social Council of Teheran Province, the existing laws and bylaws concerning the punishment of those in violation of Islamic *hejab* are as follows:

A:

1. The Islamic Law of Punishment *(ta ʿzirat)*, ratified on 9 August 1983, states in ARTICLE 102 and its corollary:

—Whoever, in public, in streets, and in public views and places, engages in exhibition of a forbidden *(haram)* act will receive up to seventy-four lashes in addition to the punishment of the act itself. If the act itself is not punishable but injures public decency, it will only receive up to seventy-four lashes.

Corollary: Women who appear in public view and streets without religiously sanctioned *hejab* will receive up to seventy-four lashes.

2. The law dealing with processing violations and punishment of vendors selling clothes of which usage in public is against religious law or injures public decency, ratified on 19 March 1987, deals with this problem in its ARTICLES 1 and 2 and 3 and 4, which is hereby reproduced:

ARTICLE 1. Whoever knowingly produces, imports, sells, or displays in public view and open places clothes or emblems marked with anti-Islamic or counterrevolutionary symbols is considered an offender. Such clothes and objects constitute contraband goods.

Corollary: Religious insignia of official religious minorities, for the followers of these religions, are exempt from the terms of this law.

ARTICLE 2. The *ta ʿzir* punishment of domestic producers and importers and sellers and users of such clothing and emblems as described in ARTICLE 1 is as follows:

1. Warning and guidance. 2. Reprimand and reproach. 3. Threat. 4. Closure of the business for three to six months in the case of sellers, a cash fine of five hundred thousand to one million rials in the case of producers and importers, and ten to twenty lashes or cash fine of twenty to two hundred thousand rials in the case of users. 5. Annulment of business permit in the case of sellers, and twenty to forty lashes or cash fine of twenty to two hundred thousand rials for the users.

The court will sentence the offender to one of these punishments, taking into account conditions and trade of the offender, the frequency, timing, and place of the offense and other circumstances.

Corollary 1: The court will require the closing down of particular production lines and their adjustment to Islamic regulations.

Corollary 2: If the offender is a government employee, in addition to one of the above sentences he or she will receive one of the following punishments:

1. Temporary dismissal from service up to two years.

2. Expulsion and dismissal from state employment.

3. A five-year ban on employment in all ministries, public and state corporations, institutes, and organizations.

ARTICLE 3. Peddlers engaged in sale and distribution of clothes and emblems referred to in ARTICLE 1 are considered offenders. On first count, the goods will be confiscated and they will be treated according to the first clause of ARTICLE 2. If the offense is repeated, the fine will be two hundred fifty thousand to five hundred thousand rials first and on subsequent occurrences it will be five hundred thousand to one million rials.

ARTICLE 4. Whoever, in public view, dresses or uses makeup in a manner that is in violation of religious law, or spreads corruption, or injures public decency, will be arrested, processed without delay (out of turn) and sentenced according to one of the punishment spelled out in ARTICLE 2.

B: Islamic dress for government employees:
The complete Islamic clothing for use of sister employees is the following:
1. Simple trousers and manteau, loose and long, from thick material.
2. Trousers and manteau must be chosen from sober colors. (Preferred colors are navy blue, brown, grey, and black.)
C: The agreement and coordination arrived at between the respectful assistant to the prime minister and the director of National Organization of Employment and Administrative Affairs with the respectful general commander of the Islamic Revolution Committee concerning the administrative punishments of violators of Islamic *hejab* in government offices and the forms proposed by the National Organization of Employment concerning moral violations on the part of the state employees.
The Social Council of Teheran Province declared the following executive bylaws concerning unveiling and mal-veiling and vulgar clothes:

ARTICLE 1. Categorization and definition of various types of mal-veiling that will be subject to arrest and delivery to the judicial authorities:
A: Unveilings related to the head:
1. Exposure of part of head hair in an exhibitive and vulgar manner.
2. Use of facial makeup, lipstick, eye shadow, in a seductive and vulgar manner.
B: Unveilings related to the torso and legs:
1. Use of clothes that leave parts of body uncovered.
2. Use of lace and see-through clothes.
3. Use of clothes that exhibit in a seductive manner curvatures of the body.
4. Use of tight trousers without a manteau.
5. Use of lace and see-through stockings without trousers or with short trousers.
6. Use of clothes that have symbols or pictures or writings that are vulgar and contrary to Islam.

Explanations:

1. The boundary of religiously sanctioned cover is to cover the whole body except for the face and the hands up to the wrists.

2. For men, usage of vulgar clothes includes what violates public decency and exhibits cultural decadence.

How to execute the Bylaws:

ARTICLE 2. All violations concerning the definitions expounded in ARTICLE 1 that are deemed inadvertent according to the judgment of officials will be dealt with through warning and guidance.

ARTICLE 3. Those cases subject to warning, guidance, and eventually a written commitment are the following:

A: When the hair shows, other than in a way specified in ARTICLE 1.

B: If the length of the hair causes its display from under a headscarf.

C: If bodily movement has caused unveiling.

D: If unbuttoning has caused the exposure of parts of the body.

ARTICLE 4. Concerning employees of government offices subject to the terms of ARTICLE 1, they should be referred to the offices of public prosecutor, through the preliminary investigatory body charged with dealing with administrative violations of state employees, according to the agreement reached between the National Organization of Employment and Administrative Affairs and the Islamic Revolution Committee, described in Chapter 2.

Corollary: In all cases of visible unveiling that occur in places the entry to which does not require a legal writ, measures should be taken according to these bylaws. A copy of the report concerning any previous offenses and follow-ups should be sent to the Office of Habitations of the Islamic Revolution Committee, so that offenders are dealt with under the Habitation Bylaws.

Appendix B

Text of the Conditions Printed into the Legal Marriage
Contract That Make It Possible for a Woman to Divorce Herself

Translated from the Persian as it appeared in *Iran Times*, 13 June 1986. Signatures of husband and wife are required after each provision because they can choose whichever provision they want to include as grounds for the wife's power to divorce herself. Notice that the legal terms do not grant the wife the power to divorce her husband but to divorce herself on his behalf.

1. During the conclusion of the marriage contract, the wife makes it a condition that if divorce is not requested by the wife, and if, according to the judgment of the court, the cause of divorce is not any breach of matri-

monial duties on the part of the wife or any immoral or ill behavior of hers, the husband is required to transfer to the wife up to half of the properties (or any equivalents agreed by the court) earned during the years of marriage.

(signature of husband and wife)

2. During the conclusion of the marriage contract, the husband grants to the wife an irrevocable power of attorney to divorce herself under the following circumstances, by going to a court and receiving proper permission. She is also given irrevocable power of attorney to accept on her husband's behalf forgoing of her *mahr*.

(signature of husband and wife)

The circumstances in which the wife, according to a court's judgment, could request permission for divorce are the following:

1. Refusal of the husband to pay living expenses *(nafaqeh)* over a six-month period, for any reason, and if it is impossible to make him pay. Also if the husband cannot fulfill other required obligations of a husband over a six-month period and if it is impossible to force him to do so.

(signature of husband and wife)

2. Ill behavior or bad social interaction of the husband to the extent that would make life unbearable for the wife.

(signature of husband and wife)

3. If the husband suffers from a hard-to-cure disease that makes married life hazardous to the wife.

(signature of husband and wife)

4. Insanity of the husband in cases where it does not provide [previously recognized] legitimate grounds for annulment of marriage (that is, when it occurs occasionally and not continuously).

(signature of husband and wife)

5. If the court issues an order certifying that the husband's engagement in certain employment is contrary to the interests of the family and to the reputation of the wife and the husband does not abide by this order.

(signature of husband and wife)

6. If the husband is condemned to five years or more imprisonment, or to monetary fines that he is not able to pay and as a result of which has to serve prison terms of five years or longer, or a combination of prison terms and fines that eventually become five years or more imprisonment.

(signature of husband wife)

7. Addiction of the husband to any harmful substance that according to the court's judgment damages the foundation of family life and makes life for the wife difficult.

(signature of husband and wife)

8. If the husband leaves family life without any justifiable reason (determination of what constitutes leaving family life and justifiable reason are up to the court), or is absent over six consecutive months without justifiable reason (to be determined by the court).

(signature of husband and wife)

9. If the husband is condemned for a crime or is punished in any other way, either of which is considered contrary to family honor and the wife's reputation—the determination of what constitutes such dishonor is up to the court, taking into account the status and circumstances of the wife and other common norms.

(signature of husband and wife)

10. If after five years the wife cannot bear a child because of the husband's infertility or other physical problems.

(signature of husband and wife)

11. If the husband disappears and six months after the wife has informed the court he does not reappear.

(signature of husband and wife)

12. If the husband takes another wife without the consent of the first wife, or if according to the determination of the court he is not treating them justly.

(signature of husband and wife)

Notes

1. Fatimah was Mohammad's daughter. A week after the four men had received their sentences, on the suggestion of the head of the supreme court of Iran, Ayatollah Khomeini pardoned them. All were reinstated in their previous jobs (*Iran Times*, 10 Feb. 1989).

2. For an attempt at such a reading, see Najmabadi 1989. For an alternative reading of the same event, see Kohan 1990.

3. I am using the concept of "political sociability" as it has been developed by Furet (1981) in the context of the French Revolution. For political interpretations of Islamic movements and the Iranian revolution, see Arjomand 1984, 1988; Burke and Lapidus 1988; and Milani 1988.

4. Since the appropriation of the concept by the Islamic Republic, many critics of the new regime have distanced themselves from it. In fact, Al-e Ahmad is in the unfortunate

situation of metamorphosing from the indigenous intellectual hero into a demon held responsible for the rise and consolidation of Islamic theocracy in Iran.

5. On the concept of the presentational symbol, see Langer 1942. I would like to thank Frances Hancock for bringing this work to my attention. Hancock, in an unpublished 1989 paper, employs this concept to discuss the significance of the veil in Islamic culture. Here I am extending that discussion to the woman's body.

6. For a discussion of the significance of the journal *Zan-e Ruz* and a content analysis of its editorials, see Saba 1991.

7. For a fuller discussion of the construction of "the woman question" in modern political discourses in Iran, see the text of my 6 April 1989 talk at the Harvard Divinity School, "Hazards of Modernity and Morality: Women in the Contemporary Middle East."

8. For protest against such incidents, see *Kayhan,* 17 Jan. 1979. For a reprint of this letter of protest and other letters and essays by women from the press of the early postrevolutionary months, see Tavakoli-Targhi 1989–90.

9. For an account of some of these activities, see the Chronology section in Tabari and Yeganeh 1982. See also Millet 1981.

10. See *Ettela ʿat,* 3 March 1986, for the full text of Dary-e Najafabadi's speech at the three-day seminar held in Karaj, 4–7 January 1986, on *Hejab va barresi-ye hoquq-e zan dar eslam* (*Hejab* and women's rights in Islam). (All translations are by the author unless otherwise noted.)

11. This point was suggested in the workshop discussions by Margaret Mills.

12. That the issue is perceived as a contest over the character of the power being shaped is perhaps best expressed in one the most popular slogans advanced by women supporters of the regime, "Islam is our doctrine; the veil is our barricade." Recent relaxations of the color code and dress modes indicate, not a de-Islamization process, but the assurance of the state that the issue of power has been settled.

13. See note 10 for full reference.

14. For the full text of Monireh Gorji's speech, delivered at the same seminar as Najafabadi's, see *Ettela ʿat,* 5 Mar. 1986.

15. The two dates are only two weeks apart. Zeynab's birthday was later adopted as Nurse's Day, presumably as a symbolic recognition of her nursing activities during the battle of Karbala, as well as the contemporary role of many women nurses and doctors in the war with Iraq.

16. See the Chronology section in Tabari and Yeganeh 1982.

17. Similar observations could be made about the issue of the woman's vote. Although in 1963 the shah's granting of the female vote was vehemently opposed as un-Islamic and a means of involving women in corrupt and corrupting social interaction, there has been no attempt to disenfranchise women in the Islamic state.

18. For a detailed elaboration of these themes, see newspaper accounts of some of Rafsanjani's Friday sermons in late 1985 and early 1986, particularly sermons delivered on 31 December 1985, 17 January, 28 February, and 4 April 1986.

19. For a discussion of educational policies of the Islamic republic, see Mojab 1987 and 1991.

20. See *Ettela ʿat,* 3 Dec. 1986, for the full text of the half-time employment bill.

10

Gender Inequality in the
Islamic Republic of Iran
A Sociodemography

VALENTINE M. MOGHADAM

Data from the 1986 National Census on Population and Housing—Iran's fourth census and the Islamic Republic's first—reveal a disquieting situation for women in contemporary Iran. An adverse sex ratio, male–female inequalities in literacy and educational attainment, a disadvantaged place for women in the labor market, and high fertility would seem to confirm what some authors (Afshar 1985b; Afkhami 1984; Nashat 1983) have argued: that Iranian women have suffered a continuing loss of economic and social status since Islamization. What is clear is the existence of marked gender asymmetry. Fertility, education, and employment patterns all point to gender inequality in the Islamic Republic.

Gender as a Source of Inequality

In social theory, the concept of gender has now reached the analytic status of class and ethnicity (Farnham 1987; Hess and Ferree 1987). Feminist scholars define gender as the social organization of sexual

Many thanks to Hanna Papanek, Hooshang Amirahmadi, Patricia Roos, Jim Jasper, and Shahin Gerami for comments on earlier drafts of this chapter. As always, I am indebted to my father for providing the data. An earlier version of this chapter first appeared in *World Development* 19 (1991): 1335–50, as "The Reproduction of Gender Inequality in Muslim Societies: A Case Study of Iran in the 1980s."

difference, or a system of unequal relations between the sexes. Oakley (1972) and Rubin (1975) are among the earliest scholars who distinguished sex as a biological category from gender as a cultural-social construct. More recently, de Lauretis (1987) has elaborated on the concept and the social fact of gender in the following way: "The cultural conceptions of male and female as two complementary yet mutually exclusive categories into which all human beings are placed constitute within each culture a gender system, that correlates sex to cultural contents according to social values and hierarchies. Although the meanings vary with each concept, a sex-gender system is always intimately interconnected with political and economic factors in each society. In this light, the cultural construction of sex into gender and the asymmetry that characterizes all gender systems cross-culturally (though each in its particular ways) are understood as systemically linked to the organization of social inequality."

Like age, gender distinctions are basic to the social order in all societies (Ortner and Whitehead 1981; Epstein 1988). A number of feminists feel that women's subordination is such a truism it is no longer necessary to "prove" it scientifically; moreover, social science has not been "innocent" in the perpetuation of gender distinctions and inequality (Nicholson 1987). Others feel that further evidence is needed (and readily available) and that gender inequality can be explained and measured in ways similar to class and racial inequalities (Beneria and Sen 1982; Chafetz 1984, 1990; Leacock and Safa 1986).

The position of women in the labor market is frequently studied as an empirical measure of women's status (Farley 1985). In many developing countries, women constitute a small percentage of the salaried labor force, but they carry out the majority of informal economic activities through Latin America, in Africa, and in much of Asia (Ward 1990). In the formal sector, widespread occupational sex typing, wage disparities, and lack of support services for working mothers are a function of discriminatory economic and ideological systems (Hartmann 1976; Reskin and Hartmann 1986).

Gender distinctions are not accidental or a fact of nature but are reproduced institutionally. The thesis that women's relative lack of economic power is the most important determinant of inequalities, including those of marriage, parenthood, and sexuality, is cogently demonstrated by Blumberg (1978) and Chafetz (1984), among others. The gender division of labor at the macro (societal) level reinforces that of the household, and this division is an important source of women's disadvantaged position and of the stability of the system. This situation is maintained juridically and ideologically. In most contemporary societal arrangements, "masculine" and "feminine" are defined by law and custom; men and women have differential access to political power and economic resources; and cultural images and representations of women are fundamentally distinct from those of men. This is the case even in societies formally committed to social (including gender) equality. Inequalities are learned and taught, and "the non-perception of disadvantages of a deprived group helps to perpetuate those disadvantages" (Kynch and Sen 1984, quoted in Papanek 1990). Many governments do not take an active interest in improving women's status and opportunities, and active and autonomous women's organizations to protect and further women's interests and rights are not widespread. In many countries and among certain social groups within societies, high fertility rates limit women's roles and choices and perpetuate gender inequality. Where the state's policies and rhetoric are actively pronatalist and where official and popular discourses stress gender differences rather than legal equality, an apparatus exists for the production of stratification based on gender. The legal system, education system, and labor market are all sites of the construction and reproduction of gender inequality and the continuing disadvantage of women.

Many contemporary researchers are now investigating the intersection of gender, ethnicity, and class in stratification, subjectivity, and political consciousness. This research is predicated on the understanding that gender (like class and ethnicity) is not a homogeneous category; it is internally differentiated and elaborated by class, ethnicity, age, region, and education. To paraphrase Mann (1986, 56), gender is stratified and stratification is gendered.

Gender in Muslim Societies

That women's legal status and social position are worse in Muslim countries than anywhere else is a common view. The prescribed role of women in Islamic theology and law is often argued to be a major determinant of women's status. Women are viewed as wives and mothers, and gender segregation is customary, if not legally required. Whereas economic provision is the responsibility of men, women must marry and reproduce to earn status (Youssef 1978). Men, but not women, have the unilateral right of divorce; a woman can work and travel only with the written permission of her male guardian; family honor and good reputation, or the negative consequence of shame, rest most heavily with the conduct of women (Fluehr-Lobban 1989).

It is true that Muslim societies are characterized by higher-than-average fertility, higher-than-average mortality, and rapid rates of population growth (Weeks 1988, 12, 46). Age at marriage affects fertility. An average of 34 percent of all brides in Muslim countries in recent years have been under twenty years of age, and the average level of childbearing in Islamic nations is six children per woman (Weeks 1988, 15, 20). The Moroccan sociologist Fatima Mernissi (1987) has explained this in terms of Islamic fear of *fitna:* social and moral disturbance caused by single, unmarried women. Early marriage and childbearing, therefore, may be regarded as a form of social control. The Muslim countries of the Middle East and South Asia also have a distinct gender disparity in literacy and education (Weeks 1988, 27), and low rates of female labor force participation (Youssef 1978; Sivard 1985; Moghadam 1993). High fertility and low literacy and labor force participation are linked to the low status of women, which in turn is often attributed to the prevalence of Islamic law and norms in these societies.

These conceptions, however, are too facile. In the first instance, the view of woman as wife and mother is present in other religious and symbolic systems. The Orthodox Jewish law of personal status bears many similarities to the fundamentals of Islamic law, especially with respect to marriage and divorce (Fluehr-Lobban 1989). Second, the demographic patterns are not unique to Islamic countries; high fertility rates are found in sub-Saharan countries today (Weeks 1988). High fertility was common in Western countries during the first stage of the demographic transition, as Tilly and Scott (1978) showed for England and France. Third, high maternal mortality and an inverse sex ratio exist in non-Muslim areas as well; in northern India and rural China, female infanticide has been documented. The low status of women is a function less of religion than of kinship-ordered patriarchal structures. In the most patriarchal regions of West and South Asia (including India), there are marked gender disparities in the delivery of health care and access to food, resulting in an excessive mortality rate for women (Boutalia 1985; Drèze and Sen 1989; Harriss 1990; Miller 1981; Weeks 1988). Papanek (1990) has argued that differential access to food, education, and health care results from "socialization for inequality," or concepts of unequal "socio-cultural entitlements to resource shares," especially in underdeveloped patriarchal settings.

There are at least three reasons why women's subordination in the Islamic world, of which Iran is a part, cannot be attributed solely to

394   VALENTINE M. MOGHADAM

Islam. First, adherence to Islamic precepts and the applications of Islamic legal codes vary throughout the Muslim world. For example, Tunisia and Turkey are formally secular states, and only Iran has direct clerical rule. Second, women's legal and social positions are quite variable, as any detailed comparative and historical study will show (see Beck and Keddie 1978; Moghadam 1993). Gender segregation is the norm and the law in Saudi Arabia but not in Syria (Ingrams 1988). In Iran and Egypt women vote and run for parliament. There are intraregional variations in patterns of fertility, education, and employment of females. In Tunisia contraceptive use is widespread, and the average age of marriage is twenty-four (Weeks 1988, 26). In Turkey the female share of certain high-status occupations (law, medicine, judgeship) is considerable (Abadan-Unat 1980). Third, gender relations in Muslim societies are determined and affected by such factors as state ideology (regime orientation), level of economic development, extent of industrialization and urbanization, and integration into the world system. The governments of Afghanistan (see Moghadam 1992) and South Yemen (see Molyneux 1985), motivated by Marxist and socialist ideology, took important steps to reduce gender inequality and increase women's rights. Areas with large Muslim populations outside of what is generally called the Muslim world, such as Azerbaijan and Uzbekistan in what was Soviet Central Asia and Bosnia-Herzegovina in the former Yugoslavia, saw improvements in all socioeconomic indicators (Bodrova and Anker 1985; Denitch 1976). Thus, to ascribe principal explanatory power to religion and culture is methodologically deficient because it exaggerates their influence and renders them timeless and unchanging.

These qualifications aside, however, there can be no doubt that where gender inequality exists in its most blatant forms in the Middle East, it claims a religious derivation and thus establishes its legitimacy. Reintroduction of Islamic legislation, including family law, in countries such as Iran, Pakistan, and Egypt has so been justified. Muslim fundamentalists in India oppose the move to a uniform civil code, because it would supersede Islamic personal law governing marriage, divorce, maintenance, adoption, succession, and inheritance (Pathak and Rajan 1989). Following the assumption of power by Ayatollah Khomeini and his clerical associates, steps were taken to abrogate modern, Western-inspired codes related to personal and family life and to institute precepts from the Shariʿah (Islamic canon jurisprudence). Early marriage was promoted, the policy of birth control dismissed, employment of young mothers discouraged, and the raising of children ("committed Muslims") lauded. As the Iran-Iraq War continued, polygyny and temporary marriage were encouraged as a way of dealing with a potential source of social and moral problems: the unmarried woman (Haeri 1989).

Muslim societies, like many others, harbor illusions about immutable gender difference. There is a strong contention that women are fundamentally different from men—and this difference is often translated into inferiority—which strengthens social barriers to women's achievement. In the realm of education and employment, as Epstein (1988) has pointed out, not only is it believed that women do not have the same interests as men and will therefore avoid men's activities, but care is exercised to make sure they *cannot* prepare for roles considered inappropriate. Women's reproductive function is used to justify their segregation in public and their restriction to the home, as well as their lack of civil and legal rights (Ghoussoub 1987). As both a reflection of this state of affairs and a contributing factor, few states in the Muslim world have signed or ratified the United Nations Convention on the Elimination of All Forms of Discrimination Against Women (CEDAW). Under such circumstances, where religion is a privileged sphere and where a more generalized discourse of equality does not exist, challenging gender inequality and discrimination against women becomes extremely difficult.

But even countries such as the Islamic Republic of Iran, whose legal system is largely based on the Shariʿah,[1] find themselves caught between the desire for ideological purity and the exigencies of global and societal changes, between cultural prescriptions and economic imperatives.[2] In Iran, women's educational attainment and employment patterns, though highly problematic, exceed the injunctions of Islamic orthodoxy. In understanding the mechanisms of gender inequality, therefore, it is necessary to examine both structure and ideology, discourses and institutions, rhetoric and statistical trends.

The gender system as it exists today is only partly "new," for many of its features are legacies of the past or inherited from the previous regime. Female physical mobility was not extensive in prerevolutionary Iran, and there were many legal and customary restrictions on women. They could not travel, obtain jobs, or rent apartments without the permission of father or husband. Moreover, male sexist attitudes and behavior were notorious, making it difficult for women even to stand for taxis or go shopping. The beneficiaries of Pahlavi-style modernization were primarily middle-class and upper-class women, whereas the majority of women from working-class and peasant households remained illiterate and poor. The 3.2 percent annual population growth rate resulted from this. The veil was not enforced but was characteristically worn by working-class, traditional lower-middle-class, and urban poor women. Most secondary schools (the exceptions being the international schools where the language of instruction was European) were gender-segregated. Universities and workplaces, however, were not. Men could be taught by female instructors (I taught English at the Air Force Language School in the early 1970s), but the matter of "appropriate dress" was always raised. Thus, there are some continuities, and some breaks, in the gender system.

A Review of the 1986 Census Data

Population, Sex Ratio, Fertility

According to the census, the population of Iran was 49.4 million in November 1986. (This was adjusted upward to 50.6 million in 1989.) As shown in table 10.1, a little over half of this figure comprises the male population (25.2 million), and women constitute 24.1 million, suggesting an adverse sex ratio (105 men to 100 women). The census shows that in all age groups there are more males than females. In a few countries of the world, males still have a higher life expectancy than females; apart from Iran, they are Bangladesh, Bhutan, India, the Maldives, Nepal, and Pakistan (Weeks 1988). This was apparently also true for Afghanistan until recent years, when the escalation of the civil war resulted in more male deaths than female.[3] An adverse sex ratio indicates the low status of women, which within the overall cultural matrix and resource constraints would mean more nutritional deficiencies suffered by females than males (Harriss 1990; Drèze and Sen 1989). Female mortality is also linked to high fertility and to poor access to health care services during pregnancy and in childbirth (Miller 1981; UNICEF 1989).

The sex ratio in Iran is curious because the census shows more male deaths than female for the years 1982–86. From 1980 to 1988 Iran was involved in a major war, which reportedly took half a million lives on the Iranian side, the vast majority of whom were the male fighters. One may well ask, as Amartya Sen has asked regarding India: Where are the missing women?

In 1976 the population numbered 33.7 million. The increase of 15 million people over a ten-year period represents a rate of population increase of 3.9 percent, and a total fertility statistic of 5.6, placing Iran

TABLE 10.1

Iran's Population, by Gender, 1956–1986

Year	Male	Female	Total	Ratio
1956	9,644,944	9,309,760	18,954,704	104 .
1966	13,355,801	12,422,921	25,778,722	108
1976	17,356,347	16,352,397	33,708,744	106
1986	25,491,645	24,365,739	49,857,384	105

Sources: National Census of Population and Housing 1365 (1986), tables A and B; Statistical Yearbook 1366 (1987), table 1; Statistical Yearbook 1367 (1988), table 2.

among the countries with the highest growth rates (UNICEF 1989, table E; World Bank 1984, 166; SCI 1987). Until recently, and like many Muslim countries, Iran had no official population control or family planning policy; indeed, family planning was frowned on. Contraceptive devices and abortions were banned after the 1979 revolution (Mossavar-Rahmani 1983; Afshar 1985b). The high rate of marriage and the promotion of childbearing, the lack of any policy of birth control and of family-planning services for older women, and the large number of women in their reproductive years has kept the birth rate high in postrevolutionary Iran (Aghajanian 1988). Accordingly, in 1986, 45.5 percent of the population was under the age of fifteen (SCI 1987, 3).

As noted by Aghajanian (1988), the social and economic consequences of such population dynamics are not consistent with the ideal goals of improving the welfare and well-being of the population. Similarly, the economic growth of the Islamic Republic is not consistent with such a high rate of population growth. Absolute poverty, inequality, and declining standards of living and quality of life have been documented (Amirahmadi 1990), suggesting the inability of the government to create jobs, provide basic needs, and invest in industry and agriculture. Besides the strain placed on a country's resources and on economic development (Menard 1987), high fertility has also been linked to maternal mortality (Weeks 1988, 31; World Bank 1987; Herz and Meacham 1987) and infant mortality (Trussell and Pebley 1984; UNICEF 1989). During 1980–87 the maternal mortality rate in Iran was 120 per 100,000 (UNICEF 1989, table 3). This may be compared to the low rates of Cuba (31) and Kuwait (18) and the high rates of Zaire (800) and Peru (310).

Rising fertility rates negatively affect women's mobility, especially educational attainment and labor force participation. Studies have shown that fertility and labor force participation are inversely related (Anker, Buvinic, and Youssef 1982; Bodrova and Anker 1985; Concepcion 1974; Sathar et al. 1988). Wage-earning and salaried women tend to have fewer children. Women who work outside the home, particularly those who earn cash incomes, are presumed to have enhanced control over household decisions, increased awareness of the world outside the home, and subsequently more control over reproductive decisions, as a recent study of women in rural Dominican Republic has confirmed (Finlay 1989). Therefore, one reason for the continuing high fertility rate in Iran is the small percentage of women in the labor force and the even smaller percentage of women workers who are wage and salary earners. Rising fertility is also linked to rising unemployment and diminishing job opportunities for women in an overall untoward economic situation. That the marriage age was lowered (from sixteen to thirteen for girls) by the new Islamic state is a further influence on the fertility rate. Another influence on fertility is female literacy and education.

Literacy and Education

In 1986 more than 7 million Iranian men and women, mostly in the provinces, did not speak or understand Persian, the principal and official language of Iran (SCI 1987, table 6.1). Of that figure, 57 percent, or more than 4 million Iranian women (17 percent of the female population) did not speak Persian. These women resided mostly in East and West Azerbaijan, Zanjan, Khuzestan, and Kurdestan. The number of men who did not know Persian was 2.9 million, or 11 percent of the male population. The male-female disparity in knowledge of Persian may be explained by education and employment disparities.

A steady improvement in literacy rates over the last twenty years is evident from the censuses: in the decade 1956–66 the literacy rate improved from 8 percent to 17.9 percent for women, and 22.4 percent to 40.1 percent for men. In 1971 some 25.5 percent of women and 47.7 percent of men were literate; the corresponding figure for the urban areas was 48.1 percent of women and 68.7 percent of men (Mirani 1983). According to the 1976 census, 55 percent of urban women were literate (Moghadam 1988). In 1986, 65 percent of urban women (and 80

TABLE 10.2

Literacy Rates for Population Six Years and Older,
by Sex and Region, Iran, 1986

	Total Literate	%	Urban Areas Numbers	%	Rural Areas Numbers	%
Men and Women	23,878,000	61.7	15,507,000	73.1	8,371,000	48.4
Men	14,052,000	70.9	8,765,000	80.4	5,287,000	60.0
Women	9,826,000	52.0	6,742,000	65.4	3,084,000	36.3

Sources: National Census of Population and Housing 1365 (1986), table 7; *Statistical Yearbook 1367* (1988), 97.

Note: Figures rounded.

percent of urban men) were literate. The rural rates were, as expected, lower: 60 percent of men and 36 percent of women were literate. Although total literacy rates improved over the decade, women's literacy rates do not compare favorably to those of men. In all age groups, more males than females were literate.

Following the launching of the "Islamic cultural revolution" in 1980, a number of steps were taken by the authorities to revise the education system (Mehran 1989). Among the most widely noted changes were the conversion of all coeducational schools into single-sex institutions; the establishment of Islamic dress codes in schools; the encouragement of Arabic (rather than English) as a second language; the elimination of private schools, including those of the religious minorities; and the revision of textbooks. A recent study of sex-role socialization in Iranian textbooks (grade school through high school) concludes that the most dramatic change in textbooks lies in illustrations. Compared to prerevolutionary Iran, visibility of women in textbook illustrations is much lower and their inclusion in lessons with a public, as opposed to a private, setting has dropped precipitously (Higgins and Shoar-Ghaffari 1989, 17). Moreover, all women in the textbook illustrations are veiled. This is consistent with the Islamic government's emphasis on the distinctiveness of male and female roles and on the importance of family life and domestic responsibilities for women. Notions of gender difference and inequality are thus created and reproduced through the medium of the school textbook.

TABLE 10.3

College Population and Fields of Study for Men and Women in Iran, 1986

	Total	Post-diploma	Bachelors	Masters	Doctorate
	181,889	60,490	96,353	10,394	14,652
Male	125,327	42,357	65,263	7,869	9,838
Percentage of Total	69	70	67.7	75.7	67
Teacher Training and Education	16,659	15,194	1,392	60	13
Health and Medicine	17,922	3,955	4,345	1,696	7,926
Engineering	34,569	8,870	22,866	2,433	400
Natural Sciences	10,271	1,958	7,522	661	230
Female	56,562	18,133	31,090	2,525	4,814
Percentage of Total	31	30	32.2	24	33
Teacher Training and Education	7,490	5,858	1,575	50	7
Health and Medicine	15,808	5,477	5,060	1,033	4,238
Humanities	6,934	1,318	5,298	183	35
Natural Sciences	6,257	931	5,011	251	64

Sources: National Census of Population and Housing 1365 (1986), table 10.2.

Note: The academic fields were selected on the basis of the greatest concentration of male and female college populations.

The 1986 census reveals that universal primary schooling has yet to be achieved, especially for girls. Both absolutely and relatively, more males than females are receiving education, at both the grade school and post-secondary school levels. The gap is narrowest at the primary school level (where boys constitute 55 percent of the student population and girls 44 percent) and begins to widen at the intermediate ("guidance") school level, where the male and female shares are 60 percent and 40 percent respectively. But it is the gender gap in the postsecondary student population that is most striking. Out of nearly 182,000 receiving higher education in 1986, just over 56,000 (or 31 percent) are female (see table 10.3). The *Statistical Yearbook 1988* (March 1988–March 1989) lists forty universities, including one all-male seminary and one all-female seminary. The only institutions in which women's enrollment equals or exceeds that of men's are the country's public health and medical schools.

One thing that has not changed since the revolution is that admission to university remains extremely difficult, for both men and women. In the entrance examination for the academic year 1986–87, 586,086 persons (383,245 males and 202,841 females) participated. Of the nearly 62,000 persons who were admitted, 19,000 were women (as against 42,000 men) (*Iran Yearbook* 1988, 627). These figures represent 9.5 percent of the women who took the entrance exams and 11 percent of the men. But it means, again, that the female share of the university population is 31 to 33 percent.

And what are women studying? Nineteen academic disciplines are listed in the census. Women are represented in all of them, including engineering (2,259), but as can be seen from table 10.3, the largest numbers of women university students are in health and medicine, teacher training, the humanities, and the natural sciences. Engineering is the most popular field for male students. In the early 1980s the Iranian authorities declared certain areas of study (technological, veterinary, and some arts programs) off-limits to women. The reasons officially cited were the limited capacity of the universities, lack of job prospects for women in those fields, and the need for women specialists in other fields. Women are discouraged from attending law faculties, because they are deemed to be by nature "too emotional." Thus, of 4,178 law students in the academic year 1988–89, there were only 485 women (Iran, MPB 1989, table 5.46). Qahreman (1988) and Najmabadi (Chapter 9) explain that for the academic year 1987–88 the booklet guiding prospective university students in their choice of academic discipline specified 65 fields out of 108 in Group I (mathematical and technical sciences) that were closed to women. In Group II (experimental sciences), 21 out of 56 fields were open only to men, whereas 2 fields were open only to women. In 7 other fields quotas under 50 percent were fixed for women. In Group III (humanities), 3 fields (out of 28) were closed to women, and in 6, quotas under 50 percent were fixed. In Group IV (arts) there were no official quotas, but numerous protest letters from students appeared in the press in the summer of 1987 indicating that a number of faculties had decided to reject female applicants, among them the graphics and painting faculty at Tehran University and handicrafts and archaeology at Isfahan University. For women to be eligible for government scholarships to study abroad, they must be married and accompanied by their husbands (Mojab 1987).

In the summer of 1989 the quotas for women at the universities were removed from many disciplines. Zahra Rahnavard, the wife of former prime minister Mir Hossein Musavi and herself a university professor, was responsible for negotiating removal of these barriers. This reversal of policy indicates that women are hardly passive in the face of official discrimination and that "Islamic feminists" such as Rahnavard can maneuver on behalf of women's rights within the confines of the existing Islamic system.

In 1986 the female share of the total university teaching staff was 17 percent, including 11 percent at Tehran University, 15.5 percent at Shaheed Beheshti University (formerly the National University), and 11 percent at Shiraz University, the three major Iranian institutions of higher learning. Again, the greater female proportions are in the medical training schools. Women are being encouraged to enter the field of health care so that women can serve women and thus avoid excessive male-female contact.

The data in the foreoing vividly demonstrate the intersection of class and gender in education. The female population is clearly stratified; one stratum (or several strata) has access to high school and university education, whereas others do not. Although one could argue that all women are equally second-class citizens under strict Islamist rule, gender inequality is very differently experienced by women of different social classes, and women's life chances are greatly determined by their place in the social class structure.

Employment

Ascertaining characteristics of a labor force can be problematic. Figures for urban areas are more reliable than those for rural areas, but even so, dealing with large informal sectors, seasonal employment, migrant workers, unstable work arrangements, and part-time employment makes enumeration difficult. Refugee populations (in Iran's case, large numbers of Afghan economic refugees work as domestics or construction workers) could also complicate enumeration. And then there is the notorious undercounting of women, a problem in all developing countries (Beneria 1982; ICRW 1980). Rural women, in particular, are frequently left out of the tabulations or are assumed to be "homemakers." The Iranian census overlooks large numbers of women, most of them rural. It categorizes fully 11 million Iranian women as "homemakers." Consequently, there is a huge disparity between the activity

TABLE 10.4

Comparison of Male and Female Economic Activities in Iran, 1986

Activity	Male	Female
Total Population	25,280,961	24,164,049
Population aged 10 and older	16,841,000	16,030,900
Employed	10,048,858	987,103
Unemployed seeking employment	1,486,138	332,602
Student	3,871,000	2,659,000
Homemaker	194,689	11,250,865
Activity rate (%)	45	8
Percentage of labor force	91	9

Sources: National Census of Population and Housing 1365 (1986), tables 16 and 27; *Statistical Yearbook 1367* (1988), tables 3.1 and 3.2; *Iran Yearbook 89/90* (Bonn: M&B Publishing, 1989), p. 17–4.

rates of men and women, and only a tiny percentage of Iranian women are calculated as part of the labor force.[4] Thus, what follows should not be regarded as exact; the description does, however, provide a picture of labor force participation patterns in Iran that accords with earlier surveys and with informed expectations.

According to the census data, the economically active population numbered 13,041,000 persons, constituting 19.3 percent of the total population over ten years of age. Of the employed population, 65 percent was engaged in the private sector and 31 percent in the public sector (*Iran Yearbook* 1988, 476). Some 990,000 women are classified as employed, which is 6 percent of the female population aged ten and over, and 9 percent of the total employed population (see table 10.4). Female civil servants numbered about 420,000 (as against more than one million men), constituting 28 percent of the total number of civil servants and 41 percent of the total employed female population (see table 10.5). The largest numbers of female government employees are in the Ministries of Education and Health. (The same is true of male government employees.) This concentration obtained in prerevolutionary Iran as well.

In the years following the revolution, female employment in modern industry decreased relative to the prerevolutionary situation and to

TABLE 10.5

Distribution of Male and Female Government Employees in
Selected Ministries: Pre- and Postrevolutionary Iran

Ministry[a]	1974–75		1983–84		1986	
	Male	Female	Male	Female	Male	Female
Total	210,389	87,474	875,735	341,155	1,104,422	419,544
Education	93,976	66,539	316,735	218,703	381,710	286,103
Health	17,747	6,152	95,490	52,707	123,967	87,102
Economics and Finance	12,556	1,660	77,982	11,277	84,562	10,130
Road and Transportation	18,814	627	54,908	2,310	58,801	2,863
Agriculture and Rural Development	12,562	1,660	41,672	2,733	47,778	2,940
Interior	5,848	638	37,333	4,844	14,132	1,126
Culture and Higher Education	6,326	4,105	31,832	14,154	26,622	6,152
Other[b]	42,560	6,093	219,785	38,878	366,850	23,128

Sources: Statistical Yearbook 2533 ("Imperial Year" corresponding to 1974–75); Statistical Yearbook 1363 (1984–85), 68; Statistical Yearbook 1367 (1988–89), 69.

[a]The ministries were selected on the basis of the greatest concentration of male employees so as better to compare female concentration distribution.

[b]For 1983–84: Prime Minister's Office, Islamic Guidance, Foreign Ministry, Commerce, Post/Telegraph/Telephone, Justice, Light Industries, Labor and Social Affairs, Housing and Urban Development, Industries and Mines, Power, Oil, Islamic Republic Media, Defense, Heavy Industries. This makes for a total of 1,216,890 employees. For 1974–75: the same, excluding Islamic agencies and including the Ministry of War. This makes for a total of 304,404 employees. In the span of a decade, there was an increase in government employment roughly corresponding to the annual growth of the population. In 1986, male participation in the Rural Reconstruction Crusade numbered 54,388, but a mere 579 women were employed there.

employment in government agencies and ministries. Women continued to work in the large industrial establishments, but their participation in modern-sector industrial activity was almost insignificant. What was left of the blue-collar female work force in the large industrial establishments was in textiles/clothing/shoes/leather, in food and beverages, and in nonmetallic minerals, machinery, and chemical industries (Moghadam 1988). In the major economic sectors, the largest number of women were in private and public services. Agriculture ranked second, with about 263,000 women, and industry third, with 216,000 women employees. But clearly, vast women were not being counted in the agricultural sector; the figure for men in agriculture was nearly 3 million. In line with the economic sectors, the occupational groups in which most women were represented are (1) professional, technical, and related workers (35 percent of employed women); (2) agricultural, animal husbandry, forestry, fishing and hunting workers (26.6 percent of employed women); and (3) production and transport workers (23.4 percent of employed women). The remaining 15 percent of employed women were spread over managerial, administrative, and clerical work (SCI 1987, table 20).

Among the most significant characteristics of the employed female population that may be discerned from the census are (1) the female share of the total labor force is still small, under 10 percent; (2) the majority of women employees in the public sector are teachers and health workers; (3) apart from carpet weaving, women's role in industrial production is extremely limited—only 14 percent of the manufacturing labor force, and mostly unwaged—rendering them marginal to the production process; and (4) a mere 19 percent of women in the private sector receive a wage for their work. (The corresponding figure for men is 27 percent—suggesting a high level of "self employment" in the private sector.) Some 42 percent of women in the private sector are "unpaid family workers" and another 35 percent are own-account workers. Most of these unpaid women are in agriculture, and a smaller number in industry (SCI 1987, table 21). As in other countries, such as Turkey (see Berik 1988; Kandiyoti 1984) and Afghanistan (see Moghadam 1993), the products of and income from their labor—agricultural goods, rugs, clothing—often accrue not to themselves but to their husbands or male kin (Afshar 1985a). Clearly, women are better off in the public sector.

These figures, and the classification system, suggest both a methodological bias and a social problem. The social problem is that women workers are subject to "double exploitation" (as workers and as women, or, to put it more analytically, by class and by gender), as fewer of them are wage earners and many more are unpaid family workers. (One may also assume that women's wages and salaries fall below those of men, although data are not available.) This social problem of the labor market (low employment and unwaged employment of women) spills into other areas of the social structure and is manifested in rising fertility rates, as discussed earlier. The methodological bias and inadequacy lies in the fact that many women are simply not counted as part of the labor force and will therefore not be considered in any employment or social policies designed by the authorities.

Besides education level and wage earning, the difference between work in the public sector and in the private sector manifests itself in age structure as well. For such occupations as scientific-technical workers and teachers, the largest numbers of women are in the age groups 20–29 and 30–39. In agricultural occupations, however, the largest numbers of women are in the age group 10–19, followed by the age group of 20–29. In "industrial" occupations (rug weaving and the like), the largest numbers of women workers are in the 10–19 age group (SCI 1987, table 22).

The data reveal internal differentiation of the female population, with marked differences between rural and urban women. In urban areas, women in the public sector tend to be largely professional, highly educated, and salaried; they are to be found mainly in education and health care; they are also less likely to be married. By contrast, a rural woman is typically married and illiterate, or has attained only primary education.

The stratification of women in Iran along education, employment, and income lines does not attenuate gender inequality as it exists systemically. Women are less likely to be in positions of power, authority, and wealth than are men, and are less likely to be powerful and wealthy (in their own right) today than in prerevolutionary Iran. This will no doubt change. In the meantime, it is gender inequality, rather than class differences among women, that is the principal "fault line" in contemporary Iran.

Implications of Gender Inequality

According to Papanek (1990), "Gender differences, based on the social construction of biological sex distinctions, are one of the great 'fault lines' of societies—those marks of difference among categories of persons that govern the allocation of power, authority, and resources." But gender differences are not the only such fault line; they operate within a larger matrix of other socially constructed distinctions, such as class, ethnicity, religion, and age, that give them their specific dynamics in a given time and place. Because of the intersection of gender with other social distinctions and because of such factors as state policy, economic development, and global communications, gender systems are not totalistic and unchanging. Gender systems may be designed by ideologues and inscribed in law, justified by custom and enforced by the police, sustained by processes of socialization and reinforced through distinct institutions. But they are not impervious to modification, change, resistance. Modern societies are too heterogeneous for a single system to remain intact without challenges. The challenges to a strictly defined gender system such as that envisioned by the early Islamist ideologues in Iran may derive from economic imperatives (such as the need to open the formal labor market to more women in a war economy or in times of economic expansion) and from the growth of the ranks of educated women who reject domestication. There is also a profound internal inconsistency in Iran's gender ideology, inasmuch as it seeks to associate womanhood with family life—with marriage and child rearing—but does not deny women education and employment opportunities (albeit limited to those deemed "appropriate") or the rights to vote and to run for parliament. In Iran today, women may be veiled, but they are found in schools, universities, government offices, factories, and the Majlis. Ideologies of gender difference and the practice of gender inequality exist, but these conditions are subject to the challenges of economic development and demographic changes, such as the growth of an educated female population. As universal schooling expands in Iran, the gender system will be further challenged.

For theorists who argue that women's economic dependence on men is the root cause of their disadvantaged and devalued status, change in the structure of labor force opportunities and rewards is the key target (Chafetz 1990; Moghadam 1993). Many studies examining the rise in female paid employment worldwide and the structure of work opportunities for women have concluded that women are better off in paid employment than in unpaid family labor (ILO/INSTRAW 1985; Lim 1983; Joekes 1987; Bruce and Dwyer 1988; Finlay 1989). Problems, unfair practices, and biases continue, however. Women are paid less for the same work, even when controlling for training and job continuity; whatever work women do tends to be devalued; and women often take jobs on appallingly bad terms (Elson and Pearson 1981; Joekes 1987; Epstein 1988). The long-term and unintended consequence of women's participation in the labor force, however, is to undermine gender inequality and gender ideology and to raise women's consciousness. Employment is a prerequisite for women's equity and empowerment.

TABLE 10.6

**Female Share of Employed Population:
Iran Compared with Other Countries**

(in percentage)

Industrialized Country	Year	Female Share	Industrializing Country	Year	Female Share
Austria	1987	40.1	Egypt	1984	18.7
Bulgaria	1985	47.7	India	1981	25.9
Canada	1986	42.9	Indonesia	1985	35.9
France	1987	43.3	Israel	1983	38.5
West Germany	1987	39.5	South Korea	1987	39.9
Greece	1986	35.5	Mexico	1980	27.8
Italy	1987	36.4	Pakistan	1980	3.7
Japan	1985	38.6	Philippines	1987	36.2
Portugal	1987	42.0	Tunisia	1984	21.3
Sweden	1987	48.7	Turkey	1980	30.0
United States	1987	45.5	Venezuela	1987	27.7
Yugoslavia	1981	38.6	Iran[a]	1986	9.0

Source: ILO, *Yearbook of Labour Statistics 1988* (Geneva: ILO), table 2A.

[a]Data from *National Census of Population and Housing 1365* (1986).

The census data pertaining to women in contemporary Iran suggest that beyond the limitations and restrictions are opportunities for women's advancement. And certainly there is much that could be improved, even within the confines of the Islamic system as it has developed in Iran. First of all, the female share of the total labor force has declined by 2 percent from previous years. When the female share of the labor force is not very great to begin with, the drop is significant. Male employment is down as well, reflecting overall untoward economic conditions. But the female share of the total labor force in Iran is exceedingly low compared to other countries (see table 10.6).

The data also reveal that men are concentrated in the high-status, high-paying occupations; the labor market is extremely gender-segregated. And it will continue to be so if the present educational patterns persist wherein male students are overwhelmingly concentrated in engineering and related fields, while women are tracked into health and medicine, the humanities, and teaching. "Men's work" and "women's work" are not "natural" but are social and cultural constructs. The market and other economic processes are not gender-neutral, nor are they divorced from political and ideological influences and noneconomic institutions (such as, in Iran's case, official interpretations of Islamic canon law). Thus, the education and employment patterns pertaining to women are neither accidental nor natural but derive from women's disadvantaged position in the stratification system and in the ideological-symbolic system.

Second, attention must be drawn to the large numbers of women in the private sector who are not receiving a wage for their work ("unpaid family workers"). Studies are needed to determine who these women are, how long they work per day or per week, what tasks they perform, how the income generated is disposed, who disposes of it, and so on. Their subordinate status as workers—determined solely by their gender—needs to be faced squarely, and steps need to be taken to improve their situation. The first step is to transform work conditions in the private sector so that women are properly compensated for their labor.

The connection between employment patterns and fertility rates has been widely noted in the development literature (Anker, Buvinic, and Youssef 1982). When women are marginalized from the productive process, they pursue strategies of childbearing either because they are unable consciously to choose fertility reduction or because they may find such a reduction economically disadvantageous. Stripped of their economic and productive role, women depend on motherhood performance for status and prestige and on children's labor as a strategy for survival (Ward 1984). The combination of low education, low employment, and the absence of a concerted family-planning strategy explains why fertility rates and population growth rates increased rather than decreased in Iran over the decade. Spiraling population growth at a time of straitened fiscal resources and increasing pockets of poverty throughout the country eventually forced the authorities within the Islamic Republic to reverse the policy on family planning. In June 1989 the government formally lifted the ban on contraceptives at state hospitals and clinics. (Still prohibited by law, however, were abortion, vasectomy, and tubal ligation.)[5] In January 1990, a seminar on population control convened in Tehran, with the result that the government is now openly favoring and encouraging family planning and the use of birth control devices.

410   VALENTINE M. MOGHADAM

Another issue that needs to be faced is the methodological problem of the undercounting of women workers, which has been the subject of many international reports and studies. How, for example, can it be possible that millions of rural women in Iran are categorized as "home-makers"? Rural women normally carry out household and field tasks that should be counted as "work" (Beneria 1982; Charlton 1984; Dixon 1982; Rogers 1980). The enumeration techniques and classification scheme need to be reevaluated and reformulated to obtain more exact answers from respondents and to present a more accurate picture of the Iranian work force.

Finally, the data reveal not only that there is a gender gap in education and employment but also that women as a group are internally differentiated; they are stratified by class and region, and further differentiated by occupation, income, education, age, and marital status. Although gender determines one's status in Islamic countries where the Shariᶜah is law, status is also elaborated by other factors (notably class and ethnicity), which in turn affect life chances. The diversity within Iran's female population, however, should not preclude steps to overturn the discrimination that all Iranian women face by law and by custom.

Conclusion

Throughout the world, policies are shaped by existing social and gender ideologies. In turn, state policies serve to reduce gender inequality or to increase it. In the first years of the Islamic Republic, the rhetoric and the policies were intended to segregate the sexes and domesticate the women (Nashat 1983). The authorities have not been successful in driving women out of public life, but they continue to see men and women as fundamentally different. Leaders of the Islamic Republic are still mired in the myth of brain size, and their thinking is distorted by the banalities of biology.[6] However, to the extent that the Islamic Republic is not autarkic and intends to be an actor on the global and regional political and economic scenes, one can expect women to take part in public life and in so doing subvert the notion of immutable gender difference.

Notes

1. The Islamic republic inherited and retained a legal system based on both Shariᶜah and the Code Napoléon.

2. This tension was a theme explored in an earlier study of women, work, and ideology in Iran; see Moghadam 1988.

3. Interview with Dr. Azizullah Saidali, Indira Ghandi Children's Hospital, Kabul, 9 Feb. 1989. See also U.N. *Statistical Yearbook 1983/84* (N.Y., 1986), table 18.

4. In the urban areas, women who are classified as "homemakers" may actually be part-time workers in the informal sector. Or they may be women whose domestic work and child care take up so much time that there is not time left for work outside the home. Other women may be bound by cultural or familial constraints; yet others may choose to stay at home. Because of the low prestige of certain occupations, some women may identify themselves as housewives rather than workers. In the absence of more-detailed labor force and household surveys, one can only speculate why the female employment figure is so low in Iran and theorize on the basis of similar patterns found elsewhere.

5. I am grateful to Professor Shahin Gerami for bringing this continuing prohibition to my attention.

6.   Ali-Akbar Hashemi Rafsanjani, president of the Islamic Republic, once opined, "A man's brain is larger. Women mature too fast. The breathing power of men's lungs is greater and women's heartbeats are faster. . . . Men heed reasoning and logic, whereas most women tend to be emotional. . . . Courage and daring are stronger in men" (*Washington Post*, 21 Dec. 1988).

11

The Consequences of State Policies
for Women in Pakistan

ANITA M. WEISS

Pakistani state policy toward women has changed dramatically with the changes in governments since independence was achieved in 1947. Class issues (as opposed to gender issues) and differences in ideological orientation emerge as considerable factors in explaining these marked shifts in state policy toward women. Political exigencies and economic realities, as well as changing social norms and ambiguities regarding women's roles, must also be taken into consideration in assessing policy shifts, for to ignore these factors is to risk seeing state action as purposeless. Such factors compel consideration in any reflection on why the government headed by Benazir Bhutto (1988–1990), the first female prime minister of a Muslim state, found itself unable or unwilling to modify existing policies toward women.

Women play important symbolic roles in every society, and it is in the interest of the state to promote a certain image of woman to serve its purposes in a given time. Mernissi (1987) argues that this promotion of feminine images is particularly prevalent in Muslim societies where the ongoing process of renegotiation of new authority boundaries and limits culminates in a subtle change in the abstract perception of women. In Pakistan, state policy toward women in different periods is derived from the symbolic representation of women in (1) redefining traditional culture; (2) affirming social identity in juxtaposition to another group (e.g., Hindus, Indians); or (3) maintaining social cohesion in the face of rapid—and potentially destabilizing—change.

In the last quarter century, state policy has been reoriented explicitly to affect the status of women. The state's legal policy regarding women—laws that were introduced and/or passed that directly affected the status of women—has been a reflection of its political ideology and has had the most significant impact. The state's economic policy has had explicit socioeconomic consequences for women; educational and other social reforms have largely been by-products of economic policies in Pakistan, as the former are an outcome of the fate of the latter. This outcome, however, has manifested differently in different periods. In the heyday of economic boom under Ayub Khan (1958–68), female literacy was promoted as a way of creating a larger work force. During the Zulfiqar Ali Bhutto era (1971–77), female literacy was promoted on ideological grounds, unconnected to the lagging economy. Female employment was also on the upswing as a means to counter the growing strength of trade unions (Weiss 1984). Under the Zia ul-Haq regime (1977–88), female literacy rates suffered severely because no real attempt was made to improve primary education. In his quest to house his actions in an Islamic ideological framework, Zia insisted on separate schools and colleges and even proposed separate universities on the basis of gender.

Government policy regarding women appears to be more concerned with economic exigencies than with gender or identity issues. Indeed, the circumstances of elite women's lives have consistently improved over the years in terms of a wide range of social development indicators, despite the orientation of state policy. It is instead the fate of poorer women that has been affected most by state policy shifts. Their lives are similar to those of most women throughout South Asia, where they are burdened by household and familial obligations, low literacy levels, and a political culture that constrains them from acting outside of traditionally mandated roles. Only an elite few have been able to break away from existing social controls in order to pursue university degrees, enter a nonfemale professions, join women's political movements, or even select their own husbands.

Approximately three-quarters of all Pakistani women continue to live in rural areas, which tend to be the most tradition-bound parts of the country, as shown in table 11.1. Life expectancy for females at birth has risen from 44 years in 1965 to 51 in 1986, which compares highly unfavorably with other lower-middle-income countries, which have seen female life expectancy rise to 61 years during this time (World

TABLE 11.1

Population of Women in Urban and Rural Areas, 1951–1981
(in millions)

Year	Urban	Rural
1951	3.9	11.7
1961	4.3	15.7
1971	7.6	22.9
1981	11.1	28.9

Source: Population Census of Pakistan, 1981.

TABLE 11.2

Life Expectancy at Birth, by Gender, 1965–1986

Country	1965		1986	
	Male	Female	Male	Female
Pakistan	46	44	52	51
India	46	44	57	56
Middle-income countries	53	56	61	65
Lower-middle-income countries	47	50	57	61
Low-income countries	47	50	60	61
Low-income countries (excluding India and China)	43	44	52	54
United Kingdom	68	74	72	78
United States	67	74	71	79

Source: World Bank 1988, 286.

Bank 1988, 286). Pakistan's female life expectancy even compares poorly to that in low-income countries, as shown in table 11.2. The female dependency ratio for Pakistan is among the highest in the world;[1] in 1981 the female dependency ratio for the young, for example,

TABLE 11.3

Population and Sex Ratios in Pakistan, 1951–1986

| Year | Population (millions) | | | Sex Ratio (females per 100 males) |
	Males	Females	Total	
1951	18.2	15.6	33.8	85.9
1961	23.0	19.9	42.9	86.8
1972	34.8	30.5	65.3	87.5
1981	44.3	40.0	84.3	90.5
1986[a]	51.9	47.3	99.2	91.0
1988[b]			107.0	

Sources: Government of Pakistan 1985; Population Census of Pakistan, 1951, 1961, 1972, and 1981.

[a]World Bank estimate, 1988.

[b]Estimated in Pakistan's Seventh Five-Year Plan.

was 188 for Pakistan, 128 for the Third World, and 111 for the global average (Mustafa, 1990).

That most Pakistani women live under extremely dire physical conditions is implicit in the markedly disproportionate sex ratio whereby there are 91 females for every 100 males in the country, as shown in table 11.3. Although females, biologically, constitute about 49 percent of all infants at birth, they eventually make up the majority of adult populations in most parts of the world (Bernard 1981). In 1985 Pakistan's male/female ratio was 111:100; the average ratio for lower-middle-income countries was 100:100; for all low-income countries 95:100, including India and China, 99:100 when excluding them; and 105:100 in the United States (World Bank 1988, 286–87). While various factors account for the inverse sex ratio in the subcontinent, such as the benign neglect of daughters, limited access of females to adequate health care, and high maternal mortality rates (Miller 1981), the significant point is that the most basic needs of women—virtually the right to life itself—have suffered immensely in Pakistan. There is consequently an urgency associated with Pakistani state policy toward women, for even a slight shift can have major repercussions on women's lives.

Legal Policies

The area where state policy has had the most profound effect and hence has had the most far-reaching implications is in the realm of law. In the early years of the Pakistan state only a few laws were passed whose aim was to affect the status of women. The two most noteworthy are the 1951 Muslim Personal Law of Shariʿat, which recognized women's right (as stated in the Qurʾan) to inherit agricultural property, and the 1956 constitution's acceptance of the principle to reserve special seats for women in the National Assembly (Mumtaz and Shaheed 1987, 56–57). Such laws, however, had scant impact on most women's lives. In the context of the state's ideological framework at the time this makes sense because the state was searching for an identity and an ideology on which to base nascent social cohesion. The demand for a Muslim state had been achieved, but the groups that now comprised it were so factionalized that it would have been purposeless to bring up a potentially divisive issue such as the place of women in society when few were clamoring for its attention.

The watershed period from which to begin an analysis of Pakistani legal policy toward women is that of the promulgation of the Muslim Family Laws Ordinance in 1961, widely regarded as the first attempt by the state to provide women some form of economic and legal protection from their husbands' unbridled libidinal capriciousness by regulating divorce and polygamy. In attempting to provide safeguards for women in the event of a divorce, the law requires the registration of all marriages and eliminates divorce solely by repudiation (talaq). The written permission of a man's wife (or wives) is supposed to be obtained and brought before an arbitration council that decides whether he may marry again, although the discretionary right to allow or disallow another marriage remains within the council and is not dependent on that written permission. While in fact minimal sanctions exist for those who circumvent the law, its passage during Ayub Khan's administration symbolized the state's attempt to provide Pakistani women with basic rights concurrently being gained by Muslim women elsewhere. The law was passed at a time when state policy was focused on establishing a secure economic base. Ideological orientation was pragmatically tied to economic growth while socially liberal forces propelled the state into action. That such a major legal reform having significant sociocultural repercussions was promulgated during a period of martial law must not be overlooked. Perhaps this action was taken to draw attention away from the lack of a public voice in the state's affairs. This fits well into Ayub Khan's ideology: the benevolent state would watch out for all its people, especially the weak, while promoting economic prosperity.

During the Zulfiqar Ali Bhutto era, there was a marked increase in women participating in politics and trade union activities, and an overall more-empowering attitude toward women. The promulgation of the 1973 constitution further advanced women's legal position; Article 25 of the Fundamental Rights guarantees that all citizens are equal under the law and prohibits discrimination on the basis of sex, and Article 27 prohibits discrimination on the basis of sex, race, religion, or caste for government employment. The constitution also reserves seats in the National Assembly for women to contest in elections and advocates the inclusion of women in all aspects of national life. In 1975 Pakistan was one of the cosponsoring nations of the United Nations Convention on the Elimination of All Forms of Discrimination Against Women.[2] Despite Zulfiqar Ali Bhutto's vocal commitment to empowering weaker groups, however, no other legal changes during this period specifically addressed the status of women.

On 5 July 1977 General Zia ul-Haq overthrew the government of Zulfiqar Ali Bhutto. It did not initially appear that this act would have any particularly severe implications for women. The military government promised to hold elections within ninety days, but kept postponing them. In its search for a basis of legitimacy, however, the government implemented a religiously based legal code unparalleled in the modern history of Islam in South Asia. For the first time in Pakistan's history, the law regarded men and women as having different legal rights, which has effectively reduced women's power and participation in the larger society.

Whereas the United Nations Decade for Women commenced in 1975 with an aim to promote the uplifting of women everywhere, Zia's legal reforms begun in 1979 had the paradoxical effect of compromising women's rights. The Zia government idealized the image of women faithful to *chador aur char diwari*—remaining veiled and within the confines of the four walls of one's home—although in reality women were becoming increasingly integrated into the public realm. Such contradictions in Pakistan have their roots in two of the strongest symbols of classical Islamic society: the Qur'an, a radical document for its time in seventh-century Arabia for empowering women through certain rights and responsibilities, and the veil, which by physically limiting women's mobility in the larger society effectively symbolizes her powerlessness. While the legal position of Muslim women is guaranteed in the Qur'an, South Asian customs and attitudes have historically contradicted these rights in practice.

The government's Islamization program initiated in February 1979 was, at the outset, fairly limited in its specific impact on women. The first hint that the government's implementation of an Islamic penal code would not favor equality of status for men and women came with the promulgation of the Offense of Zina (adultery) Act.[3] A *hadd* (pl. *hudud*)[4] punishment could be prescribed if "a [sane] adult man and a [sane] adult woman . . . willfully have sexual intercourse without being validly married to each other" (Ordinance Number 7 of 1979, Part 4). However, an adult could be proven guilty of *zina-bil-jabr* (four types of sexual intercourse without consent, e.g., rape) "with or without the consent of the parties" (Zia ul-Haq 1979, 19). Yet evidence for *zina-bil-jabr* remains the same as for any other *hadd* crime: the severest punishment (death by stoning or one hundred lashes) can only be invoked either with the accused's self-confession or by the testimony of four *salah* (morally upright) adult Muslim males. Without such evidence, the penalty is at the court's discretion.

Punishments were meted out in a highly discriminatory fashion: women's guilt could be proven through medical examinations or by their pregnancy following a rape (see Weiss 1986, 100), whereas men were often acquitted because of lack of evidence. Heated disputes erupted over this policy, for besides making a woman suffer twice, the use of illegitimate birth as a criterion for a woman's "self-confession" was discriminatory because it could not be used for a man. Without a man's verbal confession, it was nearly impossible to prove his guilt, for what four *salah* Muslim men would stand by and let a woman be raped?

The issue of evidence became central to the concern for women's legal status, not only in penal issues but in all aspects of the legal code. The Qanun-e-Shahadat (law of evidence) was eventually promulgated in October 1984—following nearly two years of protests—to modify the existing evidence law enacted during the British raj in 1872. The law would require oral testimony and attestation of two male witnesses or that of one male and two females; the witness of two or more females without corroboration by a male would not be sufficient. Opponents of the evidence law feared that women might be restricted from testifying in certain *hudud* cases, such as those in which they were the sole witness to their father's or husband's murder. The final adopted 1984 version, however, restricts the testimony of two women being equal to that of one man to financial cases; in other instances, acceptance of a single woman's testimony has been left to the discretion of the judge. However, that a woman's evidence in financial cases is not equal to that of a man's is symbolic of an ideological perspective that could not perceive women as equal economic participants with men.

The proposed law of qisas (retaliation) and diyat (blood money) had not been decreed before Zia's death and was set aside as a "back burner" issue during the tenure of the Pakistan People's Party (PPP) government, only to be taken up again as a priority by Nawaz Sharif in 1991. It would allow for a *diyat* equivalent to 30.4 kilos of silver to be paid to the family of a murdered man, but only half of that would have to be paid if the victim was a woman. If a woman was physically harmed, the compensation again would be only half that given for a man. However, this would create a situation where the punishment would be equal for male and female murderers, although the *diyat* would differ if the victim of a murder were a man or a woman. This imbalance indeed would be a strong statement by the state that a woman's value is only half that of a man.

The Zia government's final attempt at legislating social policy through legal channels had profound implications for women. In 1986 it proposed the Ninth Amendment and the Shariᶜat Bill. Although it had appeared that the government's support for both of these died along with Zia ul-Haq, the issue was revived as soon as Nawaz Sharif formed a government. Both were promulgated in early 1991.

The Ninth Amendment gives government organs the power to interpret Muslim personal law. Many of its opponents feared that it could be used to challenge the Family Laws Ordinance of 1961 and probably the Guardian and Wards Act. But the impetus behind the Ninth Amendment really derives from the Shariᶜat Bill.

The Shariᶜat Bill is perhaps the most controversial legislation of all. Five versions have been proposed since 1985, with only the latest one being passed into law (on 10 April 1991). The government contends that the Shariᶜat Bill's purpose is to give more power to interpretations of Shariᶜah (Islamic law) in all aspects of state policy, significantly widen the jurisdiction of the Shariᶜat Court, and elevate the Qurʾan and *sunnah* to be the country's supreme law.

The Shariᶜat Court's established precedence of decisions, however, often considered unfavorable to women, has caused opponents of the Shariᶜat Bill to fear that it would ultimately serve to further diminish women's power and status in the country.

Although Benazir Bhutto's 1988–1990 government was able to prevent the implementation of the Ninth Amendment and the Shariᶜat Bill

Bill during its tenure, it was less successful in its attempts to repeal some of the earlier legislation passed during martial law, given the restrictions of the Eighth Amendment. Passed in 1985 under Zia's tutelage, the Eighth Amendment essentially states that future governments cannot condemn the martial law government for its actions or repeal any of the laws that it passed without a two-thirds vote in the National Assembly.

Economic and Social Implications of State Policy

Work in many parts of Pakistan—be it making, selling, fixing, or moving something for which there is some kind of economic compensation—appears to exist in the public space of the male world. While true virtually everywhere, it is particularly important in poorer areas of Pakistan for a woman's status (as well as for that of her family) that her activities are popularly considered to be respectable. Historically, this has implied a prohibition on mixing freely with unrelated men and a marked sexual division of labor. Concerns over traditional notions of propriety have not prevented women from working for pay; instead, they often simply prevented women and their families from admitting that women engage in such work. For example, one of the reasons cited by the government of Pakistan for the comparatively low official employment rates is "the low rate of female participation in the labor force" (Government of Pakistan 1978, 173).

But underneath this public face lies a significant amount of confusion, particularly regarding the work that women do. On the basis of the predominant fiction that most women do not labor outside of their domestic chores, past governments have been hesitant to adopt deliberate policies increasing women's employment options and to provide for legal support for women's labor force participation. Official statistics discount women's labor in the formal sectors of the economy and dismiss their productive contributions in the informal, piecework, domestic, and subsistence sectors.[5] In 1988, the female labor force participation rate was only ten percent, as shown in table 11.4. By 1990, females as a percentage of males in the labor force had officially risen to 13 percent (UNDP 1992, 145). Virtually no change was documented in the absolute number of women in the work force between 1973 and 1981 (FBS 1985a, 245–246) and only 3.5 percent of all women living in urban areas were recorded as being engaged in some form of work (FBS 1985b, 248–250). An example of such low reportage of figures can be seen in the 1981 Lahore district census which assessed that 26.4

percent of persons over age ten were either working or looking for work: 48.2 percent of males and only 2.6 percent of females.

Such official assessments, however, obfuscate economic realities. Alternatively, research carried out by the Women's Division and others (Hafeez 1983; Shaheed and Mumtaz 1983; Weiss 1984; Hooper 1985) refutes the idea of low female work force participation figures.[6] Because most urban working women are engaged at home either in piecework or in contributing to family-based production, they are not engaged in formal employment, and their contributions are subsequently not counted. Rural women are generally engaged in production for exchange at the subsistence level, again not earning a countable wage. In both urban and rural contexts, women's economic contributions are often counted as part of the total family's labor, with government data crediting it to the male earner.

In a recent study that I conducted in the walled city of Lahore,[7] 56 percent of the women surveyed stated that they had some sort of marketable skill, and 32 percent said that they were currently engaged in work for which they received some sort of economic compensation. Of the 68 percent who were "not working," more than half stated that they would like to if they had the opportunity to do so. Therefore, more than two-thirds of the women surveyed either earn from their own efforts or would if they had the opportunity. The most prevalent income-earning skills women report having are sewing and embroidery, both of which are usually engaged in at home. The women, however, are dependent on a middleman for the raw materials and for marketing the finished goods. The middleman himself rarely goes to the women's homes; instead, he sends a female relative or a young boy to drop off and pick up the materials and goods. The women are fearful of asking for more payment for their labor, because the middleman might just stop coming at his whim, which would be disastrous for their families. In many instances, women working at home are doing the same kind of small-scale manufacturing as done by men working in the bazaar, although they earn appreciably less.

UNICEF recently commissioned a national study on women's economic activity to enable policy planners and donor agencies to cut through the existing myths on female labor force participation (Shaheed and Mumtaz, 1992). The study addresses the specific reasons for discrepancies and underenumeration in counting women's work in Pakistan and provides a comprehensive discussion of the range of informal-sector work performed by women throughout the country.

422   ANITA M. WEISS

TABLE 11.4

Labor Force Participation Rates by Gender, 1971–1988

	1971–72	1982–83	1987–88
Total	45.2	44.4	43.2
Male	78.7	75.2	73.8
Female	8.1	10.3	10.2

Source: Labour Force Surveys as reported in Government of Pakistan 1992, 33.

Women tend to work out of economic necessity and to withdraw from the labor force when their contribution is no longer required (Khan and Bilquees 1976; Abbasi and Irfan 1986, 179). In rural areas, although women engage in labor for their family's subsistence, few own productive resources or have an opportunity for paid employment. In urban areas, factory employment tends to be temporary and insecure, void of such luxuries as maternity leave and medical benefits. Work within the home is possible because of its anonymity—but precisely because of this, wages are unreasonably low.[8]

Urban working-class women have always played critical economic roles that have largely gone undocumented, but circumstances today require even more from them. Nuclear families have become the norm in industrializing urban Pakistan, and women are increasingly being recruited as wage earners. This is highlighted in a series of graphic portraits of working women in Lahore written by Khawar Mumtaz in various issues of *Viewpoint* between 1985 and 1987. She details the problems facing female "temporary workers" who have labored for years at a transnational pharmaceutical plant; the daily routine—as well as the hopes and aspirations—of a maidservant; and the myriad problems confronting women in the informal sector. The stark reality depicted is often more than most people would like to read: the shattered dreams of an industrial worker; the twenty-hour day of a domestic worker who returns home to six children, a tired husband, and a *kutchi abadi* (ramshackle shack) at night; and the plight of the vegetable seller in her fifties who supports her invalid husband. These are the tales left out of official statistics. Such portrayals, in circumventing problems inherent in quantitative data collection and allowing for vivid descriptions of these women's lives, argue the case for more attention to be paid to predicaments facing women.

Male emigration to the Gulf in the 1970s and 1980s affected women's labor force participation in two important ways: first, it opened up job opportunities for educated women; second, it enabled many women in migrants' families eventually to withdraw from the formal as well as the informal labor force. Abbasi and Irfan (1986, 182) have found that remittances from abroad also reduced female unpaid family work in rural areas and female low-wage employment in urban areas.

Conditions under which women work in the Punjab and Karachi—albeit limited and problematic—are vastly different from those existing outside of these relatively industrially advanced parts of the country. For example, a report for the Women's Division, based on conditions in the North-West Frontier Province, looked at the extent to which women participate in cottage and small-scale industries in the Peshawar, Mansehra, and Swat districts (Nazeer and Aljalaly 1983). Women were consistently found doing work that was an extension of tasks traditionally done at home (e.g., canning, tailoring, weaving, spinning). Essentially, women undertake work either associated with female tasks or jobs that men do not like to do. The traditional view that a woman's modesty can best be protected if she remains within the confines of her home is still reported as the main impediment to female participation in industrial employment, even at the government level. Although social customs and taboos, illiteracy, job scarcity, and lack of segregation at the workplace still serve to inhibit female participation in the North-West Frontier Province, these same factors have apparently been modified when the demands of industry, such as exist in the Punjab and Karachi, require it.

Women's economic power in the 1990s in Pakistan, and on into the next century, will most likely continue to increase; such trends are prevalent worldwide. The state of Pakistan's economy on the whole, however, will significantly affect their prospects. The structure of the economy is currently under review by both the government and the World Bank, which has voiced concern over the failure to integrate women. Despite the business orientation of the Nawaz Sharif government and its efforts toward privatization, no actual policy to pursue the integration of women into the economy ever made it to the government's agenda.

The social implications of Pakistani state policy are more problematic than the legal or economic issues. Policies existing during Zia's tenure, such as compelling women newscasters to wear a *dupatta* (a type of scarf) while on television, may have reinforced existing norms of female modesty in some segments of society, but they were ignored or ridiculed by others. That females were unable to compete in various athletic events (ostensibly so as not to risk immodest exposure) may have precluded the discovery of a world-class Pakistani athlete, but the more important issue is that the policy symbolically constrained the growth of girls' athletics and fitness at a time when this was being given worldwide attention. Although the actual consequences of such kinds of policies can only be conjectured, education and fertility are two areas in which the social implications of government policy on women are evident.

Increases in female education levels have held the promise of raising the status of South Asian Muslim women for nearly a century. The first woman who publicly articulated such demands was Chand Begum. She spoke out against the dire conditions faced by Muslim women and their lack of education at the Mohammedan Educational Congress in Bombay in 1903 when, speaking from behind a curtain, she "hailed the Reform Party, a group of Muslim supporters of female education, and hurled bitter invectives on reactionary maulvis. She called upon the Muslim women to follow fervently the female reform movement which was advocating modern education amongst Muslim women, and to say goodbye to the immovable maulvis" (from Sarfaraz Hussain Mirza, *Muslim Women's Role in the Pakistan Movement*, cited in Mumtaz and Shaheed 1987, 39). What became known as the Women's Reform Movement gathered momentum after 1904 and caused the opening of various Muslim girls' schools by 1911 (Mumtaz and Shaheed 1987, 40). Despite the popularity of promoting female education in elite circles, preindependence literacy rates for Muslim women were never above 3 percent (FBS 1985a, 161).[9]

Using the 1972 definition of literacy—"read and write a short statement in everyday life with understanding in any language"— Pakistan's postindependence record of growth in female literacy is also not heartening, as shown in table 11.5. UNESCO evaluated that 35 percent of urban women and only 7 percent of rural women were literate in 1989. Only a few years ago, World Bank economists were predicting that Pakistan was about to cross the "poverty threshold" and would be considered a middle-income country. Pakistan's economy today, however, is nowhere near those predicted levels. The UNDP argues in the *1991 Human Development Report* that an important factor contributing to this lack of growth has been Pakistan's neglect of social development issues and of incorporating women into the development process, and its failure to raise its female literacy levels.

TABLE 11.5

Literacy Rates in Pakistan, by Gender, 1951–1992
(in percentage)

Year	Male	Female	Combined
1951	17.0	8.6	13.2
1961	25.1	6.7	16.7
1972	30.2	11.6	21.7
1981	35.1	16.0	26.2
1991–92 (est.)	45.5	21.3	34.0

Source: FBS 1985a; Government of Pakistan 1992, 142.

TABLE 11.6

**Percentage of Age Group Enrolled in
Schools, by Gender, 1965–1989**

	Primary		Secondary		Tertiary	
	1965	1989	1965	1989	1965	1989
Total	40	38	12	20	2	5
Female	20	27	5	12	n.a.	2[a]

Source: World Bank 1992, 274.
[a]Estimate by National Education Council, Ministry of Education.

Pakistan's low female literacy rates are particularly confounding because these rates are analogous to those of some of the poorest countries in the world. Relatively limited resources have been allocated to education. In 1986, the government of Pakistan allocated 3.2 percent of total expenditures to education, less than 1.0 percent to health, but 33.9 percent to defense (World Bank 1988, 266). Pakistan in 1991 held the dubious distinction of being tied for fourth place in the world in its ratio of military expenditure to health and education expenditures: 279 to 1 (UNDP 1990, 162).

A significant disparity in female literacy rates exists among the provinces and between rural and urban areas. The lowest female literacy rates are found in rural areas, particularly in Baluchistan and the North-West Frontier Province. Of rural Pakistani women aged twenty-five and above, 96.5 percent have received no schooling whatsoever (Bhatti 1988, 44).

Levels of female education rose in many parts of Pakistan during the 1970s. In the Punjab, for example, government statistics reveal that between 1971 and 1978 female enrollment increased in primary schools by 32.7 percent, in high schools by 60.5 percent, and in colleges by 35.7 percent (Government of Punjab 1979, 155). The percentage of female enrollment at all levels of schooling increased between 1965 and 1985, as shown in table 11.6. When considering this increase, however, the much higher level of male participation at the primary and secondary levels must be borne in mind, although this disparity in education levels is not as marked among the elite. Gender discrepancies are lessened at the university level, where the majority of students are children of the elite. For example, Punjab University announced that 153 more females than males (6,210 females; 6,057 males) appeared in its B.A. and B.S. examinations in 1992. Female and male children of elites have equal access to education; male children of the poor are given priority for their education over their sisters.

In 1986 a report on women's conditions in the country written by the government-appointed Commission on the Status of Women condemned the government's failure to raise female literacy rates. It argues that the "appallingly low" rate in rural areas perpetuates oppressive conditions and that

> rural women tend to have an extremely low status self image. They believe themselves to have been born inferior, they curse themselves for being deficient and they glorify the males in their lives. Their fathers are often tyrants, their brothers selfish, their husbands uncaring in their attitude towards their women, and yet they dwell in a state of resignation, accepting the myth of male superiority as an important part of their perceptions. . . . Thus the average rural woman of Pakistan is born in near slavery, leads a life of drudgery and dies invariably in oblivion. This grim condition is not fantasy but the stark reality of nearly 30 million Pakistani citizens, who happen to have been born female and dwell in the rural areas of the country.
>
> (Pakistan Commission 1986, 29–31)

Although every government in Pakistan has paid lip service to the need for increasing female literacy rates, there has never been a systematic, nationally coordinated effort to improve female primary education in the country. The government of Pakistan has successfully enlisted the assistance of various international donors in its primary education efforts in the seventh Five-Year Plan (which commenced in 1988), but these efforts have not yet been evaluated adequately.

The nagging problem of high levels of female illiteracy is sobering when placed in the context of Pakistan's having one of the world's highest population growth rates. The World Bank (1988, 274) estimates that the growth rate of 3.1 percent between 1980 and 1986 will decline to 3.0 percent between 1986 and 2000. Pakistan's population in 1990 was estimated at 113 million. No more-recent statistics are available, as the Nawaz Sharif government decided to cancel the scheduled 1991 census on the grounds that holding it would create too volatile a situation, given the prevailing ethnic tensions.

A population increase rate of 3 percent will virtually guarantee that although female literacy rates may well rise, the absolute number of female illiterates in the country will also continue to rise, as shown in table 11.7. Other low-income countries have an average annual population growth rate of only 1.9 percent; India and China have growth rates of only 1.6 percent. Excluding India and China, the rate is 2.8 percent. Lower-middle-income countries have an average growth rate of 2.3 percent. Pakistan's total fertility rate (the number of children a woman is likely to have) of 6.8 in 1986 was nearly double that of the average of all low-income countries (3.9), a third higher than the average for lower-middle-income countries (4.7), and still higher than the average of low-income countries when India and China are excluded (6.0).

It is widely presumed that higher levels of female literacy have an inverse effect on women's fertility. Zeba Sathar and her colleagues (1988, 416) argue that although this is true in Pakistan, it "is open to question, however, to what extent relative educational attainment is a measure of gender inequality and whether the impact of education on fertility necessarily acts through a rise in status. One impact of educational attainment may be through marriage postponement, since even primary-level schooling is associated with delays in marriage greater than the actual additional years of schooling." Initial efforts to contain population growth rates in Pakistan were made by a nongovernmental organization (NGO), the Family Planning Association of Pakistan (FPAP), in 1952. Three years later, the government of Pakistan began to fund FPAP. In the late 1950s, the government also combined population planning efforts in hospitals and clinics. By the early 1960s there was a two-pronged program (FPAP-NGO and public sector), and the total population was 43 million.

TABLE 11.7

Number of Literates and Illiterates Ten Years and Older, by Gender, 1981

(in millions)

	Illiterates			Literates		
	Total	Urban	Rural	Total	Urban	Rural
Combined	41.6	8.8	32.8	14.8	7.9	6.9
Male	19.5	4.0	15.5	10.6	5.1	5.5
Female	22.1	4.8	17.3	4.2	2.8	1.4

Source: Population Census of Pakistan, 1981.

[a]Estimate by National Education Council, Ministry of Education.

In the mid-1960s the government's health department initiated a new program to train midwives and provide IUDs through incentive payments to hospitals and clinics. The government was able to attract many international donors to fund its efforts, but its program lost support because the targets were regarded as overly ambitious and there was allegedly rampant fictitious reporting by doctors and clinics to claim incentive payments.

The population-planning program was suspended after the fall of Ayub Khan's government and substantively reorganized. Zulfiqar Ali Bhutto's PPP government, commencing with a population estimated at 65.3 million, initiated the Continuous Motivation System program, which added a subprogram called Inundation in 1975. This latter program involved the sale of birth control pills and condoms throughout the country on the premise that increased availability would increase usage. The program failed for various reasons, although two features stand out as particular cultural faux pas: (1) the government employed as motivators young, unmarried urban girls (who presumably had little understanding of the conditions of rural women whom they were supposed to motivate); and (2) although contraceptives were supplied to a large number of shops, they were usually kept in the back (i.e., out of sight) because it was considered mannerless to expose them to all customers—thus, potential purchasers just did not know they were there.

The government's population-planning efforts were virtually canceled following Zia's coup d'état. By the early 1980s the population had reached 84.3 million. The government enlisted Attiya Inayatullah (who had received international recognition for her family-planning efforts while working earlier with the United Nations Fund for Population Activities) to play a major role in formulating a new population-planning strategy. The result was a multifaceted community-based "cafeteria" approach using family welfare centers (essentially clinics) and reproductive health centers (mostly engaged in sterilizations). Community participation finally became a cornerstone of the government's policy, which hoped to see contraceptive use go from 9.5 percent in 1982 to 18.6 percent by 1988. During the Sixth Five-Year Plan (1983–88), the Pakistan government projected the country's population at 147 million in the year 2000 if the growth rate could remain constant at 2.8 percent, and at 134 million if the rate declined to the desired low of 2.1 percent by 2000. Although the current growth rate is a topic of heated date, it is agreed that it remains at least 3 percent and that Pakistan has not been successful at all in lowering it. The Seventh Five-Year Plan (1988–93) allocated Rs 3.5 billion for its ambitious goals of raising the practice of family planning from 12.9 percent of couples to 23.4 percent and of reducing the crude birth rate from 42.3 to 38.0 per thousand by the end of the plan period. The preliminary results, however, are not encouraging. The World Bank (1992, 218) ascertained that Pakistan's mid-1990 population was 112.4 million.

The Zia government made two attempts to investigate how to improve the status of women: (1) by creating the Women's Division in January 1979 and (2) by establishing the Commission on the Status of Women in 1983.

The Women's Division was intended as an overarching organization for coordinating all endeavors relevant to women in the national development process; it was to be "a special organ of the Federal Government to substantiate the fact that upholding the status and enhancing the socio-economic role of women is a national imperative, not a condescending concession" (Pakistan, Women's Division, 1988b, 1). As a woman's advocacy organization, it has supported thousands of nationwide development projects and more than fifty research studies and has established training academies, mobile dispensaries, legal aid facilities, and small credit programs in this regard (Pakistan, Women's Division, 1988b, 9–17, 21–29). In addition to supporting greater representation of women in local government bodies, it took a stand opposing the Zia government's attempts to compromise the Family Laws Ordinance.

The Pakistan Commission on the Status of Women was established 8 March 1983. The government appointed all the commission's members, including its chairperson, Begum Zari Sarfaraz. The commission had four explicitly stated purposes:

1. To ascertain the rights and responsibilities of women in an Islamic society and to make recommendations to the federal government for effective safeguards of women's rights.
2. To advise the federal government on measures to provide education, health, and employment opportunities for women.
3. To identify what services women can render in eradicating ignorance, social evils, poverty, and disease in the country.
4. To suggest measures to integrate women of minority communities into the national life.

The resultant report begins with a discussion of the "Islamic Vision" of women, but argues that

while Islam provided for equality, justice and harmony between the sexes and emphasized that the one was complementary to the other and while it set the trend to liberate women from centuries old tyrannies, the pernicious influence of latter day political and socio-economic developments in the Islamic world ... set in the opposite trend of the enslavement of women which is totally alien to Islamic genius. Under these un-Islamic influences women along with other weaker sectors of society steadily lost ground in all parts of the Muslim world. ... Today the situation of women in Muslim lands especially in resource-poor nations such as Pakistan is deplorable. Here mass illiteracy, scientific and technological backwardness, economic decline, grueling poverty and drudgery and denial of fundamental human rights characterize the condition of the vast majority of women, they suffer from numerous disabilities and inequities, due to the unjust socio-economic systems under which they function. (Pakistan Commission 1986, 2)

The report states that although Islamic perceptions regarding the role and rights of women are "enlightened and progressive," the actual status of women in Pakistan is "at its lowest ebb. Women in general are dehumanized and exercise little control over either themselves or on affairs affecting their well being. They are treated as possessions rather than as self-reliant self-regulating humans. They are bought and sold, beaten and mutilated, even killed with impunity and social approval. They are dispossessed and disinherited in spite of legal safeguards" (Pakistan Commission 1986, 3). The report traces the source of women's abject condition, and maintains that development attempts thus far have had a detrimental impact on women, in that "the mass of women in the nation have unfortunately fallen on the wrong side of technological change and development. Introduction of new technologies and modernization has not been an unmixed blessing for the Pakistani women. The vast majority of women have consistently lost their traditional sources of personal income. They have also lost ground relative to men. Increasing disparities have been created in their access to education as well as economic opportunities. . . . Women are being pushed back to low income, low skill traditional technologies and relegated to tasks which are bound to be replaced by modern mechanized processes" (Pakistan Commission 1986, 8–9).

The report reminds its readers that the Sixth Five-Year Plan recognized the need for women's participation in national development, because no society can progress "half liberated and half shackled." Besides condemning the deplorable state of women in Pakistan, it makes a number of suggestions for improving their circumstances and advocates that the government prepare a national policy to improve women's social and cultural status. Although it was the Pakistan government that had appointed the commission members, it is no surprise that the Zia government, given the report's condemnation of previous policies and efforts to affect women's lives and its divergence from existing official policy, adamantly refused to release the commission's findings to the public.

Mobilization for Women's Rights

Women in Pakistan have rarely been able to mobilize and collectively stand up for their rights, although reference can be made to individual Muslim women (e.g., Bibi Fatima, Bi Amman) who have made public appearances for a just cause. A futile attempt was made in the 1950s to include a Charter of Women's Rights (see Mumtaz and Shaheed 1987, 56) in the 1956 constitution, although this was not on the basis of a collective group action but was rather promoted by a small group of elite women.

In response to the harshness of Zia's repressive laws regarding women, the 1980s witnessed the emergence of urban grass-roots women's movements that publicly exposed the controversy over interpretation of Islamic law. Cries of discrimination against women were initially raised in response to the proposed Qanun-e-Shahadat in February 1983, when women lifted the veil of silence that had fallen over Pakistan since the 1979 execution of former Prime Minister Zulfiqar Ali Bhutto. At the time, Syeda Abida Hussain, chairman of the Jhang District Council and the sole directly elected female member of the National Assembly, said that women in Pakistan were in the midst of fighting the biggest jihad (holy war) in history and that "Islam enjoins rights and responsibilities on Muslim women which are not subject to any dispute" (The Muslim, 17 Feb. 1983). It is, therefore, in the highly visible territory of law that women have been able to articulate their objections to certain pronouncements of the state and have been able to mobilize against their implementation. Protests organized by such groups as the Women's Action Forum (WAF) and the Pakistan Women Lawyers' Association (PWLA) were unprecedented. They prompted both private and public discourse about the position of women in Islam and women's roles in a modern Islamic state.

Since independence in 1947, the only long-standing women's organization of note in Pakistan has been the All Pakistan Women's Association (APWA), headed until her recent death by the wife of the late first prime minister of Pakistan, Begum Raana Liaqat Ali Khan. During its first thirty-five years, APWA was commonly regarded as a charity organization made up of the wives of the elite (Chipp 1980). It has been largely urban-oriented and concerned with establishing specific projects such as health and family-planning clinics, hospitals, industrial homes, and schools and colleges (see Mumtaz and Shaheed 1987, 52–56, for a discussion of APWA's social role). Although APWA has consistently acted as an interest group for promoting women, its emphasis changed in the 1970s as it began to promote women's integration into the development process and expanding work opportunities for rural women. In the 1980s, its public image underwent an added transformation as it supported activist women's groups in many of their demands for women's rights. In September 1983 Begum Ra'ana publicly opposed certain aspects of the government's Islamization program and criticized some clauses of the Ansari Commission's report as being "repugnant to the Holy Qur'an and Islam, which gives women equal rights with men in all public matters" (Dawn, 5 Sept. 1983).[10] In assessing the relevance of the United Nations' Decade for Women for Pakistan, she stated that "we the women of Pakistan find that in spite of the progress we have made, we are still dispossessed of equal rights and equal opportunities. . . . I categorically state Islam affords complete equality of men and women. That instead of being wrongly associated with total suppression, severe physical punishments and denial of human rights, in Islam every principle is to be tempered with understanding, justice, a sense of brotherhood and forgiveness. I, therefore, assert that it is necessary to repeal certain laws and to enact new legislation which will give women their due rights and a challenging stake in the destiny of Pakistan" (APWA 1985, 4). APWA took a strong stand protesting against the imposition of certain aspects of the government's program and passed the following resolutions:

> 1. 21 February 1983: opposed discriminatory laws that falsely claim to be based on Islam.
> 2. 19 May 1984: noted "with anxiety" that crimes and violence against women have been on the increase.
> 3. [No date given]: noted with regret that "despite the hopes raised by the Sixth Five-Year Plan, progress in women's literacy is appallingly slow," and that the government must implement a crash program to raise female literacy levels.

That a woman of Begum Ra³ana's stature would take such a strong stand and support the women's activist groups gave them and their demands greater credibility in the eyes of many Pakistanis. For example, at its triennial conference in Lahore in 1982, APWA supported the groups' demand that the government establish a Commission on the Status of Women; after APWA joined in, the government did so.

The WAF, an independent group, was organized in 1981 by women in Lahore, Karachi, and Islamabad in response to proposed discriminatory laws and to strengthen women's position (Mumtaz and Shaheed 1987). The first national convention was held in Lahore in October 1982, with the intention to hold the second the following October in Karachi. Owing to the protests against the Qanun-e-Shahadat held in early 1983, however, the second convention was moved ahead to July.

The WAF charter begins with a 1944 quote from Pakistan's founding father, Quaid-i Azam Muhammad Ali Jinnah, in which he explicitly supports the empowerment of women and their participation in a wide range of preindependence nationalist movements: "No nation can rise to the height of glory unless your women are side by side with you, we are victims of evil customs. It is a crime against humanity that our women are shut up within the four walls of the houses as prisoners. There is no sanction anywhere for the deplorable condition in which our women have to live. You should take your women along with you as comrades in every sphere of life" (cited by Mumtaz and Shaheed 1987, 183). The charter asserts that WAF is "committed to protecting and promoting the rights of women by countering all forms of oppression" by being a consciousness-raising group as well as a lobby cum pressure group. It would use these two foci as well as the media, meetings, workshops, and the like to create a heightened awareness of women's rights and to mobilize support for promoting these rights, as well as to "counter adverse propaganda against women."

Women of varying political and social backgrounds (most of whom were members of WAF, APWA, or PWLA) led marches in early 1983 in Lahore and Karachi protesting the passage of the Qanun-e-Shahadat in the Majlis-e Shura (consultative assembly) and its recommendation to the president. After police lathi-charged (beat with sticks) some of the female demonstrators in Lahore on 12 February 1983, the assault on the women was denounced by politically diverse groups. PWLA members argued that the proposed Qanun-e Shahadat was not the only acceptable evidence law in Islam. They contested that there is only one instance in the Qur'an, Ayat 282 (Sura al-Baqr), in which two women are called to testify in the place of one man. In addition, this is in regard to a specific financial arrangement, and the role of the second woman is to remind the first about points that she may have forgotten. They argued that the *niyya* (intent) of the law also must be taken into consideration, as it was initially intended to help women and not to discriminate against them. In numerous other *ayats* (particularly in Sura al-Noor), men and women are referred to as being equal in matters of witness. Critics of the law also noted that the testimony of Hazrat Khadija (the Prophet's business-oriented first wife), asserting that Muhammad was the Prophet of God, made her his first disciple; hundreds of *hadith* were verified on the single testimony of Hazrat Ayesha, another of the Prophet's wives; and the sole evidence of Hazrat Naila (the wife of the third caliph, Usman) was accepted by the Prophet's companions regarding the guilt of Usman's murderer. The protesters argued that criteria for witnesses as stated in the Qur'an are possession of sight, memory and the ability to communicate; as long as witnesses have these, testimony should be equally weighed regardless of gender. They also argued that a rigid interpretation of the Qur'an such as would support the Qanun-e-Shahadat—meaning "male" whenever the generic word "man" was used—would virtually exclude women from being members of the religion.

The final adopted version restricts the testimony of two women being equal to that of one man to financial cases. Otherwise, it is up to the discretion of the judge whether to admit the testimony of a single woman. WAF asserted that the state still declaring a woman's evidence in financial cases as not equal to that of a man's would constrain women's economic participation and was symbolic of an ideological perspective that could not perceive women as equal economic participants with men. They argued that for the first time in Pakistan's history, the resultant laws regard men and women as having different legal rights, and despite the rhetoric that such laws were being promulgated to protect women, they were indeed constraining women's power and participation in the larger society.

It must be recalled that women had been somewhat politicized in the 1970s. The Bhutto government had appointed some women to powerful posts: Begum Ra'ana Liaquat Ali Khan had become governor of Sind, Kaniz Fatima was the vice-chancellor of a university, and Ashraf Abbasi was elected Deputy Speaker of the National Assembly (Mumtaz and Shaheed 1987, 63). Women began entering government service in unprecedented numbers (albeit still marginally) and few could have imagined then that just a decade later a basic right—the right to testify that you had observed a person commit a crime—might be legally taken away from them.

At WAF's national convention in Karachi in July 1983, its membership reiterated the organization's aims and objectives: that, most important, it was to be a consciousness-raising group remaining nonpolitical, nongovernmental, and nonaligned. They also protested against the Sixth Five-Year Plan's failure to place adequate resources at the disposal of various development programs that focused on women. They and the PWLA later urged the government of Pakistan to sign the United Nations Convention on the Elimination of All Forms of Discrimination Against Women.

In the fall of 1983 WAF and other women's groups organized demonstrations throughout the country to protest both the Qanun-e-Shahadat and the public flogging of women. In late 1983 a disagreement over WAF's internal organization caused it to separate into chapters based in the major cities. The following year, in 1984, these same groups mounted a campaign against the promulgation of the Qisas and Diyat Ordinance, which was evidently successful, because the Zia government never enacted it.

The tradition of female activism in support of larger political goals remains very much alive in the Sindhiani Tehrik women's movement, although its class composition differs a great deal from the elite, urban composition of the WAF and PWLA.[11] Sindhiani Tehrik's rural, grassroots basis enables its membership to consist of peasant women, students, schoolteachers, educated housewives, and professional women. Allied with the Awami Tehrik in Sind, Sindhiani Tehrik endeavored to make women aware of larger provincial issues such as the question of using the Sindhi language in schools and political institutions in the province, the accelerating practice of auctioning land to non-Sindhis, and the growing Sindhi nationalism. Outreach activities promote the education of women to enable them to understand conditions of oppression of both women and the larger social system. Public action has mostly supported political issues such as the Kalabagh Dam and the repatriation of Biharis from Bangladesh, although demonstrations have also been held for "women's issues," including campaigns against early marriages, second marriages, and childhood bonds. While the movement has had an impact on the social orientations and self-consciousness of some of its members, its wider impact, particularly in the political sphere, has been limited. For example, the Sindhiani Tehrik candidate Rasul Bux Palejo lost in the November 1988 elections to his PPP opponent.

The lifting of martial law in December 1985 enabled many Pakistanis more openly to have a voice in the workings of the state. Women's groups organized protests in 1986 in the wake of the debate over the Shariᶜat Bill and the Ninth Amendment. On 1 August 1986 twenty-eight organizations representing lawyers, trade unions, cultural and literary organizations, students, and women issued a joint statement opposing the Shariᶜat Bill on the grounds that it negated principles of justice, democracy, and fundamental rights of citizens, and that it would give rise to sectarianism and serve to divide the nation. On 21 September the Shahrah-i-Quaid-i-Azam in Islamabad witnessed two simultaneous processions: more than one thousand women representing twenty-five women's groups gathered under WAF's banner protesting the Shariᶜat Bill, and about a hundred ulama (religious leaders) shouted threats and slogans against the women and demanded the bill's passage (*Dawn*, 22 Sept. 1986, 1). In early January of 1987, ten women's organizations in Lahore passed a resolution protesting against the Ninth Amendment, considering it "extremely injurious" to the rights and status of women in Pakistan (*Viewpoint*, 15 Jan. 1987, 15). They and other supporting organizations were not small, fanatical groups on the fringe of society, but rather consisted of elite women from the Business and Professional Women's Club, APWA, and the Democratic Women's Association, as well as supporters from the YWCA. In support of the agitation, Syeda Abida Hussain urged women "to unite and launch an immediate campaign to force parliament to reject the Bill" (*Viewpoint*, 15 Jan. 1967, 16).

The final years of the Zia regime found WAF members focused on protesting against the Ninth Amendment, instituting legal aid cells for indigent women, opposing the gendered segregation of universities, and playing an active role in condemning the growing incidents of violence against women and bringing them to the attention of the public.

While women's status was being lessened by proposed legislation, incidents of violence against women were on the increase throughout the country. Was it a coincidence that as women were increasingly being denied legal safeguards, they were increasingly becoming targets of violence? What kind of message was the state giving out, especially when there was the possibility that a woman's testimony alone could not condemn her rapist to a court sentence or that her murder was not "worth" the same as the murder of a man if the Qisas and Diyat Ordinance passed? An example of this violence is the case of two sisters who were kidnapped, presumably raped, and then murdered in Karachi. There were subsequent allegations that the police, on finding the bodies of the Masoom sisters and afterward, incompetently destroyed much of the evidence that could have led to a solution of the crime. The case was extended to the larger issue that the police were unable to control the mounting crimes against women, evidenced by four cases of rape occurring in Karachi in January 1987 alone (Irshad 1987). Protest riots broke out in the major cities; crowds were lathi-charged by police in Karachi; women set their veils ablaze in Lahore. At the same time, a controversial delegation led by Salma Ahmed (former secretary of the Women's Division) was in New York addressing the United Nations' Commission on the Status of Women. It was controversial in that two female members of the National Assembly had refused to join the delegation, protesting that "women had no status to speak of in the country." But the official delegation assured the United Nations that the government was working toward promotion of the full participation of women in all spheres of life. *Viewpoint*'s 14 January edition includes an account of what was occurring Pakistan while Mrs. Ahmed praised the government's efforts: "Meanwhile, the women of Lahore advanced towards the barricades again, and faced the three-deep line of riot police. Young men attempting solidarity were pushed back by raised lathis." Women protesting in front of the Sind Assembly were also lathi-charged, prompting additional public outcry.

At the time of Zia ul-Haq's death, a number of outstanding draft laws that women's groups had protested against had never been promulgated. In 1983 women's organized protests enjoyed little public support; in November 1988 the PPP government included the empowerment of women as a key theme in its manifesto. Since the PPP government, a new challenge confronts women's groups. In the past, they enjoyed the luxury of being able to protest against obviously repressive laws and policies; since 1989 they have been facing the difficult transition of becoming an influential lobby in a democracy.

The Recent Agenda Concerning Women

State policy under Zia ul-Haq was pursued within a rather complicated ideological framework. From one side, Zia was praised by some orthodox religious forces, although others felt that his Islamic reforms did not go far enough. The religious forces, however, are a small minority with a limited following and therefore win few seats in fair elections. But their support was in the state's ideological interests because it could use an Islamic interpretation as a basis for cohesiveness. From the other side, however, many people resented Zia's manipulation of religion for political purposes. His stance contradicted popular culture, in which most people are "personally" very religious but not "publicly" religious. An untoward outcome was that by relying on an Islamically based policy, the state created factionalism between groups. By legislating what is Islamic and what is not, Islam itself could no longer provide unity, because it was now being defined to exclude previously included groups. Shiʿite-Sunni disputes, ethnic disturbances in Karachi between Pashtuns and muhajirs (migrants from India), increased animosity toward Ahmediyyas, and the revival of Punjab-Sind tensions can be traced to Pakistan's having lost the ability to use Islam as a common moral vocabulary.

Following the August 1988 plane crash in which Zia ul-Haq and a number of other high-ranking generals died, many people considered that the era of women's suppression in Pakistan had come to a close. The women's political protest movement had publicly exposed the controversy regarding various interpretations of Islamic law and the role of the modern state. Significant change in popular opinion regarding women had occurred in the country by then, prompted by many things, not the least of which was the person of Benazir Bhutto as the decade-long symbolic and actual leader of the opposition to the military government. Benazir Bhutto led her party to victory in November 1988 and was subsequently invited by the president of Pakistan, Ghulam Ishaq Khan, to become prime minister and form a government. Although there was initial disagreement regarding whether she, as a female, could become prime minister under Shari ʿah law, a *fatwa* (religious pronouncement) was issued stating that as the prime minister is not the emir, or the head of the state (i.e., president), who must be a man, but is rather the head of a political party, there were no gender restrictions on who could hold the office of prime minister.

Immediately preceding the November 1988 election, the PPP released its manifesto outlining a number of reforms for the empowerment of the people of Pakistan, including provisions for securing basic human rights, employment, and political participation. In particular, it pledged to eliminate all forms of discrimination against women by promising that the new government would

> 9.1: sign the [United Nations] Convention on the Elimination of All Forms of Discrimination Against Women;
> 9.2: provide women with the right to work, to free choice of employment, to just and favorable conditions of work, to protection against unemployment, to equal pay for work of equal value, and payment of maternity leave;
> 9.3: repeal all discriminatory laws against women;
> 9.4: reform Personal Law and bring it in line with the demands of contemporary socioeconomic realities;
> 9.5: make the law-enforcing machinery effective to protect [the] modesty of women;
> 9.6: take special measures to promote the literacy of women;
> 9.7: eradicate the "curse of Jahez [dowry], a pernicious evil in our society," by enlarging social consciousness and enforcing strictly the relevant laws and Dowry Act.

One of Benazir Bhutto's first acts as prime minister was to free all female prisoners from Pakistan's jails. This was followed by the government's request in late December 1988 to the Women's Division to provide a list of all laws that were discriminatory against women. Trade unions were revived and seemed to be including a sizable number of women in their ranks. The government lifted press censorship, and there was a marked difference in the media's portrayal of women. For one, female newscasters no longer always wore their *dupattas* when reporting the news on television.

Benazir had initially been criticized by Pakistani advocates of women's rights for failing to include women in the November 1988 elections. Aside from herself and her mother, only one other woman was given a PPP ticket to contest the National Assembly election, and few women were given provincial assembly tickets. But, on 23 March

1989, Pakistan Republic Day, when Benazir expanded the federal cabinet to forty-three members, she included five women in it. Only one woman—her mother—was among the twenty-four ministers. Of the nineteen ministers of state, four were women: Begum Shahnaz Wazir Ali (minister of state for education); Begum Rehana Sarwar (minister of state for the Women's Division); Mahmooda Shah (minister of state for special education and social welfare); and Begum Khakwani (minister of state for population welfare). The symbolism of this gesture cannot go unnoticed—women were being encouraged to participate actively in public life.

In July 1989 the government took an important step by elevating the Women's Division to the level of a ministry, the Ministry for Women's Development. The new ministry, however, faced a number of formidable tasks. The government had requested that by the beginning of 1989 the Women's Division provide it with a list of laws discriminatory against women, which it did. Most of the laws that the Women's Division listed had been promulgated under Zia's Islamization program and were recommended to be either amended or repealed. The government had also requested that the Women's Division explore expanding employment opportunities for women by providing it with the following:

> 1. A list of training programs that provide skills for women (there were almost none).
> 2. Information on how the Women's Division has assisted women in seeking employment.
> 3. A completed affirmative action proposal that would enable women to be placed into decision-making positions within each ministry. From 5 to 10 percent of all posts would also be reserved for women.

The Women's Division's first publication under the PPP government was released in late December 1988 for the South Asian Association for Regional Cooperation (SAARC) summit held in Islamabad. Entitled *Solidarity: SAARC Women's Journal*, it included chapters on rural development programs for women, contributed by each of the member nations. Pakistan's chapter was a commendable, honest portrayal of life in rural areas: "The villages themselves present an unedifying picture of poverty, ill-health, alarmingly low rate of literacy, malnutrition, increasing population, poor communication, lack of institutions, low production and productivity, unemployment, migration trend to cities, low holding capacity and exploitation of the poor by landlords and petty government officials" (Pakistan, Women's Division, 1988a, 44).

Upon the Women's Division's elevation, its minister, Rehana Sarwar, immediately constituted a Women's Jail Committee to investigate the details of women's convictions, a Women's Legal Rights Committee, and a Women's Legal Aid Committee. By the end of July 1989, the government of Pakistan had allocated Rs 100 million toward the establishment of a Women's Bank, which has been hailed as "the first tangible and meaningful step towards recognizing the Pakistani woman·as an independent economic entity" (Usuf 1989, 16).

The Ministry for Women's Development hoped to establish women's studies programs at several universities in the country, and at one time was optimistic it might establish a National Centre for Research on Women. These acts were, in a sense, a culmination of the century-long campaign for women's education.

Benazir's government also inherited the Zia government's Seventh Five-Year Plan (1988–93). It acknowledges that "women have been neglected" and that "the results of this neglect in terms of low productivity, illiteracy and poor health are an unacceptable cost, both morally and economically" (Pakistan, Planning Commission, 1988, 281). The plan also pledges (1) to uplift women through the provision of full equality of opportunity in education, health, employment, and other spheres of life, and (2) to create an awareness among policymakers and the public at large of the discrimination women suffer and of concomitant socioeconomic costs. However, the ways in which the plan suggests it will "try to integrate women more fully into the development process" are vague, indeterminate, and poorly funded. For example, substantive proposals affecting women are found only in the health sphere; what is needed in other areas such as employment, cooperatives, and legal assistance is mentioned, but no ways of implementing these needs are proposed. Therefore, although the PPP government had its own manifesto from which it could derive a philosophical stance, it also remained formally tied to the former government's weak proposals for incorporating women into Pakistan's development agenda. It would have had to garner strong support to veer from the Seventh Plan's strategy, but that deviation would also have meant risking the defection of party members over the potentially controversial initiative of empowering women. It ultimately took less controversial issues to bring down the government in August 1990.

State policy toward women again shifted somewhat under the Pakistan Muslim League government of Mian Nawaz Sharif, which came to power after the October 1990 elections. As an industrialist (his family owns the Ittefaq Group of companies in Pakistan), Sharif's plans to improve Pakistan's economic condition seemed, at the outset, in accord with increasing women's literacy, lowering fertility levels, and raising female work force participation rates. Political considerations superseded such goals. For example, although Syed Fakr Imam, minister of education, aspired to improve the quality of female education, he also realized that the new education policy he and his aides offered to the government in mid-1992 would be ineffective. The government's priority emphasis was instead placed on promoting Pakistan Studies and Islamic Studies in the curriculum.[12]

This priority is indicative of the dilemma that faced the Nawaz Sharif government in that it had to appease its supporters, most of whom had been the PPP government's antagonists. Therefore, on another front, Nawaz Sharif became a champion of the Shari'at Bill, finally engineering its passage in April 1991, but without the gender-discriminatory clause that had sparked the earlier controversy. The debate over the issue of which kind of law—civil or Islamic—should prevail in the country, however, remains unresolved.

The Ministry for Women's Development remained intact, although it appears that the Sharif government placed a low priority on its activities. The women's studies programs that were to be established at universities in Islamabad, Lahore, Karachi, Quetta, and Peshawar have been disappointing either because of official backpedaling, lack of commitment, or women involved with the programs being overworked with other obligations. However, small projects focusing on such economically oriented issues as training women entrepreneurs and providing housing to working women in cities seem successful at both the national and provincial (at least in Punjab) levels.

In its preparations and deliberations for the Eighth Five-Year Plan (1993–98), the Nawaz government has enlisted representatives from women's groups for feedback on a range of important areas affecting women (Pakistan 1991) and commissioned Khawar Mumtaz to write a prescriptive paper on Women in Development for its momentous *National Conservation Strategy* (Pakistan 1992). This shift in awareness on the part of the government to include women is an important beginning; getting the state to follow through on its proposals in the Eighth Plan may prove to be more problematic.

The October 1993 elections found both of the major political parties, the PPP and the PML, advocating the advancement and empowerment of women. Increasing female literacy rates, employment options, and women's political participation—especially to become "partners in development"—were included in each party's agenda. Indeed, official policy has dramatically transformed since the demise of Zia's government, as recognition of women's needs are now being incorporated into all major documents such as the National Conservation Strategy, the annual Economic Surveys, and the Approach Paper for the Eighth Plan. Unfortunately, most observers remain pessimistic that such recognition will make much difference in most women's lives.

What might matter, however, is the change that has come about in many women's attitudes and the expansion of the women's movement. The women's movement has regrouped and shifted its focus to three primary goals: to secure women's political representation in the parliament; to work to raise women's consciousness, particularly in the realm of family planning; and to counter suppression by taking stands and issuing statements to raise public awareness on events as they occur. An as yet unresolved issue is whether the precedent of having a set number of seats in the National Assembly reserved for women will be reinstituted. Importantly, it appears that a melding of the women's movement's traditional social welfare activities and its newly revised political activism is occurring. Groups with such diverse class basis as APWA, WAF, PWLA, and the Business and Professional Women's Association, as NGOs, are supporting small-scale projects throughout the country that focus on women's empowerment. The Pakistan Women's Lawyers Association has released a series of films educating women about their legal rights; the Business and Professional Women's Association is supporting a comprehensive project inside Yakki Gate, a poor area inside the walled city of Lahore. Many women activists had their expectations raised during the brief tenure of Benazir Bhutto's first government, and now feel they must seize the initiative themselves to bring about a paradigm shift in women's personal and public access to power.

The status of women in Pakistan and state policy oriented toward changing it cannot be separated from other events that are happening in the country. Political and interethnic tensions are exacerbating the strains within civil society at virtually every level, and the ensuing social confusion has spread over into gender relations. Writing about the world in general, African social historian Ali Mazrui (1990, 63) makes an argument particularly pertinent to Pakistan: "A greater role for women is needed in the struggle to tame the sovereign state, civilize capitalism, and humanize communication." It just may be that the resultant distraction of Pakistani men to other issues may enable women to become more active in the public domain and be successful not only in empowering women but in finding solutions to the problems that are shaking the social cohesion of the nation to its foundations.

Notes

1. Dependency ratios indicate the number of persons in the dependent ages (under fifteen and over sixty-five) for every one hundred women in the active ages.

2. By the time the convention was written up and ready to be signed, Pakistan had a new government (that of Zia ul-Haq), which subsequently refused to sign it.

3. Weiss (1986) provides a complete discussion of Zina and other aspects of the Pakistan government's Islamization program.

4. The severest punishments meted out under Islamic law are for *hudud* crimes, regarded as being against God's commands. Such crimes include theft, adultery or fornication, alcohol consumption, slander, and apostasy. Such punishments as death, whipping, and loss of ligaments, however, are only applicable under specific circumstances.

5. Needless to say, this phenomenon of "not coming" women's labor contributions exists worldwide but is of particular concern in countries such as Pakistan. For further discussion on the "invisibility" of women's labor, see Beneria 1982 and Waring 1988.

6. Completed in 1983, the Women's Division report was based on responses of more than 2,000 women, 500 labor leaders, and 500 male executives from diverse sectors of industry in 30 Pakistani cities.

7. This research is part of a larger study; see Weiss 1992.

8. The wages I uncovered in my research are so low that women only contribute minimally to their household maintenance expenses. However, these families are often so poor that the average monthly income of Rs 500 (U.S. 26) can have a significant impact on their standard of living.

9. The accuracy of these data is doubtful, however, because the age categories and definition of literacy changed over the years, and these would likely be considered exaggerated if adjusted to the prevailing (1972) definition.

10. The Ansari Commission was assembled in 1982 with the purpose of informing the president of which aspects of existing laws and social mores were repugnant to Islam.

11. My knowledge of the Sindhiani Tehrik is based in large part on Khawar Mumtaz, "Khawateen Mahaz-e-Amal and Sindhiani Tehrik: Two Responses to Political Development in Pakistan," an unpublished paper presented at the annual meeting of the Association for Asian Studies, 18 March 1989.

12. This was conveyed in personal discussions with the author in 1992.

Bibliography
Index

Bibliography

Abadan-Unat, Nermin, ed. 1980. *Women in Turkish Society,* Leiden: Brill.

Abbasi, Nasreen, and Mohammad Irfan. 1986. "Socioeconomic Effects of International Migration on Pakistani Families Left Behind." In *Asian Labor Migration: Pipeline to the Middle East,* edited by Fred Arnold and Nasra N. Shah, 177–93. Boulder, Colo.: Westview Press.

Adamec, Ludwig W. 1974. *Afghanistan's Foreign Affairs to the Mid-Twentieth Century: Relations with the USSR, Germany, and Britain.* Tucson: Univ. of Arizona Press.

———. 1987. *A Biographical Dictionary of Contemporary Afghanistan.* Graz: ADEVA.

Afghanistan. Ministry of Planning of the Royal Government. [1962]. *Afghanistan: Ancient Land with Modern Ways* (photo album). Kabul: Ministry of Planning of the Royal Government of Afghanistan.

———. [1972]. *Survey of Progress: 1970–1971.* Kabul: Ministry of Planning of the Royal Government of Afghanistan.

Afkhami, Mahnaz. 1984. "Iran: A Future in the Past—The Prerevolutionary Women's Movement." In *Sisterhood is Global,* edited by Robin Morgan, 330–38. New York: Anchor Books.

Afshar, Haleh. 1985a. "The Position of Women in an Iranian Village." In *Women, Work, and Ideology in the Third World,* edited by Haleh Afshar, 66–82. London: Tavistock.

———. 1985b. "Women, State, and Ideology in Iran." *Third World Quarterly* 7 (April): 256–78.

Aghajanian, Akbar. 1988. "Post-revolutionary Demographic Trends in Iran." In *Post-revolutionary Iran,* edited by Hooshang Amirahmadi and Manoucher Parvin, 153–67. Boulder, Colo.: Westview Press.

Ahluwalia, Montek S. 1974. "The Scope for Policy Intervention." In *Redistribution with Growth,* edited by Hollis Chenery, Montek S. Ahluwalia, C. L. G. Bell, John H. Duloy, and Richard Jolly, 73–90. Oxford: Oxford Univ. Press.

Ahmad, Mumtaz. 1986. "Ideology, Power, and Protest: Toward Explaining Islamic Revivalism in Pakistan." Paper presented at the Center of Strategic and International Studies, Georgetown Univ., Jan.

447

Ahmad, Muneer. 1964. *The Civil Servants in Pakistan.* Karachi: Oxford Univ. Press.
———. 1978. *Political Sociology: Perspectives on Pakistan.* Lahore: Punjab Abbi Markaz.
Ahmed, Akbar S. 1976. *Millenium and Charisma among Pathans: A Critical Essay in Social Anthropology.* London: Routledge and Kegan Paul.
Alavi, Hamza. 1986. "Pakistan and Islam: Ethnicity and Ideology." Paper presented at the South Asian Institute, Univ. of Heidelberg, July.
Al-e Ahmad, Jalal. 1981. *Plagued by the West (Gharbzadegi).* Translated by Paul Sprachman. Delmar, N.Y.: Caravan Books.
Algar, Hamid. 1986. "Social Justice in the Ideology and Legislation of the Islamic Revolution of Iran." In *Social Legislation in the Contemporary Middle East,* edited by L. O. Michalak and J. S. Salacuse, 17–60. Berkeley: Institute of International Studies, Univ. of California.
———. 1988. "Imam Khomeini, 1902–1962: The Pre-revolutionary Years." In *Islam, Politics, and Social Movements,* edited by Edmund Burke III and Ira M. Lapidus, 263–88. Berkeley and Los Angeles: Univ. of California Press.
Ali, Chaudhri Mohammad. 1967. *The Emergence of Pakistan.* New York: Columbia Univ. Press.
Allman, J. ed. 1978. *Women's Status and Fertility in the Muslim World.* New York: Praeger.
All Pakistan Women's Association (APWA). 1985. "The U.N. Woman's Development Decade—Its Relevance to Pakistan." Victoria Printing Works, Karachi. Mimeo.
Amin, Tahir. 1988. *Ethno-National Movements of Pakistan: Domestic and International Factors.* Islamabad: Institute of Policy Studies.
Amirahmadi, Hooshang. 1988. "War Damages and Reconstruction in the Islamic Republic of Iran." In *Post-revolutionary Iran,* edited by Hooshang Amirahmadi and Manoucher Parvin, 126–49. Boulder, Colo.: Westview Press.
———. 1990. *Revolution and Economic Transition: The Iranian Experience.* Albany: State Univ. of New York Press.
Anderson, Jon. 1975. "Tribe and Community among the Ghilzai Pashtun: Preliminary Notes on Ethnographic Distribution and Variation in Eastern Afghanistan." *Anthropos* 70:596–97.
———. 1978. "There Are No Khans Anymore: Economic Development and Social Change in Tribal Afghanistan." *Middle East Journal* 32:167–83.
———. 1983. "*Khan* and *Khel:* Dialectics of Pakhtun Tribalism," in *The Conflict of Tribe and State in Iran and Afghanistan,* edited by Richard Tapper, 119–49. London: Croom Helm.
Andrus, J. Russell, and Azizali F. Mohammad. 1958. *The Economy of Pakistan.* London: Oxford Univ. Press.
———. 1966. *Trade, Finance, and Development.* Karachi: Oxford Univ. Press.
Anker, Richard, Mayra Buvinic, and Nadia Youssef, eds. 1982. *Women's Roles and Population Trends in the Third World.* London: International Labour Office.

Anwar, Raja. 1988. *The Tragedy of Afghanistan: A First-hand Account.* Translated by Khalid Hasan. London: Verso.

APWA. See All Pakistan Women's Association.

Arjomand, Said A., ed. 1984. *From Nationalism to Revolutionary Islam.* Albany: State Univ. of New York Press.

———. 1988. *The Turban for the Crown.* New York: Oxford Univ. Press.

———. 1989. "The Rule of God in Iran." *Social Compass* 34, no. 4:539–48.

Arnold, Anthony. 1983. *Afghanistan's Two-Party Communism: Parcham and Khalq.* Stanford: Hoover Institution Press, Stanford Univ.

———. [1981] 1985. *Afghanistan: The Soviet Invasion in Perspective.* Stanford: Hoover Institution Press, Stanford Univ.

Ashraf, Ahmad. 1988. "Bazaar-Mosque Alliance: The Social Basis of Revolts and Revolutions." *Politics, Culture, and Society* 1, no. 4:538–67.

———. 1989. "There Is a Feeling that the Regime Owes Something to the People." *Middle East Report* (Jan.–Feb.): 13–18.

———. 1991. "State and Agrarian Relations Before and After the Iranian Revolution, 1960–1990." In *Peasant Politics in the Modern Middle East,* edited by Farhad Kazemi and John Waterbury, 277–311. Gainesville: Univ. Presses of Florida.

Ashraf, Ahmad, and Ali Banuazizi. 1985. "The State, Classes, and Modes of Mobilization in the Iranian Revolution." *State, Culture, and Society* 1, no. 3:3–40.

Asian Employment Programme. 1983. "Employment and Structural Change in Pakistan—Issues for the Eighties: A Report for the Pakistan Planning Commission for the Sixth Five Year Plan (1983–88)." Bangkok: ILO-ARTEP.

Ayub Khan, Mohammad. 1967. *Friends Not Masters: A Political Autobiography.* London: Oxford Univ. Press.

Aziz, Abdullah. 1987. *Essai sur les catégories dirigeantes de l'Afghanistan, 1945–1963: Mode de vie et comportement politique.* Berne: Peter Lang.

Azoy, Whitney. 1982. *Buzkashi, Game, and Power in Afghanistan.* Philadelphia: Univ. of Pennsylvania Press.

Bahl, R. W. 1971. "A Regression Approach to Tax Effort and Tax Ratio Analysis." *International Monetary Fund Staff Papers* 18 (Nov.): 570–612.

Bakhash, Shaul. 1984. *The Reign of the Ayatollahs: Iran and the Islamic Revolution.* New York: Basic Books.

Banuazizi, Ali. 1988. "Martyrdom in Revolutionary Iran." Paper presented at the Iranian Studies Seminar, Columbia Univ.

Banuazizi, Ali, and Ahmad Ashraf, eds. 1978. *Shakhesha-ye ejtema'i-ye Iran* (Social indicators for Iran). Teheran: Plan and Budget Organization.

Barfield, Thomas J. 1981. *The Central Asia Arabs of Afghanistan: Pastoral Nomadism in Transition.* Austin: Univ. of Texas Press.

Barry, Michael. 1984. *Le royaume de l'insolence: La résistance afghane du grand moghole a l'invasion soviétique.* Paris: Flammarion.

Barth, Frederik. 1959. *Political Leadership among Swat Pathans.* London: Athlone Press.

Baxter, Craig, and Shahid Javed Burki. 1975. "Socio-economic Indicators of the People's Party Vote in the Punjab." *Journal of Asian Studies* (Aug.): 913–30.

Bazargan, Mehdi. 1983. *Masa'el va Moshkelat-e Avvalin Sal-e Enqelab.* Teheran: Daftar-e Nahzat-e Azadi-ye Iran.

———. 1984. *Enqelab-e Iran dar Dow Harekat.* Teheran: Daftar-e Nahzat-e Azadi-ye Iran.

Bazgar, Shah, 1987. *Afghanistan: La résistance au coeur.* Paris: Denoël.

Beattie, Hugh. 1982. "Kinship and Ethnicity in the Nahrin Area of Northern Afghanistan." *Afghan Studies* 3–4:41–42.

———. 1984. "Effects of the Saur Revolution in the Nahrin Area of Northern Afghanistan." In *Revolutions and Rebellions in Afghanistan: Anthropological Perspectives,* edited by M. Nazif Shahrani and Robert L. Canfield, 184–208. Berkeley: Institute of International Studies, Univ. of California.

Beck, Lois, and Nikki R. Keddie. 1978. *Women in the Muslim World.* Cambridge: Harvard Univ. Press.

Behdad, Sohrab. 1989. "Winners and Losers of the Iranian Revolution: A Study in Income Distribution." *International Journal of Middle East Studies* 21, no. 3:327–58.

Benazir Bhutto, the Way Out: Interviews, Impressions, Statements, and Messages. 1988. Karachi: Mahmood Publications.

Bendix, Reinhard. 1968. "Reflection on Charismatic Leadership." In *State and Society,* 616–29. Berkeley and Los Angeles: Univ. of California Press.

———. 1977. *Max Weber: An Intellectual Portrait.* Berkeley and Los Angeles: Univ. of California Press.

Bendix, Reinhard, and Guenther Roth. 1971. *Scholarship and Partisanship: Essays on Max Weber.* Berkeley and Los Angeles: Univ. of California Press.

Beneria, Lourdes. 1982. "Accounting for Women's Work." In *Women and Development: The Sexual Division of Labor in Rural Societies,* edited by Lourdes Beneria, 119–42. New York: Praeger.

Beneria, Lourdes, and Gita Sen. 1982. "Class and Gender Inequalities and Women's Role in Economic Development: Theoretical and Practical Implications." *Feminist Studies* 8, no. 1.

Bensman, Joseph, and Michael Givant. 1975. "Charisma and Modernity: The Use and Abuse of a Concept." *Social Research* 2, no. 4:570–614.

Berik, Gunseli. 1988. "Born Factories: Women's Labor in Carpet Workshops in Rural Turkey." Department of Economics, New School for Social Research, New York. Manuscript.

Bernard, Jessie. 1981. *The Female World.* New York: Free Press.

Bhattacharya, Nikhilih, G. S. Chatterjee, and Padiraja Pal. 1988. In *Rural Poverty in South Asia,* edited by T. N. Srinivasan and Pranab K. Bardhan, New Delhi: Oxford Univ. Press.

Bhatti, Mukhtar Ahmad. 1988. *Female Teachers in Rural Pakistan: Problems and Remedies.* Islamabad: National Education Council.

Bhutto, Zulfikar Ali. 1976. *Speeches.* Vol I. Islamabad: Ministry of Information and Broadcasting.

Bierstedt, Robert. 1954. "The Problem of Authority." In *Freedom and Control in Modern Society*, edited by Morroe Berger, Theodore Able, and Charles Page, 67–81. New York: D. Van Nostrand.

Blumberg, Rae Lesser. 1978. *Stratification: Socio-economic and Sexual Inequality.* Iowa City, Iowa: William C. Brown.

Bodrova, Valentina, and Richard Anker, eds. 1985. *Working Women in Socialist Countries: The Fertility Connection.* Geneva: International Labour Organisation.

Borovik, Artem. 1988. "Will Kabul Fall after Soviet Withdrawal?" *Current Digest of the Soviet Press* 40, no. 33:1–5. (Condensation and translation of "Afghanistan: Preliminary results—*Ogonyok* correspondent Artem Borovik interviews Maj. Gen. Kim Tsagolov, doctor of philosophy and chairman of the department of Marxism-Leninism at the M. V. Frunze Military Academy." *Ogonyok,* 23–30 (July, 25–27.)

Boutalia, Urvashi. 1985. "Indian Women and the New Movement." *Women's Studies International Forum* 8, no. 2:131–33.

Brandt Commission. 1980. *North-South: A Program for Survival.* Cambridge: MIT Press.

Brown, W. Norman. 1963. *The United States and India and Pakistan.* Cambridge: Harvard Univ. Press.

Bruce, Judith, and Daisy Dwyer. 1988. Introduction to *A Home Divided: Women and Income in the Third World,* edited by Daisy Dwyer and Judith Bruce, 1–19. Stanford: Stanford Univ. Press.

Burke, Edmund, III, and Ira M. Lapidus, eds. 1988. *Islam, Politics, and Social Movements.* Berkeley and Los Angeles: Univ. of California Press.

Burke, S. M. 1973. *Pakistan's Foreign Policy: An Historical Analysis.* London: Oxford Univ. Press.

Burki, Shahid Javed. 1969. "Twenty Years of the Civil Service of Pakistan." *Asian Survey* 9 (Apr.): 121–40.

———. 1971. "Interest Group Involvement in West Pakistan's Rural Works Program." *Public Policy* 19 (Winter).

———. 1974. "Pakistan: A Demographic Report." Washington, D.C.: Population Council.

———. 1980a. *Pakistan under Bhutto, 1971–77.* London: Macmillan.

———. 1980b. "What Migration to the Middle East May Mean for Pakistan." *Journal of South Asian and Middle Eastern Studies* 3, no. 3:47–65.

———. 1984. "Pakistan's Sixth Plan: Helping the Country Climb out of Poverty." *Asian Survey* 24 (Apr.): 400–422.

———. 1988a. *Pakistan under Bhutto, 1971–77.* 2d ed. London: Macmillan.

———. 1988b. "Poverty in Pakistan: Myth or Reality?" In *Rural Poverty in South Asia,* edited by T. N. Srinivasan and Pranab K. Bardhan, 69-88. New Delhi: Oxford Univ. Press.

Burki, Shahid Javed, and Robert LaPorte, Jr., eds. 1984. *Pakistan's Development Priorities: Choices for the Future.* Karachi: Oxford Univ. Press.

Burki, Shahid Javed, and Mahbub ul-Haq. 1981. "Meeting Basic Needs: An Overview." *World Development* 9.

Carroll, Lucy. 1982. "Nizam-i-Islam: Processes and Conflicts in Pakistan's Programme of Islamisation, with Special Reference to the Position of Women." *Journal of Commonwealth and Comparative Politics* 20:57–95.

Centlivres, Pierre. 1972. *Un bazar d'Asie Centrale: Forme et organisation du bazar de Tashqurghan (Afghanistan).* Wiesbaden: Dr. Ludwig Reichert Verlag.

———. 1983. "Attitudes, gestes et postures en Afghanistan: Du corps enculturé au corps modernisé." In *Le corps enjeu,* 87–112. Neuchâtel: Musée d'ethnographie.

Centlivres, Pierre, and Micheline Centlivres-Demont. 1987. "Sociopolitical Adjustment among Afghan Refugees in Pakistan." *Migration World Magazine* 15, no. 4:15–21.

———. 1988a. "The Afghan Refugee in Pakistan: An Ambiguous Identity." *Journal of Refugees* 1, no. 2:141–52.

———. 1988b. "The Afghan Refugees in Pakistan: A Nation in Exile." *Current Sociology* 36, no. 2:71–92.

———. 1988c. *Et si on parlait de l'Afghanistan? Terrains et textes 1964–1980.* Neuchâtel: Institut d'ethnologie, Paris: Maison des sciences de l'homme.

———. 1988d. "Les femmes afghanes aujourd'hui." *Afghanistan Info* 23 (Nov.): 17–19.

———. 1992. *Afghanistan: Case Study.* Geneva: United Nations High Commissioner for Refugees.

Centlivres-Demont, Micheline. 1981. "Rites de mariage en Afghanistan: Le dit et le vécu." In *Naître, vivre et mourir,* 119–34. Neuchâtel: Musée d'ethnographie.

———. 1983. "Le tailleur, le fripier et la brodeuse." In *Textilhandwerk in Afghanistan,* edited by Marie-Louise Nabholz and Paul Bucherer, 113–29. Liestal: Bibliotheca Afghanica.

Centlivres-Demont, Micheline, and Pierre Centlivres. 1984. "La societé afghane, structures et valeurs." In *Afghanistan: La colonisation impossible,* 57–80. Paris: Editions du cerf.

Centlivres-Demont, Micheline, Pierre Centlivres, Bernard Dupaigne, Etienne Gille, Alain Marigo, Jacky Mathonnat, Jean-José Puig, Gilles Rossignol, and Olivier Roy. 1984. *Afghanistan: La colonisation impossible.* Paris: Editions du cerf.

Central Bank of the Islamic Republic of Iran. N.d. *Barresi-ye tahavvolat-e eqtesadi-ye keshvar ba ʿd az enqelab* (An analysis of the economic changes since the revolution). Teheran.

———. 1981. 1984. *Economic Report and Balance Sheet.* Teheran.

Chafetz, Janet S. 1984. *Sex and Advantage: A Comparative Macro-structural Theory of Sex Stratification.* Totowa, N.J.: Rowman and Allanheld.

———. 1990. *Gender Equity: An Integrated Theory of Stability and Change.* Newbury Park, Calif.: Sage Publications.

Charlton, Sue Ellen. 1984. *Women in Third World Development*. Boulder, Colo.: Westview Press.

Charnay, Jean Paul. 1986. *L'Islam et la guerre*. Paris: Fayard.

Chehabi, Houshang. 1990. *Iranian Politics and Religious Modernism: The Liberation Movement of Iran under the Shah and Khomeini*. Ithaca, N.Y.: Cornell Univ. Press.

Chipp, Sylvia A. 1980. "The Modern Pakistani Woman in a Muslim Society." In *Asian Women in Transition*, edited by Sylvia A. Chipp and Justin Green, 204–26. Univ. Park, Pa.: Pennsylvania State Univ. Press.

Christensen, Hanne. 1988. *The Reconstruction of Afghanistan: A Chance for Rural Afghan Women*. Geneva: UNRISD.

Clawson, Patrick. 1988. "Islamic Iran's Economic Politics and Prospects." *Middle East Journal* 42, no. 3:371–88.

Cohen, Stephen. 1984. *The Pakistan Army*. Berkeley and Los Angeles: Univ. of California Press.

Concepcion, Maria. 1974. "Female Labor Force Participation and Fertility." *International Labour Review* 109, nos. 5 and 6:503–18.

Constitution de l'Afghanistan. 1964. Kabul, 1 Oct.

Constitution of the Republic of Afghanistan. 1977. Occasional Paper No. 7, Afghanistan Council of the Asia Society, New York.

Crompton, Rosemary, and Michael Mann, eds. 1986. *Gender and Stratification*. Cambridge: Polity Press.

Daoud, Zemaray. 1982. *L'Etat monarchique dans la formation sociale afghane*. Berne: Peter Lang.

Davani, Ali. 1979–80. *Nahzat-e Ruhaniyun-e Iran*. 10 vols. Tehran: Iman Reza Publishers.

de Kruijk, Hans. 1987. "Source of Income Inequality in Pakistan." *Proceedings, Fourth Annual General Meeting of the Pakistan Society of Development Economists*. Islamabad: Pakistan Institute of Development Economists.

de Kruijk, Hans, and Myrna de Leeuwen. 1985. "Change in Poverty and Income Inequality During the 1970s." *Pakistan Development Review* 24, nos. 3 and 4.

de Lauretis, Teresa. 1987. *Technologies of Gender*. Bloomington: Indiana Univ. Press.

Delloye, Isabelle. 1980. *Des femmes d'Afghanistan*. Paris: Editions des femmes.

Democratic Republic of Afghanistan (DRA). 1979. *Statistical Information of Afghanistan, 1975–1978*. Kabul: Central Statistics Office.

———. 1981a. *Statistical Year Book 1358: March 1979–March 1980*. Kabul: Central Statistics Office.

———. 1981b. *Supplement No. 1 to DRA Revolutionary Council Decree No. 8*. Decree of the Presidium of the DRA Revolutionary Council issued on 9 Aug., translated from the Pashto in Foreign Broadcast Information Service (FBIS) VIII (20 Aug.): C1–C2.

———. 1982. *Statistical Year Book 1359: March 1980–March 1981*. Kabul: Central Statistics Office.

———. 1983. *Statistical Year Book 1361: March 1982–March 1983.* Kabul: Central Statistics Office.

———. 1986. *Statistical Year Book 1362: March 1983–March 1984.* Kabul: Central Statistics Office.

Democratic Republic of Afghanistan. Information and Press Department. 1984. *Achievements of the April Revolution in Afghanistan.* Kabul: Ministry of Foreign Affairs.

Democratic Youth Organization of Afghanistan (DYOA). 1985. *Afghan Youth Fights and Builds.* Kabul.

Denitch, Bogdan. 1976. *The Legitimation of a Revolution: The Yugoslav Case.* New Haven: Yale Univ. Press.

Dixon, Ruth. 1982. "Women in Agriculture: Counting the Labor Force in Developing Countries." *Population and Development Review* 8, no. 3:539–66.

Doubleday, Veronica. 1988. *Three Women of Herat.* London: Jonathan Cape.

DRA. See Democratic Republic of Afghanistan.

Drèze, Jean, and Amartya Sen. 1989. *Hunger and Public Action.* Oxford: Clarendon Press.

Dupree, Louis. 1959. *The Burqa Comes Off.* American Univ. Field Staff, South Asia Series, vol. 3, no. 2. New York.

———. 1971. *Population Review 1970: Afghanistan.* American Univ. Field Staff, South Asia Series, vol. 15, no. 1. New York.

———. 1977. "Toward Representative Government in Afghanistan, Part II: Steps Six Through Nine; and Beyond?" In American Univ. Field Staff Reports, no. 21.

———. [1973] 1980a. *Afghanistan.* Princeton: Princeton Univ. Press.

———. 1980b. *Red Flag over Hindu Kush, Part III: Rhetoric and Reforms, or Promises, Promises.* American Univ. Field Staff, South Asia Series, no. 23. New York.

Dupree, Nancy. [1981] 1984. "Revolutionary Rhetoric and Afghan Women." Occasional Paper No. 23, Afghanistan Council of the Asia Society, New York. Reprinted in *Revolutions and Rebellions in Afghanistan: Anthropological Perspectives,* edited by M. Nazif Sharani and Robert L. Canfield, 306–40. Berkeley: Institute of International Studies, Univ. of California.

Dwyer, D., and J. Bruce. 1988. *A Home Divided: Women and Income in the Third World.* Stanford: Stanford Univ. Press.

Egger, Rowland. 1953. *The Improvement of Public Administration in Pakistan.* Karachi: Inter-Services Press.

Eisenstadt, Samuel. 1978. *Revolution and the Transformation of Societies.* New York: Free Press.

Elmi, Sayed Mohammad Yusuf. 1986. "The Impact of Sovietization on Afghan Education and Culture." In *The Sovietization of Afghanistan,* edited by S. B. Majrooh and Sayed Mohammad Yusuf Elmi, 72–141. Peshawar: Afghan Jehad Works Translation Centre.

Elphinstone, Montstuart. [1815] 1972. *An Account of the Kingdom of Caubul and Its Dependencies in Persia, Tartary, and India. . . .* Reprint. 2 vols. Karachi: Oxford Univ. Press.

Elson, Diane, and Ruth Pearson. 1981. "The Subordination of Women and the Internationalisation of Factory Production." In *Of Marriage and the Market: Women's Subordination in International Perspective*, edited by Kate Young, Carol Wolkowitz, and Roslyn McCullagh, 144–66. London: CSE Books.

Enayat, Hamid. 1982. *Modern Islamic Political Thought*. Austin: Univ. of Texas Press.

Engels, Friedrich. [1884] 1972. *Origins of the Family, Private Property, and the State*. Reprint, edited by Eleanor B. Leacock. New York: International Books.

Epstein, Cynthia. 1988. *Deceptive Distinctions: Sex, Gender, and the Social Order*. New Haven: Yale Univ. Press and Russell Sage.

Esposito, John L. 1986. "Islam: Ideology and Politics in Pakistan." In *The State, Religion, and Ethnic Politics: Afghanistan, Iran, and Pakistan*, edited by Ali Banuazizi and Myron Weiner. Syracuse, N.Y.: Syracuse Univ. Press.

Etienne, Gilbert. 1972. *L'Afghanistan, ou les aléas de la coopération*. Paris: Presses Universitaires de France.

Evans, Peter B., Dietrich Rueschemeyer, and Theda Skocpol. 1985. "On the Road Toward a More Adequate Understanding of the State." In *Bringing the State Back In*, edited by Peter B. Evans, Dietrich Rueschemeyer, and Theda Skocpol, 347–66. Cambridge: Cambridge Univ. Press.

Falcon, Walter P., and Carl H. Gotsch. 1968. "Lessons in Agricultural Development—Pakistan." In *Development Policy: Theory and Practice*, edited by Gustav F. Papanek. Cambridge: Harvard Univ. Press.

Falcon, Walter P. and Gustav F. Papanek, eds. 1971. *Development Policy II: The Pakistan Experience*. Cambridge: Harvard Univ. Press.

Farley, Jennie, ed. 1985. *Working Women in Fifteen Countries*. Ithaca, N.Y.: ILR Press.

Farnham, Christie, ed. 1987. *The Impact of Feminist Research in the Academy*. Bloomington: Indiana Univ. Press.

FBS. See Pakistan, Government of. Federal Bureau of Statistics.

"Femmes en Afghanistan." 1986. Dossier: *Femmes en Afghanistan: Les Nouvelles d'Afghanistan*, special issue, nos. 29–30, Oct., Paris.

Ferdinand, Klaus. 1962. "Nomad Expansion and Commerce in Central Afghanistan: A Sketch of Some Trends." *Folk* 4:123–59.

Finlay, Barbara. 1989. *The Women of Azua: Work and Family in the Rural Dominican Republic*. New York: Praeger.

Fischer, Michael M. J. 1980. *Iran: From Religious Dispute to Revolution*. Cambridge: Harvard Univ. Press.

Fluehr-Lobban, Carolyn. 1989. "Arab-Islamic Women: Participants in Secular and Religious Movements." Paper presented at New Hampshire International Seminar, Univ. of New Hampshire, Durham (Mar. 3).

Frommer, Gisela. 1981. *Das moderne Bildungswesen als Instrument nationaler Entwicklung: Eine Studie zur Theorie der Schule in Afghanistan*. Heidelberg: Esprint-Verlag.

Fry, Maxwell J. 1974. *The Afghan Economy: Money, Finance, and the Critical Constraints to Economic Development.* Leiden: E. J. Brill.

Furet, Francois. 1981. *Interpreting the French Revolution.* Cambridge: Cambridge Univ. Press.

Gailey, Christine Ward. 1987. "Evolutionary Perspectives on Gender Hierarchy." In *Analyzing Gender,* edited by Beth B. Hess and Myra Marx Ferree, 32–67. Beverly Hills, Calif.: Sage Publications.

Gankovsky, Yuri V., M. R. Arunova, V. G. Korgun, V. M. Masson, G. A. Muradov, G. A. Polyakov, and V. A. Romodin. 1985. *A History of Afghanistan.* Translated by Vitaly Baskakov. Moscow: Progress Publishers.

Gellner, Ernest. 1985. Introduction to *The Islamic Dilemma.* Berlin: Mouton Publishers.

Ghani, Ashraf. N.d. "Conjunctures of State, Economy, and Ideology in Afghanistan, 1950–1978." Paper presented at the Conference on Social Movements in the Contemporary Near and Middle East, Columbia Univ.

Ghoussoub, Mai. 1987. "Feminism—or the Eternal Masculine—in the Arab World." *New Left Review* 161 (Jan.–Feb.): 3–13.

Giddens, Anthony. 1987. *The Nation-State and Violence.* Berkeley and Los Angeles: Univ. of California Press.

Gilani, Ijaz, M. Fahim Khan, and Munawar Iqbal. 1981. *Labor Migration to the Middle East and Its Impact on the Domestic Economy.* Washington, D.C.: World Bank.

Gille, Etienne. 1984. "L'accession au pouvoir des communistes prosoviétiques." In *Afghanistan: La colonisation impossible,* 179–212. Paris: Editions du cerf.

Gilmartin, David. 1989. *Empire and Islam: Punjab and the Making of Pakistan.* Oxford: Oxford Univ. Press.

Girardet, Edward R. 1985. *Afghanistan: The Soviet War.* London: Croom Helm.

Glatzer, Berndt. 1983. "Political Organisation of Pashtun Nomads and the State." In *The Conflict of Tribe and State in Iran and Afghanistan,* edited by Richard Tapper, 212–32. London: Croom Helm.

Glukhoded, Vladimir. 1981. "Economy of Independent Afghanistan." In *Afghanistan Past and Present,* edited by Social Sciences Today Editorial Board, 222–45. Moscow: USSR Academy of Sciences.

Goodman, Henry Frank. 1964. *The Civil Service of Pakistan: Bureaucracy in a New Nation.* New Haven: Yale Univ. Press.

Gregorian, Vartan. 1969. *The Emergence of Modern Afghanistan: Politics of Reform and Modernization, 1880–1946.* Stanford: Stanford Univ. Press.

Grevemeyer, Jan-Heeren. 1987. *Afghanistan: Sozialer Wandel und Staat im Zwanzigsten Jahrhundert.* Berlin: Express Edition.

Guha, Amalendha. 1967. "The Economy of Afghanistan During Amanullah's Reign, 1919–1929." *International Studies* 9:161–82.

Gupta, Bhabani Sen. 1986. *Afghanistan Politics, Economics, and Society: Revolution, Resistance, Intervention.* London: Francis Pinter.

Haeri, Shala. 1989. *Law of Desire: Temporary Marriage in Shi'i Iran*. Syracuse, N.Y.: Syracuse Univ. Press.
Hafeez, Sabeeha. 1983. *Women in Industry: Phase I, Basic Survey*. Islamabad: Sponsored by the Women's Division, Government of Pakistan.
Hager, Robert. 1983. "State, Tribe, and Empire in Afghan Inter-polity Relations." In *The Conflict of Tribe and State in Iran and Afghanistan*, edited by Richard Tapper, 83–118. London: Croom Helm.
Halliday, Fred. 1978. "Revolution in Afghanistan." *New Left Review* 112 (Nov.–Dec.): 3–44.
———. 1980. "War and Revolution in Afghanistan." *New Left Review* 119 (Jan.–Feb.): 20–41.
Hamilton, Angus. 1906. *Afghanistan*. London: William Heinemann.
Hancock, Frances. 1989. "The Veil as a Presentational Symbol." Divinity School, Harvard University. Typescript.
Hansen, Henny Harald. 1983. "The Veil in Islam." *Folk* 25:147–66.
Harrison, Selig. 1981. *In Afghanistan's Shadow: Baluch Nationalism and Soviet Temptations*. Washington, D.C.: Carnegie Endowment for International Peace.
Harriss, Barbara. 1990. "The Intrafamily Distribution of Hunger in South Asia." In *The Political Economy of Hunger*, vol. 1, *Entitlement and Well-being*, edited by Jean Drèze and Amartya Sen, 351–424. Oxford: Clarendon Press.
Hartmann, Heidi. 1976. "Capitalism, Patriarchy, and Job Segregation by Sex." *Signs* 1:137–69.
Hazrati, Elias. 1990. "Didgahha." *Bayan* 1, nos. 5–6.
Herberger, Arnold C. 1977. "Fiscal Policy and Income Distribution." In *Income Distribution and Growth in Less Developed Countries*, edited by R. Frank, Jr., and Richard Webb. Washington, D.C.: Brookings Institution.
Herring, Ronald J. 1983. *Land to the Tiller: The Political Economy of Agrarian Reform in South Asia*. New Haven: Yale Univ. Press.
———. 1984. *The Politics of Land Reform*. New Haven: Yale Univ. Press.
Herz, Barbara, and Anthony Meacham. 1987. *The Safe Motherhood Initiative: Proposals for Action*. World Bank Discussion Paper 9. Washington, D.C.: World Bank.
Herz, Martin. 1964. *Some Intangible Factors in Iranian Politics*. U.S. Department of State, no. A-702, June.
Hess, Beth B., and Myra Marx Ferree, eds. 1987. *Analyzing Gender*. Newbury Park: Sage Publications.
Higgins, Patricia J., and Piroux Shoar-Ghaffari. 1989. "Sex-Role Stratification in Iranian Textbooks." Department of Anthropology and Communication, State Univ. of New York, Albany. Mimeo.
Hojjati Kermani, Mohammad Javad. 1988–89. "Fiqh va tamadon-e jadid." *Iran Times*, various issues from 4 Nov. 1988 to 24 Feb. 1989.
Homayun, Daryush. 1981. *Diruz va farda: Seh goftar dar bara-ye Iran-e enqelabi*. N.p.

Howard-Merriam, Kathleen. 1987. "Afghan Refugee Women and Their Struggle for Survival." In *Afghan Resistance: The Politics of Survival*, edited by Grant M. Farr and John G. Merriam, 103–25. Boulder, Colo.: Westview Press.

Hunt, Lynn. 1984. *Politics, Culture, and Class in the French Revolution*. Berkeley and Los Angeles: Univ. of California Press.

Huntington, Samuel P. 1968. *Political Order in Changing Societies*. New Haven: Yale Univ. Press.

Hussain, Akmal. 1985. "Pakistan: The Crisis of the State." In *Islam, Politics, and the State*, edited by Asghar Khan. London.

———. 1988. *Strategic Issues in Pakistan's Economic Policy*. Lahore: Progressive Publications.

ILO/INSTRAW. 1985. *Women in Economic Activity: A Global Statistical Survey 1950–2000*. Geneva: International Labour Organisation; Santo Domingo: United Nations International Research and Training Institute for the Advancement of Women.

Ingrams, Doreen. 1988. "The Position of Women in Middle Eastern Arab Society." In *The Middle East*, edited by Michael Adams, 808–14. New York: Facts on File.

Institute of Policy Studies. 1983. *Development Strategy for the Sixth Plan, 1983–88*. Islamabad: Institute of Policy Studies.

International Center for Research on Women (ICRW). 1980. *Keeping Women Out: A Structural Analysis of Women's Employment in Developing Countries*. Washington, D.C.: ICRW.

International Development Association. 1989. *The Evolving Role of IDA*. Washington, D.C.: International Development Association.

International Monetary Fund (IMF). *World Economic Outlook*. Washington, D.C.: International Monetary Fund. Semiannual, various issues.

Iran. Ministry of Interior (Vezarat-e Keshvar). 1960. First National Census of Agriculture: Mehr 1339 (Oct. 1960): vol. 15.

Iran. Ministry of Labor and Social Affairs. 1983. *Barresi-ye masa'el-e kolli-ye niru-ye ensani va eshteghal* (Survey of general problems of manpower and employment). Vol. 1. Teheran: Ministry of Labor and Social Affairs.

Iran. Ministry of Planning and Budget (MPB). *Annual Economic Report*. Teheran: MPB, various issues from 1981 to 1989 (in Persian).

———. 1987. *Statistical Yearbook 1986*. Teheran: Statistical Center, MPB.

———. 1988. "Gazaresh-e ʿamalkard-e budje-ye sale-e 1366" (Report on the operation of the 1987 budget). MPB, Teheran. Mimeo.

———. 1989. *Statistical Yearbook 1988*. Teheran: Statistical Center, Ministry of Planning and Budget.

Iran Yearbook '88. 1988. Bonn: Moini-Biontino Verlagsgesellschaft.

Irshad, Sairah. 1987. "A Licence to Rape?" *The Herald* (Karachi) 18, no. 2, Feb.: 93–96.

Jahan, Rounaq. 1972. *Pakistan: Failure in National Integration*. New York: Columbia Univ. Press.

Jalal, Ayesha. 1985. *The Sole Spokesman: Jinnah, the Muslim League, and the Demand for Pakistan.* London: Cambridge Univ. Press.

———. 1990a. "State-Building in the Post-war World: Britain's Colonial Legacy, American Futures, and Pakistan." In *South Asia and World Capitalism*, edited by Sugata Bose. New Delhi: Oxford Univ. Press.

———. 1990b. *The State of Martial Rule: The Origins of Pakistan's Political Economy of Defence*, Cambridge.

———. 1991. "The Convenience of Subservience: Women and the State of Pakistan." In *Women, Islam, and the State*, edited by Deniz Kandiyoti, 77–114. Philadelphia: Temple Univ. Press.

Joekes, Susan. 1987. *Women in the World Economy: An INSTRAW Study.* New York: Oxford Univ. Press.

Jones, Philip E. 1979. "The Pakistan People's Party: Social Group Response and Party Development in an Era of Mass Participation." Ph.D. diss., Fletcher School of Law and Diplomacy.

Kabeer, Naila. 1988. "Subordination and Struggle: Women in Bangladesh." *New Left Review* 168 (Mar.–Apr.): 95–121.

Kakar, Hasan. 1978. "The Fall of the Afghan Monarchy in 1973." *International Journal of Middle East Studies* 9, no. 2:195–214.

———. 1979. *Government and Society in Afghanistan: The Reign of Amir 'Abd al-Rahman Khan.* Austin: Univ. of Texas Press.

Kandiyoti, Deniz. 1984. "Rural Transformation in Turkey and Its Implications for Women's Status." In *Women on the Move*, edited by UNESCO, 17–30. Paris: UNESCO.

Kardar, A. H. 1988. *Pakistan's Soldiers of Fortune.* Lahore: Feroze and Sons.

Karimi, Setareh. 1986. "Economic Policies and Structural Changes since the Revolution." In *The Iranian Revolution and the Islamic Republic*, edited by N. R. Keddie and Eric Hoogland, 32–54. Syracuse, N.Y.: Syracuse Univ. Press.

Khan, Seemin Anwar, and Faiz Bilquees. 1976. "The Environment, Attitudes, and Activities of Rural Women: A Case Study of a Village in Punjab." *Pakistan Development Review* 10, no. 3.

Kholin, D. 1988. "Afghanistan—vzglyad iz vnutri" (Afghanistan—view from within). *Argumenty i Fakty* 27:4. ("Afghan Official on Past Mistakes, Current Issues." FBIS-SOV, 14 July, 18–19.)

Khomeini, Ruhollah. 1944. *Kashf al-Asrar.* Tehran: n.p.

———. 1978. *Velayate Faqih.* Teheran: Amir Kabir.

———. 1981. *Islam and Revolution.* Translated and annotated by Hamid Algar. Berkeley: Mizan Press.

———. 1983. *Sahifa-ye Nur.* 18 vols. Tehran: Markaz-e Madarek-e Farhangi-ye Enqelab-e Islami.

Klass, Rosanne, ed. 1987. *Afghanistan: The Great Game Revisited.* New York: Freedom House.

Knabe, Erika. 1974. "Afghan Women: Does Their Role Change?" In *Afghanistan in the 1970s*, edited by Louis Dupree and Linette Albert, 144–66. New York: Praeger.

————. 1977. *Frauenemanzipation in Afghanistan: Ein empirischer Beitrag zur Untersuchung von sozio-kulturellem Wandel und sozio-kultureller Beständigkeit*. Meisenheim am Glan: Verlag Anton Hain.

Kohan, Sara. 1990. "Bad hejabi az chashm-e sharqi va gharbi" (Mal-veiling from Eastern and Western perspectives). *Nimeye Digar* 11:3–9.

Kohli, Atul. 1987. *The State and Poverty in India: The Politics of Reform*. Cambridge: Cambridge Univ. Press.

Kravis, Irving B., Alan Heston, and Robert Summers. 1982. *World Product and Income: International Comparison of Real Gross Products*. Baltimore: Johns Hopkins Univ. Press.

Kuznets, Simon. 1955. "Economic Growth and Income Inequality." *American Economic Review* (Mar.).

Kynch, Jocelyn, and Amartya Sen. 1983. "Indian Women: Well-being and Survival." *Cambridge Journal of Economics* 7:363–80.

Laber, Jeri, and Barnett R. Rubin. 1988. *A Nation Is Dying: Afghanistan under the Soviets, 1979–1987*. Evanston, Ill.: Northwestern Univ. Press.

Langer, Susanne. 1942. *Philosophy in a New Key: A Study in the Symbolism of Reason, Rite, and Art*. Cambridge: Harvard Univ. Press.

LaPorte, Robert, Jr. 1975. *Power and Privilege: Influence and Decision-Making in Pakistan*. Berkeley and Los Angeles: Univ. of California Press.

LaPorte, Robert, Jr., and Muntazar Bashir Ahmed. 1989. *Public Enterprises in Pakistan: The Hidden Crisis in Economic Development*. Boulder, Colo.: Westview Press.

Lautenschlager, Wolfgang. 1986. "The Effects of an Overvalued Exchange Rate on the Iranian Economy." *International Journal of Middle East Studies* 18, no. 1:31–52.

Leacock, Eleanor. 1978. "Women's Status in Egalitarian Society: Implications for Social Evolution." *Current Anthropology* 19, no. 2:247–75.

Leacock, Eleanor, and Helen Safa, eds. 1986. *Women's Work, Development, and the Division of Labor by Gender*. South Hadley, Mass.: Bergin and Garvey Publishers.

Lerner, Gerda. 1987. *The Origins of Patriarchy*. Chicago: Univ. of Chicago Press.

Lewis, Stephen R. 1969. *Economic Policy and Industrial Growth in Pakistan*. London: George Allen and Unwin.

Lim, Linda. 1983. "Capitalism, Imperialism, and Patriarchy." In *Women, Men, and the International Division of Labor*, edited by June Nash and Maria Patricia Fernandez-Kelly. Albany: State Univ. of New York Press.

Lobato, Chantal. 1987. "Femmes afghanes, femmes musulmanes." *Islam, le grand malentendu*, special issue of *Autrement* (Paris), no. 95, Dec., 170–73.

Lodhi, Maliha. N.d. "Politics in Pakistan During the Bhutto Period." Typescript.

Loewenstein, Karl. 1966. *Max Weber: Political Ideas in the Perspective of Our Time*. Amherst: Univ. of Massachusetts Press.

Mackintosh, Maureen. 1981. "The Sexual Division of Labour and the Subordination of Women." In *Of Marriage and the Market: Women's Subordination in International Perspective*. London: CSE Books.

Mahdavi, Hossein. 1970. "Patterns and Problems of Economic Development in Rentier States: The Case of Iran." In *Studies in the Economic History of the Middle East*, edited by Michael Cook, 428–67. London: Oxford Univ. Press.

Majlis-e Shura-ye Islami. 1981. *Ashna ͨi ba Majlis-e Shura-ye Islami*. Teheran: Majlis-e Shura-ye Islami.

———. 1985a. *Moarefi-ye namayandagan-e Majlis-e Shura-ye Islami*. Teheran.

———. 1985b. *Surat-e mashruh-e muzakerat-e majlis: Barresi-ye qanune asasi-ye jumhuri-ye Islami*. 3 vols. Teheran: Majlis-e Shura-ye Islami.

———. *Annual Budget Bill*. Teheran: Ministry of Planning and Budget, annual, various years from 1981 to 1990 (in Persian).

Male, Beverly. 1982. *Revolutionary Afghanistan: A Reappraisal*. London: Croom Helm.

Mann, Michael. 1986. "A Crisis in Stratification Theory?" In *Gender and Stratification*, edited by Rosemary Crompton and Michael Mann, 40–56. Cambridge: Polity Press.

Mason, Philip. 1969. *The Men Who Ruled India: The Founders*. London: Jonathan Cape.

Masud, M. 1949. *Hari Enquiry Committee: Minute of Dissent*. Karachi: Government of Sind.

Mathonnat, Jacques. 1984. "Une économie impulsée de l'extérieur." In *Afghanistan: La colonisation impossible*, 143–78. Paris: Editions du cerf.

Maududi, Maulana Abdul. 1955. *Islamic Law and Constitution*. Karachi: Jamaati Islami Publications.

———. 1960a. *First Principles of the Islamic State*. Lahore: Islamic Publications.

———. 1960b. *Political Theory of Islam*. Lahore: Islamic Publications.

Mazlish, Bruce. 1976. *The Revolutionary Ascetic*. New York: Basic Books.

Mazrui, Ali A. 1990. *Cultural Forces in World Politics*. London: James Currey.

Mehran, Golnar. 1989. "Socialization of Schoolchildren in the Islamic Republic of Iran." *Iranian Studies* 22, no. 1:35–50.

Menard, Scott. 1987. "Fertility, Development, and Family Planning, 1970–80: An Analysis of Cases Weighted by Population." *Studies in Comparative International Development* 22, no. 3:103–27.

Mernissi, Fatima. 1987. *Beyond the Veil*. 2d ed. Bloomington: Indiana Univ. Press.

Michel, Aloyse A. 1967. *The Indus River: A Study of the Effects of Partition*. New Haven: Yale Univ. Press.

Milani, Mohsen. 1988. *The Making of Iran's Islamic Revolution*. Boulder, Colo.: Westview Press.

Miller, Barbara D. 1981. *The Endangered Sex: Neglect of Female Children in Rural North India*. Ithaca, N.Y.: Cornell Univ. Press.

Millet, Kate. 1981. *Going to Iran*. New York: Coward, McCann, and Geoghegan.

Mirani, Kaveh. 1983. "Social and Economic Change in the Role of Women, 1956–78." In *Women and Revolution in Iran*, edited by Guity Nashat. Boulder, Colo.: Westview Press.

Mirza, Mahmud. 1987. *Aaj ka Sind* (Today's Sind). Lahore: Progressive Publications.

Moghadam, Valentine M. 1988. "Women, Work, and Ideology in the Islamic Republic." *International Journal of Middle East Studies* 20, no. 2:221–43.

———. 1992. "Fundamentalism and the Woman Question in Afghanistan." In *Fundamentalism in Comparative Perspective*, edited by Lawrence Kaplan, 126–51. Amherst: Univ. of Massachusetts Press.

———. 1993. *Modernizing Women: Gender and Social Change in the Middle East.* Boulder, Colo.: Lynne Rienner Publishers.

Mojab, Shahzad. 1987. "The Islamic Government's Policy on Women's Access to Higher Education: 1979–85." Office of Women in International Development Working Paper No. 156, Michigan State Univ., Dec.

———. 1991. "Control-e dolat va moqavemat-e zanan dar ʿarse-ye daneshgah-ha-ye Iran" (State control and women's resistance in Iranian universities). *Nimeye Digar* 14:35–76.

Mojtahed, Ahmad, and Hadi S. Esfahani. 1989. "Agricultural Policy and Performance in Iran: The Post-revolutionary Experience." *World Development* 17:839–60.

Molyneux, Maxine. 1985. "Legal Reform and Socialist Revolution in Democratic Yemen: Women and the Family." *International Journal of the Sociology of Law* 13:147–72.

Mossavar-Rahmani, Yasmin. 1983. "Family Planning in Post-revolutionary Iran." In *Women and Revolution in Iran*, edited by Guity Nashat, 253–62. Boulder, Colo.: Westview Press.

Mottahedeh, Roy. 1984. *The Mantle of the Prophet.* New York: Simon and Schuster.

Muhammad'Ali, Maulana. N.d. *The Religion of Islam.* Cairo: The Arab Writer.

Mujahid, Sharif al. 1981. *Quaid-e-Azam Jinnah: Studies in Interpretation.* Karachi: Quaid-e-Azam Academy.

Mukherjee, Sadhan. 1984. *Afghanistan: From Tragedy to Triumph.* New Delhi: Sterling Publishers.

Mumtaz, Khawar, and Farida Shaheed. 1987. *Women of Pakistan: Two Steps Forward, One Step Back?* Lahore: Vanguard Press.

Munir, Muhammad. 1981. *From Jinnah to Zia.* Lahore: Vanguard Press.

Muradov, Ghulam. 1981. "La République Démocratique d'Afghanistan à la deuxième étape de la Révolution d'Avril." In *L'Afghanistan: Le passé et le présent*, Eastern Studies in the USSR 1, 190–214. Moscow: Academy of Sciences of the USSR.

Mustafa, Zubeida. 1990. "Rethinking in the Social Sciences." *Dawn*, 30 March, vii.

Muttahhari, Mortada. 1963. "Moshkel-e asasi dar sazeman-e ruhaniyyat." In *Bahthi dar marjaʾiyyat va ruhaniyyat*, edited by M. H. Tabatabaʾi, 165–230. Tehran: n.p.

———. 1981. *The Rights of Women in Islam.* Teheran: World Organization for Islamic Services (WOFIS).

Najmabadi, Afsaneh. 1987. "Iran's Turn to Islam: From Modernism to a Moral Order." *Middle East Journal* 41:202–17.

———. 1989. "Olgu-ye zan-e mosalman va fetwa-ye emam" (A Muslim woman's role model and Imam's *Fitwa*). *Nimeye Digar* 9:94–97.

Naqavi, Syed Nawab, Mahmood Hasan Khan, and M. Ghaffar Chaudhry, eds. 1987. *Land Reforms in Pakistan: A Historical Perspective*. Islamabad: Pakistan Institute of Development Economics.

Nashat, Guity. 1983. "Women in the Ideology of the Islamic Republic." In *Women and Revolution in Iran*, edited by Guity Nashat. Boulder, Colo.: Westview Press.

Nazeer, Mian, and Saiyeda Zia Aljalaly. 1983. "Participation of Women in Rural Economic Activities." Centre for Applied Economic Studies, Univ. of Peshawar. Unpublished report from the Women's Division.

Nicholson, Linda. 1987. *Gender and History: The Limits of Social Theory in the Age of the Family*. New York: Columbia Univ. Press.

Noman, Omar. 1988. *The Political Economy of Pakistan 1947–1985*. London: KPI.

Oakley, Ann. 1972. *Sex, Gender, and Society*. London: Temple Smith.

Ølesen, Asta. 1982. "The Musallis—the Graincleaners of East Afghanistan." *Afghanistan Journal* 9:13–19.

Ortner, Sherry, and Harriet Whitehead, eds. 1981. *Sexual Meanings: The Cultural Construction of Gender and Sexuality*. Cambridge: Cambridge Univ. Press.

Pahlavi, Mohammad Reza. 1980. *Answer to History*. New York: Stein and Day Publishers.

Pakistan, Government of. Federal Bureau of Statistics (FBS). 1985a. *Pakistan Statistical Year Book*, Karachi.

———. 1985b. *Women in Pakistan: A Statistical Profile*. Islamabad: Sponsored by the Women's Division.

Pakistan, Government of. Finance Division. 1983a. *Economic Survey: 1982–83*. Islamabad: Economic Adviser's Wing.

———. 1983b. *Pakistan: Basic Facts, 1982–83*. Islamabad: Economic Adviser's Wing.

———. 1992. *Economic Survey: 1991–92*. Islamabad: Economic Adviser's Wing.

Pakistan, Government of. Ministry of Finance. 1981. *Economic Survey 1980*. Islamabad: Ministry of Finance.

Pakistan, Government of. Planning Commission. 1958. *Second Five-Year Development Plan, 1955–60*. Karachi: Government Printing Press.

———. 1978. *The Fifth Five-Year Plan: 1978–83*. Karachi: Manager of Publications.

———. 1983. *The Sixth Five-Year Plan: 1983–88*. Karachi: Manager of Publications.

———. 1988. *Seventh Five-Year Plan: 1988–93; and Perspective Plan: 1988–2003*. Islamabad: Printing Corporation of Pakistan Press.

Pakistan, Government of. Planning Division. 1991. *Eighth Five-Year Plan (1993–98): Approach Paper*. Islamabad.

———. 1992. *National Conservation Strategy*. Islamabad.

Pakistan, Government of. Statistics Division. 1951. 1961. 1972. 1981. *Population Census of Pakistan*. Islamabad: Population Census Organization.

Pakistan, Government of. Women's Division. 1988a. *Solidarity: SAARC Women's Journal*. Islamabad, Dec.

―――. 1988b. "Women's Division: Organization and Activities." Islamabad, Sept.

Pakistan Commission on the Status of Women. 1986. "Report of the Commission on the Status of Women in Pakistan." Islamabad. Photocopy.

Pakistan Muslim League. 1949a. *An Enquiry into Land Ownership.* Lahore: Pakistan Muslim League.

―――. 1949b. *Report of the Agrarian Committee Appointed by the Working Committee of the Pakistan Muslim League.* Karachi: Pakistan Muslim League.

Papanek, Gustav F. 1967. *Pakistan's Development: Social Goals and Private Incentives.* Cambridge: Harvard Univ. Press.

Papanek, Hanna. 1985. "Gender and Class in Education-Employment Linkages." *Comparative Education Review* 29 (Aug.): 317–46.

―――. 1990. "To Each Less Than She Needs, from Each More Than She Can Do: Allocations, Entitlements, and Value." In *Persistent Inequalities: Women and World Development,* edited by Irene Tinker, 162–84. New York: Oxford Univ. Press.

Pasandideh, Mortada. 1989. "Zendaginama-ye rahbar-e enqelab-e Islami beh revayat-e baradarash." *Iran Times,* 17, 24, 31 Mar. and 7, 14, 21, 28 Apr.

Patel, Rashida. 1979. *Women and Law in Pakistan.* Karachi: Asia Foundation.

Pathak, Zakia, and Rajeswari Sunder Rajan. 1989. "Shahbano." *Signs* 14:559–82.

Poullada, Leon B. 1973. *Reform and Rebellion in Afghanistan, 1919–1929: King Amanullah's Failure to Modernize a Tribal Society.* Ithaca, N.Y.: Cornell Univ. Press.

Prokhanov, Aleksandr. 1983. "A Tree in the Center of Kabul." *Soviet Literature* 7 (Jul.): 3–129.

―――. 1988. "A Writer's Opinion: Afghan Questions." *Literaturnaya Gazeta* 17 (Feb.): 1, 9. (Condensed text translated in *Current Digest of the Soviet Press* 40, no. 8:13–14.)

Punjab, Government of the. Bureau of Statistics. 1979. *Development Statistics of the Punjab, 1978.* Lahore: Government Printing Office.

Qahreman, Shirin. 1988. "The Islamic Regime's Policy on Women's Access to Higher Education." *Nimeye Digar* 7:16–31. In Persian.

Rafsanjani, Ali Akbar. 1980. *Enqelab ya be 'that-e jadid.* Qom: Yaser Publishers.

Rahimi, Fahima. [1977] 1986. *Women in Afghanistan.* With a 1985 update by Nancy Dupree. Liestal: Bibliotheca Afghanica.

Razi, Mohammad. 1953. *Athar al-Hojja.* Qom: Borqe1 Bookstore.

Representatives of Hizb-i Islami in France. N.d. *Resistance/Renaissance Afghane.* Strasbourg: Hizb-i Islami.

Reskin, Barbara, and Heidi Hartmann. 1986. *Women's Work, Men's Work: Sex Segregation in the Job.* Washington, D.C.: National Academy Press.

Rizvi, Hassan Askari. 1986. *Military and Politics in Pakistan: 1947–86.* Lahore.

―――. 1988. "Pakistan's Political Scene in 1988: The Year of Change." *The Muslim* (Islamabad), 31 Dec.

Rogers, Barbara. 1980. *The Domestication of Women: Discrimination in Developing Societies*. London: Tavistock.

Roy, Olivier. 1980. "Afghanistan: La 'révolution' par le vide." *Esprit*, n.s., 4, no. 3 (Mar.): 78–88.

———. 1985. *L'Afghanistan: Islam et modernité politique*. Paris: Seuil.

———. 1986. *Islam and Resistance in Afghanistan*. Cambridge: Cambridge Univ. Press.

———. 1988. "Afghanistan: La guerre comme facteur du passage au politique." Paper presented at the National Conference of the Association Française de Science Politique, Bordeaux, 5–8 Oct.

Rubin, Barnett R. 1988. "Lineages of the State in Afghanistan." *Asian Survey* 28 (Nov.): 1188–1209.

Rubin, Gayle. 1975. "The Traffic in Women: Notes on a Political Economy of Sex." In *Toward an Anthropology of Women*, edited by Rayna Rapp, 157–210. New York: Monthly Review Press.

Rudolph, Lloyd I., and Susanne Hoeber Rudolph. 1987. *In Pursuit of Lakshmi: The Political Economy of the Indian State*. Chicago: Univ. of Chicago Press.

Ruhani, Hamid. 1979. *Barresi va tahlili az nahzat-e Imam Khomeini dar Iran*. Qom: Dar al-Fekr.

Saba, Manijheh. 1991. "Tahlili az dibachah-ha-ye 'zan-e ruz' dar dorah-ye ba'd az enqelab" (An analysis of editorials of *Zan-e Ruz* in postrevolutionary period). *Nimeye Digar* 14:8–34.

Sathar, Zeba, Nigel Crook, Christine Callum, and Shahnaz Kazi. 1988. "Women's Status and Fertility Change in Pakistan." *Population and Development Review* 14, no. 3:415–32.

Sayeed, Khalid bin. 1968. *Pakistan: The Formative Phase*. London: Oxford Univ. Press.

———. 1980. *Politics in Pakistan: The Nature and Direction of Change*. New York.

———. 1984. "Pakistan in 1983: Internal Stresses More Serious Than External Problems." *Asian Survey* 24 (Feb.).

Sayers, Janet, Mary Evans, and Nanneke Redclift, eds. 1987. *Engels Revisited: New Feminist Essays*. New York: Tavistock.

Schweitzer, Arthur. 1984. *The Age of Charisma*. Chicago: Nelson-Hall.

SCI. See Statistical Center of Iran.

Scott, Alison MacEwan. 1986. "Industrialization, Gender Stratification, and Stratification Theory." In *Gender and Stratification*, edited by Rosemary Crompton and Michael Mann, 154–89. Cambridge: Polity Press.

Scott, James C. 1976. *The Moral Economy of the Peasant: Subsistence and Rebellion in Southeast Asia*. New Haven: Yale Univ. Press.

Scott, Joan. 1988. *Gender and the Politics of History*. New York: Columbia Univ. Press.

Sérignan, Claude. 1960. "La condition des femmes en Afghanistan et son évolution récente." *Orient* (Paris) 4, no. 14:33–56.

Shafi Khan, Shahrukh. 1987. *Profits and Loss Sharing: An Islamic Experiment in Finance and Banking.* Karachi: Oxford Univ. Press.

Shah, Nasra N., ed. 1986. *Pakistani Women: A Socioeconomic and Demographic Profile.* Islamabad: Pakistan Institute of Development Economics.

Shah, Nasra N., and Makhdoom A. Shah. 1980. "Trends and Structure of Female Labour Force Participation in Rural and Urban Pakistan." In *Women in Contemporary India and South Asia,* edited by Alfred de Souza, 95–123. New Delhi: Manohar.

Shaheed, Farida, and Khawar Mumtaz. 1983. *Invisible Workers: Piecework Labour Amongst Women in Lahore.* Islamabad: Women's Division, Government of Pakistan.

———. 1992. *Women's Economic Participation in Pakistan: A Status Report.* Islamabad: UNICEF Pakistan.

Shahrani, M. Nazif. 1984. "Marxist 'Revolution' and Islamic Resistance in Afghanistan." In *Revolutions and Rebellions in Afghanistan: Anthropological Perspectives,* edited by M. Nazif Shahrani and Robert L. Canfield, 3–57. Berkeley: Institute of International Studies, Univ. of California.

———. 1986a. "The Kirghiz Khans: Styles and Substance of Traditional Local Leadership in Central Asia." *Central Asian Survey* 5:255–71.

———. 1986b. "State Building and Social Fragmentation in Afghanistan: A Historical Perspective." In *The State, Religion, and Ethnic Politics: Afghanistan, Iran, and Pakistan,* edited by Ali Banuazizi and Myron Weiner, 23–74. Syracuse, N.Y.: Syracuse Univ. Press.

Shaji'i, Zahra. 1965. *Namayandegan-e Majlis-e Shura-ye melli dar bist dowra-ye qanun gozari.* Teheran: Institute for Social Research.

Shari'ati, Ali. 1979. *On the Sociology of Islam.* Translated by Hamid Algar. Berkeley: Mizan Press.

Shchipakhina, Lyudmilla. 1988. "Motherland Meets Its Sons." *Krasnaya Zvezda* 22 (May): 2.

Sivard, Ruth Leger. 1985. *Women: A World Survey.* Washington, D.C.: World Priorities.

Skocpol, Theda. 1988. "Social Revolutions and Mass Military Mobilization." *World Politics* 40:147–68.

Staar, Richard, ed. 1982. *1982 Yearbook on International Communist Affairs.* Stanford: Hoover Institution Press, Stanford Univ.

———. 1984. *1984 Yearbook on International Communist Affairs.* Stanford: Hoover Institution Press, Stanford Univ.

———. 1985. *1985 Yearbook on International Communist Affairs.* Stanford: Hoover Institution Press, Stanford Univ.

———. 1987. *1987 Yearbook on International Communist Affairs.* Stanford: Hoover Institution Press, Stanford Univ.

———. 1988. *1988 Yearbook on International Communist Affairs.* Stanford: Hoover Institution Press, Stanford Univ.

Statistical Center of Iran (SCI). 1968. *National Census of Population and Housing, November 1966,* Teheran: SCI.

————. 1976. *Bayan-i amari-yi tahavvolat-i eqtesadi va ejtemai-yi Iran.* Teheran: SCI.

————. 1981. *National Census of Population and Housing, November 1976.* Teheran: SCI.

————. 1982. *Salnama-ye Amari-ye Sal-e 1360.* Teheran: SCI.

————. 1985. *Salnama-ye Amari-ye Sal-e 1363.* Teheran: SCI.

————. 1987. *National Census of Population and Housing, November 1986.* Tehran: SCI.

————. *Urban Household Expenditure and Income Survey.* Teheran: SCI, annual, various issues from 1978 to 1988 (in Persian).

————. *Rural Household Expenditure and Income Survey.* Teheran: SCI, annual, various issues from 1978 to 1988 (in Persian).

Stepan, Alfred. 1978. *The State and Society: Peru in Comparative Perspective.* Princeton: Princeton Univ. Press.

Stewart, Rhea Talley. 1973. *Fire in Afghanistan, 1914–1929: Faith, Hope, and the British Empire.* Garden City, N.Y.: Doubleday.

Strategic Issues in Pakistan's Economic Policy. 1988. Lahore.

Syed, Anwar Hussain. 1977. "Pakistan in 1976: Business as Usual." *Asian Survey* 17 (Feb.).

Tabari, Azar, and Nahid Yeganeh. 1982. *In the Shadow of Islam: The Women's Movement in Iran.* London: Zed Press.

Tabibi, Latif. 1981. "Die afghanische Landreform von 1979: Ihre Vorgeschichte und Konsequenzen." Ph.D. diss., Free Univ. of Berlin.

Tai, Hung-Chao. 1974. *Land Reforms and Politics.* Berkeley and Los Angeles: Univ. of California Press.

Tapper, Nancy. 1984. "Causes and Consequences of the Abolition of Brideprice in Afghanistan." In *Revolutions and Rebellions in Afghanistan: Anthropological Perspectives*, edited by M. Nazif Shahrani and Robert L. Canfield, 291–305. Berkeley: Institute of International Studies, Univ. of California.

Tapper, Richard. 1974. "Nomadism in Modern Afghanistan: Asset or Anachronism?" In *Afghanistan in the 1970s*, edited by Louis Dupree and Linette Albert, 126–43. New York: Praeger.

————. 1983. Introduction to *The Conflict of Tribe and State in Iran and Afghanistan*, edited by Richard Tapper. London: Croom Helm.

————. 1984. "Holier Than Thou: Islam in Three Tribal Societies." In *Islam in Tribal Societies: From the Atlas to the Indus*, edited by Akbar S. Ahmed and David S. Hart, 244–65. London: Routledge and Kegan Paul.

Tavakoli-Targhi, Mohammad. 1989–90. "Archive." *Nimeye Digar* 10:167–97; 11:96–157.

Thomas, John W. 1968. "Rural Works Program and East Pakistan's Development." Ph.D. diss., Harvard Univ.

Tilly, Louise, and Joan Scott. 1978. *Women, Work, and Family.* New York: Routledge and Kegan Paul.

Trussell, James, and Anne R. Pebley. 1984. "The Potential Impact of Changes in Fertility on Infant, Child, and Maternal Mortality." *Studies in Family Planning* 15, no. 6:267–80.

ul-Haq, Mahbub. 1974. *Poverty Curtain: Choices for the Third World*. New York: Columbia Univ. Press.

UNESCO. 1984. *Women on the Move*. Paris: UNESCO.

UNICEF. 1989. *The State of the World's Children 1989*. New York: UNICEF.

United Nations Convention on the Elimination of All Forms of Discrimination Against Women. 1985. Vienna.

United Nations Development Programme (UNDP). 1990. *Human Development Report 1990*. New York: Oxford Univ. Press.

————. 1992. *Human Development Report 1992*. New York: Oxford Univ. Press.

U.S. Department of Commerce, Bureau of the Census. *World Population 1983*. Washington, D.C.: Government Printing Office.

Usuf, Zohra. 1989. "A Woman's Bank." *Dawn Overseas Weekly*, 20 July, 16.

Valenta, Jiri, and A. Sheikh. 1987. "Afghanistan: Leninism with an Islamic Face." Paper presented at the Conference on Afghanistan and Soviet Strategies for the Muslim World, 29–30 Sept., sponsored by the Defense Academic Research Support Program, MacDill AFB.

Venkataramani, M. S. 1984. *The American Role in Pakistan*. Lahore: Vanguard Books.

Vercellin, Giovanni. 1979. *Afghanistan 1973–1978: Dalla repubblica presidenziale alla repubblica democratica*. Venice: Quaderni del Seminario di Iranistica, Uralo Altaistica e Caucasalogia dell'Universita degli Studi de Venezia.

Viollis, Andrée. 1930. *Tourmente sur l'Afghanistan*. Paris: Librairie Valois.

Wakman, Mohammad Amin. 1991. "Text of Speech of Dr. M. Amin Wakman, Chairman of the Afghan Social Democratic Party in the Council Meeting of the Socialist International, Istanbul, Turkey, 11 June 1991." *Afghan Mellat*, 2.

Walzer, Michael. 1965. *The Revolution of Saints*. Cambridge: Harvard Univ. Press.

Ward, Kathryn. 1984. *Women in the World-System*. New York: Praeger.

————, ed. 1990. *Women Workers and Global Restructuring*. Ithaca, N.Y.: ILR Press.

Waring, Marilyn. 1988. *If Women Counted: A New Feminist Economics*. San Francisco: Harper.

Weber, Max. 1946. *From Max Weber: Essays in Sociology*. Translated by Hans Gerth and C. Wright Mills. New York: Oxford Univ. Press.

————. 1968. *Economy and Society*. Translated by Guenther Roth and Claus Wittich. New York: Bedminster Press.

Weeks, John R. 1988. "The Demography of Islamic Nations." Special issue of *Population Bulletin* 43, no. 4.

Weinbaum, Marvin G., and Stephen Cohen. 1983. "Pakistan in 1982: Holding On." *Asian Survey* 23 (Feb.).

Weiss, Anita M. 1984. "Tradition and Modernity at the Workplace: A Field Study of Women in the Pharmaceutical Industry of Lahore." *Women's Studies International Forum* 7, no. 4:259–64.

————, ed. 1986. *Islamic Reassertion in Pakistan: The Application of Islamic Laws in a Modern State*, Syracuse, N.Y.: Syracuse Univ. Press.

————. 1992. *Walls Within Walls: Life Histories of Working Women in the Old City of Lahore*, Boulder, Colo.: Westview Press.

White, Lawrence J. 1974. *Industrial Concentration and Economic Power in Pakistan*. Princeton: Princeton Univ. Press.

Wiebe, Dietrich. 1984. *Afghanistan: Ein mittelasiatisches Entwicklungsland im Umbruch*. Stuttgart: Ernst Klett.

Wolfenstein, E. Victor. 1971. *The Revolutionary Personality: Lenin, Trotsky, Gandhi*. Princeton: Princeton Univ. Press.

World Bank. 1979. *Pakistan: Economic Development and Fifth Plan Review*. Washington, D.C.: Oxford Univ. Press.

————. 1980. *World Development Report, 1980*. Washington, D.C.: Oxford Univ. Press.

————. 1983. *World Development Report, 1983*. Washington, D.C.: Oxford Univ. Press.

————. 1984. *World Development Report, 1984*. Washington, D.C.: Oxford Univ. Press.

————. 1987. *Preventing the Tragedy of Maternal Deaths*. Nairobi: Oxford Univ. Press.

————. 1988. *World Development Report, 1988*. Washington, D.C.: Oxford Univ. Press.

————. 1989. *World Development Report, 1989*. Washington, D.C.: Oxford Univ. Press.

————. 1992. *World Development Report, 1992*. Washington, D.C.: Oxford Univ. Press.

Writers' Union of Free Afghanistan (WUFA). [1988]. *Life in Refugee Camps* (photo album). Peshawar: WUFA.

Youssef, Nadia. 1978. "The Status and Fertility Patterns of Muslim Women." In *Women in the Muslim World*, edited by Lois Beck and Nikki R. Keddie. Cambridge: Harvard Univ. Press.

————. 1982. "The Interrelationship Between the Division of Labor in the Household, Women's Role, and Their Impact on Fertility." In *Women's Roles and Population Trends in the Third World*, edited by Richard Anker, Mayra Buvinic, and Nadia Youssef, 173–201. London: International Labour Office.

Zaidi, Akbar S. 1985. "The Urban Bias in Health Facilities in Pakistan." *Social Service and Medicine* 20.

————. 1986. "Issues in Health Sector in Pakistan." *Pakistan Development Review*.

Zia, Shehla, Hina Jilani, and Asma Jahangir. 1982. "Muslim Family Laws and Their Implementation in Pakistan." Islamabad: Women's Division, Government of Pakistan.

Zia ul-Haq, Mohammad. 1979. "Introduction of Islamic Laws: Address to the Nation." Islamabad, 10 Feb.
Zonis, Marvin. 1971. *The Political Elite of Iran.* Princeton: Princeton Univ. Press.
———. 1991. *Majestic Failure: The Fall of the Shah.* Chicago: Univ. of Chicago Press.

Index

Anglo-Afghan wars, 362
Ansari Commission, 432
Arabic (language), 399
Araki, Ayatollah Mohammad Ali, 149
Arian, Abdur Rashid, 45
Armed forces: in Afghanistan, 47, 54,
   210; in Islamic Iran, 102, 110, 121; in
   Pakistan, 174, 270, 279, 324. *See also*
   Army; Military
Armenians, 148
Army: *in Afghanistan,* Communist rule
   and, 44–45, 59, 351, prewar era and,
   73, 201–2; *in Iran,* 240, and Iran-Iraq
   War, 250; *in Pakistan,* Bhutto and,
   164, 166, 170, ethnic makeup of,
   157–61, 182, Zia and, 174, 177
Assembly of Experts, 128, 141, 230, 261
Ataturk, Kemal, 333
Awami League, 9, 160–61, 299
Awami Tehrik, 435
awqaf, 112
Ayatollah, 113. *See also* Khomeini,
   Ayatollah Ruhollah
Ayesha (Prophet's wife), 363, 434
Ayub Khan, General: basic democracies
   and, 13, 158, 299; economic
   development and, 278, 284–86, 316,
   323–26; and muhajirs, 300, 307; and
   reforms, 297–98, 307, 317; rule of, 9,
   17, 157, 160–65, 301, 309, 318, 323–
   24; women issues and, 26, 413, 416–
   17, 428
Azerbaijan, 394
Azerbaijanis, 2, 4, 30, 148, 394–95
Aziz, Abdullah, 338

Babrak. *See* Karmal, Babrak
Bacha-Saqqa, 338
Baha'is, 148
Bakhtiar, 119
Baluchis: of Afghanistan, 36, 52; and
   Khomeini's regime, 4, 148; of
   Pakistan, 8, 271; and punjabis, 156;
   in Sind, 172
Baluchistan: Afghan refugee camps in,
   21; Bhutto and, 162, 166; discrimi-
   nation in, 21, 29, 300–301, 303;

economic development in, 285,
   294, 298–99, 302; elections in, 175;
   female literacy in, 426
Baluchi tribes, 166
Bangladesh, 271; Biharis in, 436; emergence
   of, 297, 302; female life expectancy in,
   396; Pakistan and, 283, 287, 294, 296;
   poverty in, 274, 277
Bani Sar, Abu al-Hassan, 116
Banuazizi, Ali, 147
Baqi, Abdul, 67
Baryalai, Mohammad, 64
baseej, 240
Bazaaris, 3–5; in Afghanistan, 93;
   Iranian ulama and, 130; Iran's
   Majles and, 121, 123; in revolution-
   ary Iran, 108, 116–17, 131, 134–35
Bazaar-mosque alliance, 105, 107, 113–
   14, 117–18, 130, 132, 134–35, 139,
   146, 149–50
Bazargan, Mehdi, 15, 114, 116, 119, 130–31
Bazgar, Mujahid Shah, 362
Behbahani, Ayatollah Sayyid
   Mohammad, 112
Bengal, 272, 296–97
Bengalis: economic development and,
   296, 314; Pakistani military and, 8–
   10, 160; and Punjabis, 156–57; and
   secession, 294
Bhutan, 396
Bhutto, Benazir: dismissal of, 11, 14; and
   Pakistani politics, 182–83; and
   Pakistani women, 412, 419, 439–43;
   rise to power, 16, 23, 29, 438
Bhutto, Zulfikar Ali, 4, 9, 17; distribution crisis and, 296, 314, 317;
   economic development and, 278–
   81, 283, 318, 325–26; execution of,
   173, 175, 323, 432; industrial classes
   and, 309, 312; nationalization
   policies of, 10, 21, 310, 317; and the
   opposition, 167–73; policies of, 308,
   322; and reform, 17, 164; rule of,
   284–86, 294–95, 300; and state
   formation, 161–67; and women's
   issues, 26, 413, 417, 428, 435. *See
   also* Nationalization; Pakistan;
   Pakistan People's Party
Bibi Fatima, 431

Komitehs, 19. *See also* Revolutionary
  committees
Kurdistan, 398
Kurds, 4, 148
Kunduz, 194, 360
Kuwait, 268, 398

Lahore, 171, 282, 299, 319, 420–22, 433–
  34, 436–37, 442–43
Landlords: in Afghanistan, 188, 193, 195,
  200, 205–6, 209, 216, 219–20; in
  Islamic Iran, 123; in Pakistan, 156–
  59, 162–63, 165, 168, 171–72, 295,
  302, 305–7, 441
Land Reform: *in Afghanistan*, Babrak
  and, 46, failure of, 215, and
  Parcham-Khalq struggle, 4, 6, 199–
  200, and PDPA, 190–91, 207–11, and
  the resistance, 219; *in Iran*, Islamic
  revolution and, 20, 115–16, 121, 132,
  and Muslim radicals, 232, 257,
  religious establishment and, 113,
  the Shah and, 228, Shari ͨ ah and,
  233, the U.S. and, 103; *In Pakistan*,
  21, 180, attempts at, 307–8, 325,
  Bhutto and, 163, 165–66, 168, 171,
  and Punjabi bureaucracy, 157, Zia
  ul-Haq and, 175
Latin America, 321
Law for Protection and Expansion of
  Industry, 256
Lenin, Vladimir Ilyich, 144–45
Liaqat Ali Khan, 9, 26
Liaqat Ali Khan, Begum Ra ͗ ana, 432–33
Literacy: Afghan Communists and, 42,
  191, 345–47; among Afghan
  women, 342, 344–45; in Iran, 390,
  398–99; in Muslim societies, 393; in
  Pakistan, 413, 424–27, 442

Machiavelli, Niccolò, 145
Madhya Pradesh, 287
Madrasa, 74; in Communist Afghanistan,
  85, 87, 94, 97; in Iran, 111, 121
Mahdavi Kani, Ayatollah, 377

Mahdi, 109, 149. *See also* Hidden Imam
Mahr (bride price), 25, 344
Majlis-e Shura, 176, 434
Majlis-e Shura-ye Islami, 4, 261. *See also*
  Islamic Consultative Assembly;
  Majlis; National Assembly
Majlis, 115, 120–28, 133, 135, 137–39,
  141–42, 144, 150n. 8, 369, 380, 407.
  See also Islamic Consultative
  Assembly; *Majles-e Shura*; National
  Assembly
Maknun, Soraya, 374
Malalai School, 338, 360
Maldives, 396
Mangal, Habib, 41
Mangal tribes, 337
Mao Ze-dong, 144
Maoists, 73, 75
Marriage: in Afghanistan, 191, 200, 205–
  7, 341, 343–44, 355; in Iran, 395,
  397–98, 407; in Tunisia, 394; and
  women, 391, 393, 427, 436. *See also*
  Divorce; Women
Martial law: in Pakistan, 171–72, 174–77;
  Zia ul-Haq and, 300, 306, 416, 420,
  436
Martyr Foundation, 20, 121, 129, 255
Martyrs: of Afghan war, 214, 346, 358; in
  Iran, 243
Marx, Karl, 145
Marxism, 110, 143
Marxism-Leninism, 42, 348. *See also*
  Communists; Khalq; Parcham;
  People's Democratic Party of
  Afghanistan (PDPA)
Mashhad, 110, 112
Masleha, 137–38
Masud, Ahmad Shah, 15, 67, 78, 88, 90–
  91, 93, 96. *See also* Afghanistan;
  Mujahidin; Resistance
Maternal mortality: in Iran, 377; in non-
  Muslim countries, 393, 397; in
  Pakistan, 274, 321. *See also* Infant
  mortality; Women
Maulana Muhammad Ali, 362
Mawlawi Faqirullah, 85
Mawlawi Islam, 85
Mazdak, Farid, 67
Mecca, 136

Pakistan (*continued*)
  women and Nawaz Sharif's, 442–43;
  women's organizations in, 432–33,
  435–36; Zia ul-Haq's rule in, 176–77,
  179–83. *See also* Ayub Khan, General;
  Bhutto, Zulfikar Ali; Islamization;
  Military, in Pakistan; Zia, ul-Haq
Pakistan Civil Service (PCS), 8
Pakistan Commissionate for Afghan
  Refugees, 359
Pakistan Commission on the Status of
  Women, 430
Pakistan Democratic Alliance (PDA), 183
Pakistan Industrial Development
  Corporation, 21, 284
Pakistan movement, 298. *See also*
  Muslim League
Pakistan National Alliance (PNA), 168–
  73, 179
Pakistan People's Party (PPP): elections
  and, 161, 294–95, 327, 436; and
  Islamization, 419; Muhajirs and, 16,
  301; reemergence of, 11, 182–83;
  and reforms, 164, 308, 439–40, 441;
  rule of, 2, 10, 12, 165–72, 300; social
  base of, 162; and women, 428, 437–
  40; and Zia ul-Haq, 175–77, 179;
  and Zulfikar Ali Bhutto, 163. *See
  also* Bhutto, Zulfikar Ali
Pakistan Women Lawyer's Association
  (PWLA), 432–35, 442–43
Paktin, Raz Mohammed, 67
Palejo, Rasul Bux, 436
Palwasha, Jamila, 352
Parcham: in Afghan politics, 18, 44–49, 63;
  and Daoud, 38–39; in power, 6, 43,
  45, 209; purge of, 42, 46; recruitment
  policies of, 38; and the resistance, 52;
  and rural reforms, 208; and struggle
  with Khalq, 5–6, 37, 39, 69, 415; and
  women, 25, 342–43
Pashto (language), 87, 359
Pashtuns: in Afghanistan, 36, 63, 69; and
  Hekmatyar, 75, 89; Karmal regime
  and, 53, 71n. 18; and Muhajirs, 182;
  in Pakistan, 8, 36; in Pakistani
  military, 9; and Punjabis, 156; in
  Sind, 172; transformation among,
  76, 83; women among, 357

Pashtun tribes, 199, 204
Pashtunwali, 337
Pastoralism, 192–93
Peace, Solidarity, and Friendship
  Organization, 350
Peasantry, 193, 196; and Afghan
  Communists, 40, 49, 196, 200–201,
  205–9; and Afghan resistance, 81,
  219–20; in Babrak period, 35, 46; and
  the birth of Pakistan, 295, 300, 303,
  305; Iran's Islamic Revolution and,
  115, 121, 135–36; Iran's White
  Revolution and, 103; and Zulfikar
  Ali Bhutto, 167–68
Peasant's Justice Party, 61
People's Democratic Party of Afghanistan (PDPA): and Afghan society, 2,
  6–7, 13, 18, 41; and Afghan women,
  342–43, 345–46, 350, 352–53; failure
  of, 215, 217; formation of, 37–38;
  internal conflict in, 6–7, 40, 43;
  membership in, 42, 51–52, 58, 69–70;
  and Mujahidin, 15; and Najibullah's
  regime, 56, 59–65, 68; in power, 14,
  44, 54, 58–59, 78, 187; and reforms,
  16–17, 41, 188–89, 191, 202, 215, 218;
  and Soviet Union, 30, 53, 221n. 1. *See
  also* Khalq; Parcham
People's Islamic Party, 61
Persian (language), 2, 76, 83, 90, 96, 148,
  204, 398
Peshawar, 64, 76, 81, 442; Afghan female
  refugees in, 356–59, 361–62; working
  women in, 423
Peshawar Alliance, 83, 92–94, 361–62
Philippines, 273–75
Pir, 82, 91
Politburo: of the PDPA, 45, 47–48, 54, 56,
  59–60, 63, 352; of the CPSU, 55, 63
Polygamy: in Afghanistan, 335, 337; in
  Iran, 377; in refugee camps, 358;
  regulation of, in Pakistan, 416
Polygyny, 395. *See also* Polygamy
Proletariat, 5, 105, 135–36. *See also*
  Workers
Punjab, 8, 11, 21; British India and, 272,
  306–7; economic development in,
  285, 294, 298–300; and the military,
  177; and Pakistani elections, 169,

486   INDEX

**The Politics of Social Transformation
in Afghanistan, Iran, and Pakistan**
was composed in 10 on 12 Palatino on a Mergenthaler L-300
by Partners Composition;
printed by sheet-fed offset on 50-pound, acid-free Natural Smooth,
Smyth-sewn and bound over binder's boards in Holliston Roxite B
and notch bound with paper covers printed in 2 colors
by Braun-Brumfield, Inc.;
and published by
Syracuse University Press
Syracuse, New York 13244-5160